The world of BUDDHISM

The world of

Edited by Heinz Bechert and Richard Gombrich

With 297 illustrations, 82 in colour

215 photographs, drawings and maps

BUDDHISM

Buddhist Monks and Nuns in Society and Culture

Texts by Richard Gombrich
Etienne Lamotte
Lal Mani Joshi
Oskar von Hinüber
Siegfried Lienhard
Michael B. Carrithers
Heinz Bechert
Jane Bunnag
Erik Zürcher
Robert K. Heinemann
Per Kvaerne

T&H

THAMES AND HUDSON

Endpapers: Detail of upright from stupa railing, Amarāvatī. 2nd century.

The editors and the publisher wish to acknowledge the generous advice given by all the authors on the selection of the illustrations and the wording of the captions; it must be made clear, however, that final responsibility for these picture sections remains entirely with the publisher.

Designed and produced by THAMES AND HUDSON, LONDON
MANAGING EDITOR: Ian Sutton
DESIGN: Pauline Baines
PICTURE RESEARCH: Georgina Bruckner
EDITORIAL: Mary Chesshyre; Michael Hall
MAPS by Hanni Bailey

Filmset in Great Britain by Keyspools Ltd, Golborne, Lancs.
Monochrome origination in Great Britain by DSCI, London
Colour origination in Switzerland by Cliché Lux, La Chaux-de-fonds
Printed and bound in Italy by Amilcare Pizzi s.p.a. Milan

Contents

Foreword

Buddhism is the oldest of the great 'world religions'. Like both the others – Christianity and Islam – it not only addresses itself to all mankind but has found adherents in almost all parts of the world. The founder, Siddhārtha Gautama, a nobleman born near the border between Nepal and India, achieved 'Enlightenment' some 2,500 years ago; so he was known as the 'Buddha', the 'Enlightened'. In the course of history Buddhism was forced out of the land of its origin, India, just as Christianity was forced out of Palestine. It reached all countries bordering India at an early date. To the west of India and in large parts of Central Asia it again disappeared, as a result of the spread of Islam; but it found an enduring home among the Tibetans, in large parts of east Asia as far as Japan and Korea, with Mongol peoples in northern Asia, in several countries of Southeast Asia and on the island of Sri Lanka. In 1982 I saw for myself in China that the Cultural Revolution has not permanently destroyed Buddhism in 'the Middle Kingdom'. Between 1966 and 1976 all Buddhist institutions in China were damaged or at least shut; but now that the practice of religion is again permitted, though only to a rather limited degree, it is evident that the attempt definitively to suppress the Buddhist religion proved a failure.

Buddhism is also a world religion in the sense that it has been able to adapt itself to a variety of social systems. Thus we find it today in a modern industrial society like Japan as well as in the peasant societies of Southeast Asia. Moreover, even now – according to traditional Buddhist chronology, more than 2,500 years after the Buddha first preached – its strength as a missionary religion has not been sapped. It has reached the USA via Hawaii; taken as a philosophy, it found adherents in Europe and North America by the turn of this century. Today it has become a religion practised in the Western world too; here too there are Buddhist institutions, though comparatively few. Even in India and Indonesia, countries in which Buddhism long seemed extinct, Buddhist monks and monasteries have again appeared.

The title of this book, *The World of Buddhism*, here requires an explanation. One cannot really talk of a 'world' of Buddhism in the sense in which there is a 'world' of Christianity or Islam. The Buddha's teaching is for all mankind; but its original aim was not to shape life *in* the world but to teach liberation, release *from* the world. The Buddha thus did not intend to institute a new order in the world, as Mohammed did. The world follows its own laws. Even so, one can ascertain that as Buddhism spread, the entire cultures of the countries which fell under its influence were shaped in a particular and characteristic way.

If we talk of the 'World of Buddhism', the central place in our discussion is taken by the most truly Buddhist institution, the Sangha, the Order of Buddhist monks and nuns. The Sangha is not the oldest institution of its kind, for the monastic order of the Jains, which also arose in ancient India, is surely older. Nor can one say that Buddhism exists only where the Sangha exists, for the book deals with forms of Buddhism without a Sangha in Nepal, Japan, Indonesia and the Western world. Nevertheless, the Sangha has a special significance. An often quoted traditional view has it that Buddhism has not taken root in a country till there are native monks there. That is why we considered as a title for this book 'The Sons of the Buddha', one of the many conventional designations of monks. Of course, members of the Sangha are not part of a supernatural ordination tradition; they are not consecrated in the sense in which a Catholic priest is; their true legitimacy derives not from their monastic ordination but solely from the extent to which they embody the Buddha's teaching – that is, from their conduct. Buddhists are familiar with the distinction between conventional and absolute truth; so one could say that according to absolute truth membership of the Order is only an outward sign, but according to conventional truth an almost metaphysical significance is attributed to it. It is primarily the Sangha that has transmitted the Buddha's words and maintained the tradition of meditation and thus ensured that future generations too can be shown the way to release from the world.

The problem of the relation between religious doctrine and worldly power occurs in the history of Buddhism too. We find widely differing attempts to solve it, from the hermit dwelling apart from the world and its problems to the transformation of the monk into a political ruler.

The editors and publishers have tried in this book to show this diversity. We begin with the teachings of the original form of Buddhism or, to be more precise, with the oldest form of the teachings one can derive from surviving sources (Chapter 1). We then follow its fortunes in India, its land of origin (Chapter 2), in Central Asia, which before the advent of Islam was imbued with Indian culture (Chapter 3), and in Nepal, where traditions of Indian Buddhism have been preserved without a break till today (Chapter 4). The second section is dedicated to Theravāda Buddhism, the name given to a form of Buddhism which is doctrinally very conservative and thus relatively close to the original doctrine. It reached Sri Lanka as early as the 3rd century BC; in the course of time it also came to Burma, Thailand, Laos and Cambodia (Chapters 5 to 7). We turn next to the Buddhism of the Far East, which was formed by the doctrines of the Mahāyāna, the 'Great Vehicle', themselves of Indian origin; we follow its course in China, Korea, Vietnam and Japan (Chapters 7 and 8). India itself, the motherland of Buddhism, was the point of origin for the fourth great tradition with which we deal: though Tibetan Buddhism (Chapter 10) preserved essential features of the Indian form of Buddhism, it became an independent form of religion and gave rise to one of the richest religious and literary cultures of Asia. Tibetan Buddhism penetrated not only the other countries of the Himalayas, but also the Mongols, the Manchus, and even the Kalmucks and thus the Urals, so that it reached the very borders of Europe. Our final chapter discusses how Buddhism has met the demands of our time, how it still represents a living spiritual force and how its teachings have for the first time reached the Western world (Chapter 11).

The authors of this book are 'Buddhologists' from nine countries; the diversity of approach reflects the diversity of the 'Buddhist world', a truly universal phenomenon of human culture. On 5 May 1983 Monseigneur Etienne Lamotte passed away. Professor Lamotte was acknowledged to be the greatest living authority on Buddhism in the Western world. He was kind enough, in spite of his health being already weak, to provide us with his two fundamental contributions to the present volume.

The present work results from the intensive co-operation of eleven authors, including the two editors, and the publishing house. The selection of illustrations as well as the first draft of the texts in the picture sections and the captions of the line-drawings have been the responsibility of Thames and Hudson; all these texts have, however, been revised by both editors and by the authors of the relevant sections. Most of the contributions were written in English. Chapters 1 and 2(b), originally written in French, have been translated into English by Sara Boin-Webb (who also contributed valuable editorial help); Chapters 4 and 6, originally in German, were translated by Kathrine Talbot; and Chapter 9, part of which was written in German, by J. R. Foster. These translations have been checked by the original authors and thereby authorized.

The glossary has been provided by Professor Gombrich. The bibliography was compiled by the undersigned; he would like to thank Professor Heinemann, Professor von Hinüber, Professor Kvaerne, Professor Lienhard, and Professor Zürcher for their suggestions concerning their respective sections. The index was compiled by Mary Chesshyre. The note on the pronunciation of Tibetan words was contributed by Professor Kvaerne. Both editors also wish to thank the co-authors as well as those colleagues who have given valuable information, practical help and advice; in particular we should like to mention Dr Michael Aris of Oxford University; Henry Ginsburg and Patricia Herbert of the British Library, London; Dr Heinz Braun of Göttingen University; Professor Klaus Röhrborn of Giessen University and Dr Akira Yuyama of the International Institute for Buddhist Studies, Tokyo.

HEINZ BECHERT

A note on orthography and transliteration

In rendering names and terms from Asian languages, we have wherever possible used accepted scholarly systems of transliteration; this was done in particular for Sanskrit, Pali, Sinhalese, Newari and Tibetan. For Chinese we have used the Wade-Giles system. For Burmese and Thai, however, we use conventional transcriptions which are based on the pronunciation of these languages, since there is as yet no generally accepted system for their Romanization.

Buddhist terms are quoted in their Sanskrit form in the Introduction and in Chapters 1–4, while preference has been given to their Pali forms in the chapters dealing with Theravāda Buddhism.

The names of historical persons and historical places, as well as Buddhist and other religious and technical terms, are regularly written in the scholarly transliteration with diacritical marks. The only exceptions are a few words which have become generally accepted in modern English. These are found in the glossary in exact transliteration. Some modern place names (e.g. Rangoon, Calcutta) as well as names of people of our times and of the recent past (e.g. Bandaranaike, Gandhi) are spelt in the conventional orthography generally used today.

The pronunciation of Tibetan words

The orthography of Tibetan was fixed in the 9th century. Like English, however, the pronunciation has changed over the centuries, so that most words are now pronounced rather differently from the way they are spelt. The following rough guidelines may aid the reader in pronouncing Tibetan words more or less according to the rules of modern Central Tibetan (the various *tones* of this dialect will not be taken into account).

Words frequently contain *initial consonant clusters*. These are simplified to *one* consonant sound. If *r*, *l*, or *s* comes first, it is silent (*sngags-pa* = ngakpa, 'tantrist'). If *r* is the second element, the whole cluster is pronounced like d with a very faint r following (a 'retroflex' d, e.g. *bsgrubs* = dup, 'achieved'). An exception, however, is the cluster *sr* which is pronounced s (*Srong-btsan-sgam-po* = Songtsen-gampo, one of the early kings of Tibet). If *l* is the second element, it alone is pronounced (*bla-ma* = lama, 'Lama').

There are five letters which are not pronounced when they are in an initial position ('prefixed'): *g*, *d*, *b*, *m*, and *'* (*gtum-mo* = tum-mo, 'internal, mystic heat'). There also occur *final* consonant clusters in which *s* is the last letter; in that case, *s* is not pronounced (see *sngags-pa*, above). The vowels *a*, *u* and *o* are subjected to an 'umlaut' (vowel modification) when the following and final consonant is *d*, *l* or *s*, and are then pronounced (very roughly) as e, ü, (French 'u') and ö (French 'eu'). The following consonant (*d*, *l* or *s*) is then usually silent (*Bod* = bö, 'Tibet', *Mi-la-ras-pa* = Mi-la repa, name of a Tibetan yogin).

Introduction: The Buddhist Way

RICHARD GOMBRICH

THIS BOOK IS ABOUT ONE of the three world religions. The other two, Christianity and Islam, have always demanded an exclusive allegiance: 'Thou shalt have no other God but me.' They have concerned themselves with both this world and the next. Buddhism makes no such demand and has other concerns. Monotheists believe that the world has been created by God, so that it must have some religious value, or at least significance. They also believe that God is relevant – to say the least – to man's salvation. Buddhists believe neither of these things. Buddhism is not concerned with God or the world, though of course it has views about both. Buddhism is concerned with man, or rather with all living, suffering beings. Buddhism is about morality, meditation and gnosis.

Half a millennium before Jesus, more than a millennium before Mohammed, the Buddha found Enlightenment, and out of his infinite compassion taught the way to salvation which he had discovered. The world, including all its heavens and hells, is a place of suffering, if for no other reason than that its joys are transient and all lives (including those in heaven) end in decay and death. Into this arena of suffering all creatures are constantly reborn in an endless cycle. Salvation consists in getting off the treadmill. How is that to be done?

What binds one to the treadmill is desire. Desire in turn rests on a false perception of our condition, a perception intuitive but wrong. We think that we have some enduring essence (some call it a soul), a Self which is the subject of our experiences. But, said the Buddha, this so-called Self is nothing but a bundle of physical and mental constituents kept going by desire. It is desire alone which leads to rebirth, for there is really no Self to be reborn, no substantial entity which could pass from one life to another. Gnosis is to realize this and behave accordingly.

To eliminate desire and attain salvation we must purify our minds. The first stage of that purification is ethical: we must restrain our appetites and be kind, both to ourselves and others. Since there is no Self, there is no basis for selfishness; the Buddhist aims to love without attachment and hence to love all equally. All living beings are equally entitled to sympathy and respect. But each is responsible for his own acts, his own mind and ultimately his own salvation.

The Buddha urged those who wished to escape from suffering to follow his example and renounce the world. Free from social and family ties, and from the need to earn a living, they should devote themselves to a life of meditation. To make such a life as easy as possible, the Buddha founded a monastic Order. This organization was to be an association of convenience for men – and in due course for women – seeking as autonomous individuals to make progress towards their own salvation, whether the ultimate gnosis would be attained in this or a future life. On ordination as monks and nuns, men and women shed all their social ties and ascriptions, even their families. They were their own company, sons and daughters of the Buddha.

The position of the monastic Order in Buddhism is even more dominant than that of the church in Christianity. Buddhists believed that where the Order dies out, Buddhism itself is dead. This is for two reasons. Firstly, Buddhists have traditionally believed that for a layman to attain salvation is virtually impossible; it just is not practically feasible. Secondly, it is the Order that preserves the scriptures; without the scriptures the true Doctrine will soon be forgotten, and so for want of a guide no one will be able to attain salvation.

This view realistically recognizes that the Buddha's saving Doctrine is difficult and abstruse. At another level, as a moral message to the laity, Buddhism has proved simple and appealing. Its supremely civilized ethos of benevolence, honesty and self-control appealed to merchants and rapidly spread along trade routes. Buddhism is not tied to community or locality, but is a universalistic religion residing in men's hearts. The Order requires a broad lay base both as a recruiting ground and for its material support. Only a few, perhaps, can bring themselves to renounce the world. The material support of a few monks and novices is normally not beyond the resources of any village, so that it is as a 'donor' that the average lay villager sees himself or herself as doing something positively Buddhist. But the large monasteries which could serve as centres of Buddhist learning usually depended on the wealth, whether derived from trade or from land, which is concentrated in cities. History has shown the importance for the Order of the favour of kings and governments.

Thus, however fast Buddhism might travel, Buddhists do not consider that it has taken root in a country until the Order is established there. We may add that for reasons not peculiar to Buddhism it is at the great monastic centres that Buddhism remains most recognizably Buddhism; the further one travels from court, capital and monastic university the greater will be the influence of the local culture of a country to which Buddhism, an Indian religion, comes as an alien import. Buddhist influence has been vast in extent, but sometimes thinly spread.

In 1877 the Society for Promoting Christian Knowledge published *Buddhism* by T. W. Rhys Davids, the first scholarly book on the subject in English, many times reprinted and still worth reading. The first chapter begins:

> Several writers have commenced their remarks on Buddhism by reminding their readers of the enormous number of its adherents; and it is, indeed, a most striking fact, that the living Buddhists far outnumber the followers of the Roman Church, the Greek Church, and all other Christian Churches put together. From such summary statements, however, great misconceptions may possibly arise, quite apart from the fact that numbers are no test of truth, but rather the contrary. Before comparing the numbers of Christians and Buddhists, it is necessary to decide, not only what Christianity is, and what is Buddhism; but also, as regards the Buddhists, whether a firm belief in one religion should or should not, as far as statistics are concerned, be nullified by an equally firm belief in another. The numbers are only interesting in so far as they afford a very rough test of the influence which Buddhism has had in the development of the human race.

Rhys Davids then estimates that of approximately 1¼ billion people in the world, 500 million or 40 per cent were Buddhists, as against 20 per cent Christians and 12½ per cent Muslims. He immediately adds that these figures 'are vitiated by the attempt to class each man's religion under one word'. We repeat them here merely to remind the reader that the Buddhist Order has been one of the most enduring and most influential institutions in human history.

To give an idea of the part that the Order has played in history and culture is the aim of this book. This project is an analogue to describing 'the world of Islam'. There is no 'world of Buddhism' in the sense that there is a 'world' of Islam or of Christianity, for two reasons. The first, as Rhys Davids indicated, is the attitude and relation of Buddhism to other religions. Since Buddhism concerns itself only with salvation, and defines that as escape from the cycle of rebirth, it has no axe to grind with any religion which has other concerns. In Asian countries Buddhism has thus coexisted with other religious systems; the best-known are the Confucianism and Taoism of China and the Shintoism of Japan, but the statement is just as true of Southeast Asia. Nor is Buddhism's capacity to tolerate other religions confined to those which deal mainly with life in this world. Sri Lankan Buddhists infuriated early missionaries by raising no objection to the Christian veneration of Jesus, denying only that one's stay in heaven can be forever and that one can be saved by God. Rhys Davids wrote of them: 'many . . . take their oaths in court as Christians, and most of them believe also in devil-worship, and in the power of the stars. Their whole belief is not Buddhist; many of their ideas are altogether outside of Buddhism; their minds do not run only on Buddhist lines' (*Buddhism*, p. 7). Thus Buddhism, though of paramount importance in various countries at various times, shares territory with other religions.

The second reason is related. Buddhism as such is not about this world. Such spheres of human activity as the arts and sciences are not part of its concerns. The concern of Buddhism is the welfare of all living beings, but the material aspects of that welfare have a purely moral purpose: men whose families are starving cannot be expected to be virtuous, let alone to meditate. It is even difficult to feel confident that there is such a thing as a Buddhist society. Spread by traders and protected by kings, through most of its history Buddhism has flourished among peasants; indeed, most of the chapters in this book deal with rice-growing agricultural economies. Do these societies where Buddhism has taken root have less in common with other agrarian but non-Buddhist cultures than they do with Japanese industrial society? No: if Buddhism can be socially located, it is in the monastery, where the Doctrine is kept alive.

The fortunes of Buddhism as a historical phenomenon, then, are the fortunes of the Order. This book follows them through time and space, from the founding of the Order in north-eastern India 2,500 years ago to contemporary America, attempting in its arrangement to combine the historical and geographical dimensions. For more than a thousand years Buddhism spread through Asia, travelling first south, then mainly north and east. By the time it reached Japan it was declining in India, and when Thailand, now one of the most thoroughly Buddhist countries, was converted, in the 14th century, Buddhism no longer existed in northern India; Muslim invaders had extinguished it by sacking the monasteries. In this century the Order has all but disappeared from China, been brutally suppressed in Tibet, shown new life in India, and established its first monasteries in the New World.

Throughout this period, about as long as European recorded history, and in so many different countries and cultures, the Order has preserved its essential organizational features and its ultimate purpose – the salvation of its members. But of course the monastery is a human institution; monks and nuns are not abstract embodiments of Buddhist principles but living people who are Buddhists. Very few are exempt from secular concerns; some have made great contributions to secular culture.

The need to preserve and spread the Doctrine has brought literacy to millions and was responsible for the invention of printing. Monks and nuns, some of them among the most educated and cultivated members of their societies, have been active in every field of artistic and intellectual endeavour. Not all members of the Order have lived up to its ideals, for men and women are subject to desire and ignorance. Some have become involved in the worlds of politics and commerce. In Tibet monks have been rulers; in China monasteries have been markets; in Japan there have even been soldier-monks. The history of the Order is a varied subject, and we have asked our contributors to deal with each area as seems appropriate to the topic, so as to give some idea of that variety. But however varied their actual behaviour, the sons and daughters of the Buddha represent an ideal. Their goal is invisible, its attainment a private experience. This book can only illustrate some of their achievements along the way.

The background to Buddhism

Buddhism is a way to salvation which is open to all and depends for its attainment neither on faith nor on divine grace, but only on understanding 'the way things really are'. Such understanding, it says, can be achieved only after careful moral and psychological preparation. Salvation consists in a state of blissful calm so long as this life lasts and no rebirth when it comes to an end. This goal is something for individuals to aim at and reach, and is essentially independent of culture. However, in its understanding of the world (which the true Buddhist wishes ultimately to leave) Buddhism has carried on its journey through history a certain amount of cultural baggage from its Indian origin. The most important item in this baggage is Buddhism's central institution, its monastic Order. Both this and other features of Buddhism can best be appreciated with some knowledge of their Indian antecedents. This section will therefore introduce some basic Buddhist concepts, essential elements in the Buddhist view of 'the way things really are', by briefly explaining the context in which Gautama the Buddha preached.

Gautama Buddha was born on the fringe of Indian civilization, on the Nepalese side of the present frontier between India and Nepal, in the 6th or 5th century BC – we cannot be sure just when. Nearly a thousand years earlier, nomads speaking an Indo-Aryan language, an early form of Sanskrit, had entered the Indian subcontinent from the north-west, probably through what is now Afghanistan. They slowly spread down through the Punjab into north-central India and gradually took to stock-keeping and then to agriculture. They settled into villages and somehow co-existed and amalgamated with the local population.

The society of these settlers was stratified into hereditary status groups who were normally not allowed to intermarry. The highest status was that of Brahmin. Brahmins were 'gods on earth', and only they had the right to officiate in the sacrificial cult they brought with them and continued to elaborate for several centuries. There were certainly other cultures in India at the time, and other religious beliefs and practices, but we only know about the Brahmins because only they composed texts. Brahminism, as we now call it, was the only articulated ideology. In their village society, Brahmins practised domestic rituals for themselves and for high-status non-Brahmins, and more public rituals for the local rulers to legitimize and magically sustain their rule.

The bulk of the early brahminical texts preserved (I refer not to the earliest one, the *Ṛg Veda*, but to texts dating approximately from 1000 to 500 BC) speculate on the meanings of the rites they prescribe. Those speculations are of crucial importance for the history of all Indian religions, including those, like Buddhism, which reacted against them. In brahminical ideology, the ritual action of the fire sacrifice is the prototype of *all* meaningful or significant action. The Sanskrit word for it is *karman*. Why does sacrifice work? Because every *karman* has its consequences, results which come about through a causation of which the operation is invisible but built into the system of the universe. No Indian religion was ever to lose this idea of *karman*.

The original sacrifice, said the Brahmins, was of the creator-god sacrificing himself – for there was nothing else to sacrifice. That sacrifice sustained the cosmos. All subsequent sacrifices have the same function of sustaining the world, and indeed attempt to replicate the original sacrifice, except that the mortal human performing a sacrifice substitutes other things for his own person as offerings. There is a detailed religious equivalence between the parts of the sacrifice, the parts of the (human) sacrificer, and the parts of the cosmos. The latter pair is familiar in many cultures as equivalence between microcosm and macrocosm. The brahminical texts evolved the doctrine that the essence of success in the sacrifice (and hence in life in general) lay not so much in correct ritual action – though that too was essential – as in understanding the esoteric equivalences which were presented as the rationale for the ritual.

The creator-god, the original sacrificer, was sometimes seen as a personification of the spirit infusing the universe, a kind of primal universal soul, immanent in everything. (This doctrine veered between pantheism and monism.) Similarly, man too had an eternal essence, which resided in the space within his heart. The principle of equivalence between microcosm and macrocosm revealed in the later texts (called *Upaniṣads*) that one's individual soul was the same as the soul of the universe. Realizing this secret would lead to some kind of bliss (as well as power) in this life; at death the soul of the enlightened man was physically reabsorbed into the soul of the universe, thus reverting to its true nature.

Doctrines about what happened after death had evolved slowly. At first, the life well led (for the Brahmin, correct sacrifice) was thought to result in an afterlife in heaven. Then came the idea that the next life too was transient. Probably not very long before the Buddha came the notion of *saṃsāra*, which literally means 'keeping going': perpetual rebirth. The arena for these endless rebirths became a complex universe with many heavens above us and many hells below us. The good went to heaven, but not forever. One could only avoid rebirth by the gnosis which caused one's individual soul to be reabsorbed at death into the ground of the universe.

The Brahmin was normally a householder, a married man sacrificing daily in the fire of his own hearth. He was also a villager, who by his rites maintained a village-centred universe. The system of that universe was called *dharma*. *Dharma* designates at once the way things are and the way they have to be; ultimately those two must coincide. Everyone and indeed everything in the world has its station. It is as much the *dharma* of the sun to shine and the grass to grow and be eaten by cattle as it is the *dharma* of the Brahmin to perform rites and of his wife to cook his dinner.

But there were also holy men (and women?) outside this village world. Whether the first of them were dropouts from the social system or rather intruders from another culture we do not know. They were celibate wanderers, without families or other social ties, playing little or no part in the economy as either producers or consumers. Some of them went naked. They kept no fire and so could play no part in sacrifice as either patron or officiant.

The Buddha was such an outsider. Certainly he chose 'to leave home for homelessness' and encouraged his followers to do the same. Maybe he was also predisposed to this form of religious life by coming from a society on the margin of brahminical civilization. He began his very first sermon, *The Turning of the Wheel of the Law*, by saying: 'Avoid these two extremes: attachment to the pleasures of the senses, which is low and vulgar, and attachment to self-mortification, which is painful; both are unprofitable.' He goes on to characterize his own way as the Middle Way. This term came to have several applications in Buddhism, but the first was to a mean between the sensual life of the ordinary householder, perhaps exemplified by the village Brahmin, and the extreme asceticism of other religious wanderers, exemplified by such contemporary sects as the Jains. The Buddhist Order institutionalizes that Middle Way: Buddhist monks and nuns are to lead a life of simplicity but not of actual discomfort.

In intellectual terms we could see the Buddha's most fundamental move as a reinterpretation of *karman*. Though the *Upaniṣads* had perhaps recently begun to generalize the concept of *karman* from ritual to ethics, it remained primarily an *act*, the quality of which depended on context: what was right for one man to do was wrong for another. The Buddha declared *karman* to be purely an ethical matter, of thought, word or deed; and the quality of a *karman*, good or bad, virtuous or evil, lay solely in the intention behind it. The quality of an act depended only on the motive, regardless of who did it. The Buddha's ethic was thus a simple moral dualism, applicable to all beings (including animals, gods and demons).

This intellectual move interlocked with a social attitude. The Buddha denied all authority to the Brahmins and their scriptures. Brahminical rites – indeed all rites – were useless and pointless. He ridiculed both the idea of an omnipotent creator-god and that of a cosmic soul (the impersonal form of the same idea), and directed his analysis to showing that man too had no soul.

At the same time, he left much of the brahminical world-view in place. He accepted most of the detail of its cosmology, including the gods, denying only their ultimacy. He also accepted the reality of its social world, including the existence of the caste system, denying only the latter's relevance to salvation. Caste, a social creation, could be avoided by leaving society and joining his Order. He accepted also that a life of action (*karman*) in the normal social world of the home and village would lead you to a good or bad rebirth somewhere in the world, and that the only escape from *saṃsāra* lay in a gnosis to be achieved by understanding an essential Truth. He even called that Truth, the system of the universe as he had understood it, the Dharma. Only his Truth was objective, involving the same duties and the same realization for all.

Moreover, though he did not put it in this way himself, the historian can see in the Buddha's teaching an important trace of the brahminical equivalence between microcosm and macrocosm. Where the Brahmin had to discern the true identity between his own soul and the world soul, for the Buddha the emptiness in the centre of man – his 'no soul', *nairātmya* – corresponded on the macrocosmic level to the lack of any supreme omniscient god and indeed to the absence of any religious significance in the world as such. Thus it is no chance that when Buddhists took to philosophy in ancient India their attention rapidly shifted from the *nairātmya* of the individual to the *nairātmya* of everything in the world.

As Steven Collins has shown, even the Buddha's metaphor for salvation was an answer to Brahmin symbolism. Fire, always negative in Buddhism, symbolizes both the passions and the Brahmins' sacrificial fire. The latter one leaves behind on leaving home. One's goal is Nirvāṇa, which means 'blowing out': the blowing out of the fires of greed, hatred and delusion. As for the Brahmin, release is in two stages: after extinguishing the fires of passion one lives in peace till the fire of one's life force has no more fuel to burn.

The Three Jewels

We have been talking of 'Buddhism' as if the term were unproblematic. But of course the Buddha did not think of himself as founding 'Buddhism' and there is no word in his language which that term translates. He saw himself as simply preaching the Dharma. How are we to translate this word? As explained above, Dharma both describes a state of affairs and is a programme for action: since the world is fleeting, unsatisfactory and devoid of any abiding essence we must hasten to put out the fires of passion and find the coolness of release. Like 'natural law' (a concept now obsolescent in the West), the Dharma is both prescriptive and descriptive. To stress its normative aspect we can translate it 'Law'; to stress its veridicial aspect we can translate it 'Truth'; to stress that it is what the Buddha taught and Buddhists believe we can translate it 'Doctrine'. We may warn the reader that all this applies only to Dharma in the singular, which we are spelling with a capital letter; unfortunately the Sanskrit word has many other meanings too.

The reader of the first part of this section may still not be satisfied. If Buddhism is so accommodating and Buddhists may believe and practise so many different things, how do we know who is a Buddhist?

The answer is that a Buddhist is anyone who 'takes refuge' in the Three Jewels: the Buddha, the Dharma, the Sangha. 'Taking refuge' means that the Buddhist declares his reliance on these three things (hence also known as the 'Three Refuges') for release from the suffering inherent in life as we know it. For worldly goals he may turn elsewhere – to the gods, the stars, to magic or modern science – but for salvation he relies on the Buddha, the Dharma and the Sangha.

None of these three terms is quite simple to explain. Buddha means 'Enlightened' and as well as a description is here a title; for further detail see the next chapter. Dharma is discussed above. The term Sangha we have so far been translating as 'Order', though 'Community' might be closer to its original meaning. This requires explanation.

In the earliest Buddhist scriptures the term Sangha had two main uses. In its wider sense, it referred to all who had accepted the basic premises of the Dharma; we might say to all Buddhists. This was the 'fourfold Sangha': monks, nuns, laymen and laywomen. It is however the narrower sense which has become common and will be used in this book: the Sangha consists of all those ordained, both monks and nuns. In fact in the Theravāda Buddhist countries (Sri Lanka and most of continental Southeast Asia) the Order of nuns in the strict sense has died out. There are women in those countries who lead cloistered lives and behave like nuns, but for lack of a valid ordination tradition they remain outside the Sangha in the usual, strict sense. In those countries, therefore, the term Sangha is generally understood to refer only to monks and male novices. We do not know exactly why or when the Order of nuns disappeared from medieval Ceylon. Nuns are formally subordinate to monks in the Order; but their contribution to Buddhist life and to Buddhist spirituality was great in ancient times, just as it remains important in Mahāyāna countries today.

The Sangha in history

Our opening paragraphs may have warned the reader that Buddhism is so different from the religions with which we are familiar in the West that to understand it we may need to abandon some assumptions about what a religion is and how its adherents behave. The matter of exclusive allegiance is a case in point. Another is the 'no soul' doctrine: some Westerners have found this so strange that they have asserted that Buddhism is not a religion at all, but a philosophy. Perhaps they have been misled by Buddhism's ability to co-exist with other religions. But anyone who has seen a Buddhist society will find the proposition that Buddhism is not a religion ludicrous. If a way to salvation is not a religion, what is?

A further assumption we must jettison is that there must be a connection between doctrine and religious organization. Membership of a Christian sect or denomination is defined by a shared body of belief. Not so with the Sangha. As will be more thoroughly explained below (pp. 77–89), Buddhist sects in the strict sense are produced only by fissure in the monastic Order, and fissure occurs through differences in practice, not in doctrine or belief. Strictly speaking, there is no heresy: no Buddhist can be expelled from the Order – let alone from the wider community of Buddhists – for holding an unpopular opinion. But certain *acts* merit, indeed entail, expulsion. The Christian church split over whether the Holy Ghost proceeds from the Father or the Father *and* the Son. That could not happen in Buddhism. But the Buddhist Order has divided over whether to shave the eyebrows or whether to wear the outer robe over one shoulder or both. The social psychologist may surmise that either kind of quarrel and rupture may be reduced to a question of loyalties, that the same kind of group dynamics is at play everywhere, whether articulated in terms of orthodoxy, as in the West, or of orthopraxy, as in the East; but if we turn from looking at motives to looking at consequences we find the results very different.

The Buddhist Order is truly one of monks and nuns, not of priests. The distinction between monk and priest was clear in early Christianity, but today so many monks are also ordained as priests that even some Christians are hazy about it. A monk has joined an organization and accepted its discipline in order to devote his life to the search for his own salvation. A priest is one whose training and commitment entitle him to perform religious services (especially sacraments) for others. Monks tend to seclusion, whereas priests must have frequent contact with those they serve. The priest fulfils essentially a functional role; a monk *per se* has no function.

When Christian missionaries encountered Buddhist monks, they often criticized them for not behaving like priests. In 1892 the Anglican bishop of Colombo reported with evident scorn on his visit to a rural Sinhalese monastery where he talked to a villager: 'We ask whether the monk does any good in the place: and the answer is, "No, why should he?"' Was it because Buddhist monasteries are scattered through the Sri Lankan countryside rather like village churches in

Europe that Bishop Copleston expected the monks to behave like country parsons?

Monks preserve Buddhism; but it is not their function to provide religious services to the laity. The life crises of Buddhists (birth, puberty, marriage) are mostly either treated as secular events or solemnized by specialists in the religious systems which co-exist locally with Buddhism. There are however quite a few exceptions to this general principle. The major one is death: Buddhist monks everywhere officiate at funerals. That is no doubt because death is at the centre of Buddhist religious awareness, so that death ceremonies are the ideal occasion for preaching.

Acquaintance with the Dharma through preaching and other forms of teaching is what the monks directly give the laity in return for their material upkeep. This 'gift of the Doctrine' is held infinitely to outweigh any possible physical gift, which is disparagingly referred to as 'the gift of raw flesh'. Yet monks also confer benefit on the laity by the mere fact of being available as recipients for generosity – a priestly function if you like, for it is directly inherited from the Brahmin. The Sangha is described as 'the supreme field of merit'; a gift sown there will yield the greatest harvest.

Buddhism is sometimes presented in the West as if the religion of the laity on the one hand and of the clergy on the other were discontinuous, completely separate. That is wrong. Morality is the prerequisite for spiritual progress, and doctrine holds that the morality of an act lies in its intention. Generosity is considered the basis of morality. Laity and clergy must all practise generosity to the best of their ability and the more generous they are in spirit, the purer their minds will become. But it must be admitted that in practice this doctrine is sometimes compromised. Givers – not necessarily lay givers – do sometimes hope by well-placed gifts to buy a seat in heaven or a prosperous rebirth on earth. Not everyone is immediately interested in Nirvāṇa.

Are the relative roles of Sangha and laity the same in all kinds of Buddhism? The reader will see in this book that there is some variation from country to country; yet in general the relation we have described holds for Mahāyāna as well as for Theravāda countries. Early Mahāyāna seems to have been a monastic development. The predominance of the Sangha has been compromised in just two kinds of Buddhism. In tantric Buddhism, a form of Mahāyāna which began round the middle of the first millennium AD, the structural position of the Sangha somewhat changes. The second great change has begun in our century, for the most part very recently, with the first prolonged contact between Buddhism and modern urban society.

As will be explained below, the term *tantra* refers primarily to a ritual system which, with accompanying meditative practice, is thought by its practitioners to be the most rapid and efficacious means to salvation. What concerns us here is that *tantra* introduced into Buddhism (from Hinduism) a new system of statuses. Access to tantric rituals and the meditations based on them is given by initiation (*dīkṣā*), or rather by a graded series of initiations, imparted by teacher to pupil. Laymen too may be initiated and in due course themselves become teachers and initiators; and women may be hierarchically superior to men of the same social category; *tantra* thus has a different status system from earlier Buddhism, and one which on the ground may cross-cut the clerical/lay distinction.

Though most tantric rituals have no sexual component, their theory revolves round a central sexual metaphor, which on certain solemn occasions is put into literal practice. In Buddhist *tantra*, the metaphor is that skilful Means (*upāya*) – which in Sanskrit is a masculine noun – penetrates Wisdom (*prajñā*) – which in Sanskrit is feminine – to attain the Great Bliss of Enlightenment: the Wisdom which is the subject and content of the early Mahāyāna scriptures is personified, not only at the theoretical level. To enact the ritual which concretizes this experimence the practitioner, who may be and often is a monk or nun, has intercourse with a partner. Since in the traditional Discipline sexual intercourse is a disbarring offence, non-tantrics find this scandalous. In some tantric traditions monks do not literally have female partners or enact sexual rites; in others they do. Outsiders often refer to these female partners as 'wives', but the partners themselves do not consider that they are 'married', and their own languages (e.g., Newari, Tibetan) preserve the distinction. There can be no such thing as a married monk or nun. On the other hand, this tantric practice has led in Tibet to a further stage of development: there are men who live much of the time as married laymen, and at certain regular times go to monasteries and behave like traditional monks. In this case we find blurred the distinction between monk and layman which is so clear elsewhere. The final stage of this development may be observed in Nepal; among the Newari no monks remain, only tantric masters (*vajrācārya*).

The Sangha is also less important in the Buddhism of contemporary Japan. In that country a powerful movement, Amidism, has preached that salvation lies in faith alone and all rules of conduct are irrelevant. This has led to a preponderance of married clergy, a development which accentuated the Japanese tendency for monks to assume a priestly role concerned with this life. Some of the modern Japanese Buddhist sects are lay movements with no place for the professional religious specialist, whether monk or priest. The individualism characteristic of economically developed, urbanized societies probably leads everywhere (first among the middle class) to greater stress on the responsibility of each adherent and less on the role of a religious élite. Thus there are signs that in the West too Buddhist laymen are not leaving religious leadership to the Sangha, and we may perhaps expect lay Buddhists to play a more important part in every Buddhist society if economic growth continues.

The Path to Enlightenment

1

The Buddha, His Teachings and His Sangha

The Buddha, the Dharma and the Sangha constitute Buddhism. They are the Three Jewels, the Three Refuges of every Buddhist.

The Buddha was called Gautama and known as Śākyamuni, 'the Śākyan sage'. Born among the Śākya people in what is now Nepal in the middle of the 1st millennium BC, he was a prince who was brought up in sheltered luxury, married and had a son. When he became aware of old age, disease and death he left home for the forest and became an ascetic. But extreme asceticism brought him no insight. Only on taking proper food again did he realize the Truth of the Middle Way. Thus, at the age of 35, he became Enlightened, which is what 'Buddha' means. He realized *Nirvāṇa*, the 'blowing out' of greed, hatred and delusion. He thus no longer clung to existence or to the notion that he had an enduring essence. There was nothing left of him to be reborn. His death, at the age of 80, was the mere cessation of his body, the Final Nirvāṇa.

The Buddha was no god, merely a man who has seen the Truth, the Dharma. In the whole world, populated with all kinds of beings who are endlessly reborn – even gods included – nobody could help him to find salvation. It was exclusively by his own efforts that he discovered the Truth that everything, from men to mountains, is unsatisfactory, impermanent and devoid of enduring essence.

The Buddha's first sermon was the Turning of the Wheel of the Doctrine. In it he formulated his discovery as Four Noble Truths: all is suffering; suffering has a cause: desire; suffering can be ended; there is an eight-stage path to end it. In a later formulation, the path leads from morality to meditation, from meditation to wisdom.

To traverse this path is barely possible for one who has to live in this world, with its economic cares and emotional distractions. Therefore the Buddha institutionalized his 'Middle Way' between luxury and asceticism by founding a monastic order, the Sangha. In that respect he followed the example of contemporaries who lived as wandering ascetics, alone or in small groups. The members of the Buddhist Sangha, monks and nuns, work for their own salvation, but they also preserve the Buddha's Dharma so that others can follow it.

The Three Jewels – Buddha, Dharma and Sangha – are symbolized in this detail from a Tibetan *tanka*, painted on cloth. The central figure is Śākyamuni, the Buddha, the Enlightened One. Above him flowers the lotus, a common symbol of the Doctrine. And from the lotus rises a small figure of a monk, the Sangha, the means by which mankind participates in the Dharma. The Buddha is himself shown holding a begging bowl and there are other monks on either side. 'The Buddha is the great physician; the Dharma is the remedy; the Sangha is the nurse who administers the remedy.' (1)

The Three Jewels shown in wheel form. The wheel itself is a symbol of the Dharma in its universality and power. This relief is from Gandhāra in modern Pakistan, where Greek cultural influences met Indian. (2)

Accounts of the Buddha's life were handed down in oral tradition for several centuries but the first written versions date back only to the 1st century BC. Certain episodes were soon regarded as key events. Four were signalized by earthquakes: his birth, Enlightenment, first sermon and death. Before his birth, according to legend, his mother Queen Māyā dreamed that her son entered her womb in the form of a white elephant, as shown in this 2nd-century BC relief (*below*) from Bhārhut. (3)

The hidden Buddha

For some time after the Buddha's Final Nirvāṇa, Buddhists out of respect avoided depicting him. In the iconography of the time the presence of the Buddha or of the Bodhisattva (the future Buddha) is left to be inferred from the scene depicted.

Haunted by his discovery of old age, disease and death, Śākyamuni decided one night to renounce his comfortable and secure life and live as a religious mendicant seeking wisdom in meditation. A relief from Amarāvatī portrays the moment when he leaves through the ceremonial gateway of the palace. The horse is shown riderless, but a god holds a royal umbrella over the place where the Buddha is. (4)

Preaching, Enlightenment and Final Nirvāṇa are all represented here through symbols. The Buddha's Enlightenment (*above*) is signalled by showing the tree under which he sat when attaining it. This tree is known as the Bodhi (or Bo) tree, the 'Enlightenment' tree. Here is shown the seat on which he attained Enlightenment, with his footprints below it. *Above right:* the Buddha's first sermon, preached in a deer park at Benares. The wheel symbolizes the Dharma, and so the Buddha himself. The same imagery is used in another relief (*below*) from Nālandā. His Final Nirvāṇa (*below left*) took place as he lay under trees flowering out of season while the gods rained garlands. At his cremation the pyre was miraculously quenched by water rising from the ground. (5–8)

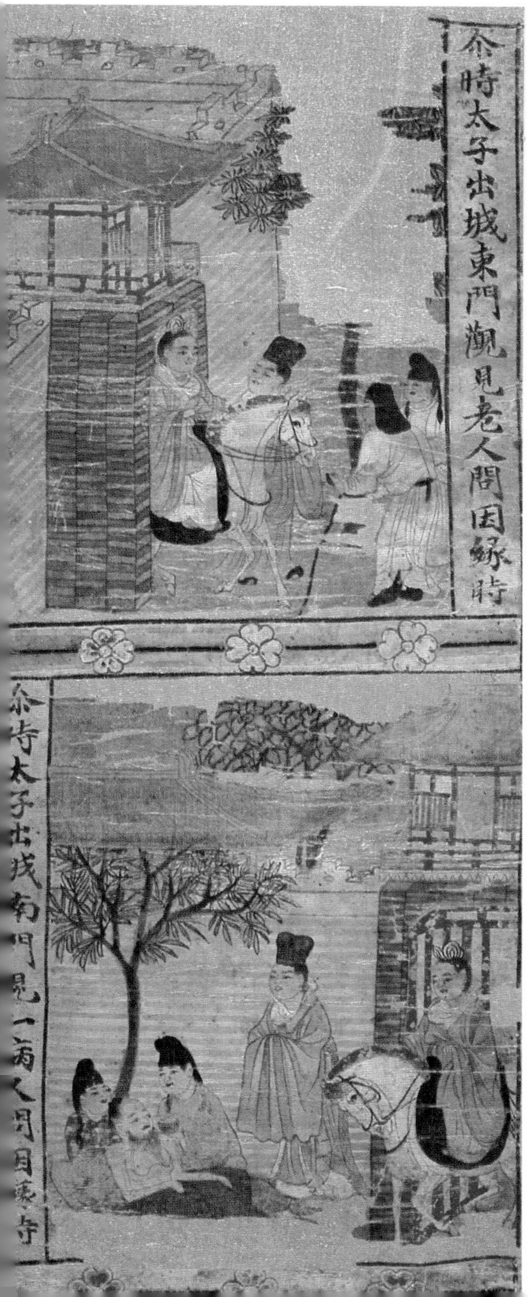

The Buddha made manifest

As Buddhism spread to almost all of Asia north and east of India, scenes from the Buddha's life were represented with increasing realism and drama.

The birth of Śākyamuni (*opposite*): from Tibet comes this crowded and exuberant scene. At the top appears the white elephant who entered the womb of Queen Māyā, as shown on the previous page. In the centre Queen Māyā stands, holding a sal tree with her right hand. The Buddha is born from her right side. He is received by the greatest gods of his time, Brahma and Indra, and takes his first steps on lotus blossoms. (9)

The Bodhisattva (the future Buddha) leaves his palace in order to devote himself to the search for Enlightenment, a 19th-century painting from Burma. In the foreground Śākyamuni takes a last look at his sleeping wife and son. In the background he is riding away followed by his attendant Channa, with celestial beings holding the horse's hooves so that they shall not wake the sleeping guards. (10)

The Bodhisattva encounters old age and sickness (*left*), from a Chinese painting on silk. In each scene he is shown leaving his palace attended by servants, coming first upon an old man with a stick and then upon a sick man lying on the ground. (11)

Enlightenment came to Śākyamuni after six years of asceticism, as he sat under the tree which was to become known as the Bodhi tree near Gayā. This was the supreme moment when he achieved Buddhahood, and it is understandably the most frequently chosen for painting and sculpture at all levels. This postcard is typical of the religious art available in Thailand today. (12)

Final Nirvāṇa

For forty-five years after his Enlightenment the Buddha travelled through the region of the middle Ganges explaining his Doctrine and founding religious communities. At the age of 80 he died 'like a flame which goes out through lack of fuel'.

The Buddha's death was not like the death of unenlightened beings, for whom it is only one more stage in the cycle of rebirth and suffering. Having, after innumerable existences in divine, human and animal form, attained Enlightenment, he was released from that cycle. What happens to an enlightened person after death is a question the Buddha refused to answer. None of the categories of human thought apply to the Tathāgata, the 'Perfect One', and therefore this question makes no sense.

The recorded sayings of early monks and nuns unmistakably show that Nirvāṇa is experienced as a state of ineffable calm, a joyous tranquillity. The Buddha said: 'There is a sphere which is neither earth, nor water, nor fire, nor air, which is not the sphere of the infinity of space, nor the sphere of the infinity of consciousness, the sphere of nothingness, the sphere of neither perception nor non-perception, which is neither this world nor the other world, neither sun nor moon. I deny that it is coming or going, enduring, death or birth. It is only the end of suffering.' (*Udāna* 80)

It is one of the wonders of Buddhist art that painters and sculptors have succeeded in conveying this ineffable state through the image of the Buddha meditating on his deathbed. Among the most renowned masterpieces is this rock-carving in the caves of Ajaṇṭā, *c.* 6th century AD. (13)

The fleeting world

The transience of the body and of physical pleasures is a commonplace of all mystics, East and West. Buddhists hold that absolutely everything is transient, arising from prior causes, only to fall away again. The aim of meditation is to penetrate the apparent solidity of the world and see things 'as they really are' – unsatisfactory, impermanent, devoid of essence.

The path of earthly life which ends in death is reproduced in this 'meditation walk', used by Sri Lankan monks today. (15)

Death was one of the three experiences (with disease and old age) that persuaded the Bodhisattva to abandon the pursuit of earthly happiness and search instead for truth. As the end to life, it is paradigmatic for the transience of all joys. *Left:* monk meditating on a skull, a wall-painting from Qizil, Central Asia, *c.* AD 500. (14)

The dancers of Bhutan perform a sort of *danse macabre*, wearing skull masks, beating drums and clashing cymbals, to express death's universal dominion. The entire world of our normal experience is held to be under the sway of Death and Desire, which are but two sides of the same coin. (16)

Child monks

Although a boy may be placed in the care of a monastery with the idea that he will become a monk, no formal step will be taken until he is about eight, when the lower ordination, a ceremony called Going Forth, takes place. The boy is now a novice. Full ordination must wait until he is twenty.

Novices mourn (*below*) over the coffin of the Buddha, an early carving from Gandhāra. (19)

The young disciple is represented in the early Chinese monastic complex of Tun-huang. This painted clay figure dates from the 6th century. *Below:* a novice from Gandhāra, holding the corner of his robe in his left hand. (17, 18)

From Burma comes this appealing sculpture of a novice carrying a begging bowl. It is of marble and dates from the early 19th century. (20)

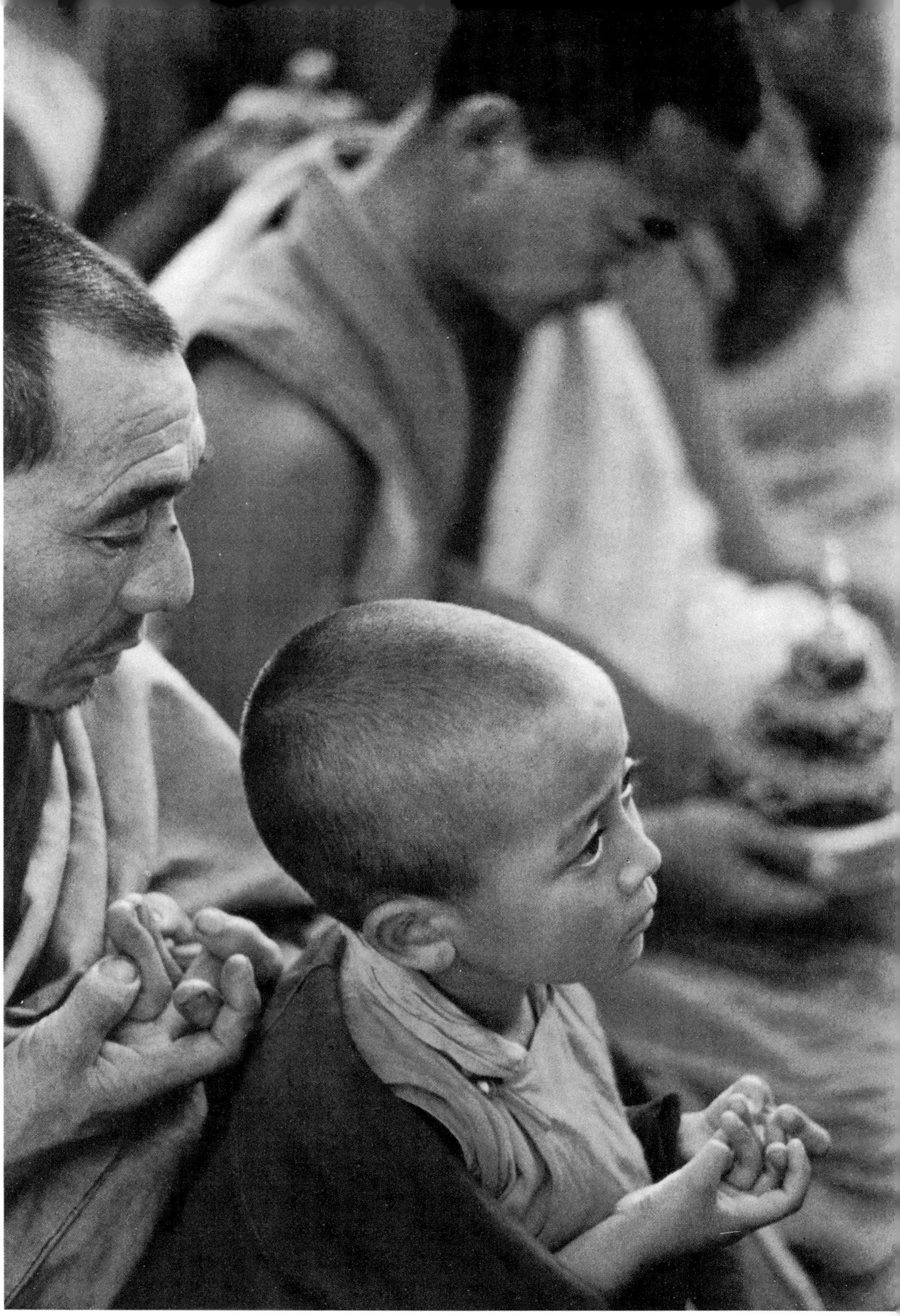

A Tibetan child (*above*) learns one of the hand gestures (*mudrā*) used in prayer and meditation, in this case the so-called '*maṇḍala*' *mudrā* symbolizing the universe. In Tibet the Buddhist doctrine of reincarnation is given a very specific application. Not only is each Dalai Lama thought to be a reincarnation of the last – as well as a manifestation of a bodhisattva – but many other abbots are also seen as reincarnate monks. (21)

The Path and the Wheel

For the Buddhist, the universe is a place of delusion and suffering, in which living beings – who are, if they but knew it, mere collections of 'aggregates', forever fickle and changing – are condemned by their passions to an endless cycle of rebirths.

The upward Path to Enlightenment is represented in this Tibetan mural from the monastery of Likir in terms of child-like simplicity. The elephant is the human spirit, driven along the path by the Discipline whose halter is attentiveness and whose goad is insight. At first the elephant is completely black and is accompanied by worldly concerns, symbolized by a monkey and a hare (on his back). But as they mount, all three change from black to white. (22)

The Buddha's own progress towards his final incarnation entailed an infinite number of previous existences, in which he accumulated moral qualities. At the feet of many previous Buddhas (twenty-four in the Theravāda tradition) he made the resolve to become a Buddha. The series of twenty-four previous Buddhas with 'our' bodhisattva at their feet is depicted in many temples in Sri Lanka. (23)

This Tibetan painting (*opposite*) represents one of the most essential tenets of the Buddha's teaching – the chain of dependent origination (*pratītya-samutpāda*). The outer ring symbolizes the twelve links of this chain. The main register of the circle contains the six spheres of existence – going anticlockwise: the realm of the gods, of the *asuras* or rebel gods, of the ghosts, of the hells hot and cold, of the animal world and finally of the human beings. The half-circles show those who deteriorate spiritually and end in hell, and those who advance towards Nirvāṇa. In the centre are the three cardinal faults: passion (the cock), hatred (the snake) and delusion (the pig). Māra, the personification of death, holds the whole in his grasp. (24)

Transmitting the Doctrine

To memorize, preserve and preach the words of the Buddha are the greatest services a monk performs for others. A monk should not preach unless requested three times, but should give access to the Dharma to any who so ask. Till about a century ago, monks also acted as schoolteachers in Ceylon and Southeast Asia and were the main preservers of high culture in all Buddhist countries. They have lost their monopoly of these roles but some qualify themselves as educators in the modern world.

Śākyamuni himself, in this as in every other respect, provided the model for the monk to imitate, and his preaching pose, with the hands held in the appropriate *mudrā*, is one of his commonest images (*far left:* from Sārnāth, 6th century). A detail from a cave-painting at Qizil in Central Asia, *c.* AD 500 (*left*) gives us a charming incidental story. Rapt in the sermon, a listening cowherd accidentally squashed a frog, but the latter's consciousness was so pure at that moment that he was reborn in heaven, i.e. as a god. (25, 26)

The monks of today continue the preaching tradition both at large public meetings and at small gatherings in temples and houses. *Right:* a sermon in the Namtok monastery, Shan States, Burma; the monk is hiding his face behind a fan so as not to be distracted by women in his congregation or in turn to distract his listeners by over-personalizing his message. *Below right:* a scene in Burma, with the offerings of the laity placed before the monk's chair. (28, 29)

The mission to preach and to convert has inspired epic tales in every Buddhist country. Here (*below*) the Japanese evangelist Ryōnin Shōnin converts people from all classes and walks of life. Ryōnin lived in the 12th century; the painting is of the 14th. (27)

Preserving the word

To guard the Canon of the scripture is perhaps even more important than to preach, since without the scripture there could be no Doctrine. Its translation from Indian languages into the various languages of eastern Asia was a massive task, but essential if Buddhism was to reach new converts.

The great libraries of Tibet have been destroyed, but those of its neighbour Ladakh survive. At Lamayuru (*above*) one still finds shelves of books stored in the traditional way. Each book consists of long narrow strips of paper, written or printed on both sides. They are covered with a silk cloth fastened between two boards of wood. A piece of brocade hangs down with the title and the volume number on it. *Left:* a closer view of an illustrated Tibetan manuscript, written on native paper. (30, 31)

Engraved on marble: to establish a definitive text of the scriptures was the aim of scholars throughout history. In 1871 the devout Burmese King Mindon convened the Fifth Buddhist Council at Mandalay for this purpose. After the texts had been finally verified by this assembly, they were engraved on 729 stelae and erected within the precincts of the Kuthodaw pagoda at Mandalay (*opposite*), where they remain. (32)

Lower Ordination in Burma is a happy and not too solemn occasion. Most children will only spend a week or so in the monastery and will not go on to be full-time adult monks. *Above:* novices about to assume the yellow robe gather in front of a temple; the ceremonial umbrellas allude to Śākyamuni's royal rank. *Below left:* proud fathers carry their young sons to the ceremony where, imitating the Buddha, they will put off their rich clothes and receive the few possessions that a monk is allowed. *Below right:* a boy's head being shaved before ordination. (33, 34, 35)

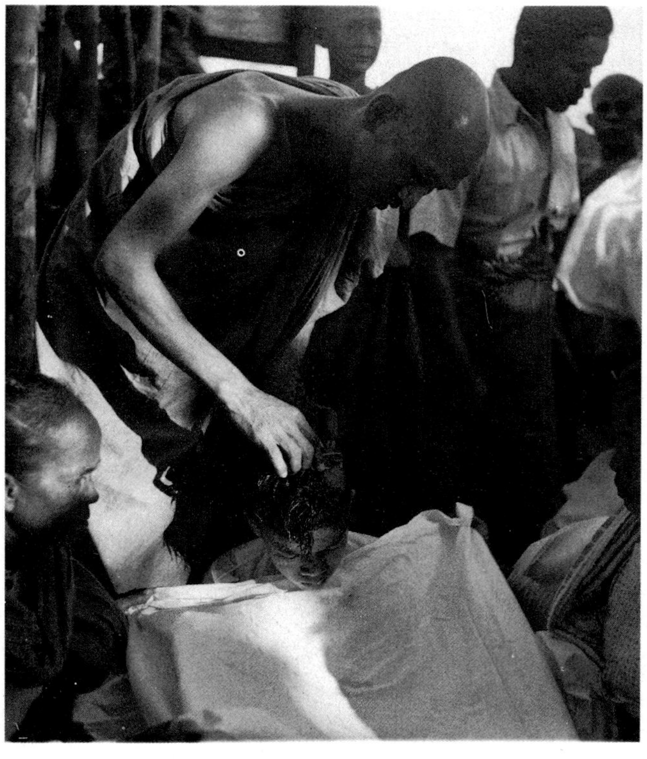

Entering the Sangha

To become a monk should be the final goal of every sincere Theravāda Buddhist, since only through the monastic life can he hope to achieve salvation. Mahāyānists too attach great value to monastic life. First or Lower Ordination (facing page) is normally taken as a child and in Southeast Asia almost all boys expect to spend a few weeks in a monastery. The more serious commitment, the Higher Ordination (this page), takes place on reaching maturity.

Three novices of the 18th century, a wall-painting from an ordination hall in Pagan, Burma. The central figure is praying; those on his left and right hold ordination texts of the type illustrated underneath. This example, with its cover, is 19th-century Burmese. It contains extracts from the Canon used for ceremonies of monastic life such as ordination, bestowal of robes and demarcation of boundaries. (37, 38)

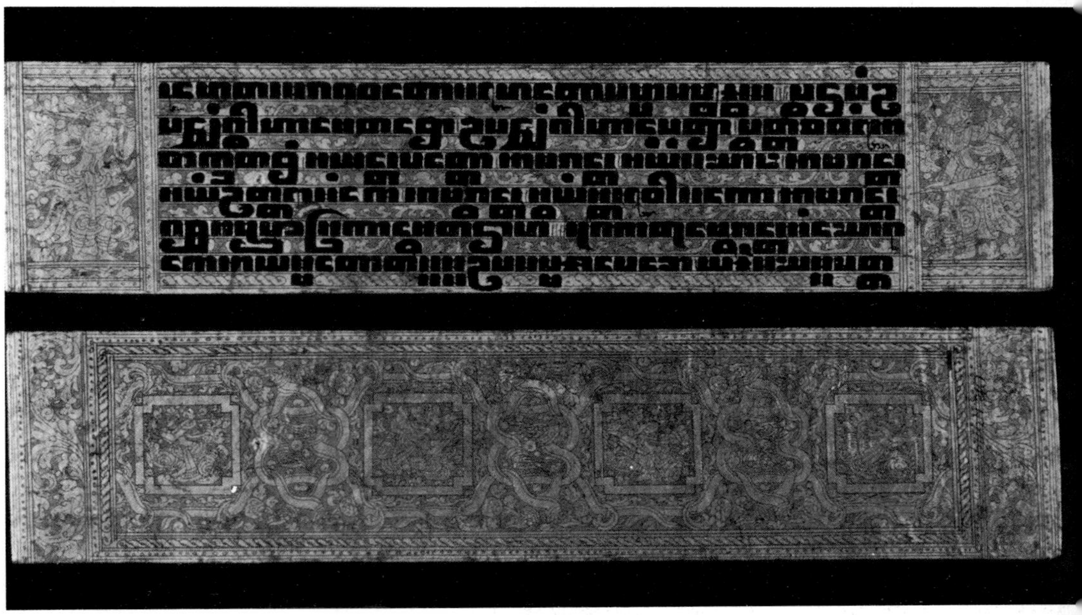

The world and the Sangha. *Below:* a Sri Lankan man wearing his pre-ordination robes, traditional finery of a Kandyan nobleman, which symbolize the luxury he must now abjure. *Below right:* in Thailand, having renounced the world, the monk, wearing the white robe of lay piety, greets his new brothers and receives the saffron robes that he will wear henceforth. (36, 39)

The layman's contribution

In the secular world, surrounded by its cares and temptations, a man can give little attention to spiritual advance. What he can and should do, however, is to lead a moral life. And just as morality is the foundation for Buddhist spirituality, it in its turn is grounded on generosity. The worthiest recipient of generosity, 'the supreme field' in which to sow the seeds of merit, is the Sangha.

The layman gives and the monk returns the gift a thousandfold by preserving the Doctrine and preaching the way to Enlightenment. Incidents in the life of the Buddha showing him accepting gifts are popular subjects for illustration, as also are stories showing the generosity of individual donors. In a Burmese painting (*below*) the Buddha, at the head of a band of disciples, receives alms in his bowl from the same rich merchant who gave him the park which became the first permanent monastery. (40)

The rich give food, money, even monasteries. The life of the Buddha again provides the prototype and examples. This Burmese manuscript (*above*) shows two separate scenes of donation. On the left the Buddha and his disciples are fed, and later receive homage; they sit in a row at the back of the courtyard while gifts are presented in the foreground. (41)

In Rangoon today a woman drops an offering into the bowl of a mendicant monk. She is handing him a small bundle of rice wrapped in a green banana leaf. (44)

The poor contribute whatever they can. Villagers are expected to give something from their own meagre provisions, and to make travelling monks welcome in their homes. These details (*above*) are from a Thai folding book. Monks who rigorously observe the rule live entirely on food they beg each day on alms rounds, but laymen often bring the food to established monasteries and some monasteries even have their own stores. (42, 43)

Within the Sangha

Communal ceremonies (especially the obligatory Confession once a fortnight) knit monasteries together, but personal links between masters and disciples often determine the character of the monastery and the succession of offices.

Monks chanting in the Tibetan monastery of Gyantse. In this photograph taken in the 1930s, when Tibet was still a totally Buddhist state, we can catch a rare glimpse of the community functioning as it had done since the Middle Ages. Note the elaborate decoration of the prayer hall, the books stacked on shelves at the back, the large *maṇḍala* behind them and the young monks with their backs to the camera in the foreground. (45)

Teacher and pupil developed a close spiritual relationship, since only thus could meditation techniques and the higher levels of Buddhist wisdom be transmitted. *Below:* a young monk paying honour to a seated teacher, from a 10th-century Central Asian fresco. (46)

In Korea (*above*), in Thailand (*left*) and in Sri Lanka (*below*) – all over the Buddhist world – the technique of instruction is basically the same. The Thai example is from a 19th-century illustrated manuscript. The Sri Lankan monk on the far right is a 'forest-dweller', a man held in particular esteem for the simplicity of his life and his renunciation of those comforts enjoyed by the monks of urban and village monasteries. (47, 48, 49)

1

The Buddha, His Teachings and His Sangha

ETIENNE LAMOTTE

THE BUDDHA IS ONE OF THOSE exceptional beings who see the truth, expound a doctrine and found a religious order. The Buddha, the Dharma and the Sangha are the Three Jewels in which beings take refuge in order to find deliverance.

The Buddha is the great physician; the Dharma is the remedy; the Sangha is the nurse who administers the remedy. The foundation of a religious order is part of the work of the Buddhas: when the master attains complete Nirvāṇa, he can do nothing more for beings, and his Doctrine would not last long if there were no community to collect and perpetuate it.

The Buddha

The last Buddha to appear in the world for the welfare and happiness of the many and to destroy suffering, disease, old age and death was named Śākyamuni.

According to unanimous tradition, Śākyamuni lived for eighty years, but the date of his Final Nirvāṇa, that is his decease, has still not been established with certainty. Nowadays, the Buddhists of Sri Lanka, Burma, Thailand, Kampuchea and Laos place that Nirvāṇa in the year 543 BC. This date has, however, been rejected by the majority of Western and Indian historians, because the date of the Nirvāṇa is tied to that of the consecration of the Emperor Aśoka, an event which cross-checking with Greek sources enables us to place about 268–267 BC.

Two independent chronologies are used in the old documents: the 'long' chronology which places the Final Nirvāṇa 218 years before Aśoka's consecration, i.e. in 486 BC, and the 'short' chronology which locates the same event 100 years before the consecration, i.e. in 368 BC.

For the sake of simplicity, I shall base myself here on the more generally adopted long chronology, although nowadays there is a tendency drastically to bring forward the date of the Buddha's Nirvāṇa.

The Buddha was born to the noble warrior Śuddhodana and the Princess Māyā, about the year 566 BC, in Kapilavastu, the main town in what is now the Nepalese Terai. He was a member of the Śākya tribe belonging to the Gautama clan. His forename was Siddhārtha ('Aim Attained'), but he was more commonly known as Gautama, or as Śākyamuni, 'the sage of the Śākya tribe'. His followers addressed him as Bhagavat, 'Lord' or 'Blessed One'. He usually referred to himself as Tathāgata, an enigmatic epithet meaning 'he who has gone [to the Truth] in the same way as his predecessors'. Until the night of his Enlightenment which was to make him a Buddha, Śākyamuni was only a bodhisattva, that is, a 'future Buddha'.

His youth passed in comfort and pleasure; he married at the age of sixteen, and his wife, Yaśodharā, bore him a son who received the name of Rāhula.

However, the great mysteries of an existence subject to old age, disease and death filled Śākyamuni with disgust for the world and, like many young people of his time, he resolved to win Immortality (*amṛta*). To his mind, this was not so much a question of eternal survival as of a definitive end to *saṃsāra*, the long series of existences which involve beings in suffering. In 537 BC, at the age of twenty-nine, he secretly left the town of Kapilavastu and adopted the life of a wandering religious mendicant (*parivrājaka*, *śramaṇa*).

Making his way southward, he reached the kingdom of Magadha (now southern Bihar) where King Bimbisāra was then reigning; he studied with two yoga masters and under their direction devoted himself to the practice of meditation and similar techniques which put him in contact with the higher spheres of existence, but these still did not guarantee him Immortality. Disappointed by the teachings of his masters, Śākyamuni decided to apply himself to the 'great effort'; he withdrew to Uruvilvā, where five mendicants came and joined him. For six years (537–532) he devoted himself to strict asceticism, with prolonged

---

The possessions permitted to a monk were laid down by Śākyamuni himself. The earliest list consists of eight items. For monks outside India ('the middle country') the number was increased because of the cold climate. Some items from this larger list of thirteen items are illustrated in this stylized painting from the monastery of Samskar in Ladakh. There are shoes, rugs to sit on, two white towels, robes, a staff, an alms bowl and a filter for straining living organisms from drink in order to avoid taking life. Not shown, but also in this ancient list, are a razor, a needle and thread and a belt. Most modern monks use, of course, a much larger number of requisites in their daily life. (50)

Śākyamuni as an ascetic, his body emaciated by the privations he underwent in the quest for Enlightenment – a stone sculpture from Gandhāra, 2nd century AD. After six years, convinced that such austerities served no purpose, he evolved the doctrine of the Middle Way.

fasting and holding of the breath, which endangered his life. All these efforts were in vain, since such mortification did not even enable him to acquire psychic powers. He therefore gave them up; at which, his five companions left him and went to the Deer park in what is now Sārnāth, near Benares (Vārāṇasī).

Now alone, Śākyamuni was close to his triumph. A substantial meal and a bath in the river Nairañjanā restored his strength. In the evening, he went to Bodh-Gayā and sat down near a fig-tree (called a bodhi tree after his Enlightenment) in order to meditate. He directed his mind no longer towards the heavenly spheres and spheres beyond normal consciousness which his masters had taught him, but to the mysteries of death and rebirth in the world of appearances. During one memorable night (531 BC) he reached that Enlightenment (*bodhi*) which brings Buddhahood, Enlightenment of the higher degree (*abhisaṃbodhi*), supreme and perfect Enlightenment (*anuttarā samyaksaṃbodhi*).

During the watches of that night, Śākyamuni won three knowledges: remembrance of his former lives, knowledge of the birth and death of beings, and the certainty of having finally cast off the ignorance and passion which until then had bound him to the world of becoming and led to successive rebirths. This threefold knowledge brought with it perfect insight into the mechanism of Dependent Origination and Destruction (*pratītya-samutpāda*), the cycle of the causation of all the psycho-physical phenomena of life. The Buddha mentally examined, first forwards and then in reverse, the twelve causes (*nidāna*) or 'links' which condition that origination and destruction, and thus acquired the certainty of having himself escaped from the whirling wheel of rebirths and of living his very last life.

Having continued his meditations at Bodh-Gayā for four (or seven) weeks, the Buddha, enlightened and compassionate, conceived of a doctrine capable of opening the doors to Immortality, of putting an end to suffering and of ensuring peace, Nirvāṇa. This doctrine received the name of Dharma, 'Doctrine' or 'Law', a doctrine of deliverance, not of salvation by any external agency. It is profound, difficult to envisage and difficult to understand; it was not without hesitation, and only after the intervention of the great god Brahmā, that the Buddha decided to expound it. He went back to Benares, to the Deer Park. There, before the five mendicants who had witnessed his mortifications, he expounded his Discourse 'Turning the Wheel of the Doctrine' (*Dharmacakrapravartanasūtra*), in which are set out the Four Noble Truths (*āryasatya*) (see below), a discourse soon followed by a homily on the 'No-Self' (*anātman*) which proclaims the impersonality of all living phenomena of existence: there is no Self, nothing belongs to a Self.

The Discourses at Benares inaugurated the public ministry which the Buddha carried out for forty-five years (531–486). He travelled through the region of the middle Ganges in all directions, expounding the Doctrine, refuting his adversaries, making converts and recruiting those inclined into the religious order of monks (*bhikṣu*) which he had founded as one more of the many religious communities which existed at that time.

Worn out by age and fatigue, the Buddha resolved to relinquish his life forces and, leaving the town of Rājagṛha (Rajgir), by successive stages he reached the town of Kuśinagarī in the Malla country. An attack of dysentery compelled him to stop just outside the town, in the Upavarta Grove. There, lying between two trees, he went through a long series of meditative states and, 'like a flame which goes out through lack of fuel', reached the peace of complete Nirvāṇa. The Mallas of Kuśinagarī performed his cremation, and the neighbouring population shared out his relics, which they placed in commemorative monuments known as stupas.

The above historical sketch is not exactly identical with the mythical life of the Buddha as it is conceived by Buddhists. This myth is a biographical stereotype which, with a few minor differences, applies as well to the Buddhas who preceded him and to those who will follow him. The wonders and prodigies which, according to tradition, marked the events of his life from conception to cremation have been passed over in silence here in order to present the biography in a more rational light. But it is not sufficient merely to discard the wondrous in order to reach historical truth. History cannot be based on legends. Moreover, my sketch makes no concessions to the Indian point of view, according to which beings are reborn for all eternity, assuming in turn hell-born, animal, human and divine forms; a complete biography, relating all the lives of a given individual, is therefore impossible. It could thus be objected that the sketch is only concerned with Śākyamuni's last life; it was then that he became a Buddha, but for that he first had to equip himself with knowledge and merit over a vast series of lives in human, animal and divine form. From this point of view, the story of Śākyamuni really began when, long long ago, he aroused the Thought of Enlightenment (*bodhicittotpāda*) and formed the resolve one day to attain supreme and perfect Enlightenment for the welfare and happiness of all beings. He then committed himself to the career of a bodhisattva (literally, Enlightenment-Being) – a future Buddha. This career, the stages of which were only fixed by later doctrine, was very long and stretched over at least three incalculable eons (*asaṃkhyeya kalpa*). During the first of these, Śākyamuni made the resolve to become a Buddha; at the end of the second, he communicated his decision to the Buddha Dīpaṃkara and the latter predicted success for him; during the third, he was assured of never slipping back; finally, for another ninety-one shorter eons, he performed meritorious actions which were to earn him the thirty-two physical marks of a Great Man which characterize both universal monarchs and fully and perfectly Enlightened Buddhas.

For Buddhists no being has any enduring essence or personality; all, the Buddha included, exist in name only. What receives that name is merely an assemblage of *skandhas*, 'Aggregates' or 'groups of psycho-physical elements' which arise and perish from instant to instant, carried along for all eternity on the whirling wheel of lives. Contrary to what is asserted by the Brahmins, the Self conceived as a permanent, stable, eternal and unchanging entity does not exist anywhere; there is no Self and nothing belongs to a Self.

Thus Śākyamuni, like all other beings, throughout time (for time has no beginning) was constantly reborn into the triple world (the earth, the heavens above and the hells beneath) in the form of a series of five Aggregates: form or corporeality; feeling; perceptions; volitions; consciousness. These Aggregates are impure (*sāsrava*) in that they are defiled by passion and ignorance, which bind them to the triple world. After becoming a bodhisattva, Śākyamuni progressed in morality, concentration and wisdom, aiming both for the deliverance which would free him from the world of existences and for the omniscience which would make him a Buddha. Through the practice of the perfections (*pāramitā*), especially generosity, he developed within himself elements of holiness which correlated with the five impure Aggregates constituting his 'false' personality. These elements of holiness, called pure (*anāsrava*) *skandhas* or Aggregates, are five in number: morality (*śīla*), mental concentration (*samādhi*), wisdom (*prajñā*), deliverance (*vimukti*), and the knowledge and vision of deliverance (*vimukti-jñāna-darśana*). The bodhisattva gradually perfects them but does not yet possess them in their fullness.

After his Enlightenment, Śākyamuni was still a man, because the five impure Aggregates, fruits of his previous actions, persisted in him, but he was also a Holy One (*arhat*) and a fully Enlightened Buddha (*samyaksaṃbuddha*). He was a Holy One in that he was freed from the impurities: he was possessed in full of the five pure Aggregates which culminated in conscious deliverance. Many were to be the disciples who, after him, reached that same deliverance and, in this sense at least, were the equals of their master since 'between one deliverance and another, there is no difference (*M.* II, 129; *S.* V, 410; *A.* III, 34).* All the same, the Enlightenment (*bodhi*) which they reached does not equal the full and perfect Enlightenment (*anuttarā samyaksaṃbodhi*) of the Buddhas.

If Śākyamuni was fully and perfectly Enlightened, he owed this to the knowledge (*jñāna*) and merit (*punya*) he had accumulated for incalculable eons. At the moment of his Enlightenment, that merit was transformed into the corresponding attributes of a Buddha, especially omniscience (*sarvajñatā*) and great compassion (*mahākaruṇā*). His omniscience knows the particular and general characteristics of all things; his great compassion extends to all beings and seeks to free them from *saṃsāra*. In fact, if three things, birth, old age and death, were not to exist, the Tathāgata would not appear in the world; since, however, they do exist, he manifests himself in it (*A.* V, 144; *NidSa.* 205).

When shortly after his Enlightenment, Śākyamuni was going to Benares, he met the ascetic Upaka on the way and said to him: 'There is no master for me, no one is comparable to me; in this world I am the only fully Enlightened One; I have attained perfect and supreme Enlightenment; in this world I have overcome all and am omniscient; here, I am defiled by nothing. Having abandoned everything and being free from desire, I am delivered; having reached Enlightenment by myself, whom could I call master? None is like me, I have no equal; by instructing myself, I have attained Enlightenment. I am the Tathāgata, the teacher of gods and men, omniscient and endowed with all powers. In this world I am the Holy One; in the worlds of gods and men, none surpasses me; in those worlds with all their gods I have vanquished Māra, I am the conqueror. . . . Like me, those who have attained the destruction of the impurities are conquerors; I have conquered evil things; that is why I am the conqueror' (*Sanghabh.* I, 132; *C.P.S.* 128, 443; *Vin.* I, 8; etc.).

* A list of abbreviations of the titles of texts quoted in this chapter appears on p. 58.

Śākyamuni devoted forty-five years of his last life to expounding the Doctrine, founding a community of religious mendicants (*bhikṣu*) and a fellowship of devoted lay people. Having accomplished his Buddha work, he attained complete Nirvāṇa (*parinirvāṇa*), Nirvāṇa without a remainder of conditioning (*nirupadhiśeṣa nirvāṇa*). The five Aggregates which constituted his false personality disappeared without a trace: 'Just as all the mangoes attached to a stem bearing a bunch of mangoes undergo the fate of that stem if it is broken, so the body of the Tathāgata has broken what leads to existence. As long as his body lasts, gods and men will see him. On the breaking up of the body, at the end of his life, gods and men will see him no more' (*D.* I, 46). 'Just as the flame touched by the wind goes towards stillness, goes from sight, so the sage delivered from his names and bodies [or the five impure Aggregates] enters stillness, goes from the sight of all. . . . He who has attained stillness, no measure can measure, to speak of him there are no words. What the mind might conceive vanishes. Thus every path is closed to discussion' (*Sn.*, verses 1074–6). At the moment of the Final Nirvāṇa of the Buddhas or of their great disciples, the series of the five pure Aggregates which were the cause of their holiness also disappear.

Thus when the Buddhas have left the world of becoming, the pure and impure elements which constituted their personalities disappear without a trace and are nowhere to be found. So it is for the Holy Ones. When the noble Godhika, who had attained the summit of perfection, stabbed himself and entered complete Nirvāṇa, a veil of smoke and darkness spread in the ten directions: it was Māra, the Malign One who rules over the world of desire, who had gone off in search of Godhika's consciousness; but he did not find it anywhere, for the Holy One was in complete Nirvāṇa and his consciousness had found no place (*S.* I, 121–2).

What then remains of a Buddha in Final Nirvāṇa? A corpse, a few relics with which the monks were not to be unduly concerned. To Ānanda, his attendant monk, who asked him what to do with the body of the Perfect One, the master replied: 'Do not waste your time, O Ānanda, in paying homage to my body; but concern yourself, with all diligence and application, with your own spiritual welfare. There are, O Ānanda, among the nobles, Brahmins and householders, wise men who believe in the Perfect One; they will pay homage to the body of the Perfect One' (*D.* II, 141).

The Buddha held his body in low esteem even though it was adorned with the thirty-two marks of a Great Man and surrounded by a brilliance a span in width. His disciple Vatkali was too attached to him and, worn out by his constant attentions, his master sent him away with these words: 'What good to you is this body of filth? He who sees the Dharma sees me.' (*S.* III, 120.)

The Dharma, that is, the Doctrine, is the only heritage the Buddha left to his disciples: 'Have the Dharma as an island', he said to them. 'Have the Dharma as your refuge and seek no other help' (*D.* II, 100–1). But, as we have seen, the Buddha did not merely expound a doctrine; he also founded a religious order, the Sangha, comprising four assemblies: monks (*bhikṣu*), nuns (*bhikṣuṇī*), laymen (*upāsakā*) and laywomen (*upāsikā*).

In this 2nd-century AD relief from Amarāvatī, India, the central stupa stands for the Buddha's Final Nirvāṇa; two intertwined snakes (nagas, or serpent divinities) are coiled round the dome, and the umbrellas on either side are signs of honour. The elephants kneel in worship; they commonly symbolize royalty or supremacy and are a conventional sign of good fortune.

A community does not appear out of nothing, outside a setting in time and place; the Buddhist monastic Order came into being as part of an established category of Indian religious renunciates who were not strictly recluses, but rather wanderers and mendicant monks. The Buddha and his disciples were aware of belonging to a wider Indian religious world and had no hesitation in claiming its titles inasmuch as they devoted themselves to the practice of higher morality, higher thought (concentration) and higher wisdom. In the Buddhist Doctrine and Discipline there are a large number of tenets and institutions which have parallels in Hinduism and Brahminism. This by no means implies that the Buddha and his disciples swallowed them whole: they evaluated them for their true worth and made a judicious selection. The Buddha declared: 'It is not I who argue with the world, it is the world that argues with me. What is accepted in the world of the wise, I adopt' (*S.* III, 138).

Buddhism met with rivals among the Brahmins and religious of the time and, on occasion, did not spare them from criticism. If it triumphed over them, this was due less to polemics than to the quality of its doctrines and practices. The Buddha limited his teaching to what would lead to calming, knowledge, Enlightenment, Nirvāṇa. All the rest is but speculation which he refused to discuss, because it did not contribute to deliverance.

Another quality conducive to the success of the Dharma was the rejection of extreme positions. The Buddha condemned both a life given over to pleasure and a life of austerity as unworthy and useless (*Vin.* I, 10). On points of doctrine which were not directly concerned with deliverance, he kept to the middle way, at an equal distance between realism and nihilism (*S.* II, 17, 21–24).

Moreover, the Good Doctrine is tolerant. The disciple who has entered the Path to Nirvāṇa is not expected to renounce the beliefs and practices inherited from his environment. While it is true that the traditional rites (*śīlavrata*) have no great efficacy, they are not absolutely forbidden. Whatever their origin, the Hindu, Vedic and Brahminic deities (Maheśvara, Brahmā, Indra, the four Divine Kings, etc.), the countless throng of demi-gods (Devas, Nāgas, Yakṣas, Gandharvas, Asuras, Garuḍas, Kiṃnaras, Mahoragas, Kumbhāṇḍas), not to mention the divinities of trees, water and jungle, all have their place in Buddhist mythology and play an important part in the life of the Buddha himself. None of them, however, accede to the rank of an eternal, stable and unchanging god, since they are subject to the vicissitudes of rebirth. Nevertheless, they have a right to respect and consideration: they honour those who honour them and they esteem those who esteem them (*Vin.* I, 229).

The Dharma

The Buddha's Word is good in the beginning, in the middle and at the end, perfect in meaning and letter, homogeneous, complete and pure (*Vin.* I, 35, 242; *D.* I, 62; *M.* I, 179). From the night of the Enlightenment until the night of the Final Nirvāṇa, all that the Buddha uttered and taught is true (*D.* III, 135; *A.* II, 24; *It.* 121). The sky will fall with the moon and stars, the earth will rise up into the heavens with the mountains and forests, the oceans will dry up, but the great sages say nothing untruthful (*Divy.* 268, 272). The Good Word of the Buddhas is distinguished by four characteristics: it is well spoken; it is agreeable and pleasant; it is in conformity with welfare; it is truthful (*Sn.* 78).

The Buddha honoured the Dharma he had discovered. A few weeks after his Enlightenment, when he was meditating under the goatherd's banyan tree, Śākyamuni sought to discover an ascetic or Brahmin in the world whom he could revere and serve. Finding no one superior to himself, he resolved to devote himself to the Dharma which he had himself discovered in order to honour, respect and serve it (*S.* I, 138–40).

The Doctrine of Dependent Origination, the norm governing the arising and passing away of all phenomena, constitutes the leading theme of the Dharma. It is discovered and taught from age to age by the Buddhas, but it was not created either by the Buddhas or by anyone else (*Nid.Sa.* 164) and, whether or not the Buddhas appear in the world, it remains constant and invariable (*S.* II, 25; *A.* I, 286).

He who sees Dependent Origination sees the Dharma, and he who sees the Dharma sees Dependent Origination (*M.* I, 190–1). The law of causality – the chain of causes and effects – is something difficult for humanity to grasp. Equally difficult to grasp is the attainment of peace of all compounded things, the detachment from earthly things, the extinction of covetousness, the cessation of desire, the end, Nirvāṇa (*Vin.* I, 5). Fearing his efforts might be useless, Śākyamuni hesitated to expound the Dharma but, yielding to the request of the god Brahmā, he went to Benares and 'set turning the wheel of the Doctrine'.

The Buddha put forward his Teaching, but did not impose it as a truth requiring the assent of faith. Undoubtedly, in order to be able to receive it one must be to a certain degree well disposed, but a mere act of faith is not enough to bring about true conversion. The Truth is only emancipatory to the degree that it is based on spontaneous conviction. Although the whole of Śākyamuni's biography is imbued with marvels, the master never had recourse to miracles in order to demonstrate the cogency of his teachings. He abhorred and execrated wonders which had no conclusive value (*D.* I, 213). He condemned as vulgar and unworthy the hundreds of forms of charlatanism by which ascetics and Brahmins of his time made their living (*D.* I, 9–12); he excommunicated certain monks who falsely claimed psychic powers (*Vin.* III, 92); he severely reprimanded one of his disciples who, for a trifling reason, had risen into the air and walked above the crowd, for that, he said, was the conduct of a courtesan exhibiting herself for a few coins (*Vin.* II, 112). Śākyamuni sought a

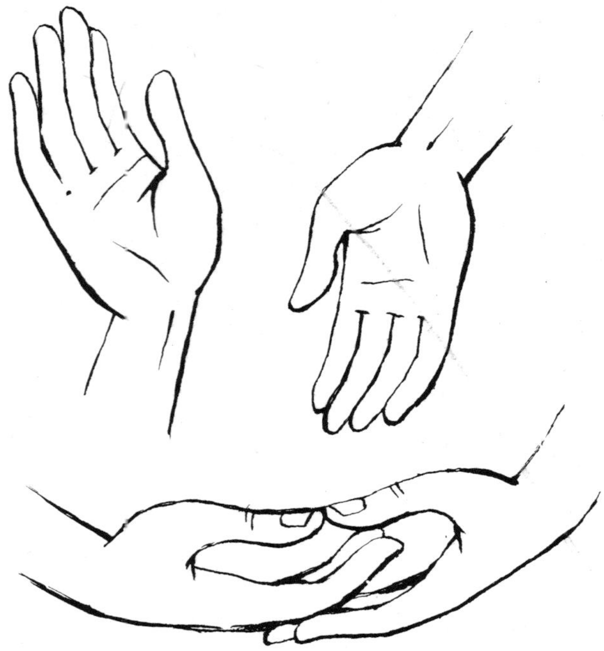

Buddhism took over from Hinduism a complex vocabulary of hand-gestures ('mudrās') to symbolize spiritual ideas. The selection shown here is taken from a Tibetan source; preaching (open hand upright); generosity (open hand pointing downwards); and meditation (hands folded on lap).

spontaneous conviction from his monks on certain points of doctrine:

'And now, monks, that you know and think thus, are you going to say, "We honour the master and through respect for the master, we say this or that"?'

'We shall not say it, Lord.'

'What you assert, is that not what you have yourself acknowledged, you yourselves seen, you yourselves grasped?'

'That is just so, Lord.' (*M.* I, 265).

The Dharma, which the Buddhas penetrate so perfectly in depth and detail that they hardly differ from it, is independent of time (*akālika*), and is communicated to mankind by the Buddhas from age to age and by various means. The Buddhas are alike in knowledge, might, bodily perfection and the services they render beings, but they differ in life-span, caste and clan, bodily dimensions, the length of duration of the Doctrine they promulgate, etc. Śākyamuni, for instance, lived for eighty years, was of the Kṣatriya caste and the Gautama clan, and he prophesied that his Doctrine would last only for a thousand years.

It might be expected that the Omniscient One would teach us everything, but it was not so. He was not unaware of the great problems which disturb the human mind, or of the solutions proposed by the ascetics and Brahmins. Is the world of beings transitory or eternal, finite or infinite? Is the life-principle the same as the body or different from it? Does the Holy One exist after death? Śākyamuni refused to express an opinion on these questions, because the knowledge of such things does not lead to any progress on the paths to holiness, because it does not lead to peace or to Enlightenment (*M.* I, 430–1). These problems, forever discussed by pundits, provoke endless arguments. Śākyamuni did not take part in such discussions. The true reason for the Buddha's silence is that the problems in question are wrongly put; to answer them in the affirmative or the negative is to fall within the extreme views of eternalism or nihilism. On this matter, Śākyamuni took a middle way, at an equal distance between affirmation and negation, and he recommended his disciples to do the same: 'Consider as undeclared that which I have not declared; consider as declared that which I have declared' (*M.* I, 431).

The Buddha did not teach everything to his disciples and did not pretend that he had. One day, when he was staying in Kauśāmbī in the Śiṃśapā Wood, he took some *śiṃśapā* leaves in his hands and said to the monks:

'What do you think? Which are more numerous, these leaves or the leaves of all the trees in the wood?'

'Few are the leaves the Lord holds in his hands; very numerous are the leaves of all the trees in the wood.'

'Similarly, O monks, much have I learnt; very little have I taught you. Nevertheless, I have not acted like those teachers who close their fists and keep their secrets to themselves; for I have taught you the Four Truths. That is what is useful; those are the principles of the religious life; that is what leads to disgust, renunciation, destruction, stilling, peace, superknowledge, perfect Enlightenment, Nirvāṇa. That is why I have taught it.' (*S.* V, 437–8)

The Word of the Buddha has only one flavour (*rasa*): that of deliverance. Its aim and effect is to end universal suffering (*Vin.* II, 239; *A.* IV, 203; *Ud.* 56). It is not, properly speaking, an encyclopaedia of religious knowledge but a way of deliverance discovered and proposed by the Buddha. His teaching is public, not secret (*A.* I, 283); he addressed all beings without distinction and showed them the Path to Nirvāṇa. Nevertheless, it did not depend on him to make the traveller follow his indications. He was merely 'he who points the Way' (*mārgākhyāyin*), the Path to follow in order to reach the goal (*M.* III, 6).

Invariable in essence, the Dharma varies in its expression. In his great compassion, Śākyamuni adjusted his Teaching according to whether he was concerned with a non-believer, a lay person, or a monk. The truth cannot be presented to everyone at the same time and in the same terms; it needs to be communicated with care if it is to suit an astute person capable of assimilating it; it can be harmful to an ignorant person incapable for the moment of grasping it. Some of the Buddha's hearers could understand his Teaching; others did not even hear his voice. Śākyamuni was the good sower who spread the seed in different ways depending on whether he was sowing a field of higher, middling or poor quality (*S*. IV, 315). He multiplied skilful means in order to lead beings to deliverance; through their flexibility and variety, his teachings sometimes pose awkward problems for exegetes, but they are all marked by his great compassion. It even happened that he seemingly contradicted himself. Phālguna, who believed in the existence of a soul and personality, asked: 'What is the being that touches, feels, desires and grasps?' The Buddha replied: 'I deny that there is any being that touches, feels, desires and grasps.' Conversely, when Vatsagotra, who no longer believed in the existence of a soul, asked whether it were true that the Self did not exist, the Buddha refused to answer in the negative, 'in order not to confirm the doctrine of the ascetics and Brahmins who believe in annihilation' (*S*. II, 13; IV, 400).

Manifold in its unity, unique in its manifoldness, the Dharma is a doctrinal code in which are set out truths which the Buddha did not originate, but of which he had a pure knowledge and which he transmitted to his disciples. Śākyamuni's fleshly body (*māṃsakāya*), adorned with the thirty-two marks and surrounded by pure brilliance, is not longer visible to gods and men, and it would be useless to look for it anywhere: it is not his essential body. The Dharma which he expounded and which, by the most various of means, guides beings towards deliverance is, metaphorically speaking, the true body of the Buddhas, for it is independent of time. If its brilliance is sometimes obscured, this is due to man's incomprehension; the truth itself undergoes no eclipse. The sun shines in daytime; the moon at night; fire shines day and night, but sometimes here and sometimes there; among all lights the Buddha is the incomparable light (*S*. I, 15).

Consequently, without denying the historicity of the Buddha Śākyamuni, one should see him above all as a light and a guide. His adherents commemorate him by saying: 'Indeed, that Blessed One is worthy of homage, fully and perfectly enlightened, endowed with knowledge and practice, well-come, knower of the world, supreme leader of men – those beings to be tamed – teacher of gods and men, the Enlightened One, the Blessed One' (*A*. III, 285).

The content of the Buddha's Teaching

The Dharma, that is, the Buddhist Doctrine, is condensed in the Four Noble Truths (*āryasatya*) expounded by the Buddhas, and especially by Sākyamuni in his Discourse at Benares (*Vin*. I, 10; *Sanghabh*. I, 137–8):

(i) Everything is suffering (*duḥkha*).

(ii) The origin of suffering (*duḥkhasamudaya*) is desire (*tṛṣṇā*).

(iii) There exists a Nirvāṇa, an end to suffering (*duḥkhanirodha*).

(iv) A Path, defined by the Buddha, leads to Nirvāṇa.

'Everything is suffering'

Everything is suffering, in the sense that the psycho-physical phenomena of existence are suffering and the existences in which these phenomena develop are themselves suffering. By examining a man in an empirical and immediate way, there can be noted in him five categories of phenomena which are basically distinct but so closely united that the categories are called Aggregates (*skandhas*). They are:

(i) Form or corporeality (*rūpa*), made up of the four great elements (earth, water, fire, wind) or a subtle matter derived from those four elements.

(ii) Feeling (*vedanā*), which can be pleasant, unpleasant or neutral. Feelings result from contact between six internal organs (*indriya*) and six external objects (*viṣaya*) which together form the twelve Bases of Consciousness (*āyatana*):

Internal organs	*External objects*
1 Eye	7 Sight
2 Ear	8 Sound
3 Nose	9 Odour
4 Tongue	10 Taste
5 Body	11 Touch
6 Mind	12 Mental object

The first five organs each have their own object: the eye is concerned with sight, the ear with sounds, etc.; the mind (*manas*) is concerned with not only its own object, namely, mental objects (*dharma*), but also the objects of the first five organs.

(iii) Perception (*saṃjñā*), related to the six external objects.

(iv) Volition (*saṃskāra*), the reaction of the will to the six objects.

(v) Consciousness (*vijñāna*), which grasps the characteristics of the six objects. There are six kinds of consciousness which are added to the twelve Bases of Consciousness and are called Elements (*dhātu*):

13 Visual consciousness
14 Auditory consciousness
15 Olfactory consciousness
16 Gustatory consciousness
17 Tactile consciousness
18 Mental consciousness

So the whole field of living experience can be defined in the terms of the five Aggregates (*skandha*) or of the twelve Bases of Consciousness (*āyatana*) or of the eighteen Elements (*dhātu*). These three classifications, which are interchangeable, appear in the early canonical sources, but the first is the most widespread. Other classifications were added later.

The five Aggregates, inasmuch as they arise from causes and conditions, are conditioned things (*saṃskṛta dharma*), also referred to as 'Formations' (*saṃskāra*). They are endowed with the three or four characteristics of conditioned things (*saṃskṛta lakṣaṇa*) – arising (*utpāda*), disappearance (*vyaya*), duration-and-change (*sthity-anyathātva*) – by the terms of which they arise, endure and disappear (*A*. I, 152; *S*. III, 37; *NidSa*. 139).

Each Formation (*saṃskāra*) has its own essential nature (*svabhāva*) or particular characteristic (*svalakṣaṇa*), but all are marked by the seal of impermanence, suffering and impersonality (*M.* I, 138–9; *S.* II, 244–6; *M.* III, 271–3):

'What do you think, O monks – are the Aggregates, Bases of Consciousness and Elements permanent (*nitya*) or impermanent (*anitya*)?'

'Impermanent, Lord.'

'But that which is impermanent, is it suffering (*duḥkha*) or happiness (*sukha*)?'

'Suffering, Lord.'

'So, therefore, of what is impermanent, suffering and subject to change, can it be said, when this is considered: That is mine, I am that, that is my Self?'

'It cannot, Lord.'

The Formations are seen as follows:

(i) They are transitory because they arise and perish in a perpetual changing. Subject to birth, disease, old age and death, the body changes from instant to instant. Feelings, perceptions and volitions follow each other and do not resemble each other. As for the mind or consciousness, it appears and disappears in a perpetual changing, day and night, like a monkey gambolling in a forest and leaping from branch to branch (*S.* II, 94–5).

Let us suppose the Ganges sweeps along a mass of foam and that a man with keen sight perceives, observes and attentively examines it. He will find that the ball of foam is empty and insubstantial, with no real essence. In the same way, if it is observed, corporeality will be seen to be empty and insubstantial, with no real essence, and it is the same with the other four Aggregates: 'Form is like a ball of foam, feeling is like a bubble of water, perception is like a mirage, volition is like the trunk of a banana tree [i.e. without a core, like an onion] and consciousness is like a ghost' (*S.* III, 140–2). It is undeniable that all that is subject to arising is also subject to destruction (*S.* IV, 47).

(ii) The Formations are suffering precisely because they are transitory. Three principles of suffering exist: suffering in itself (*duḥkhaduḥkhatā*), experienced as such; suffering resulting from the fact of being conditioned (*saṃskāraduḥkhatā*); and suffering arising from change (*vipariṇāmaduḥkhatā*) (*D.* III, 216; *S.* IV, 259). All that is felt is felt in suffering (*S.* IV, 216); nothing arises but suffering and nothing is destroyed but suffering (*S.* I, 135).

If all the psycho-physical phenomena of existence – Aggregates, Bases of Consciousness and Elements – are stamped by impermanence and marked by suffering, it follows that the various forms of rebirth and the world in which they develop share the same defects.

Saṃsāra, or the round of rebirths, continues for all eternity: 'It is impossible to discover a beginning from which beings, led astray by ignorance, fettered by the thirst for existence, wander aimlessly from birth to birth' (*S.* II, 179). According to the Buddhist conception, the roots of which reach into ancient Indian traditions, *saṃsāra* occurs throughout the five forms of rebirth (*pañcagati*) and the Triple World (*traidhātuka*).

The five forms of rebirth are those of the hell-born, animals, ghosts (*preta*), mankind and gods. The first three are qualified as bad, and the last two as good (*M.* I, 73). In the first three there is more suffering than happiness; in the human, the two are balanced; in the divine, happiness transcends suffering. However, whatever blisses may be in store for them, all existences are basically suffering because they are transitory, and happiness destined to disappear is suffering. Vitiated by impermanence, existences are merely an infinitesimal point in the long series of suffering: 'While, on this long journey, you wander aimlessly from birth to birth, there have been more tears shed for you than there is water in the four oceans' (*S.* II, 180).

The five forms of rebirth are spread throughout a receptacle-world called the Triple World. It consists of:

(a) The world of desire (*kāmadhātu*), in which beings enjoy the five sense-objects (colours, sounds, odours, tastes and tangible objects). This world of desire includes the rebirths of the hell-born, animals, ghosts and mankind, plus some of the gods, namely, the six classes of lesser gods who are still subject to sense-pleasure.

(b) The world of form (*rūpadhātu*), inhabited by the seventeen classes of Brahmā gods, who are endowed with subtle form, detached from sense-pleasure but experiencing the joyful effects of the four meditative absorptions in which they dwell.

(c) The formless world (*ārūpyadhātu*), appertaining to the higher gods, who are formless, exist in the shape of 'pure mentality' and are plunged in the blisses of the four formless attainments (*samāpatti*) in which they contemplate the infinity of space, the infinity of consciousness, the infinity of nothingness and the summit of existence (*bhavāgra*), a psychic sphere transcending the limits of consciousness.

(iii) Transitory and painful, the Formations are not a Self and do not belong to a Self. Buddhism is the doctrine of the No-Self (*anātmavāda*) and is thus the reverse of Brahminism and Hinduism, which believe in the existence of a permanent, stable, eternal and unchanging Self.

The Buddha explained that the five Aggregates are not the Self because if corporeality, feeling, perception, volition and consciousness were the Self, they would not be subject to disease, and they could be controlled at will – in the case of corporeality for instance by saying: 'May my body be so, may my body not be so' (*Vin.* I, 13; *S.* III, 66–8), and so on.

Since the Self and what belongs to the Self do not exist in truth or with certainty, is it not sheer folly to claim: 'The world of the Aggregates is my Self; after my death, I will be permanent, stable, eternal and unchanging' (*M.* I, 138)?

Led astray by a belief in a personality (*satkāyadṛṣṭi*), the ignorant ordinary man considers bodily form as the Self, the Self as possessing form, form as present in the

After his Enlightenment the Buddha, with those followers who had witnessed his mortifications, went to a Deer Park near Benares and preached his first sermon, in which he announced his discovery of the Four Noble Truths and expounded his doctrine of deliverance. His discourse became known as 'Turning the Wheel of the Doctrine' and is one of the most frequently represented scenes in Buddhist art. This relief is from Ali Masj'd, in what is now Afghanistan. The two deer at the bottom allude to the Deer Park.

Self, and the Self as present in form. And he does the same with the other four Aggregates (*M.* I, 300; III, 17). The ordinary man thus nourishes four misconceptions concerning each of the five Aggregates, so the belief in a personality is compared to a twenty-peaked mountain chain.

It should be admitted that the belief in a personality is not a defiled view in the sense that it is not directly a cause of wrong-doing and hell. In fact, the man who believes in the Self wishes for happiness after death and, in this belief, practises giving, observes morality: all good actions ensuring rebirth in the world of mankind or in heaven.

However, the belief in an 'I' is incompatible with Buddhist spiritual life, the uprooting of desire and the reaching of Nirvāṇa. Taking a tiny ball of dung between his fingers, the Buddha said to a monk: 'The belief in the existence of a permanent, stable, eternal and unchanging Self, be it as tiny as this ball of dung, would ruin the religious life which culminates in the perfect destruction of suffering' (*S.* III, 144); he also said: 'With regard to this, I see no adhesion to that view which would not engender in him who adheres to it grief, lamentation, suffering, anguish and despair' (*M.* I, 137–8).

In popular language, which the Buddha himself did not hesitate to use, the terms 'being', 'man', 'person' or 'self' (*ātman*) are used. These are mere labels for convenient reference to a complex of conditioned, impermanent, suffering and impersonal phenomena. Just as when the parts of a chariot, once assembled, are called 'chariot', in the same way, wherever the five Aggregates are to be found, it is usual to speak of a 'being' (*S.* I, 135). In truth, no so-called soul or spirit, no Tathāgata, is any of the five Aggregates, can be found in them or elsewhere, or is an assemblage of the five Aggregates and yet separate from them. Therefore, even in the present life, the Tathāgata is not acknowledged as a real being (*S.* III, 111–2; IV, 383–4).

An objection naturally comes to mind: how can early Buddhism, which denies the existence of a transmigrating entity, affirm the reality of rebirth? The answer is simple. What passes from existence to existence is not a permanent, stable, eternal and unchanging soul (which is nowhere to be found), but a series of five transitory, suffering and impersonal Aggregates, ever subject to change and rebirth.

The Truth of suffering affirms the reality of the Aggregates alone (*skandhamātravāda*) and rejects the Self (*nairātmyavāda*). It is a series of psycho-physical phenomena, real but impermanent, which passes from existence to existence during the long night of *saṃsāra*, but those phenomena are not a Self and do not belong to a Self. 'The world is empty (*śūnya*) of a Self and anything belonging to a Self' (*S.* IV, 54). Here appears for the first time the notion of 'Emptiness' (*śūnyatā*) to which Buddhist thinkers have always been drawn and which was to be taken to great lengths.

'The origin of suffering is desire'

The phenomena of existence, the Aggregates, Bases of Consciousness and Elements, are transitory, suffering and empty of a Self or anything belonging to a Self, but they do not occur by chance; they originate in desire (*tṛṣṇā*). Their appearance and disappearance are ruled by Dependent Origination (*pratītyasamutpāda*), by virtue of which arising (*utpatti*) is due to action (*karman*) and action is due to passion (*kleśa*).

Saṃsāra, which has no beginning, is like an infinite sequence of existences. From this series, let us take at random a group of three rebirths, respectively past, present and future, and examine how the five Aggregates appear in them. We note that they are subject to the mechanism of the twelvefold Dependent Origination, each 'fold' or link of which is the cause, or more exactly, the condition of the next. This interdependence is traditionally indicated in the following way: 'This being, that is; from the arising of this, that arises; and conversely, this not being, that is not; from the destruction of this, that is destroyed' (*S.* II, 28; *C.P.S.* 102–4).

Each of the twelve links is a complex of five Aggregates, but it takes its name from the most important phenomenon (*dharma*) All of them, including ignorance, which starts the list, are of equal importance: impermanent, conditioned and dependently arising, they are doomed to destruction, disappearance, detachment and suppression (*S.* II, 26).

The formula of Dependent Origination is as follows (*S.* II, 2–4). Through (1) ignorance (*avidyā*) are conditioned the (2) Karmic Formations (*saṃskāra*), i.e. rebirth-producing volitions; through the Karmic Formations is conditioned (3) consciousness (*vijñāna*); through consciousness are conditioned (4) name and form (*nāmarūpa*), i.e. mental and physical phenomena; through name and form are conditioned the (5) six Bases of Consciousness (*ṣaḍāyatana*), which have already been explained; through the six Bases of Consciousness is conditioned (6) contact (*sparśa*), i.e. contact between the internal organs and external objects which leads to the six kinds of consciousness; through contact is conditioned (7) feeling (*vedanā*); through feeling is conditioned (8) thirst, or desire (*tṛṣṇā*), i.e. an impassioned reaction to what has been felt; through thirst is conditioned (9) clinging (*upādāna*), or attachment to the five Aggregates; through clinging is conditioned (10) becoming (*bhava*), or action which produces rebirth; through becoming is conditioned (11) birth (*jāti*), the appearance of the five Aggregates and internal organs; through birth is conditioned (12) old-age-and-death (*jarā-maraṇa*).

These twelve links describe the Dependent Origination of the five Aggregates in the course of three successive existences: ignorance and the Karmic Formations occur in the past existence; eight links, from consciousness to becoming, occur in the present existence; and birth, old-age-and-death in the future one. Taken forwards this explains the arising of the phenomena of existence; in reverse, their destruction.

The links involve a process of activity (*karmabhava*) and a process of birth (*utpattibhava*); they are therefore both cause and result. Moreover, ignorance, thirst and clinging are passions (*kleśa*); Karmic Formations and becoming are actions (*karman*); and the links from consciousness to feeling inclusive, birth, old-age-and-death are results (*vipākaphala*) or birth (*janman*), in that they continue existence in *saṃsāra*. This shows that the wheel of life has no beginning: passions and actions lead to birth which leads to passions and actions which lead to birth, and so on. However, 'everything that is subject to arising is also subject to destruction'.

In simple terms, the system of Dependent Origination comes down to three things: (i) passion, (ii) action and (iii) result; passion vitiates action and action causes a retributive result.

(i) Passion, also designated ignorance (*avidyā*), thirst (*tṛṣṇā*) and clinging (*upādāna*), is a mental state composed of delusion and desire. The word thirst is taken here in its widest meaning: (1) the thirst for sense pleasures (*kāmatṛṣṇā*) – the desire which awakens and takes root in the presence of agreeable and pleasant objects; (2) the thirst for existence (*bhavatṛṣṇā*) and, especially, for existences in the higher worlds, i.e. the world of form and the formless world; (3) the thirst for annihilation (*vibhavatṛṣṇā*), from the point of view of the belief that everything ends at death (*Vin.* I, 10). Desire, with all the delusions it presupposes, is a fetter (*saṃyojana*) which is difficult to break. It is pernicious to delight in sense-pleasures and even more pernicious to nurture in oneself an impossible ideal of eternal survival or total annihilation.

Passion vitiates action by means of the threefold poison of craving (*rāga*), hatred (*dveṣa*) and delusion (*moha*): 'There are three causes of the origin of actions: craving, hatred and delusion' (*A.* I, 263). 'Consumed by craving, enraged by hatred, blinded by delusion, overwhelmed and despairing, man contemplates his own downfall, that of others, and both together' (*A.* I, 156–7).

(ii) Action (*karman*) is a volition (*cetanā*) which is translated into bodily, vocal and mental acts (*A.* III, 415). Some Indian thinkers have considered action to be a material substance, a virus infecting the organism. Buddhism's great step was to place action in the mind, and this new position conditioned and determined the whole development of Buddhist philosophy. Action is only truly action, only of any significance, if it is conscious, reflected on and willed. Action is strictly personal and incommunicable. Actions are the property of beings, their inheritance, their formative mould, their kin and their refuge (*M.* III, 203). Man is the inheritor of the actions he carries out (*A.* III, 186). 'This bad action which is yours was not done by your mother or your father or by anyone else. You alone have done this bad action, you alone will reap its fruit' (*M.* III, 181).

In fact, action separates beings by distributing them

According to Buddhist doctrine, life is vitiated by three things: craving, hatred and delusion. They are represented in the centre of a Tibetan tanka by the cock, the snake and the pig (see also p. 29, pl. 24). The Buddha laid great stress on individual moral responsibility: 'This bad action which is yours was not done by your mother or your father or by anyone else. You alone have done this bad action, you alone will reap its fruit.' Only by overcoming craving, hatred, and delusion can one achieve Enlightenment.

throughout the different good and bad forms of rebirth (*M.* III, 203).

(iii) Ripening or fruition (*vipāka*) of actions takes place exclusively in the Aggregates, which are reborn throughout the destinies in *saṃsāra*: 'Done (*kṛta*) and accumulated (*upacita*) actions do not ripen in earth or in water or in fire or in wind but in the phenomena of existence – Aggregates, Bases of Consciousness and Elements – which their enactor has acquired (*Sanghabh.* II, 1–2). Since the Aggregates are suffering, and since the *saṃsāra* in which they develop is suffering, all the fruits of actions are suffering.

Whether its consequences are pleasant or unpleasant, all action is deleterious in as much as it prolongs the long sequence of *saṃsāra*. The only way to interrupt the series of rebirths and put an end to suffering is to neutralize action by eliminating the delusions and passions which vitiate it. Non-action alone leads to the destruction of action (*A.* II, 232).

It remains to be seen whether it is possible to destroy suffering and, if so, of what this destruction consists. The third Noble Truth answers this question.

'There exists a Nirvāṇa, an end to suffering'

The first two Truths are exclusively concerned with the world of becoming. The third Truth is located on a diametrically opposite plane: that of the unconditioned (*asaṃskṛta*), especially Nirvāṇa, devoid of arising, disappearance, duration and change, and avoiding the paths of speech and thought: 'No eye, no tongue, no thought can perceive the Holy One who is in complete Nirvāṇa' (*S.* IV, 52–3).

Nirvāṇa is presented to us in the following way:

(i) It is the destruction of desire and the basic passions which are craving, hatred and delusion (*A.* II, 34; *S.* IV, 251). The destruction of the passions neutralizes actions and prevents them from yielding any result.

(ii) Nirvāṇa is the disappearance of the five Aggregates and the end of painful rebirth. The Holy One, freed from the Aggregate of form, from the Aggregate of feeling, from the Aggregate of perception, from the Aggregate of volition and from the Aggregate of consciousness, is as profound, immeasurable and unfathomable as the great sea. In him the Aggregates are destroyed, uprooted and unable to generate (*S.* IV, 378–9). He who has reached complete Nirvāṇa is indefinable. The disappearance of the passions does not prevent the Holy One from continuing his last existence; his Aggregates go on existing for some time longer; this is known as a 'Nirvāṇa with a remainder of conditioning' (*sopadhiśeṣa*) continued in the present existence (*dṛṣṭadharma*). However, after the decease of the Holy One, all his Aggregates, impure and pure, disappear, and the Holy One is no longer to be found anywhere; he has reached complete Nirvāṇa; this is what is called 'Nirvāṇa without a remainder of conditioning' (*nirupadhiśeṣa*) (*It,* 38).

(iii) Nirvāṇa is the end of suffering. Remote from becoming, Nirvāṇa marks the end of suffering, but this

Worn out by age and fatigue the Buddha achieved Final Nirvāṇa at the age of 80, lying between trees – a 10th-century relief from eastern India. His body was cremated and his relics placed in commemorative stupas; one is represented above him.

final end is not a paradise; it is outside space and time and, in truth, is nowhere to be found: 'There is a sphere which is neither earth, nor water, nor fire, nor air, which is not the sphere of the infinity of space, nor the sphere of the infinity of consciousness, nor the sphere of nothingness, nor the sphere of either perception or non-perception, which is neither this world nor the other world, neither sun nor moon. I deny that it is coming or going, enduring, death or birth. It is only the end of suffering' (*Ud.* 80).

(iv) Nirvāṇa is supreme happiness (*parama sukha*). Secure from birth, disease, old-age-and-death, Nirvāṇa is supreme happiness (*M.* I, 508), but since feeling is absent from it, what causes the bliss of Nirvāṇa is precisely the absence of bliss (*A.* IV, 414).

(v) Nirvāṇa is unconditioned (*asaṃskṛta*). Free from arising, disappearance, duration and change, Nirvāṇa is an unconditioned thing in direct contrast to the conditioned (*saṃskṛta*) Aggregates which arise, disappear, endure and change. Early Buddhism accepted the reality of conditioned things and hence deduced the reality of the unconditioned, especially Nirvāṇa – which led to the saying: 'There is an unborn, unarisen, uncreated, unconditioned; if there were no unborn, there would be no release for what is born, arisen, created, conditioned' (*It.* 37).

'A Path, defined by the Buddha, leads to Nirvāṇa'

The fourth Noble Truth deals with the Path which leads to the extinction of suffering (*duḥkhanirodhagāminī pratipad*): it is the destruction of the delusions and passions and brings release from the world of becoming, the world of suffering. It is called the Noble Eightfold Path (*āryāṣṭāṅgamārga*): right view, right resolve, right speech, right action, right livelihood, right effort, right mindfulness and right concentration (*Vin.* I, 10); but the eight limbs in fact come down to three basic elements: morality (*śīla*), concentration (*samādhi*) and wisdom (*prajñā*) (*D.* II, 81, 84; *It.* 51). All three are indispensable but the most important is wisdom, by means of which the mind is freed from impurities (*āsrava*).

(i) Morality (*śīla*) consists of conscious and willed abstention from misconduct of body (taking the life of living beings, theft, sexual misconduct), of speech (falsehood, slander, harsh and useless speech), and of mind (covetousness, animosity, wrong views). Its aim is to avoid any action which might harm someone else. The observation of morality increases in value when it is sanctioned by a vow or commitment: it is then called morality of restraint (*saṃvaraśīla*). Based on the same fundamental principles, it nevertheless varies with different ways of life: the obligations of a monk are stricter than those of a lay person.

(ii) Concentration (*samādhi*) is the fixing of the mind on one point. In practice it is much the same as the absence of distraction (*avikṣepa*) and as mental tranquillity (*śamatha*). Concentration normally involves nine successive stages of meditation; these are well defined in the texts (*D.* II, 156; III, 265, 290; *A.* IV, 410), but too detailed to go into here. At the beginning of their practice the mind still exerts all its natural activity, namely seeking both an object of meditation and a well-thought-out judgment on that object. In the course of the practices the mind gradually frees itself from its various activities and becomes increasingly clear. Finally, it penetrates the ninth and last stage, the contemplation of the destruction of perception and feeling (*saṃjñāvedayitanirodhasamāpatti*), where the practitioner's passions are destroyed by knowledge and he attains Enlightenment, or, to use the exact expression, Nirvāṇa in this world.

The practice of concentration, eventually completed by insight (*vipaśyanā*), puts the practitioner in possession of six higher spiritual powers called superknowledges (*abhijñā*), five of them worldly and the sixth transcendental. These are psychic power, the divine eye of immense farsightedness, the penetration of others' thoughts, divine hearing, the remembrance of former existences and, finally, the destruction of the impurities which ensures liberation in this life (*D.* III, 281).

A set of four spiritual practices, called *brahmavihāra*, known and practised at all times by Indian meditators, is particularly recommended although, in the economy of the Path, they appear somewhat ancillary. They consist of the projection of thought filled successively with goodwill (*maitrī*), compassion (*karuṇā*), altruistic joy (*muditā*) and perfect equanimity (*upekṣā*) in all directions, and enveloping the whole world in these infinite states (*D.* II, 186; III, 223–4).

(iii) Wisdom (*prajñā*) is the ultimate and main element of the Path. The practice of concentration is not capable of completely purifying the mind; in order to ensure quiescence, peace and Nirvāṇa, wisdom is also necessary. This is not a gnosis of vague and imprecise content, more emotional than intellectual. It is a question of clear and precise vision, embracing the Noble Truths and penetrating in depth the general characteristics of things – impermanence, suffering and the impersonality of phenomena – as well as the peace of Nirvāṇa.

There is a distinction between wisdom arising from teaching, from reflection, and from repeated practice (*bhāvanā*). This last, if it is pure (*anāsrava*), i.e. completely free from delusions and wrong views, sees in depth the true nature of things (*dharmatā*) – which is, according to early Buddhism, nothing more or less than Dependent Origination – severs the final bonds with the world and ensures 'deliverance of mind through wisdom' (*cetovimukti* and *prajñāvimukti*). The Noble One whom this Enlightens becomes aware of his deliverance and declares: 'I have realized the Noble Truths; ended are rebirths; I have lived the pure life; what had to be done has been done; henceforth there will be no further rebirth for me.'

The Sangha

The formation of the Sangha during the Buddha's lifetime

The Buddhist Sangha is composed of four assemblies: monks (*bhikṣu*), nuns (*bhikṣuṇī*), laymen (*upāsaka*) and laywomen (*upāsikā*). The religious are distinguished from the laity by their dress, way of life and particularly by their spiritual faculties. All are children of the Buddha and aspire to deliverance. The religious will reach this quickly by using the Path to Nirvāṇa; the laity, more slowly, by committing themselves at first to the Path to the Heavens. A close collaboration between these various groups is indispensable to the smooth running of the community: 'They pay you great service, O monks, the Brahmins and householders who give you clothing, alms, seats, couches and medicines. You also pay them great service when you teach them the Good Doctrine and the pure life (*brahmacarya*). Thus it is through your mutual help that the religious life, which causes the crossing over beyond rebirth and puts an end to suffering, can be practised. Each relying on the other, householders and homeless cause the Good Doctrine to prosper. The latter are protected from need, since they receive clothing and the rest; the former, having practised the Doctrine in this world, the Path which leads to good forms of rebirth, delight in the world of the gods possessed of the blisses' (*It.* 111).

The superiority of the religious state over that of the laity has never been contested, but there is a striking contrast between the passive virtues of renunciation and detachment practised by the monks and the active virtues of generosity and kindness practised by the laity. Among the latter appeared the tendency to claim rights equal to those of the religious. When it became no longer a question of attaining Nirvāṇa but of acceding to Buddhahood – an ideal adopted by the Mahāyāna – the career of the future Buddhas was open to the laity as well as to the religious. Nevertheless, at the first stage of this career, the adherent leaves the world and becomes a monk in the Tathāgatas' Order (*Tr.* V, 2390).

The *Skandhaka*, which is the second part of the *Vinaya*, the book of monastic Discipline, narrates the conversions carried out by the Buddha in Benares, Uruvilvā and Rājagṛha during the weeks that followed his Enlightenment. It was then that the first lay followers and monks appeared. Five years later, nuns were received into the Sangha. Differences between the various recensions of the *Vinaya* that have come down to us can be observed, but all the conversions followed the same format. The Buddhas make use of many means in order to convert beings; Śākyamuni mainly resorted to instruction. The group of five monks who had assisted the future Buddha during his years of austerity and who had later abandoned him were converted during the Discourses at Benares. After the account of the Enlightenment, one of them, Ājñāta Kauṇḍinya, obtained the first fruit of the religious life, that of 'Stream-Entry' (*srotaāpatti*) and requested entry into the Order; after the description of the Four Noble Truths, Kauṇḍinya became an *arhat* or Holy One, while his four companions discovered the first fruit of the religious life and asked for ordination; finally, after the Homily on the No-Self, his companions became Holy Ones in turn. Thus there were, including the Buddha, six Holy Ones in the world.

After the Discourses at Benares and in varying circumstances, the number of Holy Ones reached sixty-one. According to Sanskrit sources, Yaśa became a Buddhist layman before becoming a Holy One and entering the Order. Yaśa's four brothers and his fifty companions asked for and received ordination before reaching holiness, while his mother and wife became the first Buddhist laywomen. Other people who had benefited from the same teachings declared themselves as lay followers: they understood the Noble Truths, but their minds were not yet freed from the impurities.

Except for the group of five monks, conversions took place in the following way. The Buddha instructed the candidate by communicating to him the gradual teaching (*anupūrvīya dharmadeśanā*), the terms of which are fixed and allow of no variety: 'To the candidate sitting at his side, the Blessed One communicated the gradual teaching, namely, a discourse on giving, a discourse on morality, a discourse on heaven, and explained to him the peril, vanity and depravation of the sense pleasures as well as the advantages there are in renouncing them. When the Blessed One realized that the candidate's mind was prepared, pliable, free of hindrance, joyful and well disposed, then he taught him in full the excellent doctrinal account of the Blessed Buddhas (of the past), namely, the Four Noble Truths: suffering, its origin, its extinction and the path leading to its extinction.'

Enlightened by these teachings, the candidate understands the Four Noble Truths, penetrates the mechanism of Dependent Origination, and the Eye of the Doctrine (*dharmacakṣus*) without dust or stain arises in him, which means in scholastic terms that he obtains the first fruit of the religious life, Entry into the Stream of Nirvāṇa (*srotaāpattiphala*). This result is rendered by the following formula: 'Just as clean fabric, without any black stain, can exactly hold the dye, so in this candidate, still in the same position, arose the Eye of the Doctrine without dust or stain, and he knew that everything that is subject to arising is also subject to perishing.'

The candidate who is possessed of the Eye of the Doctrine can either become a lay follower (*upāsaka*) or request ordination (*upasampad*). The candidate who professes to becoming a lay follower expresses this in the following way: 'It is wonderful, Lord! As if what had fallen has been straightened, as if what was hidden has been found, as if the path was shown to one who had strayed or as if a lamp was placed in darkness for those who have eyes to see the visible, so the Doctrine has been explained by the Blessed One in many a way. I myself take refuge in the Buddha, in the Dharma and in the Sangha of monks. May the Blessed One consider me as a lay follower from this day for as long as my life may last.' Such a commitment was entirely unilateral and was accepted by the Buddha in silence.

The lay man or woman is expected to accept five rules (*śikṣāpada*) of moral restraint (*pañcaśīla*); although in translation they are often called 'the Five Precepts', they have the form of undertakings. He says: 'I undertake to refrain from taking life', and makes similar promises regarding stealing, unchastity (defined according to the situation), lying and taking intoxicants which make for carelessness (and hence for breaking the other four rules). On certain holy days pious laymen traditionally undertake five further abstentions: from all sexual activity, from eating after midday, from the use of perfumes, unguents and personal adornment, from seeing public entertainments, from the use of grand beds; their vow is known as 'the Eight Precepts' (*aṣṭāṅga śīla*)

The ceremony of admission into the Sangha is quite different if, instead of becoming a lay follower, the candidate requests entry into the Order. During the lifetime of the Buddha, it was obtained in a rather informal way. 'The candidate, having seen the Doctrine, acquired the Doctrine, known the Doctrine and been immersed in the Doctrine, having cast out doubt, dispelled uncertainty and having, without the help of anyone else, placed his confidence in the teaching of the master', requests ordination in the following terms: 'May I, O Lord, in the presence of the Blessed One, receive the 'Going forth' from home (*pravrajyā*), receive ordination (*upasampad*). May I, in the presence of the Blessed One, practise the pure conduct (*brahmacarya*).' To the request put to him the Buddha answered with a summons: 'Come, O monk; the Doctrine has been well expounded; practise pure conduct in order to put a definitive end to suffering.'

Often the Buddha had no sooner uttered those words than the candidate miraculously found himself shaved, dressed in the religious cloak and holding in his hands the begging bowl and water pot, with a week's growth of hair and beard – as though he were a monk who had been ordained for a hundred years (see *Divy*. 37).

The summons 'Come, monk', which can be addressed to one man or several, is one of the ten kinds of ordination in use in Buddhism. It does not necessarily culminate in a fruit of the religious life, but it marks the beginning of pure conduct and brings about monkhood.

The monk still has to practise and exert himself before attaining holiness (arhatship) which constitutes the final fruit. It is only after right thought, eventually provoked by further instruction from the Buddha, that 'his mind is, through detachment [from the world], freed from impurities'.

'After his ordination, the monk remains alone and solitary, diligent, vigorous and master of himself. And soon, in this very life, through his own comprehension and realization, he attains the supreme culmination of pure conduct, for which the sons of good family rightly pass from life at home to homelessness, and dwells there. He acknowledges: "I have realized the Noble Truths; ended are rebirths; I have lived the pure life; what had to be done has been done; henceforth there will be no further rebirth for me."'

The conversion of the first sixty Holy Ones was extremely quick. They passed directly from the first to the fourth and culminating fruit of the religious life. The teaching of the Noble Truths gave them possession of the Eye of the Doctrine without dust or stain; they requested and obtained ordination; then, following a further discourse from the Buddha, their minds were freed from impurities and they attained holiness. The Buddha's career was longer and more complicated, because he had to discover the Truths without the help of a master and he had a much more perfect understanding of them: the Enlightenment of the *arhats* penetrates the general characteristics of things, but the Supreme Enlightenment of the Buddha includes an omniscience which extends as far as the particular characteristics of all phenomena.

The first sixty *arhats* did not attach themselves to the master's person and did not follow him on his peregrinations. Later, during his journeys in the middle Ganges basin, the Buddha was regularly accompanied by a Sangha of 1,250 monks made up of the three Kāśyapa brothers, 1,000 former matted-haired ascetics (*jaṭila*) and the 250 wandering mendicants (*parivrājaka*) led by

Śāriputra and Maudgalyāyana. The Buddha, who abhorred miracles, nevertheless converted these matted-haired ascetics by a long series of wonders. Once possessed of the first fruit of the religious life, they requested ordination and this was conferred on them with the formula, 'Come, monk'. Some time after, in Gayāśīrṣa, they heard the Fire Discourse, and their minds were freed from impurities.

Śāriputra and Maudgalyāyana had from a tender age been in search of the 'Immortal'. They first attended the school of the sectarian master Sañjaya, who had an entourage of five hundred wandering mendicants. One day, in the streets of Rājagṛha, Śāriputra met Aśvajit, one of the first five monks converted in Benares, and heard from his lips the famous stanza which summarizes the Buddhist Doctrine in four lines: 'Of all phenomena arising from a cause, the Tathāgata has told the cause; he also revealed their extinction; he was the great Ascetic.' Śāriputra immediately acquired the Eye of the Doctrine without dust or stain. He told the stanza to Maudgalyāyana, who in turn was possessed of the first fruit of the Path. Taking with them 250 of Sañjaya's wandering mendicants, the two friends went to the Buddha. At their own request, they received ordination with the 'Come, monk' formula. At that very instant the minds of the 250 wandering mendicants were freed from impurities and they became *arhats*. The two who had led them to the Buddha took longer to reach the same result: Maudgalyāyana became a Holy One seven days after his ordination and Śāriputra another week later. Śāriputra became 'first of those of penetrating intelligence', Maudgalyāyana 'first of those who have magic powers', and together they were known as the 'foremost pair' (*agra yuga*) of the Buddha's disciples, his 'right hand' and 'left hand' disciple respectively.

Five years after the Buddha's Enlightenment, his aunt Mahā Prajāpatī Gautamī accompanied by five hundred Śākyan women went to the Lord in Vaiśālī and requested permission for women to leave home for the homeless life of the Doctrine and Discipline so well expounded by the Tathāgata. The Buddha refused three times. Gautamī and her companions cut off their hair, dressed in the yellow robes and went to the Buddha. Ānanda, the Buddha's cousin and attendant monk, interceded for them, but three times more the Buddha refused his permission. Later on, he conceded that if a woman were to accept eight strict rules (*gurudharma*) this would replace ordination (*upasampad*) for her, and she could obtain the four fruits of the religious life. Gautamī and the five hundred Śākyan women joyfully accepted this proposition and were thus ordained (*Vin.* II, 253–6; *A.* IV, 274–7).

However, this new status did not immediately confer the fruits of the religious life on them. It was only later, when they heard the religious instruction communicated twice to them by the monk Nandaka, that they had access to these attainments; even the favoured nun only achieved the first, Stream-Entry (*M.* III, 277).

The career of the monks and nuns after the Buddha's decease

The Order is open to all those who are free to dispose of themselves and who do not suffer from the impediments of crime or contagious disease. No account is taken of caste distinctions, although Śākyamuni preferred to recruit his monks from among 'noble young people who leave home to lead a life of wandering' (*Vin.* I, 9). The obligations taken on by the monk do not commit him for ever; he is not forbidden to leave the Order and return to lay life (*Vin.* III, 23–7).

Entry into the Order is made through two distinct ceremonies, which were clearly differentiated soon after the Buddha's decease: 'Going Forth' (*pravrajyā*) and ordination (*upasampad*). Nowadays these are sometimes referred to in English as lower and higher ordination respectively. The candidate cannot be admitted to the 'Going Forth' before the age of eight. He acquires two patrons, a preceptor (*upādhyāya*) and a master (*ācārya*), whose companion (*sārdhavihārin*) and pupil (*antevāsin*) respectively he will become. Having put on the yellow robe and having had his hair and beard cut off, he prostrates himself in front of the preceptor and announces three times that he takes refuge in the Buddha, the Doctrine and the community of monks. After this purely unilateral action, the master teaches him the ten rules (*daśa śikṣāpada*). These are practically the same as the Eight Precepts undertaken by pious Buddhists on holy days, mentioned above (see p. 54); the only difference is that the novice also forswears accepting gold or silver. After 'Going Forth', the candidate is still only a novice (*śrāmaṇera*); he only becomes a regular member of the community, a monk, after higher ordination (*upasampad*), which cannot be conferred on him until he is twenty.

Ordination is fixed down to the smallest detail by the ritual texts called *karmavācanā*. It is conferred by a chapter of at least ten monks. Supplied with a begging bowl and three robes, the supplicant requests ordination three times. The celebrant ensures that he is free of impediments and enquires for his name, his age and his preceptor. Then the ordination proper follows: this is an ecclesiastical act in which the 'motion' is fourfold (*jñapticaturthakarman*). It in fact consists of a motion (*jñapti*) followed by three propositions (*karmavācanā*) concerning the admission of the motion by the chapter.

First, the motion: the celebrant asks the chapter: 'May the community hear me: so-and-so, here present, desires, as the pupil of the venerable so-and-so, to receive ordination. If this pleases the community, may it confer ordination: such is the motion.' Then follow the three propositions; the celebrant continues: 'May the community hear me: so-and-so, here present, desires, as the pupil of the venerable so-and-so, to receive ordination. The community confers ordination on so-and-so, with so-and-so as preceptor. He who is of the opinion that ordination should be conferred ..., may he remain silent. He who is of the contrary opinion, may he speak.' This proposition is repeated

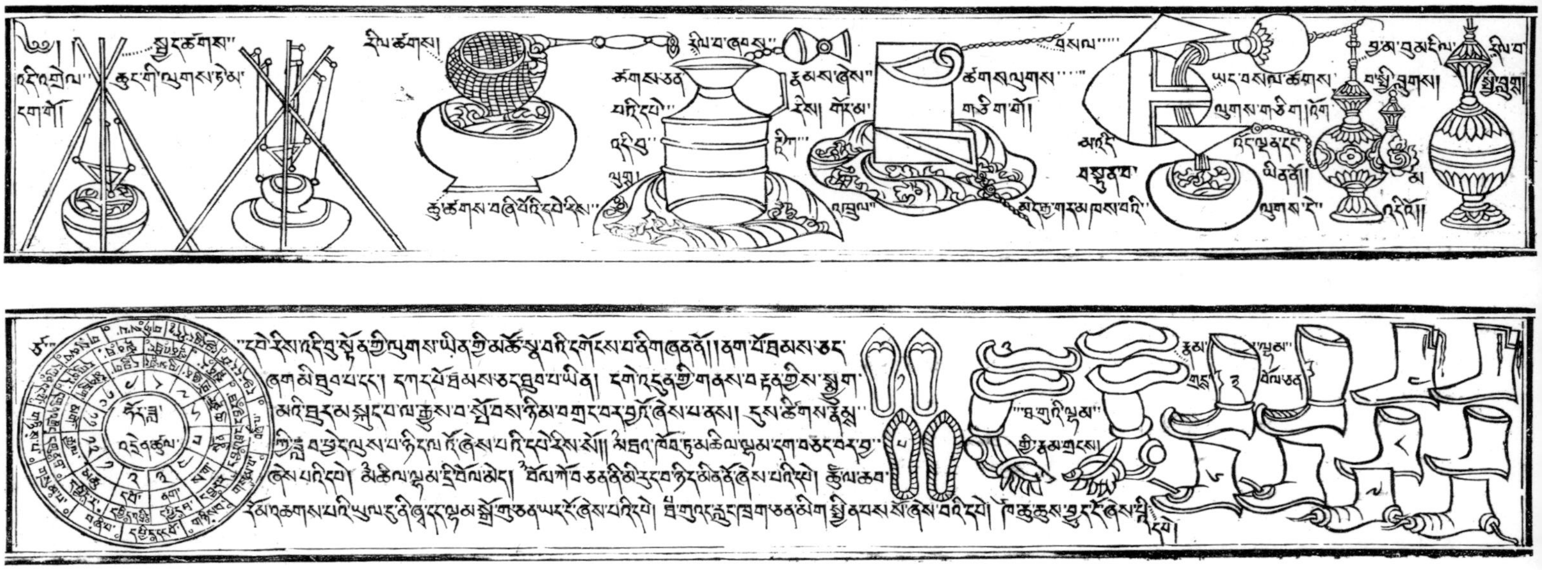

The monk's possessions – two leaves from a Tibetan series of blockprints now in Japan. The upper leaf is devoted to the various water-strainers used by monks to prevent them from inadvertently killing insects, and flasks containing water to rinse their mouths after meals. The lower leaf shows, on the left, a mnemonic diagram of the months and seasons and, on the right, the various shoes and boots allowed and forbidden to monks.

three times. After the third proposition, if the chapter remains silent, the ordination is accepted and the celebrant declares: 'So-and-so has received ordination from the community with so-and-so as preceptor. The community is of this opinion, that is why it remains silent: it is thus that I hear it' (*Vin.* I, 22, 56, 95).

After which, in order to determine the new monk's rank, the day and hour of his ordination are noted. He is informed of the four rules of monastic austerity (*niśraya*) which he may observe in his outward life, and he is told of the four great prohibitions (*akaraṇīya*) the violation of which would in itself exclude him from the community: sexual intercourse, theft, murder, and false or self-interested usurpation of the spiritual perfections.

The career of the nun is closely modelled on that of the monk. However, before being accepted for ordination, girls aged under twenty and women with more than twelve years of married life are subjected to a probationary stage which lasts for two years. During that period the female probationer (*śikṣamāṇā*) must observe six rules which correspond to the first six of the novice's rules: to abstain from murder, theft, impurity (i.e. sexual activity), falsehood, intoxicants, and meals outside the right time (*Vin.* IV, 319–23).

At the time of her ordination, the future nun, supplied with a begging bowl and the fivefold robe, presents herself, with her preceptress (*upādhyāyikā*) and instructress (*ācāriṇī*), first before the chapter of nuns and then before the chapter of monks, and receives ordination from this twofold assembly. Eight strict canonical provisions place the nun in complete dependence on the monks. The main ones are that she cannot go into retreat where there is no monk; that every fortnight she must go to the community of monks and receive instruction, but that she herself can neither instruct a monk nor admonish him; that the ceremonies of ordination, of the end of the retreat and of confession are repeated before the community of monks (*Vin.* II, 271–2).

The collection of the detailed regulations for the conduct of the fully ordained monk and nun is called the *Prātimokṣa*. The monks' code consists of more than 220 rules which are arranged in categories according to the penalty prescribed, in decreasing order of gravity. The first four offences, which are so grave that they entail automatic dismissal from the Order, have already been mentioned. The discipline to which the nun is subjected is stricter than that of the monks. Her regulations consist in principle of five hundred articles, double those of the monks, but in practice their numbers vary between 290 and 355.

Equipment and life of the monks

The Buddhist Sangha is a mendicant order. The monk renounces all possessions, cannot practise any lucrative career, or receive gold or silver. He expects lay generosity to provide the supplies necessary for his subsistence: clothing, food, shelter and medicines.

The monk has the use of three robes (*tricīvara*): an outer garment (*uttarāsaṅga*), an under garment (*antaravāsaka*) and a cloak (*saṃghāṭi*) (*Vin.* I, 94, 289); in addition to these, the nun also wears a belt (*saṃkakṣikā*) and a skirt (*kusūlaka*) (*Vin.* II, 272). These clothes are yellow or reddish (*kāṣāya*) in colour. The monk is permitted to wear clothing given by the laity or made of rags which he has collected. Shoes are considered a luxury, but the use of fans is allowed. The monk's equipment also includes a begging bowl, a belt, a razor, a needle, a strainer, a staff and a tooth-pick; with his robes, these seven items constitute the Eight Requisites (*aṣṭa pariṣkāra*).

The monk lives on the food which he begs daily during his morning alms-round. In silence and with lowered eyes, he goes from house to house and places in his bowl the food which is held out to him, usually balls of rice. Towards midday, his meal time, he withdraws in solitude and eats his food: bread, rice, with water to drink. The use of intoxicant drinks is strictly forbidden; that of flesh or fish is only permitted if the monk has not seen, heard or suspected that the animal was killed on his behalf (*Vin.* I, 238). Ghee (clarified butter), butter, oil, honey and sugar are reserved for the sick and can be taken as medicine (*Vin.* I, 199). A meal eaten at the wrong time, that is, between midday and the morning of the following day, entails a penance. Monks are permitted to accept invitations and have their meal in the homes of the laity.

As to lodgings (*śayanāsana*), the monks have no fixed residence: some live in the open air in mountains and forests, sheltering under a tree; others, more numerous, set up their residence, *vihāra*, near a village or town: a hut of leaves (*parṇaśālā*), a tower (*prāsāda*), a house made of stone (*harmya*) or a cave (*guhā*). In principle the *vihāra* only houses a single monk. *Vihāras* can be grouped in lesser or greater numbers and can shelter some tens of monks. When the complex takes on importance, it is called a convent or monastery (*saṃghārāma*) and may be built of stone, bricks or wood.

During the three or four months of the rainy season, usually from the full moon of the month of Āṣāḍha (June–July) to the full moon of the month of Kārttika (October–November), the Buddhist monk, like the adherents of other non-Brahminical sects of the time, is compelled to go into retreat (*varṣopanāyikā*) and remain in a set place (*Vin.* I, 137). At the end of the retreat, he can continue his wanderings, but is not compelled to do so. Monastic life must have been organized early on, since the buildings put at the disposal of the community by kings and wealthy merchants had to be administered all year round. Today every monastery of any importance has its own officers in charge of food and drink and its own gardener; other monks are in charge of the storerooms, wardrobe, water supplies, begging bowls, voting tickets (*śalākā*), etc.; a superintendent is in charge of the novices.

The daily life of the monk is regulated in every detail. The monk rises very early and devotes himself to meditation. At the appropriate time, he dresses to go out, takes his wooden bowl in his hands and goes to the nearest village to beg for his food. Having returned to the monastery, he washes his feet and, a little before noon, eats his meal. Then he settles on the threshold of his cell and gives instruction to his spiritual sons. When this is over, he withdraws in seclusion, most often to the foot of a tree, there to pass the hot hours of the day in meditation or semi-somnolence. Sunset signals the hour for the public audience, open to all comers, to which flock sympathizers as well as the merely curious. The darkness of the night brings calm to the monastery once again. The monk may take his bath, then again he receives his disciples and engages in edifying conversation with them which continues well into the first watch of the night.

Twice a month, on the days of the full and of the new moons, the monks who live in the same parish, as well as visiting monks, are obliged to assemble and together celebrate the *poṣadha*, Observance Day – a day of fasting and particularly strict respect of the observances. The Buddhists borrowed this custom from other sects. Each alternate celebration of the *poṣadha* concludes with a public confession between monks. The monks take their places on low seats which have been reserved for them in the assembly area. The senior monk chants a preliminary formula, and invites his brethren to acknowledge their misdeeds; he questions the monks and asks them three times if they are pure of such misdeeds. If everyone remains silent, he proclaims: 'Pure of these misdeeds are the Venerable Ones, that is why they keep silent; thus have I heard it.' Anyone guilty who remains silent would be perpetrating a voluntary falsehood, and would violate his solemn commitments.

Some festivities break the monotony of the days. They vary according to the region. However, a festivity celebrated by all the communities is that of *pravāraṇā*, which marks the end of the rainy season and the conclusion of the retreat. This is the occasion for offering gifts to the monks, inviting them to a meal and organizing processions. Then follows the *kaṭhina* festival during which the laity distribute raw cotton cloth (*kaṭhina*) to the members of the community: the monks immediately make clothing out of this which they dye yellow or reddish.

The ideal of the monk

The ruling which imprisons the monk in a network of detailed prescriptions tends to make him a fully self-denying person: gentle and inoffensive, poor and humble, continent and perfectly trained.

He cannot take the life of any living being, and refuses to use water in which there might be the tiniest creature. Being unable to practise any lucrative profession, he depends on the generosity of the laity for his food and clothing. Nevertheless, he can accept no gold or silver from them and, if he does touch a piece of jewellery or some precious object, he can only do so to return it to its owner.

It is in this spirit that the *prātimokṣa*, the disciplinary code, forbids the monk to be alone with a woman, to share her roof, to walk in her company, to take her hand, to tease her, or even to exchange more than five or six sentences with her. The monk cannot accept food or clothing from a nun who is not related to him. He should, in all circumstances, adopt a correct, humble and vigilant attitude.

However, the obligations imposed on the monk, the

burdens with which he is entrusted, must never be so heavy and absorbing as to deprive him of the faculty of thought and turn him into a mere machine. Each preserves his own personality and aims towards the supreme goal according to the method of his choice. He can, like Musīla, apply himself to the understanding of phenomena (*dharma-pravicaya*) or, like Nārada, devote himself to the ascetic and meditative disciplines of yoga.

It is possible that the exclusive search for personal holiness is not always conducive to giving the monk a charitable heart, making him benevolent towards his brothers and devoted to the wretched. Nevertheless, in the mass of disciplinary prescriptions an article with a truly human ring can be discerned here and there. One day Śākyamuni found a monk who was suffering from an internal disorder, lying in his own urine and excrement. Since he was no longer of any use, his colleagues took no further care of him. The Buddha washed him with his own hands, changed his bedding and placed him on his bed. Then, addressing the monks, he said: 'O monks, you no longer have a father or mother to take care of you; if you do not take care of each other, who will? Whoever wishes to take care of me, should take care of the sick' (*Vin.* I, 301–2).

Nevertheless, for anyone who wishes to eliminate desire down to its root, brotherly charity is itself not without danger. It is up to each one to work towards his own holiness without being occupied or preoccupied with his neighbour. It is not by any means through love for his brothers that the monk finds his joy and happiness, but in the observance of his vows and rules, in study, meditation and the penetration of the Buddhist truths.

Generally, the monk leaves to the laity the practice of active virtues, which are just advantageous enough to ensure wealth and long life during future rebirths. Personally, he confines himself to the passive virtues of renunciation and imperturbability which alone lead him to holiness in this world and, in the other world, to the destruction of suffering, to the end of *saṃsāra*, and to Nirvāṇa.

The absence of an authority

Such were the Holy Ones whom the Buddha had trained when he deceased. We should add, since it was to affect the whole history of Buddhism, that he left them without a master or hierarchy. He believed that man cannot constitute a refuge for man, that no human authority can be usefully exerted over minds, and that adherence to the Doctrine should be exclusively based on personal reasoning, on what one has oneself acknowledged, seen and grasped.

In the Buddhist monasteries, particular duties were entrusted to the monks capable of fulfilling them, but this conferred no authority on them over their colleagues. The only precedence allowed was that of seniority calculated from the date of ordination.

If the Buddha refused to establish a functional hierarchy in the monasteries, still less did he intend to give the whole community a spiritual leader. Seeing him aged, his cousin Devadatta offered to replace him as head of the Sangha: 'Lord,' he said, 'attend calmly, then, to the delightful meditation of the Doctrine and entrust the congregation to my keeping; I will care for it.' Śākyamuni rejected this self-interested offer: 'I would not even entrust the congregation to Śāriputra and Maudgalyāyana. Even less to you, Devadatta, who are of no account and so contemptible' (*Vin.* II, 188).

Shortly before his master's decease, gentle Ānanda expressed the hope that the Blessed One would not leave this world before having given his instructions to the community and having designated a successor. The Buddha answered him in substance: 'What does the community expect of me, O Ānanda? Never having wished to direct it or subject it to my teachings, I have no such instructions for the Sangha. I am reaching my end. After my decease, may each of you be your own island, your own refuge; have no other refuge. Acting in this way you will set yourselves on the summit of the Immortal' (*D.* II, 100).

Abandoned by their master, the disciples had to continue the work by themselves and devote the attention they had paid to the Buddha to the Doctrine alone.

List of abbreviations

Unless otherwise indicated, references are to volume and page of the original Pali and Sanskrit texts of the scriptures.

A. *Anguttara-Nikāya* ed. R. Morris and E. Hardy, 5 vols, London 1885–1900

CPS. E. Waldschmidt *Das Catuṣpariṣatsūtra* 3 vols, Berlin 1952–62

D. *Dīgha-Nikāya* ed. T. W. Rhys Davids and J. E. Carpenter, 3 vols, London 1890–1911

Divy. *Divyāvadāna* ed. E. B. Cowell and R. A. Neill, Cambridge 1886

It. *Itivuttaka* ed. E. Windisch, London 1889

M. *Majjhima-Nikāya* ed. V. Trenckner and R. Chalmers, 3 vols, London 1888–99

NidSa. C. Tripathi *Fünfundzwanzig Sūtras des Nidāna-saṃyukta* Berlin 1962

S. *Saṃyutta-Nikāya* ed. L. Feer, 5 vols, London 1884–98

Sanghabh. *The Gilgit Manuscript of the Sanghabhedavastu* ed. R. Gnoli, 2 vols, Rome 1977–8

Sn. *Suttanipāta* ed. D. Andersen and H. Smith, London 1913

Tr. E. Lamotte *Le traité de la grande vertu de sagesse de Nāgārjuna* 5 vols, Louvain 1944–80

Ud. *Udāna* ed. P. Sternthal, London 1885

Vin. *Vinayapiṭaka* ed. H. Oldenberg, 5 vols, London 1879–83

The Indian Tradition

2

Buddhism in Ancient India

3

Expansion to the North:
Afghanistan and Central Asia

4

Nepal: the Survival of Indian Buddhism
in a Himalayan Kingdom

THE SANGHA ESTABLISHED BY THE BUDDHA had taken root at the time of his death. When he attained Final Nirvāṇa, five hundred senior monks met to codify his teachings. They lived in monasteries in and around the modern Indian state of Bihar, a name which actually means 'Buddhist monastery'. These monks and nuns gradually spread through northern India; but the great expansion of Buddhism came under its imperial patron, Aśoka (268–239 BC). From surviving edicts he had engraved on rocks and pillars we know that Aśoka was converted to Buddhism early in his reign and propagated it throughout the Indian sub-continent and far beyond. His own son, Mahendra, headed the mission that officially introduced Buddhism into Sri Lanka.

Buddhism never had a central authority or enforced doctrinal orthodoxy. The Sangha, however, was liable to schism over interpretations of its Rule, the more so as communities came to be separated by vast distances and cultural barriers. Buddhist 'sects' are monastic divisions. On the other hand, soon after the time of Aśoka began the great movement in thought which became known as the Mahāyāna, or 'Great Vehicle'. This movement is characterized on the learned level by the doctrine of two truths, that the world of appearances has only provisional reality and is ultimately insubstantial, and on the popular level by devotion to a host of Buddhas and bodhisattvas, some of whom are treated almost as gods who can bestow favours.

Early in the first millennium AD began Buddhist tantra, a movement heavily influenced by Hinduism, which accepted Mahāyāna philosophy but sought salvation largely through ritual. With tantra Buddhism became esoteric and the Sangha lost its primacy, in that the spiritual élite consisted of initiates who could be clerical or lay.

Buddhism in India was at the height of its influence from 250 BC to the middle of the 1st millennium AD. Maybe both tantra and popular devotionalism weakened Buddhism by making it seem like a form of Hinduism; maybe the accidents of royal patronage, on which the great monasteries always have depended, were adverse. The Muslim invasions into India, sacking the monasteries, substantially destroyed Buddhist culture by the 13th century, though vestiges remained in India till nearly AD 1500.

In Central Asia too, Buddhism was finally supplanted by Islam. Aśoka's missions introduced it there, and it throve under the patronage of the Kuṣāṇa King Kaniṣka (*c.* 2nd century AD). The importance of Buddhism in Central Asia has become fully appreciated only in this century, as both documentary evidence and monastic remains have come to light in unexpected profusion. Now what used to be the 'forgotten chapter' of early Buddhist history is proving to be one of the most revealing.

The interest of Nepal, on the other hand, is that here alone Indian Buddhism survives in a tradition of unbroken continuity. The Buddhist Newars of the Kathmandu Valley practise a tantric Buddhism which stems directly from the form of Buddhism which must have existed when Buddhism was extinguished in India, but which has continued to undergo Hindu influence.

The face of the Buddha was conceived by the sculptors of the Gandhāra school in realistic as well as spiritual terms, the compassion of his quest on behalf of humanity softening the remoteness that he attained in Nirvāṇa. In the regions of Haḍḍa and Taxila artists evolved a technique of working in stucco, using methods imported via Iran from the eastern Mediterranean. Buddhists seem to have come to Haḍḍa, where this head was found, about the 1st century AD. Stucco sculpture reached its peak about the 3rd century; much of it was painted. But its fragility compared with stone has left few intact examples. This life-size head was part of a full-length figure. (1)

The stupa: monument and mnemonic

Stupas were originally funeral mounds built to contain the remains of kings and great men. After the Buddha's death his relics were divided and a number of stupas raised to hold them. By the time of Aśoka the stupa was already the accepted symbol of his Final Nirvāṇa, and the main Buddhist cult object.

As a focus of devotion within the monastery, the stupa serves both a practical and a spiritual function (see p. 94–5). *Above:* the inner courtyard of a Nepalese monastery, from a manuscript dated AD 1015 – a highly stylized representation that reduces the monastery to four cells and a stupa. *Below left:* adoration of a stupa, from Gandhāra, 2nd–3rd century AD. (2, 3)

The form of the stupa is subject to regional variation. In Nepal (*right*) the vertical feature almost dominates the hemisphere. This is at Svayambhunath – placed on a hill overlooking Kathmandu. The stupa, dedicated to Svayambhūnātha, the 'Self-Existent Lord', is surmounted by *toraṇas* (portal-like decorations) and an umbrella in burnished gold. One of its main features is the great pair of eyes painted on each side of the square base of the spire. (4)

The greatest Buddhist monument is Borobudur, in Java. Built in the mid-9th century, the central stupa is surrounded by three circles of stupas and supported on five square terraces, 33 metres (108 feet) high and 123 metres (403 feet) square at the base. Every level is faced with a carved frieze, showing that the base stands for hell and the lower world, with the terraces rising through the earthly to the celestial regions, the whole forming a vast three-dimensional *maṇḍala*. (5)

Sacred sites

For a thousand years Buddhism had followers in almost every part of India. The monasteries and monuments that were built throughout that long period include some of the grandest examples of Buddhist art and architecture anywhere in the world, though nearly all of them now stand desolate and ruined.

Bhājā is a rock-cut monastery dating from the early 2nd century BC. Its main stupa stands inside a huge excavated *caitya* hall, as at Kārle (see pl. 13), but there are rows of smaller stupas against the exterior cliff. (6)

Nālandā was a monastic university and one of the most splendid Buddhist centres in India, described at length by the pilgrim Hsüan-tsang in the 7th century. Rows of monasteries have been excavated (*below*), with small cells opening off an inner courtyard. One of the stupas (*left*) is unusual in having a two-storey base, with niches holding statues of Buddhas and bodhisattvas, and an octagonal top. (8, 9)

Bodh-Gayā's Mahabodhi temple marks the spot where the Buddha attained Enlightenment. The present structure dates essentially from the 12th century AD, though restored in the 19th. Sārnāth (*below*) was the scene of the Buddha's first sermon. Its ruined stupa (*c.* 5th century AD) gives some idea how these great monuments were built; the hemispherical dome has disappeared and only the substructure remains, with niches surrounded by relief carving. (11, 12)

Sāñcī is the site of the earliest surviving stupas in India. Uniquely, it preserves not only the stone fence encircling the base (defining the path of ritual circumambulation) but also the four carved gateways (*toraṇas*) at the cardinal points. The whole arrangement as seen today (*below*) dates from the end of the 1st century BC, but in origin it may go back to the days of the Emperor Aśoka; a stupa there contained relics of monks whom he had sent as missionaries. Each gateway consists of three horizontal beams with spiral ends. The inner face of the East Gate (*above*) includes representations of the throne under the Bodhi tree, the stupa being venerated by goddesses (second panel of the uprights) and by elephants (lowest horizontal). (7, 10)

Temples in the rock

The practice of excavating sanctuaries out of the solid cliff began in western India. Surviving examples preserve features from wooden prototypes now lost.

Kārle (*left*) is the largest of these early cave sanctuaries containing stupas or *caityas*. Two rows of columns with figural capitals and bases like water-jars lead to a semicircular ambulatory containing the stupa. (13)

Ajaṇṭā and Ellora, about 100 miles apart in the hills of the northern Deccan, are both sites built up over several centuries. Cave 19 at Ajaṇṭā (*above left*) has an elaborate façade leading into a *caitya*-hall similar to but smaller than that of Kārle. The date is 5th century AD. At Ellora the façade of Cave 10 (*above right*) fronts a pillared hall containing a colossal seated Buddha. (14, 15)

Far to the north, at Bezeklik in northern Turkestan (*below*), are cave temples resembling those of India but containing paintings of the 8th–10th centuries in a specifically Central Asian style. (16)

The heart of Asia

Buddhist missions began penetrating the barriers of the Hindu Kush and Himalayas in the 1st century AD. Vast and populous monasteries arose in what is now Afghanistan, adorned with frescoes and sculpture and visited by pilgrims on their way to and from India. Soon the wide regions of Chinese Turkestan were open to Buddhism.

In the rich valley of Bāmiyān, at the foot of the Hindu Kush, Buddhist monks founded a centre from which to evangelize Central Asia. Cells and temples were hollowed out of the cliff face, and two huge images of the Buddha were carved at either end. This one is 54 metres (177 feet) high, the largest stone statue in the world. The drapery folds are constructed by suspending thick ropes from dowels fixed into the rock and coating the whole with plaster. Contemporary frescoes inside the caves are equally memorable. The valley was devastated and the monuments defaced in AD 1222 by Jenghis Khan. (17)

The men who evangelized Afghanistan and Turkestan, who converted kings, administered monasteries and translated texts, were changing the whole face of civilization in Central Asia. Buddhism was able to gather into itself all the intellectual currents of the age, uniting ideas from the Greco-Roman world of the West and China in the East. At Mirān (*above left*) lively wall-paintings from about AD 300 show a group of monks, one of them holding a fan, depicted according to the conventions of Sassanian art. The withdrawn gaze of the monk (*above*) signifies inner contemplation, the prolonged mental effort to attain Enlightenment. This stucco head is from Srinagar, Kashmir, another of Aśoka's monastic foundations. (18, 19)

Haḍḍa, once a teeming city and one of the leading monasteries of Central Asia, was totally forgotten until its ruins were rediscovered in the 19th century. It has since been partially excavated, yielding fragments of stucco and painting of high quality and similar in style to those of Mirān and Bāmiyān. Most, however, have been removed to museums and the site is now returning to the desert. (20)

The monk's life

Discoveries by Sir Aurel Stein in the early part of this century give us an unexpectedly vivid glimpse into the daily life of a Buddhist monk in Central Asia during the 9th and 10th centuries. These wall-paintings are now in the British Museum, London. Others from the same site are in the National Museum in Delhi.

Writing was one of the monk's most important occupations. Every new mission meant laborious copying and often translation. *Left:* a monk, his hands in the horizontal position of adoration, kneels before another who makes a gesture of protection. A third monk seems to sweep down from the clouds. The corner of a water tank appears bottom left. *Opposite:* here an aged monk holds a pen and a *pothi* leaf while younger monks kneel in front of him. The pen is held like a brush, and from its position it has been possible to deduce that a vertical script is being used, i.e. Chinese or Uigur. A celestial being floats down from the sky, scattering flowers. *Below:* seven monks sit in a rocky cave writing with pen-like brushes on *pothi* leaves. A small inkpot or vase is suspended bottom right. The caves have arched entrances suggesting masonry. Outside the cave on the right is a pool. (21–24)

A new ideal: the Mahāyāna

The teachings of the Buddha centred around the ideal of the monk striving for his own deliverance. Mahāyāna, in contrast, works for the salvation of all living beings. This is the ideal of the bodhisattva who forsakes Final Nirvāṇa until he has contributed to the redemption of other beings from suffering. By this way, many new bodhisattvas and mystical Buddhas found their way into the pantheon of Mahāyāna Buddhism, and they are represented in numerous works of art. For the laity they were supernatural beings who would help the faithful on their way to salvation. At the same time, the philosophers of the Mahāyāna tradition stressed the 'emptiness' (*śūnyatā*) of all phenomena in the world.

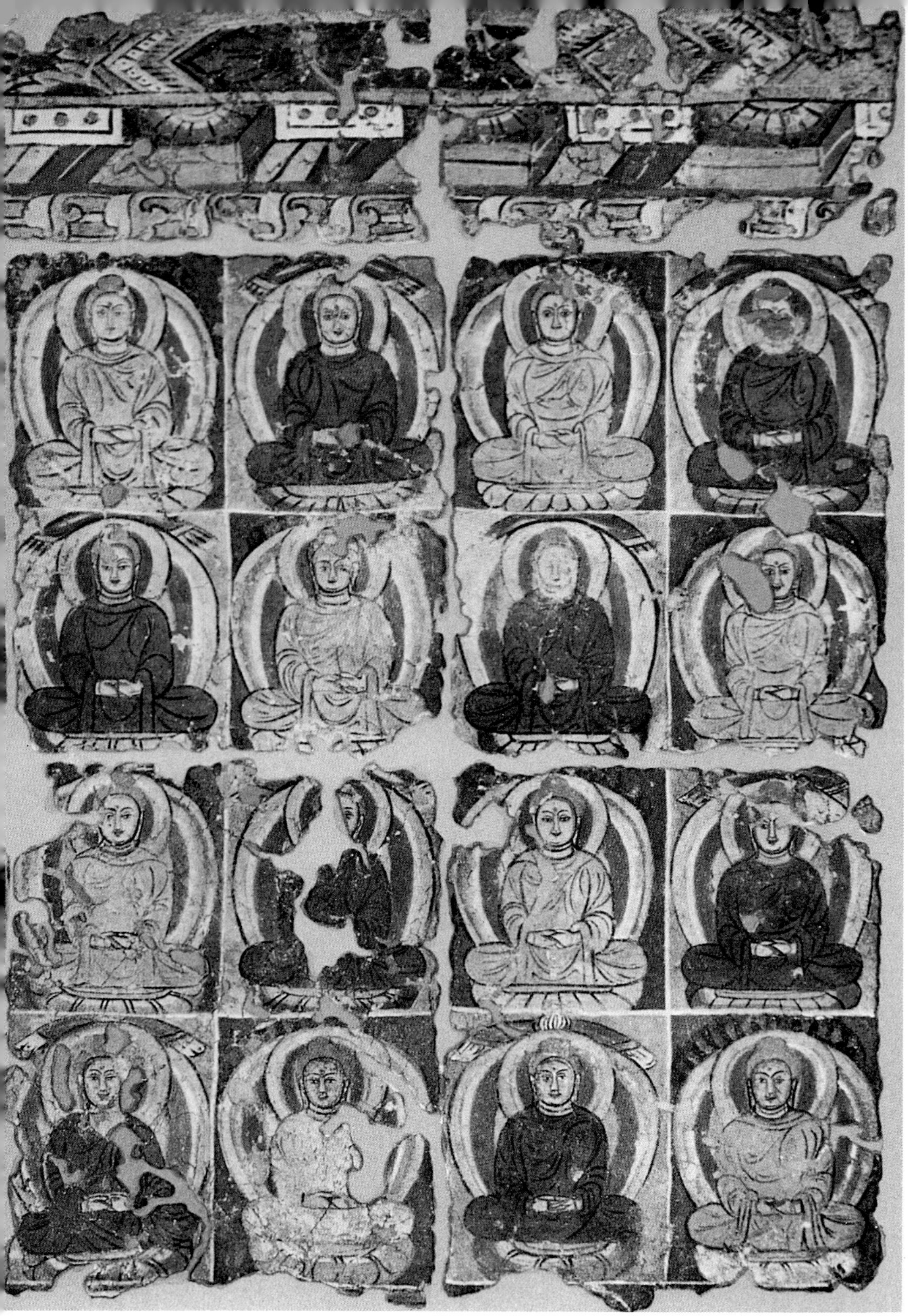

The reduplication of Buddha images occurs in the traditional earlier forms of Buddhism, foreshadowing the emergence of Mahāyāna beliefs. This wall painting is (like pl. 16) from the Central Asian monastery of the Sarvāstivāda sect of early Buddhism at Bezeklik. Each figure has his hands in the *mudrā* of meditation, resting on the lap with palms upward. In Mahāyāna ritual the repetition of prayers and actions is given prime importance. Sheer numbers acquire a mystical efficacy, and Halls of a Thousand Buddhas reinforce the worshipper's faith. (25)

Some bodhisattvas watch over human destiny like guardian angels. One of the greatest, Mañjuśrī, is shown in a 10th-century Indian palm-leaf manuscript (*right*), sitting in a shrine with two worshippers, his hands in the gesture of teaching. (26)

'Royal ease' is the name given to the languid pose that often characterizes bodhisattvas, conveying effortless power, harmony and benevolence. *Above:* Kuan-yin bodhisattva, seated by the sea-shore – a wooden statue from China, late 13th century. Kuan-yin is the Chinese form of Avalokiteśvara (see p. 92) – conceived as female instead of male. Here she wears a jewelled chain with pendants and a diadem decorated with lotus flowers. (28)

Wrathful deities keep the forces of evil at bay. These guardian figures are a feature of tantric iconography. Here, in an 18th-century terracotta from Tibet, Mahākāla, the Power of Devouring Time, wears a flaying knife in his headdress and carries a skull cup full of blood. (30)

Wise, compassionate and beautiful, the bodhisattvas are among the most familiar Buddhist images. This example from Sri Lanka dates from the 11th century when there was Mahāyāna influence. Head-dress and girdle are studded with gems. This period was the apogee of the fine south India tradition of bronze casting; large figures have been found in northern Ceylon, which was conquered by Tamils. (27)

Mañjuśrī again – this time from Japan, seated on a lotus and riding an elephant. (29)

The crossroads

It is easy to forget that for much of the 1st millennium Central Asia – roughly Afghanistan and east and west Turkestan (now divided between Russia and China) – placed as it was on the Silk Road between East and West, was at the centre of world culture, a region where currents from China, Byzantium, Islam and India could meet and mingle.

Takht-i-Bahi, in present-day Pakistan, is among the most impressive remains of Buddhist monasticism during its first period of expansion, the 1st century AD. Around a large courtyard are shrines containing stupas and statues. Behind it is the monastery proper, with more shrines, cells for the monks and a meeting hall. Only vestiges remain of a row of colossal Buddhas. Here too are clear signs of Greco-Roman influence, including columns surmounted by Corinthian capitals. (31)

Faces that betray their origins in widely scattered parts of the continent bear witness to the cosmopolitan character of Central Asian Buddhism. *Above:* monks or disciples in a wall-painting from the Ming-öi, near Šorčuq; 8th–9th centuries, strongly Chinese in physiognomy and style. *Right:* detail from a Bezeklik painting, 8th century, showing pilgrims mourning the death of the Buddha. From various indications, three at least can be identified as Arab, Chinese and Persian. (32, 33)

Nepal, the heir of India

The form of Buddhism which survives in Nepal has been undergoing Hindu influence for many centuries, especially under Hindu kings. Hindu and Buddhist concepts and practices are so intermingled that it is often impossible to draw a distinct line between them. Here Buddhism is no longer in the hands of a monkhood drawing voluntary recruits, but of gurus who form a Hindu-type high caste.

The typical vihara in Nepal consists of a courtyard surrounded by monastery buildings and by the main temple. *Left:* entrance to the Golden Vihara (*Hiranyavarṇamahāvihāra*) in Patan, showing the bell struck by the faithful and a pagoda-like shrine containing a thunderbolt (*vajra*) on a pedestal. (34)

'Diamond Masters', *vajrācāryas*, are the heirs of the tantric tradition of Nepal, learned in Sanskrit and revered as teachers. Many of the rituals that they carry out are close to Hindu models. This detail from a long picture-roll painted in 1837 shows a *vajrācārya* performing the *aṣṭamīvrata,* i.e. sacrifice on the eighth day of the lunar fortnight in honour of the bodhisattva Avalokiteśvara. (35)

2

Buddhism in Ancient India

RICHARD GOMBRICH ETIENNE LAMOTTE LAL MANI JOSHI

THE EVOLUTION OF THE SANGHA

The scriptures

'Go monks and travel for the welfare and happiness of the people, out of compassion for the world, for the benefit, welfare and happiness of gods and men. No two of you go the same way. Teach the Doctrine, monks, which is fine in its beginning, middle and end, with its meaning and letter, sheer and whole, and proclaim the pure holy life. There are beings, naturally of little passion, who are languishing for lack of hearing the Doctrine; they will understand it.'

With these words, according to the traditional account, the Buddha despatched the first sixty monks he had converted and ordained. Generosity is the first Buddhist virtue. The laity can make the Sangha only material gifts ('raw flesh', as they are not very politely called); in turn the monks and nuns give them the Doctrine. 'The gift of the Dharma is superior to all others.'

The first function and duty of the Sangha was to preserve the Doctrine and thus preserve Buddhism as such. Preserving the Doctrine meant in effect preserving the scriptures, the Canon and its commentaries. The Canon accepted by all Buddhists consisted of 'Three Baskets' (*tri-piṭaka*) of texts, a large collection which is the equivalent of the Bible for Christians or the Koran for Muslims. This Canon claims to be 'the Word of the Buddha', but it is of course composed by monks. When we say that an early Buddhist text is 'composed' we must remember that we are dealing with an oral tradition. We cannot know just when or where the first Buddhist text was written down, but it was probably centuries after the Buddha. The first time the Canon was committed to writing was in Sri Lanka in the 1st century BC; that was in its Pali version, preserved by Theravādin monks. There is a tradition that the Canon was written down in a Sanskrit version at a council organized in Kashmir under the auspices of the Emperor Kaniṣka. Kaniṣka was a ruler in the Kuṣān dynasty, who had invaded India from Central Asia. Unfortunately the dating of the Kuṣān dynasty, and hence of Kaniṣka, is still controversial, but it is reasonable to guess that the council Kaniṣka organized (which is sometimes known in the literature as the Fourth Buddhist Council) took place in the 2nd century AD. Even after that, Buddhist texts were preserved primarily by memorization and recitation; manuscripts were mainly mnemonic aids. Outside the monasteries, perhaps only a minority of the Buddhist laity were literate.

The early versions of the scriptures were in various dialects of Middle Indo-Aryan, that is, languages derived from Sanskrit. So long as they were orally preserved, their language no doubt fluctuated. Around the turn of the Christian era, some of these dialects had diverged so far that they were not mutually intelligible. To preserve the unity of Buddhist culture it was necessary to find a *lingua franca*. Within India, this *lingua franca* was Sanskrit, the language which throughout the pre-Muslim period and to some extent to this day has been the language of learned discourse. Buddhist texts were first translated into and composed in a kind of Sanskrit which deviated from the classical norm, remaining very close to the Middle Indo-Aryan dialects (which are also called Prākrits); this language is nowadays called Buddhist hybrid Sanskrit, and it was used in the early centuries of the Christian era and perhaps a little earlier. Buddhists also came to use good classical Sanskrit. But it is not simply the case that the later the text, the better the Sanskrit; it also depends on the kind of text. Original works were free to use classical Sanskrit, while works translated from or closely modelled on earlier scriptures usually stuck more closely to the earlier linguistic forms. Thus, the more strictly religious (as against philosophical or literary) a text, the more likely it was to be in a distinctively Buddhist form of Sanskrit.

The question of the language of a text is relevant to its function, preservation and diffusion. The Buddhist Canon alone, even without its commentaries, is so large that only very gifted individuals could memorize the whole of it. Its oral preservation was therefore organized into specialisms; monks in a particular pupillary

This fragment, inscribed across the skirt 'The King of Kings, his majesty Kaniṣka', is among the few memorials of one of the most powerful rulers of early Asia. Kaniṣka is credited with having organized the Fourth Buddhist Council, in the 2nd century AD.

succession would regard it as their primary duty to memorize one particular part of the Canon. But when translations of the Canon were needed, it became awkward to depend on oral transmission. Whether this problem arose with the first translations, those into Sanskrit, we have no idea, because we have absolutely no record of the circumstances in which those translations were made. But the next need for translations arose for a very remote market: China. The first translators of Buddhist scriptures into Chinese were two Indian monks who travelled to China in AD 68. Maybe they took manuscripts with them; certainly their successors did. At that period the Chinese were more used than the Indians to depending on books. Oral transmission cannot have been very satisfactory when what was wanted was the systematic translation of an entire corpus of sacred literature. Some of the Mahāyānist texts which were already translated into Chinese in the 2nd century AD were enormous. A succession of Chinese Buddhist monks came to India in search of manuscripts; the most famous are Fa-hsien (travelled 399–413), Hsüan-tsang (in India 630–44) and I-tsing (travelled 671–95), all of whom left accounts of their travels which are among our most important sources of information on ancient India in general and Indian Buddhism in particular.

Most of the important Buddhist scriptures were translated into Chinese several times and in different versions. Later, from the 7th or 8th century on, they were also translated into Tibetan. These translations are of crucial importance now because many of the originals, in Sanskrit and other Indian languages, have been lost: they were preserved orally by monks and in writing in monastic libraries, but the monks were killed and dispersed and the libraries burnt by Muslim invasions between the 8th and the 13th centuries. Thus the literature of Indian Buddhism is now available mainly in Chinese and Tibetan translations. Though the Chinese translations are more numerous and were generally made earlier, the Tibetan ones are usually the best for reconstructing the Sanskrit originals, because they were made almost mechanically, word for word, rather creating their own dialect of Tibetan 'translationese' than attempting to conform to a pre-existent language.

The largest body of Buddhist literature to survive in an Indian language was that preserved in Sri Lanka by the Theravādin school. Its language is an early form of Middle Indo-Aryan called Pali, a word which until comparatively modern times actually meant '(Buddhist canonical) text' – as distinct from commentary. This Pali literature includes the only complete version of the Canon to come down to us in an Indian language; as we have seen, it was committed to writing in the 1st century BC. The form of Buddhism which depended on this version of the Canon came to use Pali very much as Indian Buddhists came to use Sanskrit or indeed as the Roman Church used Latin: as a sacred language which enabled monks to transcend local differences. It was in Pali that Theravāda Buddhism spread from Sri Lanka to the mainland of Southeast Asia early in the present millennium. It is interesting to note that whereas the Chinese first used printing to multiply Buddhist texts, and printed their entire Canon in the 10th century, the first time that a complete edition of the Pali Canon was printed was by order of King Chulalongkorn of Siam in 1893. In India itself, since Buddhism had all but died out, the Buddhist Canon was not printed till after Independence. Modern scholars have generally depended on the version of the Pali Canon printed in London in roman characters by the Pali Text Society, which was founded in 1881.

Several times in Buddhist history, hundreds of learned monks have assembled to rehearse the Canon (and its commentaries). Though these assemblies are referred to in English as Councils, they are really Communal Recitations. The most recent such occasion was the Sixth Buddhist Council held in Rangoon in 1954–56, which was convened to produce an authoritative printed edition of the Pali scriptures. This Council was, however, called the Sixth only in the Theravādin enumeration; Buddhist schools differ in the Councils they recognize. Only the first two are recognized by all schools.

The First Buddhist Council was held at Rājagṛha

(modern Rajgir in Bihar) within a few months of the Buddha's Final Nirvāṇa; the Second at Vaiśālī (also in Bihar) a century later. The function of the First Communal Recitation was to establish the Canon for the first time. The meeting was presided over by Mahā Kāśyapa, the senior monk alive, and the Canon was in effect created by his questioning other monks about what the Buddha had said. Upāli expounded the *Vinaya Piṭaka* – the Discipline – and Ānanda, the Buddha's personal attendant, expounded the *Sūtra Piṭaka* – the 'Basket of Religious Discourses', the Buddha's sermons and sayings. That is why each *sūtra* begins 'Thus have I heard': Ānanda is speaking. The third Basket, the *Abhidharma*, consists of scholastic elaboration of the Doctrine.

There can be no doubt that the Pali *Abhidhamma Piṭaka* is apocryphal in the sense that it does not date from the First Council. Although all Buddhist schools and traditions share the *Vinaya* and *Sūtra Piṭakas*, the texts of the Theravādin *Abhidhamma Piṭaka* are peculiar to that school; each school of Buddhism came to possess its own texts of *abhidharma* (systematic philosophy). The situation with the more central part of the Canon, the Discipline and Discourses, the modern historian sees as rather more complicated. Broadly speaking, the essential contents of both are shared by all early Buddhist traditions. (The Mahāyāna paid less attention to the original Canon but never denied its authenticity.) Comparison between the various versions of texts that have survived (usually in Pali, Chinese and Tibetan; very occasionally in Sanskrit) shows that in both the *Vinaya* and the *Sūtra Piṭakas* one can distinguish between a shared core, which is much the larger part, and a divergent periphery. For example, traditions disagree about the occasions on which particular sermons were delivered, while keeping the sermons themselves intact. In the case of the *Vinaya Piṭaka*, some minor rules have variously been added to a larger body of rules which is undoubtedly original.

We can thus be fairly sure that the fundamental Buddhist texts, which are long enough to fill several hefty volumes, go back to a time before the Sangha divided, an event which can be dated to some time after the Second Council. It seems that this Second Communal Recitation may have been rather more creative than a mere repetition of the texts established at the First Council. Professor Frauwallner has given us good reason to believe that at the Second Council a systematic biography of the Buddha and the beginnings of a Buddhist church history were created, in order to give the *Vinaya* rules a charter and a historical setting. This scholarly deduction may be applied to the *Vinaya* as a whole. One part of that scripture concerns the *prātimokṣa*, the rules governing the monks' individual lives; the other concerns their ceremonies and communal life. Each rule and most subsequent adjustments are put in the mouth of the Buddha and related to some exigency which arose and demanded his intervention. The stories of most of these exigencies are minimal, formulaic, no more than is logically required for the promulgation of the rule. Clearly the anecdotes are historical fictions; such exigencies may have arisen, but the author of the text before us has no record of what they were. Moreover, the *Vinaya Piṭaka* documents changes in monastic life and discipline greater than are likely to have occurred during the Buddha's lifetime. It is therefore possible that the *Vinaya Piṭaka* as we have it owes at least as much to the Second Communal Recitation as to the First. Many scholars would regard this hypothesis as too bold in its precision, but would be prepared to accept that the *Vinaya Piṭaka* records, in a rather ahistorical manner, the development of the Sangha over its first one-and-a-half centuries. This view is, incidentally, half way between that of the most orthodox tradition, which gives the *Vinaya* forty-five years to develop (i.e., the period between the Sangha's founding and the Buddha's Final Nirvāṇa), and that of the most sceptical scholars, who would close this part of the Canon during the reign of the Emperor Aśoka, which, on the long chronology (see p. 41), would mean two to two-and-a-half centuries after the Buddha's decease.

We return to our statement that the creation and preservation of the scriptures are the work of monks. These scriptures fall into three categories: canonical, commentarial and pseudo-canonical. The Canon, we have seen, is ascribed to named Buddhist elders, repeating at the First Council the Buddha's words; the commentaries and pseudo-canonical works are almost entirely anonymous, though we can be sure that they

The Second Buddhist Council is represented on a terracotta plaque from Burma, made in the 19th century but traditional in style. The Second Council, held about a hundred years after the Buddha's death, probably saw the beginning of a biography, in the context of the codification of rules for the monastic life.

Palm-leaf manuscript containing part of one of the so-called 'Perfection of Wisdom Sūtras'. The manuscript was written in Bihar between 1150 and 1175. This text was not part of the original Buddhist canon but was probably composed around the start of the Christian era. It was among the early Mahāyāna sūtras that reached China with the first missionaries and which were fundamental to Chinese Buddhism. This leaf has a painting of the Buddha's Nirvāṇa in the centre.

too were composed by monks. The commentaries were not written down till long after the Canon, but that does not mean that they are not very old. We must remember that the texts were preserved orally. That means that when a monk taught his pupils, and *a fortiori* when he preached to the laity, he recited a text he had learnt by heart, and no doubt explained it as he went along. Texts would simply not have been available without such exegesis. In due course some of these commentaries were stabilized and systematized, and themselves memorized. Commentaries on the central parts of the Theravādin Canon were written down in Pali in Sri Lanka early in the 5th century AD by Buddhaghosa, a monk from India, but he was merely an editor, working on a body of material which had probably been closed in the 2nd century AD and was for the most part much older; the Theravādin tradition that the commentaries came to Sri Lanka with the first Buddhist missionaries in the 3rd century BC is probably too simple but not very wrong in its general tenor.

Pseudo-canonical works were apparently produced in India throughout the first millennium AD. They fall into two main groups: the early Mahāyānist literature and the Buddhist *tantras*. The largest single part of the early Mahāyānist literature is the collection of texts called 'The Perfection of Wisdom' (*Prajñā-Pāramitā*). Some of these texts, such as the *Diamond Sūtra* and the *Heart Sūtra*, and some other early Mahāyāna sūtras such as the *Lotus Sūtra* (*Saddharmapuṇḍarīka*, 'The Lotus of the True Doctrine') were among the Buddhist texts early to reach China and have been extremely popular with most Far Eastern Buddhists. This is the body of literature which contains the doctrinal changes referred to on pp. 90–93. Though the texts are religious, not philosophical, their ontology is that so brilliantly argued for by the great philosopher Nāgārjuna (2nd century AD) and known as Madhyamaka – 'Centrist', holding to a 'Middle Way' between affirmation and denial.

Each major doctrinal shift produced its own apocrypha: the 'Consciousness Doctrine' (*Vijñāna-vāda* – see p. 86) is enshrined in the *Laṅkāvatāra Sūtra*, which Professor D.T. Suzuki's translation and articles made accessible to the West fifty years ago. But the largest body of Buddhist apocrypha after the Wisdom Literature was that produced by the Buddhists who founded and practised the 'Diamond Vehicle' (*Vajrayāna*) or 'Spell Vehicle (*Mantrayāna*), two terms for what is also called tantric Buddhism.

All pseudo-canonical works were ascribed to a Buddha or one of his immediate disciples, with no trace of their real authorship; but it is reasonable to think that all or almost all must have been by monks. The philosophical works which accompanied and initiated developments in doctrine were by named authors, writing in Sanskrit; so far as we know, all these philosophers were monks. A few of the secular works written by Buddhists were written by laymen – King Harṣa, the 7th-century ruler of northern India who was also a major Sanskrit playwright, is a striking example – but the Buddhist contribution to Indian culture, immense as it was, was virtually the Sangha's contribution: the laity just paid for their upkeep.

Oral transmission and anonymity may be connected: the first named Buddhist authors date from the 2nd century AD, which is also likely to be the period when the texts were first written down. Certainly oral transmission must be partly responsible for another feature of early Buddhist literature – its highly repetitious style. Many of the canonical and pseudo–canonical texts can be decocted for content to a fraction of their size, as they are full of repetitions: if the Buddha says something about, for instance, the Five Aggregates, he is made to say it in full about each of the Aggregates in turn. Moreover, the prose portions of the Canon (they form its greater part) are chock-full of the kind of formulae and stock expressions familiar from oral literature the world over, and the later pseudo-canonical texts tended to imitate this feature. Such repetition assisted memorization; and maybe the rehearsal of repetitive texts, requiring little thought, was felt to be a kind of meditation, a training in calming and concentrating the mind.

Early development and structure of the Sangha

We mentioned above that the *Vinaya Piṭaka* quietly records considerable changes which took place during the Sangha's formative years. Most of these changes can be seen as a move away from asceticism. The Buddha had begun his first sermon by proclaiming a Middle Way between the sensual life of the ordinary householder and the mortification of the extreme ascetic.

Probably in his mind the former was exemplified by the brahmin householder, the latter by the Jain ascetics, who wore nothing but a loincloth and for most of the year were not allowed to spend two consecutive nights in the same place. The Sangha, though initially peripatetic, came to settle down for all or most of the year in fixed residences; moreover, though the possessions of individuals were stringently limited, the possessions of communities were not. The guiding idea is that one should treat oneself well enough not to be distracted from the spiritual life by hunger, and moderately enough not to be distracted by over-indulgence. But obviously one man's moderation may leave another man hungry and give a third man indigestion. The general tendency of early developments was towards an easier life for monks, the severer practice being retained as an option open to the zealous. The stricter practice or style of life could be undertaken temporarily or for life. Moreover, such asceticism was undertaken as a matter of individual choice: there is no evidence that one sect was in general more austere than another, though particular communities have sometimes fallen into lax ways.

At the end of a monk's ordination he is formally told of four austere practices called 'resorts': eating only alms-food gained by going out to beg; wearing only rags garnered from refuse heaps; living at the foot of a tree; using fermented cows' urine as medicine. The *Vinaya Piṭaka* says that the Buddha refused to make any of these practices compulsory. Later in Sri Lanka, and probably in India too, they were elaborated into a set of thirteen ascetic practices (*dhutaṅga*), any or all of which an individual monk could undertake if he felt inclined; they represent a kind of limit of permissible asceticism. Buddhist monasticism has in this regard shown a recurrent dynamic, at least in India and neighbouring countries: the more austere the way of life of a monk or group of monks, the more lay veneration and charity they attract; the charity in turn usually mitigates their austerity. It has often happened that a monk settles down to live in a forest cave, to find the cave rapidly equipped by admiring laity with 'all mod. con.'

Monks generally regarded themselves as having a dual function: to strive for their own Enlightenment, and to preserve the Doctrine so that others could do likewise. There was naturally a tendency towards specialization, so that those who went off to live in forests as hermits – though not necessarily alone, as our word implies – were regarded primarily as meditators, while those who lived in monasteries were primarily teachers and scholars. This correlation is not hard and fast but there must have been a considerable coincidence between style of life and primary function. Actual evidence for it in ancient times comes from Sri Lanka, but one may deduce that conditions in India were similar, because it is a matter of the Sangha's internal logic. Of course no member of the Sangha can have been allowed to remain ignorant of the scriptures: in modern times we can observe that the ordination ceremony includes an oral examination on selected scriptures. Nor was any member of the Sangha thought to be somehow exempt from the duty of meditation, for this was a 'duty' owed to no one but himself. It is important to stress both aspects of monastic life, because whatever may have been the shortcomings of individuals, especially those who passed their lives far from centres of learning and tradition, one is unlikely to form a correct appreciation of the works of the great Buddhist philosophers unless one remembers that they were steeped both in Buddhist literature – especially the Canon – and in a tradition of meditative practice.

There are very few Buddhist monastic rites or ceremonies, and only two are of critical importance: the higher ordination (*upasampad*), and the communal recitation of the Disciplinary code (*prātimokṣa*) and confession of faults. The ordination is so important because it must be valid to convey the authentic tradition – the Buddhist equivalent of apostolic succession. Traditionally there is no synchronic authority; all authority flows diachronically, from the Buddha himself. (This book will show that this ancient state of affairs has not survived everywhere.) A certain quorum of monks, themselves with valid ordination and innocent of any of the four disbarring offences, must be present; a competent monk of at least ten years' standing must preside; the candidate must truthfully state himself to be free of various potential disqualifications; and the correct forms must be observed. The higher ordination originally established formally who the ordinand's teacher was; this has since become more complicated, and in the Theravādin tradition the teacher who really counts is usually the monk who gives one the lower ordination to become a novice. In most Buddhist countries the line of pupillary succession has been of great importance because it establishes legal rights to residence in a monastery, to monastic property, etc. The relationship between teacher and pupils is explicitly modelled on that between father and sons, with the emotions such a bond implies; one may perhaps surmise, however, that to a young novice his teacher has to be both father and mother.

The Buddhist monastery is not organized as a spiritual hierarchy. It is an association of individuals seeking their own salvation and that of others. One corollary of this is the principle that decisions on matters of monastic discipline should be taken unanimously; another is that monks owe no obedience. Since early days there have however been officials, from abbot down, to deal with a monastery's daily life and temporalities. In many Buddhist countries the headship of a monastery has traditionally passed from an abbot to his eldest pupil, much like a temporal inheritance.

The importance of the communal *prātimokṣa* recitation in Buddhist history cannot be overemphasized. When the ritual was first established it seems to have been instrumental: monks went into it aware of faults they had committed and publicly confessed to them when the appropriate point in the

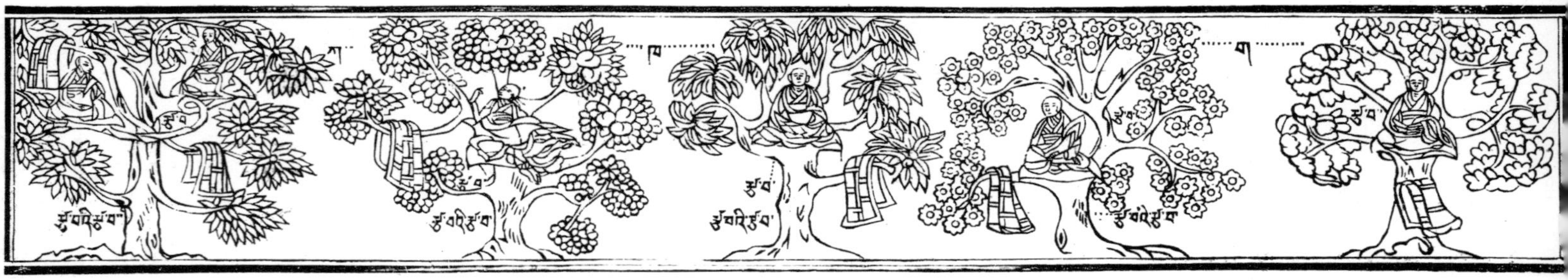

A set of Tibetan block-prints illustrate aspects of monastic life. These two strips show the various postures adopted by monks who

catalogue was reached, thus declaring their intention of submitting to the specified penalty – which, for many faults, is no more than the admission itself. Very soon, however – perhaps in the Buddha's own lifetime – the ritual became expressive of the Sangha's purity. All faults are confessed privately by one monk to another before the ceremony begins. Attendance is an indication that one has nothing left on one's conscience. The catalogue of faults is recited by the senior monk present (nowadays, at least, often in abbreviated form) while all are silent and thus declare their moral integrity.

It is absolutely essential that every monk present within a given area, defined by a formally established monastic boundary, must personally attend such a *prātimokṣa* ceremony once a fortnight, unless he is too ill to be moved, in which case he must confess on the spot and declare his purity by proxy. This is the concrete meaning of 'the unity of the Sangha', a recurrent expression in the *Vinaya*. That unity must be preserved. If monks in the same place hold separate *prātimokṣa* ceremonies, the Sangha is split into sects *ipso facto*. Splitting the Sangha is regarded by Buddhists as utterly deplorable; in theory it is just as bad as parricide.

Serious misunderstandings have arisen in the West among scholars who have grown up in monotheistic cultures, because we are accustomed to thinking of a sect as a body of opinion, a heterodoxy. Buddhist sect formation has nothing to do with doctrine or opinion; it is a matter of *vinaya*, and in particular of the *prātimokṣa*. Since the minimum number for holding a valid *prātimokṣa* ceremony is four, the Sangha can split when there is a minority of not less than four. Such splits occur only when there is formal dissent on a matter of discipline, on orthopraxy. So *Mahāyāna is not a sect*: it is a religious movement which affected monks regardless of their sect. For example, the 7th-century Chinese pilgrim Hsüan-tsang writes how in the great monastic university at Nālandā, which was a congeries of monasteries, Mahāyāna and Hīnayāna monks lived in the same monasteries. There is no such thing as a Mahāyānist *Vinaya*: all monks follow one of the *prātimokṣa* codes which (with one probable exception) were formulated long before the Mahāyāna arose. Doctrinal schools indeed proliferated, but that is quite a separate topic – of which more later.

Sects, holding separate *prātimokṣa* ceremonies and hence separate ordinations, have not only arisen because of *dissensions* over practice. It seems that most of the major sects arose simply because of geographical distance. When a group of monks lived in isolation, it happened that their *prātimokṣa* code acquired extra rules tagged on at the end, which meant that when they met other monks they could no longer celebrate the *prātimokṣa* together. And even when the formal codes were closed, differences in custom still arose with the same result. The first group to split off from the main body of monks and acquire a separate identity, the Mahāsāṅghikas, happen to have the shortest *prātimokṣa* code, with only 219 rules. It was among the Mahāsāṅghikas that Mahāyānist ideas about the nature of Buddhas and bodhisattvas seem to have originated, whereas we see that in Discipline they were the most conservative of all the sects. The Theravādins, whom modern historians sometimes label conservative, have 227 rules; the other sects all have more.

The diffusion and extinction of the Indian Sangha

The greatest figure in the history of Indian Buddhism after the Buddha himself is undoubtedly the Emperor Aśoka (268–239 BC). From his capital at Pāṭaliputra (modern Patna) Aśoka ruled over the whole of northern and central India, more than two thirds of the subcontinent and probably the largest empire that India was to see for two millennia. Aśoka left a set of edicts, engraved on rocks and pillars, recording his exploits, opinions and wishes. The idea of having such inscriptions made may have come to him from the Achaemenid empire; but the tone of what he had to say is utterly different. He tells us that early in his reign he was converted to Buddhism; he calls himself a lay follower (*upāsaka*). For a while he was not zealous, but after a successful military campaign the thought of the suffering his war had caused gave him great pain. The thirteenth major rock edict, in which he records his remorse, is a document probably unique in history and deserves to be read by everyone (it is translated in N. A. Nikam and R. McKeon's *The Edicts of Aśoka*). In other inscriptions Aśoka records the restrictions he imposed

meditate in forests.

on killing animals and his exhortations to his subjects to lead kind, tolerant and orderly lives.

In the best tradition of Indian kingship, Aśoka supported all religions; though he put it on public record, his Buddhist piety was a personal matter. Two of his inscriptions, however, are addressed to the Sangha. In one of them (extant in three versions) he warns them that if they do not hold the *prātimokṣa* together and observe unity he will have the laggards disrobed. Buddhist chronicles claim that he carried out a massive purification of the Sangha in Pāṭaliputra, expelling many bad monks. Though this is not corroborated by any inscription, and indeed the account seems garbled, the episode (whatever really happened) was influential in Buddhist history. The image of Aśoka as the ideal monarch who upheld Buddhist values and took an active interest in the purity of the Sangha shone as a model and as an inspiring example before every later Buddhist king.

Aśoka did more than any other individual to spread Buddhism. Buddhist tradition has it that in the middle of his reign, about 250 BC, monks set out from central India to travel in all directions towards and beyond his borders. Some scholars connect these missions with Aśoka's own statement in his edicts that he sent emissaries to foreign rulers and conquered them by 'righteousness' (*dharma*), Unfortunately, it may not be possible to match the destinations of the emissaries with those of the alleged missions. There is reason to be sceptical about the traditional story, though what may well be true is that a mission led by the monk Mahinda, who was a son of Aśoka, brought Buddhism (in its Theravādin form) to Sri Lanka. For the rest, the tradition may be over-simple in presenting various visits of monks to outlying regions as a simultaneous and co-ordinated enterprise. But there can be no doubt that it has a symbolic truth in recording how Aśoka's patronage enabled Buddhism to spread and the Sangha to establish itself in ever wider territory.

Several Indian kings patronized Buddhism; but no Buddhist state was ever established in India. The Indian tradition, to which most kings adhered, was that the king should protect all religions, whatever his personal convictions. Sri Lanka was the first, and for a long time the only, Buddhist state.

We must remember that in Buddhist estimation the Doctrine is only established where the Sangha is established, and, in turn, that is considered to be the case only when a monastic boundary has been duly established, for without such a boundary no formal act of the Sangha, whether *prātimokṣa* or ordination ceremony, can take place. The establishment of a monastic boundary requires lay support: the land has to be given to the Sangha. Alternatively, Buddhism can be considered to have taken root somewhere only when a local recruit has been properly ordained there. These considerations would apply just as much to the spread of Buddhism within India as to its diffusion into foreign parts. The latter is also a part of the history of Indian Buddhism, if only because our fragmentary evidence strongly suggests that in ancient times, as now, all sects established monasteries in the heartlands of Buddhism in north-east India and participated in maintaining such central institutions as its major pilgrimage sites and the great university at Nālandā.

Buddhism spread into southern India in the time of Aśoka and lasted there longer than in the north; evidence is fragmentary, but we hear of a Theravādin monk being invited from Kāñcī (Conjeevaram) in Tamilnadu to Sri Lanka as late as the early 14th century, about a century after the Muslims had delivered the *coup de grâce* to Buddhism in northern India by sacking the monastic universities of Bihar and Bengal. By land Buddhism spread first into eastern Iran and Central Asia and then along the caravan routes into China. Striking evidence that the move north-west out of India began early is the Aśokan inscription in Greek and Aramaic found at Kandahar (now in Afghanistan). By sea it spread from the east coast, in the middle of the first millennium AD, to continental southeast Asia and Indonesia. Some of the greatest Buddhist monuments, notably Borobudur in Java and temples in Angkor in Kampuchea, are due to this seaborne expansion. To parts of Central and most of southeast Asia the Buddhist missionaries brought or helped to bring their first system of writing, the Indian script in one or other of its variants, and many other aspects of Indian civilization.

The nearest thing we have to a census of monks and monasteries in ancient India is the record compiled by

The most famous of the early Chinese pilgrims was Hsüan-tsang, who visited India in the 7th century and left a valuable record of his travels. This painting at Tun-huang, dating from only a century later, shows him travelling through mountains with a horse and elephant.

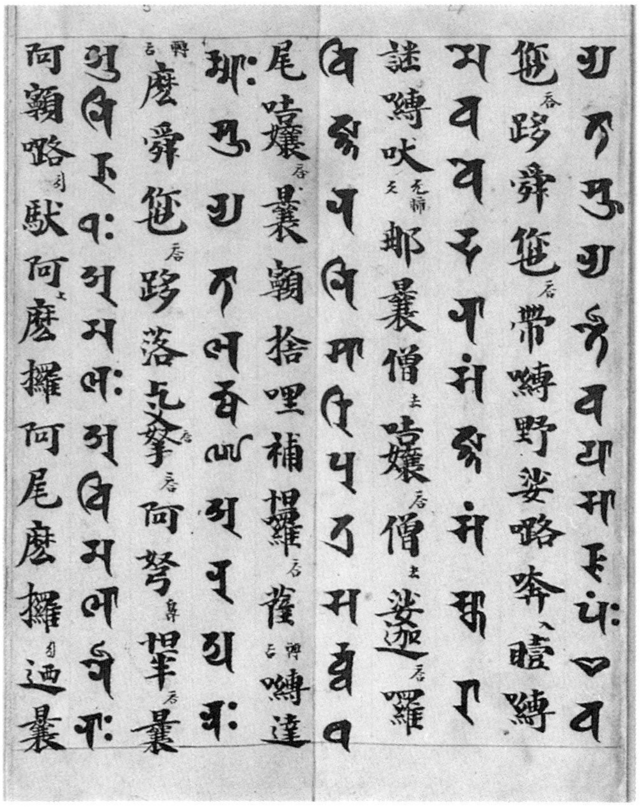

Hsüan-tsang between AD 630 and 644. He listed them by area. India for him included Sri Lanka, what is now Bangladesh, much of what is now Pakistan and Afghanistan, and a bit of modern Nepal. If we exclude Sri Lanka (with 20,000 monks), his totals come to about 115,000 Hīnayāna and about 120,000 Mahāyāna monks; however, about half of the latter also studied Hīnayāna (maybe this just means that they belonged to one of the older *vinaya* sects). The Hīnayāna had about 2,000 monasteries and the Mahāyāna about 2,500.

Hsüan-tsang sadly noted that in some areas there were many ruined monasteries. Buddhist monasteries were tempting targets for invaders, and occasionally also for rapacious local rulers, because many of them were rich. A monastery would attract donations, but monks who observed the Discipline could consume very little. So all they could do with their wealth was to invest it. Often they invested it in real estate: they could own whole villages, and indeed their inhabitants. In the western Deccan (modern Maharashtra) the great monastic temples cut into the rock, culminating in Ajaṇṭā, seem to have been paid for by traders whose businesses they in turn financed. The evidence is only indirect, but it does seem likely that Buddhist monasteries were among India's earliest and most important capitalists.

Around AD 1200 Nālandā was sacked for the last time. A Tibetan monk, Dharmasvāmin, has left us a tragic vignette of the extinction of the Sangha in the area where once the Buddha trod. Visiting Nālandā in 1235, he found that not one manuscript remained. A single monk, in his nineties, was teaching Sanskrit grammar to a class of seventy pupils. Dharmasvāmin studied under him. When they were warned that Muslim soldiers were approaching, he carried his teacher on his back, like Aeneas saving Anchises from the sack of Troy. The two monks hid until the raid was over, then returned and finished their course.

The Sangha and Buddhist thought

The achievements of Buddhist philosophy must lie outside the scope of this volume, but a few paragraphs about doctrinal developments are necessary to make other aspects of Buddhist history intelligible. Opinions which intimately affected views of their religious life and its goal naturally caused controversy in the Sangha, and were more likely to divide adherents of opposing views (*vāda*) into different camps or schools than were views on more abstruse topics such as logic and epistemology (to which Buddhists made great contributions). A tradition grew up that round the end of the 3rd century BC there were eighteen Buddhist schools; in fact the names of rather more are known. Sources

The Buddhist scriptures were translated into Chinese at an early date – a vast and intellectually very impressive undertaking – and in some cases these Chinese versions are the only ones to survive. This page from the 'Heart Sūtra' (left) contains the Sanskrit text in phonetic Chinese transliteration.

record about five hundred points of disagreement; the great majority would seem to outsiders to be trivial. These eighteen schools pre-date the rise of Mahāyāna reinterpretations of Doctrine far more radical than any previously known. The number eighteen as the tally of Buddhist schools of thought became conventional, a fact for which India offers many parallels. If the Sangha had developed eighteen schools by the late 3rd century BC, it stands to reason that divergences would have multiplied in the succeeding centuries; but the Chinese pilgrims in the 7th century AD still report that there are eighteen schools, which they arrange into four groups. These are all Hīnayāna schools; moreover, some Hīnayāna monks belong to none of them. One can only deduce that in fact no one tried to make a realistic enumeration of the schools of Buddhist thought after the rise of Mahāyāna; the subject had grown out of hand. Moreover, since the Sangha did not split along doctrinal lines, the schools of thought were to some extent an abstraction, comparable to bodies of opinion among Western secular philosophers rather than to Christian sects. The doctrinal works of named Buddhist authors which have come down to us seldom correspond exactly to the positions of the schools. The *Vinaya* allows monks full freedom of thought so long as they are sincere in the views they propound. Since monks live in groups and are human it frequently happened that there was a coincidence between Discipline and Doctrine: monks sharing an ordination tradition and Disciplinary code also shared a view on a point of doctrine. The history of Theravāda in Sri Lanka, better known to us than that of any other ancient sect, clearly shows that after a power struggle had split the Sangha the dissident parties, now separate sects in the strict sense, sometimes espoused different doctrinal opinions. But essentially views were held and propounded by individuals, not by groups.

Doctrinal points were continually debated in monasteries; maybe it is no coincidence that the word *vāda* can be translated not only as 'view' or even 'school of thought' but also as 'debate'. Debate was part of monastic education – in Tibetan monasteries the tradition is still alive – and sometimes there were big public debates between Buddhist monks or between Buddhists and non-Buddhists. In 792–94 a controversy raged in Tibet: did Enlightenment arrive suddenly, as Chinese teachers said, or gradually, as Indians claimed? A debate was held between a monk from each camp and the Indian, Kamalaśīla, won. As recently as 1873 a Sinhalese Buddhist monk defeated a Methodist minister in a three-day public debate near Colombo, and the report of his victory in the newspapers caused enthusiasm which had momentous consequences; it could be said to have initiated the modern Buddhist revival.

A book in the Theravādin Canon called 'Points of Controversy' summarizes the refutations of various Buddhist opponents by a Theravādin elder at a debate held in Aśoka's capital, Pāṭaliputra, in about 250 BC. This book gives us a picture of the issues (over two

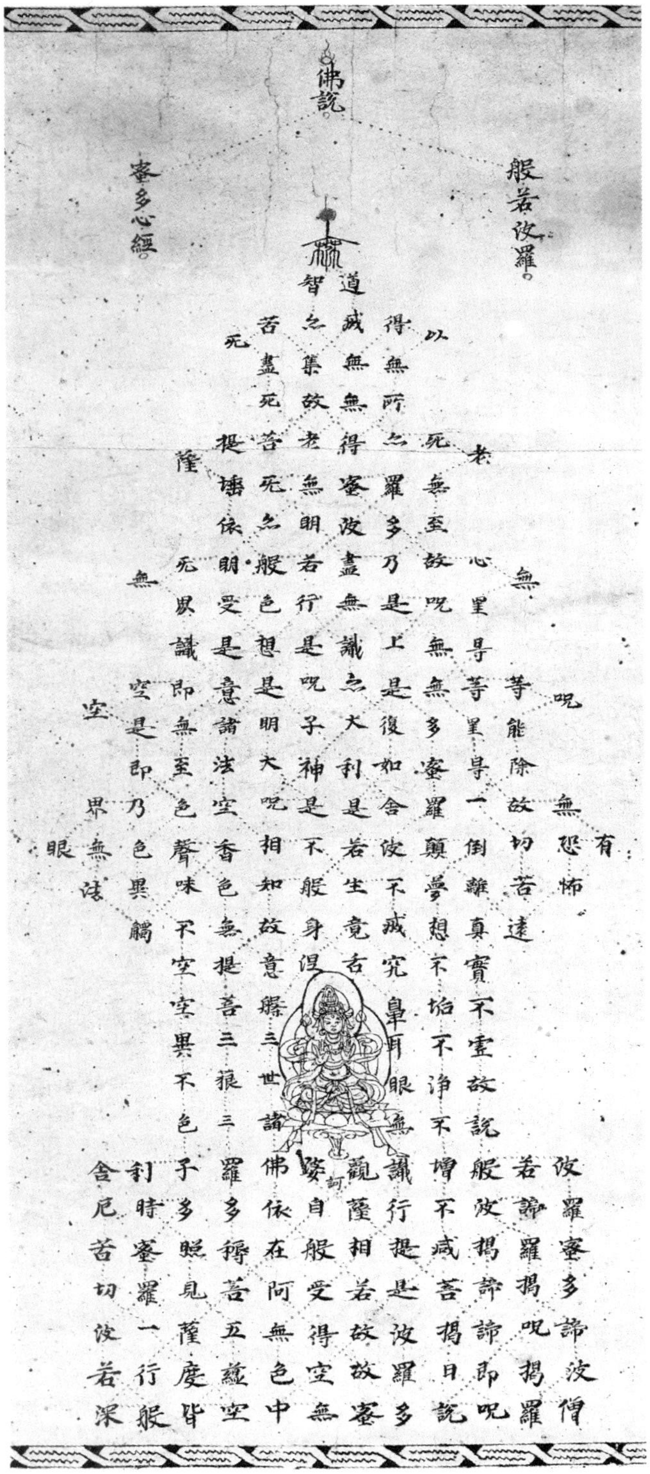

In this 8th-century Chinese manuscript, the 260 Chinese characters of a particular Prajñāpāramitāsūtra ('Perfection of Wisdom Sūtra') are arranged to form a five-storeyed stupa. A thin line of dots (almost invisible here) lead from character to character giving the order in which they should be read. The text begins below the image of the bodhisattva Kuan-yin.

hundred are listed) over which Buddhists argued in that period. A serious problem was the precise character of the Enlightened person, the *arhat*. For instance, was he (it was always a he) omniscient, or did he still suffer from normal ignorance on such worldly topics as someone's name or how to get to a certain village? Could he still have a nocturnal emission? These questions aroused such strong feelings that, according to some traditions, they occasioned the first great schism, but in what sense there was or could have been a schism is unclear. Perhaps there was just a terrible row.

The central problem which puzzled Buddhist thinkers and generated new philosophical developments was exactly what intrigues everyone who encounters Buddhism: the Doctrine of No Self. Everyone jibs at this doctrine initially, whatever their more considered reaction, because it is counter-intuitive: sane people in all cultures unreflectingly believe that they have some enduring essence, however exactly this may be named or conceptualized. In addition to this universal attitude, Buddhist monks had the more particular problem that they believed as a central and fundamental principle in the law of *karman*, moral cause and effect. Buddhism is at bottom an ethical religion, for morality is held to be a prerequisite for any spiritual progress: morality, concentration and wisdom form a hierarchy in ascending order. The very first step on the Noble Eightfold Path, Right Views, is in fact taken to mean belief in the law of moral causation: the belief that by an impersonal law of nature good acts will be rewarded and bad acts punished – if not in this life, then in a future life. On the other hand, if there is no Self, will the agent be the same as the reaper of the result?

The classical Buddhist answer to this problem is found in the Doctrine of Dependent Origination: the two are neither the same nor different, for at each moment what appears as a person is causally determined by what appeared as the same person a moment ago, the volitional element in this cluster being largely a matter of free will. The history of Buddhist controversy shows that not everyone found this answer satisfying. There was a recurrent search for something more substantial to serve as a medium through which *karman* could act; one might compare it to the way in which Western physicists for a time posited ether as a necessary medium to explain apparent action at a distance. Thus rose and fell various deviant doctrines (the word 'heresy' would wrongly imply the possibility of excommunication) positing some kind of 'individual' to be the responsible moral agent.

The basic Mahāyāna approach – rather than solution – to this problem was to undercut the Selflessness of the moral agent by ascribing the same kind of Selflessness to everything. This led (see below, p. 93) to the doctrine that there are two levels of truth, so that conventional morality, like all conventional appearance, could be left in its place as a necessary but provisional stage. The only Mahāyānists who reverted to tackling the problem head on were the school variously known as Vijñānavāda ('Consciousness Doctrine') and Yogācāra. As the former name implies, they assigned a central position to consciousness (one of the canonical Five Aggregates) and speculated how a moral act left traces or stains in it. It can hardly be a coincidence that at the same period – the 4th and 5th centuries AD – Hindu philosophers too were constructing analogies between the workings of *karman* and known physical processes. The Yogācāra reverted to the ancient tradition that all the senses, including mind, work by 'grasping' or apprehending their objects, so that the six consciousnesses are by that token impure; they assigned a fundamental role to what they termed 'appetitive consciousness' (*ālaya-vijñāna*), the workings of which must be reversed to attain Nirvāṇa.

The origins of Buddhist *tantra* are still very obscure. Its philosophy is Madhyamaka, i.e., mainstream Mahāyāna. But as a practical religion it shares more with Hindu *tantra* than with other forms of Buddhism. Some Buddhist texts containing clearly tantric features were translated into Chinese in the early 4th century AD; no early Hindu tantric text is so securely dated. On the other hand, tantrism seems not to have been a major movement in Buddhism before the late 7th century. When we say that Buddhist *tantra* must have borrowed more from Hinduism than vice versa we are not arguing on chronological grounds, which would be guesswork, but because Buddhist *tantra* is so much more discontinuous with earlier Buddhism than Hindu *tantra* is with earlier Hinduism. The term *tantra* refers primarily to a system of ritual action which is believed to lead the practitioner towards salvation – and also towards magical power. (Only the value put on this magical power is new: Buddhists have always held that certain magical powers accrue to the meditator as a by-product of spiritual progress, but they were earlier supposed to attach no importance to them.) The rationale for this ritual action is extremely complex and involves the visualization of a whole pantheon of deities. In theory these deities symbolized – often personified – elements of Buddhist Doctrine; in practice they acquired an imaginative life of their own which betrays to the historian their antecedents in older cults. Any emphasis on ritual was utterly alien to earlier Buddhism. As in Hindu sects, access to salvation for Buddhist tantrics is handed down from teacher to pupil by initiation, not through an impersonal institution (see above, p. 53 ff.). By the same token, the content of what is handed down is esoteric. Though outsiders can nowadays acquire copies of tantric texts, their meaning is obscure to non-initiates, and the study of *tantra* is still in its infancy. That this is changing is mainly due to the Tibetan diaspora: Tibetan refugees from the Chinese invasion of the 1950s have begun not only to publish texts and translations (sometimes in collaboration with foreign scholars) but also to explain their contents. The fact that *tantra* is full of spells (*mantra* and *dhāraṇī*),

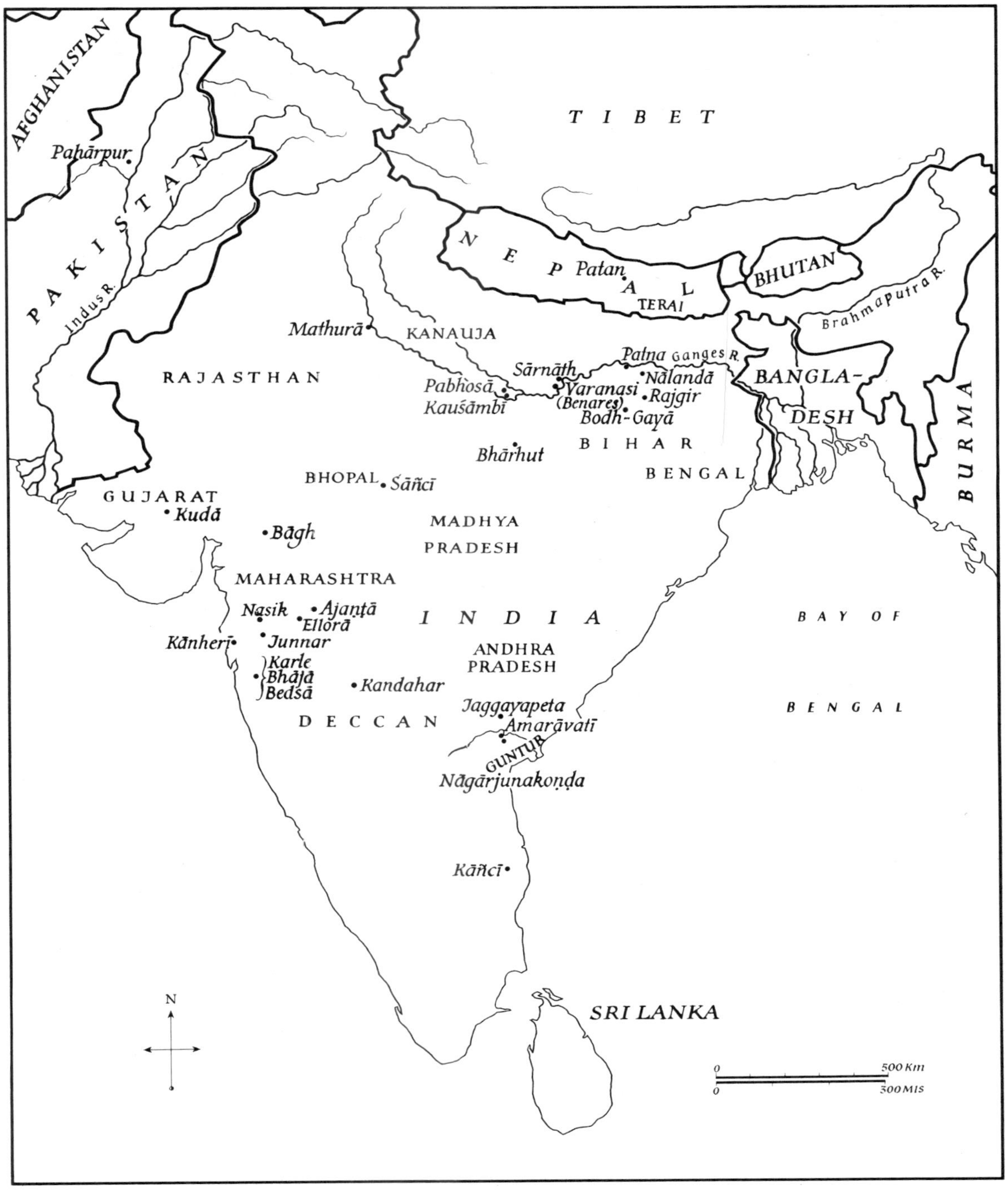

India, showing the main sites mentioned in this chapter.

cosmograms (*maṇḍala*) and ritual gestures (*mudrā*) does not mean that it is a mass of unintelligible hocus-pocus; the elements of the rituals have precise symbolic meanings which are revealed to practitioners. As in all religions, they are differently understood by those of greater and lesser sophistication.

The Sanskrit term for Buddhist tantrism is *Mantrayāna* ('Spell Vehicle') or *Vajrayāna* ('Thunderbolt (or Diamond) Vehicle'); the thunderbolt is a symbol for ultimate reality, the void. There is an ambiguity here. Those who wish to divide Buddhism into two classify Vajrayāna Buddhism as falling within Mahāyāna; that is not incorrect, inasmuch as Vajrayāna uses philosophical concepts found elsewhere in Mahāyāna. On the other hand, those like the Tibetans who practise Vajrayāna as a way to salvation see a hierarchic progression in three stages: Hīnayāna, Mahāyāna, Vajrayāna. Each succeeding revelation by the Buddhas affords a quicker and surer way to the goal.

The Sangha and literature

Buddhists made great contributions to Indian literature. The Pali Canon contains several books of verse. One is an anthology of verses composed by the first generations of monks, another a similar anthology of verses by nuns. The two most famous books of verse (both of which also existed in related languages) are the *Dhammapada* and the *Sutta-Nipāta*; both are didactic, intended to inculcate Buddhist values, and we may be sure that to the anonymous authors (unless one ascribes them to the Buddha) and to their audiences their content was far more important than literary grace. Nevertheless, the *Sutta-Nipāta* marks a major development in Indian lyric metre, and both anthologies contain many fine verses. Here are a few verses from the first chapter of the *Dhammapada* in the famous translation by Max Müller, which he published in 1881 in his *Sacred Books of the East* series:

> 1. All that we are is the result of what we have thought: it is founded on our thoughts, it is made up of our thoughts. If a man speaks or acts with an evil thought, pain follows him, as the wheel follows the foot of the ox that draws the carriage.
> 2. All that we are is the result of what we have thought: it is founded on our thoughts, it is made up of our thoughts. If a man speaks or acts with a pure thought, happiness follows him, like a shadow that never leaves him.
> 3. 'He abused me, he beat me, he defeated me, he robbed me,' – in those who harbour such things hatred will never cease.
> 5. For hatred does not cease by hatred at any time: hatred ceases by love, this is an old rule.
> 9. He who wishes to put on the yellow dress without having cleansed himself from sin, who disregards also temperance and truth, is unworthy of the yellow dress.
> 13. As rain breaks through an ill-thatched house, passion will break through an unreflecting mind.

From the *Sutta-Nipāta* we quote part of the poem 'On Kindness' (*Metta Sutta*), because it is perhaps the most famous poem of all among Theravāda Buddhists. Not only do numberless Buddhists learn it by heart; its recitation with full awareness of its meaning constitutes one of the commonest meditative practices. (We see that 'meditation' need be nothing so very recondite.)

> May all beings be happy and secure; may their minds be contented. Whatever living beings there may be – feeble or strong, long or tall, stout or medium, short, small or large, seen or unseen, dwelling far or near, born or yet to be born – may all beings, without exception, be happy-minded!
>
> Let no one deceive another or despise any person whatever in any place. In anger or illwill let not one wish any harm to another.
>
> Just as a mother would protect her only child even at the risk of her own life, even so let one cultivate a boundless heart towards all beings.
>
> Let one's thoughts of boundless love pervade the whole world – above, below and across – without any obstruction, without any hatred, without any enmity.
>
> Whether one stands, walks, sits or lies down, as long as one is awake one should maintain this mindfulness. This they say, is the Sublime State in this life.
>
> Not falling into wrong views, virtuous and endowed with Insight, one gives up attachment to sense desires. Verily such a man does not return to enter a womb again.

Sanskrit secular literature developed mainly after the turn of the Christian era. Its beauty and sophistication are hard to convey in translation. One can plausibly claim that the earliest Sanskrit poetry to have survived which has the full polish of the classical style is that by Aśvaghoṣa, a Buddhist monk who probably lived in the 2nd century AD. His lengthy poems on Buddhist themes are elaborated in the best courtly manner. The balance and antithesis sometimes recall Ovid. Here is an extract from his 'Life of the Buddha' (*Buddha-carita*). Siddhārtha, seated under the Bodhi tree, is striving for Enlightenment. Buddhist tradition always gives an allegorical account of this episode: the Buddha is assailed by Māra, who personifies both Death and Desire (especially Lust), which for Buddhists are but two sides of the same coin. Suddenly a voice from the sky addresses Māra:

> Māra, do not tire yourself in vain. Stop trying to do injury and go home. For you can no more shake this man than the wind can shake Mount Meru.
>
> Fire may lose its heat, water its fluidity, earth its solidity, but he has accumulated good deeds for many eons and can never abandon his resolution.
>
> His determination, his valour, his force of character, his compassion for all creatures are such that he will not rise without attaining the truth, as the thousand-rayed sun will not rise without slaying the darkness.
>
> By rubbing sticks one gets fire, by digging the ground one finds water; nothing is impossible if one persists; by method everything is acquired, everything achieved.
>
> So this great physician, pitying the world as it lies ill with the diseases of passion, is not to be hampered in his struggle for the medicine of wisdom.
>
> While the world is carried off on many wrong roads he toils to find the right one. It is improper to interfere with him, as it is with a good guide when a caravan is lost.
>
> All beings are lost in deep darkness and he is a being made into a lamp of wisdom. It is as wrong to blow him out as to quench a lamp lit to blaze in the dark.
>
> He has seen the world sunk in the flood of *saṃsāra*, unable to find a way to the further shore; he

has undertaken to bring them across; what decent man could wish him harm?

The tree of wisdom has fibres of forbearance, deep roots of steadfastness, flowers of virtue, branches of awareness and enlightenment, and yields fruit of *dharma*; thriving, it should not be uprooted.

His desire is to free creatures whose minds are held fast by the snares of delusion. How misplaced is your wish to harm him as he toils to free the world from its bonds!

For the acts he has performed for enlightenment the destined hour has arrived. Thus he sits on this spot, just like the earlier sages.

For here the navel of the earth's surface has power entire and supreme. No other spot on earth can bear the power of his concentration.

So do not grieve, be peaceful. Do not be arrogant, Māra, in your might. Fortune is inconstant, not to be relied on. You are on unstable ground, heading for bewilderment.

As a last and contrasting specimen, here is a short extract from the *Bodhicaryāvatāra* by Śāntideva, a Mahāyānist scholar and poet of the 7th century.

For the sake of things unloved and things loved have I sinned these many times; and never have I thought that I must surrender everything and depart. They whom I love not, they whom I love, I myself, shall be no more, naught shall remain. All the things whereof I have feeling shall pass away into a memory; like the vision of a dream, all departs, and is seen no more. The many whom I love or love not pass away while I stand here; only the dire sin wrought for their sake remains before me. I understood not that I was but a chance comer, and through madness, love, or hatred I have wrought many a sin. Unceasingly through night and day the waning of vital force increases; must I not die? Lying here on my bed, or standing amidst my kin, I must suffer the agonies of dissolution alone. Whence shall I find a kinsman, whence a friend, when the Death-god's messengers seize me? Righteousness alone can save me then, and for that I have not sought. Clinging to brief life, I have been blind to this terror, heedless; O my Masters, grievous guilt have I gathered. He who is taken to be maimed of his limbs at once withers away; thirst racks him, his sight is darkened, the world is changed to his sight. How then will it be with me when I am in the charge of the Death-god's hideous messengers, consumed by a fever of mighty terror, covered with filth, looking with timid glances to the four quarters of heaven for aid? Who will be the friend to save me from that awful terror? I shall see in the heavens no help, and sink back into madness; then what shall I do in that place of horror? Now, now I come for refuge to the mighty Lords of the world, the Conquerors eager for the world's protection, who allay all fear; to the Law learned by them I come with all my heart for refuge, and to the Congregation of the Sons of Enlightenment. . . . Whatsoever guilt I have gathered in my foolishness and delusion, alike the wrong of nature and the wrong of commandment, I confess it all as I stand before the Masters with clasped hands, affrighted with grief, and making obeisance again and again. May my Lords take my transgression as it is; never more, O Masters, will I do this unholy work.

(ii, 35–49, 64–66, trs. L. H. Barnett)

Richard Gombrich

MAHĀYĀNA BUDDHISM

During the first five centuries of its history, Buddhism progressed considerably; nevertheless, it had to face both external and internal difficulties because of the divergent tendencies which formed at the heart of the community. Some monks questioned the authenticity of the early scriptures and claimed to add new texts to them; others leaned towards a more lax interpretation of the rules governing their life; the scholastic treatises, continuously increasing in number, became more and more discrepant; finally, and above all, the laity, considering the monks' privileges to be excessive, tried to win equal religious rights for themselves.

Thus it was that shortly before the beginning of the Christian era there appeared a new form of Buddhism which, in opposition to what is called *Śrāvakayāna* 'Vehicle of the Listeners' (*śrāvaka*, i.e. the disciples of the Buddha) or Hīnayāna, 'Small Vehicle', took the name of Mahāyāna, 'Great Vehicle', also called *Bodhisattvayāna*, i.e. the 'Vehicle of the bodhisattvas or future Buddhas'. It is distinguished from the former by a more ambitious religious ideal, a more complex Buddhology and, especially, more radical philosophical positions.

The ideal of the bodhisattva

The *Śrāvakas*, i.e. 'the Listeners', the first disciples of the Buddha, sought to detach themselves from the world in order to enter Nirvāṇa as quickly as possible; the Mahāyānist aspires to become a Buddha and attain omniscience in order to devote himself to the welfare and happiness of all beings.

Arhatship, for which the follower of *Śrāvakayāna* aims, consists of *personal* holiness entailing the eradication of delusions and passions and a certain form of Enlightenment (*bodhi*) or wisdom (*prajñā*) concerned with the three general characteristics (*sāmānya-lakṣaṇa*) of things: impermanence, suffering and impersonality. The death of the Holy One is followed by Nirvāṇa, the ending of painful rebirths. The Holy One who disappears in this way passes from the contingent domain to that of the absolute and definitive. In order to reach this final goal, he is compelled to tread, in the robe of a monk, the Path to Nirvāṇa, the three essential elements of which are morality, concentration and wisdom.

This ideal of holiness, clearly defined by Śākyamuni and his disciples, could be pursued by monks withdrawn into solitude or confined within the enclosures of monasteries; this was out of reach of the lay person living in the world and subjected to its worries. Accustomed to supporting their fellow-men and especially to supplying food, clothing and lodging to the community, the laity had more respect for the *active* virtues which they willingly undertook than for the *passive* virtues which the monks exemplified. In literature as in art, the predilection of the male and female laity for active virtues was clearly shown. Thus in the Jātakas, which are stories of former lives of the future Buddha Śākyamuni, we witness that deeds of generosity, morality, patience and vigour had multiplied, thus demonstrating the altruistic virtues of which he was capable. It was therefore him, rather than the formal and solitary monk, whom the laity took as a model, with the secret hope that by acting like him they too would reach Buddhahood. The Mahāyāna sanctioned these profound aspirations by inviting, not only the monks and nuns, but also the 'sons and daughters of good family' to commit themselves to the career of the bodhisattva (future Buddha).

The prerogative of the Buddhas is not only holiness, but the possession of supreme and perfect Enlightenment (*anuttarā samyaksambodhi*) thanks to which they ensure the welfare and happiness of all beings. For the adherent who commits himself to the bodhisattva career, there are two crucial moments: (i) the arousal of the Thought of Enlightenment (*bodhicittotpāda*), by which the bodhisattva solemnly commits himself to win Supreme Enlightenment so as to devote himself to the welfare of all; (ii) the attaining of Supreme Enlightenment which will transform him into a Buddha. A long interval separates these two moments, since the bodhisattva indefinitely delays his entry into

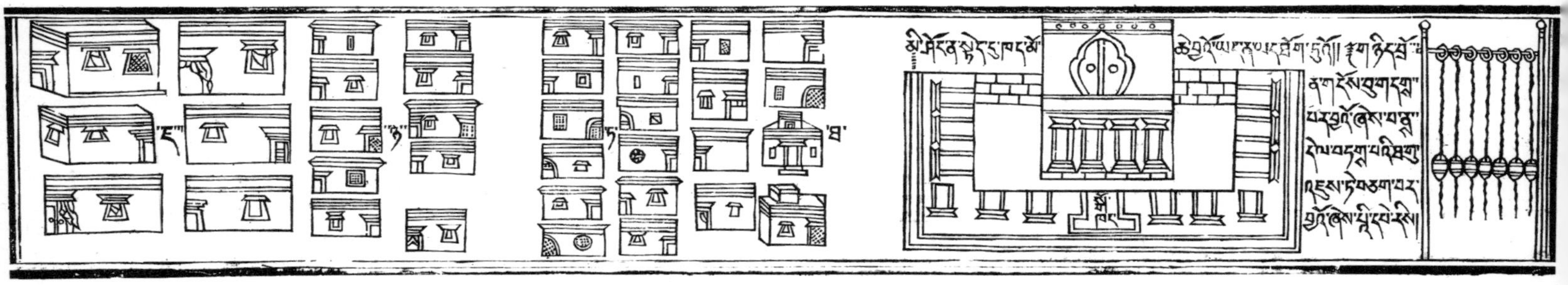

Another leaf from the Tibetan block-book illustrated earlier. This one is concerned with the different monastic cells which are variously permitted or forbidden by the rules.

The Buddhist scriptures, and in particular the Mahāyāna texts, enumerate many Buddhas who have existed in the infinite ages before 'our' Buddha was born. It is common to find halls dedicated to the Thousand Buddhas. The invention of printing made it easy to multiply Buddha images as often as one pleased. This 9th-century Chinese roll juxtaposes images made by repeated impositions of the same wood block.

Nirvāṇa in order to carry out his liberating activity as long as possible. He knows, in fact, that once he has entered Nirvāṇa he can do nothing more for anyone.

Thus during three, seven or thirty-three incalculable eons, he accumulates meritorious actions by practising the six perfections (*pāramitā*) of his state: (i) generosity, (ii) morality, (iii) patience, (iv) vigour, (v) meditation, (vi) wisdom. To these six perfections are sometimes added: (vii) skilfulness in liberating means, (viii) the aspiration for the Enlightenment and welfare of beings, (ix) strength, (x) knowledge.

The practice of the perfections is spread over ten stages, also known as 'grounds' (*bhūmi*). They were eventually designated as follows: (i) stage of rejoicing, (ii) stage free from impurity, (iii) luminous stage, (iv) stage of brilliant wisdom, (v) stage hard to conquer, (vi) stage of presence, (vii) far-reaching stage, (viii) immovable stage, (ix) stage of unerring wisdom, (x) stage of the Cloud of the Doctrine.

Within the framework of the philosophical conceptions which will be described below, the practice of the perfections increased in quality throughout these ten stages.

(i) In the course of the first six stages, the bodhisattva still has a notion of beings and things.

(ii) In the seventh, he endeavours no longer to perceive objects.

(iii) In the eighth, he definitely acquires the certainty that phenomena do not arise (*anutpattika-dharma-kṣānti*) and, since his mind is no longer troubled by objects and notions, he is certain to pursue an irreversible (*avaivartika*) career and to attain Buddhahood rapidly.

(iv) In the ninth, he acquires his ability to change form and teach according to the dispositions of his hearers.

(v) In the tenth, he receives from the Buddha's hands the consecration in omniscience which will make him nearly the equal of a Buddha. Immersed in ineffable mystic concentrations and endowed with limitless psychic power, he mechanically and without being aware of it ensures the welfare and happiness of all beings in several cosmic systems at once. Perfect altruism is that of which one is unaware.

Multiplication of the Buddhas and bodhisattvas

Even when acknowledging in the Buddha a series of prerogatives and powers, the *śrāvakas* for a long time kept him on the human plane. They claimed him to be the pre-eminent Master endowed with knowledge and practice, the instructor of gods and men, but were not unaware that once he had entered Nirvāṇa, he was invisible to gods and men, could do no more for them and had abandoned them to their fate, with his Doctrine as their only heritage. According to them, the appearance of a Buddha was a very rare occurrence – as rare as the blossoming of a flower on a fig-tree – and humanity remains without a guide and advisor for long periods.

A god 'dead since his Nirvāṇa' – as H. Kern defined it – could just suffice for monks; it could not satisfy popular aspirations which clamoured urgently for a supreme spirit, a pantheon, saints, a mythology and a cult. The vulgarization of the Good Doctrine and its penetration into the masses had the effect of transforming the 'Instructor of gods and men' into a 'God superior to the gods' and of surrounding him with a host of minor and major deities as well as powerful disciples. The Hīnayānist 'sects' (*nikāya*) or 'schools' (*vāda*) had already given support to this process of sublimation: the Sarvāstivādins by padding out the legend of Śākyamuni with marvels, the Mahāsāṅghikas by consigning his historical career to the field of fictitious phenomena. As the need for efficacious protectors had become more pressing, the Listeners had already conceived, alongside the historical Buddha, a compassionate Messiah, the future Buddha Maitreya, and some *arhats*, immortalized for the needs of the cause, always ready to fly to the help of the faithful.

These developments remained only isolated cases in *Śrāvakayāna*, but the followers of Mahāyāna had no hesitation in infinitely increasing the number of Buddhas and great bodhisattvas. Bursting through the narrow limits of the old cosmology, the Mahāyānists conceived at the heart of the cosmos a considerable number of universes, each ruled over by a Buddha assisted by one or more great bodhisattvas. The Buddha is already possessed of Supreme Enlightenment, while the great bodhisattvas – those of the tenth stage – are merely 'close to Enlightenment'. Apart from this difference, the Buddhas and bodhisattvas, inspired by a similar beneficence, convert the beings in the universes which are theirs and often appear simultaneously in manifold forms and in different universes.

Śākyamuni, whose historical existence cannot be doubted, was soon to see an infinite number of peers and emulators lined up beside him. He was to remain the best known of the Buddhas but he was no longer to be the only one. The scriptures of Mahāyāna mention many Buddhas and bodhisattvas hitherto unknown.

Among these Buddhas should be noted: Amitābha or Amitāyus, luminous and of infinite life-span, ruling over the Sukhāvatī, the Western Paradise; Akṣobhya, the immovable, located in the east, in the Abhirati universe; Bhaiṣajyaguru, the master physician, also holding sway in the east. Among the most famous bodhisattvas are: Maitreya, waiting in the Tuṣita heaven to succeed Śākyamuni; Avalokiteśvara, dwelling on Mount Potalaka before manifesting himself in China in the form of the female deity Kuan-yin; Mañjuśrī, of sweet majesty, the bodhisattva of wisdom.

For those with deeper understanding, these Buddhas and bodhisattvas are merely manifestations of the wisdom and compassion of the Buddhas. The Buddhas are identical in their essential body (*dharmakāya*), which is none other than the Doctrine, the truth discovered and expounded by them; they are enthroned in paradises, in the midst of an assembly of gods and Holy Ones whom they enchant with their luminous 'Enjoyment-Bodies' (*saṃbhogakāya*). Finally, they send to this world as deputies likenesses of themselves, fictitious bodies (*nirmāṇakāya*) which expound the Doctrine and convert beings. This vast undertaking would be impossible if the Buddhas were not possessed of the Dharma, the Truth, and if that Truth were not to lead to the end of suffering, to detachment and to peace.

The twofold non-existence of beings and things

Faithful to the teaching of Śākyamuni, the followers of *Śrāvakayāna* had proclaimed the non-existence of the person (*pudgala-nairātmya*); the Mahāyānists took a step further and proclaimed the non-existence both of the person and of things (*dharma-nairātmya*). Belief in the person is the greatest of delusions since it plants in the mind all forms of desire, the destruction of which is the indispensable condition of deliverance. *Śrāvakas* and Mahāyānists are in agreement in condemning the belief in a Self (*ātma-graha*) and the belief in anything belonging to the Self (*ātmīya-graha*): whatever may be the term which designates it – soul, living being, man, person, agent – it does not exist; men, Holy Ones, bodhisattvas, Buddhas are but names, corresponding to nothing substantial.

However, though the *Śrāvakas* deny the Self, they acknowledge a certain reality in things. The Hīnayānist schools of the Sarvāstivādins and Sautrāntikas drew up long lists of conditioned phenomena – material entities, thoughts, mental functions, associated factors – which last only momentarily or infinitesimally, but which nevertheless are possessed of an essential nature (*svabhāva*) and characteristics (*lakṣaṇa*): they are fugitive and transitory realities, but realities all the same.

Conversely, for the Mahāyānists, phenomena, through the very fact that they are conditioned, do not exist by themselves or in themselves: they are empty of essential nature (*svabhāva-śūnya*) and of characteristics (*lakṣaṇa-śūnya*). From this emptiness three corollaries follow:

(i) things (*dharma*) do not arise and do not perish, because empty things arising from empty things do not in reality arise and, since they do not arise, they never perish;

(ii) things, being without arising and without perishing, are originally calm and in complete Nirvāṇa, Nirvāṇa being nothing other than calm;

(iii) things, being simultaneously calm and in Nirvāṇa, are all equal and do not have any duality. That is why the adherent of the Mahāyāna, the bodhisattva, does not perceive phenomena and, as a text of the Great Vehicle says, 'if he does not perceive them it is because of their absolute purity. What is that purity? It is non-arising, non-manifestation, non-activity, non-existence (*anupalambha*).' (*Pañcaviṃśatisāhasrikā Prajñāpāramitā-sūtra*, 146).

It follows that the Four Noble Truths expounded at Benares by the Buddha Śākyamuni must receive a new interpretation. The Buddha said: 'All the phenomena of existence are suffering', but those phenomena do not exist. He said: 'The origin of suffering is desire', but since nothing arises, one cannot speak of an origin. He also said: 'There is an extinction of suffering, namely, Nirvāṇa', but since suffering never existed, Nirvāṇa is acquired at all times, and *saṃsāra* (painful re-birth) is the same as Nirvāṇa. Finally, the Buddha said: 'There is a path which leads to the extinction of suffering', but that path has always been trodden since there is nothing to be extinguished. Faced with the emptiness (*śūnyatā*) of beings and things, the attitude of the wise man consists of no longer doing anything, no longer saying anything, no longer thinking anything: that is the secret of peace.

Emptiness

Some Western interpreters have tried to see a sort of negative absolute in Emptiness, but when the Mahāyānists say that beings and things are empty, they are not attributing any characteristic to them. They refuse to hypostatize an Emptiness which is nothing at all (*akiṃcid*), 'mere non-existence' (*abhāva-mātra*). It is not that by virtue of Emptiness beings and things are empty: they are empty because they do not exist. The very notion of Emptiness is only of provisional value: it is a raft which is abandoned after crossing the river, a medicine which is thrown away after the cure. That is why the Mahāyānists are not nihilists: nihilists deny what they see but the Mahāyānists do not see anything and, consequently, neither affirm nor deny anything.

Conventional truth and absolute truth

An objection naturally comes to mind: on the one hand the Mahāyāna nourishes a high ideal of kindness and altruism, and multiplies the Buddhas and bodhisattvas whose activities and careers it describes; on the other hand it clearly affirms that beings do not exist and that things are empty of an essential nature and of characteristics. One must choose: either the Buddhas and bodhisattvas convert beings, or nobody converts anybody.

The Mahāyānists posed this objection to themselves and discovered the answer to it in the theory of the two truths: conventional or provisional truth (*saṃvṛti-satya*) and absolute truth (*paramārtha-satya*). Without having lived everyday life according to conventional standards, profound reality cannot be perceived; and it is just this that must be perceived in order to reach Nirvāṇa. It is therefore necessary, at the starting point, to bow to convention, because it is the means of reaching Nirvāṇa, just as whoever wants to draw water makes use of a receptacle.

At the beginning of his career, the bodhisattva, still not fully enlightened, who sees beings and perceives things, should practise normally the six perfections required by his state: practising giving, observing morality, being patient, developing vigour, concentrating the mind and clarifying wisdom. That is a worldly and provisional way of practising the perfections. However, when his mind is open to absolute truth and he has understood the twofold emptiness of beings and things, he practises the same perfections in a supramundane way and in conformity with deep truth: he gives while no longer making a difference between giver, beneficiary and thing given; he observes morality while ceasing to distinguish merit from fault; he is patient while considering sufferings as non-existent; he is vigorous without displaying any bodily, vocal or mental effort; he concentrates while considering meditation and distraction as identical; he is wise while ceasing to oppose truth to delusion. The culmination of the bodhisattva's career is 'the stopping of all speech and all practice' (*sarva-vāda-caryoccheda*), and since this attitude corresponds to reality it is more efficacious than feverish activity inspired by vain preconceptions.

By admitting from the point of view of conventional truth what it denies from the point of view of absolute truth, and vice versa, the Mahāyāna stands at an equal distance between affirmation and negation, between the view of existence and the view of non-existence. This is the Middle Way (*madhyamā pratipad*) in which it avoids every objection.

Etienne Lamotte

A Nepalese maṇḍala dedicated to the bodhisattva Mañjuśrī. Altogether 220 divine figures are included in the design. In the popular mind these are gods to be invoked and placated; more philosophically they are manifestations of the wisdom and compassion of the Buddha.

THE MONASTIC CONTRIBUTION TO BUDDHIST ART AND ARCHITECTURE

Apart from their writings, the main monuments that the Buddhist monks of India have left to us are architectural and artistic. Indian artists and architects have until modern times been anonymous craftsmen, and the names of the makers of the Buddhist monuments are hardly ever known to us. Works are never signed. One must admit that for the most part we cannot even be sure whether, for instance, the carvers of the great gateways at Sāñcī or the painters of the murals at Ajaṇṭā were themselves Buddhists. We can only extrapolate from modern observation and surmise that the subjects depicted were probably suggested by the monastic incumbents, and that occasionally some gifted monk himself contributed paintings or sculptures. Though some Buddhist monastic traditions are rather indifferent to the visual arts, none are actually hostile to their practice; and a couple of Indian inscriptions do name monks as artists. For instance, on inscriptions at Bhārhut one monk is described as a sculptor and another as a superintendent of construction. But inscriptions usually record donors not artists. Although royalty and merchants played the leading part in providing the funds for monasteries and monuments, it is notable that frequently monks and nuns are named as donors. They may have either given money they possessed before ordination, or passed on what was supplied to them by lay supporters.

The early Buddhist monument *par excellence* was the stupa (see pp. 62–63). The Buddha's relics were distributed in these large burial mounds, and according to the authority of a canonical text he recommended the laity to obtain religious serenity by worshipping them. The physical remains of Buddhist monks were often deposited under monuments of this shape, and stupas containing the relics of those who were held to be great saints were venerated. Miniature stupas were made as portable reliquaries. The earliest stupa of which we have incscriptional record (though no remains) is mentioned by Aśoka; he had been on pligrimage to a stupa which he believed to contain the relics of a former Buddha. Buddhist legend credits Aśoka with having erected 84,000 stupas; for example certain stupas still standing at Patan in the Kathmandu valley of Nepal are locally believed – not very plausibly – to have been erected by him.

One may wonder how so many stupas could be supplied with relics. The answer is threefold. Firstly, although monks were cremated, their bones were not thereby entirely destroyed, and the tiniest fragment of bone or hair is considered sufficient to qualify as a relic; moreover, objects that Holy Ones had used – such as robes or begging bowls – were also classed as relics. Secondly, recourse was had (perhaps not in the first centuries) to the Buddha's dictum that 'he who sees the Dharma sees me'; his Dharma body, consisting of the scriptures, or rather in fact a section of them, sometimes inscribed on a precious metal, could be used as a doctrinal equivalent to a corporeal relic. Thirdly, not all stupas did in fact contain relics; the stupa was itself classed as a relic, a 'reminding relic', its mere shape serving by association to remind the beholder of the Buddha's Final Nirvāṇa. Indeed, though scholars and most Buddhists have tended to use the Sanskrit words *stūpa* and *caitya* interchangeably, a passage in the Mahāsāṅghika *Vinaya* (preserved in Chinese) says that it is called a *stūpa* when it contains relics of Holy Ones and a *caitya* when it does not.

Stupas were built by laymen and were primarily objects of lay religiosity; at first they had no connection with monasteries. But it seems that by the 2nd century BC monastic quarters were sometimes built next to stupas (or vice versa); and by the 1st or 2nd century AD we find Buddhist texts which present the stupa homiletically as a meditational aid. Thus the ground on which it rests is said to symbolize generosity (the basic Buddhist virtue, first in any list of good moral qualities); the stupa's base symbolizes moral restraint (as in the Five Precepts); and so on up to the top node of the spire, which symbolizes the Buddha's great compassion. The parts of the stupa, considered from the ground upwards, thus serve as a mnemonic aid to a monk who is striving for spiritual progress or who wishes to describe such progress in a lecture or sermon.

Stupas are found throughout the Buddhist world and have taken many different shapes. Indian stupas in the 1st millennium AD acquired up to thirteen discs or 'umbrellas' round the central spire – the number in theory indicated the importance of the saint buried there. These umbrellas were so conspicuous that they dominated the appearance of Far Eastern stupas, which the West knows as pagodas. The pagoda acquired other symbolic meanings, but at the furthest point of its diffusion from India, in Japan, the stupa has retained its original function as a relic depository and memorial monument.

Originally the Buddha was not depicted, perhaps because 'he who sees the Dharma sees me': after his Enlightenment the Buddha is simply 'like that' – indescribable. The earliest literary mention of a Buddha image is in the Ceylonese chronicles compiled in the 5th century AD; they refer to a Buddha image in Ceylon in the late 3rd century BC. Scholars tend to regard this as an anachronism because it is so much earlier than the oldest Buddha images found in India itself; those come from Mathurā and are usually dated to the 1st century AD. Such scepticism may be justified; however, the same chronicle gives an extremely circumstantial account of the contents of the relic chamber built into the Great Stupa (the Ruvanväli sāya) by King Duṭṭhagāmaṇī in the early 1st century BC, and that too is said to contain a Buddha image. By far the largest number of Buddha images surviving are from Gandhāra (straddling the modern Pakistan–Afghanistan border). Under Greek influence since its invasion by Alexander the Great, Gandhāra produced a great quantity of Buddhist sculpture.

Unfortunately it is almost impossible to date. Experts now incline to place it between the 1st century BC and the 5th century AD inclusive, but, since it is reasonable to suppose that Buddhism came to Gandhāra in the reign of Aśoka, the earlier limit may well be too cautious.

The function of the Buddha image runs parallel to that of the stupa. Images intended for worship were actually relic-containers in the first instance; then, however, the image itself came to be classed as a 'reminding relic'. The stages and timing of these developments are still obscure. A text taken to China in AD 148 says that 'a true disciple of the Buddha venerates his image evening and morning and often lights a lamp before it to honour it'. Perhaps Buddha images were used as cult objects before they figured in narrative scenes depicted for decorative purposes.

Let us now look more closely at some of the most notable sites of Indian Buddhism. The existence of thousands of monasteries in classical India is attested by literary records and archaeological remains. Besides the ravages of time, human vandalism – practised first by Brahmanical Hindus and later on by invading Muslims – was responsible for the destruction of numerous Buddhist establishments in most parts of India. Archaeological explorations at many places suggest that Hindu and Muslim structures were built on Buddhist sites with materials taken from Buddhist buildings.

A large number of monasteries flourished in north-west India. The well-known sculptures of the Gandhāra school of art were produced between 100 BC and AD 500 in the monasteries of this region. The ruins at Taxila and Manikiālā near Rawalpindi, at Charsadā and Shāhjī-kī-Ḍherī near Peshawar, at Takht-i-Bāhī, Sahrī-Bahlol and Jamālgaṛhi near Mardan, and at Mīrpurkhās in Sindha, seem once to have been among the architectural wonders of Asia. In the 6th century the Hūṇa king Mihirakula caused the demolition of 1,600 Buddhist establishments in north-west India. Hsüan-tsang (AD 629–645) recorded that in former days 18,000 monks lived in 1,400 monasteries in Uḍḍiyāna in the Swāt valley. The names of four monks, Saṅghamitra, Bhava, Nāgadatta and Dharmatrāta, are preserved in

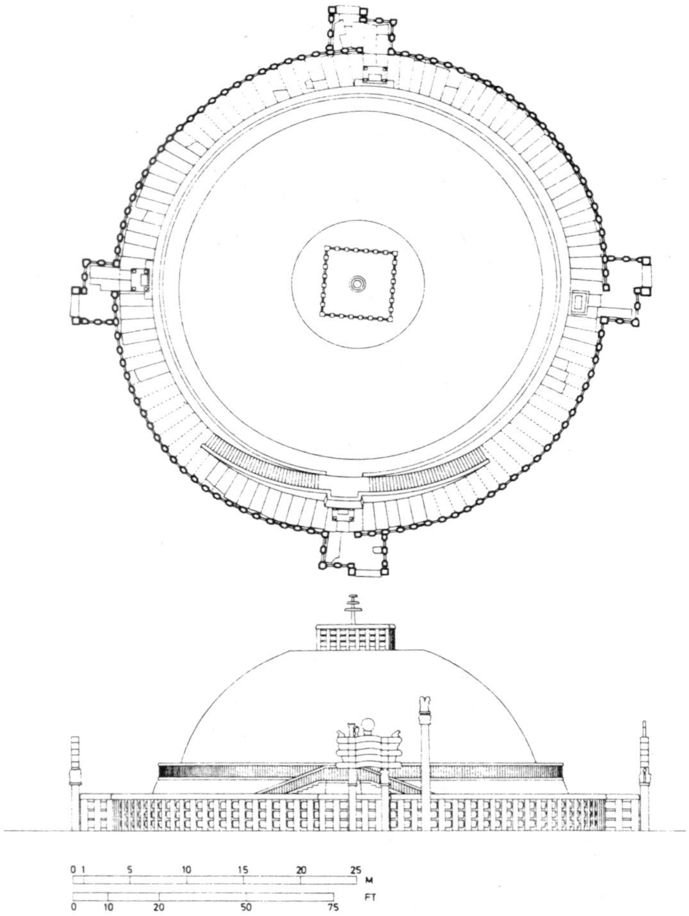

Plan and elevation of the Great Stupa at Sāñcī; the central mound is surrounded by a stone palisade with four ceremonial gates. This is one of the most famous examples of the stupa tradition, which was to generate such diverse forms throughout Asia, culminating in the Chinese and Japanese pagoda (below: the Hōryūji pagoda, Japan).

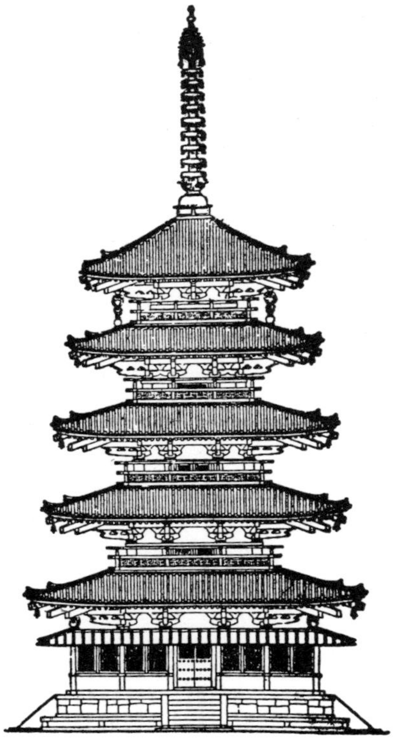

Lion capital from Sarnath, erected by Aśoka about 250 BC. Seven feet tall, crowning a column that was over thirty feet high, it is the most elaborate of Aśoka's column-capitals. The lions originally supported a large wheel – the Doctrine – and there are four smaller wheels on the base.

inscriptions of the 1st century AD discovered in this region.

Many monastic establishments existed in Mathurā between 300 BC and AD 600. Śaka and Kuṣāṇa monarchs patronized Buddhist monks and their monasteries and promoted Buddhist art in Mathurā, Śrāvastī and Sārnāth. Life-size figures of some of these monarchs and some of the finest images of the Buddha were made in Mathurā. Inscriptions of the 1st and 2nd centuries AD found in Mathurā reveal the names of nuns (Buddhamitrā and Dhanavatī) and of monks (Buddhadeva, Buddhila, Bala, Buddhavarmā and Saṅghadāsa). Fa-hsien (AD 399–411) reported the existence of 20 monasteries and 3,000 monks in Mathurā. The famous Jetavana monastery at Śrāvastī continued to be a centre of Buddhism till the 12th century, when Buddhabhaṭṭāraka was the head of the Sangha there. Among the ruins of monasteries and temples at Kuśīnagara was found a 20-feet-long stone figure of the Buddha in the posture of Final Nirvāṇa which was made in the 5th century AD.

One of the largest monastic settlements of India was Sārnāth, just outside Benares. Ruins of numerous large and small monasteries can still be seen there. Two of the first Buddhist monasteries were built at this site in the time of the Buddha. Aśoka had some monasteries and stupas built and set up a monolithic pillar surmounted by a lion-capital. Its figures of four roaring lions facing the four cardinal directions symbolize the Buddha's preaching, which is likened to a lion's roar. This remarkable sculpture has been adopted by modern India as her state emblem. Inscriptions refer to certain monks as donors. Sārnāth, like Mathurā, was a major centre of Buddhist religion, art and literature. One of the masterpieces produced here is the Buddha figure seated in preaching posture. The Dhamekha stupa is another imposing monument. Kumāradevī, a Buddhist queen of the Brahmanical king Govindacandra of Kanauja, built the Dharmacakrajinavihāra, one of the last monasteries to be founded in medieval India. The soldiers of Muhammad Ghorī killed most of the monks and destroyed the monasteries of Sārnāth in AD 1194.

A rock monastery lay in Pabhosā, near Kauśāmbī, in which *arhats* of the Kāśyapīya sect lived in the 1st century BC. Buddhamitrā, a nun, had a Buddha image set up near the Ghoṣitārāma monastery at Kauśāmbī in the 1st century AD. Hūṇas ransacked this city in the 6th century.

No ancient monastic building has been preserved at Bodh-Gayā, the site of the Buddha's Enlightenment. Meghavarṇa, a king of Ceylon, had a large monastery constructed here in the 5th century for the use of Ceylonese monks. Śaśāṅka, a Brahmanical king of Bengal, is reported to have persecuted Buddhism in and around Bodh-Gayā early in the 7th century. The most important monument here is the Mahābodhi Temple, which now again stands in its magnificent grandeur, having been restored in the 19th century. Bodh-Gayā was subjected to violent vandalism by Muslim invaders at the beginning of the 13th century.

Nālandā was the greatest centre of Buddhist monks and scholars in ancient Asia. Traces of earlier monasteries have disappeared but the extant ruins give a continuous history of monasteries, sculptures and patronage from about the 7th to the 12th century. The accounts of Chinese pilgrim-scholars Hsüan-tsang and I-tsing reveal something of the greatness of its Buddhist university. They mention its thousands of scholars, numerous temples, monks' hostels, libraries, observatories and prayer halls. Nālandā inscriptions preserve the names of the two disciples Śāriputra and Maudgalyāyana, and eminent monks such as Vasumitra, Maitreyanātha, Pūrṇendrasena, Mañjuśrīdeva, and Vīradeva. The monasteries, libraries, and temples of Nālandā were devastated in the closing years of the 12th century by Turkish armies under Ikhtiyar Khilji, who slaughtered most of the monks living there. Dharmasvāmin (1197–1264) from Tibet spent some months in Nālandā in the early years of the 13th century when he found only two out of eighty-four monasteries in good condition.

The rulers of the Pāla dynasty (AD 800–1200) established at least four great monasteries which developed into centres of Buddhist learning and literature. All of them were destroyed by Muslim armies in the 12th and 13th centuries. The ruins of Odantapura Mahāvihāra are still buried in Bihār-Shariff near Nālandā; the site of Vikramaśilā Mahāvihāra has so far not been located, although it seems to have been in the Bhāgalpur District of Bihar. The ruins at Pahārpur in East Bengal represent the site of Somapura Mahāvihāra. The last monastery built by a Pāla king at Vārendra in north Bengal was founded by Rāmapāla and called Jagaddala Mahāvihāra. A large number of learned Buddhist monk-scholars associated with Nālandā university and colleges of the Pāla monasteries are known to us from Chinese and Tibetan sources.

Two sites in central India deserve mention here for their remarkable architectural and sculptural wealth, Bhārhut (District Baghelkhand) and Sāñcī (District Bhopal). Both had monasteries and sanctuaries dating from the 3rd century BC. At Bhārhut only ruins of a monastery and mutilated sculptures belonging to a great stupa have survived. About 140 short inscriptions exist on stones which once formed part of the great shrine. Names of several monks and nuns figure among donors; some of the monks were reciters of scriptures while others were masters of particular Sūtras or of five collections of Sūtras. A monk named Buddharakṣita is described as a sculptor, while another named Ṛṣipālita is referred to as a superintendent of construction. Some of the other names mentioned in these inscriptions are those of nuns and monks.

Some of the oldest and finest stupas still exist at Sāñcī; the gateways to these shrines are masterpieces of both architecture and sculpture. Around these stupas are the ruins of several monasteries. Sāñcī was a major centre of Buddhist monasticism, art and culture during the period between 200 BC and AD 600. A noteworthy feature of the monuments of Sāñcī is the existence of several hundred short inscriptions; one is an edict of Aśoka prohibiting schism among monks and nuns. Mahendra, who converted Ceylon, is associated with the Vedisagiri monastery of Sāñcī. Names of numerous monks and nuns of 200 BC to AD 200 are recorded among donors of different parts of the stupas. Another important feature of this site is that the relics of a large number of eminent 'sons of the Buddha' were enshrined here. The inscriptions refer to the relics of Kāśyapagotra, the teacher of Haimavatas, Madhyama, Maudgaliputra, Maudgalyāyana, Śāriputra, Hārītiputra, Kauṇḍinīputra, Kauśikīputra, Gauptiputra, and Vātsi-Suvijayita. These inscribed relic caskets corroborate the evidence of the Pali chronicles, which name several of these monks as leading missions to outlying parts during Aśoka's reign. The sculptures of Sāñcī are thus an important source for Buddhist history, faith and mythology.

A large number of monasteries and shrines existed in Andhra Pradesh. Ruins of monastery buildings and stupas have been excavated at Bhaṭṭiprolu, Jaggayapeṭa, Amarāvatī, and Nāgārjunakoṇḍa, all in District Guntur. Tradition associates the emergence of Mahāyāna sūtras and tantric doctrines with south India. A powerful school of Buddhist art flourished in Andhra from the 2nd century BC to medieval times. The great stupas at Amarāvatī and Nāgārjunakoṇḍa were active centres of several sects of Mahāsāṅghikas and Sthaviravādins. The Bhaṭṭiprolu relic casket inscription refers to a conference of *arhats*. The decline of Buddhist monks and monasteries in south India had begun after the 7th century, but Buddhist icons continued to be made and revered till the 15th. A 14th-century inscription at Kandy in Sri Lanka refers to one Dharmakīrti's repairs to a Buddhist temple at Amarāvatī.

Buddhist monasteries and temples in Sindha were demolished by Arab invaders under Muhammad Kāsim in AD 712. His soldiers slaughtered a large number of 'samanis' (*śramaṇas*) who 'shaved their heads and beards'. Another report says that Kāsim had spared 1,000 Buddhist monks in Sindha, ruled over by King Candra who was a Buddhist monk. Toward the end of the 8th century the Arabs swooped down upon the prosperous monasteries of Gujarat and destroyed the Buddhist University at Valabhī on the sea coast. Inscriptions of Maitraka rulers of Gujarat belonging to the period AD 500–700 mention about one dozen spacious monasteries in Valabhi where learned and virtuous monks lived.

Excavation of rock monasteries for the use of Buddhist monks and nuns started on a large scale early in the 2nd century BC in the mid-south-west of India; the latest were dug in the 9th century AD in Rajasthan. The most important centres of rock monasteries are in Maharashtra, Madhya Pradesh, Gujarat and Rajasthan. The total number of them in India exceeds 1,000. Those at Kārle, Bhājā, Bedsā, Kānherī, Kondāṇe, Junnar, Kudā, Nasik, Ajaṇṭā, Pītalkhorā, Ellorā, Aurangabad and Bāgh have been studied in some detail. These rock-cut halls contain a marvellous wealth of architecture, sculpture and painting, but no Buddhist monk now lives in any of them. A complete rock monastery has three functional features: a series of small rooms with rock beds and rock pillows for use of monks (*bhikṣugṛha*), a pillared hall (*maṇḍapa*) for conducting religious ceremonies and holding meetings of the Sangha, and a sanctuary (*caitya*-hall), usually containing a rock-cut

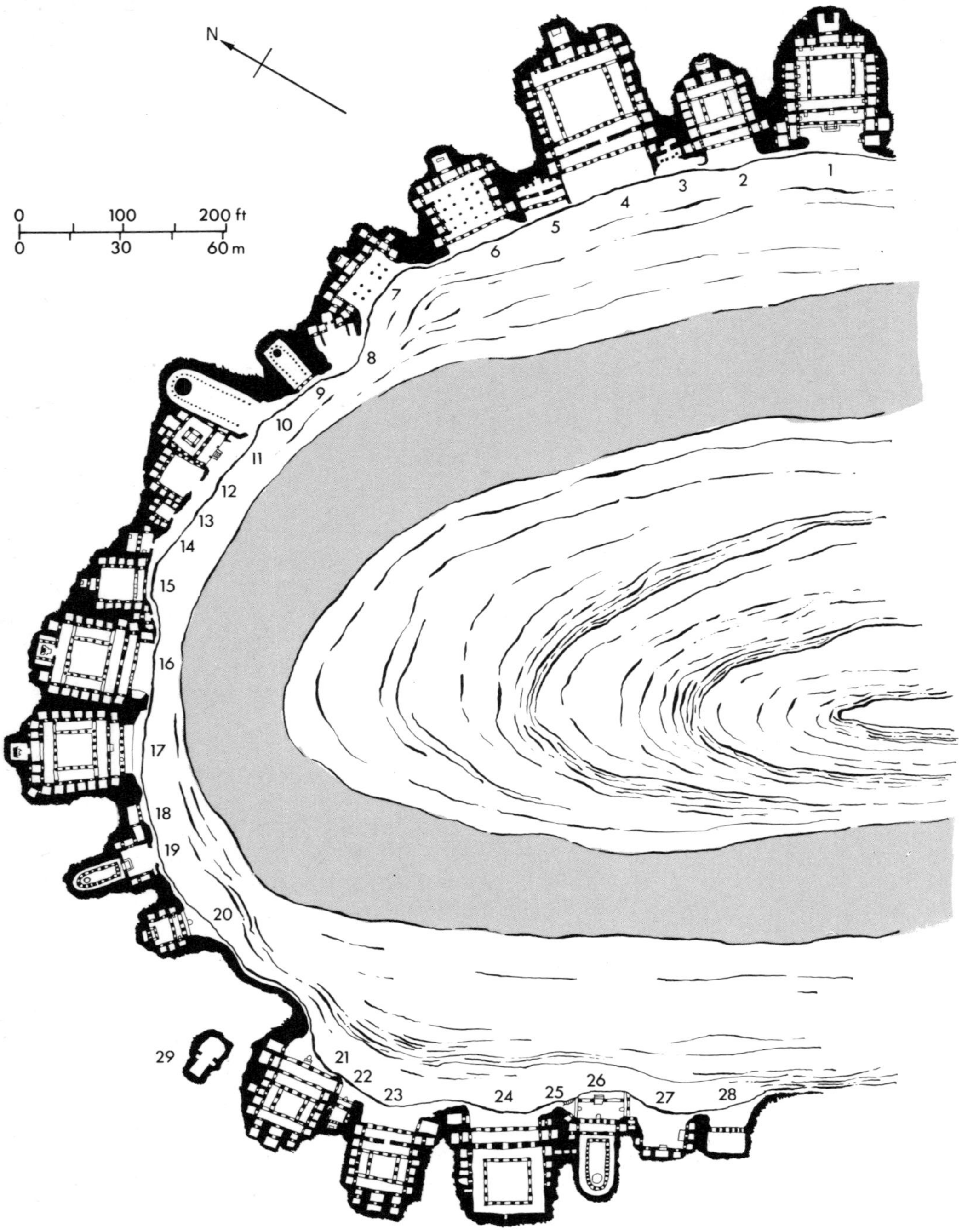

Plan of Ajaṇṭā and its rock-hewn caves. In the horseshoe of cliffs forming one bank of the Wagora river, twenty-eight cave-temples were dug between the 2nd century BC *and the 7th* AD. *The earliest seems to be Cave 10, a caitya-hall similar to that of Karlē shown on p. 66, pl. 13. Most of the caves, however, were vihāras, or monastic quarters, with cells grouped round a central courtyard – all carved from the living rock, often with elaborate façades and containing paintings and sculptures that make Ajaṇṭā a treasure-house of early Buddhist art. Their preservation is due to the fact that by the time Buddhism disappeared in India they had been abandoned and forgotten, and were not rediscovered until 1817.*

stupa or *caitya*, sometimes with figures of the Buddha on it. Much of the decorative art found in these monasteries and shrines illustrates the life of the Buddha and subjects drawn from folk mythology.

Very little is known about the life of the monks and nuns who inhabited these monasteries. Inscriptions mention the names of a few: one at Bedsā refers to a stupa in memory of Gobhūti who is called 'a forest-dweller' (*āraṇyaka*) and 'one living on alms' (*paiṇḍapātika*). This shows that some monks were known for their ascetic practices. At Junnar there was a nunnery of the Dharmottarīya sect. An inscription in the oldest rock monastery at Kārle tells us that 'this rock monastery, the best in the whole of India, was established by Bhūtapāla, the banker'. Among the donors mentioned in epigraphic records are monks, nuns, kings, queens, princes, ministers, officers of the state, physicians, merchants, goldsmiths, fishermen, brāhmaṇas, kṣatriyas, Greeks and Śakas. The records impress the reader with the religious zeal and the pious hopes of donors who seem to have vied with each other in offering 'righteous gifts' for the use of monks and nuns, for the good of all, and with a view to earning religious merit.

LAL MANI JOSHI

3

Expansion to the North: Afghanistan and Central Asia

OSKAR VON HINÜBER

THE SETTING OF Central Asian Buddhism consists of a region roughly from 32° to 42° N and 60° to 93° E. It stretches from the eastern end of the Silk Road (whose two branches, embracing the Takla Makan desert and following the old oases, meet at An Hsi), through the Karakorum and Hindu Kush regions, Kashmir, parts of present-day Pakistan and northern Afghanistan, up to the Oxus and as far west as Merv. Neither geographically nor politically is it a unit. Our only reason for treating it as one is that Buddhism flourished here among many different peoples and changing political forces during the first millennium AD.

Up to the middle of the last century hardly anything was known about the easternmost part of this region, Chinese Turkestan. Even when a few daring travellers, mostly geographers and scientists, began to investigate it, they paid little attention to its cultural history. This situation was changed dramatically in 1889 by a lucky coincidence, when a Captain Hamilton Bower happened to arrive in Kučā in pursuit of the murderer of the English merchant and traveller Andrew Dalgleish. Here he was offered, and bought, an old Sanskrit book written in Brāhmī characters on birch bark. It proved to be a medical text, still famous today under the name of the Bower Manuscript, and was at that time by far the oldest book in Sanskrit known to have survived. But before long a still older manuscript turned up – this time a Buddhist text: the Gāndhārī version of the *Dharmapada*. It was acquired by the French cartographer and naval officer Dutreuil de Rhins shortly before he too was murdered in 1893. These finds created widespread interest and were the direct cause of a number of expeditions to investigate the culture of Chinese Turkestan. Sir Aurel Stein inaugurated a new era of research in the Tarim Basin when he set out on his first journey of 1900–1. The two highlights of these expeditions were Stein's discovery in 1907 at Tunhuang of a whole library full of Buddhist scriptures that had lain untouched for nearly a thousand years, and the German excavations at the Turfan Oasis.

The antiquities recovered by archaeologists in this area, mainly before the First World War, are today divided between the British Museum in London, the National Museum in New Delhi and the Museum für Indische Kunst in Berlin. They are one of the bases for our knowledge of monks and monasteries in Chinese Turkestan. The other basis is the literature written as reports on the 'Western Countries' by Buddhist Chinese pilgrims to India, travelling along the Silk Road on their way to Gandhāra or Gilgit, where many inscriptions by Buddhist pilgrims have been found in recent years.

The report of one of these pilgrims, Hsüan-tsang, who travelled outside China between 629 and 645, was so detailed that Sir Aurel Stein could use it almost as a guide-book. Such accounts by pilgrims give valuable information on the number of monks and monasteries and the prevailing schools of Buddhist thought. Where accounts are silent, as they are for large parts of western Central Asia, we have to rely entirely on archaeology. Ruined stupas and monasteries, and especially the reliefs and wall-paintings that they contain, often enable us to draw conclusions about Buddhist monastic life during the period when Buddhism was spreading and flourishing.

Ancient Buddhist sites in Afghanistan and on the territory of what is now Pakistan have been known since the beginning of the 19th century. Systematic research, however, began only after the First World War, when the Délégation Archéologique Française en Afghanistan was founded in 1922. During the time of British India Sir John Marshall excavated Taxila (now in Pakistan) as director of the Archaeological Survey of India. After the Second World War Italian archaeologists took up work in Swāt.

Numerous sites on what is now territory of the USSR, for instance Kara Tepe near Termez, have been excavated by Russian archaeologists during the last decades. Among the many surprising finds was a voluminous, still unpublished complete Sanskrit manuscript on birch bark containing Buddhist texts from the 6th to 8th centuries AD. In recent years Chinese archaeologists have excavated in Chinese Turkestan with spectacular though still hardly known success.

Although most texts have been recovered in a more fragmentary state, scholars have been able to piece many of them together, often from very tiny pieces, and so recover large parts of the original Sanskrit versions of writings known previously only from Tibetan or Chinese translations. Texts in Central Asian languages have also been found. Besides Buddhist scriptures, there have been documents shedding light on the political, economic and religious situation in Central Asia.

The new faith from India

It is obvious that the first Buddhist missions to Central Asia must have started from the north-west of the Indian subcontinent. According to legend, it was a pupil of Ānanda who brought the teaching of the Buddha to Gandhāra only fifty years after Śākyamuni's death. Neither archaeological evidence nor anything recorded by the Greek historians who followed Alexander the Great's expedition to India supports this tradition. But from the time of the Maurya empire (about 300–150 BC) such evidence does become available and surviving remains prove the presence of Buddhist monks in the north-west.

Aśoka's inscriptions in Kharōṣṭhī characters at Shāhbāzgaṛhī and Mānsehrā, and those in Greek and Aramaic, bear witness to his missionary zeal. He seems to have been the first to build stupas here; that of Dharmarājika in Taxila, dating back to the period of the Maurya empire, became a centre of Buddhist scholarship. The pilgrim Hsüan-tsang records several stupas in the Punjab area, and archaeology confirms that they go back to Mauryan times. Legends relating to the building of these stupas mostly refer to episodes in the former lives of the Buddha, so that the north-west became associated with his previous existence, as east India was associated with his last.

Greco-Bactrian kingdoms founded by Alexander's successors governed this region after the collapse of the Mauryan empire. It is difficult to say how far Buddhism influenced them. A Pali text, the 'Questions of King Menander', expounds Buddhist Doctrine in the form of a dialogue between the Buddhist monk Nāgasena and the Indo-Greek king Menander; it seems to point to a vivid Greek interest in the religion of the Buddha, and certain ceremonies held after Menander's death, described by Plutarch, recall the scriptural accounts of the Buddha's death. Neither Menander nor any Greek king, however, rose to a position comparable to that of Aśoka or later Kaniṣka. Buddhism was certainly not suppressed, but neither was it promoted by the rulers as part of official religious policy.

Several invasions by Iranian tribes now disturbed the region, and Buddhism suffered a series of setbacks, though these proved to be temporary. In the 1st century BC the Greek kingdoms were conquered by the Śakas (Scythians); a hundred years later they in their turn were overturned by the Pahlavas (Parthians), who built up shortlived kingdoms in the north-west. Both Śakas and Pahlavas began by destroying Buddhist monuments, stupas and monasteries, but their attitudes quickly changed. Taxila was rebuilt on the lines of Greek town-planning, thus showing the survival of Greek cultural influence even after the political change. The Dharmarājika stupa founded by Aśoka was enlarged, and inscriptions record extensive building activities and rich gifts to the Sangha. From now on Buddhism flourished and expanded steadily, the Kuṣāṇa empire was founded at the beginning of the 1st century AD, and from its centre at Bactria pushed its frontiers across the whole of north India and parts of

One of the ink sketches discovered by Sir Aurel Stein in the region of Tun-huang. It shows rich patrons worshipping at a shrine, men on the left and women on the right. Nearly all the faces are left blank, but head-dresses are represented in some detail, probably an indication of rank.

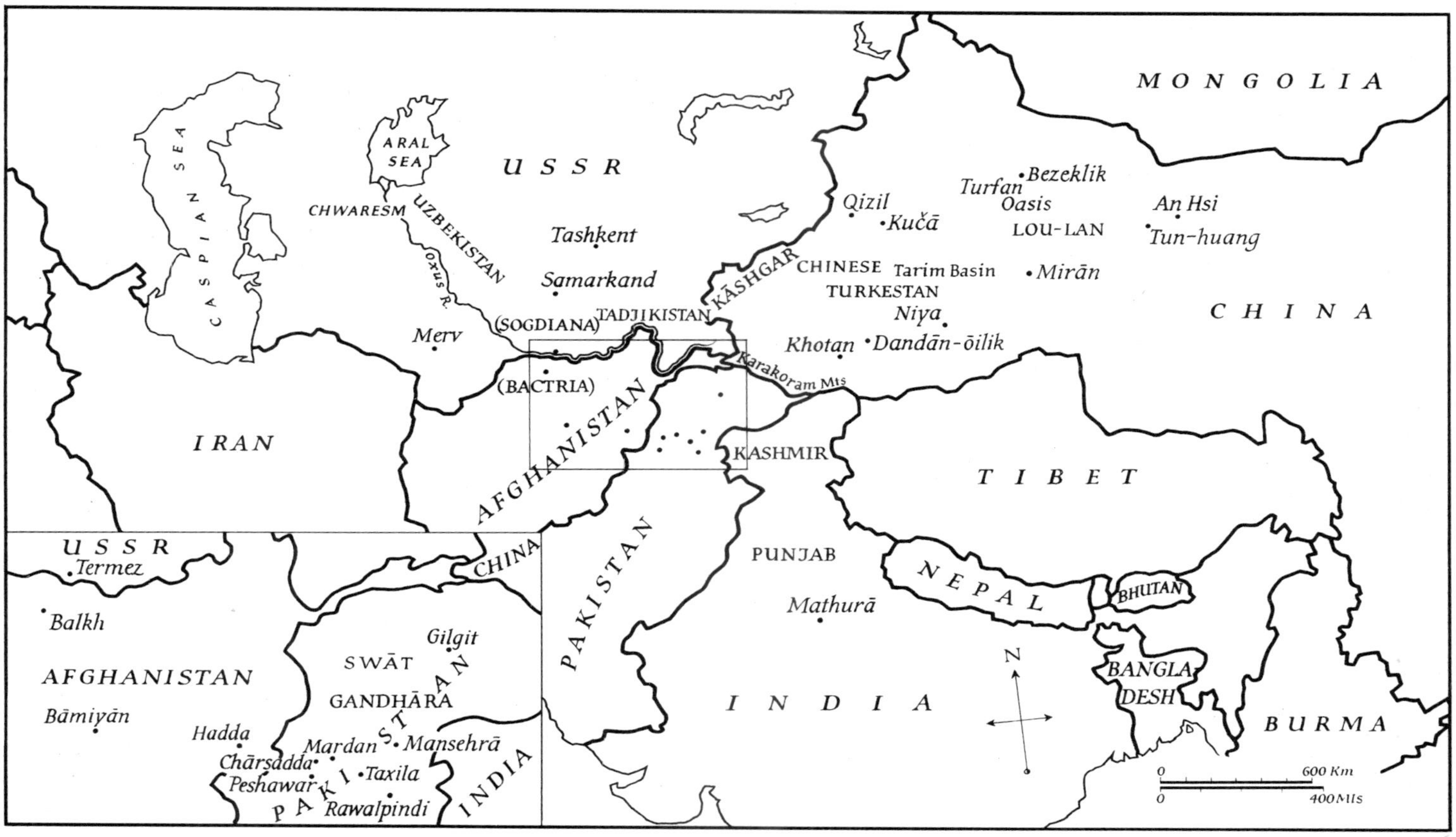

Central Asia: the area of Buddhist expansion discussed in this chapter.

Chinese Turkestan and Afghanistan, eventually taking in Uzbekistan and Tadjikistan as far west as Chwaresm.

From the comparatively few records of the huge empire available today – chiefly coins and archaeological evidence – we can piece together a picture of a strong political power embracing a wide territory and bringing peace and prosperity to the greater part of Central Asia. Wealth, stability and secure conditions for travel were favourable to the spread of Buddhism, and Buddhist tradition gratefully recognized a second Aśoka in the greatest of the Kuṣāṇa emperors, Kaniṣka. He certainly built large stupas near his own city of Puruṣupura (modern Peshawar), much admired at the time and later by Chinese pilgrims; but the tradition that he organized a Buddhist council there seems to be at variance with history. Nor did Buddhism conquer Bactria and north-west India during his reign quite so triumphantly as was once believed. Only a comparatively small number of the monasteries so far excavated in Afghanistan, for instance, go back to the early Kuṣāṇa period, although foundations like Kara Tepe near Termez (now in the USSR) do originate from that time.

During the 3rd century the emerging power of the Sassanians in Iran became a growing threat to the Kuṣāṇas. Gradually they were driven back from west to east, though why and when the empire finally collapsed is a matter of conjecture. The religion of the Sassanians was Zoroastrianism, but they seem to have continued a policy of relative tolerance towards Buddhism.

After the fall of the Kuṣāṇa empire we find a collection of petty kingdoms, all apparently fairly prosperous and friendly to Buddhism. Kings embellished their capitals with temples, monasteries and stupas. Between the 3rd and 5th centuries the beautiful stupa at Jauliān in Taxila was erected and enlarged, the heavily decorated stupas of Haḍḍa were built, and the cave monasteries were dug into the mountain at Bāmiyān.

This was the zenith of Buddhism in western Central Asia. It encountered a severe check with the invasion by White Huns (also called Hephthalites), who conquered Gandhāra and Taxila on their way into India during the second half of the 5th century. But just as the image of Kaniṣka seems to be exaggerated on the positive side by Buddhist tradition, so the White Huns do not seem to have been quite such ferocious persecutors of Buddhism as they are depicted by Hsüan-tsang. Here, too, archaeology tells its own story: the White Huns in fact seem to have shown different attitudes towards Buddhism in different regions. Although it is true that Taxila and Gandhāra were damaged considerably, in the more western areas monasteries hardly suffered at all. There had, however, been a marked decline of Buddhism by the time Hsüang-tsang visited this region in the early 7th century: in Haḍḍa he found a pious Buddhist laity but so few monks that they were hardly able to look after the large monasteries properly. But this rather points to a *general* decline in economic prosperity leaving laymen with few funds to feed a large community of monks.

A second and perhaps even more decisive factor in the decline was the revival of Hinduism, a pressure which made itself felt in the border regions after it had gained ground in India proper at the time of the Guptas. The numerous Śāhi dynasties who ultimately inherited the Kuṣāṇa empire in Afghanistan and further west mostly professed Hinduism. Not exclusively, however: some were Buddhists. The Paṭola Śāhis of Gilgit, only recently emerging from the darkness of history, evidently favoured Buddhism. Some of them are named as donors in manuscripts unearthed from two small stupas at Naupur near Gilgit. Peculiarities of orthography and names mentioned in the colophons at the end of these manuscripts, moreover, show that there were manifold connections between the Buddhists of Gilgit and those of Khotan, one of the centres of Buddhism in Chinese Turkestan during the 7th century.

In contrast to the situation in western Central Asia, material for the history of Chinese Turkestan is somewhat richer. Ancient, if fragmentary, literary sources supplement the archaeological evidence. Since the territories along both branches of the Silk Road, avoiding the Takla Makan Desert to the north and the south, were well known and from time to time even ruled by the Chinese, the 'Western Countries' are mentioned rather frequently in their imperial annals.

After the collapse of the Kuṣāṇa empire in this area, the kingdoms of Kāshgar, Khotan and Lou-lan (Shanshan or Kroraina) emerged as local powers in which the influence of Indian culture continued to be felt even after the direct political connection had been disrupted during the 3rd century AD. Documents discovered by Sir Aurel Stein at Niya are written in an Indian language and script, thus proving that a north-western form of Middle Indo-Aryan continued to be in use in Khotan and in Lou-lan for administrative purposes long after the fall of the Kuṣāṇas. Still stronger and more durable was the Indian impact on religion: Buddhism prevailed from early in the Christian era.

The kingdom of Lou-lan collapsed in the late 4th century. Whether this was due to the invasion of the White Huns remains doubtful. At the same time disaster seems to have struck Khotan too and there is a break in its history; afterwards the Indian language was replaced by a local Iranian one, though still written in an Indian script.

The kingdom of Khotan, as well as other regions of Chinese Turkestan, later suffered twice from the expansion of Tibet – once in the late 7th century and again from 783 to 866. Although the Tibetans were themselves Buddhists, the political turmoil and economic decline left their mark on the Buddhist Sangha in Khotan. When recovering from this setback Khotan formed close diplomatic ties with China, with the result that new religious inspiration came to the kingdom from China during the T'ang dynasty.

The Tibetan expansion also made itself felt in the Buddhist centres along the northern branch of the Silk Road and during the 7th and 8th centuries the southern road became increasingly impassable east of Khotan. At Kučā a local dynasty managed time and again to maintain or regain political independence. The presence of Buddhism here from the 1st century AD onward was no doubt responsible for Kučā's close cultural contact with India: the Indian Brāhmī script was adopted for the local Indo-European language, Tokharian, and there is a strong Indian influence in the wall-paintings preserved at the 'Thousand Buddhas' cave monastery at Qizil. Farther east, in the Turfan Oasis, on the other hand, it was Chinese political influence that prevailed until the middle of the 9th century, when Uigur Turks founded the kingdom of Qočo. The prosperity of Buddhism during this period is well documented – for instance, by the rich paintings in the monasteries of Bezeklik.

Missions and tongues

According to Hsüan-tsang, Buddhism was brought to Bactria by Trapuṣa and Bhallika, two merchants who were the first to offer food to the Buddha after his Enlightenment and became the first lay followers. This legend, which is evidently based on a popular etymology identifying the name Bhallika with the town of Bahlika (Balkh), does at least show that not only monks but travelling merchants as well were presumed to be capable of spreading Buddhism. One remembers, for instance, how Soghdian merchants established small colonies all the way from Samarkand to China, though they never built up a powerful kingdom.

We shall never know in detail about the coming of Buddhism to western Central Asia. Archaeology can give us a rough date for the foundation of a monastery, but no personality of any monk emerges from its ruins, and we are left merely with a few names in inscriptions or manuscripts. Yet there was clearly a wave of missionary zeal throughout the area. Most of the early translations of Buddhist texts into Chinese are attributed to monks from western Central Asia, among them Iranians such as Parthians and Soghdians. Indeed the very beginning of the period of translation into Chinese is marked by the arrival of the Parthian missionary An Shih-kao at the Chinese capital Lo-yang in AD 148. At about the same time or a little earlier other Buddhist missionaries reached Chinese Turkestan, where Buddhism was officially adopted at Kāshgar. Archaeological evidence suggests a similar date for the introduction of Buddhism into Khotan, even though Hsüan-tsang records the legend of a monk from

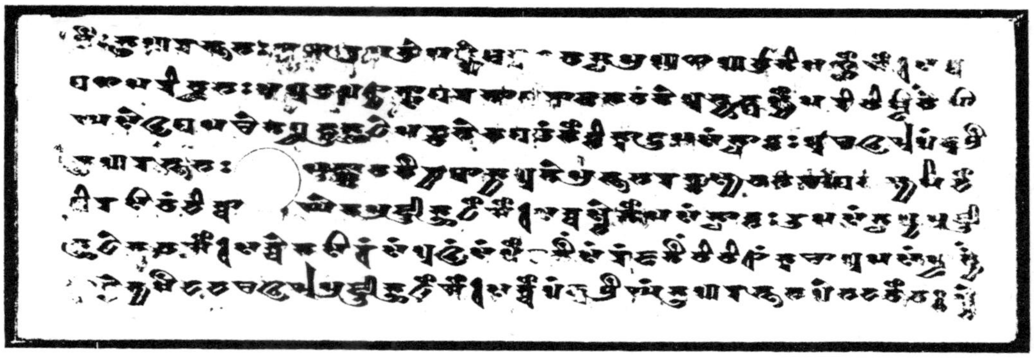

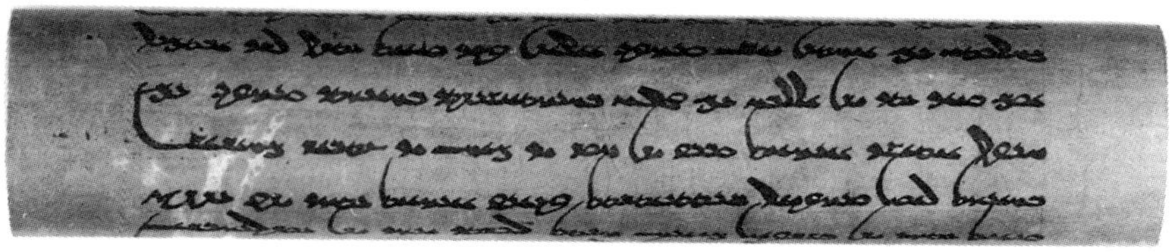

Three of the scripts used for the diffusion of Buddhist texts: (top) a leaf of a Central Asian manuscript in Sanskrit of the Saddharmapuṇḍarīka or Lotus Sūtra in Central Asian Brāhmī script, found at Kāshgar; (centre) an Uigur manuscript of a work on Buddhist Tantrism, dated 1350; (bottom) part of a Sogdian scroll containing charms and spells invoking a goddess of good fortune.

Kashmir arriving there as early as the reign of Aśoka. Maybe it reached Kučā and Turfan, on the northern branch of the Silk Road, in the same period; but the hard evidence for it there (in the Chinese sources) goes back only to the 3rd century AD. Later still it reached the Turkic tribes of eastern Central Asia. There is virtually no direct evidence for the Buddhist missions among peoples of Turkic origin, but linguistic data can provide some clues: loanwords taken over to express Buddhist terminology often betray the language, and consequently the home, of the missionaries.

Language, in fact, was one of the most formidable obstacles to the propagation of the faith. As soon as they left the area of the Indo-Aryan languages (Sanskrit and its derivatives), the missionaries found themselves amid the vast linguistic diversity of Central Asia. If they came from north-west India they spoke Gāndhārī Prākrit up to the first centuries AD, when it gradually gave way to Sanskrit. Although only one Buddhist text in Gāndhārī survives (the fragmentary *Dharmapada*, half of which was bought by Dutreuil de Rhins, the other half by the Russian consul Petrovsky in Khotan in the late 19th century), there is plenty of evidence for it as a major language of Buddhist missionaries. The documents from Niya, referred to earlier, and other stray finds in the Kučā region indicate that it was still in use as late as the 7th century along the northern branch of the Silk Road. The evidence is tenuous but fairly conclusive, for it is possible to show, from the Indian words that were transcribed and thus preserved in Buddhist texts translated into Chinese, that the translators were working from copies of Gāndhārī, and not in Sanskrit as was once erroneously assumed by Western scholars. The earliest Indian loanwords in the local Central Asian languages point in the same direction. And inscriptions found at Termez, in western Central Asia, prove that Gāndhārī was in use there during the times of the Kuṣāṇas.

The monks using Gāndhārī probably belonged mainly to the school of the Dharmaguptakas, and this seems to have nearly disappeared in the 7th century. Hsüan-tsang found none of them in India proper and only small groups in Central Asia. With the decline of this school the Gāndhārī language seems to have died out, to be replaced by Sanskrit when another school, the Sarvāstivādins, gained the dominant position. Towards the end of this period, the Dharmaguptakas themselves probably adopted Sanskrit, under pressure from the more powerful school; a few fragments from a Dharmaguptaka Canon in Sanskrit have been found at Qizil.

Buddhist texts in Sanskrit are still being discovered in western Central Asia. One of the most spectacular finds came from Naupur near Gilgit. Here some shepherds digging a mound (which was perhaps a kind of library and not a stupa, as generally assumed) unearthed by chance about sixty manuscripts, mostly on birch bark but some on a special kind of paper and one on palm leaf, containing nearly fifty different texts. They included an almost complete copy of the *Mūlasarvāstivāda-Vinaya* in Sanskrit, besides texts of Mahāyāna Buddhism. These manuscripts date from the 6th and 7th centuries. Names of donors given in the colophons include Khotanese and probably Chinese names together with others from as yet unidentified, perhaps local, languages. Close connections between the Buddhists in Gilgit and those in Chinese Turkestan show up in many ways, not only from these manuscripts. Inscriptions in Kharoṣṭhī writing, in Sanskrit, Soghdian and Chinese, engraved on the rocks in the Gilgit region by travelling Buddhists, give a vivid picture of the journeys made during the centuries along this road into and out of India. Many of these inscriptions have been discovered since 1979 and are still unpublished.

By the time of the Gilgit manuscripts the literary scene at Khotan had changed fundamentally. The local Iranian language, Khotanese, and in some degree Sanskrit also, had superseded Gāndhārī. Besides Buddhist texts translated from Sanskrit the remains of manuscripts show some traces of a flourishing local literary production by Buddhist monks. The famous 'Book of Zambasta' preserved at Leningrad and named after the patron for whom it was written expounds the 'Khotanese' variety of Buddhism, a subject that still awaits investigation.

The Khotanese language was recovered and deciphered only at the beginning of this century; other languages known from fragmentary manuscripts found at Kučā and Turfan are still in the process of being interpreted. One of the many surprises to scholars was the discovery of Tokharian, an Indo-European language spoken in the ancient kingdoms of Kučā and Agni (Karashahr). Still further east the influence of Chinese Buddhism was predominant, and many Uigur texts written in a variety of the Soghdian script adopted by the Uigur Turks were translated from Chinese, as were the remnants of Soghdian Buddhist literature, and not from Sanskrit, as the Tokharian Buddhist literature was. Besides canonical texts, *avadānas* and *jātakas* were highly popular. In addition to several texts long known to Western scholars of Buddhism, the *Sanghāṭa Sūtra* now emerges as a Mahāyāna scripture held in high esteem by Buddhists at Gilgit and in Khotan, as is shown by the quite exceptional number of manuscripts preserved. The reason for its unusual popularity, which is further stressed by a recently identified Soghdian fragment of this text, may be its simplicity, which could appeal to the religious feelings of both monks and laity.

Art and imagery

These *sūtras* belong to Mahāyāna Buddhism, which flourished in north-west India and especially in Khotan, which was considered one of its centres. Although it is not possible to connect the origin of Mahāyāna with any definite school or even geographical area, north-west India seems to have played a prominent role in its development. The oldest dated monument apparently attesting Mahāyāna Buddhism is an image of the Buddha flanked by two bodhisattvas, probably Maitreya and Vajrapāṇi. It is found in Gandhāra and dated to the year five of Kaniṣka, that is, the late 1st century AD; its inscription seems to mention the transfer of merit, which is typical of Mahāyāna. Bodhisattvas on the other hand are by no means alien to Hīnayāna either, and the mere presence of Maitreya or Vajrapāṇi, who both frequently appear in sculptures from Gandhāra, does not prove the Mahāyānistic character of this art.

Vajrapāṇi ('He who carries a thunderbolt') often stands beside or behind the Buddha himself ready to terrify or to crush his opponents with his thunderbolt (*vajra*). Similarly Maitreya, the future Buddha, is a protector of Buddhism and especially of missionary monks, which may be one of the reasons for his popularity in Central Asia, where monks were often exposed to alien religions and hostile people. Texts describing Maitreya's future exploits to re-establish Buddhism have been found in the Tokharian and Uigur languages and in Khotanese in Chapter 22 of the 'Book of Zambasta'. Such features as his identification with the sun and his epithet 'Invincible' have led scholars, perhaps erroneously, to think he was influenced by the Iranian god Mithra, also called 'Invictus', a hypothesis encouraged by the popular etymology connecting the names Mithra and Maitreya. Iranian influences on the treatment of bodhisattvas and on other Buddhist religious concepts are certainly possible, especially during the time of the Kuṣāṇas, which was the formative phase of Central Asian Buddhism when Iranian and Indian religions came into close contact. The so-called 'Persian Bodhisattva' from Dandān-ōilik near Khotan furnishes an example of the blending of Indian and Iranian concepts: this image of the patron deity of weaving and silk-making resembles at the same time a bodhisattva and the Iranian hero Rustam.

Iranian influence may be found in some aspects of the bodhisattva Avalokiteśvara as well. He was widely worshipped in India too, but figures prominently in Central Asia. He is invoked by people in distress to save the believer and to lead him into the presence of the Buddha Amitābha, whose image Avalokiteśvara bears

Khotanese painted panel, c. 8th century AD: the four-armed figure is a deity of silk-weaving holding the tools of that profession. Stylistically it resembles a bodhisattva and shows at the same time a strong influence from non-Buddhist Persian art.

in his head-dress. Amitābha was not known to Hīnayāna Buddhism and little evidence for him can be collected in India, although recently a votive inscription from Kuṣāṇa times mentioning him has been discovered at Mathurā. But in Central Asia the cult of Amitābha grew enormously, eclipsing all other Buddhas. His association with light and with endless life recalls the Iranian god of time, Zurvān. Amitābha was believed to keep Buddhists on their way to Nirvāṇa in uninterrupted bliss and happiness in his paradise Sukhāvatī located in the 'western region'. Sometimes pious Buddhists were said to be brought there by the bodhisattva Kṣitigarbha, whose cult perhaps was introduced from China to Turfan where it seems to have won great popularity among the Uigur Buddhists of Qočo. Where texts are not available, evidence for these bodhisattvas can sometimes be deduced from sculptures and wall-paintings. When these are preserved *in situ* they provide valuable information on the chronological sequence and the geographical distribution of different forms of Buddhist faith and worship.

Monks themselves do not seem to have indulged much in artistic activities, but those propagating Buddhism in Central Asia were soon followed by artists from north-west India. A Buddhist text speaks of an artist travelling from Puṣkarāvatī (Chārsadda) to the neighbourhood of what is today Tashkent to embellish a monastery. In Mirān, in eastern Chinese Turkestan, the name of a painter is mentioned as Tita, apparently identical with the Latin Titus, thus showing Western connections.

Such connections must certainly have existed, and at Gandhāra Hellenistic traditions combined with influences from India and Iran to bring about one of the turning points of Buddhist art. Up to this period the Buddha himself had not been represented naturalistically. A footprint, a parasol, a *bodhi* tree had been used to indicate his presence. But at Gandhāra and the other important centre of Mathurā the image of the Buddha as a man appears for the first time. Numerous reliefs representing the Buddha and his previous lives appear all over the north-west, in a variety of styles. In the first phase (1st-4th centuries AD), stone (schist) is the commonest material. From the 3rd to the 5th centuries stucco too was used. Then the White Huns' destruction of Buddhist monasteries put an end to Gandhāran art.

No paintings survive in Gandhāra, but the influence of the school was felt in Chinese Turkestan as far as Kučā, where numerous wall-paintings found at Qizil deserve special mention. Nothing comparable is available from western Central Asia, although, thanks to the successful efforts of Russian archaeologists, evidence for painting in this area is growing. It is already clear that, whereas at Kučā the technique of painting and the fair complexions of the monks and laymen depicted all betray Western influence, those of Qočo look definitely Chinese – a distinction that might have been predicted on linguistic grounds, since the inhabitants of Kučā spoke the Indo-European language Tokharian.

The monk in his monastery

The decoration of the cells of cave monasteries in these areas affords a glimpse of the daily life of the Buddhist monk. For besides subjects taken from scripture we find many depictions of monks, some even named portraits; and lay donors are shown in various local costumes. The pictures show that the monks' robes were patched together so as to appear produced from cloth collected from rubbish heaps. Laymen holding flowers or vessels with incense are shown worshipping images of the Buddha and of bodhisattvas, very much as they are depicted on old book covers found near Gilgit.

The richness and the high artistic quality of most paintings show the prosperity of the Buddhist community. For the 7th century this can be corroborated by the statistics given by Hsüan-tsang for monks and monasteries on the southern branch of the Silk Road and in north-west India, although these are of course rough estimates only. He found about one hundred monasteries in Khotan inhabited by five thousand monks, all adhering to Mahāyāna. By contrast, he was

Races of Central Asia depicted in Buddhist paintings. Above are two details of frescoes at Qočo. Left: two worshippers, the one on the left a Syrian, the one on the right a Śaka, a Scythian people originally from the area north of the Aral Sea (the same head-dress appears in Khotanese Jātaka pictures).

Right: a monk from a distant country visiting a Qočo monk. The latter conforms to the Chinese ideal of beauty; the foreign visitor has somewhat grotesque features (e.g. traces of beard). Below: Uigur and Tokharian monks, from frescoes in the Kučā region.

hardly able to find a single monk in Gandhāra, a further indication of the disastrous consequences of the invasion of the White Huns for this part of the Buddhist world.

Yet even in ruin the monasteries are impressive as architecture and evocative of the life of the monks. Jauliān shows a ground plan with a stupa standing in the middle of a courtyard, richly decorated as the main object of worship (the gates and railings used at Bhārhut and Sāñcī to depict scenes from the lives of the Buddha have now been superseded). Around a second square courtyard were the cells where the monks lived, if they did not prefer an even more secluded life in caves, as at Bāmiyān or in the cave monasteries of Turfan. Although not much is known yet about the architecture of monasteries in Khotan a different type seems to have been prevalent there, with houses for monks built in a more or less arbitrary way round a stupa, without any clear plan. This architecture suggests that perhaps the Buddhist monks of Khotan participated much more in worldly affairs than did their confrères elsewhere in Central Asia.

Besides art and architecture, there are manuscript remains to help reconstruct the picture of daily life in a monastery. The survival of accounts for daily food expenses in a Tokharian bill is particularly fortunate, but fairly numerous fragments of text relating to the formal acts of the Sangha shed light in other ways. In Khotan the *prātimokṣa* was recited in Sanskrit, as can be deduced from a passage in the 'Book of Zambasta', although *sūtras* and *avadānas* were translated into Khotanese. This was the case also in the Uigur kingdom of Qočo. In Kučā the *prātimokṣa* was translated into Tokharian. But even here fragments of this text in Sanskrit with Tokharian rubrics show that the sacred Indian language was kept, side by side with Tokharian. In the legal acts executed by the Sangha, Sanskrit also prevailed although there is evidence that Tokharian and Khotanese were used too.

The position of laymen in Afghanistan and Central Asia seems to have differed in some respects from their position in India. A special custom among the laity attested by manuscripts in Uigur and Tokharian but not known from India is the confession of sins, in which the laymen ask forgiveness not only for their individual sins but for all kinds of misdeeds committed by people past and present. This may have developed under Iranian influence, and significantly the oldest known formulary of this kind was brought to China by an Iranian prince in the 2nd century AD. It is, however, not altogether impossible that these confessions were influenced by the 'confessions' made at the beginning of their career by those setting out to become bodhisattvas.

The decline of Central Asian Buddhism

Although Buddhism had survived several ups and downs caused by political changes, a real threat to its very existence arose in the west after the Arab defeat of the last Sassanian ruler in AD 642, when the way into Central Asia lay open to the Arab military leaders.

The encounter between Buddhism and Islam did not, however, result in the immediate destruction of monasteries or in anything like the horrible massacres of monks that occured later in northern India. Buddhism and Islam existed side by side for centuries in many places, for instance at Bāmiyān, where the ruler embraced Islam during the late 8th century, but where, nevertheless, Buddhist monasteries were still functioning more than a hundred years later. Even long after the coming of Islam a remarkable revival of Buddhism was possible at Merv in the days of the Mongol invasion of the 13th century. Indeed, close contacts seem to have persisted between the two religions over a long period of time. Only recently Buddhist texts have been identified that were translated into Persian by a Muslim author of the 14th century, thus showing that Buddhism was still alive at that time in Iran. In the field of architecture, Buddhism even influenced some of the characteristic building types of Islam. The theological schools (*madrasah*), for instance, seem to have developed on the model of Buddhist monasteries. But, nonetheless, as in other areas of western Central Asia, the year 1000 does roughly mark the beginning of a steep decline of Buddhism, and the great Muslim scholar Al Bīrūnī (973–1050) was able to witness and to describe only the last traces of the vanishing religion.

In the east, in Khotan, news of the Arab conquest seems to have alarmed the local monks as early as the 8th century, when some of them fled into Tibet. But it took another two centuries before Islam finally reached Khotan itself, via Kāshgar, and the Khotanese ruler embraced the new religion in about 950. Thus here, too, Buddhism had vanished by the year 1000; monasteries were deserted; and Buddhist literature slowly fell into oblivion, together with the Khotanese language.

On the northern branch of the Silk Road Buddhism continued to exist, though no longer to prosper. In the late 10th century the Chinese government ordered the monks to leave the Sangha and to return to secular life. Many refused and were killed; hundreds of their mummified bodies were found in a temple in Qočo by the second German expedition to Turfan. When the ruler of this city assumed the title of *sultan* in 1469, thus withdrawing official support from the Sangha, the sand of the desert finally began to bury (and at the same time conserve) the last vestiges of the once flourishing Buddhist culture of Central Asia, a culture not to be rediscovered until the 19th century.

4

Nepal: the Survival of Indian Buddhism in a Himalayan Kingdom

SIEGFRIED LIENHARD

In the temperate zone of Nepal, between the high mountains of the outer Himalayas in the north and the Mahabharat range in the south, lies the pleasant valley of Kathmandu. This small basin, which is also known as the Nepal valley and is even sometimes simply called Nepal by its inhabitants, enjoys a climate which is both uncommonly mild and very constant. While the nights are cool and can become cold in the latter part of December and in January, the daytime temperature, in the hottest summer, seldom exceeds the maximum found in Mediterranean countries. Thick forests once covered the hills and mountains surrounding the valley, but their terraces, slopes and fields are now agricultural land. Fruit and vegetables flourish in the fertile soil, as well as rice and various kinds of grain crops.

Though it is impossible to give precise dates, it can be assumed that Hinduism and Buddhism were introduced into the Nepal valley from nearby India at a very early date. Once they were established, both these great religions existed side by side, and their stability was doubtless assisted by the fact that both religions considered this small Himalayan kingdom a region of special religious significance. For Nepal was not only the source of several tributaries of the sacred Ganges, but also the native country of the historical Buddha, Gautama Śākyamuni, who came from the Indo-Nepalese border country. A Buddhist legend links the origin of the Kathmandu valley with the arrival from the east of the bodhisattva Mañjuśrī, the protector of the arts and sciences. It was said that he arrived riding on a lion, and that it was he who, with one blow of his sword, drained the deep water of Lake Nāgavāsa which is supposed to have filled the valley in the distant past. Though this legend is thought to be relatively ancient, it has several Hindu variants which link the origin of the central part of Nepal with Viṣṇu-Kṛṣṇa or with a hero of India's great epic the *Mahābhārata*, Bhīmasena, who was deified there.

In view of the Kathmandu valley's geographical position it is not surprising that the two most important peoples in the history of the Nepalese kingdom settled there. They were the Newars, strongly Indianized Mongols who migrated from the north or north-east, and the Gurkhas (or Gorkhas) who came from Rajasthan and were originally pure Aryans but in the course of time interbred with various tribes, especially those from the west Nepalese mountain region. While the Gurkhas speak Nepali (also called Gurkhali), an Indian language which is now the recognized official language of Nepal, the Newars speak Newari (usually called Nepālbhāṣā), a language of Tibeto-Burmese origin with many Indian words borrowed both from Sanskrit and from modern Indian languages. There is a rich Newari literature, mostly religious, narrative and didactic, which has so far been little explored.

The ancestors of the present-day Gurkhas fled to Nepal mainly because of the Muslim onslaught on India and brought with them from their homelands their old Hindu faith, which was predominantly based on an ethical code appropriate to warriors. Though this faith had not reached either the spiritual or emotional intensity of some Indian sects, it slowly began to play an important political and national role, especially from the beginning of the 19th century, when it was reinforced by brahminical influences.

While the Gurkhas were exclusively Hindus, some of the Newars were adherents of Hinduism; others were adherents of late Buddhism, and others of a religious syncretism, characteristic of the Nepal valley, of which the dividing lines cannot be precisely defined, but in which Buddhist, Hindu (chiefly Śaiva tantric) and popular religious elements mingled. There is every reason to believe that the earliest Newars were, in fact, predominantly Buddhists, and that later, too, in the Middle Ages, the majority of the Newars followed the Vajrayāna, the third great Buddhist school of thought. Though the Newars were neither politically nor militarily particularly active, and though they are today a minority of a little more than half a million, it was they who gave the Nepal valley its special character, for they have long been the cultural élite of the country.

Like the Gurkhas, the first Newars were immigrants into Nepal, but they arrived too long ago for us to know when. Their descendants apparently integrated very quickly, but without losing their own individuality, into the life of the Nepal valley, which had always been open to the cultural influence of India. It was indeed the Newars who determined the intellectual life and culture of the country at least as early as the time of the first Malla kings (about AD 1200 to 1480). This was especially true during the era of the Malla kingdoms of about AD 1480 to 1768 which centred around the three cities of Kathmandu, Patan (Lalitpur) and Bhatgaon (Bhaktapur), so that medieval Nepal can be called the Nepal of the Newars. Its present-day religious composition seems to have been the same in the distant past: while Patan, the cultural centre of Nepal until the time of King Jayasthiti Malla (AD 1382–95) was mostly Buddhist, and Bhatgaon in the west of the valley almost totally Hindu, Kathmandu, the most recent of the three cities of the Nepal valley – it became politically important only after 1500 – always contained both predominantly Buddhist and predominantly Hindu communities. Political power always lay in the hands of Hindu rulers who were not of Newar descent and who modelled their courts on India, but the kings, especially the later Mallas, were mostly keen to advance both the Newars' religious life and their rich art and literature. However, the conquest of 1768 of the Malla states (which had at times been at war with each other) by the Gurkhas who had settled in the west of the country brought about a radical change. Śāh Pṛthivī Nārāyaṇ (1768–75) was the first of the dynasty of Śāhs who still rule today; he created the Nepal of the Gurkhas, who until their invasion of the Nepal valley had owned only an unimportant principality in the small town of Gurkha. With him began an era of attempts to Hinduize the valley, which led at times to rigorous repression of the Newars.

The Kathmandu valley was the centre of not only the political and economic, but also the intellectual and religious life of the kingdom. The term 'Nepalese Buddhism' usually refers solely to this heartland and centre of Nepal and to the particular form of Buddhism which was developed in this tiny area. Such a usage can however, be disputed, since one meets various forms of Buddhism, or a religion close to Buddhism, in other parts of Nepal. Just as the countryside and climate of the kingdom are very diverse, so the ethnic and religious distribution of the population presents a varied and even confusing picture. A number of peoples of Tibeto-Burmese origin have developed religions which show various degrees of assimilation to forms of late Buddhism, and the Sherpas in the North-east (who have become famous as mountaineers and mountain guides), as well as the Bhotiyas who live in the high mountain regions on the borders of Tibet, are adherents of Lamaism, the Tibetan form of Mahāyāna/Vajrayāna.

The first references to Buddhism in historical times concern the Emperor Aśoka. Two edicts found inscribed in southern Nepal and the four stupas named after the emperor in Patan, as well as the insistent tradition that Aśoka married his daughter Cārumatī to a nobleman from Nepal, are a reminder of the extent of the influence of the Indian emperor and show a direct connection between him and the Kathmandu valley. However we evaluate this unauthenticated tradition, it seems reasonable to suppose that the teaching of Buddha was introduced into Nepal either during or soon after the reign of Aśoka, around 268–232 BC. Since then Buddhism has developed uninterrupted in the Nepal valley, under the Hindu dynasty and side by side with the Indian or Hinduized sections of the population, and flourishes, though much altered, to the present day. For a long time the religious situation in the valley of Kathmandu was similar to that of pre-Islamic India. There were many schools and sects of late Buddhism at work in Nepal, and the country experienced a great – and final – influx of Buddhist forces in the 12th and 13th centuries, when Islam invaded northern India and Buddhism finally ceased on Indian soil. The centre of Nepal now became a sanctuary for many monks, scholars and artists from India, who had a crucial effect on both the religious and the artistic life of the Buddhist Newars.

Through the centuries Indian immigrants of the most diverse faiths and sects had brought Indian culture to the Nepal valley, but the stream of devout Buddhists dried up completely after Muslim rule had been firmly established in India. While Hindu courts and successive groups of new immigrants ensured not only the survival but the constant renewal of the Hindu faith, a spiritual revival of Buddhism through external forces was from then on denied to Buddhism in the Kathmandu valley. It was in fact probably the growing isolation of Buddhist Newar communities which existed alongside a Hindu faith constantly strengthened and nourished by new stimuli that led to the peculiar development of the Nepalese form of Buddhism. Its chief characteristics are on the one hand a strong blending with elements of Hinduism, especially of Śaiva tantra, and on the other hand the far-reaching laicization of the monks and monasteries. Many Nepalese monasteries, especially those of Patan, probably the oldest Buddhist city in the valley, were widely renowned as places of learning and instruction and attracted Buddhist monks from foreign countries. The 7th-century Chinese pilgrim to India Hsüan-tsang, though he never visited the country himself, heard from others that, in his time, around two thousand Buddhist monks of both the Hīnayāna and the Mahāyāna studied in Nepal. Hsüan-tsang also recorded in his 'Report from Western Countries' that in the Nepal valley Buddhist and Hindu buildings stood side by side. But whereas the Hīnayāna, unable to establish itself firmly among the broad mass of the population of Nepal, lost ground and finally disappeared, the Vajrayāna, which was easily assimilated and open to Hindu influences, continued to prosper. Since the beginning of the 20th century Hīnayāna missionary activity has begun again with the arrival of Sinhalese monks who are working to introduce Theravāda Buddhism, but their success has been limited.

The nature of Nepalese Buddhism

Buddhism in Nepal has come a long way from its older forms in India and elsewhere. While at his death Gautama Buddha left a community of monks and nuns subject to a rigorous discipline, in the Kathmandu valley more than 1,500 years later the Order of the Sangha, so important for the preservation of the Doctrine, disintegrated. This disintegration further weakened the already loosely drawn dividing line between the world of the monks and that of the laity. Monks and nuns had originally only stayed in monasteries (*vihāra*) during the rainy season. These *vihāra* were now not only permanently inhabited, but had become the true family homes of monks, who were married and lived there with their wives, children and other relatives. This great change did not, of course, happen suddenly, but came about slowly, and did not clearly occur until after the isolation of Nepal from India. In the 17th century Patan still had about twenty-five monasteries in which the monks, pledged to the older rule, kept strictly to celibacy.

Hinduization exerted a lasting influence not only on the social structure of the Nepal valley but also on the Buddhist pantheon and its rituals, which became more and more important and more or less took the place of the Doctrine. Like all Hindu courts, those of Nepal depended on the support of Brahmins and Hindu officials, but, while there can be no doubt that the ruling dynasties represented a powerful rallying point for orthodox Hinduism, the growth of Hinduism in Nepal as a completely conscious trend aiming at national prestige appears, as mentioned above, to have begun only with the era of the Śāhs. At the time of the early Mallas and the three Malla kingdoms, the increasing acceptance of esoteric Vajrayāna Buddhism, with its concepts and practices taken from Śaiva tantrism, began to erode the core of Buddhist Doctrine. We know that schools of late Buddhism on Indian soil, especially in Bihar and Bengal, which adjoin Nepal, had already borrowed many elements from Hinduism. The decay of the old Buddhist monasteries in Nepal and their transformation into living quarters for whole families must be attributed less to the deteriorating financial position of the monasteries than to the development of the schools of tantric Vajrayāna which flourished in the Middle Ages, especially since many tantric rituals were open to both men and women, and to celibate monks as well as to fathers of families.

While it is essential to Hinduism that its adherents are inexorably subject to the strict hierarchy of the caste system, Buddhism (which had originally been essentially a road to salvation for monks) remained indifferent to social structure. But in the Kathmandu valley a social hierarchy very like the Hindu caste structure emerged in the course of time among the Buddhists. This process had no doubt begun long before the 15th century, but it accelerated when, as we have seen, more and more Hindu religious observances became absorbed into the largely ritualistic Vajrayāna of the Nepal valley. Towards the end of the 14th century King Jayasthiti Malla (AD 1382–95), aided by five learned Brahmins, codified the social order and arranged the Buddhist Newars too in a hierarchic system of professional groups – the final phase of a long development. The professional categories fitted only loosely into the classical pattern of the four great Indian classes: Brahmin, Kṣatriya, Vaiśya and Śūdra; but, as in India, the highest rank was exclusively reserved for the priesthood. The second rank was that of the nobility, i.e. members of the ruling house, the military aristocracy and the civil service, while the succeeding ranks included certain classes of tradesmen and the main sections of the population, i.e. a descending scale of representatives of intermediate and humble trades, and workers and peasants. Outside this order stood those who followed various 'unclean' professions, the 'untouchables': butchers, shoemakers and fishermen. Since most of the Gurkhas did not come to the Nepal valley until much later, this professional and caste structure at first affected chiefly the Newars, whose higher castes were either Śaivites or Vajrayāna Buddhists.

The ranks of priesthood

In this short account we are only concerned with the priestly classes of the Newars who, as can easily be established, were all the descendants of Buddhist monks who had married. It is significant that they did not owe their spiritual rank to their own decisions and efforts, but only to their descent. There are two distinct groups of monks whose names clearly indicate their original place in the spiritual hierarchy. The first and higher category comprises scholar and teacher priests who are in Sanskrit called *vajrācārya*, 'Diamond Master', while the less learned and lower-ranking priests are called *bhikṣu*, 'monk', or more accurately *śākya-bhikṣu* (recalling the Buddha's Śākya origin). These statuses conform very closely to Hindu models, and indeed the establishment of a hereditary priesthood among the Newars marks one of the final and crucial phases of the gradual assimilation of Nepalese Buddhism to a Hinduism that embraces the whole of society and assigns every section of the population a definite position. The wish to emulate Hindu priests, as well as material considerations, led Buddhist clerics to aspire to privileges like those of the Brahmins, and we may assume that the considerable shortage of Hindu priests in the distant past made it easier for *vajrācārya* and *bhikṣu* to assimilate their social position to that of the Brahmin.

There are some interesting similarities between the Newar priest and the hereditary Brahmin. Just as the Brahmin, beside his function as a priest, has the authority of a learned pandit, well-versed in the scriptures, so the *vajrācārya* appeared to the faithful primarily as an erudite teacher familiar with the scriptures. He was an adept in the *mantras* and *dhāraṇīs* (spells and incantations), the tantric *caryā* songs (esoteric mystical poetry) and many rituals, some public, some secret. Above all he was, until well into the last century, an expert in and custodian of Buddhist scholarship and knowledge. His very name shows this, for *ācārya* is Sanskrit for 'teacher'; the prefix *vajra* ('diamond' or 'thunderbolt') defines him as a teacher of the Vajrayāna. The *vajrācāryas* were in effect also *bhikṣus*, but because they were considered gurus and possessed a higher grade of ordination, or rather initiation, they were not considered merely 'monks' in the ordinary sense, but priests of a higher order. In accordance with Brahmin custom *vajrācāryas* and *bhikṣus* led in adulthood an ordinary family life, and their Buddhist education, like the priesthood, was handed down mainly on a hereditary basis. The *bhikṣu* fulfilled a more limited number of sacred functions but was addressed as *bandya* ('your honour') in accordance with his standing as a former monk.

While in Hīnayāna and Mahāyāna Buddhism the admission into a monastic order (lower ordination) and the full ordination of monks were predominantly occasions within the monastic community, the rites carried out for *vajrācāryas* and *bhikṣus* in Nepal seem to have become part of the life-cycle of ceremonies which again are obviously copied from Hindu models. Like the Hindus, the Buddhists of Nepal undergo a succession of prescribed rituals of personal purification, beginning with cutting of the umbilical cord, ritual purification after birth, naming of the child, the first feeding, etc. An important life-cycle ritual for all high-caste Hindu and Buddhist boys is the tonsuring which is carried out in early childhood, amongst Buddhist Newars mostly in the third, fifth or seventh year. In Nepalese Buddhism this has taken the place of ordination (*pravrajyā*). This is a counterpart of the Hindu initiation which, granted only to Brahmins, Kṣatriyas and Vaiśyas, symbolizes a second birth, and has served as the model for various forms of tantric initiation and for introduction into some sects. The ceremony is carried out in the same *vihāra* in which a boy's father and forefathers have been ordained. After his head has been shaved and a sacrifice has been performed in the *vihāra*, the boy puts on the monk's habit, and for four days goes begging for alms. At the end of this time his guru releases him from the pledge to renounce all worldly things, which in our time is too difficult to fulfil. Though the boy has been ordained as a monk, he abandons now the hard life of a *bhikṣu* and, after having adopted the career of a layman, returns for the rest of his life to the bosom of his family.

The consecration of a *bhikṣu* is confined to this ritual. *Vajrācāryas*, on the other hand, receive initiation into the mysteries of the Vajrayāna. It is in keeping with the esoteric nature of the *Vajrayāna* that Newar Buddhists have to keep all rituals connected with this important act strictly secret. After a sacrifice has been performed in the courtyard of the *vihāra*, the candidate shows reverence for his spiritual leader in a secret place and receives the initiatory *mantra* at an auspicious hour of the night. The consecration is followed by the handing over of the ritual vestments and insignia of a *vajrācārya*: a magnificent crown, a splendid pair of ritual garments and finally the two most important religious implements, the thunderbolt (*vajra*), always held in the right hand, and the bell, always held in the left. While the latter is the symbol of the feminine principle and thus of transcendent, salvific Wisdom (*prajñā*), as well as of the phenomenal world and its transience, the thunderbolt symbolizes on the one hand active, masculine power and thus the teaching which is the means to salvation, and on the other absolute Thusness and Emptiness, indestructible as a diamond.

The consecration of monks in Nepal was greatly influenced by Śaiva tantrism, which has a similar ceremony modelled on the Indian consecration of kings. Paintings and sculptures produced as late as the beginning of the 19th century show that elements of ancient royal symbolism survived in the ritual of the Buddhist Newars; the head-dress and regalia of the officiating *vajrācārya* often made him look like an Indian king, while the priest assisting him is made to look like a minister. But in everyday life these descendants of former monks appear in civilian dress; they wear the robes and insignia of religious office only when performing religious duties.

The caste system has done much to keep alive the way of life and the traditions of the lay-monks of the Newars; though much weakened, it continues to the present day. But recently both the proficiency of the priests, and the cultivation of the various arts and sciences which was once the proud responsibility of many Nepalese monasteries, have unfortunately suffered a rapid decline. However, even today the monastery and the buildings surrounding the *vihāra* house only *vajrācāryas* and *śākyabhikṣus*. The communities of some *vihāras* consist of either solely *vajrācāryas* or solely *śākyabhikṣus*, while those of other *vihāras* are mixed, that is, comprise *vajrācāryas* as well as *śākyabhikṣus*. *Vihāras* are not open to other groups of Newar society such as, for example, the Buddhist *tulādhars*, an important merchant caste.

Inside the vihāra

The early builders of the Nepalese *vihāras*, which usually consist of four buildings of two or more storeys surrounding an inner courtyard, presumably copied the architecture of the Buddhist monasteries of Bihar and Bengal. The visitor enters the monastery through a gateway surmounted by a tympanum (Sanskrit: *toraṇa*) and flanked by two lions. This leads into a kind of entrance hall in which are stone statues of various deities, protectors of the monastery and of Buddhism. On each side of the entrance there are open niches with seats on which pilgrims can rest; in recent years they have also been used as platforms for groups of singers and musicians who, on certain evenings, make music in front of the *vihāra*. From this entrance hall the visitor

The festival of the Red Matsyendranātha of Patan is probably the most spectacular in all Nepal. The image of the deity (identified with the bodhisattva Avalokiteśvara) is paraded through the streets in a great ceremonial carriage. This drawing dates from the late 19th century but the festival still takes place with unabated splendour.

enters the inner courtyard surrounded by the monastery buildings. The structure opposite the entrance houses the shrine of the Kvāthapāla Deva, i.e. the non-tantric deity of the monastery, usually Śākyamuni, Avalokiteśvara, Dīpaṃkara or Maitreya. This wing is either a pagoda or carries a pagoda-like structure on its roof. In many *vihāras* the '*Āgama* House', the shrine of the esoteric tantric deity, is situated in the same building, above the Kvāthapāla Deva shrine. The main temple sometimes stands in the middle of the courtyard. A large bell near the entrance to the shrine of the chief deity of the monastery serves to attract the attention of the public; the faithful strike it now and then while performing their religious devotions. Like the monastery gateway, the shrine of the chief deity has a tympanum. It is open to all worshippers. To the secret *Āgama* House only the elders are admitted. This often has two rooms, one of them being used for meetings of the *vajrācāryas* or for exhibiting statues.

The container for the sacrificial fire is kept in the courtyard of the *vihāra* in a rectangular block of stone often decorated with a lotus pattern. On a pedestal nearby, a thunderbolt stands as the *dharmadhātumaṇḍala*, the mystic diagram symbolizing Thusness and Emptiness. Also in the monastery courtyard stand one or more small stupas, statues of both Buddhist and Hindu origin, and pillars bearing animals and other figures. The sloping roofs both on the side facing the street and on the side facing the courtyard are usually supported by slanting rafters carved with figures of the late Buddhist pantheon painted in bright, often luminous colours and executed in accordance with the iconographic rules.

We know from inscriptions and documents that there were *vihāras* in the Kathmandu valley at least as far back as the 5th century AD, but only a very few survive from before the 14th century. Most of the *vihāras* are of later date, after celibacy had long been abandoned and small apartments, store rooms, etc. had taken the place of the monks' cells. Since the families of the married *vajrācāryas* and *śākyabhikṣus* constantly increased, the monasteries were frequently enlarged, either by adding new monastery buildings and courtyards to an old *vihāra*, as was done at the Itum Bahāla, one of the oldest *vihāras* of Kathmandu, or by building branch monasteries separate from the main monastery. There are also

the so-called 'monasteries of the outsiders', which do not house *vajrācāryas* and/or *śākyabhikṣus* but belong to members of Buddhist mixed classes who have been ordained as Bandyas of low status.

Life and worship

Important *vihāras* observed, as some still do today, the custom of worshipping a *kumārī* (virgin) with elaborate rituals. A girl, often very young, who must be sexually immature and without physical defect, is chosen by a strict rule from the Bandya families to become the pure 'virgin' protectress of the monastery. Though of Śaiva origin, this institution of the 'living goddess', who is identified with one of the eight mother goddesses of the Hindus, flourished in Vajrayāna and the religious life of the Nepalese monasteries. The numerous temples especially sacred to the Newars, for example those of Brahmāṇī or of Indrāṇī, show that other Śaiva goddesses worshipped as 'mothers' either become attached to the Vajrayāna or were incorporated in it as Śaktis (feminine principles personifying the powers of male deities). Though they were not different in character, a distinction must be made between the Kumārīs of the monasteries and the state or royal Kumārī who, from the times of Pṛthivī Nārāyaṇ, was closely linked with the Śāh dynasty and protected the king and kingdom of Nepal.

We may assume that in the transitional period celibate monks lived in certain *vihāras* while married monks lived in others. During the earlier period, fathers of families were no doubt still closely bound to their own monasteries, but it is quite usual today for *vajrācāryas* and *bhikṣus* to follow a non-clerical profession outside the monastery. *Śākyabhikṣus* are usually craftsmen and workers in copper, silver and other metals. Their continued secularization has led to the terms '*vajrācārya*' and '*śākyabhikṣu*' slowly becoming family names, which then of course also belong to the female members of the families, and their priestly functions are nowadays often merely a sideline. Since the monasteries cannot provide enough space, most *vajrācāryas* and *bhikṣus* no longer reside in the buildings around the inner courtyard of their *vihāra*. They dwell in houses surrounding the monastery and live more or less secular lives. The ordained male inhabitants of all the houses belonging to a *vihāra* constitute its community, its Sangha.

Despite this secularization, many monasteries are still active centres of Newar religious life. Many of the faithful visit, often daily, the *vihāra* they belong to and its shrines, and at certain periods *vajrācāryas* read aloud from various devotional works, especially the *Prajñā-*

pāramitā and stories of the Buddha's former births, recite *dhāraṇīs* or sing *caryā* songs. Recitations are acts of piety and also take place when a family or individual asks a priest versed in the Buddhist scriptures to read from the texts. These readings occur most frequently in the first month of the rainy season. The priest is rewarded in cash or kind, as he is for other services. The distribution of religious duties among the elders of the *vihāra* is generally a matter for the monastery elder. While the daily worship is mostly the duty of the *vajrācāryas* or *śākyabhikṣus*, who take it in turns, the sacrifices within the walls of the monastery, always bloodless, are invariably performed by the *vajrācāryas*. Some deities demand blood sacrifices, but these always take place, as is shown by the statues of these deities, outside the actual *vihāra*. Some of these practices and observances are unmistakably based on Hindu models and have either been taken over completely or have been copied, with their meaning changed, from Hindu rituals. An outline of the main rituals of Nepalese Buddhism, written in Sanskrit by the *śākyabhikṣu* (later *vajrācārya*) Amṛtānanda in the 19th century, distinguishes between daily, monthly and annual rituals. Daily ritual comprises the divine services to be performed in the morning, afternoon and evening. Important parts of the morning service are worship of Kvāthapāla Deva, washing of his face, painting a small vermilion mark on his forehead, swinging of oil-lamps, sprinkling of flowers and rice-grains, reciting, and finally the singing of hymns. One of the monthly rites is the worship of the bodhisattva Amoghapāśa-Lokeśvara or the goddess Vasundharā (the Earth) who, when suitably honoured, prevents poverty. Annual rituals include celebrating the anniversary of the manifestation of Svayambhū (the 'spontaneously arisen' Buddha, who appeared at the birth of the Kathmandu valley) on the fifteenth day of the light half of the month of Kārttika, and the processions on fixed dates to sacred river fords for ritual bathing.

The chief deities worshipped in the various shrines are looked after with great care, a custom taken from Hinduism. They are, as we have seen, paraded, bathed, clothed, bejewelled and have their faces painted in accordance with elaborate rituals. The cult which has grown up around the god-'saint' Matsyendranātha is especially lavish. This 'saint', who is identified with the bodhisattva Avalokiteśvara-Lokanātha, embodies in his complex constitution elements of Buddhism, Hinduism and popular religion. The cult of this great bringer of salvation to Nepal has several variants, notably the Red Matsyendranātha of Patan and the White Matsyendranātha of Kathmandu. The festival of the former, which lasts many weeks, is famous. During the festivities this deity, who promises salvation and brings rain, is paraded on a magnificent high carriage. The climax of the procession comes when the shirt of Matsyendranātha is exhibited at the end of the festival. The eighth day of the month of Pauṣya, which falls at the beginning of January, is dedicated to the ritual bathing of his counterpart, the White Matsyendranātha, who is worshipped in the Matsyendranātha *vihāra* in the centre of Kathmandu. Ritual dances by the *vajrācāryas*, sacrifices and *caryā* songs precede the ceremony, which is watched by many spectators; first cold water, then warm, is poured three times over the deity. A frisson of delight runs through the assemblage when the water flows over the statue; then the priests sprinkle the drops which have been sanctified by their contact with Matsyendranātha over the crowd.

The blurring of the dividing line between Buddhism and Hinduism is recognizable not only in the widespread worship of Matsyendranātha, but also in numerous other deities in Nepal. Some of these have been taken direct from Hinduism, and some have been assembled by a process of syncretism and therefore represent a smaller Hindu-Buddhist pantheon which exists side by side with specifically Buddhist or Hindu deities. In spite of these interactions of the two great religions, life in the communities of the Newar *vihāras* has until now remained intrinsically Buddhist and, therefore, contrasts with the way of life of other, non-Buddhist groups in the Nepal valley.

Theravāda Buddhism

5

'They will be Lords upon the Island':
Buddhism in Sri Lanka

6

'To be a Burmese is to be a Buddhist':
Buddhism in Burma

7

The Way of the Monk and the Way of the World:
Buddhism in Thailand, Laos and Cambodia

THAILAND, BURMA AND SRI LANKA are now the most solidly Buddhist countries in the world. In Thailand, Buddhism is the state religion, in Sri Lanka it is the faith of the majority of the people. Laos and Cambodia could until recently have been included in the same description, but the present regimes there are bent on the destruction of the Sangha. With the virtual disappearance of Buddhism in India and its suppression in Tibet and China it is thus to these countries that we must look to see Buddhism as a living force today, though it is very much a living force in Japan too.

In principle, Theravāda Buddhism concerns itself only with the Path to Enlightenment through the teachings and techniques outlined in Chapter 1. Those who continue to live in the world acquire merit by supporting the Sangha and by other good works and purify their minds by cultivating love and sympathy for all forms of life. In practice, religious and social usages have become very closely connected and the Buddhist monastic ideal of withdrawal from the world has not been wholly sustained. In Sri Lanka monks have acted as advisers to kings and ministers. In Thailand not only is the Sangha organized as a hierarchical system like the civil service, but it actually acknowledges the secular power (the king has the right to appoint the supreme patriarch); spiritual matters are institutionalized, even progress towards Enlightenment being assessed by examinations.

This promotes a high degree of participation by the laity in religious affairs. Thailand, Burma and Sri Lanka may be called 'Buddhist societies' in a sense that cannot be applied elsewhere. Many stages of public and private life are marked by a religious ceremony. Monks enjoy respect and veneration from the whole population. And in Burma and Thailand probably half the adult men have spent some time in a monastery as temporary monks.

The monk's real life is that of the mind. However vividly one describes and illustrates the monastic setting – the architecture, the ceremonial, the externals of preaching and meditation, the daily sights and sounds of the Sangha – one is still leaving out the most vital ingredient: thought. Perhaps as close as we can come to the essence of Buddhism in a visual image is the face of a monk in meditation – here in a monastery in Bangkok. (1)

The tranquil mind

Southeast Asia and Sri Lanka are notable for the extent to which monks take part in social and political life, but this should not be emphasized to the point of ignoring the practice of study and meditation that continues in these countries. In Sri Lanka, as in the other countries, the 'forest monks' are the heirs of a tradition going back to the Buddha himself.

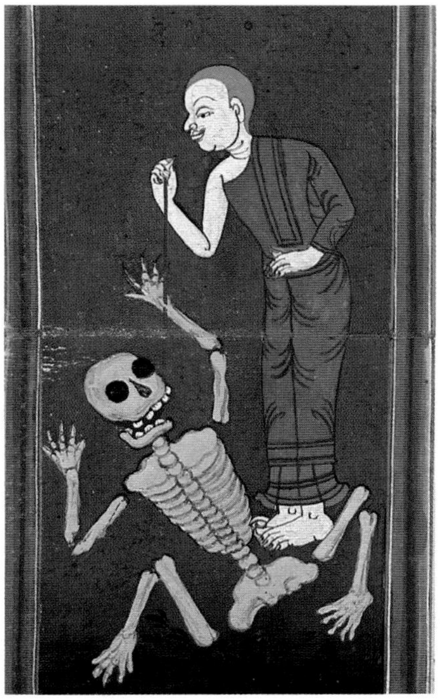

The many techniques of meditation have a long history and are not easily learned. These coloured discs (*above*) in a Sri Lankan monastery are used to concentrate the mind and to render it wieldy and clear. A Thai meditation manual (*right*), on the other hand, has a very explicit reference – the inevitability of death. (2, 3)

In the remote forests of Sri Lanka (*above* and *right*), monks have sought to revive the original ideals of Buddhist monasticism, living a life of absolute poverty, devoted chiefly to meditation. The movement, which has grown in strength since Independence, is in part a protest against village and urban monks, who are thought to take too active an interest in worldly affairs. In the popular mind these forest monks have a particular holiness. Pilgrims make long journeys to visit them, to give them alms and to listen to their sermons. (4, 5)

Sangha and society

In the past, monasteries were criticized for taking too much from society; today they are more likely to be criticized for giving too much to it.

Among the riverfolk of Bangkok, a monk makes his rounds for alms – a custom still kept up, although most monasteries now have an assured income from money donations. (6)

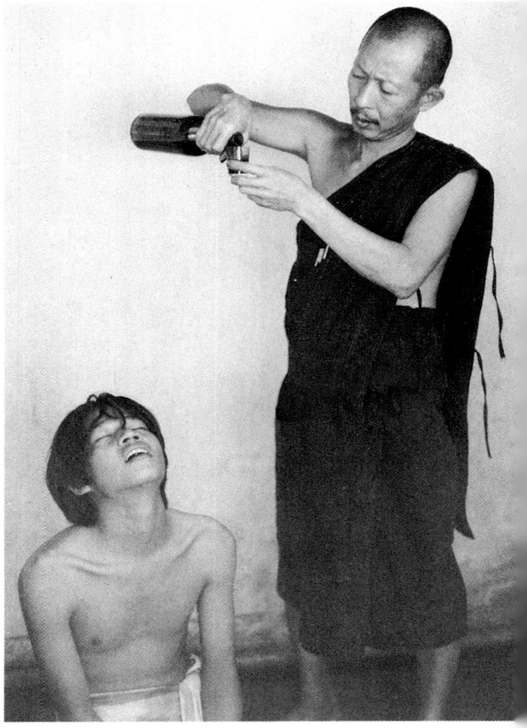

The monk's presence lends solemnity to the important events of life, and is essential to funerals. (Traditionally they must not attend weddings because they symbolize the renunciation of earthly joys.) At the municipal cemetery in Colombo, Sri Lanka, (*above left*) three monks at a funeral are given new robes. The monk touches the package to indicate acceptance. But in modern Thailand monks are to be found doing work that would have been forbidden by earlier rules – from building their own monasteries (*left*) to running centres for the cure of drug-addicts (*above*). (7, 8, 9)

The monk as teacher: in the past monks were the sole teachers and schools were normally in temple compounds. During the 19th century Thai monks began to organize primary schools in the provinces. But with the establishment of state schools they have had to choose between giving up this aspect of their work and adopting more secular standards. The decision of many to devote themselves to this and other works of service to the community has aroused bitter debate. One monk of the old school has said: 'Monks should concern themselves with helping people *spiritually* .... This is an incomparable service, far better than a monk who applies for a job in social work or joins in such work as kitchen gardening' (*below*). The Rule does indeed explicitly forbid the monk to dig the earth or to have someone else dig the earth for him. Yet in the past, in both Sri Lanka and Thailand, monks owned and administered vast agricultural estates. (10, 11)

Pomp and ceremony

Burma and Thailand, where Buddhism as the state religion for centuries received munificent patronage from generations of rich and powerful kings, still possess temples, shrines and monasteries of unsurpassed splendour.

Ayudhya flourished in the 15th and 16th centuries under a series of progressive Thai kings. Characteristic of its monuments (*left*) are bell-shaped stupas in a style taken from Sinhalese models. (12)

Golden images of the Buddha shine in the darkness of the Shwedagon pagoda in Rangoon, Burma. According to legend, this is one of the oldest sacred sites of Buddhism, but it was raised to its present height in the 15th century. (13)

Wat Phrathat Doi Suthep is situated on a hill above Chiang Mai in northern Thailand. A stupa was built there in 1371 to enshrine a Buddha relic which was brought by the elder Sumana to the kingdom of Chiang Mai when he came there from Sukhotai, the ancient capital of the Siamese (central Thai). The temple was rebuilt in its present form in 1545 and its main stupa (*right*) is surrounded by ceremonial umbrellas at the four corners. (14)

Building for merit

A new temple is thought to win more merit for the builder than the maintenance of an old one. The result is a proliferation of temples; the more notable are kept in repair because of their antiquity and associations, but the rest are allowed to decay while resources are poured into the provision of new ones. It is estimated that the Burmese spend a quarter of their income on religious donations.

Temple landscapes bear witness to the piety and pride of the past. On the shores of Lake Inle, Shan States, Burma (*above left*), a group of crumbling stupas crowd together, their circular forms rising to umbrella-like tops. (15)

At Prome, the Shwesandaw pagoda (*left*) is like a small town; the main structure, constantly regilded and enlarged throughout its history, is surrounded by eighty-three temples, also gilded and adorned with complicated roofs. (16)

Pegu is another ancient city in Burma, once famous for its magnificent temples. It reached its peak in the 16th and 17th centuries. The Kyaikpun pagoda (*below*) has four seated Buddhas, back to back, nearly 30 metres (100 feet) high, representing Śākyamuni and his three immediate predecessors. (18)

Pagan (*above*), traditionally founded in AD 849, was the capital of Burma for 250 years. Before Kubilai Khan occupied it in 1287 it was said to contain nearly 13,000 pagodas; remains of some 5,000 can still be seen, extending for 20 miles along the bank of the Irrawaddy. Modern Pagan is little more than a village. (17)

The endowment of monasteries by private patrons is still a living tradition in Buddhist countries. Subscription lists and fund-raising by communal action are common, as among Christians in the West. Here (*below*) a foundation stone is laid in Kandy in Sri Lanka, the modest ceremony attended by monks and laymen. (19)

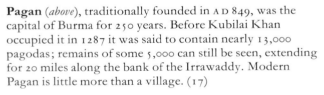

The privilege of giving

Donations by the laity to monks are not something for which the monks need to be grateful; indeed it is they who are conferring the benefit, by allowing the laymen to acquire merit in this way. The theory holds true at every level. In every Buddhist country the monarch was always the leading patron. Some modern Buddhist governments have taken over this role.

Gold leaf is applied to the great Shwedagon pagoda in Rangoon (*below*). When the scaffolding is removed the whole dome will glow with renewed splendour. (20)

Royal donations to a monastery at Amarapura (the capital of Burma between 1783 and 1857) are vividly illustrated in this painting of 1856, almost a pictorial inventory of the monk's needs throughout the year (compare pl. 50, p. 40). According to the Discipline he should have three robes, a needle, a belt, a begging bowl, a strainer for his drink and a razor. An accompanying text tells that the monastery on this occasion received manuscripts (wrapped in white cloth), two cupboards to hold them, towels, blankets and other items. In the foreground the gifts are being prepared. A later section of the manuscript goes on to show the presentation of the gifts. (21)

11 Movement. The elephant of Maligawa bearing the dato or small of bones in the Karandowa made with Gold &

A lotus blossom is one of the traditional gifts to monks, in return for their gift of the Doctrine. This illustration (*right*) is from a 19th century Thai manuscript featuring the story of a monk who travels through heaven and hell. The same offerings, along with incense-sticks and candles, are still prominently displayed today outside temples, for the faithful to buy before entering. Flowers are laid before Buddha images as symbols of transience, reminding the worshipper that his body too will fade. (22, 23)

Sangha and state

Links between the secular and religious authorities in Burma and Sri Lanka go far back into history. Kings have seen themselves as servants of the Buddha, and the Buddha has assumed many of the attributes of kingship.

A novice, says one legend, having been sent for by King Aśoka, seated himself on the throne and began to preach, while the king and his whole court listened. A modern mural (*above*) shows the continuing lesson of the story – the most junior novice is superior in status even to a king. (24)

The charismatic King Mindon of Burma (1853–78) made it his aim to be the pattern of a Buddhist monarch. The Dharma permeated all his acts and thoughts. In this picture from a contemporary folding book (*below*) his army and court go in procession to the pagoda at the foot of Mandalay hill. *Right:* the Buddha, crowned and bejewelled, as ruler of the world. This kind of Burmese image reflects the identification of Buddhahood and ideal kingship. (25, 26)

Buddhism and the state. Another Sri Lankan mural tells the story of how an 18th-century monk was accorded the title of king of the Sangha. Links with the state have remained close. *Below:* Mrs Bandaranaike, as prime minister, offers devotion at the Temple of the Tooth, in Kandy. On the right is the lay custodian of the Tooth in the traditional dress of a Kandyan chief. *Bottom:* a meeting in 1961 passes a resolution urging the government to make Burma a Buddhist state. (27, 28, 29)

Devotion and pageantry

The great popular festivals of Burma, Thailand and Sri Lanka unite monks and lay people. Many of them centre round relics or images of the Buddha, or commemorate religious events.

Every year a fantastic barge representing the mythical Karavika bird sails across Lake Inle in upper Burma bearing images of the Buddha to all the villages on its shore. These images (*above right*) have been venerated for so long and covered with so many layers of gold leaf that they have lost their original form and become shapeless lumps. The same process can be seen at an early stage (*top right*) in Thailand, where small areas of gold leaf are being applied to the base of a Buddha image. (30, 32, 33)

The 'sacred tooth' of Kandy, in Sri Lanka, is perhaps the most famous relic of the Buddha. No Sinhalese king was regarded as fully legitimate unless he had it under his protection, a belief which still has its resonances (see pl. 28). It is said to have been brought to the island in the 4th century AD. The Portuguese who occupied Ceylon in 1505 claimed to have taken it to Goa and destroyed it, but pious Buddhists believe it miraculously saved itself. Its custody today is shared between the elected lay custodian and the heads of Kandy's two chief monasteries (*left*). The splendid ceremony held annually in its honour takes place for a week in July or August. Up to a hundred elephants, magnificently caparisoned, take part. An 18th-century painting (*right*) shows it essentially as it remains to this day. (31, 34)

the elephant of Maligawa bearing the dalada or small

5

'They will be Lords upon the Island': Buddhism in Sri Lanka

MICHAEL B. CARRITHERS

THE BUDDHISM OF SRI LANKA (Ceylon, as it used to be called) and of Southeast Asia is the School of Elders, Theravāda. 'School of the Elders' indeed: it would best be thought of as that school which, as Buddhism grew and expanded, continually inclined toward the conservative choice, the preservation of an archaic view of Doctrine and of the Order of monks, the Sangha. This view of the Doctrine is crystallized in the commentaries to the Canon, which were finally edited in Sri Lanka in the 5th century AD. These are devoted to rejecting change, to certifying the original sense of every word of the Buddha. In the same spirit, the Sangha is conceived as a fraternity observing, in the minutest detail, its original way of life as conducted under the Buddha.

In this stern and uncompromising attitude there is little place for the idea, developed in other schools of Buddhism, that laymen may achieve Enlightenment, or that Enlightenment may be achieved without the monastic code, the Discipline. The highest ideal is that of the *arhat*, the monk who attains Enlightenment for himself by following meticulously the Path laid down by the Buddha. And in this view the Sangha is radically different from, and superior to, the life of the layman. For the monk has *attained* the Discipline, that is, his spiritual training in the Discipline is the first hard step towards that wisdom so difficult to discern amidst the unregulated sensual confusion of lay life.

In fact, if one were to seek *one* theme, *one* idea, which could be said to underlie the Theravāda Sangha, it would be the Discipline: a word applied both to the monastic code and to the moral purity embodied in the code. This is so in several senses. First, the attributes of the monk – shaven head, robes, begging bowl – and the monk's deportment – reserved, upright, calm, eyes downcast – are the outward expression of the monk's inner commitment to follow the Discipline, which itself prescribes this behaviour. In another sense, each rule can be consistently reasoned on grounds that it conduces in one way or another to mental calm, and therefore to spiritual insight. An eminent Sri Lankan forest-monk once told me that the whole of the Buddhist teaching could be summarized as a commentary upon the Discipline.

The end of one cycle of earthly existence, perhaps the last? In about 1900 this monk's funeral was photographed in Burma. The body lies on a bier with high pagoda-like superstructure, all of which is consumed by the flames. (35)

'A nation at prayer'

In these senses, therefore, the Discipline is the guiding principle of the Sangha. But there is another meaning given to the Discipline in Theravāda; and this, despite the efforts of the elders to preserve the original, does represent a substantial change. In ancient India the Discipline had been codified as part of the spiritual Path of a small body of religious mendicants, acquainted with each other face-to-face, each seeking his own salvation. Discipline was significant to the Buddhist ascetics only. But then came the change: for as Buddhism came to Sri Lanka – it is impossible to trace the process closely – Discipline became the guiding principle of an established religion, of a nation 'at prayer', of what Heinz Bechert aptly characterized as one of the most ancient nation-states, with its common religion, common language, common culture and common polity all within a single territory. (The language is Sinhalese, and the majority of the people are Sinhalese Buddhists.)

The significance of this is revealed in the commentarial legend of the conversion of Sri Lanka by the missionary monk Mahinda in the mid-3rd century BC. According to that account, the king of Sri Lanka eagerly accepted the new faith, and enthusiastically went to work building great monasteries and shrines – the appurtenances of established Buddhism, as churches and cathedrals are the appurtenances of the established Church of England. After a good deal of building, the king asked the missionary whether Buddhism could now be considered established. Mahinda replied that it was established, but would not take root until a Sri Lankan, born of Sri Lankan parents, took the robes in Sri Lanka, learned the Discipline in Sri Lanka, and recited it in Sri Lanka. In other words, no Buddhism without the Sangha, and no Sangha without the Discipline. And indeed Sinhalese historians, who were always monks, tended to add: no Sri Lanka without Buddhism.

So the monk became a figure with public responsibility, guiding the morals of a nation. Much of later Sri Lankan history concerns the efforts of kings to keep the Sangha 'pure', well Disciplined, fit for its task; and even the prosperity of the nation ultimately depended upon its morality. This public duty might be thought to conflict with that of the monk seeking his own salvation. But the Sinhalese commentators and later Sinhalese monks were able to satisfy their appetite for consistency. For them the monk, though passive and chiefly concerned with his own Discipline, nevertheless acts as an exemplar. He is, in the words of a contemporary monk, a street-light, going nowhere, doing nothing, but enabling the laity to see their way in this dark world of moral confusion. In the commentarial literature the monk's morality is a fragrance, permeating the universe. Right down to the present this master image of the Sangha has remained bright and untarnished in the Sri Lankan imagination: it is the image of a stern and upright monk, unrelenting in his asceticism, retiring from the world but unequivocal in his moral judgments of the world. But at the same time it must be borne in mind that it is an *ideal*: if all monks were perfect, there would be no need for it.

This is not, however, merely a matter of human frailty. For the process that brought Buddhism to be the religion of a nation was accompanied by other equally profound changes in the Sangha. Monks acted in new roles, and though every effort was made to assimilate these to the Discipline, they were often quite contrary to it. In the rest of this chapter, I will describe the development of these roles and their consequences for the Sangha. There are four: the monk as literate ceremonial specialist, as landlord, as politician, and as reforming forest-dweller. A good deal of the material will be drawn from the classical period of Sinhalese Buddhism, before AD 1214, when a brutal and especially oppressive invader from India broke the ancient order of Sinhalese civilization, which never fully recovered. The Sangha of today in Sri Lanka, and in Southeast Asia, took on its most important features in the one-and-a-half thousand years before that invasion.

The monk as teacher, preacher, and priest

To return to the Sangha's beginning: the Sangha held one view of itself from very early days which was even stricter, and certainly more archaic, than that of the passive moral exemplar. This was the image of the solitary and peripatetic monk, bound both by specific Disciplinary rule and by the whole tenor of his philosophy to eschew the productive (and reproductive) activities of the householder. The monk must produce neither his own food, nor his own garb, nor may he house himself. These prohibitions have indeed always been relevant to the monk in his role as passive exemplar. But, for that original ascetic, his well cultivated desire-for-little, *alpecchatā*, rendered these prohibitions not into social responsibility, but into freedom, that is, independence of other people. Hence, 'like the moon, he is a stranger among families'. He begs silently from house to house for his food, he gathers his robe from scraps of cloth left with corpses on the charnel ground, he lives in caves and beneath trees. He has truly 'gone forth into homelessness'.

Yet this perfect moral economy of poverty has probably always been less the norm than the ideal, practised only by a very few. Even in the ancient canonical writings it appears chiefly in exhortations and pious reminiscences, while the more circumstantial accounts suggest that, even then, laymen invited monks for meals, gave them robes, and built them shelter: this is rather more likely to be the norm in an institution, because it provides security, and need not *in itself* temper the asceticism. But it has a further corollary. If the monks received something of value from the laity, the laity received something of value from the monks: 'the gift of the Teaching is the best gift'. The Canon is full of stories of laymen and laywomen hearing a sermon, being converted, and then piously supporting the Sangha – and not only the Sangha in general, but particular monks for their particular virtues. The relationship between monks and laymen, though then as today neither contractual nor exclusive, was more or less enduring, and might reasonably be phrased as a long-term exchange: spiritual good for material support. The history of the Sangha is the gradual unfolding of the implications of this exchange.

Let us follow one chain of implications: what precisely did the laity receive from the monks? They received merit. In its purest sense merit simply refers to that which is psychically wholesome and therefore good. This of course goes with the view that the monk imparts wisdom to the laity, and the laity gratefully and generously offer him material necessities. But already in the Indian, canonical period, merit was also curiously substantial, and could be accrued, for three purposes. It could be stored up by oneself for a better rebirth; it could be given to dead relatives for their future welfare; or it could be given to gods so that they would help one in some worldly aim. These correspond very roughly to the three chief services provided for the laity by monks in Sri Lanka today, and probably since the earliest days: preaching, presiding at funerals, and chanting *pirit*, texts designed to improve one's material and physical state. Some sort of meal or gift for the participant monks accompanies each of these ceremonies, and it is this exchange of wise and powerful words for a meal (in Sinhalese *dānaya*, originally lay 'generosity', but now just 'monk's meal') that is the source of merit and the core of further ceremonial elaborations.

This ceremonial service, however, created a role for the monk which is quite different from that of strict world renouncer – in fact, the Sangha became the body of literate ceremonial specialists *for* society who form its majority today. Though the logic of this development is clear, its history is not. For the period before the 5th century AD in Sri Lanka the commentaries reveal that the chanting of *pirit* was a recognized ceremony;

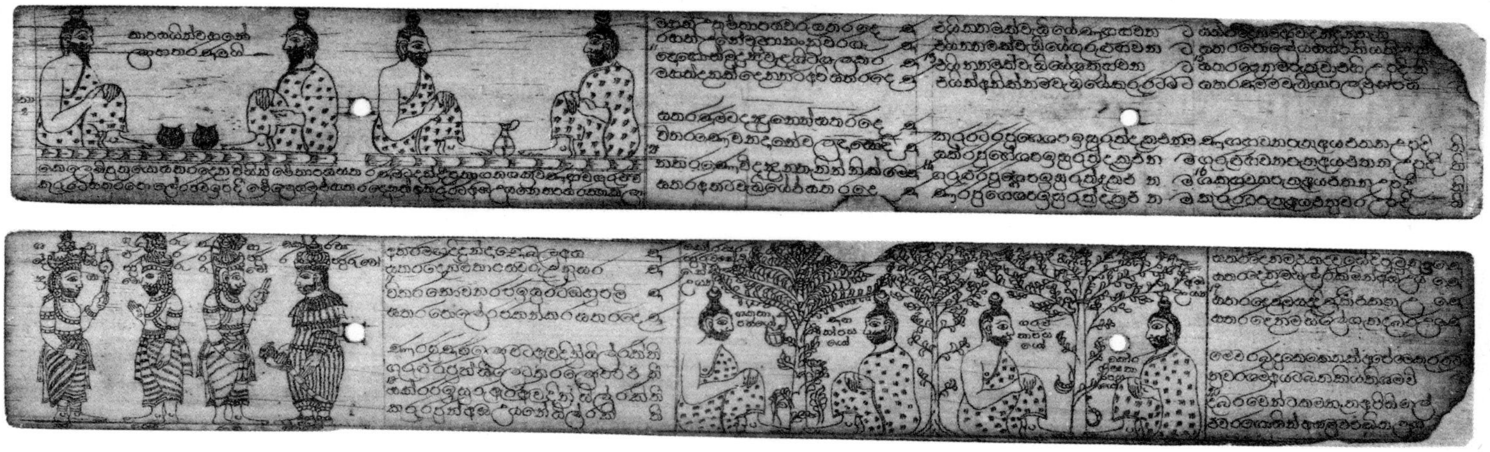

The jātaka stories, tales of the Buddha's previous lives, constitute a corpus of folklore with a moral for the Buddhist. This 18th-century palm-leaf manuscript illustrates the popular tale of the 'Vidhura-paṇḍita Jātaka'. In this episode, four kings meditate in a forest.

monks probably attended funerals; and the number and nature of tales about sermons imply that they were a major activity, even a major public entertainment. The real evidence lies in monastic education, though, for it is the education of monks chiefly, if not solely, for a ceremonial role that bears witness to the predominance of ceremony in monastic life in latter-day Sri Lanka.

There is one brief passage in the commentary to the Discipline which reveals at what stage it was thought appropriate for a monk in early Sri Lanka to give up learning and become a 'scholar of the world, able to live under his own mastery wherever he likes'. This was perhaps the basic instruction for the monks of the countryside. They had to learn the basic 227 Disciplinary rules, the rules of legal procedure within the Sangha, and one subject of meditation. Beyond this rather elementary preparation they had three tasks. First, they had to memorize one of a list of pious stories 'in order to regale those present', certainly laymen. Second, they had to learn three formulae, one for reciting when invited for a meal, another for auspicious occasions, and a third for inauspicious occasions. Today the auspicious occasions are sermons and *pirit* ceremonies, the inauspicious are funerals, and they must have been the same then. Third, the monks had to learn 'four sections of scripture for announcing the Teaching'.

This is certainly an education for the preacher, and indeed from the Buddha's own day till the present preaching has been one of the main activities of monks. What developed in Sri Lanka was a number of elaborations, among which may be counted more or less large-scale public performances, in which two or more monks took part. A more significant change is traceable in the *pirit* ceremony. It is certainly present in ancient India and early Sri Lanka, but it is difficult to decide from this account of early Sangha education whether it was yet important. From other evidence we may infer that it gathered importance, however, and by the 10th century AD it was a chief part of monastic education: for by then the 'four sections' certainly referred to a primer consisting of some basic catechistical material, but above all of texts for *pirit* chanting. Indeed, we learn from a king's inscription of that century that suppliants were to know this primer by heart before entering the Sangha. By the Kandyan period, the 17th century and later, the primer contained most of the knowledge necessary for an ordinary monk in the Kandyan kingdom. It is still a central part of monastic education today.

It is not only that the Sangha was gradually and insensibly entangled in ritual services for laymen. The effect was much deeper: it became inconceivable that the Sinhalese laity could live a civilized, human life at all without the Sangha to make their merit and bury their dead. It is no wonder that by far the majority of extant Sinhalese art, architecture and literature is explicitly Buddhist, either devotional or homiletic. Most of the literature is by monks; most of the architecture is for monks or influenced by monks; and most of the painting and sculpture is executed under the tutelage of monks. Indeed – one could cite the famous Toṭagamuvē Srī Rāhula, an elder of the 15th century – even quite secular verse, celebrating the beauty of women and the glory of kings, was penned in the monastery. On the other hand, the fire-and-brimstone sermons of the preachers must have worked a terrible mastery over the minds of layfolk – scenes of otherworldly torture still enliven the walls of temples today. In traditional Sri Lanka, cultural hegemony lay in the hands of the Sangha, and the exercise of this hegemony became for most monks their chief or only concern.

Other literate specialities, such as the teaching of reading and writing, fell to the Sangha's lot very early. Some monks even practised medicine, a very literate skill, and astrology. Of course they also kept the chronicle history of Sri Lanka, since, in their view, the history of Sri Lanka is the history of Buddhism, and a good deal of the Buddhist theory of the kingdom must be laid at their door. Much of this is against specific Disciplinary injunction, but it would have been impossible for Buddhism to become the religion of a people without this entanglement of the Sangha in their affairs.

Nor does it go unjustified. The inner sense that draws these different vocations together is that they are all *lō väḍa*, work for the welfare of the world. Preaching, teaching and scholarship for the welfare of lay minds, *pirit* and medicine for their bodies. This is, to be sure, an active ideal, quite different from the passive moral ideal, but it is founded on the monk's fitness to be a teacher. The English scholar Rhys Davids reflected the view of learned Sinhalese elders nicely when he wrote that the Sangha's mission was to 'devote their lives to the acquisition of the highest wisdom, and fit themselves to teach and guide others out of the pleasant path leading towards misery into the harder path that leads towards true happiness and liberation'. In this sense both the chanting of *pirit* and the writing of the national chronicle were 'for the pious joy of the faithful'.

The difficulty arises when in practice the monks' fulfilment of these traditional duties becomes an end in itself; then they act as a traditional class in society, rather than for a moral principle. This is exacerbated by monks becoming landholders or landlords.

The monk as landlord

The development of the role of literate ceremonial specialist – parish priest – implied a corresponding development of enduring arrangements to feed, clothe and house the Sangha. At the most modest this meant that the monk became the incumbent of a small dwelling with the surrounding ground, and his food and robes might have been seen to, as in poor rural temples today, by the arrangement of a rota among his villagers. At the least modest the Sangha became lords and heirs of vast estates, encompassing not only land and villages, but also irrigation, reservoirs, canals and plantations. By the end of the great period of Sinhalese civilization, monks had been so long and deeply embroiled in the political economy that a Sri Lankan king's genealogy (that of the 13th-century king Parakkamabāhu II) was traced proudly to an ancient lineage of lay temple functionaries.

The logic of this grander development derives not only from the exchange of support for spiritual services, but also from the encounter of the Sangha with an agrarian, hierarchical social order. That the society was agrarian simply meant that the Sangha, to ensure perennial support, had to control its own farm land. That society was hierarchical meant that it had to control the labourers, the people who worked the land. In other words, far from remaining outside society as renouncers of the world, monks came to stand at the very centre, with the attributes and status of great feudal lords. As usual, the logic of this is clearer than the history, but four periods in the development may conveniently be distinguished. The first is the ancient Indian period of the Canon, when the process had already begun and Disciplinary rules were laid down against it. The second is the early period in Sri Lanka down to the 2nd century AD, in which the peculiarly Sinhalese features of monastic landlordism emerged. Third, in a transitional period lasting roughly until the 9th century AD society grew larger and more complex, and the Sangha's involvement grew deeper. In the last period, from the 9th century until the 12th, the monasteries were arguably the greatest landlords in Ceylon.

To begin with the canonical period: it is clear that the basic components were already present. In the Canon one reads of land being given to the Sangha, though this is usually unproductive land, a forest or park. More significantly, there is a brief mention of how much of a crop is due to the Sangha if someone plants on Sangha land, and how much is due to the Sangha if its seeds are used. And there is the puzzling story of the monk Pilindavaccha, to whom King Bimbisāra, the Buddha's contemporary, gave a village of five hundred monastery servants. The bare details of this lend themselves to various interpretations, but there is no doubt that the tale looks forward to the feudal Sinhalese Sangha, rather than back to the homeless and propertyless monks depicted in other parts of the Canon.

Indeed, the rules of the Discipline may be read as a systematic attempt to ward off the consequences that these developments entailed. The rules provide that monks should neither dig the earth nor have someone else dig the earth; neither cut living plants nor have someone else cut plants; and not be given uncooked rice, the staple food. Furthermore, monks should receive their cooked food from the hands of laymen. Thus the Discipline attempts to ensure that the monks do not engage, nor engage others, in productive activity, so preserving the status of religious beggars. But material wealth was given to the Sangha, and the Discipline was forced to recognize a category of lay people to look after it, as servants in the monastery. It also recognized a category of persons interposed between the material goods and the monks, whose function was to hand over the necessities of life to monks at the appropriate time – when, for example, the monks needed new robes, and not before. These lay functionaries were called 'those who make fitting', a legal classification which came in Sri Lanka to cover a whole microcosm of laymen attached to monasteries, from high nobility to slaves.

The early period in Sri Lanka may conveniently be assumed to run from Buddhism's arrival in the mid-3rd century BC down to the 2nd century AD. In this period irrigation reservoirs remained relatively small – at the end of the period the first reservoirs were built with perimeters measured in miles – and we may infer from this and other more direct evidence that society was still

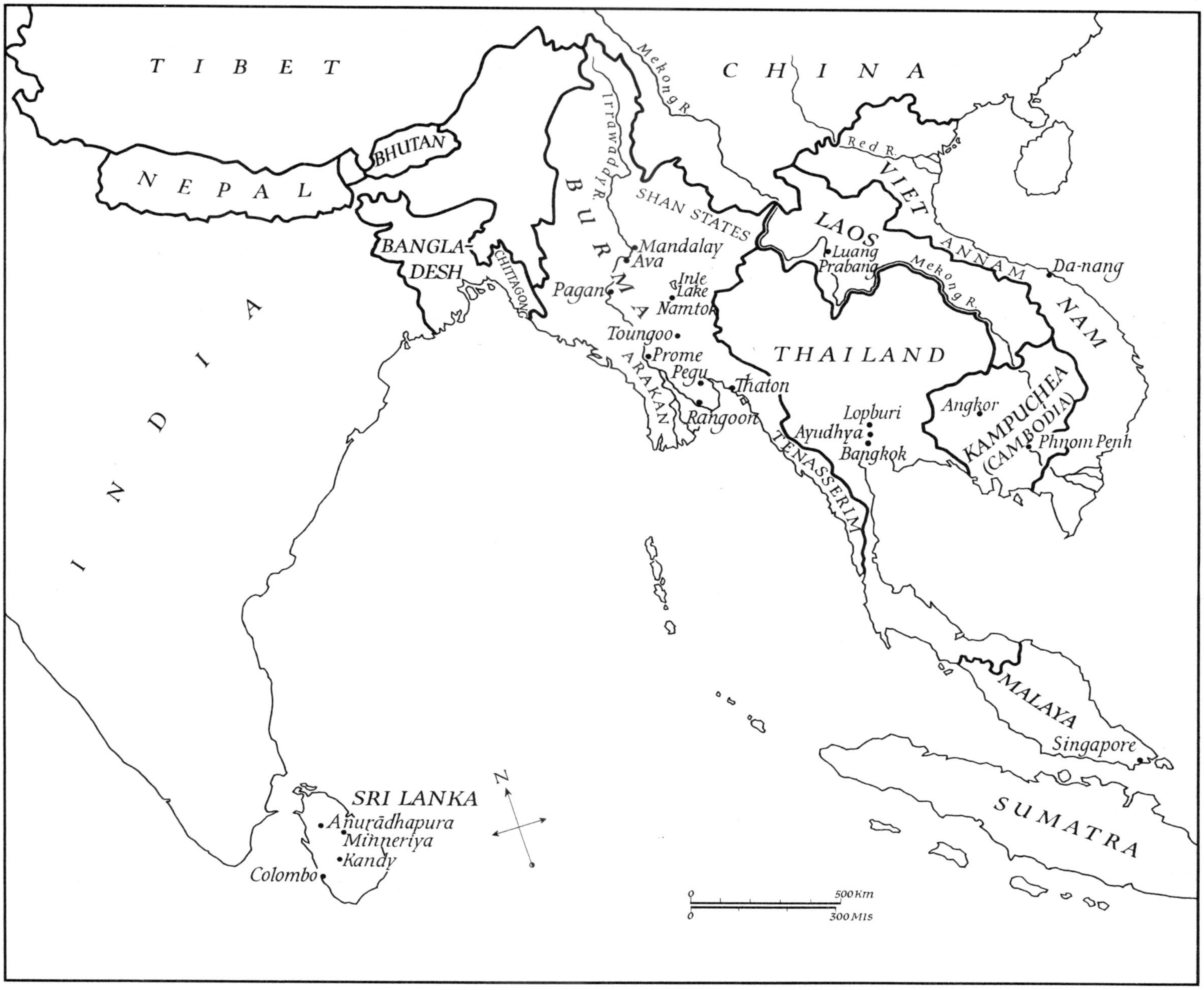

Southeast Asia and Sri Lanka, showing the sites mentioned in this section.

relatively simple. Yet two characteristically Sinhalese developments in this period are clear: first, the monks were given a status very like that of lay lords, and second, the monks were quite practically involved in irrigation, that is, in the management of reservoirs and the people who depended upon the reservoirs.

The monks' attainment of lordship status is signalled by a shift in the terms that were used to refer to them. In the Canon, though the Buddha or monks might occasionally be likened to persons of secular power, it is clear that they were thought of as having a quite different kind of respectability, and this is reflected in the terms used for monks as opposed to laity. Sri Lankan sources, however, gradually began to blend the two. Thus, for example, the commentarial account of the Sangha's arrival in the island has soothsayers exclaiming of the monks, 'they will be lords in the island!' The word for 'lords', *issarā*, has an unmistakably secular significance; and though in the immediate context the reference is merely to the ascendancy of Buddhism in Sri Lanka, it portends quite a new way of regarding the Sangha. Another source, the earliest stone inscriptions of Sri Lanka, shows the same honorifics being used interchangeably for monks and laymen. In later Sri Lanka, monks, lords and kings were always referred to in very similar terms.

This was not merely a matter of language. Many of the earliest stone inscriptions, belonging to the first four centuries of Buddhism in Ceylon, record gifts of caves, which were prepared as dwellings for monks. Many of these were given by ostensibly noble persons . . . but others were given by monks. While the amount of labour involved in preparing a cave may not have been very great, it nevertheless betokens the power of a monk to command laymen. Monks had already become local notables of the peasant landscape. The commentaries reflect such a figure indirectly in the description of the 'great elder of the residence', the monk who takes executive responsibility for a monastery.

It was only natural that monasteries in fact be given to individual monks, though this was a contravention of the letter and the spirit of the Discipline. The convention in ancient India and Sri Lanka had been that monasteries or dwellings be given to 'the Sangha of the four quarters'. This legal fiction presupposed that the Sangha was effectively separated as a corporate body from the laity. Yet it must have been the case that many of the gifts to 'the Sangha of the four quarters' were in fact to a local 'great elder of the residence'. The national chronicle first records a gift in this spirit for the reign of King Vaṭṭagāmaṇī (89–77 BC), who gave a presumably grand monastery to the monk Mahātissa, who had helped the king in adversity. Later Sinhalese monks saw this as the beginning of a long and morally dubious process, but it was more likely just a recognition in name of something which, in form, had been going on for generations, or centuries.

But it was the Sangha's involvement with productive agriculture which set the seal on the monks' entanglement as landlords in Sinhalese society. Many of the gifts recorded in the early inscriptions are interests in, or ownership of, reservoirs, fields and villages. Indeed they are very nearly the same thing, for the reservoir irrigates the paddy (rice) fields in a small valley, and the villagers who live at the edges of the field live from it, give a proportion of the crop to the monks, and maintain the reservoir. Sometimes the grants were merely a portion of the dues which were paid by the villagers to the lord who had built, owned or oversaw the maintenance of the reservoir. On other occasions, however – as in an inscription attributable to the same King Vaṭṭagāmaṇī of the 1st century BC – a reservoir and attached villages were given to a particular monastery.

A less laconic source is the commentaries, which tally very well with the evidence from inscriptions. Their witness is chiefly in the form of extensions of Disciplinary rulings to cover new cases, and they attempt wherever possible to maintain the formal separation of monks from property and productive activities, in the face of growing involvement *de facto*. Thus, for example, the commentary states that the Sangha may not accept a reservoir . . . unless it is offered with the formula that it is intended to provide the Sangha with the four requisites: alms-food, robes, shelter and medicine. Slaves are to be accepted, not as such, but as 'those who make fitting', or as servants of the *monastery*. And money – which was used by monks in a slightly later period to buy land, according to one inscription – can be handed over to 'those who make fitting' for the monastery, or for the four requisites, but the monks must not touch it.

In fact the commentaries are quite circumstantial in their directions concerning land management by monks. Thus, the Discipline forbids a monk to order someone to dig the earth; but the commentary explains that if the monk says, 'dig a *pond*' – for a pond is that which is *already* dug – it does not transgress the rule. Sometimes the advice is quite practical. The monk is told how to see that everyone cultivating a set of paddy fields gets a fair share of water; and, when one set of tenants leaves because oppressed by the king, and is replaced by another set who do not pay rent to the monks, the monks are justified in withholding water . . . but only in the ploughing season.

At this very early period, therefore, all the characteristics of monastic landlordism were present. There must have been, then as now, a considerable difference between the relatively large landed monasteries of the capital and the small village temples with, perhaps, no more than a few coconut trees on the grounds. But the Sangha as a whole must have been coloured by these developments. No doubt the provision of permanent support could have had the intended effect of allowing monks simply to go about their ascetic business securely. Landholding, however, tended generally to draw the Sangha closer to the laity in attitude and social position, to domesticate the Sangha, to render it no longer, in any sense, 'homeless'.

This process must have continued through the third, transitional, period. By the 3rd century AD more village tanks had been built, from which we may infer a population increase; and in the next century some of the greatest public works were erected: the vast Minneriya reservoir of King Mahasena (AD 274–301), and the huge Jetavana Stupa, with a diameter of 112 metres (367 feet). From this period onward the irrigation works grew more extensive, and the order of society, without altering its fundamentally hierarchical character, grew more complex. The architecture of monasteries in the capital, Anurādhapura, reflected this change – they grew grander and more decorated – and so too did the social organization of the Sangha.

Hence, by the greatest period of Sinhalese civilization, the 9th to the 12th centuries, the Sangha, encrusted with privilege, was an ancient and central organ of an ancient and highly complicated society. This is the fourth and final period of the Saṅgha's development as landlords, when it is very likely that the monks, taken together, owned more land in the island than the Crown or any other class. We owe a good deal of our knowledge of this period to especially informative stone inscriptions. Dynasties had come and gone;

relations between sectors of society had altered and been adjudicated; and rights in land and labour had been claimed, lost, and re-established. Against this too evident flux, kings and ministers took to cutting the details of grants, property rights, even laws, in stone. Frequently on the stones appeared the sun and moon, expressing the command that the grant or law should last as long as those heavenly bodies. Or they might bear the image of a dog or crow, to remind anyone, including the next king, that if the grant were violated or the monastery despoiled, the perpetrator would be reborn as such a disgusting animal.

As complex as the arrangements of society were the arrangements of the Sangha. This may be glimpsed through the Jetavanārāma Sanskrit inscription of the 9th century. The inscription lies within the grounds of what was then a large monastic establishment in the capital: it prescribes that one hundred monks be supported within the monastery. The inscription, of which only a portion survives, mentions by name eight villages owned by the monastery, but many more are alluded to, directly or indirectly. Though overall administration must have lain ultimately in the hands of the 'great elder of the residence', in subsidiary monasteries in the villages themselves lived monks who were delegated to oversee the collection of income. Thus: 'the three monks who live with two novices in Lahasika Monastery will oversee properly [the villages] Lahasika, Urulgonu and the villages for [supplying] monastery repairs and robes. They will have the revenue from the householders [in the villages] brought to the [chief] monastery. Having had the accounts exhibited by the assistants and accountants to monks appointed by the Sangha, they shall live at will with blameless attendants.' Even in this bald summary the scale of things is clear: the many villages, the monks posted as overseers, the accountants, the villagers, the attendants, the central administration. On the one hand, there is a division of labour within the Sangha – some oversee the property, others administer, while yet others pursue their studies within the main monastery. On the other hand, there is a complete order of lay society arranged around the monks: the inscription mentions not only villagers, accountants and assistants (probably the same as attendants, and possibly drawn from the villages themselves), but also skilled stonemasons and carpenters, overseers and a chief lay administrator who seems to have been given some acres of paddy land in each village: he would have been a rich and powerful man. And there is evidence that several thousand monks in the capital were supported by one such cluster of monasteries or another.

The real strength of this vast edifice of monastic landholding is revealed in its statutory autonomy, its possession of legal power. A general feature of the ancient Indian and Sri Lankan kingdoms was that, though final recourse to force, and nominal spiritual ownership of land, lay always with the king, lesser lords enjoyed power over land and people which was in effect a copy of the king's power. In practice this was embodied in the form of the grants of villages given to nobles, to the Sangha, or to religious institutions (such as the Temple of the Tooth, the great relic-shrine of the Buddha). Such grants were accompanied by lists of immunities which guaranteed that the king's officers would not interfere in the villages, and such lists were often set on a stone at the village boundary. The provisions were often quite specific: royal officers of this rank and that, archers, guards, tax-collectors, and so forth, should not enter a certain village, nor should goods, corvée labour or livestock be demanded from the villagers. Such inscriptions sometimes also included clauses implying that monastery functionaries were responsible for the administration of justice as well, if not for capital punishment. These large monasteries in the capital, in other words, held lordship over small kingdoms within the kingdom.

By the end of this period the Sangha had come to be written about as wholly composed of eight such 'establishments' (*āyatana*) – though there seem to have been more than eight – and this usage reveals how greatly their political and economic significance had influenced the monks' conception of themselves. The elders in such establishments were lords indeed, and in many contexts acted as lords: one inscription of the late 10th century records the grant, by such an elder, of about nine hundred grains of gold to provide beverages for the monks of an establishment monastery in the capital. Later, in the 13th century, this had gone so far that a monk was found endowing the Sangha with land! And it is not surprising that monks acting with such royal prerogative were often themselves royal by birth. Those legends of the origins of the establishments that have come down to us record that their founding elders were relations of royalty or retired kings who, in renouncing the world for this sort of monastic life, found a vocation befitting their birth. It would be fair to speak of 'princes of the church'.

Indeed, the final sign of the interpenetration of the lay order with the Sangha was the close link in kinship between lay lords and the great elders. In the 12th century this complex monastic civilization enjoyed a silver age under the brilliant and ruthless Parakkamabāhu I, but at the beginning of the 13th century a brutal invader from south India systematically reduced its social edifice to rubble, dispersing the monks and enslaving the nobility. The next Sinhalese king to enjoy undisputed power was Parakkamabāhu II (1236–70), who attempted to restore the previous glory of the landed Sangha by proclamation. In so doing he had explicitly to legislate matters that had usually remained in the sphere of unrecorded custom, so that by reading his proclamation we can gather what that Sangha had been – a traditional body ruled at the top by a *de facto* hierarchy of family privilege and caste monopoly. (It is only fair, however, to note that within these bounds, or in spite of them, the ancient ascetic philosophy of the Discipline lived on.)

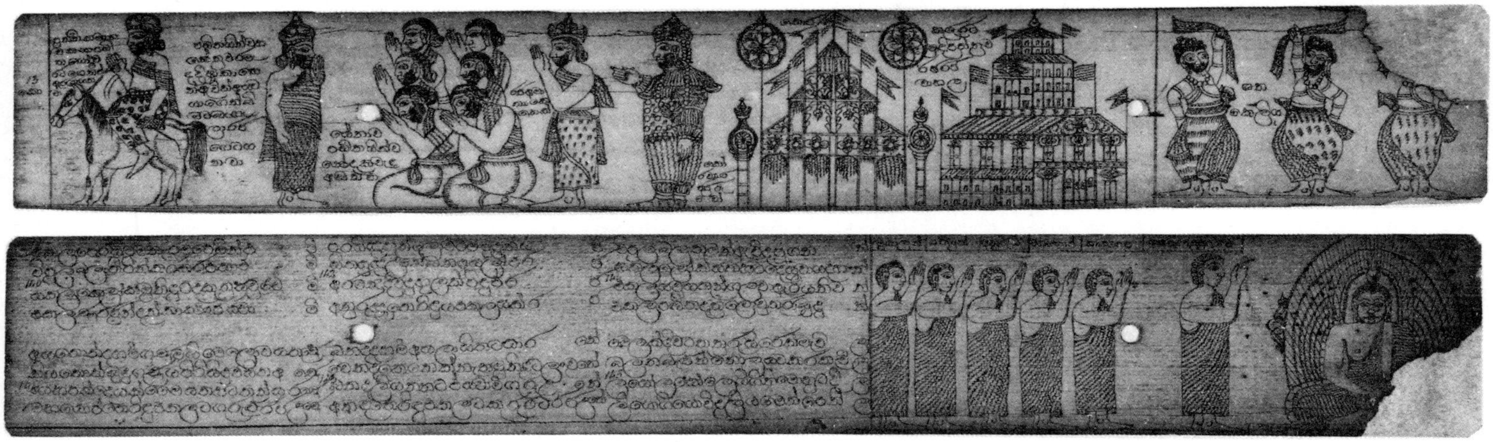

Two more sections of the palm-leaf manuscript illustrated on p. 135. The upper leaf shows the wise Vidhura, the future Buddha, returning in triumph to his royal master. In the lower, six disciples, leading monks, worship the Buddha.

In the next centuries, following the depredations not only of the Indian invader but perhaps also of the malaria mosquito, Sinhalese civilization was confined chiefly to the hills and less irrigable western plain. In the last period, that of the Kandyan kingdom of the 17th and 18th centuries, the Sinhalese held sway only in the interior, while Europeans ruled the coasts. In the Kandyan period the Sangha retained its privileges as landlords. Indeed, monks were sometimes *only* landlords, for the ordination tradition died out three times and, since only fully ordained monks could ordain new monks, elders had to be brought from Southeast Asia to ordain the holders of monastic grants. By this time such grants were held openly by families. This may have been the case for centuries, but only in this age of decline did it become official. Temples were passed ideally from uncle to nephew, so that one brother in every generation could be reserved for the Sangha. By disrobing while still potent, however, or by taking the robes only after a fruitful marriage, one could pass a temple on to one's son. It is from this period that is preserved the oldest really colourfully scandalous evidence of the changes wrought in the Sangha by landholding. Heirs of this tradition still have their seats in the Kandyan highlands today.

Though this is rather distant from the Discipline, it was not impossible to draw together the Sangha's moral ideal with the fact of landholding; it was even necessary that this be done, for the Sangha's endowments depended ultimately, in theory, upon their moral fitness. Ananda Coomaraswamy, in his great book on Sinhalese Kandyan art, did in fact pen a sketch of the 19th-century landholding Kandyan monk which allows us to see how the two might be reconciled. The sketch, though romanticized and in a foreign, Western, idiom, is fair to the best in the Kandyan monastic heritage:

> The principle duties of a Buddhist priest, beside the observance of the ten precepts, are to care for the *vihāra* (Buddhist temple), keep it clean, and offer flowers daily, meditate and study; receive the offerings of worshippers, administer [precepts to laymen on festival days]; explain the teachings of the Buddha when required; read and expound the scriptures . . . on special occasions . . .; perform *pirit* when required; superintend repairs to the *vihāra* buildings, and generally oversee the service of tenants; often also they taught the children and practised medicine; the priest in fact should be, often was, and sometimes still is, the intellectual centre of the village.

But at the same time it is clear that the monk adheres only to the ten Disciplinary rules of the novice, not the 227 of the full monk; and certainly the most necessary practical tasks, without which the temple could not exist as conceived, are those of worship, repair, preaching and supervision. Meditation and study take second place, and with them careful consideration of the Discipline. Those who transcend these natural limitations are remarkable men.

Monks in politics

The Sangha's involvement with Sri Lankan hierarchical order may be seen not only from the bottom, in relation to the land and villagers, but from the top, in relation to the king; and though these are but two views of the same relationship, in this latter, political, perspective a special theory of the role of the Sangha emerged, and emerged very early. In fact, the Sangha and kingship may be said to have arrived in Sri Lanka together. It was the great Indian Emperor Aśoka who sent instruments for royal consecration to the then leader of Sri Lanka; and later the emperor sent his son, the monk Mahinda, to convert the Sinhalese to Buddhism. One cannot help thinking that, whatever else the Sinhalese king found in Buddhism, he must have seen some political advantage in adopting a creed so favoured by the great ruler in the north; and the Sangha has been embroiled in politics ever since.

The theory of the king's relation to the Sangha is deducible from two premises. First, he is a layman like other laymen, earning merit by his gifts to the Sangha and owing them obeisance because of their moral superiority. Second, he is the lord, owner, husband and enjoyer of the land, all rights flow from him, his is the ultimate recourse to force and the ultimate duty to preserve the institutions of society. He is, in other words, the state. Hence, the state, the entire Sinhalese nation, owes obeisance to the Sangha, through the person of the king.

The sense of this theory is embodied vividly and forthrightly in the commentarial tradition, really an origin myth, which describes the conversion of the Emperor Aśoka himself to Buddhism. The emperor, says the Sinhalese account, was gazing out of the window of his palace when he espied a monk walking on his way, gazelle-like, beautiful, wrapped in the magnetic intensity of well Disciplined meditation. Drawn by this compelling vision of spiritual virtue, the emperor sent for the monk; when he entered the palace the monk unselfconsciously handed the emperor his begging bowl, stepped up to the throne, and seated himself. 'The very moment the emperor saw him approaching the throne he thought to himself, "Now, today itself, this monk will be master of this house."' And the monk proceeded to preach, converting the emperor to Buddhism.

In other words, over the political realm the monks reign both as exemplars and as preachers. The precedence awarded the Sangha betokens the precedence of their moral principles, so that the king rules by the Good Law, *Dhamma*. And under his moral sovereignty, backed by the Sangha's moral sovereignty, Sri Lanka is the Island of the Good Law, *Dhammadīpa*. The monasteries were to act as advisors to the king, and their preservation of the national chronicle of kings, the *Mahāvaṃsa* (Great Chronicle'), was, in this light, but an aspect of their advisory duty.

Furthermore, both the institution of kingship, and any particular king, were legitimated by this relation to the Sangha. This was expressed variously in the ceremony surrounding kingship and in the ceremonial acts and statements of kings. For example, the clay bowls which held the materials for royal consecration in the early period included earth taken from beneath the doorstep of several monastic institutions in the capital. King Saddhātissa (137–119 BC) is said to have offered the kingdom to the Sangha in the person of a famous monk, who returned it, saying, 'O great king, you have expressed your sense of devotion. We, on our part, return the kingdom given us. O great king, rule justly and righteously.' Other kings through the ages offered the kingdom or the symbols of sovereignty to the Sangha, only to have them returned: no theocracy for Sri Lanka. By the height of Sinhalese civilization the theory had led to even more baroque interpretations: a 10th-century inscription speaks of kingship being 'bestowed by the Sangha to protect the alms-bowls and robes of the Buddha', i.e. the Sangha and the Buddhist religion.

So far the theory. The practice entailed a number of consequences not entirely in keeping with the exemplary morality attributed to the Sangha, and these consequences appeared very early in Sinhalese history.

First, monks became the patrons of nationalism. When the early 2nd-century BC king, Duṭṭhagāmaṇī, went to war with a Tamil invader, he hung a relic of the Buddha on his spear and invited the Sangha to accompany him as a blessing. They responded, too, by telling him, after the bloody victory, that in reality only one-and-a-half human beings had been killed, a Buddhist and a partly converted Buddhist. The rest were no better than animals. It is a precedent called on, more today than for centuries, to justify bloodshed in the name of Buddhist nationalism.

By the end of the 2nd century BC the monasteries had revealed themselves in a second role, that of kingmakers: for they joined with a deceased king's ministers to pass over an elder son and confer the crown on a younger son. The elder son, Lañjatissa (119–109 BC) recaptured the throne and slighted the Sangha, but in the end relented and acted his proper part by bestowing gifts on them. The role of kingmaker stayed with the Sangha, as did the role of nationalist patron, throughout Sinhalese history. When one considers that the monks in the capital were becoming lords, and for that matter were often related to kings and ministers, these developments seem inevitable.

So the Sangha – or at least the monks of the capital – meddled with kings. But kings meddled with the Sangha, drawing it deeper into political matters and changing its internal constitution. To understand the significance of these changes, though, we will have to return briefly to the early Indian Sangha as depicted in the Discipline.

There we find clearly worked out a system of Sangha self-government based on two principles: the precedence of age, and the ratification of important decisions by total consensus. Thus, on the one hand, daily affairs, teaching, and administration rested in the hands of elder and (the emphasis was here) *wiser* monks, to whom the younger deferred. Authority was paternal, that is, in a way, generally similar to many traditional societies throughout the world. On the other hand, this paternal authority was balanced by a recognition that the whole Sangha – a body of men training themselves to make up their own minds and find their own salvation – had to agree on important points, among which were numbered the admission of new members, the censure of erring monks and the settlement of Disciplinary disputes. The procedure in such matters was this: the elders would put a proposal to the assembly of all fully ordained monks of an area three times, and that proposal was passed if the assembly remained silent all three times. It was an authoritarian system, but it allowed for individual judgment and dissent.

This was its weakness. Such an organization can, by its nature, only succeed in small face-to-face groups, for its strength depends on the personal kin-like authority of elder over younger, and it demands that a consensus be continually maintained. There is no way to prevent schism; and schism had occurred before Buddhism came to Sri Lanka. In Sri Lanka, in the countryside, other problems came to the fore: monks were spread among the peasantry, and among the peasantry they were less concerned about consensus within the Saṅgha than about consensus with their parishioners.

In the capital, change took a different and more dire form: competition. For in the capital there was one layman, the king, whose resources and powers, and therefore ability to help or hinder, set him above all others. In the reign of King Vaṭṭagāmaṇī, in about 85 BC, twenty or so years after the Sangha had interfered in Lañjatissa's succession, the significance of the king's power and largesse became clear.

After driving out another Tamil invasion, the king bestowed a landed monastery in the capital on a monk, Mahātissa, from outside the capital, who had helped him in adversity, partly by settling a dispute between him and his generals. At that time perhaps the only monastery in the capital was the Mahāvihāra, the Great Monastery, founded a century-and-a-half before by the original missionaries; and the inhabitants of the Great Monastery were deeply incensed over this gift within their bailiwick, and perhaps also over the influence wielded by this interloper. They gathered to impose expulsion on Mahātissa, on the grounds that he was 'frequenting the families of laymen', i.e. enjoying the confidence of the king. Mahātissa's pupil, Tissa, protested. He in turn was suspended. Tissa thereupon went with a large following of monks to the monastery – Abhayagiri – given to his teacher, and carried on, despite the Great Monastery, with the patronage of the king.

This series of events set a pattern that was to persist throughout the history of Buddhist Sri Lanka: Saṅgha involvement in politics, royal involvement in the Sangha, competition. The Great Monastery–Abhayagiri split lasted more than a thousand years, until another king, the draconian Parakkamabāhu I (AD 1153–86) effected a reconciliation among a weakened Sangha, who had lost much of their old structure. The Great Monastery tradition, which alone survives, would have us believe that the Abhayagiri were heretics, but this is almost certainly a vast exaggeration. The only list of actual disagreements records several minor points of Discipline, and on that evidence the Abhayagiri seem to have been slightly more strait-laced. No, it was schism over competition, sheer competition and competition for the king's favour.

In this dispute the king might merely have played the passive part of a well-intentioned but over-generous donor. On other occasions, however, the precedent was set for kings to intervene actively to settle disputes which the Sangha's archaic constitution could not handle. Thus, about a hundred years after the fatal gift to Mahātissa, King Kanirajānu (AD 29–32) came to settle a dispute at Mihintale, near the capital, apparently by actually entering the assembly of monks itself. Sixty monks did not accept the king's ruling, however, and plotted to kill him on the spot. He had them thrown in a dungeon. Kings did not always have their own way, though; Sīlameghavaṇṇa (617–626 AD) later tried and failed to resolve the Great Monastery–Abhayagiri split, and the Great Monastery elders simply ignored him. Angered, he betook himself to the south of the island, and there died, as the national chronicle puts it, 'without having asked the pardon of the Sangha'. Though there were other occasions on which the king intervened but failed to impose his will, in general lay authority, lying ultimately with the king, came regularly to apply to the Sangha where its own sanctions were weak or non-existent.

In fact, this activity of the monarch was raised to a duty: the duty to purify the Sangha. The precedent goes back in legend to the Emperor Aśoka, who disrobed the lazy, corrupted gourmet monks and upheld the Disciplined bearers of the true Theravāda. Many previous interventions of the king in Ceylon have later been interpreted in this light, but the first mention of it being done in a sytematically legal way is in the reign of Moggallāna I (AD 491–508). From descriptions of subsequent purifications it appears that the king actually stood in the assembly while the Sangha carried out the Act of Law according to its ancient method: proposal and assent by silence. These Acts of Law were of several kinds, but they had basically one of two effects. Either they expelled the offending monk, or they forced him to become legally the pupil and dependant of another monk.

The Sri Lankan sources are unequivocal in stating that this was always a matter of cleansing the Sangha of un-Disciplined monks; and no doubt principle frequently played a part. But two other motives should be noted. First, competition: if the Great Monastery–Abhayagiri split was any indication, those who were cleansed from the Sangha might have justifiably held the view that they were no less Disciplined than the cleansers, but that they were simply of the wrong party. Second, a purification may have had other effects, such as the freeing of property, which had accumulated over generations in the hands of the Sangha, to the Crown. In supporting the party of Discipline, therefore, the king's conscience and his best interests may have pointed in the same direction.

The monk as forest-dweller

The cumulative effect of the Sangha's embroilment with lay life was therefore in many ways contrary to the strict ideal of moral purity. Yet the norms of the thus domesticated Sangha never fully replaced the ascetic ideal, which lived on, at least in texts and folklore, and

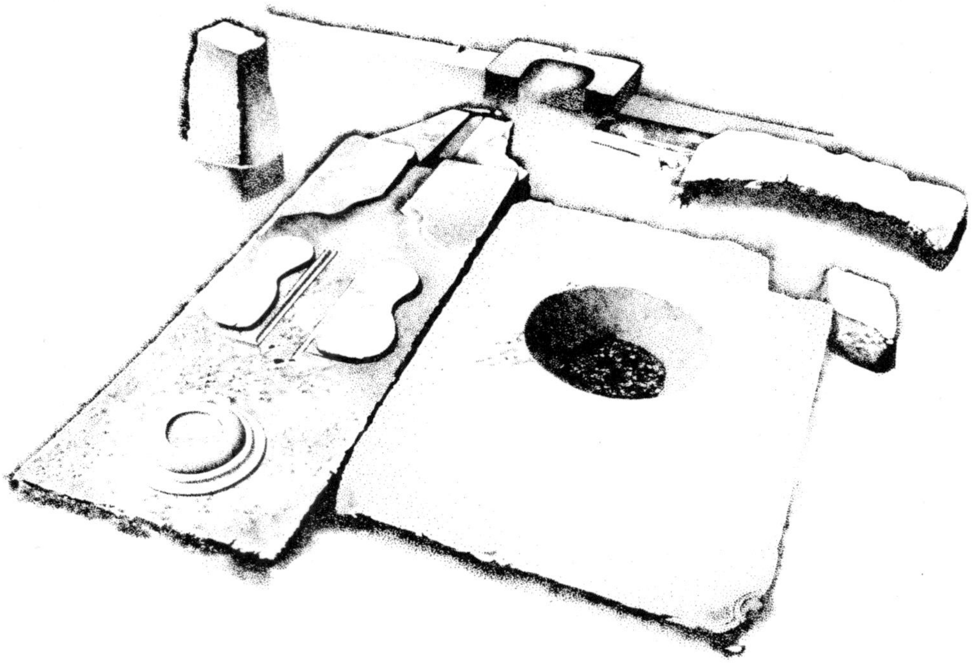

A urinal stone from the Jetavana monastery, Sri Lanka. Some of these stones have been found carved with the likenesses of palatial buildings, indicating the contempt felt by the forest-dwelling monks for worldly riches.

often in the flesh. What did happen, however, was that the Sangha came to be seen as being composed of two parties. There are different formulations of these parties, corresponding to slightly different conceptions, but one is clearly the village Sangha: preachers, teachers and scholars and village-dwellers. The other consists of ascetics, meditators and forest-dwellers. Ascetic, meditator, forest-dweller: this is wholly in keeping with the ideal of the monk as passive exemplar, and even suggests that more archaic image of the solitary ascetic, glowing with spiritual strenuousness. What is clear, however, is that from very early on they were defined in opposition to the village Sangha, rather than as the original Sangha still preserved. Two pieces of evidence illustrate this very well.

First, the *Visuddhimagga*, i.e. *Path of Purification*, a 5th-century compendium of doctrine written as a manual for meditators, prescribes the steps to be taken by a monk intent on his own salvation; and, far from assuming that the monk has joined the Sangha with salvation in mind, it presupposes that he is already a member of a Sangha with quite different preoccupations. It advises, for example, that the renouncer cannot simply go to find a meditation teacher, but must first leave his monastery in good hands, finish any building in progress, and find a teacher for his pupils. And he must take care to avoid busy monasteries, popular monasteries, monasteries near (read 'owning') cultivated land. Meditation, in other words, was clearly a special vocation, an alternative to the established village Sangha.

The second piece of evidence is archaeological. In Anurādhapura and elsewhere there exist the ruins of a type of monastery used by the meditating monks. In keeping with these monks' strict simplicity, the monasteries are very simple, in contrast to the ornate decorations of more worldly monasteries. They are very simple in every detail, that is, save one: for found among the ruins are large flat stones, carved elaborately with the likeness of palatial buildings of the sort then built for ordinary monks in the capital. The stones have holes drilled through them, and there is no doubt about their use. They are urinals. Such was the disdain the ascetics felt for the glories of monastic civilization.

So the landed ceremonial specialists dominated; but the national chronicle holds many brief references to ascetics, meditators, or forest-dwellers, and they were undoubtedly there almost continuously, a usually silent minority – living evidence of the Sangha's original heritage.

From contemporary evidence it is possible to suggest that, though from principle they attempted to avoid intervening in lay affairs, they must have exerted one significant effect: they must have held before the eyes of the Sinhalese a pure picture of the Discipline, which was elsewhere commingled with quite different sorts of behaviour. It is also possible to suggest that, far from being an unbroken tradition, asceticism and meditation continually disappeared and reappeared. On the one hand, monks and laymen, inspired by the voluminous literature on the subject, frequently started ascetic movements. On the other hand, such movements, with the passage of time, recapitulated the history of the Sangha as a whole, and gradually those who belonged to them became village ceremonial specialists, settled on their own fruitful land. This is the historical source of the peculiar pattern, found in other Theravāda countries as well as Sri Lanka, that some groups of monks identify themselves as 'forest-dwellers' or as ascetics, whereas in fact their practice is indistinguishable from that of ordinary monks around them.

Indeed it is possible to show this process in the life of a single monk whose career is a fitting summary for this discussion of monks' roles, since it illustrates how easily one version of the Sangha blends with another. The monk, Välivița Saranaṃkara, was born at the end of the 17th century in the Kandyan kingdom. He became a novice in adolescence, and his youthful idealism and energy were set a formidable task, for there was no longer a higher ordination tradition in Sri Lanka. The incumbents of the landed temples had ceased even to wear the yellow robes, and their morality consisted, as did that of the landed Sangha at the time of an earlier reform, in supporting their wives and children. The young Saraṇaṃkara had to revive the tradition of learning so that he could discover what the Discipline had been; and, though not properly ordained, he and the band of fellow ascetics who gathered around him tried to live by all 227 rules. In their fervour they insulted the landed temple incumbents on account of moral laxity.

It was not a wise move. The only person who had the authority to bring monks from abroad to renew the higher ordination tradition that Saraṇaṃkara so fervently desired was the king, but among the king's ministers were such incumbents. Saraṇaṃkara's noble birth gave him access to the king, so he went to court to plead his cause. But his rivals had got there first. He was banished to a very wild backward region, along with his fellows.

In a sense he might have been better advised to remain in exile, for only the jungle fastnesses could have preserved his apolitical ascetic purity. But he was somehow reinstated, and served as tutor to the next king. It was not until the reign of the following king, however, that his dream was realized: monks came from Thailand in 1753 to ordain Saraṇaṃkara and his followers, as well as the landed temple incumbents. That was the beginning of the Siyam Nikāya, the largest line of pupillary succession in Sri Lanka today, accounting for well over half the monks in the island. (This group is divided into 'forest-dwellers' and 'village-dwellers', though there is no difference in their practices.) And Saraṇaṃkara had other successes as well: he was appointed Sangharāja, King of the Sangha, an honorary title with little real power; and he received monasteries with lands.

But the journey from homeless ascetic to worldly involvement did not end there. For he was later implicated in a conspiracy to murder the king. The reason for this is obscure, but may well have been that the king, though a supporter of Buddhism for political reasons, was in fact a Tamil Hindu.

What is remarkable is the relative ease with which Saraṇaṃkara moved from one role to another. Once he wished to act decisively for Discipline, he could only go to court; and once at court all else followed. Saraṇaṃkara is unusual in the energy which took him through the full spectrum of possibilities, from ascetic to would-be kingmaker. Yet the spectrum exists, even today, for all monks, according to their abilities, inclinations and opportunities; so closely entwined in Sinhalese Buddhism are the different conceptions that have grown up of the monk. Few monks fall wholly into one type, whether ascetic or politician, landlord or scholar.

The modern Sangha

Today there are very approximately 20,000 monks in Sri Lanka, of whom about 600 are listed in a government census as genuine forest-dwellers. The forest monks exist chiefly as the founders or descendants of a reform movement that swept the island in the late 1940s and early 50s, and they are still relatively much more strict than the village-dwelling monks in general. The latter number among themselves many types, from the landed incumbents of the old Kandyan monastic estates (some of whom call themselves 'forest-dwellers'), through learned English-speaking scholars in the universities, to young monks in country temples more interested in leisure than in chanting *pirit*. Though this variety is largely explicable in the terms already discussed, there have been two changes which lend a particularly modern flavour to the contemporary Sangha. The first came about through the British conquest of Ceylon in 1815, the second through national Independence in 1947.

The first change was the development of the modern *nikāyas*, a word which might be best translated as 'family of pupillary succession'. All the monks of a *nikāya* trace their lineage back to a particular elder – and through him, of course, back to the Buddha. The oldest *nikāya* in Sri Lanka now is the Siyam Nikāya, which traces its lineage back to the eldest of the monks who came from Thailand in 1753 to renew the higher ordination tradition. The last Kandyan kings decreed in effect that all monks must be of this *nikāya*, by commanding that all monks must be ordained in Kandy by the monks of that line. This was to insure the purity (at least in caste, for all monks were to be of the highest caste) and the unity of the Sangha, under the king's control, although even at the best of times kings never long retained such control. On the British-controlled coast before conquest, and throughout the island after conquest, monks started other *nikāyas*, either by simply holding their ordinations elsewhere, or by bringing a new ordination tradition from Southeast Asia. In 1803 the Amarapura Nikāya began, and sheltered under its name more and more *nikāyas* until at present there are about twenty-six under its aegis. The Siyam Nikāya itself subdivided, and the third great *nikāya*, the Rāmañña, began in 1865. Just as the Sangha had once been spoken of as 'the eight establishments', it is now spoken of as 'the three Nikāyas' . . . though each of those is subdivided into smaller 'families'. They differ chiefly by the region, the caste and/or the Disciplinary purity of their monks.

Some modern monks have complained that it was the British refusal to regulate the Sangha that resulted in this, in their words, 'schism' and 'decay'. But in fact the modern Sangha may have thereby come rather to resemble the early Sangha, before the intervention of a Buddhist king: many small fraternities, each its own family, so to speak, but united by very similar observances of Discipline – or by similar lack of Discipline – and enjoying very similar positions in society. No longer do monks compete for the largesse of a king. Rather, they compete for a clientèle in their immediate area who support them on a small-scale, nearly day-to-day basis. They must not be seen to depart *too* spectacularly from the Discipline; and fresh reform movements springing up frequently, especially in the south, act as their conscience. The Sangha probably does better without a king.

The second change was more recent. National Independence in 1947 signalled a metamorphosis in the Sri Lankan political order, and with it a reinterpretation of the Sangha's role for some monks. Under the democratic constitution, politics was opened as a legitimate arena for everyone's participation; and the public welfare likewise became everyone's affair in a way never possible in the ancient Order. These changes bore on Sangha affairs in many ways, of which two may be singled out: a new idea of the monk's political responsibilities was born; and therewith the idea of the monk's social responsibilities was expanded.

First, monks in politics: in the ancient Order, and still to a large extent under the British, the involvement of individual monks in politics depended upon their connections with the king or with powerful families. It is indeed the way the landed aristocratic Kandyan monks still operate. With the new democratic order, however, and with the influx of liberal, socialist and Marxist views from the West, it became possible for anyone to consider himself a political animal, and to organize for political ends. In this atmosphere there appeared a new category of monk, the 'political' monk. In 1946 the Venerable Walpola Rahula, a monk from the intellectually and religiously active south, wrote an apology for this new role. He cited the precedents of Sangha involvement in the ancient kingdom, but interpreted that involvement as public-spirited responsibility for the nation as a whole – a complicated sentiment, compounded partly of modern democratic values, partly of ancient nationalism and the old view of the Sangha as compassionate teacher to the world.

This view, in one form or another, took hold, and many monks today regard it as part of their duty to guide their parishioners politically. They also began with Independence to form into political pressure groups. Only in one election, however, that of 1956, could the Sangha be regarded as having had a specific political effect in its own right. That was the year of the 2,500th anniversary of Buddhism, an occasion long heralded by prophecies of revival. What this meant in practice was that the Sangha (or rather less than a quarter of it) aligned itself to reject the relative ascendancy of Christian Sinhalese and Tamil Hindus in

A modern Buddha image made of coconut palm-leaves and carried in procession at Vesak, the anniversary of the Buddha's birth, Enlightenment and death.

government, to foster Sinhalese as the national official language, and to make of Sri Lanka the Buddhist nationalist state it once was. These issues were of such appeal that the Sangha came as close as it ever has to uniting behind a single opinion. The election of their candidate, S. W. R. D. Bandaranaike, brought about some of the desired changes, and led to the adoption of the idiom of Buddhist nationalism in many spheres of government. That some things had not changed since Kandyan times, however, was revealed when a monk very active in electing Bandaranaike was convicted of assassinating him.

On second glance, in fact, the actual conduct of present-day political monks is not so different from that of their traditional role as politicians. True, the new institution of elections widens their sphere of activity, but it is still by virtue of prestige and through personal ties that most monks influence government. And their one effective deed, the promotion of Buddhist nationalism, has a precedent 2,000 years old in the monks who encouraged King Duṭṭhagāmaṇī. Today the Sangha pressure groups have split along party lines and represent partisan political opinion, and the laity is quite sensitive to this demeaning of the Sangha's apolitical ideal. The very term 'political monk' is in many circles pejorative; and when a monk ran for the National State Assembly in 1977, he lost his deposit. Monks will no doubt continue to appear on election platforms, but in so doing they will always be vulnerable to criticism from the viewpoint of Discipline.

Many of these same moral ambiguities attach to the wider conception of the Sangha's active ideal, its 'work for the world', which accompanied the new Western ideas embodied in electoral democracy. A new phrase was found, 'social service'. Social service includes most of the sort of activities a public-spirited clergyman might undertake in the West: ministering to the poor, commenting on public morality, even helping to set up co-operatives. Many temples have allowed their grounds to be used to set up local weaving schools, and temple buildings are often used for meetings of local cultivators' groups of various kinds. Most conspicuous among these services is education. On the one hand, some monastery schools receive government grants to provide primary education. On the other hand, monks have been taken into the national education system as schoolteachers, and into the university system as lecturers. In fact two universities have been set up in association with two advanced seminaries for monks in the capital, Colombo, and the Venerable Walpola Rahula has acted as vice-chancellor of one of them.

Yet the criticism of these new roles has been severe. Certainly the Discipline does not envision allowing monks to receive salaries as schoolteachers. Nor does it seem proper to conservatives that a monk should go to university to learn subjects, such as geography or sociology, that have nothing to do with the monk's position. One may imagine their reaction to monks who have actually gone to work in the paddy fields with their bare hands. One limit to the social service of the Sangha was recently drawn by a judge. A monk, trained in law at one of the university campuses, applied to practise at the bar, causing a well publicized uproar. The matter was finally settled when the judge ruled that he could not practise without the traditional garb of white shirt, dark tie and suit!

In fact, from the viewpoint of Discipline, these new roles and the problems that go with them are not very different from the old. In an inscription of the 12th century, for example, a king found it necessary to decree, according to Discipline, that monks should not accept pay for teaching. The same inscription proclaimed that monks should enter villages only on business such as begging alms or preaching, and only with the strict permission of the monastery head. This was a version of the Disciplinary rules against 'frequenting the families of lay folk': a charge once laid against King Vaṭṭagāmaṇī's favourite monk, Mahātissa, and still laid against 'political' monks today. Nor is this the mere application of outmoded standards in a modern world: the monk is still defined by separation from lay society, the higher morality, the value of self-salvation from suffering. Any individual monk may act differently, but the Sangha as a whole cannot think of itself in any other way. The duty to laymen must still stand on the duty to Discipline.

For many laymen today, this double duty of the Sangha is vividly dramatized every year. For, on ordinary occasions, they support their local monk, and call on him for merit making; but once a year they travel in a busload to one of the centres of forest-dwelling monks, and there spend a day worshipping, giving alms, listening to the monks' words, and imbibing the spirit of forest asceticism. For the laymen it matters little that their village monk may have as much Discipline as the forest monks. And the village monks, too, venerate the meditative, ascetic ideal. As one put it: 'In this life it is enough that I work here in the village. How else would the villagers hear the Buddha's word? Perhaps with the merit [acquired in this work] I'll be able to go to the forest in my next life.' In this broad compassionate view, can there be any doubt that the Sangha has room for all?

6

'To be a Burmese is to be a Buddhist': Buddhism in Burma

HEINZ BECHERT

THE PROVERB THAT gives this chapter its title is an indication of the deeply Buddhist nature of the Burmese people. There is indeed no other country where even today the visitor is so immediately struck by the way the country and people have been shaped by Buddhism. For centuries Theravāda Buddhism has been the country's only form of Buddhism. As its holy scriptures are written in Pali, this became the key language of religion and education in Burma.

History

Theravāda Buddhism had already spread through the area of present-day Burma before the country was settled by the Burmese. Some of its earlier inhabitants, the Mons, were Theravāda Buddhists. Mon or Talaing was the language of a people which at a very early stage came under the influence of Indian culture and had settled in large areas of present-day lower Burma and central and northern Thailand, but which was driven back by the Burmese and Thais in the course of the centuries. Mon is now only spoken in a small area in the region of Moulmein in Burma and a few places in Thailand. The Mon language is related to the language of the Khmer or Cambodians, and together they form the Mon-Khmer languages.

There is a tradition in Burma, as there is in Sri Lanka, that the Buddha himself visited the country. The earliest historical record of the spread of Buddhism into present-day Burma is the account in the Ceylonese chronicles according to which King Aśoka sent a mission consisting of Theras Soṇa and Uttara into the 'Land of Gold' (Suvaṇṇabhūmi) to disseminate the Buddhist religion. This country can be identified as the country of the Mons. But the Mons do not appear to have been finally converted to Buddhism until several centuries after Aśoka, having previously adopted Hindu cults of Indian origin side by side with Buddhism.

Unfortunately we know little of the history and culture of the Mons, although, as one of the great civilized nations of Southeast Asia, they produced important works of art, architecture and literature. The oldest known inscription in the Mon language is from around AD 600 and was found near the stupa of Nakorn Pathom. This, the tallest Buddhist building in Thailand, situated 37 miles (60 kilometres) west of Bangkok, was founded by the Mons. Mon art and culture first flourished at the time of the kingdom of Dvāravatī (*c.* 6th–10th centuries AD) in the region of present-day Thailand, and the Dvāravatī style is named after it. It seems that hardly anything of the old Thaton or Sudhammavati, the capital of the Mons in Rāmaññadesa – which is the part of what is now lower Burma that they have inhabited since the 5th century – has been preserved, although no systematic excavations have as yet been carried out there.

The ancestors of the Burmese moved gradually from the north into the Irrawaddy plain from the mountainous country east of Tibet. Together with Tibetan and Newari, the old language of Nepal, Burmese belongs to the so-called Tibeto-Burmese group of languages. The earliest Tibeto-Burmese states in the area of present-day Burma were the state of the Pyu in central Burma, which has been in existence since the 3rd century AD, and the kingdom of Arakan in the north-west coastal regions of Burma, which was founded soon after. Śrīkṣetra, the capital of the state of Pyu, lay near the village of Hmawza in the neighbourhood of Prome. The Pyu and Arakanese were originally greatly influenced by north Indian culture and became adherents of the Hindu Viṣṇu cult and of Mahāyāna and tantric Buddhism. The study of texts belonging to the Sarvāstivāda School of Hīnayāna Buddhism was also pursued there.

The Pyu state was conquered in 832 by the rulers of the princedom of Nan Chao which was also Tibeto-Burmese. The real Burmese or Mranma (called Myamma today), who were related to the Pyu, had already penetrated into the Irrawaddy plain where they were said to have founded their capital Pagan in 849. Although they still followed their old 'animist' tribal religion, they soon came under the influence of tantric Buddhism which the Pyu had adopted. Their priests carried out complicated rituals, indulged in magic and practised alchemy.

The introduction of Theravāda in the Burmese state by King Anuruddha or Anawrahta (1044–77) was the crucial turning-point in Burma's religious history. The

Shin Arahan, represented as a donor in an early 12th-century statue in the Ānanda Temple, Pagan. Shin Arahan was a Mon monk who according to tradition converted the Burmese king Anuruddha and was thus responsible for introducing Theravāda Buddhism into the Burmese state.

Burmese chronicles report that Anuruddha was converted by a Mon monk called Shin Arahan, but that there were no copies of the holy scriptures and no relics in Pagan. The Mon king refused the Burmese king's request for a copy of the holy scriptures and some relics. It is unlikely that this was the real reason for war as the texts claim; Anuruddha at any rate conquered Thaton in 1057, took the Mon king captive, and brought him, his family and many monks and skilled workmen to his capital Pagan, together with manuscripts of the sacred scriptures of Theravāda Buddhism. With them Mon culture and Theravāda Buddhism reached the Burmese. The supremacy of the tantric monks was now broken, and though their doctrine survived for a time, particularly in the border territories of Burma, their influence diminished steadily while orthodox thought soon prevailed in all parts of the country.

The kingdom of the dynasty of Pagan which created the most magnificent of the Burmese temples was destroyed by the invasion of the Mongols from China under Kubilai Khan in 1287. In the years that followed, during which the country disintegrated into small states, the Shan tribes which linguistically and ethnically belong to the Thai peoples settled in large areas of Burma, while the Mons regained their independence in the south. Pegu, the former Haṃsavatī, now became their capital. Their great king Dhammaceti (1472–92) introduced an important reform in the Buddhist Sangha which will be discussed later. At the beginning of the 15th century the Burmese dynasty of Toungoo extended its rule quickly throughout the Burmese heartlands. King Bayinnaung (1551–81) conquered the mountain regions inhabited by the Shan tribes. A long sequence of bloody wars between Burma and Siam (present-day Thailand) which severely unsettled both countries started in the 16th century.

In 1752 the Burmese king Alaungpaya (1752–60) put a bloody end to the last attempt of the Mons to restore their state. Alaungpaya, founder of the Konbaung dynasty, which was the last Burmese dynasty, was an exceedingly warlike and cruel monarch. He launched the massive expansion of Burmese rule which later led to clashes with the British and therefore indirectly to the downfall of the Burmese empire.

One of the most remarkable Burmese kings of the last dynasty was Bodawpaya (1781–1819). Upon taking office he first eliminated all possible rivals and quelled some revolts, then improved the administration of the country with the help of a general census and the imposition of higher taxes. In 1784 the Burmese conquered Arakan, but they were not in a position to pacify this region properly, and the frequent use of mass-deportation as a weapon in the suppression of revolts led to the flight of many Arakanese into the region of Chittagong, an area administered by the British East India Company. The tensions to which this gave rise later led to the first Anglo-Burmese war.

According to some sources, Bodawpaya finally succumbed to a kind of religious mania, claiming to be the Buddha Maitreya whose coming had been prophesied by the historical Buddha. According to Burmese belief, the advent of the future Buddha was to be preceded by the establishment of a *cakravartin* or world-ruler. Bodawpaya seems to have tried to apply these two religious expectations to his own person, but the majority of the monks did not recognize his claims.

In 1826, after the first Anglo-Burmese war, Burma had to cede Arakan and Tenasserim, and in 1852, after the second war, all of lower Burma was handed over. The kingdom, now limited to upper Burma, experienced another cultural flowering under its penultimate ruler, Mindon (1853–78). It was his aim to rule in accordance with the ideal of a Buddhist king of peace, and the revival of the Buddhist religion was especially close to his heart. He convened the Fifth Buddhist Council in 1871 to carry out a revision of the holy scriptures. When the texts had been verified by this assembly, they were engraved on 729 marble tablets and erected within the precincts of the Kuthodaw pagoda in Mandalay, the new capital founded by Mindon in 1857. These and other reforms made Mandalay at this time the spiritual centre of Theravāda Buddhism.

Under Mindon's successor, Burma's last king, Thibaw (1878–85), all hopes that Burma might be preserved as an independent buffer state were finally shattered. After the third Anglo-Burmese war, upper Burma was, in 1885, incorporated in the British Indian Empire.

The kingdom of Burma had to a large extent cut itself off from the outside world. Much of domestic as well as all foreign trade was a state monopoly. At the time of its incorporation into the British Empire, the country was opened up and radically reorganized without any period of transition. Since Burma was administered as a province of India, a great many Indians from all parts of the sub-continent poured into the country, ruthlessly using the advantage they had gained from their more protracted experience in dealing with modern economic methods. Many of the inexperienced Burmese peasants found themselves tenant farmers of Indian rentiers. Rangoon became a city predominantly inhabited by Indians, and Indians held most of the new jobs created by the colonial administration on the railways, in the postal service, etc.

Royal patronage of the monastic Order had been so important a part of the religious community in the old kingdom of Burma that many Burmese thought the elimination of the dynasty would be a heavy blow to religion itself. But Burma's centuries-old identification with Buddhism prevented it from falling into decay as the Christian missionaries had hoped. Long before 1885 Buddhism had proved its power of resistance in the coastal provinces which had been annexed by Britain. Howard Malcolm, in his book, *Travels in Southeastern Asia* (Vol. 1, p. 321) published in 1839 reports,

> In the British provinces, the national faith, being robbed of the support of the secular arm, seems to be cherished so much the more by national feeling. Expectancy that the religion of the new rulers may spread, seems to awake greater vigilance that it may not. Pagodas, *kyoungs* [i.e. monasteries] and priests are well supported, and the clergy seem anxious to propitiate popular favour, to stand them in stead of government patronage.

Since interference in political affairs had been strictly forbidden in the kingdom of Burma, most Buddhist monks continued to remain outside politics after the British had taken the country over. Religious concepts did nevertheless play an important part in rebellions against British rule as early as the 19th century. In this connection, the risings connected with so-called messianic movements must be mentioned particularly, expressing the popular hope for the early advent of a *cakravartin* or *Setkya Min*, the ideal world ruler, and of the future Buddha Maitreya. Pretenders to the throne who considered themselves incarnations of the *cakravartin* tended to follow in the wake of such movements, as did magicians, astrologers and the rituals and solemn vows characteristic of secret societies. Rebellions of this kind had already occurred in times of crisis in the old Burmese kingdom, and in 1839 such a revolt broke out under the leadership of an alleged *cakravartin* in Pegu against King Tharrawaddy. Similar revolts were reported in British occupied lower Burma in 1855 and 1860. Some monks also took part in attempts to rid the country of British rule. In 1886 the colonial government offered a reward of 5,000 rupees for the capture of a monk who was considered to be the leader of the revolt in eastern Burma, and who, when apprehended, was publicly hanged.

Burma was conquered by the British in three wars, the last ending in 1885. This engraving, based on a sketch made on the spot, shows troops advancing on a fortified village, the unmistakable Buddhist stupas rising in the background.

The identification of the Burmese with their hereditary religion was still further strengthened by the fact that the British conquerors and Indian immigrants belonged to other religions (Christianity, Hinduism and Islam). It is therefore not surprising that the saying 'To be a Burmese is to be a Buddhist' is a very good description of an essential feature of Burmese efforts to preserve national self-determination. This was the reason why, from the beginning, Buddhist revival movements and Burmese independence movements were closely linked. In 1906 the Young Men's Buddhist Association (YMBA) was founded in Rangoon. It was modelled on the YMBA which had been in existence in Ceylon since 1898, and which, in its turn, had taken the corresponding Christian society, the YMCA, as its model. The society, which was at first almost exclusively formed of Buddhist laymen, turned its attention in 1917 to some of the crucial issues of the modern Burmese

The 'Shoe Question', a source of intense anti-European resentment around 1917–19, turned on the Buddhist prohibition against the wearing of shoes in sacred precincts. A contemporary Burmese cartoon ridicules foreigners who would rather be carried than take their shoes off.

national movement. It fought segregation on the railways, which provided compartments for 'Europeans only', and the sale of land to foreigners, and it took up the so-called 'Shoe Question'.

The Shoe Question involved the protest against European disregard for Burmese culture and Buddhist religion, which had found expression in an insistence on wearing shoes within the precincts of temples and stupas. It became a symbol of the first phase of the struggle for the restoration of Burma's national freedom. Since the Shoe Question symbolized this struggle in such a simple and clearcut way, and since the close link between Burmese nationalism and the Buddhist religion could hardly have been demonstrated more clearly, it was the perfect point of departure for the unification of the most diverse trends in the Burmese national movement. Here modernists and traditionalists could cooperate without reservations. In 1919 the colonial government had no alternative but to capitulate with certain qualifications.

A considerable number of monks joined the politico-religious agitation in connection with the Shoe Question. The famous monk and scholar Ledi Sayadaw wrote a detailed treatise on the subject, called *The Impertinence Of Wearing Shoes Within The Precincts Of The Pagoda*. There were some violent incidents. On 4 October 1919 outraged monks attacked a group of Europeans who had entered the precincts of the Eindawya pagoda at Mandalay wearing shoes. Four monks were convicted; their leader, U Kettaya, was found guilty of attempted murder and given a life sentence.

In 1920 the umbrella organization of all the existing YMBA branches was renamed the General Council of Burmese Associations. During this period there were a good many predominantly non-violent confrontations arising from popular resistance to the colonial power. The bitterness generated by governmental support of Christian mission schools, where missionaries lacked all consideration for the religious feelings of the Burmese, was expressed in a general school strike. Probably the most important figure of the nationalist movement of the time was the monk U Ottama. He had travelled to Japan in 1907, had studied at Indian universities, and had come to know the methods of the Indian nationalist movement. He returned to Burma in 1921. To rouse the entire Burmese people he gave the political independence movement the character of a movement for religious liberation. U Ottama was repeatedly arrested and convicted for incitement to rebellion. He died in prison in 1939, probably the most popular martyr of the Burmese independence movement.

The political activities of large groups of monks who joined together in monks' associations were of considerable importance between 1920 and the Second World War; no Burmese politician could do without their support. They often spoke at election meetings and many of the more radical among them were arrested. U Wizaya went on hunger-strike because monks had been forbidden to wear monks' robes in prison. He died in 1929 after 163 days on hunger-strike and became a national martyr.

The heavy political involvement of large sections of the Sangha of course provoked criticism on the part of many devout Buddhists who considered this involvement a violation of the monastic rules. In addition the monk-politicians lost some of their influence because of disunity amongst the various splinter groups. The reputation of the politically active monks was further damaged by the participation of some groups of monks in the anti-Indian Indo-Burmese riots of 1938. The collapse of the last great traditionalist rebellion in Burma, the so-called Saya-San revolt, which took place between 1930 and 1932 , also contributed to influencing the course of events into a different direction.

After the Japanese occupation and the short rule of the government of Dr Ba Maw (1942–45) under a Japanese protectorate, Burma received full independence in 1948 under the leadership of the Anti-Fascist People's Freedom League (AFPFL). In a country ravaged by war, the new government was faced not only with great economic problems but also with numerous revolutionary movements. The Burmese AFPFL government owed its survival to the fact that the separatist revolts of the various national minorities and communist groups remained uncoordinated.

The AFPFL had evolved from the pre-war nationalist Thakin movement. In its first period its undisputed leader was General Aung San, but he was murdered on 19 July 1947. His pre-war experiences had led him to demand a complete separation between religion and politics. His successor, and the first prime minister of a free Burma, was U Nu. He tried at first to achieve national unity through a left-orientated policy, but his Leftist Unity Plan of June 1948 failed because of the intransigence of the communists.

After 1949 the attitude of the government of U Nu changed in favour of a greater role for religious elements in the national politics of Burma. The socialists inside the AFPFL put forward the theory that Marxist doctrines were only acceptable in Burma in so far as they were not in conflict with Buddhist teaching. This led to an experiment in a fusion of Marxist and Buddhist doctrines, a so-called 'Marxist-Buddhist syncretism' which was formulated in the book *The Burmese Revolution* by U Ba Swe, published in 1952. The Burmese socialists took up the old concept of the dualism of truth: while Marxist doctrine represented the lower truth, necessary for the resolution of secular economic conditions, Buddhism embodied the ultimate truth.

At this time U Nu tried to bring about a fundamental regeneration of Burma through the Buddhist religion. At his instigation parliament passed laws to systematize the ecclesiastical jurisdiction of the Sangha (1949), to control the monastic education system (1950), and to create the Buddha Sāsana Council, a council for the coordination of Buddhist activities (1950). The attempt to revitalize Burmese Buddhism was most clearly shown to the rest of the world in the Sixth Buddhist Council (1954–56) which was held in an artificial cave (Mahāpāsāṇaguhā) beside the 'World Peace' pagoda, the Kaba-Aye, in Rangoon. Monks from all Theravāda Buddhist countries gathered here to carry out a thorough revision of the canonical texts.

But the attempt to form a central organization to supervise the whole country's Sangha foundered on the opposition of a large majority of the monks. After a split in the party in power, U Nu was forced in 1958 to hand over power to Ne Win, the commander-in-chief of the army, in order to prevent general chaos. Ne Win then re-established order in the country and organized free elections.

U Nu, for his part, put religious policies right into the foreground and promised, if elected, to make Buddhism the state religion. When he took over the government on 4 April 1960, he immediately began to act in accordance with his promise. The idea was not new. Burma's president during the Japanese occupation, Dr Ba Maw, had already tried, in 1942, to re-establish the relationship between state and Sangha which had existed at the time of the monarchy. As far back as 1956 U Nu himself had taken up the question of a state religion in a declaration of principle. The discussions about the proposed change in the constitution to make Buddhism the state religion, which was finally passed by parliament in a solemn session on 26 August 1961, led to general unrest and to political activities of militant monks' associations, which reminded many Burmese unpleasantly of the part monks had played in the politics of pre-war days. On the one hand, it was found to be impossible to fulfil the demands of radical groups of monks, while on the other the partly non-Buddhist minorities became further alienated from the state. The original aim of this legislation for a state religion, which had been to give the state the opportunity to reform the Sangha, was not achieved.

U Nu's unrealistic policy had thus brought about a situation which practically invited intervention by the military leadership. On 1 March 1962 General Ne Win took over the government once more. His aim this time was to govern indefinitely. The controversial religious laws were repealed, the political parties were dissolved, and a new official party, the Burma Socialist Programme Party, was founded. At first it seemed to those who knew the country well that U Nu's 'Buddhist socialism', which had been more concerned with ideals than the conditions in the real world, had been replaced by 'the success of efficiency criteria against the symbols of Buddhist democracy' (E. Sarkisyanz, *Buddhist Backgrounds of the Burmese Revolution*, p. 229). But matters developed differently. Brigadier Aung Gyi, who favoured a pragmatic economic policy, resigned from all his posts in February 1963 and retired to a monastery.

Ne Win now fell back on the philosophy of the party he had founded, which Buddhist monks had extensively collaborated in formulating. It was to represent a 'middle way' between Burmese traditionalism and Western socialism. Though it was described as a 'purely secular and human doctrine', it took over all the essential elements of Buddhist cosmology, using a terminology which closely followed the texts of the *Abhidhamma Piṭaka*. Closer examination of Burma's socialist economic policy since 1962 shows that the concepts which form the basis of its radical nationalization of most branches of the economy can be found in the old Burmese tradition rather than in Marxism. The Burmese kings (i.e. the state) had a monopoly of foreign as well as a large part of internal trade and general economic life, and these monopolies have been restored. And, also like today, a not inconsiderable part of the commercial activities in the country were carried on in a grey zone outside the official national economy, so that despite many shortages on the official market, one could and can live reasonably well in Burma.

In 1963 conflicts arose with groups of monks who protested against the abolition of the religious laws. At first the government persisted in maintaining that religion was now once again a private matter. When the government attempted to implement secular administrative measures to protect historic monuments within the monastic precincts of the Mahamuni Pagoda in Mandalay, the monks strongly and successfully protested against this interference in their affairs. Attempts in 1964 and 1965 to impose a general registration of monks and monks' associations, and other measures for the restoration of the internal order of the Sangha, came to nothing. A long period of abstention from religious politics followed. As anyone who visited Burma throughout these years must have noticed, there was a great upsurge in religious activities in the country even at a time of considerable economic

The Upali Thein (Upāli-sīmā) is an ordination hall which was built in order to serve the reform movement introduced into Burma from Sri Lanka and called Sīhalasangha. The foundations of the building go back to the 13th century; its present form belongs to the 18th century.

difficulties. The discontinuation of government subsidies to the religious bodies was more than compensated for by the donations made by Buddhist laymen.

Since the end of 1979, the Burmese government has made another attempt at an active religious policy which will be discussed at greater length later.

The structure of the Burmese Sangha

At first sight it seems as though the structure of the Sangha was more or less the same in all Theravāda Buddhist countries since it is based on the same canonical texts of the *Vinaya Piṭaka* and on the *Samantapāsādikā* which is a 5th-century commentary on it by Buddhaghosa. The Theravāda Buddhists have always insisted on the authority of these texts and rejected any specific change in the rules. But, in practice, different historical conditions brought about different developments in the structure of the Sangha in the various countries.

The medieval history of Burma is rich in controversies between different schools of thought within the Sangha. As we have already seen, Theravāda Buddhism, which had already been established among the Mons, gained acceptance among the Burmese after 1057, taking the place of the tantric Buddhism that had previously predominated. By the end of the 12th century the Sangha of Ceylon had gained such a high reputation, after the reforms carried out by King Parakkamabāhu I, that a group of Burmese monks travelled to Ceylon, adopted the local tradition of ordination, and introduced it into Burma. The 'Sinhalese Sangha' founded by them traced back the tradition of its ordination to that of the tradition of the Ceylonese Mahāvihāra founded by Mahinda (see above p. 142), and began to compete with the indigenous Burmese Sangha whose origin went back by way of Shin Arahan to the missionaries Soṇa and Uttara who had been sent to Burma by Aśoka. The influence of the Sinhalese Sangha grew rapidly, though it split off into several sub-groups. As in medieval Ceylon (see above p. 142), and a little later in Siam, the Araññavāsin, the forest-dwelling monks who concentrated on meditation, broke away from the majority group of the Sangha at about the same time.

Burmese Buddhism owes the most important subsequent reform to King Dhammaceti of Pegu (1472–92), who came from the country of the Mons, had been a monk and had helped Queen Shin Sawbu to escape from Burmese captivity in Ava. She became the ruler of Pegu in 1453. When she decided to retire into spiritual life in the precincts of the Shwedagon pagoda, she appointed Dhammaceti her successor. He left the monastic Order but worked for its thorough reform when he became king. This reform was much needed in 15th-century Burma, since many monks had contravened the rules of the Order, for example, by amassing wealth for themselves, or by practising astrology and other secular arts.

Since King Dhammaceti had belonged to the Sinhalese Sangha, it was natural for him to combine the revival of monastic Discipline with the introduction of ordination traditions from Ceylon. At the beginning of 1476, he sent a delegation of twenty-two monks on two ships to Ceylon. In July 1476 they were re-ordained in the Sinhalese tradition in the river Kälaṇigaṅga (Kalyāṇīgaṅgā) on Ceylon's west coast. After their return, the ordination hall, called Kalyāṇīsīmā, after the Sinhalese river, was erected in Pegu, and the native monks were invited to submit themselves to re-ordination. The Kalyāṇī inscriptions there bear witness to these events to this day.

The validity of a Buddhist monk's ordination depends on an uninterrupted line of valid ordinations going back to the Buddha himself. Since serious transgressions against the monastic rule incur automatic expulsion from the Order, the validity of the succession can only be assured if the way of life of the monks who belong to the Order is morally irreproachable. This explains why the formalities of the re-ordination were so important as a prerequisite for the general reform of the Order.

Though the kingdom of Pegu was conquered and destroyed by the Burmese in 1539 and again in 1551, the reform initiated by Dhammaceti was successfully carried out in all parts of the country, and all present-day Burmese monks trace back their ordination to the Kalyāṇīsīmā tradition. A serious dispute divided the Sangha in the 18th century, when a group of monks maintained that covering both shoulders with the monk's robe outside the monastery was in accordance with the original laws, while the rest of the monks wanted to cover only one shoulder. The dispute was not settled until 1784 when an assembly of monks under the supervision of King Bodawpaya decided in favour of covering both shoulders (which, from a historical point of view, is wrong). To this day this way of wearing the monk's robe is characteristic of Burmese monks and of the members of the Amarapura Nikāya and Rāmañña Nikāya, the two branches of the Sangha of Sri Lanka which are based on Burmese tradition.

These events show to what an extent the Burmese kings had brought the Sangha under their control. They exercised this control through a central clerical administration which was headed by a Sangharāja or Thathanabaing. The Sangharāja was appointed by the king, on whose death or overthrow the validity of his appointment would cease, and he was supported by a council of eight to twelve monastic elders termed *Thudama* (*Sudhamma*) *Sayadaws*. A *Gainggyok* and a *Gaingok* were responsible for the administration of the Sangha in the various provinces and districts respectively. The *Gainggyoks* and *Gaingoks* worked in close collaboration with the secular administration and controlled appointments in the ecclesiastical hierarchy and ecclesiastical judiciary, the supervision of monastic property, the registration of the monks, and the annual examination of their knowledge of Pali.

Since the proper operation of this system depended on the effectiveness of the power of the government, it broke down completely with the annexation of Burma by the British. This breakdown was much more complete in Burma than in Ceylon, since the Burmese Sangha – at least under the last dynasty – had lost most of its tradition of self-government, while there had always been a higher degree of administrative autonomy in the Sangha of Sri Lanka.

Hence the Burmese Sangha lost its organizational structure after 1885, when the colonial government turned the religious authorities into mere courts of arbitration. Though the Taunggwin Sayadaw was elected as the new monastic head in 1903, after the interregnum following the death of the last Thathanabaing, who had been appointed by a king, his office continued to diminish in importance. In 1935, three years before the death of the Taunggwin Sayadaw, Burma's religious jurisdiction was deprived of its remaining importance through a decision by the high court in Rangoon. The court did not recognize the authority of the Thathanabaing on the grounds that his office was not mentioned in the *Vinaya Piṭaka*. The office finally lapsed in 1938.

There have, however, been numerous reform movements within the Sangha since the beginning of colonial times, such as the Shwe-gyin Nikāya and Dvāra Nikāya which were formed as far back as the middle of the 19th century. These self-governing bodies were modelled on the reform-*nikāyas* which had been founded in Ceylon in the 19th century. But various more cohesive groups, such as the so-called 'Pakkoku' and 'Ngettwin' sects, were also created within the majority group which after the collapse of the Burmese monarchy was largely 'non-organized' and which, to distinguish it from the small reform groups, was called Sudhamma Nikāya, after its religious council which remained in existence until 1938.

Since around 1920, monks' associations with political or cultural objectives have been created to exist side by side with the traditional Sanghas. They are similar to such organizations in Ceylon. Though the official hierarchy of the Sudhamma Nikāyas and the reform-*nikāyas* took the view that political activity was incompatible with the monastic rule, the dignitaries of this hierarchy, in particular those of the Sudhamma Nikāya were unable to impose this view on other monks. This made it possible for those monks' associations whose structure corresponds to that of secular socio-political societies to become pressure groups and to exert considerable influence, especially between 1920 and 1930, and again between 1950 and 1962.

One gathers from contemporary accounts that there were few cases of serious misconduct against monastic Discipline in the 19th and early 20th centuries. Where these did occur, the offenders were expelled from the Sangha in disgrace. But since the turn of the century the number of complaints about the decline of standards in the Sangha has increased. There were accusations that large sections of the Order took part in political activities, as well as charges of misuse of monastic property, neglect of spiritual duties, and other misdemeanours. This led to an increasing demand for a new and thorough reform of the Sangha.

U Nu's attempt between 1950 and 1962 to attain this objective by once more setting up ecclesiastical jurisdiction, by instigating the registration of monks and the election of a Sangha parliament, etc., came in the end to nothing. The ecclesiastical courts did not work properly, and several of the other plans were doomed to failure from the start, foundering on the opposition of groups of monks who were against reform.

The present Burmese government started on a new phase of active religious policy in 1979 before which it had hardly concerned itself with politico-religious matters. As a first step, the Minister of the Interior and Religion, Brigadier Sein Lwin, requested a large number of *sayadaws* (p. 156) to prepare for a general Sangha conference. They formed a working committee of sixty-six *sayadaws* for this purpose. The general conference of the Sangha took place from 24 to 27 May 1980 in the cave near the Kaba-Aye pagoda in Rangoon where the Sixth Buddhist Council had taken place in

1956. Delegates from all sections of the Sangha in Burma were invited to the conference; one delegate was sent for every hundred monks. Since there are 123,450 fully ordained monks in Burma, 1,235 delegates were selected and 1,219 were actually able to take part in the congress. They belonged to all ten groups within the Sangha (Thudama Nikāya, the three sections of the Dvāra Nikāya, Shwe-gyin Nikāya, Veluvan Nikāya, Maha-Yin Nikāya, Ngettwin Nikāya, Ganavimutti Nikāya and Yun Nikāya). The purpose of the congress was to form an organization to govern the country's entire Sangha. Only those submitting to this authority would be allowed to be a *bhikkhu* (fully ordained monk) in Burma. Central to this was the registration of all monks, which was to be carried out in close co-operation with the civil authorities, as well as the re-establishment of a properly functioning ecclesiastical jurisdiction. The details of the new organization were worked out by a central working committee of 300 members from which, in turn, thirty-three Sanghanāyakas were chosen to form the actual leadership of the Sangha. This leadership would consist of three departments: scholarship, jurisdiction and 'miscellaneous'.

A general amnesty was proclaimed on the occasion of the Sangha convention which particularly benefited political offenders and refugees. U Nu, who had been a determined opponent of the present Burmese government while he was in exile, was now called back to Burma and appointed president of the newly founded Piṭaka Translation Society, whose task it is to produce a new English translation of the Pali Canon for the use of the Buddhist world mission.

There can be no doubt that the government of Ne Win is carrying on the tradition of the Burmese kings as well as the religious policy of U Nu. This is not altered by the fact that Ne Win – to maintain at least the symbolic separation between religion and state which he had previously advocated – did not personally take part in the Sangha convention, and that all decisions were taken by the Sangha and not, as under U Nu, by government institutions. Visitors to Burma also noticed that the government of Ne Win was able, with this new religious policy, to gain the sympathy of a large part of the sections of the population that had so far disapproved of government policy. But it is of course too early to judge the success of this reform of the Sangha.

Monks and laymen

The study of the holy scriptures (*pariyatti*) and the revelation of the road to salvation (*paṭipatti*) are the traditional tasks of the monks. Through the centuries the study of the holy texts has been pursued particularly intensively in Burma. Thus it is no accident that we owe the best tradition of these texts to that country. As long ago as the 12th century, a thorough revision of the Pali texts was carried out at the instigation of King Kyanzittha of Pagan (1086–1112). Also in the 12th century the scholar-monk Aggavaṃsa wrote the *Saddanīti*, the most important work of traditional Pali grammar and philology. The textual revisions made by the Fifth and Sixth Councils have already been mentioned. That the texts have come down to us so accurately is also thanks to the monks' having learnt large sections of the holy scriptures by heart. A centuries-old system of monastic examination, by which ecclesiastical titles are conferred on those who can recite certain parts of the Canon or indeed the whole thing, exists to this day.

It is the study of the *Abhidhamma Piṭaka*, which represents to the Burmese the most exalted wisdom and knowledge, that enjoys the highest reputation in Burma. It is said of the three great Theravāda Buddhist countries that it is Sri Lanka that gives precedence to the study of the *Vinaya* and Thailand to that of the *Suttas*, and that Burma's special study is the *Abhidhamma*. Not only monks but many laymen take part in *Abhidhamma* classes. This wide interest in questions of systematic philosophy may well explain why ideology is, to Burmese Buddhists, of such paramount importance in politics and sociology.

Nowadays meditation is practised in Burma by monks as well as by large groups of laymen. The traditions of Buddhist meditation seem to have survived particularly well in Burma, and modern reformers have revived long-forgotten forms of meditation on the basis of the study of the scriptures. This is true, for example, of *satipaṭṭhāna*, the method used in the Sāsana Yeiktha Monastery in Rangoon. Many Buddhists from Europe and the United States visit Mahasi Sayadaw, the abbot of the monastery, to receive instruction in the practice of this form of meditation. Sunlun Sayadaw is another of many famous teachers of meditation.

The widespread custom in Burma whereby laymen may become members of a monastic community for a limited period explains the especially close link between the Sangha and the lay community. The Buddha is known to have left it to the members of the Sangha to withdraw from the Order at any time if they did not feel equal to the spiritual life. Anyone who left the Sangha of his own accord, and not because of an offence against the basic rules during his life as a monk, could be ordained again without difficulty. In Burma (as also in Thailand, Laos and Cambodia) this meant that every male Buddhist joined the Sangha at least once, but more often several times in his life for a limited time. When a boy was first admitted to a monastic community as a novice the *shinbyu* ceremony was celebrated with a great feast.

These customs have brought about some differences between Southeast Asian and Sri Lankan Buddhism. In the latter, because of social prejudices, it became very difficult to leave the Sangha, and the monks have developed into a kind of priestly caste. There is, of course, in Burma as elsewhere a special class of permanent monks who have a strong influence on the development of the internal relationships in the Sangha. But the fact that so many Burmese are temporarily members of the Sangha means that there is a considerable amount of interplay between the Sangha and the lay community, and that the religious experience of a large proportion of laymen is increased. Many Burmese prefer to enter the Sangha at certain times of the year, especially during the so-called Buddhist rainy season, and this results in the fluctuation in the total number of monks in the country, the average being around 120,000.

Women are at least partly excluded from these experiences, for the tradition of valid ordination of nuns is regarded as having ended in AD 456 in Theravāda Buddhist countries. Women cannot therefore be nuns (*bhikkhunī*) but only *meithila-shin*, lay members who have taken at least ten vows and who wear the monastic robe. Though the revival of Buddhism has brought more women and girls into this community of women ascetics than before, the number is still very limited.

The women of Burma play a special role in the Nat cults in which the pre-Buddhist religion of Burma survives. As in other Buddhist countries, the cults of deities and spirits were allowed to survive as long as their objectives were purely for this world, and not like the Buddhist religion concerned with the escape from the cycle of life, for such deities and spirits are thought to belong, like men, to the transitory world. Burmese popular deities are called Nats, and the various Nats are allocated to the different sections of society. There are Nats of the family, of the village, of the region, and, finally, of the nation. The holy mountain of the Nat cult is the extinct volcano Popa not far from Pagan, and a rock which lies before it has become a very important place of pilgrimage in Nat worship. To establish a link between these Burmese deities and the old mythology of canonical Buddhist texts, a thirty-seventh Nat, the Indian 'king of the gods' Thagya Min (Indra or Śakra) was set above the thirty-six national Nat deities.

The Nat cults have important social functions. They bind members of a family together and village communities to their home. Their origins can largely be found in social conflicts, for new Nat cults were created to avert the consequences of wrongs that had been committed. All thirty-six national Nats are tragic figures; thirty-five of them are deifications of people who died violent or at least unnatural deaths (most of them were murdered by Burmese rulers). Besides these there are the Nats who are tutelary gods of cities, pagodas, and so on. In earlier centuries it was not unusual to kill someone during the erection of large buildings and to bury them under the structure. The spirit of the dead person became a Nat to whom a cult was dedicated to protect the building. The most important priestly functions in the Nat cults were carried out by the mother of the family, but there were also professional Nat priestesses.

These cults are also connected with a system of astrology that is not unlike its Indian counterpart. The cult of tutelary gods for the various days of the week is particularly striking. Its statues are erected around such buildings as the larger pagodas.

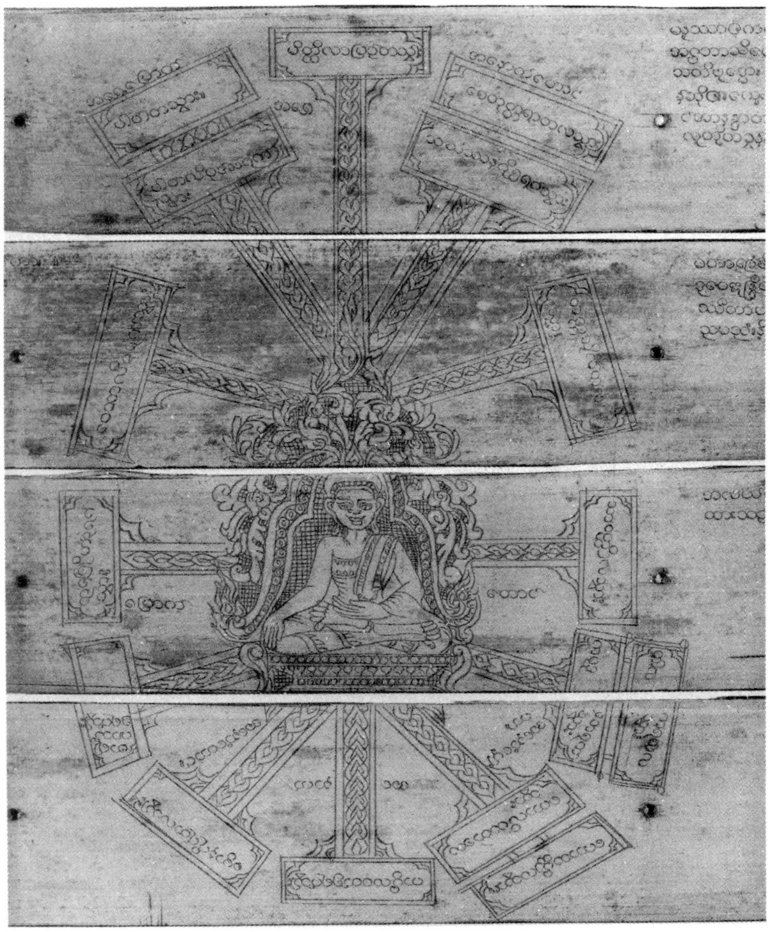

In this composite drawing, made up of four palm-leaves, the Buddha sits in the middle and the places associated with his life on earth are indicated in the panels around him. It was produced in Burma during the 19th century.

Buddhism and the Nat cults were able on the whole to coexist quite independently and peacefully because of their different objectives. According to the rules of their Order, monks were not supposed to take part in the cults of deities and spirits. Occasionally, however, difficulties did arise when Buddhist reformers objected to what they considered the excessive influence of the Nat cults, and sometimes they even demanded their complete abolition.

While the object of the Nat cults was purely that of material well-being or the aversion of dangers, the true aim of Buddhism always remained, at least in theory, the attainment of Nirvāṇa. But in practice this is much too remote and abstract an objective to be understood by the average Buddhist, monk or layman, or to be even his chief matter of concern. Religious practice concentrated therefore, much as in Sri Lanka, Thailand, etc., on the gaining of merit (*puñña*), and in this acquisition of merit the cooperation of monks and laymen plays an important part. The most usual Burmese name for a monk is therefore *pongyi*, i.e. he who has great merit and is the means for procuring it for others. An elder of the Order is given the honorary title of 'teacher' (*saya* or *sayadaw*). The everyday relationship between the Sangha and the lay population is characterized by copious gifts from laymen to the monks and monasteries, and invitations to the monks to take part in important functions such as funerals. In return the monks give religious addresses, especially formalized commentaries on the basic ethical laws, and readings of holy texts, and, above all, they carry out on important occasions and holy days the ceremonial recitation of the *Paritta* texts, deliver sermons, etc. In this way both acquire merit. Obeying the ethical laws is itself, of course, also a means of acquiring merit. The great majority of monks and laymen practise their religion in this way, but there are also some monks who concentrate completely, through asceticism and meditation, on *paṭipatti*, the way of redemption. Although the predominant view in the Theravāda Buddhist countries today is that it is impossible in our time to become an *arhat* (an enlightened person) in this world, there is still a belief in Burma that there are Buddhist saints in our century. U Kavi Mahathera, who died in 1952, is regarded as an *arhat*, and many Burmese believe that Webu Sayadaw, who died in 1977, was also a saint.

There is a widely held expectation in Burma of an imminent millennium. Since the 2500th anniversary in 1956 of the Buddha's Final Nirvāṇa (according to the Theravāda calendar) which was celebrated by the Sixth Buddhist Council, the arrival of a world saviour has been expected. This expectation of the imminent appearance of the next Buddha Maitreya and an ideal Buddhist ruler (the *cakravartin*) is very popular in Burma today. So-called *gaings*, cult-groups who await the arrival of the saviour, have been formed in a great number of places. Many *gaings* only share their knowledge with those whom they have taken into their community. They believe in the effectiveness of 'perfect' magicians (*bodaw*), who, like Bo Bo Aung and Bo Min Gaung have reached an incorporeal existence as *weiktha* or *zawgyi*. There are repeated reports of their miraculous appearances, and they are believed to live in a mysterious world until they attain Nirvāṇa after the coming of the next Buddha. The affinity of such teachings with the ideas of tantric Buddhism leads one to believe that the remains of the latter, superseded by the introduction of Theravāda in the 11th century, live on in these non-orthodox traditions. Other popular beliefs also confirm that Buddhist traditions from the time before the introduction of Theravāda continue, for example that of Shin Upagut, which is common in Burma and is a cult of Upagupta, the patriarch of the Sarvāstivāda School, who lived at the time of Aśoka. He is regarded in Burma as a giver of rain.

These beliefs and cults are mostly considered not to run counter to orthodox Theravāda today, and *gaing* cults are practised in many monasteries. Supernatural powers are attributed to some monks as they are to some abbots in Thailand, for example Shin Saddhammasiddhi, who lives near the holy mountain Popa. The undecayed body of one such miraculous abbot can be seen in the Alingahse temple in Rangoon.

Temples and monasteries

In Burma it was the Sangha that transmitted literary culture. It was not only a question of handing down the holy scriptures, but, to help the monks with the study of these scriptures, philological sciences like grammar, lexicography, metrics and rhetoric were cultivated. These disciplines, which were originally an Indian tradition, were developed independently and creatively by a great number of monks. Many Pali works were provided with Burmese commentaries or translated into Burmese, and hundreds of works of Buddhist literature were written in the Burmese language. Monks in particular had time and leisure to keep up this cultural tradition. It is their industry that has produced millions of manuscripts on palm leaves – Burmese Buddhist literature was not printed on paper until the end of the last century, and in the humid and hot climate it is not nearly as permanent as the prepared leaves of the fan-palm.

The monks passed on their knowledge to the people in the villages. As in ancient Sri Lanka, the monastery was the school for the children of the village, and for this reason the word *kyaung* (school) is still the most common Burmese name for monastic settlements. Reading and writing and basic religious knowledge were taught there, and the students were introduced to culture and the knowledge of life with the help of old

A standing Buddha, his feet resting on a lotus, made of lacquered and gilt wood in the Mandalay style. 19th century.

Two glazed terracotta panels of the 12th century, from the Ānanda Temple, Pagan, illustrating episodes from the jātaka stories, tales of the Buddha's previous existences that were immensely popular throughout Southeast Asia.

texts. One of the texts used was *Lokanīti* ('World Law'), a selection of Indian maxims, of which there were a great many.

Beside the old elementary schools attached to the monasteries, which were replaced by state schools during the colonial era, there is a purely monastic school system which to this day has looked after the preservation of traditional Buddhist scholarship in Burma. There are examinations to establish the students' attainments, and degrees are conferred on successful candidates. As we have seen, large sections of the canonical texts are often learned by heart.

There is an unusual characteristic of popular Burmese Buddhism which has contributed to the fact that there are more pagodas and temples in Burma than anywhere else in the world. It is a popular belief that the restoration of a religious building gains merit for the original founder and not for the donor of the restoration. Many pagodas were therefore preserved by the next generation of the family of the donor, but they were then allowed to fall into decay. In the relatively short era when Pagan flourished, thousands of temples were built, and the later capitals – Ava, Amarapura and Mandalay – are full of stupas, temples and monasteries, many of them half ruined. The same is true of many other parts of the country. The wealth of religious buildings contributes very much to the great beauty of Burma.

But the greatest national shrines of the country are always carefully looked after, restored, enlarged, and, above all, newly gilded. One of them is the Shwedagon pagoda in Rangoon which, according to old legends, was built over relics of the hair of the Buddha. Among the many temples of Pagan, the Ānanda pagoda, originally named not after the favourite disciple of the Buddha but after the symbol of his infinite (*ananta*) wisdom, is most deeply venerated. The most important place of pilgrimage in Mandalay is the Mahamuni pagoda. Its central figure of worship is a very old statue of the Buddha which was brought to Mandalay by King Bodawpaya in 1784 after the conquest of Arakan. The Kyaik-htiyo pagoda, which stands on an overhanging rock near the old city of Thaton, attracts many pilgrims. The list of famous temples and monasteries could be extended almost indefinitely, and the worship of the Buddha has found expression in countless works of art in all parts of Burma. Every important pagoda has an annual feast to commemorate its first consecration. The worship bestowed by the laity on statues of the Buddha exhibits traits reminiscent of the anthropomorphic practices of the worship of Hindu deities. For example, water is poured over statues of the Buddha in the hot season, symbolizing a refreshing bath.

The whole village community traditionally looks after its monks and the upkeep of its monasteries. The female inhabitants of the various parts of the town or village take turns in distributing alms-food, for in Burma most monks still go daily to beg for food. In larger towns, these tasks are nowadays carried out by various societies, so-called pagoda associations, who, as well as providing for the monasteries, are also in charge of the care and preservation of the larger shrines.

The Burmese form of Theravāda Buddhism was adopted early by the Shan, who belonged to the Thai peoples and can be found in the Burmese Shan states as well as in the frontier regions of China and Thailand. Burmese immigrants also founded monasteries in Lampang in Thailand. In the course of the last centuries several ethnic groups in the Indian federal states of Assam and Arunachal Pradesh were converted by Burmese missionaries. In the Chittagong district of East Bengal (now Bangladesh), the history of Theravāda Buddhism goes back at least to the 16th century. The Buddhists there are called Baruas. Though they form only a small minority amongst the predominantly Muslim Bengalis of the region, they have contributed considerably to the Buddhist revival in the late 19th century. Finally, the Magh (Arakanese immigrants) and the Chakmas who live in the Chittagong Hill Tracts district are also followers of the Burmese Theravāda tradition.

The Buddha's footprints (buddhapāda) have been from earliest times a symbol of his presence. Around them, especially in the Theravāda countries, cults developed, becoming increasingly elaborate and monumental. This stone slab from northern Burma, over a metre long, is covered with the 108 signs of good omen with which, according to traditional lore, the soles of the Buddha's feet were imprinted. It was carved in the 19th century.

7

The Way of the Monk and the Way of the World: Buddhism in Thailand, Laos and Cambodia

JANE BUNNAG

THERAVĀDA BUDDHISM IS THE STATE RELIGION of Thailand, as it has been until very recently of Laos and Cambodia. In all these countries it is the religion of the great majority of the population, and to be Buddhist has been considered a badge of national identity.

The source and sequence of religious influences in the area known as Thailand are much debated; I have outlined below the trends about which there appears to be general agreement.

Buddhism comes to Thailand and Laos

The original inhabitants of Thailand were the Mons; their cultural centres were at Lvo or Lopburi and further south at Dvaravati, in what is now central Thailand. Archaeological remains of cult buildings and religious objects clearly show contact with Indian Brahminism and Buddhism. Buddhism seems to have been the more popular and widespread, although portrayals of the Hindu gods Brahmā, Indra, Gaṇeśa and Viṣṇu have also been found. This may indicate that aspects of Vaiṣṇavism and Śaivism also flourished within the Dvaravati type of Buddhism.

In the reign of King Sūryavarman of Angkor (AD 1010–50) the plains of central Siam came under Cambodian domination, which lasted in full force for over two centuries and in attenuated form for about a century more. It is clear from Buddhist temples and statues found in Lopburi and in other western provinces of (then) Cambodia that Mahāyāna Buddhist and Hindu influences were rather strong during these centuries. It was at that time that the Thais slowly moved from their home in southern China into most parts of present-day Thailand (Siam), Laos and the Shan hills of eastern Burma. Their descendants are the Siamese (central Thai), the Thai Yüan (northern Thai) and the Lao and the Shan peoples. All these groups gradually accepted Theravāda Buddhism, most probably under the influence of the earlier Mon inhabitants of the country where they settled.

In about 1260, the kingdom of Sukhotai freed itself from Khmer overlordship. King Rāma Khamheng (*c.* 1275–1317) made Theravāda the official religion in his kingdom. His stone inscription of 1292 is the oldest document written in the Thai script, which was developed from Khmer writing.

The grandson of Rāma Khamheng, Lü Thai (acceded as viceroy *c.* 1340, as king 1347), invited monks famous for their learning and austerity from Ceylon (some of them coming through lower Burma) to strengthen the purity of the Thai Sangha. The successive visits of Sinhalese monks not only gave a great fillip to learning in Pali literature both sacred and secular, but also gave Buddhism in Sukhotai a church organization or government on the Sinhalese model.

The heritage of Sukhotai was taken over by the Thai kingdom of Ayudhya, which existed from 1350 until 1767. During that time Cambodia became a dependency of the Thai kings, but the Thais themselves were deeply influenced by Khmer culture. A good deal of the customs and ritual later labelled 'court Brahminism' probably dates back to the reign of King Trailok (1442–87), who re-organized his kingdom's administration on the model of Angkor.

Other kings of Ayudhya also concerned themselves with affairs of the Sangha. Songdharm (1610–28) was interested in safeguarding the purity of the canon and made a royal edition of the *tri-piṭaka*; he also built near Saraburi a shrine to the footprints of the Buddha which still draws pilgrims both monk and lay.

In the reign of Maha Dhammarāja II (1733–58) Buddhist culture seems to have flowered in Ayudhya, producing a bloom the fame of which reached Ceylon. The Sinhalese king Kīrti Śrī sent three missions to Ayudhya in about 1750 to bring Siamese monks to his kingdom to give ordination to Ceylonese monks. Of these three missions only the last was successful. It was warmly received by the king, who sent a delegation of monks to Ceylon under Phra Upāli. The monks remained in Ceylon for three years and in 1753 ordained monks who formed the nucleus of the sect known as the Siyam Nikāya (see p. 144).

In 1767 the city and the kingdom of Ayudhya were destroyed by Burmese invaders, but King Taksin (1767–82) restored Thailand's independence. He made Thonburi, on the Menam river, his new capital city. He was, however, dethroned by the first king of the present Chakri dynasty, Rāma I (1782–1809) who moved the capital across the river to Bangkok. Both these rulers initiated reforms of the Sangha and they caused a collection of the scriptures to be made. Rāma I also

Part of the inscription of the Thai King Rama Khamheng, dating from 1292. The script is a modified form of Khmer. All four sides of a stela are taken up with the inscription, which bears witness to the predominance of Theravāda Buddhism in 13th-century Thailand.

issued regulations for rituals in order to ensure that such practices did not contravene Buddhist tenets.

The greatest reformer of Thai Buddhism was, however, King Rāma IV or Mongkut (1851–68) who had been a *bhikkhu* (monk) for 27 years before he became the king of Siam. When he was still a monk, he started a reformist group in the Sangha which was called Dhammayuttika-Nikāya and followed a stricter discipline than the majority of the Sangha, which was called Mahānikāya. When Mongkut became king, the Mahānikāya was also subjected to a thorough reform. After that, state and religion in Thailand became even more closely associated than before, and attempts have been made to justify government policy by Buddhist principles, e.g. when the Supreme Patriarch made an allocution to explain Siam's entry into the First World War in 1917.

The earliest traces of Buddhist influence in Laos date back to the 12th century, but it was only with the creation of the kingdom of Laos around 1350 that Theravāda became the official religion. The man who accomplished this coalescence of several small states into one kingdom, Fa Ngum, is said to have been brought up at the Angkor court and to have married the daughter of King Jayavarman Parameśvara (1327–*c.* 1353). It is said that Jayavarman, in whose time Cambodia had come under the influence of Siamese monks, exhorted his son-in-law to rule his kingdom according to Buddhist principles, and sent to him a party of monks bearing the Pali scriptures and a Ceylonese statue of the Buddha, called the Luang Prabang. This statue was installed at Fa Ngum's residence at Muong Swa, which is now called Luang Prabang after this image. Theravāda has remained the religion of the Lao people ever since.

When the Communists took over in Laos in 1975, the Sangha lost its traditional influence. It seems, however, that at least some of the monasteries are still allowed to exist, though under various restrictions. The aged Supreme Patriarch of Laos fled across the Mekong river into Thailand in 1979; soon afterwards the government declared a new policy under which the Sangha is expected to provide support and validation for the new political order.

Buddhism in Cambodia

Cambodia – an area of seventy thousand square miles in the Mekong valley – has a sparse population of which the Khmers make up seventy per cent. Ethnically related to the Mons of Burma and Siam, the Khmers were the makers of Cambodian history.

The story of Cambodia for the nine centuries prior to the abandonment of Angkor in 1431 has been reconstructed by the patient labours of French scholars and archaeologists. The Khmers themselves had no tradition of historiography and left no chronicles like those of Ceylon or Burma. The events of the six centuries when Angkor was capital of Cambodia are, however, amply documented by the large number of stone inscriptions found there.

Together with Burma and Thailand, Cambodia is part of that large area of Southeast Asia in which Indian cultural influence was the sociologically dominant and formative force. The states within this bloc have been described by Coedès as 'Hinduized States'. Their ancient kings bore Sanskrit names; their government and administration followed the norms of Hindu polity and Brahminical jurisprudence. In these states Brahminism and Mahāyāna Buddhism appear to have flourished, but later on Theravāda Buddhism became predominant.

Much of the considerable resources of Cambodia in its heyday was spent in glorifying and maintaining the so-called *devarāja* ('divine king') cult in which the ruler was identified with the god. Large sums were used for temple building, for maintaining enormous numbers of attendants for rituals, for elaborate ceremonial and the upkeep of seminaries and places of religious learning. Most of these elements of Cambodian civilization were derived from Hindu India. According to one theory the *devarāja* cult was introduced by Jayavarman II early in the 9th century.

Several of the kings of Angkor professed Mahāyāna Buddhism in its Indian form, which seems to have been merged both conceptually and in its ritual with Hindu Brahminical religion. In the inscriptions left by these Angkor kings the Buddha is often invoked along with Brahminical deities. The Angkor pantheon was a mixture of Hindu and Buddhist deities and deified persons, exemplified by the Devarāja. The temples which enshrined these religious beliefs are breathtaking. The most famous are Phra Viharn, Angkor Wat, and the Bayon. But the drain on the country's resources caused by building and maintaining these and numerous other temples was eventually disastrous. The last of them were built at the close of the 14th century. All the state's resources both human and material had been channelled to this end, and the resultant social injustice gave rise to two serious revolts during the 'classic' period of Angkor. Cambodia was ripe for the egalitarian teaching of Theravāda Buddhism.

The date of the beginning of Cambodia's conversion to Theravāda Buddhism is not known, although it is first documented by an inscription in a private temple conjecturally dated AD 1230 in the reign of Indravarman II. The religion's progress in the country is obscure, but once introduced it appears to have made vigorous headway among the common folk of Cambodia. King Jayavarman Parameśvara came to the throne in 1327, embraced the new religion, and Sanskrit was replaced by Pali as the language of religious rituals and sacred texts.

It has been assumed by many that Siamese monks were the pioneers of Theravāda in Cambodia, although this cannot be verified. Later on, there were close connections between Buddhists of both countries, and in 1864 the Dhammayuttika-Nikāya was introduced from Siam as a reformist group within the Sangha. A hierarchy was instituted in the Sangha after the model of Siam.

When the Khmer Rouge took over in 1975, traditional Khmer Buddhism was completely destroyed and most monks were murdered. It was only after the Vietnamese invasion in 1979 that religious life was allowed again and a few monasteries were reopened.

Sangha and State

A distinctive feature of traditional Buddhism in Thailand, Cambodia and Laos is the organization of the Sangha as a national institution virtually under State control. In Thailand, for example, the first Administration of the Buddhist Order Act, which came into force in 1902, during the reign of Rāma V, stated that religious affairs were as important as the administration of the state, 'in that systematically administered they will be sure to attract more people to the study and practice of Buddhism under the guidance of Buddhism, thereby leading them to the right mode of living, in accordance with the Buddha's instructions'.

Following this legislation a hierarchy of ecclesiastical offices was created along the lines of the Thai civil administration. The Supreme Patriarch stands at the apex of the ecclesiastical pyramid, but the king has the final authority and appoints the Patriarch.

The civil authorities therefore have ultimate right of control over and intervention in Sangha affairs. Conversely a strong and respected Sangha is regarded as an indication and affirmation of the king's role as Defender of the Faith. One result of this close association and identification is that in times of political crisis in these societies millennial movements have emerged, led by monks themselves, which have sought to establish – or re-establish – utopia in place of the prevailing chaos. It is only at such times of crisis, however, that the Buddhist lay public would accept militant action by monks.

This institutionalization has some important implications for the role and function of the Sangha in each of these countries, which may to some extent distinguish the monks of Thailand, Laos and Cambodia from their brothers in Burma and Sri Lanka.

One important consequence is that study and understanding of the Dhamma or Word of the Buddha, leading ultimately to Enlightenment, has also been institutionalized and is measured by success or failure in the ecclesiastical examination system. This in its turn leads to laying less emphasis on non-measurable spiritual activities such as meditation.

This is not to say that there have not been charismatic monks who have tried to promote a new interpretation of the Buddha's Word, but the position of such leaders is precarious, as the civil authorities have the power to disrobe a monk whom they regard as offensive or disruptive.

Since King Mongkut's above-mentioned reform the Sangha consists of two sections, the Mahānikāya ('Great Group') and the Dhammayuttika-Nikāya or Reform Group. What distinguishes these two factions is not doctrine but the strictness with which they interpret the basic rules of conduct laid down in the *Vinaya* and the different emphasis they give to various facets of the role of the monk. As a whole the monks of the Reform Group place greater emphasis on study and meditation in the quest for Nirvāṇa and less on pastoral and parish activities than do their brothers in the Mahānikāya.

In terms of outward appearance the monks of the two nikāyas are normally indistinguishable. The emblems originally adopted by the Reform Nikāya, namely particular ways of carrying a begging bowl and of wearing the robes, have largely been abandoned in favour of more comfortable and convenient earlier practices.

The practical implications of this rationalization of the Sangha in Thailand have been aptly summed up by Yoneo Ishii in his article 'Church and State in Thailand' (in *Asian Survey*, vol. 8, 1968), and similar observations would doubtless hold true for Laos and Cambodia. Ishii writes that:

> The adoption of this system to give the monks an official status by State examinations helped to strengthen the State control of the monks. This system, which aimed at deepening the monks' knowledge of Buddhism, enforced a sort of orthodoxy by banning free interpretations of the Buddhist doctrines which are liable to bring about schism within the Buddhist Order. Thus the Thai monks' understanding of Buddhism became stereotyped and the monks' subjugation to the state was strengthened.

Today the political prominence of Thailand, Laos and Cambodia has rendered them vulnerable to the kind of journalistic half-exposure which disseminates misinformation. The Buddhist monk with his shaven head and eyebrows and saffron robe has been an obvious 'case for treatment'! The interpretation of his role and the understanding of 'religious' commitment for a Theravāda Buddhist society have been peculiarly difficult for Western observers to grasp. Buddhist monks have been variously expected to be more numerous, more ascetic, more political, more inflammatory and more inflammable than is in fact the case. The rest of this chapter will show how and why the Buddhist monk in Southeast Asia can be both sacred and accessible; and how the transition from sacred to profane need require little in the way of qualification or preparation. And we shall look at the tension and potentialities for power-play that the interdependence of monk and layman creates. Without attempting to look for causal relationships or to draw facile parallels between religious ethics and social behaviour, knowledge of Theravāda Buddhism and its social implementation does help us to understand other aspects of the societies concerned.

According to orthodox Theravāda Buddhism, only a monk – which is to say a man who has given up secular society – can have any hope, though far from a guarantee, of achieving Nirvāṇa. The layman who remains rooted in the material world can entertain no aspirations to reach Nirvāṇa in this life. In practice, it seems that few monks consider Nirvāṇa a realistic goal, and tend to limit their ambitions to achieving a better rebirth by doing good and avoiding evil, by making merit and avoiding the reverse.

The primary merit-making activity is the study of the Word of the Buddha – the Buddhist scriptures. The monk avoids demerit by observing the religious rules of the *Vinaya*, which define his role and conduct very precisely. Pastoral services provide a second source of merit-making which in theory is much less important, although in many cases it becomes the primary activity.

For laymen, Buddhism provides a special but much less exacting ethical code contained in essence in the Five Precepts (see p. 54) which he should observe if he is to avoid demerit. The layman's store of merit towards his future rebirth is increased by his performing various charitable activities, the most rewarding of which is to support materially those members of society – namely the monks – who have renounced the material world.

The theory of *karman* (see p. 11) provides a very general causal theory for the vicissitudes of life, but a theory far too general to be entirely satisfactory. At no time does an individual know what his merit balance is nor when the results of his actions, good or bad, will take effect.

However, as in all cosmic systems, there are alternative theories of causation – chance, luck and so on – which supplement the 'official' system of causation. In the Theravāda Buddhist societies with which we are presently concerned, Hindu and animistic elements to some extent have this function. With regard to the theological position, it is interesting to see that the Buddha did not deny the existence of the deities of the Hindu pantheon, nor of ghosts, spirits and other supernatural phenomena, but simply regarded them as irrelevant to the pursuit of Nirvāṇa and therefore a hindrance to Enlightenment. In theory monks should have no truck with unorthodox or non-Buddhist religious elements. In practice, however, many of the most famous and credible astrologers and fortune-tellers are monks, although there is a line on the religious-magical spectrum beyond which few monks would be willing to go. Monks rarely have dealings with house-spirits or with seances and rites of exorcism associated with animistic beliefs. It must be admitted, nevertheless, that they may implicitly sanction non-Buddhist practices on the part of their parishioners in the course of their activities. They often appear to maintain a dual standard, in that they give their tacit approval to religious behaviour which in reality they consider to be inefficacious. For example, scattered throughout these countries are shrines housing replicas of the Buddha's footprint, and it is commonly believed that frequent visits to these shrines reduce or eliminate the risk of going to Hell, regardless of one's bad actions. Most monks, in fact, spend the majority of their time performing merit-making rituals for laymen at critical points in the life cycle. The basic ritual elements of these ceremonies – lustral water and the sacred thread – are clearly non-Buddhist.

The life of the monk

The role or 'job-description' of the Buddhist monk is defined by the 227 rules of the *pāṭimokkha*, which order his behaviour in all its aspects from rules of sexual conduct to table manners. One of the most significant differences between a monk and his lay counterparts is that sexual activity of any kind is forbidden to the monk on pain of immediate expulsion from the Order. This does not mean that married men or widowers cannot be ordained but it does mean that they must remain celibate while in the Order. Women, as the source of sexual temptation, constitute the chief obstacle to remaining a good monk. Curiously, though in theory regarded as being a difficult rule to observe, in practice it seems to be no more difficult or tiresome than abstaining from one's evening meal – an object-lesson in different cultural expectations of sexual activity. Of course if the saffron robe becomes 'too hot' the monk can and should rejoin the lay world. It is better to become a good layman than to remain a bad monk, and a man is honoured for staying in the Order for a long time, rather than stigmatized for leaving it.

A second major austerity relates to dietary practice, the rule being that monks should take no nourishment after midday. The first meal is taken at around seven a.m., after the monk has collected his food from the householders on his begging-round, and the second meal is timed to finish just before noon. After this time he is allowed to smoke or chew betel or to drink liquids which are unsweetened or which do not contain milk. In practice this often means that the monk takes liquid to which he has not himself added either sugar or milk, so that, for instance, Coca Cola and manufactured drinks are not prohibited.

A third criterion separating the way of the monk from the way of the world is pivotal. The monk does not earn his living but subsists on presentations of food made by householders who live along the route he takes on his daily alms-round. At some of the larger monasteries, charitable funds have been established to provide food for the community throughout the year. This relieves the inhabitants of the real need to go on the alms-giving round, but they may still continue this activity for its symbolic significance. The monk should not handle or own worldly things, in particular money, nor should he cultivate the soil for fear of damaging organisms within it. Furthermore his primary function vis-à-vis the layman is to give the latter the opportunity to make merit by accepting 'alms' – food and the basic

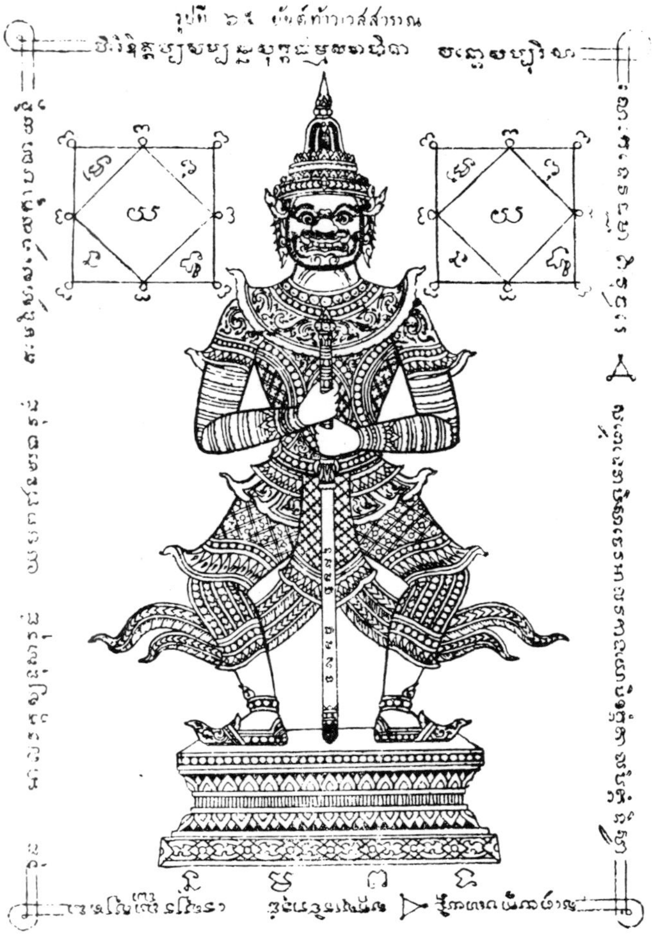

Vessavana, lord of the benevolent demons – a good luck amulet put on a child's cradle to protect it. The script is Cambodian.

necessities of life. Thus there is a basic conflict in the monk's position, the resolution of which is the integrating factor in monk-layman relations. The further implications of this paradox will be explored below. Suffice it to say here that monks must be very circumspect in their dealing with worldly possessions; they are obliged to accept them since in so doing they confer merit on the giver, but they themselves must maintain a distance, whenever possible sharing the benefits of goods received by making them common property of the monastery. In addition to the Eight Requisites (see p. 56) most monks own such items as a quilt, pillow, mosquito net, umbrella and eating utensils. Beyond this, a monk's collection of worldly artefacts – which can include even cars and refrigerators – is largely a function of the regard in which he is held by the laity.

The monk's special station in society is most visibly marked by his saffron robe, and by his shaving off his hair and eyebrows at his ordination and once each month thereafter. Monks are also expected to be more dignified in deportment than laity. Indeed the rules of the *pāṭimokkha* enjoin him not to 'eat stuffing out the cheeks like a monkey' nor to 'sit laughing loudly in inhabited areas'. The significance of correct outward behaviour cannot be overemphasized, as many monks owe their eminence more to their conformity to this stereotype of the calm and passive monk than to their knowledge of the scriptures or their preaching skills.

The superior status of the monk over the layman is acknowledged in many ways. One is by linguistic usage: there are terms of address and reference used only for and by monks in Thai, Lao and Cambodian, as well as a special vocabulary of terms to describe ordinary actions – eating, washing, sleeping – when performed by monks. Laymen and women accord to all monks of whatever age or seniority special forms of greeting, and women – as the official major obstacles to a man's renunciation of the world – must be particularly circumspect and avoid all physical contact even of an indirect nature. One implication of this avoidance is that a woman who has to pass any object – a book or a glass of water – to a monk must do this indirectly by placing it on a cloth which he carries for the purpose. Furthermore on all trains and buses special seats are reserved for monks to minimize the risk of their having physical contact with female passengers. This ban on physical contact with women should not however be misunderstood and overemphasized. It does not prevent women from making daily food offerings to monks or from attending ceremonies at the monastery.

Entering the Sangha

Who are the men able and willing to assume this most prestigious role in society? How much flexibility is allowed for different interpretations of that role and what are the implications of those differences for an individual monk's relations with laypeople?

One very important point to be borne in mind is that although 'monastic vows' can be taken for life, they need not be so. Many young men go into the monastery prior to marriage, for one 'rainy' season – July–October – in order to become 'ripe' adults. These men naturally have only a limited period of service in mind, though some of them may stay longer than they at first intended.

On the basis of national statistical estimates it would appear that on average during the 'rainy' period approximately 1 per cent of the total male population is ordained and resident in a monastery. However, anywhere between 25 and 40 per cent of those may be considered temporary and due to leave at the end of the season. It is probable that approximately half of the adult male population in any of these countries has spent *some* time at least in the monastery.

Other men may enter the Order for a variety of reasons – advancing age, unhappy marriage and other vicissitudes of life as well as interest in the spiritual aspects of monkhood – and may have no very clear idea when they will leave the Order, if they plan to leave at all. As we have seen, there is absolutely no stigma attached to leaving the Order – indeed having been a monk has a 'halo effect' which is carried over into lay life, bringing prestige to the ex-monk.

Do the procedures of entry into the Order to any extent constitute a mechanism of selection, serving to limit entry to a particular type of monk? The candidate for ordination requires the backing of a number of lay people. The ceremony requires that he be provided with the material paraphernalia necessary for a monk – the Eight Requisites and other objects of daily use mentioned above – and that the appropriate offering of money and goods (typically toothpaste, soap-powder, books, writing materials etc.) be provided for the monks who officiate at the ceremony.

The spiritual or educational requirements for entry into this most prestigious role are minimal. The candidate must complete a form – to be countersigned by three other laymen – which guarantees that he is twenty years of age or over and in good health; that he is not in debt or guilty of any crime; and that his parents and his wife, if he has one, have given their consent. He is expected in addition to be able to read and write so that he can at the very least pursue the ecclesiastical study courses available. The candidate's preparedness is very generally measured by his ability to learn the Pali responses that he must make during the ceremony, though vigorous prompting throughout by an older and more experienced relative is by no means unknown. The ordination ceremony, then, constitutes a mechanism for selection in that it requires public affirmation and the approval of a number of laymen, but the demands on the ordinand are not great and neither his intellectual ability nor his spiritual commitment are very severely screened.

What of the reverse conditions? Are there any factors that might make this role more attractive to some men than to others? Here we leave aside those young men for whom entry into the monkhood is openly a *rite de passage* prior to achieving adult status, and the very old who have retired into the Sangha.

The interesting feature about the monkhood in this regard is that it can and does provide a channel of mobility for ambitious individuals on the lower rungs of the social ladder. In addition to the other benefits associated with becoming a monk it is also possible through being ordained to receive a first-rate education in lay as well as religious subjects, which can then be turned to advantage in the lay world. Joining the monkhood can, in essence, be a way of stepping into the 'fast lane' of social mobility, giving individuals from poor rural backgrounds educational opportunities which enable them to rejoin lay society at a higher level than the one they were born to. Some individuals may manipulate the system more consciously than others.

As mentioned above, a certain degree of structural tension is inherent in the institutionalization of the ascetic way of life: the religious mendicant's abstinence from worldly activity renders him permanently dependent for his material subsistence upon those who remain in the world. The monk, who has renounced the world in order to strive for Enlightenment, often spends the best part of his time, willingly or unwillingly, ministering to the spiritual needs of the surrounding lay community.

To examine this assertion more closely, let us regard the monk's role as having three main facets: personal, monastic and pastoral.

Personal aspects of the monk's role

Those activities which are most centrally entailed in becoming a monk – at least according to the ideal – namely the study of and meditation upon the Pali texts, form the *personal* category of actions. According to Buddhist doctrine, study and meditation are progressive steps on the path to Nirvāṇa or Enlightenment, in that techniques of meditation are used to gain insights into teachings which have been absorbed intellectually. In practical terms the decision whether to pursue these personal activities at all, and to what level, rests with each individual monk. Many monks regard meditation, in theory the primary activity, as less important than the study of the Pali texts – perhaps because the latter is more easily assessed in terms of academic degrees and certificates, and therefore more concrete and provable. Many Thai monks have exhibited a kind of male chauvinism about meditation, regarding it as something more appropriate to nuns, magicians (*saiyasat*) or pilgrims (*thudong* monks).

We must here discuss the custom of making pilgrimages to Buddhist shrines, though it is marginal to the monastic vocation. The Thai word *thudong* is derived from the Pali term *dhutaṅga* meaning 'austere practices', of which there are thirteen mentioned in classical texts on discipline (see p. 81 above). In Thailand the term is most commonly used to refer to those monks who leave the monastery and go on foot to visit the various Buddhist shrines scattered throughout the country. During this period the monk observes the *Vinaya* code with more than usual austerity, which means in particular that he takes only one meal each day and eats it directly from his alms bowl without discrimination. At night he sleeps in the open under a large umbrella-like shelter (*krot*) which is equipped with a mosquito-net and can be folded for carrying on his back during the day. It is usual for two or three monks to *doen thudong* (go on pilgrimage) together, though they would talk to each other as little as possible, proceeding in single file along the road and separating each night to pitch camp so that each can meditate in solitude.

Interestingly enough, in the highly institutionalized monastic systems under consideration here, there is much ambivalence towards the monk who renounces the system, however temporarily. Conventionally the pilgrim is admired as an exceptional individual capable of enduring the loneliness and physical hardship of journeys of up to several hundred miles, punctuated by sedentary interludes of up to four or five days at each shrine on the itinerary. Nevertheless, few monks will admit to, or freely talk about their experiences as *dhutaṅga* monks. In some sense the *dhutaṅga* monk –

Prints like this are widespread in Southeast Asia as amulets to bring good fortune. This cosmogram has the Buddhist wheel in the centre and eight Buddhist arhats, or saints, presiding over the points of the compass.

whose way of life in theory corresponds most closely to the mendicant ideal of the early Buddhists – is regarded with suspicion. Neither belonging to lay society nor being properly integrated into the monastic community, *dhutaṅga* monks are in danger of being equated with tramps, beggars and other social derelicts.

Traditionally the season for monks to *doen thudong* in Thailand, Laos and Cambodia is during February and March when they leave their monasteries to pay their respects at one or more of the well-known places of pilgrimage. Laymen and women also take 'day trips' by road and rail to various shrines – footprint shrines may be particularly appropriate – to offer candles and incense-sticks to images of the Buddha and to press small squares of gold leaf to their surfaces. Particularly pious householders visit monks encamped in special parks in the vicinity of the shrines and make merit by presenting them with food. Among lay people, however, the *dhutaṅga* role is not highly respected and consequently attracts monks with relatively little interest in earning the good opinion of society. *Thudong* monks encountered by the author seem to be of two main types: elderly men who have retired into the Order; and younger, probably relatively uncommitted, monks out on a spree. It is nevertheless interesting that the religious action which it is most difficult, if not impossible, for an outsider to measure – namely

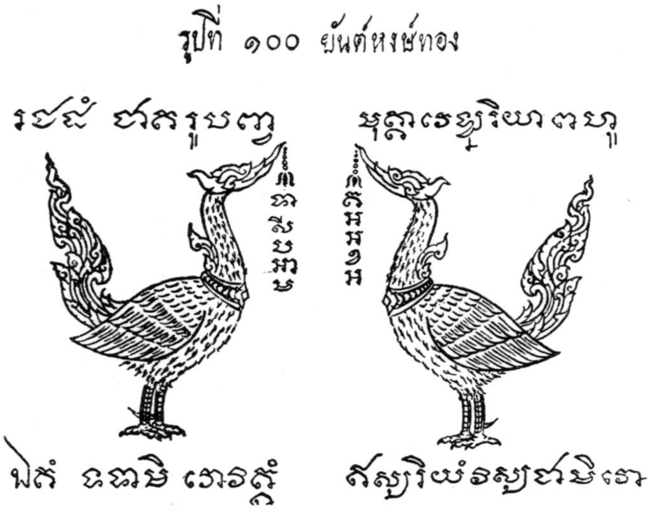

Another amulet for obtaining one's wishes: two mythical birds called haṃsas carry garlands of letters in their mouths.

meditation – is often regarded as being the special domain of monks who occupy a somewhat ambivalent position, either because they *doen thudong*, and thus temporarily are not clearly located spatially or hierarchically, or else because they specialize in other unorthodox techniques, such as healing and astrology.

An interesting development in recent years, however, particularly noticeable in Thailand, is that monks are leaving the official monastery and monastic structures and setting up simpler communities in remote rural areas where more emphasis is given to meditation and a life of austerity. The Venerable Buddhadāsa, who established Suan Mokkha (meaning the Forest of Liberation) in Chaiya, Province of Surat Thani, Southern Siam, is one of the most famous of the Thai monks who have tried to return to a simpler way of life. It may be significant that he views another current, but opposite, development of the monks – namely their role in social work and community development – with complete disfavour. In an interview in 1967 he said: 'I entirely disagree with the idea [of social work]. Monks should concern themselves with helping people to develop *spiritually*. . . . They must not be involved in making material things for people themselves, but should be the protection of people from unhappiness. . . . Man is usually defeatist – defeated by greed or love of gain. . . . Monks should not directly go in and help him in his work, but should make him wise in fighting against greed and delusion. . . . This is an incomparable service to him, far better than a monk who applies for a job in social work or joins in such work as kitchen gardening.'

The other main activity to be characterized as 'personal' – the study of the Dhamma – is more amenable to institutionalization and external measurement of success than is meditation. Indeed, an essential part of the institutionalization of the Sangha in all the countries under discussion is the establishment of an examination system which charts progress in the study of the Word of the Buddha – as well as covering secular topics.

There are two basic levels of ecclesiastical examinations. The syllabus of the first covers such topics as the previous lives of the Buddha, the basic tenets of his teaching, and the rules of conduct set out in the Monastic Code (the *Vinaya Piṭaka*). This course of study is designed to inculcate a general Buddhist education rather than to produce scholars of a high standard of academic expertise. Students of the higher level are required to study Pali and Sanskrit as well as to acquire some familiarity with the doctrinal issues debated in the Pali scriptures. Honorific titles and insignia in the form of fans serve to indicate success in these examinations, which continues to have a 'halo' effect should the student return to the lay world. Prestige is assured and often also employment in the civil service for the well-educated monk.

Monastic aspects of the monk's role

Monastic communities in Laos, Thailand and Cambodia can number anything from five to several hundred inhabitants. The basic categories are monks (permanent and temporary), novices, monastery boys and in a few cases nuns.

The larger and more prosperous monasteries are usually found in urban areas; in addition to being places of pilgrimage housing relics and Buddha images, they may also have attached to them schools for monks and novices or even universities where secular as well as religious subjects are taught. Monasteries which have teaching facilities normally house a higher proportion of novices and young monks eager to study, and because of their usually superior accommodation may provide hostel space for temple boys from outlying areas who are attending schools in town. On the other hand, and especially in rural areas outside the 'rainy' season (mid-July to October), some monasteries may be little more than hostels for elderly men who have taken refuge from the world in their declining years. During these months most communities swell in size to accommodate temporary monks or novices.

What are the implications for the individual monk of belonging to a monastic community? What are the privileges and what are the constraints? According to the Administration of the Sangha Acts, all monks must be attached to a monastery and have permanent residence, and before ordination a man must obtain permission from the abbot of his chosen monastery to take up residence there. A number of factors may influence a man's choice: he does not by any means always enter the monastery nearest to his house. He may decide on the basis of educational or other facilities offered by that monastery; or because it is the residence of a talented or well-known monk or someone he knows.

The residence of any monk is recorded on the identity card with which he is issued on ordination. During the 'rains', a period of intensified religious activity, a monk must spend every night in his monastery if he is to count that season towards his seniority in the Order.

Outside the official rainy season, however, there is considerable movement between monasteries both for pleasure and for educational and other official purposes. *Dhutaṅga* monks, as we have seen, may leave the community altogether and go on pilgrimages to visit shrines throughout the country. Moreover it is easy for a monk to change his permanent residence; this is an essential part of upward mobility through the Sangha.

The abbot is the head of a monastery, which is the smallest unit of ecclesiastical administration. The degree of control he has in that community varies very considerably, and is largely dependent on his personal interpretation of his very broad mandate. His primary responsibility is to grant or refuse permission to individual monks or novices to live in the *wat* (or monastery), or to transfer residence. He should also be informed if any monk intends to stay away from the *wat* for a long period of time, and may allow a monk to be absent from the *wat* for up to seven days during the rainy season under special circumstances. Beyond this he may be involved in the instruction of the newly ordained, and in such matters as settling the monks' routes on the alms-giving circuit.

The abbot is responsible for ensuring that communal acts of the Sangha are conducted at appropriate times, especially those that reaffirm community adherence to the Rules of the Order. The most important of these services is the recitation of the *pāṭimokkha* held on *uposatha* day (see above p. 57). Perhaps most important, the abbot provides the link between his community and the outside world, i.e. the higher ecclesiastical authorities and the lay community. Degrees of authority among other monks depend largely on age and seniority of ordination. In larger monasteries the residents may be organized into formal or informal groups centred on senior monks, although this means a certain delegation or duplication of the abbot's domestic authority. For instance, the senior monk in such a group may have charge of the instruction of the junior members; decide on their alms-giving rounds; provide them with places to sleep; or share with them donations of food or goods received from the laity.

Boys are often enlisted to handle cash transactions for individual monks, for example, in the market or when travelling, and in a similar way a committee consisting of the abbot, several leading laymen and one or more junior monks is normally established to handle monastery property. Like the temple boy for the individual monk, the monastery committee provides for the community a partial solution to some of the problems inherent in the institutionalization of the Sangha, handling financial affairs from which monks should remain aloof.

The monastery is also a centre of religious activity for the lay community. On *uposatha* days for example, many lay people visit their local monastery to pay their respects to the Buddha image there and to give the monks food for their morning meal. On these days particularly devout householders may spend the night at the monastery, usually sleeping on the floor in one of the pavilions. For the duration of Holy Day they undertake to observe three precepts or commandments additional to the five normally adhered to by Buddhist laymen: not to use jewellery or cosmetics to adorn their bodies; not to sleep on a bed or a soft couch; and, most importantly, not to take an evening meal.

These Eight Precepts are also observed as a matter of routine by the so-called Buddhist nuns. There are no ordained nuns in the strict sense of the word, because the tradition of the ordination of nuns has been lost in Theravāda countries (see p. 155) so that they may be regarded as belonging to the lay rather than to the religious section of society. There is no nation-wide hierarchical organization of nuns in any of the countries under consideration. But it is the practice for small groups of nuns to take up residence in the outlying buildings of certain monasteries where they normally perform some domestic duties – cleaning and cooking – for the monks.

Pastoral aspects of the monk's role

Let us now examine the monk's pastoral activities. These consist essentially of transactions between the monk and the householder by which the monk confers merit upon the layman, and the layman in turn expresses his gratitude and respect by offerings of money, food and other items both mundane (toothpaste, washing powder etc.) and ritual (candles, lotus-buds). Sometimes the layman gives land. Monks are, however, not allowed to cultivate land themselves because agriculture involves killing small organisms.

Obeyesekere has discussed the tension inherent in the condition of the *thudong bhikkhu*, the monk who tries to 'escape from the society of the monastery by isolating himself from the world. ... Pious laymen are attracted by the special charisma which surrounds these monks and pursue them with gifts of alms, attempt to build living quarters for them and so on.' But this tension is indeed inherent in the monkly role as a whole.

For the layman, the highest ethical value is placed upon giving without thought for oneself; it is therefore felt to be more meritorious to give alms to monks with whom one has no personal ties or to a group of monks or the monastic community as a whole without discrimination than to monks who are also relatives or friends.

This ideal of impersonal giving is perhaps most fully realized in that quintessential act of alms-giving, the daily presentation of rice to the monks. Each monastery has several alms routes and its residents may receive rice from any of the householders whose houses line these routes. This relationship should have little or no personal content – or at least none should be in evidence. 'Merit' is automatically conferred by the monks' acceptance of rice and other food.

Although this ideal of impersonal giving is most perfectly realized in alms-giving, there are other ceremonies performed by monks for laymen which are generally regarded by both parties as representing a more significant aspect of pastoral relations. These take place at critical moments in the layman's life, moments corresponding to the *rites de passage* common to all cultures.

The most crucial and hence more meritorious of these are probably the ordination ceremony, whereby a man crosses over from lay society into the world of the monk, and the ceremony of cremation, which accomplishes the transfer of the deceased from this world to the next. But monks are also usually invited to recite *parittas* or merit-making chants on other occasions, such as the wedding ceremony, entry into a new house, or the opening of a school or business.

A layman who wants to host or hold a merit-making ceremony usually invites a number of monks to come to his house from one or more monasteries on the appointed day. The central activity of the merit-making ceremony is the recitation by the monks of one of the appropriate Pali chants, in the memorizing of which a good part of the time may be spent. At the end of the ceremony the host presents each of the monks with the traditional offering – typically three incense sticks, two candles and a lotus bud – all items to be used in worship of the Buddha image; items of everyday use may be added – packets of tea and sugar, washing powder and cigarettes as well as a small sum of money, or a chit which can be cashed by the lay bursar of the monastery.

Any individual monk is likely to be invited to merit-making ceremonies by relatives and friends from his former lay life, but will also receive invitations simply by virtue of his residence in a particular monastery. It is considered more meritorious for a layman to invite monks impartially, although it would also be considered a breach of form not to invite monks who are relations or friends.

One can visualize each individual monk, then, with his 'parish' of lay supporters who support him in a variety of ways: there are the householders along his alms-giving circuit giving rice more or less regularly; there are friends and relations who invite him because of the prior bonds between them; and unrelated, even unknown, laymen who contact him as a resident of a particular monastery.

Until this century monks had an important role as teachers, as all schools were in the temple compound. However since the establishment of the State School system the monk's role has been usurped.

There are a number of other possible activities, however, which may be regarded as optional, in that only a few monks choose to specialize in them, but through which those monks are brought into contact with a wider range of the public. Some monks, for instance, are regarded as saintly simply because of their venerable appearance and demeanour. Very often the possessors of this rather diffuse charisma are believed to have the power to confer health and happiness and to consecrate objects such as amulets of the Buddha. Their services may be in great demand to inaugurate schools or businesses; often they make and distribute images and amulets of themselves. The sale of such amulets, perhaps depicting famous monks resident in a particular monastery, may be an important part of its fund-raising for upkeep of the buildings and so forth. Amulets derive their power to protect the wearer from their association with sacred things, but it is usual to consecrate them further. The most common form of consecration is the chanting of a Pali formula over the image by a monk, and monks who are renowned for the strength of their vocation and charisma are invited occasionally by groups of laymen to consecrate their amulets.

In Thailand, amulet collecting has become a fine art, particularly among men, whose traditionally more prominent place in the outside world exposes them to greater dangers than their womenfolk are subjected to. There are many different kinds of amulets – ranging from tiger's teeth and strange *objets trouvés* to auspicious diagrams and tiny images of the Buddha, or likenesses of revered monks. The tiny Buddha images are the amulets most seriously regarded by the collector and the large number of Thai magazines devoted to amulet collecting give the bulk of their space to them. Amulets of this kind are usually worn round the neck.

Another form of amulet is the tattoo. Monks, unlike lay experts, may tattoo only the upper parts of the body and the head. Most often the monk will tattoo sacred syllables and mystical signs and symbols or motifs from the Hindu epic, the *Rāmāyaṇa*.

Amulets are thought not only to bring good luck and to help the wearer to avoid catastrophe but also to endow the wearer with an immediate sense of well-being and a desire to behave well towards others which in turn causes reciprocal reaction in them and so enhances his general prosperity.

Images may be cast from various metals, stamped in clay or moulded from compressed vegetable matter. Recipes are jealously guarded, and some amulets contain scraps of plaster or bronze from famous images or stupas, or even pieces from ancient manuscripts destroyed by fire. As important a factor in efficacy as the ingredients of the amulet are the reputation and charisma of the maker. The amulets most sought after are made by monks with special powers who, in many cases, have acquired the charms of consecration and the recipe from other specialists.

In addition to the formulas uttered by the monk while he makes the amulet and when he hands it over to

Three typical amulets of the sort worn on clothes or carried as decoration: they are all enlarged about four times. In Thailand many monks make and consecrate such amulets, usually images of the Buddha or famous monks.

the layman, a more elaborate ceremony may be held in a temple to reinforce its power. On the day of such a ceremony – Tuesday or Saturday are regarded as being particularly auspicious for it – the amulets are placed near monks, and are often connected with the chapter by a sacred thread. The monks then chant in unison for up to five hours and meditate; these acts generate beneficial power which is transmitted to the amulets. The sacred thread used in this ceremony can also be cut into pieces which are amulets in themselves.

The power of the amulet is fragile and must be conserved by appropriate behaviour on the part of its owner and wearer. An amulet must never be put in a low position where it could be stepped on. When washing or relieving himself a man may place his amulet in his mouth to avoid offence. A woman's lower garments are particularly offensive and dangerous to the power of her own amulets or to those of any man she is in contact with. The exception to this is the sarong of a man's mother, a piece of which may even be given to him to wear as an amulet.

Other popular amulets, aside from Buddha images, are amulets showing monks, kings or healers. One group depicts a many-armed monk covering his eyes, ears and other bodily orifices to close off the senses, a requirement for concentration on Nirvāṇa. On the back of these images is usually to be found a small diagram or *yantra* whose arrangement of letters and numbers has mystical significance. More brahminic than Buddhist in origin, these diagrams are often worn as amulets by themselves. They can be printed on cloth, painted on buildings or cars, or tattooed across a monk's chest or back.

An additional category of amulets is comprised of natural objects credited with supernatural power. Tamarind seeds, cat's-eye gems and tiger's teeth are amongst the most common.

Unique to Thailand and Laos is another class of amulets, usually worn round the waist and never round the neck. These are phallic amulets or *phlad khik*. Traditionally they were given to small boys to protect them from dog or snake bites and to ward off evil spirits. Today, they are worn by Thai men of all ages and are nearly as common as Buddha images. Interestingly enough these phallic amulets also derive their power from being consecrated by monks or spirit doctors, and help to keep the wearer free from harm. The association of the phallus with fertility and strength is extended to the belief in its power to give prosperity and protection. Ideally, of course, a Thai will follow the precepts of the Buddha, which will bring him immediate and long-term benefits, but many Thais feel that it is better to be safe than sorry and that a strong talisman or amulet will provide added protection.

Some monks are experts in herbal cures and famous for their recipes. Others may function as seers and astrologers; this kind of expertise, although not forbidden, is outside the strict bounds of Buddhist orthodoxy. As we have mentioned earlier, monks sometimes bless houses, shops and business enterprises, power plants, highways and hotels, but this blessing should be sharply distinguished from active co-operation in their establishment and functioning.

In recent years some new and more activist trends have emerged in monk-layman relations. The monks who embrace this new thinking believe that they have a duty to make a return – in kind – to lay society and that they should recover their lost roles as educators and moral leaders of laymen. The Thai government's programme of national and community development is a striking implementation of this new mode of thought. Under a series of national development programmes to improve environmental sanitation in the more deprived areas of the country, the potentially strategic position of the monks has been put to use without causing apparent damage to their special status. The capacity for mixing cement, plastering and bricklaying to be found in most well-run and self-sufficient monasteries has been tapped by the programme officials by using the monks as teachers of these trades to the villagers who must construct and maintain wells and latrines. Furthermore, the authority of the monks and the *wat* has been utilized by establishing Revolving Loan Funds with credit from the monastery. Although these funds are administered by the monastery's lay committee, the fact that they belong to the monastery makes laymen extremely reluctant to default on their debts. The rate of repayment on these loans has been extremely high, in striking contrast to the rate of repayment on government loans.

There is a trend, most noticeable in Thailand, towards greater activism among young academic monks in the Buddhist universities; they cite 19th-century precedents when monks acted as missionaries to take primary education to the provinces in the reign of King Mongkut.

In theory the monk's pivotal role in the community would seem to fit him for leadership in a variety of fields; but, as we have seen, many people resist or disapprove of the monk's dirtying his hands – both literally and figuratively – with community development and national development programmes. His strength lies essentially in being in but not of the community, which maximizes the value of his moral support, but minimizes his practical usefulness.

In the 1970s, revivalist Buddhism developed under the charismatic leadership of Kittivuddho Bhikkhu, whose preaching attracted a mass audience. His supporters contributed vast sums to the construction of his Buddhist boarding school, Jittabhawan College, nor far to the southeast of Bangkok. During the period of great political instability between 1973 and 1976 Kittivuddho Bhikkhu became the spokesman for orthodox Buddhist anti-Communist feelings. His most famous saying was that it was no more a sin to kill a Communist than to kill a fish or a fowl to offer to a monk. Identified with the extreme right-wing regime of Prime Minister Thanin Kraivixien, he has since fallen into disrepute.

We have examined the role of the Buddhist monk in Thailand, Laos and Cambodia. We have looked at the variety of interactions between the monk and the lay people or householders who support him, and have seen that the monk is not in fact the solitary recluse dedicated to self-improvement but that in a variety of ways he ministers to the needs of lay society. He can however only maintain his semi-divine status by remaining as aloof as possible from the fruits of the world he has left behind. It is this peculiar tension and paradox in his position which makes an extension of his traditional role into new areas – community or national development – particularly problematic. It may well be that any serious modernization of the monk's role would be detrimental to his unique and prestigious social position.

Buddhism in East Asia

8

'Beyond the Jade Gate':
Buddhism in China, Vietnam and Korea

9

This World and the Other Power:
Contrasting Paths to Deliverance in Japan

Ancient Chinese legends tell how one of the Han emperors, in response to a divine summons during a dream, sent envoys into India to inquire after a god named Buddha. Several years later they returned with a white horse and the text of the *Sūtra in Forty-two Sections*; whereupon the emperor founded for them the Monastery of the White Horse, near Lo-yang, and Buddhism took root and flourished in China.

The real story is less picturesque. Elements of Buddhism seem to have percolated into China around the beginning of the 1st century BC and at first played only a marginal role in intellectual and religious life, its ideas mingling with those of Taoism and not easily distinguished from them. It was propagated at a low social level and hardly noticed by the cultured élite.

After AD 300 Buddhism began to penetrate the educated minority of aristocrats and scholar-officials. Monasteries were organized, led by monks well trained in the tradition of Chinese classical literature and scholarship. The next three centuries were an age of political upheaval, but Buddhism expanded, finding converts among all classes from the emperor downwards, and including even 'barbarian' invaders from outside. The Sangha grew in numbers, wealth and influence, leading to tensions between the clergy and secular authorities.

The next phase, corresponding to the Sui and T'ang dynasties, lasted from 589 to 960. A number of specifically Chinese Buddhist sects arose, although contact with India remained close and there was an outburst of translation activities. Chinese Buddhism reached its highest level during this period. But with the enormous wealth amassed by the monasteries came further clashes with the state, resulting, around the middle of the 9th century, in severe repression, a blow from which the Sangha never fully recovered.

For a whole millennium, Buddhism in China existed as a positive but continually declining force. Within China it was threatened by revived Confucianism; India could provide no fresh inspiration; and in Central Asia it had capitulated to Islam. By the end of the 19th century Buddhism had lost its appeal to the élite and had been reduced to meditation and popular devotionalism.

The history of Chinese Buddhism in our century has seen much change. Soon after 1900, a Buddhist revivalist movement gained momentum and had considerable success. During the long period of external and internal strife, China's religious communities suffered greatly. After the founding of the People's Republic in 1949, and particularly during the Cultural Revolution, Buddhism was suppressed in mainland China. Since the restitution of religious freedom, however, many temples and even some monasteries have been reopened. In Taiwan, Hong Kong and Singapore Buddhism remains very much a living force, and in Taiwan there are monasteries of all the major traditions that had existed in mainland China, some of them large and flourishing institutions.

The case of Japan is in some ways simpler, in some ways more complex. Introduced from Korea in the 6th century, Buddhism was at first regarded as a universal version of a theistic religion, Buddhas and bodhisattvas being invoked as benevolent deities. Such attitudes are still recognizable in popular Buddhism today. But what has chiefly distinguished the story of Buddhism in Japan has been the continuity of all schools or sects, co-existing side by side to the present day. The process of founding sects began in the 7th and 8th centuries. The teachings of these sects concentrated on metaphysical points usually too sophisticated for ordinary people to understand. From the 9th century there evolved a highly systematized esoteric Buddhism that gradually degenerated into magical practices and was adopted by the court as a religion 'to protect the state'. In the 12th and 13th centuries new sects were founded. Their simplified practice and dogma made it much easier for the people to participate actively in the religious life. Amidism, Zen and Nichirenism are the three great currents of Japanese Buddhism that originated in this period. Today Buddhism continues to flourish in all its forms, at one end of the scale hardly distinguishable from superstition and magic, but at the other end there are two elements: a highly intellectual study, whose repercussions have been felt all over the world, and profound spiritual discipline.

Amid the forest a monk of the Japanese Kegon sect sits meditating in a tree. The Kamakura period (1185–1333) was one which sought spiritual progress in quiet, simple surroundings, reacting against the pompous ceremonial and magical practices of the preceding Heian period. In the process the world of nature – trees, flowers and gardens – became strongly associated with meditation, as it still is. The monk shown here, Myōe-Shōnin, was popularly known as Chōka-Shōnin, or 'Reverend Bird's Nest', because of his fondness for this position.(1)

The legacy of the caves

Many of the cave sanctuaries of northern China have survived the vicissitudes of Chinese history. The construction of cave temples, which was already practised in ancient India, became popular in China at a quite early period, and some of them were constructed along the so-called silk route to Central Asia. For a thousand years (4th–14th centuries) these shrines were enlarged and extended, and today constitute a storehouse of painting and sculpture.

Giant Buddhas gaze down from the cliffs and caves of Yün-Kang. The tradition of rock-cut shrines comes from India and Central Asia (compare Bamiyan) and many of the artistic conventions are Indian. But the iconography is Mahāyāna, with double and multiple Buddhas and hosts of bodhisattvas, minor gods and demons. One of the largest figures (*right and below left*) is 44 feet high and flanked by bodhisattvas. Behind him, carved in relief, are previous Buddhas. (2,3,4)

The dim light and vast scale of the carvings enhanced their religious effect. Lung-mên, the second of the great cave complexes of northern China, consists of hundreds of shrines hollowed into the sandstone cliffs of a river gorge.

Above left: a group from one of the interiors. *Below:* part of the exterior; the figure on the left is a bodhisattva, those on the right are guardians of the temple. *Above right:* part of the Rock of the Thousand Buddhas, Ch'ien-fo yai. (5,6,7)

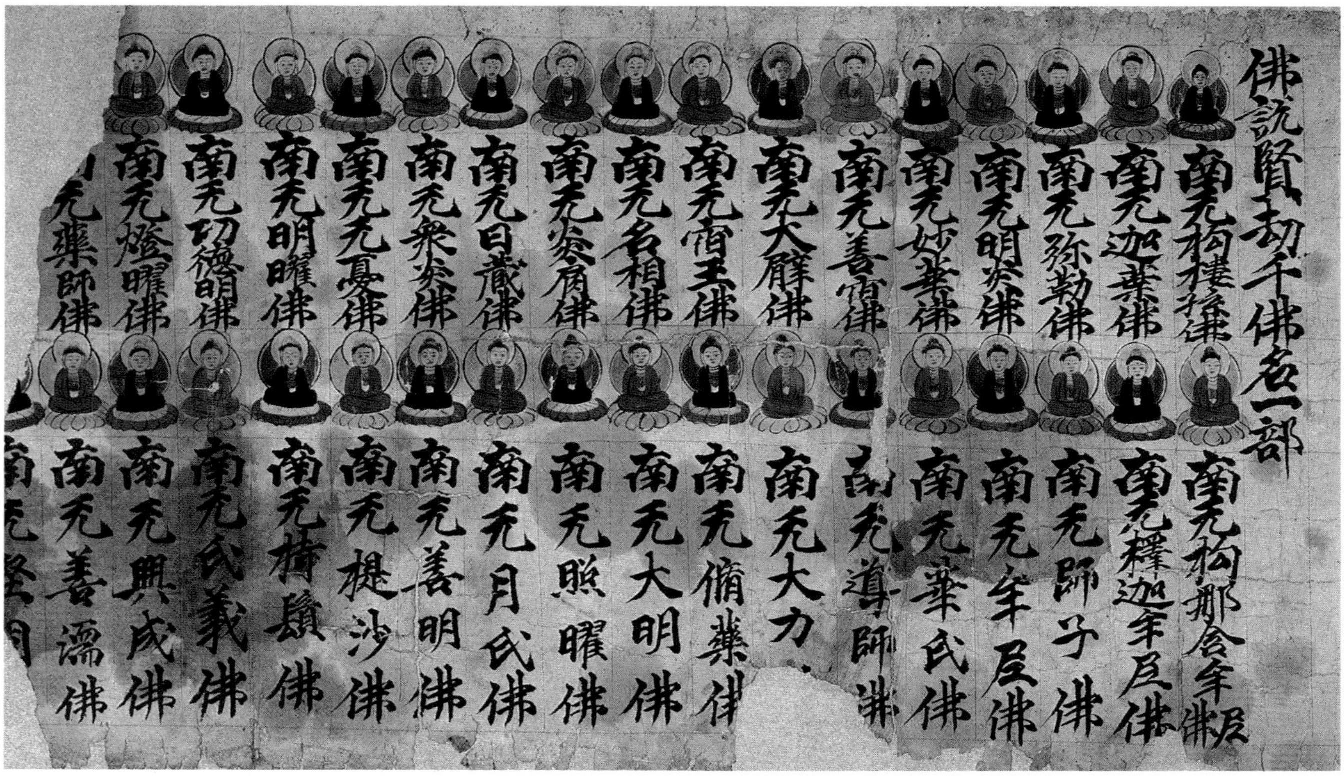

佛說賢劫千佛名一部

南无拘樓孫佛
南无迦葉佛
南无弥勒佛
南无明炎佛
南无妙華佛
南无善宿佛
南无大臂佛
南无宿王佛
南无名相佛
南无炎肩佛
南无日藏佛
南无衆炎佛
南无无憂佛
南无明曜佛
南无切德明佛
南无燈曜佛
南无藥師佛

南无拘那含牟尼佛
南无釋迦牟尼佛
南无師子佛
南无牟尼佛
南无華氏佛
南无導師佛
南无大力佛
南无脩藥佛
南无大明佛
南无照曜佛
南无月氏佛
南无善明佛
南无提沙佛
南无持鬘佛
南无氏義佛
南无興成佛
南无善濡佛
南无堅月

The Words of the Buddha

An essential basis for the spread of Buddhism in China was the collection of sacred texts and their translation into Chinese. Both represented formidable problems. But slowly, over the 3rd, 4th and 5th centuries, a series of intrepid travellers made the journey to India and back, and the work of translation was organized professionally.

Laden with precious scripts, the illustrious 7th-century pilgrim Hsüan-tsang arrives back in China after his journey to India. He was reported to have brought back seventy-five texts with him. Here, on a silk scroll from Tun-huang, the horses are led into a temple, followed by men bearing gifts. The road is lined with priests and officials, while at the side of the road the people prostrate themselves in reverence. In another painting from Tun-huang (*right*), Hsüan-tsang is shown making his way across mountains and rivers, carrying scrolls on his back and holding in one hand a fly-whisk for driving away evil spirits and in the other the *khakkhara*, the attribute of the monk. A serpent writhes beneath his feet and by his side walks a tiger. In the clouds above, watching over his journey, sits the Buddha on a lotus. (8,10)

Some rare texts survive from this heroic period of Chinese Buddhism. *Left:* part of the Thousand Buddhas of the *Bhadra Kalpa*, with two Buddhas in every vertical line. The linguistic problems were enormous; the original contained a host of specialized terms for which there were no Chinese equivalents. (9)

Power and patronage

In both China and Japan the Buddhist church has wielded considerable power, but it has been exercised through a ruling secular élite, not exerted directly by the monastic order in its own right.

Princely patrons appear frequently in the cave reliefs of the 6th century (*left*). In the first, the donor is represented with his attendants bearing fans and umbrellas. In the second, two donors, each with a servant holding an umbrella, sit in little pavilions on either side of an elaborate incense-burner. The third shows an empress and her court ladies bringing offerings to a shrine. (11, 12,13)

A giant bronze image symbolizes the identity of church and state in the Japanese mind. *Right:* the 'Great Buddha of Nara', the central Buddha of the 'Universe of the Lotus Treasure', stands for the totality of all being and at the same time for the centralized, unified Japanese state. It is the largest metal image in Japan, 14·25 metres in height and weighing 380 tons. Originally cast by order of the Emperor Shōmu in 749, it has been much damaged in the course of history and in its present form, apart from a few petals of the lotus flower and part of the seat, is the work of artists of the Edo period (1603–1868). (16)

Larger still, towering more than 50 metres from the ground, is the huge figure of Kannon, the Buddhist Goddess of Mercy (known as Kuan-yin in China), erected as a war memorial in the late 1950s. It crowns the top of Ōtsuka-hana hill, southeast of Tokyo. (17)

In Japan ties with the state were still closer. Prince Shōtoku (574–622), regarded by the Japanese people as the man who introduced Buddhism into their country, is still looked upon with respect. His portrait (*above*), the original of which is attributed to a 7th-century artist, is reproduced on the 10,000 yen banknote. (14,15)

Peaceful coexistence

Buddhism, Confucianism, Taoism and Shintoism are not mutually incompatible, and their devotees have freely borrowed ideas, sacred symbols, even gods, from one another. At a popular level, veneration is, or was, paid to the shrines of all religions. Such opposition as Buddhism encountered was more social and economic than theological.

Lao-tsu and Confucius protect the infant Śākyamuni, the future Buddha. This charming allegory, painted on silk in the 14th century, reflects the tolerance between all three religions, a tolerance that was only disturbed when religious doctrines threatened to undermine the institutions of the state. (18)

Shintō deities moved easily into the world of Buddhism without losing their identities. *Left:* a 14th-century *maṇḍala* from the Shintō shrine of Kasuga. Sacred deer are a feature of the shrine and the strips of paper are prayers to Shintō gods. The gods themselves, however, shown in the golden mirror supported by the tree, are given their Buddhist forms. *Above:* a late 14th-century Shintō *maṇḍala* from Kumano. Again, the deities are represented as avatars (manifestations) of Buddhas and bodhisattvas. (19, 20)

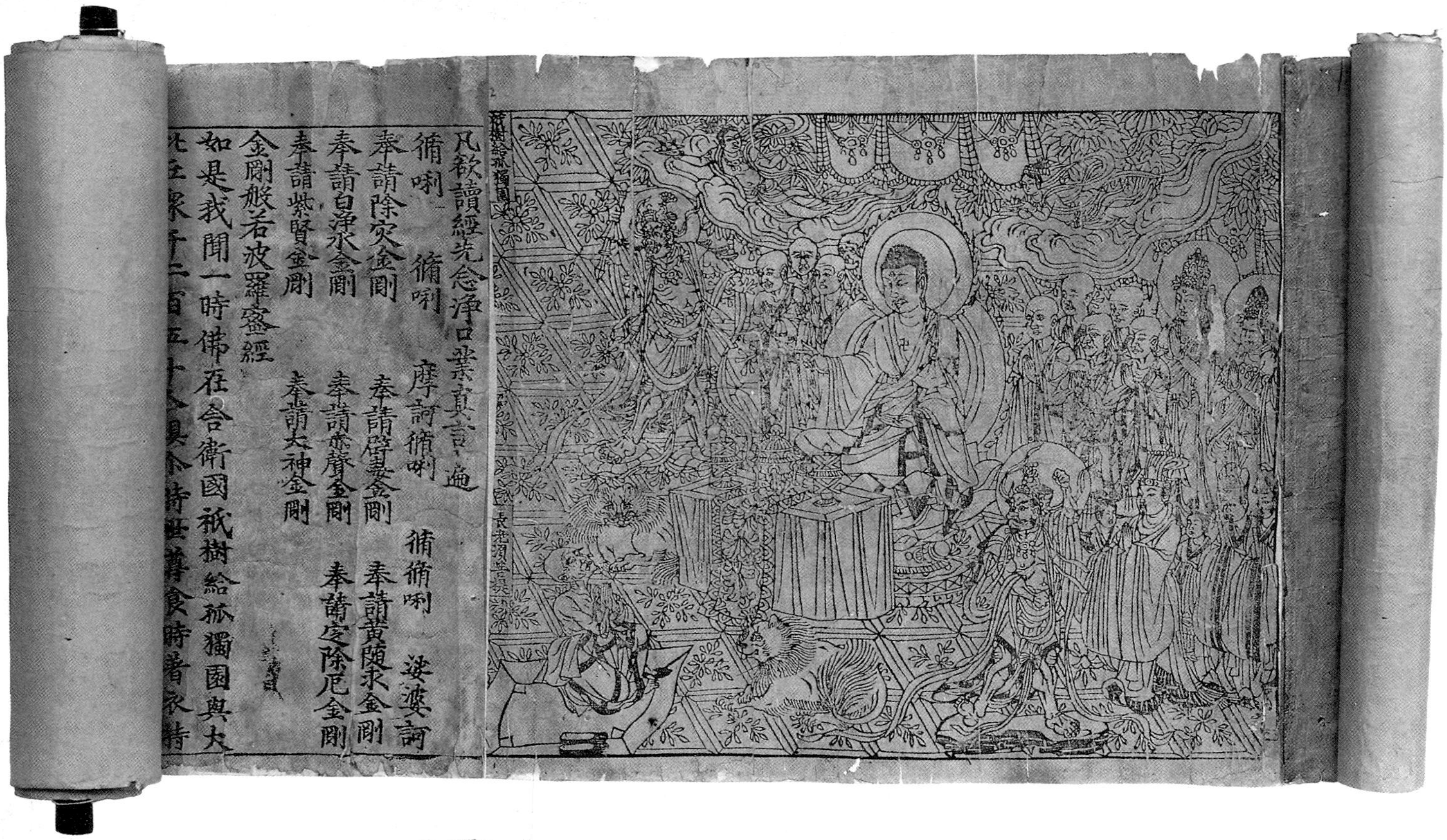

The oldest printed book in existence is a copy of the *Diamond Sūtra* dated 868. The text was carved on several wooden blocks, the picture on one. (21)

Folding books are still in use today, as we have seen in Burma and Thailand. This early Chinese example is held together not only by the folds at the back but also by a thread going through a hole in every page and tied across the cover. (22)

A Korean library (*below*) has since 1398 preserved the 81,000 engraved wooden blocks needed to print the sacred texts of Buddhism. (23)

In the octagonal library of Peking (*right*) books were kept in wooden drawers – some are shown standing empty – with Buddha images carved on the ends; the lengths differ according to the space in the octagon to receive them. (25)

Ceremonial wood-block held by a Korean monk (*below*). It was from blocks of this sort that those used for printing books evolved. *Below right:* a wood-block with a picture of the seated Buddha, recovered from the caves of Tun-huang. As in the West, printed pictures preceded texts. (24, 26)

The birth of printing

Previous chapters have stressed the importance of copying the sacred texts. It was the Chinese Buddhists who took the momentous step of using wooden type-blocks to duplicate them. Originally invented to reproduce pictures or short texts, they were already being used to print whole books by the 9th century.

In the quiet precincts of a pre-war Chinese monastery a travelling monk studies the sūtras (*right*) and librarians care for shelves of old printing blocks (*below right*). Such photographs, taken in the 1930s, vividly convey a way of life that was destined not to survive the Communist revolution. (27, 28)

引路菩

After death

The mythology of Mahāyāna stands in marked contrast to the austere doctrines preached by Śākyamuni. In Chinese and Japanese popular belief death was often the prelude not to non-existence but to prolonged happiness or torment.

The promise of salvation, expressed in the image of the bodhisattva Avalokiteśvara leading souls to paradise, would be suspended at deathbeds before the eyes of the dying person. In this 10th-century hanging scroll from Tun-huang the soul is represented as a small fashionably dressed woman. The bodhisattva carries a lotus and a censer. Falling blossoms signify blessings. (29)

Amida Buddha appears from behind the mountains to meet the dying man and lead him to paradise: a Japanese scroll of the 13th or 14th century. (30)

Eight levels of hell awaited the sinner, and Japanese artists exhausted their imaginations in depicting the torments that lay in store. In this painting of the 11th or 12th century, the king of the underworld, Enma-ō, judges the dead. (31)

From its ceremonial entrance to its innermost shrine, the layout of a Chinese and Japanese monastery has a satisfying logic. *Above:* the main gate of the great monastic complex of Anchin, China. *Left:* Nichiren priests paying homage in front of the altar of the Honmonji, the main temple of the sect, at Ikegami, Japan. Nichiren, the founder of the Nichiren sect, died here in 1282. (32, 33)

An ordered world

Architecturally the monasteries of China and Japan have little in common with those of other Buddhist countries. Logically organized in mainly single-storey buildings, each part has a clearly defined function.

Three monasteries of Buddhist China (*right*). At the top: Nanking, with monks outside the Hall of the Law. *Centre:* main hall of the Ling-yen monastery, founded only in 1937 and one of the few still fulfilling its purpose. *Bottom:* aerial view of the main hall (*ta-tien*) and library of the Chin Shan monastery, Chinkiang. (35, 36, 37)

One of the first great monasteries of Japan was that of Hōryūji, at Nara, founded by Prince Shōtoku in 607 (see pl. 14); in its present form it still contains the oldest wooden building in the world. In this bird's eye view we are looking from the southeast. In the left foreground is the Middle Gate, leading into the enclosure, where stand the Pagoda and the Main Hall. The little building behind the Pagoda is the Sūtra Repository. Corresponding with it across the courtyard is the belfry. Between them, in the background opposite the Middle Gate, is the Kōdō, or lecture hall. (34)

Paths to Enlightenment

The adaptation of Buddhist values to the new social and political situation in medieval Japan led to the foundation of numerous schools or sects, each devoted in its own way to recovering what it saw as the original doctrine of the Buddha and each based on the teachings of a charismatic 'founder' who was often revered later as a bodhisattva. It is these sects which are still the most noticeable feature of Buddhism in present day Japan.

Nichiren searches for a temple site (*left*), a 15th-century scroll painting. Nichiren lived in a turbulent period of Japanese history, the 13th century, and the sect he founded was based on absolute faith in the teaching of the *Lotus Sūtra*. Accused by his opponents of being aggressive and intolerant, Nichiren nevertheless won many adherents and his sect is now among the most popular in Japan. (38)

The Tendai sect, which places supreme value on the experience of the identity of mind and universe and on Enlightenment that does not flee from mundane reality, was established by Dengyō Daishi in the 9th century. Also known as Saichō, he spent many years of study and meditation on Mount Hiei, a practice enjoined upon his followers. A coloured print of the 14th or 15th century (*left*) shows him conversing with a semi-mythical character, En-no Gyōja, on Mount Ōmine. One of the rituals still performed today by the Tendai sect is the esoteric 'fire ceremony' (*right*), depicted here as part of an extremely severe ascetic exercise called 'walking around the mountain top'. For a thousand days the devotee prays and carries out special rites with a minimum of sleep and nourishment. The fire symbolizes purification of all worldly defilement. (39, 40)

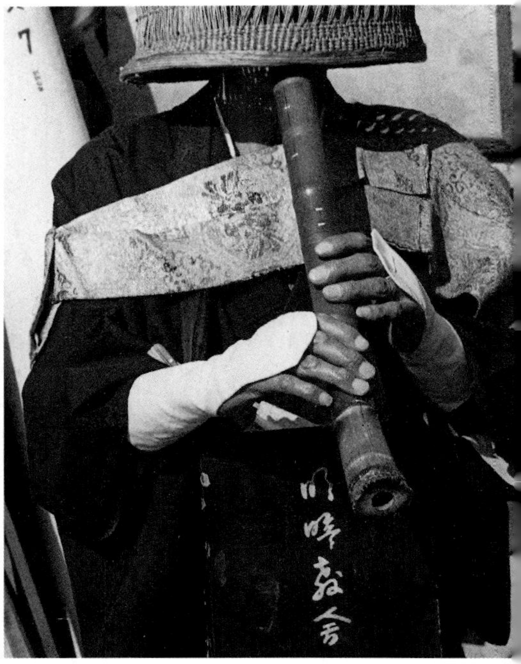

The Jōdo sect places all hope of salvation in Amida Buddha, who is regarded as a saviour, leading those who believe in him to paradise. The Procession of the Nine Buddhas (*above*) is an annual ceremony performed by members of the sect at the Kuhonbutsuji, Tokyo. (41)

The Fuke sect is a particular branch of Japanese Zen dating from the 13th century. Here a *komusō* (literally, a 'priest of emptiness') wanders about playing a *shakuhachi* (Japanese bamboo flute). His head is entirely covered so that he cannot be recognized when begging for food. (42)

The mind's release

Zen is one of the main Buddhist meditation techniques designed to free the mind from slavery to reason and logic (which find propositions such as 'neither being nor non-being' difficult to accept) and to open the way to Enlightenment. By rejecting all expressible convictions, it draws closer to the reality which cannot be expressed.

The discipline of Zen makes an intriguing contrast to the anti-discipline of its message. Here (*far left*) Zen novices clean the garden of the Manpukuji, a temple near Kyoto. Such physical work is seen as an opportunity to become aware of the concrete realities of life. *Left:* young schoolgirls practising Zen meditation under the supervision of Zen priests. They carry sticks; if a girl seems to be dozing or daydreaming the teacher strikes her gently on the shoulder. (43, 44)

The laughter of Zen makes it approachable for the Westerner more directly than the other sects. These three drawings (*above*) are typical of the way in which Zen masters deliberately disowned the idea that they were especially holy or worthy of reverence. *Left to right:* Bodhidharma in meditation, drawn by Hakuin, an 18th-century Zen sage; Kenzō, who lived by catching prawns – a 14th-century drawing; and Kanzan and Jittoku, two happy Chinese eccentrics of the Tang dynasty, one a poet, the other a kitchen sweeper: the drawing is of about 1650. (45, 46, 47)

The beauty of Zen: gardens that enshrine calm and peace, abstract compositions of rock and raked sand, help the mind to lose itself in meditation. *Right:* part of the garden of the Nanzenji, a Rinzai temple in Kyōto, a stone rising from the sand like an island amid the sea. (48)

8

'Beyond the Jade Gate': Buddhism in China, Vietnam and Korea

ERIK ZÜRCHER

THE EARLIEST TRACES of the existence of Buddhism in China date from the beginning of the Later Han dynasty (AD 25–220), and all evidence, both literary and archaeological, indicates that it reached China via Central Asia. The date and the way of transmission are certainly not coincidental. In the first two centuries of our era, the trade route that crossed the empty heart of the continent connected two powerful empires. At its eastern end, the Han empire ruled over most of what is now 'China proper', and at times also exercised a kind of military protectorate over the oasis kingdoms along the Silk Road. At the other end, the Yüeh-chih or Indo-Scythians had extended their sway over a large part of western Central Asia, from Sogdiana to northern India and Afghanistan. Central Asia was thus exposed to domination and cultural influence from both sides, and the small kingdoms along the branches of the Silk Road – Kāshgar, Kučā and Turfan on the northern route, Khotan on the southern one – were becoming centres of a hybrid Sino-Indian culture. Buddhism must have been introduced into this cosmopolitan world from the Kuśāna empire and from Parthia, further west, probably by monks who attached themselves to the trading caravans, or by pious laymen who were well versed in Buddhist scriptures – both appear to have played a role in the earliest propagation of Buddhism in China. We may assume that the spread of Buddhism throughout Central Asia was a gradual process that did not encounter great obstacles – the states were small, and their geographical position had made them receptive to foreign influence.

For the common people of Japan, remote from philosophical subtleties, Buddhism remained a creed bound up with spells to procure material benefits, the pacification of angry ghosts and the achievement of paradise after death, a creed that merged easily with their ancestral Shintō. This photograph dates from the early years of this century and represents a way of life that has virtually disappeared. A poor pilgrim stands in reverence before Buddha images at Nikkō, a popular shrine just north of Tokyo belonging to the Tendai sect, famous for its natural beauty and its ancient Shintō-Buddhist associations. The first Buddhist temple was erected here in 767. Its syncretist tradition remains to this day. The majority of Japanese are Buddhist and Shintoist at the same time. (49)

However, the situation became quite different for Buddhism once it had crossed the 'Pass of the Jade Gate' at the western end of the Great Wall. After the colourful diversity of Central Asia, it was now confronted with another, not always friendly, world: a colossal empire and a millenarian civilization, dominated by very clearly defined political and social ideas and norms that had taken shape in the course of centuries. It was ruled by an educated élite in which the feelings of cultural identity and superiority were very strongly developed, and it was based on the ideal of a total political and social order that left little room for the propagation of a doctrine of individual salvation, especially if the latter was of 'barbarian' origin. This tension between Buddhism and the Chinese dominant ('Confucian') tradition of socio-political thought, or, at the institutional level, between the Buddhist Sangha and the Confucian state, was to become a constant and supremely important factor in the whole history of Buddhism in China. It is certainly no coincidence that when in AD 220 the Han empire fell, Buddhism had existed on Chinese soil for at least one and a half centuries without ever becoming more than an absolutely marginal phenomenon, and that its development and growth into a powerful religious movement took place in the period of disunity (311–589), when the empire had disintegrated, and large parts of Chinese territory were ruled by weak and unstable 'barbarian' dynasties. It gained force in a context of political chaos and polycentrism, when the official ideology, by its very nature bound up with the ideal of imperial unity and universal power, had obviously failed to fulfil its promise. When the empire was reunified (589), the most important formative phase of Chinese Buddhism had been completed; spiritually, economically and even politically, the Buddhist 'church' had become a factor to which the rulers of the Sui and T'ang dynasties (589–906) had to pay due consideration.

But the power of the Chinese state was not the only conditioning factor, and perhaps not the most decisive one. Even at the time of national disintegration, the basic ideals and norms of traditional Chinese 'political theology' and the moral principles derived from these were kept alive by the large majority of the cultured élite. The Confucian utopia was based on a very old and universally accepted myth: the world of man forms a single organic whole together with heaven and earth; the ruler, who is sanctified by the 'Mandate of heaven', has the obligation to maintain the cosmic equilibrium by the perfect performance of his ritual, ethical and administrative duties. Therefore the authority of the imperial government is, in principle, unlimited: it embraces the whole public and, if necessary, also the private life of all its subjects. The ideal society is one of two classes, in which the mass of the productive population is ruled, in a paternalistic but authoritarian way, by an élite of 'scholar-officials' who, on account of their ethical qualities and literary accomplishments, are entitled to monopolize all power, prestige and higher culture. The basic values are those of stability, hierarchical order, harmony in human relations and painstaking observances of the ritual rules of behaviour, to be inculcated by persuasion and moral education and, if necessary, by force.

It is clear that Buddhism by its very nature was bound to come into conflict with this prevailing ideology. In general, the traditional Chinese world-view was essentially pragmatic and secular, in spite of its theological implications: its ideals are to be fulfilled in this life, and doctrines are appreciated according to their practical applicability and socio-political effectiveness rather than for their metaphysical qualities. This also holds good for the major non-Confucian indigenous tradition of religious and philosophical thought in China, that of Taoism, which was, in a more individualistic way, directed towards tangible goals: the acquisition of bodily immortality, and harmony with the concrete forces of Nature. Popular religion shared in this general attitude: the ancestral cult was naturally integrated with the family and the clan, as was the cult of the local earth god as the deified ancestral soil. The Buddhist rejection of all existence, and especially the Mahāyāna doctrine of the utter unreality of all phenomena was easily regarded as a kind of morbid nihilism and identified with *yin*, the principle of darkness and death. Ideas such as *karman*, rebirth and individual salvation, which in India had been universally accepted parts of religious culture, in China became bizarre novelties, fundamentally different from, and not seldom incompatible with, well-established Chinese notions. And, in general, Buddhism pursued aims of a metaphysical order – Enlightenment, Nirvāṇa, Buddhahood – which, because of their abstract and 'impracticable' nature, could hardly meet with approval in Confucian circles.

But the tensions were even more evident at the institutional level. Since its very beginning, Buddhism was indissolubly connected with a monastic ideal that, on account of its rejection of all social ties and obligations (and especially those related to family life), would inevitably conflict with the most fundamental principles of Chinese social ethics, according to which the first duties of man consisted in filial piety and engendering the offspring needed to continue the family line. In view of the importance attached to productive labour and, consequently, the social stigmatization of beggars, vagrants and other 'parasites', the Chinese traditional system was hardly prepared to accept the existence of a clerical community, the members of which were not allowed to perform agricultural labour, were supposed to spend part of their lives wandering and had to earn their food by begging. And, to top it all, the fact that the Buddhist Sangha regarded itself as an unworldly body, free from the obligation due to the secular powers (including the duty to perform corvée labour and to pay taxes), exempted from military service and not liable to government supervision, ran counter to the Chinese conception of government authority which in principle was all-inclusive.

This tension between Buddhism and indigenous Chinese ideology eventually led to a situation of precarious coexistence, in which Buddhism was allowed to play certain roles, within certain limits. At best, Buddhism was accepted by the authorities as a useful or even venerable addition to Chinese culture, a kind of metaphysical complement to the social and political teachings of Confucianism; it was at all times valued as a magical protection for the dynasty, the state and society. But, generally speaking, it was tolerated rather than extolled, and periodically the tension discharged itself in violent persecutions. Even at the time when Buddhism reached its zenith, in Sui and early T'ang times, China never became a 'Buddhist country', as Thailand or Burma eventually came to be – Buddhism always had to develop in the shadow of the Chinese central tradition.

However, Buddhism would not have been able to develop into one of China's major religions if the environment had been totally hostile. Apart from the areas of tension and conflict mentioned above, Chinese civilization also contained many elements that more easily lent themselves to the influence of Buddhism. The very special character of Chinese Buddhism cannot only be explained as a 'deformation' under the pressure of a hostile environment, but also, and perhaps even more so, as the result of an extremely complicated process of convergence and hybridization, in which elements of Buddhist origin were grafted upon, and amalgamated with, ideas, practices and institutions of Chinese origin with which they had (or seemed to have) a certain affinity. This may have been the main source of its extraordinary creativity, for it was especially in those areas that Buddhism was able deeply to influence and to enrich Chinese civilization. We shall meet many cases of such convergence and 'grafting' in our survey: the monastic ideal and Chinese eremitism; Buddhist meditation and the Taoist union with Nature; the Mahāyānist belief in the 'transfer of merit' and the cult of the ancestors; Buddhist lay congregations and traditional peasant associations; tantric rites and Taoist magic, and many more. Thus, 'change under pressure' and 'hybridization' can be recognized as the two main processes that, in ever varying combinations, helped to

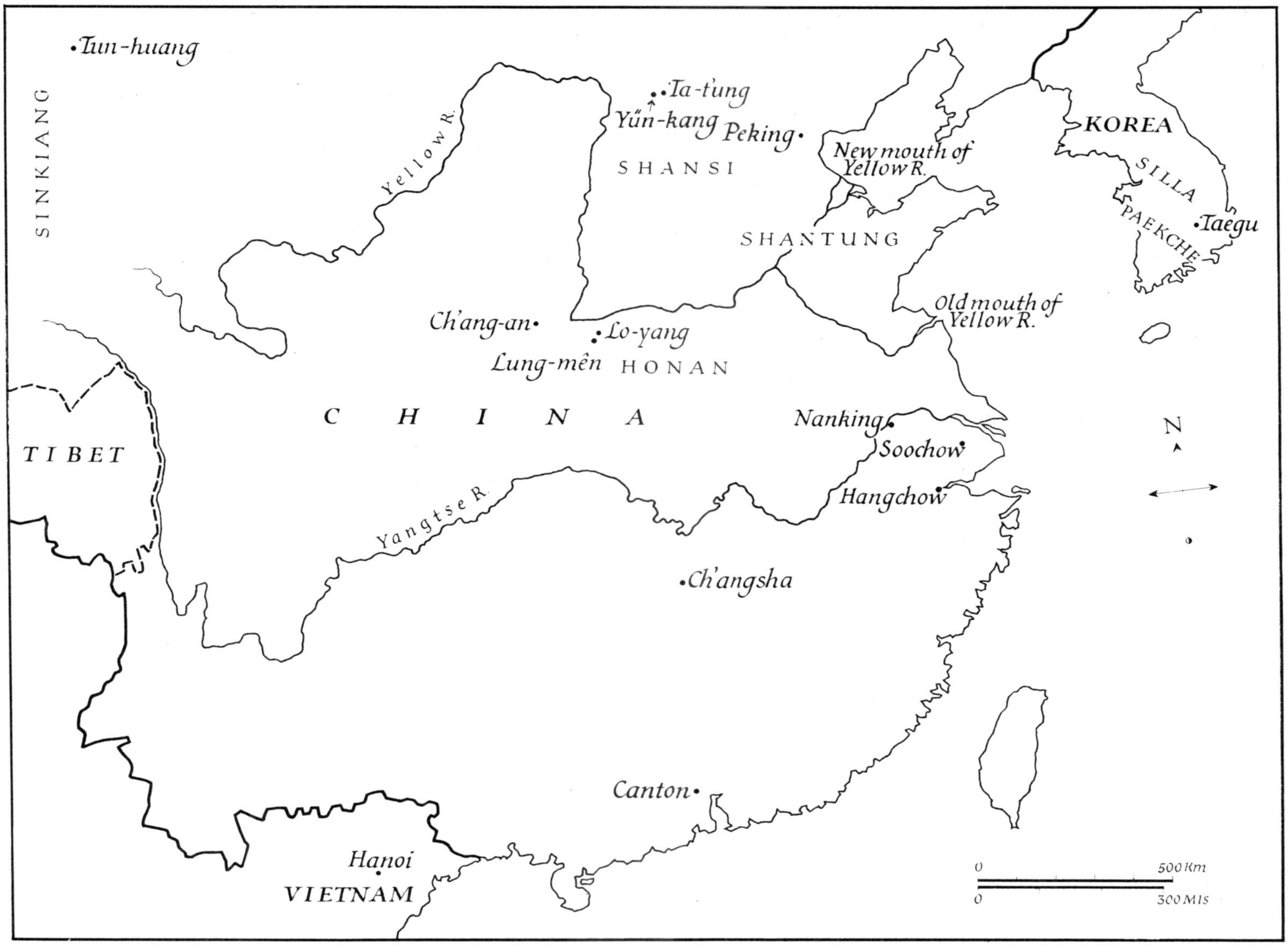

China, showing the chief sites mentioned in this chapter.

shape Chinese Buddhism. They will also be the two main themes in our survey.

Another conditioning factor of great consequence was the geographical situation, in which Central Asia played a key role. Buddhism reached China also along the southern route (by sea from Tāmralipti, Sri Lanka and Indo-China to Canton, and from there overland via Ch'angsha, or along the coast, to the lower Yangtse region) at least since the 3rd century. However, those contacts can in no way be compared to the constant influx of missionaries, with their scriptures and icons, along the Silk Road that connected northern China with Buddhist centres such as Kashgar, Kučā, Turfan and Khotan, and, beyond present-day Sinkiang, with the more distant regions of Sogdiana and north-west India.

This geographical situation deeply influenced the development of Chinese Buddhism, particularly in its formative phase, when the whole of northern China was ruled by non-Chinese dynasties. It has led to a typical regionalization in Chinese Buddhism, because the centres in northern China were constantly exposed to new impulses from the 'Western Countries'. In the north, there was a greater awareness of the foreign origin of the creed – a fact that may have contributed to the conversion of the non-Chinese rulers in northern China, and, consequently, to the close relations between court and clergy under those dynasties. It was also in the north that most of the translations of Buddhist scriptures were made. In the southern half of China, which in that crucial period was ruled by Chinese dynasties, we find the development of a much more Sinicized Buddhism, only indirectly influenced by Central Asia and India, and much more focused on the interpretation of Buddhism on the basis of the indigenous religious and philosophical traditions.

Another consequence of China's position on the eastern fringe of the Buddhist world was the fact that over a period of a thousand years it was successively exposed to the influence of different Buddhist schools or movements that had developed in India: *Prajñāpāramitā* – Doctrine of Emptiness – in the 2nd

According to tradition, Buddhism was introduced into China by envoys who had been sent to India by one of the Han emperors around AD 65. They returned with two Indian masters, a white horse, a Buddha image and the text of the 'Sūtra in Forty-two Sections'. The story was still a subject for popular illustration in the 19th century, when this drawing was made.

century; Madhyamaka scholastics around 400; Yogācāra 'idealism' around 600; tantric Buddhism in the 8th century – schools and movements that travelled like waves over the Asian continent, finally to be absorbed by Chinese Buddhism. That process of absorption finally created great problems for the Chinese Buddhists themselves, who were confronted with the most diverse, and sometimes even conflicting, ideas and practices. The diversity within Buddhism was, moreover, aggravated by the fact that it did not come to China from one region, but from a great many centres of diffusion, as distant from each other as Samarkand and Nālandā. This ever growing doctrinal diversity eventually has led to some of the most original doctrinal developments in Chinese Buddhism, either by harmonizing and integrating all known Buddhist teachings into an all-embracing system of 'periods and levels' of revelation, or a radical rejection of the whole scriptural tradition and the propagation of a direct, 'worldless' way to Enlightenment. Both movements, that of the indigenous scholastic schools and that of Ch'an (Zen), are among the most characteristic and impressive creations of Chinese Buddhism.

Buddhism comes to China (1st century to *c.* 300)

According to a famous story, the Han Emperor Ming (ruled 58–75) once had a dream in which a divine being appeared to him in the shape of a 'golden man'. After having been told that this must be the foreign god named Buddha, he sent envoys to India, who after several years returned with one (or two) Indian masters, a white horse and the text of the *Sūtra in Forty-two Sections*. The emperor lavishly entertained them, and founded for them the Monastery of the White Horse near the capital Lo-yang. Modern scholarship has proved the apocryphal nature of this picturesque tale. In actual fact, Buddhism did not enter China triumphantly. It was not introduced from India, but rather from the Kuṣāṇa empire, Parthia and Central Asia, and from there is must have gradually filtered in along the eastern extension of the Silk Road. However, the legend does contain some bits of information that are confirmed by historical evidence. The first reliable mention of Buddhism in a historical record refers to acts of Buddhist piety performed by an imperial prince in AD 65, which proves that some kind of Buddhist cult existed in China in the middle of the 1st century, and, moreover, that it was known in court circles under Emperor Ming. The *Sūtra in Forty-two Sections* is only known to us in later recensions, but a few quotations indicate that the original version was very archaic, and possibly dates from the same period. And the Monastery of the White Horse, still shown to visitors as the cradle of Buddhism in China, is mentioned in early 3rd-century sources, although the present buildings are much later.

Apart from the passage dealing with the Buddhist activities of an imperial prince in AD 65, historical literature of the later Han contained a few other stray references to Buddhism in connection with the Han court. They all indicate a very close connection between the cult of the Buddha as a divine being and religious Taoism, i.e. the study and practice of Taoist arts which were supposed to lead to bodily immortality and the cult of certain Taoist deities that had achieved such immortality and were believed now to guide the destiny of their believers from the paradise-like regions in which they were dwelling. The Taoist inspiration appears to be so strong that we may regard this kind of cult as an exotic variant of Taoism – a conclusion that is confirmed by some interesting archaeological data: a Han relief in which the Buddha figures together with the Taoist gods, surrounded by cosmological symbols, and a representation of a six-tusked elephant – a theme popularized by some archaic Buddha biography – amidst other supernatural creatures from Chinese mythology. Religious Taoism obviously functioned as a channel through which some Buddhist ideas made their first entrance into China. The association was by no means unnatural, in view of a number of superficial resemblances between Buddhist and Taoist ideas and practices, and the frequent use of Taoist terms in archaic Buddhist texts to render Buddhist ideas only served to confirm the misunderstanding. In fact, the founders of the two religions were regarded as identical: a Han source contains the first reference to the remarkable theory that Lao-tzu after his departure to the west (an old legendary theme) went to the 'barbarians' and manifested himself there as the Buddha, in order to convert them to a primitive doctrine of his own making, a kind of 'Taoism made easy', adapted to the low intellectual level of Indian savages. It seems that this theory of the 'conversion of the barbarians' originally was not intended polemically – it simply served to explain the seeming resemblance between the two religions, and may have been welcome to the growing Taoist church as well as the first Buddhist communities, because it justified both the incorporation of Buddhist elements into Taoism and the propagation of Buddhism in China as a 'foreign branch of Taoism'. But in later centuries, when Buddhism and Taoism had become rivals, it became one of the basic arguments in anti-Buddhist propaganda, expounded in an ever expanding literature about Lao-tzu's manifestations in the western regions. The controversy lasted more than a thousand years, finally to be resolved in favour of the Buddhists in the 13th century.

The first Buddhist community on which we have some concrete information was quite different from the Buddho-Taoist vagaries of the Han court. Its history can be traced back to AD 148, when the arrival of a Parthian missionary, An Shih-kao, marked the beginning of intense activity. From the middle of the 2nd to the first decade of the 3rd century, a number of Buddhist teachers and translators were working at Lo-yang; together they produced a great number of archaic Chinese translations of Buddhist scriptures, about thirty of which have been preserved. The foreign masters formed a cosmopolitan company that included Parthians, Indo-Scythians, Sogdians and even three Indians.

Practically all we know about this first community is connected with the work of translating Buddhist texts – clear proof of the fact that Buddhism had started to spread among the Chinese. It marks the beginning of a great translation activity, the results of which were one of the most impressive achievements of Buddhist culture in China for more than a thousand years. Needless to say, it was beset with great difficulties: the linguistic problems were enormous; Chinese equivalents for the innumerable specialized terms had to be created, or to be borrowed from Chinese traditional (mainly Taoist) terminology, and direct translation was usually impossible, since the foreign missionaries seldom were fluent in Chinese, and very few Chinese knew Sanskrit or Prākrit. The solution was found in the 'translation team', the foreign master reciting the text and making, mostly with the help of a bilingual interpreter, a crude translation, which was written down and afterwards revised and polished by Chinese assistants. Until the late 4th century, such teamwork remained a modest private undertaking carried out by a foreign missionary with his disciples, both monks and laymen. But from the early 5th century, when Buddhism had come to enjoy the patronage of the court and the highest aristocracy, it occasionally grew into huge 'translation projects' involving dozens of people. By that time, the successive efforts of many generations had resulted in the formation of a special kind of Buddhist 'translationese': a sort of simplified literary Chinese mixed with vernacular elements, in which the borrowings from Taoist vocabulary that characterized the earliest versions had been replaced by more accurate, newly coined Chinese equivalents. Thousands of Buddhist scriptures (*sūtra*) and scholastic works (*śāstra*) were thus translated, and often re-translated; already in 730 their number had grown to more than two thousand texts, some of which existed in four or five successive versions.

The range of texts selected for translation in the late Han 'church of Lo-yang' was rather limited. Much attention was given to short texts dealing with *dhyāna*, the ancient Buddhist system of mental exercises that outwardly resembled certain Taoist mental and physical techniques of trance and breath control. But we also find the first Chinese versions of Mahāyāna scriptures: devotional texts dealing with the glory and saving power of Buddhas and bodhisattvas, and scriptures preaching the Doctrine of Emptiness or universal unreality of all phenomena – a doctrine that was to have an immense impact on Chinese Buddhist philosophy in later ages.

Little is known about the actual organization and social composition of the first Buddhist communities on Chinese soil. There are indications that in the 2nd and 3rd centuries Buddhism was still largely a religion of foreigners – in fact, the only material relic of the 'church of Lo-yang' is a partially preserved votive inscription which is not in Chinese but in a middle Indian idiom. The Sangha still was rudimentary; in any case no Chinese version of the monastic rules (*vinaya*) was produced before the middle of the 3rd century. The most basic rules probably were transmitted orally, and for the relatively small number of monks and novices that may have been sufficient. One striking feature is the important role of the laity in the propagation of the Doctrine that would remain characteristic of Chinese Buddhism. As far as the Chinese believers are concerned, the available information suggests an urban, moderately literate public of limited education, at that time still completely outside the sphere of the cultural élite – one might think of a milieu of small traders, clerks, copyists and more or less Sinicized members of ethnic minorities. Han Buddhism still was a somewhat exotic, 'subcultural' kind of creed, comparable to the Orientalizing religions that around the same time spread throughout the Roman empire. Considering the intellectual climate of late Han times – a kind of *fin-de-siècle* sentiment mixed with despair and uncertainty, as was only natural at a time when the Han empire was crumbling and rebellions and warlordism raged over the country – it seems probable that the basic attraction of Buddhism lay in its insistence on the transience of all things, on the vanity of all existence, on the 'fleeting life', with all its dangers and sorrows, and on mental discipline and purification as the only way to escape from it. Compared with the ritual obligations of Confucian social ethics and the big magic of religious Taoism, it was a comparatively simple way, and those who trod it knew themselves protected by powerful and compassionate supernatural beings, who were ready to respond to prayers and to the observance of the basic moral rules and periodic fasting performed for the sake of the individual, his family and, in a general way, 'for all living creatures'. The monks, in addition, were supposed to observe celibacy and to practise the yoga-like techniques of trance (*dhyāna*) or mental concentration in order to 'control their mental activities' and gradually to eliminate all forms of attachment. In many respects, this has remained the fundamental content of Buddhist religious life in China through the centuries; philosophical speculations, scholastic learning and spiritual refinement have always been restricted to a tiny minority, even within the Sangha. In this early period, such a spiritual and intellectual superstructure did not yet exist, and it would only take shape towards the end of our first period, around the end of the 4th century, when Buddhism started to penetrate into the cultured upper strata of Chinese society.

In the meantime, however, the political scene had changed dramatically. In AD 220 the Han empire finally fell, after decades of disintegration and civil war. It was followed by about half a century of incessant warfare between three competing centres of political power (the Three Kingdoms, 220–265/280), and the reunification of China under the Western Chin (265–316) was short-lived and unstable. For Buddhism this situation was, in a way, favourable, because its spread was stimulated by political polycentrism. As far as we know, Han Buddhism had been limited to northern China; it now was disseminated to other parts, notably to the lower Yangtse region, the fertile and populous triangle between present-day Nanking, Soochow and Hangchow. In the north, the propagation of Buddhism and the founding of monasteries were mainly due to the activities of the great translator and missionary Dharmarakṣa, a Sinicized Indo-Scythian from Tun-huang, who with the help of his disciples is said to have made large-scale conversions among the population in the second half of the 3rd century.

At this time we observe the emergence of the typical pattern of geographical differentiation which has been referred to in our introduction: the contrast between a northern type of Buddhism, situated in the plains and loess-lands of the old heart-land of Chinese civilization, watered by the Yellow river, and a southern type, developing along the middle and lower reaches of the Yangtse and further south – vast regions that in the 3rd century were only in the first phase of exploitation, and that were destined to play an ever growing role, economically and culturally, in Chinese history. In the north, Buddhism was constantly nourished and stimulated by fresh impulses from Central Asia and beyond: the main Buddhist communities grew up along the eastern extension of the continental highway, from Tun-huang in the west to Lo-yang and Shantung in the east. In spite of all political turmoil, trade and traffic continued; the large cities in the north housed important colonies of foreign merchants. It is also no coincidence that we find, around 260, the first example of a Chinese pilgrim going to the western regions in search of Buddhist scriptures – the journey of the pioneer Chu Shih-hsing, whose journey to Khotan paved the way for the much more extensive exploits of such later illustrious pilgrims as Fa-hsien in the 5th, and Hsüan-tsang in the 7th century. It was also in the north that translation activities were pursued on a large scale: Dharmarakṣa alone is credited with the production of about 150 Chinese scriptures, among which we find some of the most important 'classics' of the Mahāyāna. Of momentous importance was the first complete version of the 'Scripture of the Lotus of the True Doctrine' (*Saddharma-puṇḍarīka-sūtra*). The *Lotus Sūtra*, with its doctrine of the 'One Buddha-vehicle' that to all believers opens the way to Buddhahood, its stress on the eternity and omniscience of the Buddha and its extraordinary wealth of images and parables, soon became by far the most popular and most venerated scripture in Chinese Buddhism. As a special revelation that claimed to transcend all other Mahāyāna doctrines, it was felt to hold a unique position – a view that found its final expression in the T'ien-t'ai sect of the 6th century, where the *Lotus Sūtra* came to be regarded as the highest fulfilment of the Law, the fifth and most complete exposition of the Truth.

Another indication of the growth of clerical communities in northern China is the appearance, around the middle of the 3rd century, of the first Chinese version of *vinaya* treatises, apparently because by that time the need was felt for a more authentic and detailed code of rules for the monastic life.

In the lower Yangtse region the situation was quite different. There is no sign of any contact with Central Asia, and the emphasis on monastic Buddhism is much less marked. In fact, the most prolific translator in the south, Chih Ch'ien, was a Chinese layman of Indo-Scythian descent, and most of the texts that he produced were 'polished' versions, aiming at literary elegance and readability rather than at accuracy. Among these texts, two may be singled out because of their extremely important role in Chinese Buddhism. Chih Ch'ien was the first to translate the fundamental scripture of the cult of Amitābha, the compassionate Buddha of the 'Western Paradise' (*Sukhāvatī*, in later Chinese devotionalism generally referred to as the 'Pure

Land'), to which every believer would be admitted who with utter sincerity focused his mind on Amitābha and repeated his holy name. The other fundamental scripture, which likewise had a special appeal to lay believers, was the 'Scripture of the Teaching of Vimalakīrti' (*Vimalakīrti-nirdeśa*), one of the masterpieces of Mahāyāna literature, which became so popular that it was translated seven times into Chinese. Its central figure is a pious and wealthy layman, who, because of his deep insight into the transcendent, 'empty', nature of all phenomena, was able to vanquish even the most illustrious saints in a series of metaphysical debates. From the 4th century it came to play a very important role in the Buddhism of the cultured laity, to whom it appealed by the nature and status of the main personage, by its high literary quality and by the depth of its philosophical arguments.

The emerging contrast between northern and southern Buddhism is also brought out by the latter's contacts with the extreme south of the empire, the region of present-day Hanoi. The northern part of present-day Vietnam had been incorporated into the Han empire in 111 BC; it was the beginning of about a thousand years of Chinese rule, in the course of which a mixed Sino-Vietnamese aristocratic élite emerged, which became thoroughly Sinicized. After the fall of the Han, this region theoretically remained the southernmost province of the empire, but all through the early medieval period the Chinese governors were virtually independent of the far-away capital. The process of Sinicization was stimulated by the constant influx of Chinese refugees, who in those centuries of turmoil made their way to this tranquil semi-colonial region.

But the Chinese territory inhabited by the Vietnamese people did not extend beyond present-day Da-nang. In the southern half of what is now Vietnam, two Indianized states had arisen: the kingdom of Funan, which covered the Mekong delta and most of present-day Kampuchea, and that of Champā, which ruled over the south-east part of Indo-China. Thus the basin of the Red river, which formed the centre of the Chinese province, was a borderland halfway between the centres of Chinese and Indian civilization. It is also from that area that we have one of the most interesting documents of early Chinese Buddhism: a 3rd-century polemical treatise, written by an otherwise unknown 'Master Mou', in which he defends Buddhism against the attacks of his traditionalist opponent. It vividly illustrates the negative reactions to Buddhism in Confucian circles, and also the tenacity of such stereotyped anti-Buddhist arguments, for we find the latter repeated again and again throughout a voluminous polemical and apologetic literature that accumulated in the course of the following centuries.

The anti-Buddhist arguments are mainly anticlerical, i.e. directed against the nature and claims of Buddhism as a monastic institution; to some extent they also attack Buddhism as a religious belief by branding it as 'barbarian', superstitious and misleading for simple people, with its promises of heavenly rewards and infernal punishments, but such doctrinal considerations have only occasionally played a major role. In general, polemical literature reflects the basic tension described in our introduction: the ideological conflict between the views and interests of the Buddhist clergy and those of the temporal authorities.

Roughly speaking, we can recognize three types of anticlerical argumentation: moral, utilitarian and political–economic. The moral argument contended that by its rejection of family duties the monastic life meant an unnatural violation of the sacred canons of social behaviour. From a utilitarian point of view, the monk's life is condemned as unproductive and useless for the community: 'for every commoner who does not plough or weave, other people will suffer hunger and cold'. Finally, the Sangha's claim to form an autonomous body is politically unacceptable, and also dangerous, because monasteries could easily become havens of refuge for criminal and anti-social elements, while their fiscal privileges and wealth undermined the economic basis of the state. The accusations were fundamental and threatening, because they questioned the Sangha's very right to exist, and time and again Buddhist 'defenders of the Faith', both monks and laymen, felt obliged to take up the challenge and to provide counter-arguments. This was no doubt most difficult in the case of the moral issue, for nobody could deny that the monk by joining the Sangha (or 'leaving the household', as is said even more explicitly in Chinese) indeed severed his family ties, and thereby deviated from the most basic principle of Chinese traditional ethics. The apologists exhausted their wits in proving that in the last analysis there was no contradiction between Buddhist and Confucian teachings, as both aimed at the perfection of man, or that the immense karmic merit gathered by the Sangha was of benefit to society as a whole, and therefore indirectly helped to maintain the moral order – but especially on this topic their arguments remained weak. The attack on utilitarian grounds was more easily countered: the monastic life is not useless, even if its fruits – saintliness and spiritual emancipation – are not of this world. And has not Confucius himself said that man should strive for virtue, and not for profit? And, finally, as a standard answer to the equally stereotyped political and economic charges: the monks are loyal and law-abiding, even if they are not subjected to temporal authorities; in fact, their church assists the ruler in maintaining peace and prosperity. There always will be occasional abuses of power and wealth, but the clergy as a whole cannot be blamed for the misconduct of a few of its members.

Such were the main themes in a debate that was never really concluded, one way or the other. It is remarkable that, to judge from Master Mou's defence of Buddhism, Buddhism had already become controversial as early as the 3rd century.

The conversion of the élite (*c.* 300–589)

Around 300 war and chaos spread over the country and shortly afterwards northern China fell under the rule of non-Chinese dynasties. When the exodus of the élite to the south started, many monks went too, no doubt because they had already established relations with the upper class. The latter fact was of capital importance for the whole further history of Buddhism in China. The penetration of Buddhism into the cultured élite led to the formation of a typical hybrid high-class Buddhism which in the early 4th century was transplanted to the lower Yangtse region, and soon came to play an important role in the intellectual life of the aristocracy.

The ruling class in medieval China consisted of a small number of 'great families': wealthy and powerful hereditary clans, the leaders of which monopolized the highest offices in the bureaucracy, dominated the court and manned the lesser posts with their relatives and clients. In those circles, Confucianism had lost much of its influence. The intellectual atmosphere was that of a sophisticated leisure class with little interest in practical politics. There was a vivid interest in metaphysical and philosophical problems; both philosophical Taoism and Taoist religion had gained many followers among the élite, and abstruse discussions were *à la mode*. It was in this atmosphere that Mahāyāna Buddhism, and particularly the profound Doctrine of Emptiness, found a ready audience. Scholar-monks such as Chih Tun (314–66) explained the mysteries of the Mahāyāna in terms of traditional Chinese thought, and thereby laid the foundations of a typically Chinese Buddhist philosophy.

The appearance of such learned and respected monks constitutes a turning point for the Sangha itself. Before that time, Buddhism had mainly been propagated by more or less Sinicized foreigners. We now see the formation of a clerical élite of Chinese monks, sometimes even from prominent families, as a cultural and social vanguard of the Sangha, moving in a milieu that was theirs by birth and education, and preaching with the authority of Chinese scholars.

Many of them may have joined the Order for spiritual reasons, because Buddhism seemed to them related, and yet superior, to their own philosophical tradition. But to others the monastery may have seemed a new form of the 'retired life': the ancient Chinese ideal of a life of reflection and quiet study, led by the 'gentleman-in-hiding' to escape the dangers of the official career and the vanity of worldly affairs. And finally, in medieval Chinese society with its rigid class barriers, the Buddhist Sangha, which in principle did not recognize such social distinctions, must have been attractive to members of cultured but relatively poor families. As a result, we see how from the 4th century onward some large monasteries developed into centres of learning and culture.

In the course of the 4th century, this type of Buddhism flourished in the lower Yangtse region, and branched out to other parts of the eastern Chin territory. The translation of Buddhist scriptures played only a secondary role, and could in no way be compared to the enormous productivity of some masters in the north such as Kumārajīva and his school in Ch'ang-an. Among the southern translators we may mention the pilgrim Fa-hsien (AD 317–420) who in the course of his stupendous journey to collect scriptures spent six years in India, and who left an invaluable account of his travels. Imperial favour (in about 380 the Chin emperor was the first Chinese ruler formally to accept the lay precepts) and the support of the aristocracy made Buddhism flourish: around 400 the Chin territory counted more than 1,700 monasteries and 80,000 monks and nuns. But there also was a growing opposition in conservative circles, in which all the well-known arguments were used, and occasionally some attempts were made to 'screen' the Sangha or to put it under state supervision. However, under the southern dynasties this never led to forceful repression, as it sometimes did in the 'barbarian' north. Under the later southern dynasties the growth of the clergy continued; in 550 the number of monks and nuns had risen to 82,000.

It was much stimulated by imperial patronage, which reached its absolute record under the fanatically Buddhist Emperor Wu (reigned 502–49) of the Liang dynasty, who consciously took the famous Aśoka as his model. He prohibited Taoism, solicited huge sums from his courtiers for temple-building, repeatedly served in temples as a menial (to be 'ransomed' by public subscription), and organized vast religious assemblies at which he personally took the 'bodhisattva vow' and explained the scriptures. It goes without saying that the imperial zealot has been as highly praised in Buddhist literature as he was condemned as an irresponsible fool in Confucian historiography.

Under the northern dynasties Buddhism was, for various reasons, patronized by most non-Chinese rulers. They welcomed Buddhist monks as a new type of court-magician, able to ensure their prosperity and military victories by means of prayers and spells. They also employed monks as counsellors, using the foreign doctrine as a means to counterbalance the influence of Confucianism – for throughout Chinese history 'barbarian' conquerors were always torn between the opposing aims of preserving their own cultural and ethnic identity and complete assimilation, and the Confucian socio-political doctrine was perhaps the most powerful force of Sinicization. This led to a close connection between state and church: government patronage on a grand scale, but also supervision of the Sangha by means of monk-officials held responsible for the activities of the clergy. Taoism had become a powerful rival competing for the favour of the ruler, and the machinations of Taoist masters contributed to outbursts of anticlericalism and to some ruthless persecutions.

Doctrinally, the most important event was the arrival in 402 of Kumārajīva, the great missionary and

Secular donors to monasteries often commemorated themselves by pictures and inscriptions. This inscription, from one of the Lung-mên caves near Lo-yang, records the gift of an image of the Buddha by a prince of An-ting, AD 511.

translator from Kučā, at Ch'ang-an, then the capital of a fervently Buddhist ruling house of Tibetan origin. He introduced Madhyamaka philosophy into China and produced a huge number of Chinese versions with the help of the largest state-sponsored 'translation team' known in history.

Imperial patronage and state supervision reached their apogee under the rulers of the (probably proto-Mongolian) Toba-Wei, who dominated the whole of northern China and part of Central Asia, first from their frontier capital in northern Shansi, and after 494 from the ancient capital of Lo-yang – a shift that symbolizes their complete acceptance of Chinese culture.

There was an outburst of temple-building of various types. In 518 one-third of the surface of Lo-yang was occupied by more than 1,300 Buddhist buildings. Of such temples none has survived, for they were built according to the tradition of Chinese monumental wood architecture, which in spite of its impressive size made them fragile and vulnerable. Contemporary descriptions of the large monasteries show us a picture of enormous wealth and extravagance, with pagodas and temple halls that would have dwarfed even the biggest medieval cathedral. Pagodas – a hybrid form based on both Chinese and Indian prototypes – were the show-pieces of such complexes; the most famous one, at Lo-yang, rose to almost two hundred metres (650 feet).

But other equally impressive monuments still remain: the huge cave temples, the most famous of which are situated near the two successive Toba-Wei capitals: the Yün-kang caves near Ta-t'ung, and the Lung-mên complex near Lo-yang. The practice of hollowing out such sanctuaries in steep cliffs, no doubt inspired by Indian and Central Asian examples, and of lavishly adorning them with wall-paintings and statues, some of gigantic size, had started around 400 at Tun-huang in the extreme north-west. Under the Wei and later dynasties it was continued on a much larger scale, at dozens of sites all over northern China: veritable treasure-houses of religious art that combine Chinese with Indian and Central Asian elements.

For the Sangha, the combination of patronage and state control was at least materially profitable. The economic foundation of the church was strengthened by a kind of monastic tenancy called 'Sangha households' and 'Buddha households', consisting of great numbers of peasant families and serfs allocated to the large monasteries to work the temple fields and to do menial work. The system provided the temples with a regular income and an enormous increase in tax-free landed property, and before long the largest monasteries had developed into veritable monastic estates engaging in land reclamation, financial activities and various types of commercial enterprise. The Sangha underwent an explosive growth: in 477, the Wei empire counted about 6,500 monasteries and 77,000 monks and nuns; forty years later their numbers had increased to 30,000 and 2,000,000 respectively. Needless to say that it also had its disadvantages. It often led to excessive this-worldliness, pursuit of material gain and political machinations. It also made the church vulnerable to attack, both from 'hard-core' Confucian traditionalists and from Taoist rivals, both of whom played a role in the severe persecutions known as the 'first' and 'second catastrophes' of Buddhism, of 446 and 574.

It must be stressed that official sponsorship only concerned a privileged minority: the largest monasteries led by an élite of cultured monks and clerical managers. The Sangha had come to consist of two very unequal parts: an upper layer of top-grade institutions entertaining close relations with the court and the ruling êlite, and a vast body of small temples and chapels, each manned by a few monks working among the common people. At that level, Buddhism merged with local non-Buddhist cults and religious movements. Doctrinally, they had very little to do with the world of scriptural studies and intellectual debates – in fact, most of them may have been hardly literate. Here, other types of Buddhist religion evolved: simple forms of devotion and exorcism; Buddhist rites mixed with the ceremonial of traditional ancestor worship; and also popular messianic movements, often based on the belief that the suffering world could at last expect the appearance of the future Buddha Maitreya who would establish an ideal world of prosperity and justice. Such movements could easily become politicized: many insurrectionist movements throughout Chinese history were led by charismatic leaders – sometimes even monks – who posed as prophets or incarnations of Maitreya; no less than nine such Buddhist-inspired rebellions are recorded in the 5th and early 6th centuries, all of which were fiercely suppressed.

Of course such clearly seditious sects remained an exception; in general, the Sangha at a popular level quietly performed its peaceful work. But in the eyes of the government, the enormous mass of small, not officially recognized, or even 'clandestine' temples remained elusive, uncontrollable and therefore, in principle, suspect. The social polarization of the Sangha created a situation to which the government responded in two ways: towards the élite of big monasteries with patronage combined with institutional control and, occasionally, severe restrictive measures of an economic nature; towards the mass of the Sangha with a mixture of *laisser-faire* (for no pre-modern bureaucracy has ever been able really to control society at village level) and continuing distrust. This situation has basically persisted till modern times.

The growth of Buddhism in the early medieval period also led to its introduction into Korea, which at that time still was divided into three independent kingdoms. It had far-reaching consequences, not only for Korea itself, but also on a wider scale, since Korean monks were to play a very important role in the earliest spread of Buddhism in Japan. In the late 4th century Buddhism was introduced at the various Korean courts from both the 'barbarian' states in northern China and the Chinese territory in the south, apparently as a by-product of diplomatic relations. In the northern kingdom of Koguryŏ the king immediately patronized the new doctrine, which he made the official religion in 392. The two other Korean kingdoms, Paekche in the south-west and Silla in the south-east, received the first missionaries in the same official way, but from the Chinese court at Nanking: Paekche in 384, and Silla, which culturally and politically lagged behind its two rivals till the 6th century, in 528. Of course such dates merely indicate the moments at which the foreign religion made contact with the court, and therefore were recorded in historical literature; the actual penetration probably was a gradual process that may have started earlier.

In Korea, as somewhat later in Japan, Buddhism functioned not only as a religious movement, but also as a great civilizing force – a channel through which Chinese culture was introduced into a rather primitive tribal society. Its most important contribution in this field was no doubt the introduction of the Chinese script, which enabled the Koreans to absorb the great tradition of Chinese classical literature. The adoption of Buddhism as the official state religion in all of the three Korean kingdoms no doubt also implied their willingness to absorb Chinese culture as a whole.

We do not yet notice a parallel development in northern Vietnam. As we have seen, Buddhism had become part of the upper-class culture in that remote part of the Chinese empire, but there are no indications that it spread among the mass of the people. It is also possible that ethnic tensions played a role. In that it came from the north, Buddhism was associated with a Chinese semi-colonial administration that was hated by the common people – in fact, the first anti-Chinese revolt already broke out in AD 39, and the Chinese authorities had regularly to cope with indigenous resistance during the thousand years of their rule. It is therefore probably no coincidence that the real floresence of Buddhism in northern Vietnam only took place after the Vietnamese made themselves independent, in the 10th century.

The reunification of China in 589 after centuries of political fragmentation marks the end of the formative phase of Chinese Buddhism. Both in the north and in the south, Buddhism had come to permeate Chinese society at all levels. The Sangha had grown into a social class of its own, with considerable spiritual and material influence. Doctrinally, the most important scriptures, scholastic treatises and *vinaya* collections had been translated, and the Chinese masters had begun to elaborate their own doctrinal system on that basis. Thus the foundations had been laid for the following phase of independent creative development, that of the Sui and T'ang period, which in many respects constitutes the apogee of Buddhism in China.

Buddhism under the Sui and the T'ang (589–906)

Under the Sui (589–618) and T'ang (618–906) dynasties, medieval Chinese civilization reached its zenith, and passed over it. Once more, a strong central government extended its power over Central Asia and imposed its suzerainty upon surrounding vassal states such as Korea, Annam and Tibet. The capital Ch'ang-an (the present Sian) was rebuilt into a symbol of universal rule: a huge rectangular metropolis with a million inhabitants that housed the palace complex and the central administration of one of the largest bureaucratic systems the world has ever known. But until the 9th century the general picture is still medieval: an agrarian economy regulated through a system of *per capita* land allotments, and supporting a state that still was dominated by an élite of aristocratic clans with large land estates.

In this world, Buddhism flourished as never before. Most emperors patronized the Buddhist church, sometimes clearly for political reasons. Thus the founder of the Sui consciously posed as a *cakravartin*, 'Turner-of-the-wheel', the saintly ruler of Buddhist tradition, and the famous (and notorious) Empress Wu, who for fifteen years (690–705) ruled China as a capable but ruthless despot, used Buddhism to justify her seizure of power by claiming to be an incarnation. Successive rulers maintained a system of 'state temples' established to perform rituals for the well-being of state and dynasty, and some of them entertained close relations with famous Buddhist masters, as did many members of the aristocracy. But, as under the Toba-Wei, patronage was always combined with attempts to place the Sangha under bureauratic control – in T'ang times even exercised by lay officials – to restrict its size, and to ensure its 'purity' by a system of clerical examinations.

Once more under Chinese control, Central Asia retained its function as a transit zone between China and India until the late 7th century. This led to an upsurge of Chinese pilgrimage in the early T'ang, the most famous representative of which is Hsüan-tsang (*c.* 596–664), an exceptional figure in Chinese Buddhism, not only because of his stupendous journey (629–45) and the quality of his observations, but also because he was a great scholar and translator, and one of the very few Chinese ever to have mastered Sanskrit. The products of Hsüan-tsang's translation team mark the highest point of Chinese activities in this field, both in terms of quantity and of quality. In the late 7th century, the Arab conquests obstructed the overland route to India, so that more and more pilgrims chose to go by sea, from the south China coast to Tāmralipti (near modern Calcutta) and Sri Lanka.

Buddhism was by far the most creative movement in the religious and intellectual life of the era. Some of the schools or sects that flourished from the 6th to the 9th centuries were directly inspired by India: Hsüan-tsang founded the Chinese counterpart of Indian 'idealistic' (Yogācāra) Buddhism, and somewhat later various types of esoteric tantric Buddhism were introduced by Indian masters. But other schools were basically Chinese. All of them, whether transplanted or developed in China, gave rise to an immense exegetical literature, partly based on translated scriptures, and partly consisting of independent theories of great originality.

Some sects, such as the Ching-t'u ('Pure Land') School, were devotional, propagating faith, surrender to the mercy of Amitābha and repentance as means to reach salvation. Other schools were based on the principle of *p'an-chiao*, 'classification of doctrines': the idea that one particular scripture contained the highest truth, and that all other scriptures belonged to a sequence of preliminary stages of revelation, each using a different teaching method and being addressed to a different audience. Thus the T'ien-t'ai sect recognized a scheme of five levels of teaching, the whole culminating in the 'One Vehicle' Doctrine of the *Lotus Sūtra*, as the equally influential Hua-yen sect did with the *Hua-yen* or 'Garland Scripture' (*Avataṃsaka-sūtra*).

The 'Meditation School' (Ch'an, Japanese Zen) as an organized movement arose in the 7th century as a unique blend of Chinese (notably Taoist) and Mahāyāna notions and practices. It holds that the universal 'Buddha-nature' is immanent in ourselves and must be realized 'directly', in a mind-to-mind communication between master and disciple, without relying on canonical texts or rational theorizing. To effect this, all reasoning must be broken down: hence the characteristic use of unconventional means to evoke in the disciple the sudden and 'wordless' experience of Enlightenment: perplexing meditation themes, paradoxes, baffling answers; even yelling and beating are used to let 'the bottom of the tub fall out' and to plunge the practitioner into a state of 'no-mind'. In this state no distinction is made between holy and profane, between the religious career and the simple tasks of everyday life: 'the Highest Truth is contained in carrying water and chopping firewood'.

In accordance with the typically Chinese predilection for genealogical filiation, several schools afterwards rewrote their early history as a succession of 'patriarchs'. This tendency was very marked in Ch'an, which traced its spiritual genealogy in China to the semi-legendary Bodhidharma (early 6th century), and further back to the Buddha himself. It eventually led to a bewildering variety of sects and sub-sects within Ch'an.

It is not known how large the clergy in T'ang times was, in spite of some official figures. When in 729 all monks and nuns were forced to be registered at prefectural level, the clergy numbered 126,100 monks and nuns in 5,358 monasteries, and at the time of the great persecution (842–5) the official sources speak of 4,600 monasteries and more than 40,000 small temples and shrines; at that time the number of monks and nuns compelled to return to lay life is stated to be 260,500. But those figures probably only refer to fully ordained monks and nuns, and the number of 'monks among the people' who often had entered the Order in irregular ways (sometimes even by buying an ordination certificate – a disastrous practice that started in T'ang times) may have been ten times as great.

In any case, the social hierarchization within the Sangha – a very small élite of cultured monks moving in the higher strata of society, and a vast majority of common priests active among the population – was perpetuated under the T'ang, as was, in institutional

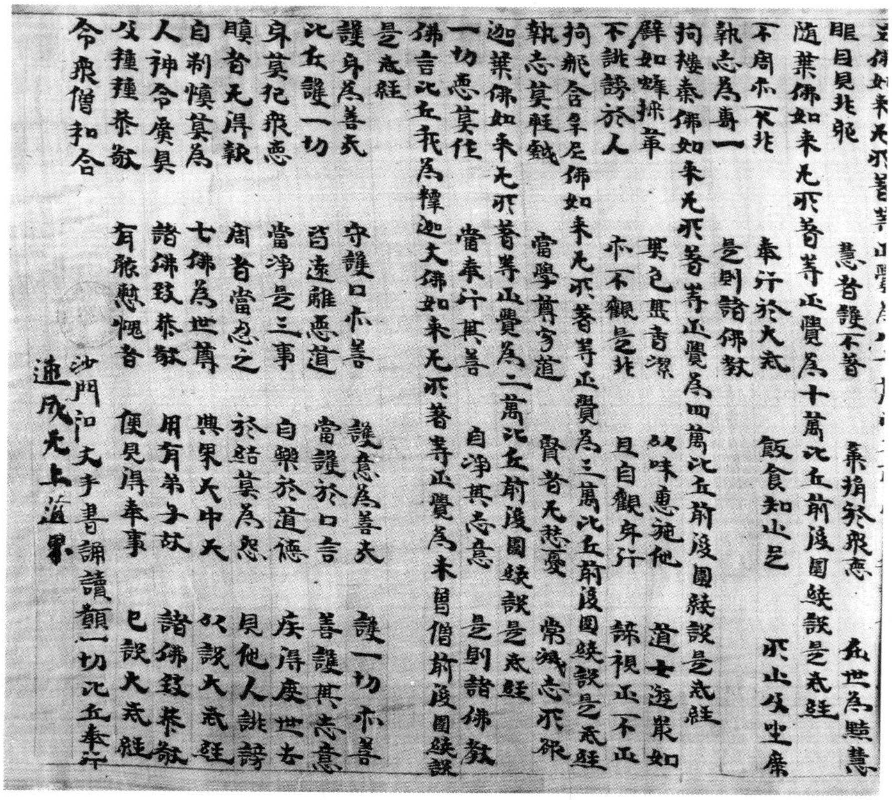

Among the early documents of the Sangha in China is this text concerned with monastic discipline, written in black ink on yellow waxed silk. Texts such as this survive from the early 5th century AD; this one dates from the 6th century.

terms, the difference between an 'establishment' consisting of the largest and richest monasteries with their landed estates, their sumptuous buildings peopled with hundreds of monks, and their labour force of temple serfs and slaves, and, on the other hand, the innumerable small temples and shrines served by only a few priests. In this respect the position of the Ch'an School is very interesting, as its opposition to the Buddhist establishment – notably the rich T'ien-t'ai monasteries – was not only doctrinal (the utter rejection of scholastic speculations) but also institutional. Around 800 the Ch'an master Huai-hai (also named Pai-chang) had formulated a new set of monastic rules for the Ch'an communities, which at least in T'ang times were small and strictly hierarchical: a master surrounded by a number of personal disciples. A striking feature was the introduction (in complete defiance of the traditional *vinaya* rules) of manual labour which each Ch'an monk had to perform. The monks had to work the fields, or, as a famous Ch'an dictum said: 'One day no work – one day no food.' Ch'an monachism thus escaped from the charge of being 'parasitic' – which, as we have seen, was one of the standard objections to the clergy.

In T'ang times, the Sangha had come to play a very important role in social life. Religious societies in which both monks and laity took part flourished everywhere, with their curious combination of devotion, good works, and down-to-earth 'mutual help'. The Mahāyāna idea of charity, reinforced by the traditional Chinese preference for concrete, this-worldly action, inspired a whole range of public welfare activities, set up by monasteries and lay societies: hospitals, dispensaries, aid for the poor, and food distribution in times of famine. Monks occasionally even engaged in establishing public facilities such as roads, bridges, wells and bathhouses. Buddhist festivals and processions became part of popular folklore; Buddhist temple fairs (originally limited to the sale of religious articles such as incense and icons) developed into regular markets, and thus contributed to the disintegration of the strictly regulated and government-controlled market system of the early T'ang. Culturally, by far the most important material contribution of Buddhism to Chinese – and indeed to world – culture was the invention of printing. It was first developed in Buddhist circles as a cheap and effective way to reproduce charms, sacred images and eventually also complete scriptures. The invention was made in the 8th century, or even earlier, for the oldest printed book in existence, the *Diamond Sūtra* of AD 868, exhibits a technical perfection which can only be the result of a long previous development. The first printing of the whole Buddhist Canon was done by imperial order in 972; around the same time the new technique started to be used for secular purposes.

This great and positive role of the Buddhist church in society can hardly be dissociated from economic activities that in the eyes of contemporary critics were less laudable. All the time, the wealth of the large monasteries continued to grow. It was primarily based on landed property and the exploitation of agrarian man-power attached to the temple fields. Some of it had been acquired legally, as government allotments or donations. But it was continuously expanded by less legal means such as the creation, by rich landowners, of purely formal 'merit cloisters' to escape taxation, and the purchase of land by the monastic manors, in spite of the theoretical prohibition of the sale of land according to the early T'ang regulations. The large monasteries amassed great wealth in the form of what was called an 'Inexhaustible Treasury' – a kind of collectively owned capital that was used for such mundane purposes as moneylending and pawnbroking (Chinese monasteries have played an important role in the development of banking in China), and various kinds of commercial enterprise such as the exploitation of water-powered rolling mills and oil presses. A practice that was much criticized was that of hoarding copper and precious metals in the form of religious statues and ritual objects; already in 715 the government ordered the confiscation of all copper and bronze images in order to turn them into cash.

Around the middle of the 8th century, the T'ang state had been shaken by a disastrous civil war from which it never recovered. The state was impoverished and eager to use any means to replenish the treasury, and this certainly became a factor in the mounting tension between the government and the Buddhist church in the 9th century. But economic considerations were by no means the only ones. The late T'ang witnessed a general change in the intellectual climate – a tendency to return to the basis of Chinese tradition, which was no doubt strengthened by the ever increasing importance of the Confucian examination system as the only respectable way to an official career. In such a climate, the old argument of the 'barbarian' origin of Buddhism gained new force.

Under Emperor Wu-tsung (841–7) the final confrontation took place. The nature of the measures taken shows clearly that the main motivation was economic: it was a radical attempt to break the power of monastic Buddhism and to confiscate its wealth. The persecution took the form of a long series of restrictive and repressive measures that started in 842 and reached their climax three years later; in Buddhist sources it is known as the 'third catastrophe' of the Doctrine.

In 845, order was given to destroy all Buddhist establishments, to secularize all monks and nuns, to free all temple slaves (150,000 were emancipated), and to confiscate all temple lands and other material possessions of the Sangha. The edict was rigorously carried out, at least in the central provinces.

The suppression of 842–5 was directed against the organized clergy, and not against lay believers; at no time was the Buddhist religion as such prohibited. It was, moreover, of short duration: within a few years Wu-tsung's successor revoked the anti-Buddhist edicts, and the Sangha started functioning again. It is true that the persecution was a blow from which the church never quite recovered – but apart from the effects of material destruction, the general decline of Buddhism after the late 9th century also had other, and more fundamental, causes. They are closely related to the great processes of economic, social and cultural change which by that time started to gain momentum. Those processes gradually undermined and transformed the structure and institutions of medieval Chinese society, of which the Buddhist Sangha at the time of its greatest prosperity was an integral part. Buddhism as it had developed under the Sui and T'ang was far too powerful to be crushed in one blow, by imperial decree. Its decline was a gradual process – it petered out and slowly lost its intellectual vitality and creativity, and its social status, in a world in which the educated élite more and more turned away from it, and in which the best minds were attracted to the examination hall rather than to the monastery.

Before turning to the next phase, we must once more return to T'ang Buddhism and place it in a wider context, by considering the powerful influence which it exerted upon neighbouring countries in eastern Asia. Since the late 6th century, the Japanese court had embarked upon a cultural reform movement aimed at a massive borrowing of Chinese civilization, and Chinese Buddhism played a central role in it. Hosts of Japanese monks went to T'ang China to collect scriptures and to study under famous masters, and T'ang Buddhism was transplanted to Japan in all its diversity. Korea, since the 7th century united under the royal house of Silla (668–935), presents a similar picture. This period and the first centuries of the Koryŏ dynasty (936–1392) form the classical age of Korean Buddhism. Korean monks regularly went to T'ang China for study, and some of them even travelled to India. Many Chinese-style temples and monasteries were built, impressive remains of which survive, notably near Kyŏngju (east of Taegu): the cave temples of Sokkur-am and the famous 'Monastery of the Buddha-realm', both of which date from the 8th century. In the Silla period all schools of Chinese Buddhism were introduced into Korea, and flourished in a congenial atmosphere – for there, unlike T'ang China, where the Sangha always had to cope with the pressure of a hostile state ideology, Buddhism was maintained as the official religion, much patronized by the royal court, and it held that position till the end of the 14th century. Official sponsorship also led to the huge undertaking of bringing out a complete printed edition of the Buddhist Canon in the 11th century. It was repeated in the years 1237–51, and the more than 80,000 printing blocks that were needed to produce it are still preserved in the Haein Monastery near Taegu. In the course of the Koryŏ period, Ch'an Buddhism became very popular, and gradually absorbed most other schools.

In what is now Vietnam, Buddhism reached its golden age somewhat later, after the realization of national independence around the middle of the 10th century. Royal sponsorship of Buddhism started under the short-lived Dinh dynasty (968–80) and reached its apogee in the following period of stability and progress under the Ly dynasty (1009–1224). In spite of the continuing struggle against the powerful northern neighbour, the Dai Viet state established by the Ly rulers was closely patterned after the T'ang, and the influence of Chinese culture dominated all spheres of life. The royal court lavishly patronized the Sangha and financially supported the building of monasteries. At the same time Buddhism was spread among the population, where it thoroughly mixed with local creeds and customs, notably the cult of spirits and divine village patrons. In one respect the Ly rulers went much farther than the T'ang ever had done: prominent monks were admitted to the administration of the kingdom and came to play an important political role. It logically led to the elevation of Buddhism to the rank of official state religion in the middle of the 12th century. Since this state-sponsored Buddhism was of Chinese origin, it was exclusively Mahāyānist, with a special emphasis on Ch'an and Pure Land Doctrines.

Buddhism in pre-modern China (10th–19th centuries)

In the 10th century, the great processes of growth and change, out of which a new type of civilization was to emerge, had gained sufficient thrust to effect large-scale transformations. The semi-feudal system dominated by the aristocracy gradually gave way to a bureaucratic one, in which government posts were filled by members of a much larger group recruited through a highly competitive examination system – the 'gentry'. This new upper class was largely urban in its way of life and cultural expression. In the late T'ang, trade and industry had broken through the barriers imposed by the dirigistic, agrarian-oriented state and had developed into large-scale enterprises, including the creation of regional trade networks, banking and international shipping. In the same period, the economic centre had gradually shifted from the arid and war-stricken north to the rich rice-growing regions of central and south-eastern China. The huge cities witnessed the development of a characteristic urban culture, shared by the élite of gentry and rich merchants. It was the typical expression of an upper class, the attention of which is focused on literary pursuits and the arts of peace – there is no greater contrast than that between the warlike early T'ang aristocrat on horseback and the delicate but somewhat bloodless gentleman-scholar of late imperial China: the Confucian gentleman surrounded by his books and curios, entrenched in his own world of literary studies, bureaucratic ambitions and moral maxims. Confucian values and attitudes ever more predominated. The 11th and 12th centuries witnessed a powerful 'Neo-Confucianist' revival in which the older system of moral and political thought was expanded into an all-embracing scholastic doctrine, a *summa theologiae* that in the 14th century became the official orthodoxy. The family and clan system, with its typically Confucian code of behaviour, spread throughout the population; in late imperial times Chinese society became thoroughly Confucianized.

The general picture of pre-modern China is one of surprising continuity and stability, especially as regards political institutions. Apart from a tendency towards autocracy or absolutism at the very top, the basic structures of government were maintained throughout this whole period; with the exception of the short and rather atypical intermezzo formed by the period of Mongol domination (Yüan dynasty, 1276–1368), the conception of law and legal procedures remained the same, and the examination system, in an ever more petrified form, survived till 1905.

Periods of territorial expansion practically coincide with those in which China was ruled by dynasties of foreign origin. The native Sung (960–1279) was weak and defensive, and eventually even had to abandon northern China to alien conquerors ('Southern Sung', 1126–1279). Under the Mongols, Peking was the residence of the great khan, who theoretically exercised a kind of overlordship over the other parts of the Mongol world empire, and Khubilai also embarked on an ambitious, if unsuccessful, policy of further conquest. Under the native Ming dynasty (1368–1644) the empire was again almost reduced to 'China proper', whereas the last dynasty (Ch'ing, 1644–1912), established by the Manchu conquerors from the north-east, again succeeded in extending its power over the steppe zone and Central Asia. The latter region had long since been Islamicized. However, the exercise of Chinese suzerainty over Tibet, and, under the Ch'ing, over most of the Mongol tribes, eventually provided China with a 'Buddhist hinterland' dominated by Lamaism. In the late 18th century a general process of decline, mainly due to dramatic population increase coupled with economic stagnation, set in. Imperial China entered the 19th century in a state of malaise, aggravated by widespread corruption and devastating rebellions. It was in such a situation of internal crisis that China became exposed to the impact of Western expansion, and under that combined pressure the old order started to disintegrate.

There can be no doubt that Buddhism steadily declined in the course of this whole period. The most important factor in this decline probably was ideological: the resurgence of Confucianism as a universal doctrine, a vast synthesis that came to dominate the intellectual life of the cultured upper class. This Neo-Confucian orthodoxy became the basis of the examination system, and, consequently, the standard ideology of the gentry. Another factor was the ongoing tendency to return to the traditions of Chinese antiquity as the sole source of inspiration. Paradoxically, the Neo-Confucian synthesis owed much to Buddhist influence: some of the most basic metaphysical conceptions that had evolved in various Chinese Buddhist schools were incorporated into it, albeit in socialized and politicized forms. Confucianism took over, but it did so by

Monks welcoming a superior

Monks studying under a master

Introducing a novice to his master

Chanting the sutras

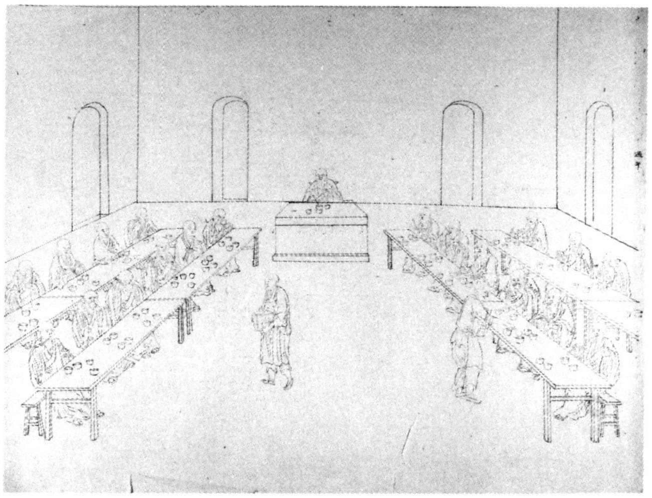

Midday meal in a monastery

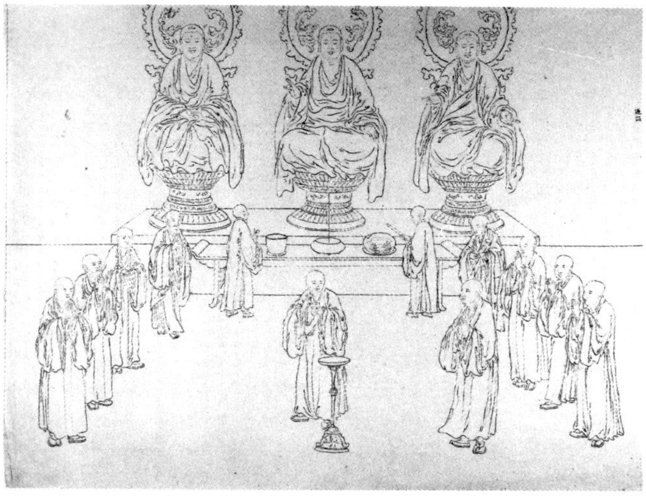

Worship in front of three Buddha images

A series of drawings made in the 19th century and now in the British Museum, London, gives a vivid glimpse into the daily activities of a Buddhist monastery in China. These are six examples from the series.

An engraved design on a stela in the Shao-lin temple, near Lo-yang, Honan, expresses one of the most characteristic features of late Chinese popular thought, the 'Unity of the Three Religions'. Here the central figure is a combination of the Buddha, Lao-tzu and Confucius.

digesting some of the strongest points of its rival. In that sense the greatest contribution of Buddhism may have been the way in which it helped to shape the Neo-Confucian ideology that was to dominate Chinese intellectual culture till modern times.

It is a remarkable fact that the triumph of Confucianism was not limited to late imperial China – it can also be observed in the surrounding countries, and appears to have been a general trend in Far Eastern history. In Japan, the Tokugawa shōgunate, which in 1603 imposed its military overlordship on the whole country, officially sponsored Confucianism and subjected the Buddhist clergy to rigorous government control. In Korea, the reaction had started earlier, and was directly inspired by the Chinese example. Under the Yi dynasty (1392–1910) Confucianism became the official ideology, and the Sangha, long since undermined by sectarian struggles and political machinations, was abandoned by the cultured élite, expelled from the cities, and exposed to a severe anticlerical policy. As in China, the decline of Korean Buddhism has continued till recent times.

To complete the picture, Le Thanh-ton, the strongest ruler of the Vietnamese later Le dynasty, in the 15th century reorganized his state into a close copy of the Ming empire, with Confucianism as the official ideology. Here also, Confucian indoctrination was practised intensively and effectively, and Buddhism slowly declined. In the 18th century there was, however, a certain revival of Buddhism which resulted in the rise of indigenous Vietnamese sects.

In China, the general decline of Buddhism did not show in quantitative terms. Popular religion flourished among the common people as it had always done; religious sects – sometimes of a clearly 'seditious type', such as the religious rebels that helped to overthrow the Mongol regime – were at times very active; the size of the Sangha hardly decreased, and temples and monasteries continued to be established, at all levels, the biggest ones not seldom under imperial patronage. The decline was, in the first place, intellectual, as a result of the 'brain-drain' caused by the attraction of Confucianism, coupled with the Confucianization of society in general. The lowering of the intellectual status and social respectability of the clergy is shown in many ways. Official proclamations and, at a lower level, 'family instructions' and clan rules often refer to Buddhism as to something close to 'opium for the people'. In popular literature monks and nuns are usually described as greedy and ignorant, and monasteries as places of moral corruption. Thus, Confucianization had a threefold negative effect: as intellectuals rarely became monks, the status of the Sangha declined; thus socially degraded, the Sangha more and more adapted itself to the demands of an uncultured public; and, finally, this situation in turn discouraged serious scriptural studies and scholarly activities.

Another factor was, of course, the disappearance of Buddhism from India and Central Asia, which put an end to fresh impulses, and to the activities of foreign missionaries in China. The last outburst of translation activities, undertaken by an official 'translation bureau' manned with Indian monks and Chinese assistants, took place in the late 10th century; after that ambitious but rather artificial attempt to revive the glories of T'ang Buddhism, the great tradition of translation work came to an end.

But the doctrinal impoverishment of Chinese Buddhism is even more clearly shown by the disappearance of most of the schools that had developed in Sui and T'ang times. There was a general tendency towards syncretism and mutual borrowing, and finally only two basic forms survived: Ch'an Buddhism and popular Pure Land devotionalism. But syncretism was not limited to trends within Buddhism – the old idea of the 'Unity of the Three Religions' (Confucianism, Buddhism and Taoism) gained great popularity. Thus Buddhism was losing much of its rich diversity, and even something of its identity as a whole.

In many cases, particularly under the Ming and Ch'ing, such syncretistic theories were developed by laymen, whose role became more important as that of the Sangha declined. There were countless religious groups and clubs, and Buddhism became closely associated with family life, as Buddhist priests performed rituals for the benefit of ancestors, at weddings and funerals, to pray for rain, and to exorcise evil powers. One of the most popular Buddhist festivals, that of 'All Souls' on the fifteenth day of the seventh month, was devoted to a great ritual in which laymen and monks together 'transferred' the merit generated by the ceremonial to rescue all suffering souls. Such salutary action was even extended to animals, as is witnessed by the widespread custom of *fang sheng*, i.e. buying animals and setting them free. Many large monasteries even contained a fish-pond for that purpose.

Religious policy was at all times still characterized by the combination of dirigistic control and occasional patronage. But in general (with the exception of the Mongol period) it was less dramatic in its manifestations: large-scale persecutions were no longer undertaken, and, on the other hand, imperial sponsorship (often connected with the idea of magical protection) never reached excessive proportions. A special role in religious policy was reserved for Tibetan, and, somewhat later, Mongolian Lamaism, which was regularly patronized under the last three dynasties, to a large extent for political reasons.

The phenomenon of secret and 'subversive' sects continued throughout this period. They often were branches of the notorious 'White Lotus Society', a messianic sect of the 12th century that played an important role in the anti-Mongol rebellions at the end of the Yüan; in the course of the following centuries it branched out into a whole range of secret societies, some of which even exist today. In Ming and Ch'ing times, the religious character of such movements was still very marked: it was not without reason that martial 'monk-heroes' (notably those of the famous Shao-lin Monastery in Honan, where a special type of fighting technique called *kung-fu* was practised) figure in the founding myths of secret societies, and that the 'fighting monk' became a favourite theme in popular lore. Revolts, partly inspired by Buddhist messianism, harassed the imperial authorities in both Ming and Ch'ing, and the great rebellions that in the first half of the 19th century almost toppled the Ch'ing dynasty actually started with a massive uprising of the 'White Lotus rebels', which it took the government ten years (1796–1805) to suppress.

If not much can be said about high-level doctrinal and philosophical developments in late Chinese Buddhism, this loss is somewhat compensated for by the fact that for this period there is much more information about Buddhism as it functioned in actual practice, both within the monasteries and among the population at large. Our picture of monastic life, largely based on the invaluable observations of modern Western and Japanese scholars, is fairly complete – with one deplorable exception. As the reader may have noticed, 'nuns' have so far only been mentioned in passing, and not without reason. Due to the extreme inaccessibility of convents – for in China the original restrictions which the *vinaya* imposed upon nuns have been reinforced by the strictness of Confucian norms concerning women and sexual morals – the female Order still is practically a *terra incognita*. Popular literature contains many scenes situated in nunneries, which generally are depicted as places of vice and debauchery, but such descriptions, written by and for representatives of an extremely male-oriented culture, actually tell us more about the authors' prejudices and fantasies than about reality.

The late imperial period marks the final stage in the absorption and transformation of Buddhism. This is most clearly demonstrated by some typically Chinese developments in the representation of divine beings and the lore connected with them. The gruesome tortures of the Buddhist hells became a favourite topic in popular religion, and Yama, the infernal judge of Buddhist mythology, naturally assumed the features of a Chinese magistrate with mandarin cap and gown. Kuan-yin, originally the Chinese equivalent of the bodhisattva Avalokiteśvara and one of the attendants of the Buddha Amitābha, assumed a female form and became immensely popular as a kind of Buddhist madonna, saving people from all kinds of distress, danger and disease, and as a giver of – preferably male – offspring. The Buddhist messiah Maitreya underwent an amazing transformation: in popular imagination he became identified with a 10th-century eccentric monk called Pu-tai, 'Hemp Sack', who in his time had posed as a manifestation of Maitreya – and, as a result, the slender and majestic figure that we know from so many early sculptures changed into the familiar 'laughing Buddha', a pot-bellied *bon-vivant* with a broad grin. In such cases, divine beings assumed typically Chinese forms. But in other figures the foreign character was stressed. Bodhidharma, honoured as the Indian patriarch who introduced Ch'an into China, was invariably represented as a formidable, dark-skinned 'barbarian' master with a fierce expression and big rolling eyes, and in the *arhats* (*lo-han* in Chinese), the original disciples of the Buddha who in China were believed to act as protectors of the Buddhist religion, the outlandish features were even more stressed. Any monastery that could afford it had its *lo-han* hall containing up to five hundred life-size statues representing the stern Fathers of earliest Buddhist tradition in different postures, often wildly gesticulating, and with almost grotesque facial expressions.

At a more sophisticated level, Ch'an Buddhism maintained itself, but it was also much changed, both doctrinally and institutionally. Since Sung times, Ch'an became more and more formalized and codified. Paradoxically, the 'wordless doctrine' developed a huge

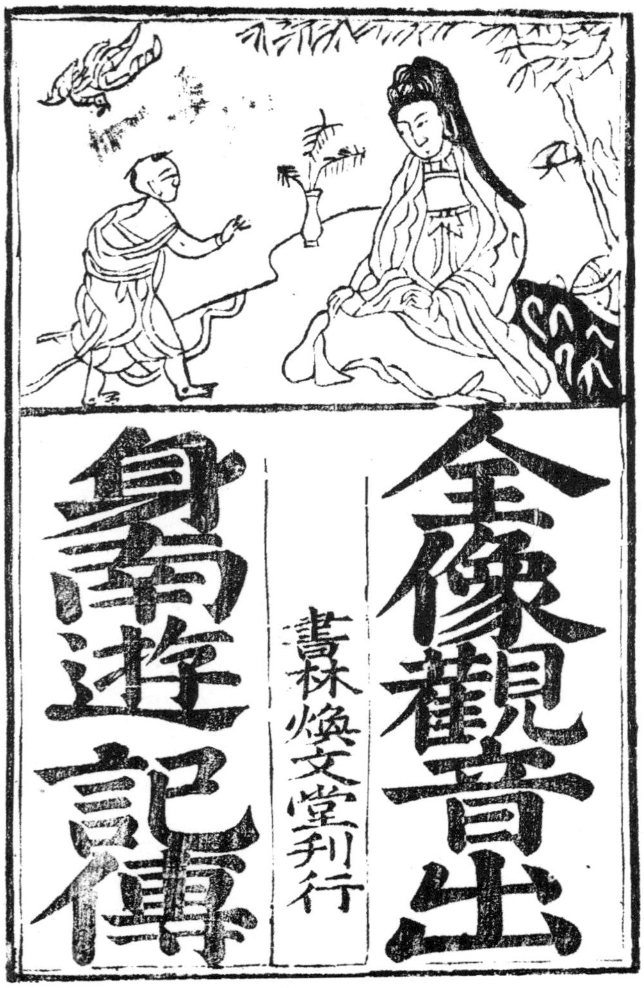

Title page of a collection of stories, printed about 1800, concerning the bodhisattva Kuan-yin, the Chinese name of the Indian bodhisattva Avalokiteśvara. In Chinese mythology he was transformed from a male into a female divinity (she is the Japanese Goddess of Mercy, Kannon). The name means literally 'taking heed of the sound', so she is often represented – as here – as one who 'takes heed of the sound', i.e. the cries of the world, a compassionate deity to be invoked in times of trouble. The good deeds and miracles attributed to her often involve Taoist and Confucian ideals like filial piety.

and highly specialized literature of its own – an aestheticized 'literary Ch'an' which deeply influenced contemporary poetry and painting. Ch'an monasteries often became big institutions peopled with hundreds of monks and with an elaborate clerical hierarchy. In such monasteries, centred around the meditation hall, Ch'an was practised as a completely formalized technique of mental concentration in which every detail was exactly regulated: the meditation 'themes' (*kung-an*, 'cases'; *kōan* in Japanese); the 'questions and answers' exchanged by master and disciple; the bodily postures and movements; and the schedule of daily activities (even meals are completely ritualized), punctuated by a curious code of signals given by drums, bells, hollow 'wooden fish' and sounding-boards.

This development was by no means fortuitous. It reflects, in the religious sphere, one of the most fundamental features of Chinese civilization, particularly in late imperial times: the ideal of *li*, the carefully defined norms of social behaviour, outwardly expressed in an extremely ritualized code of conduct.

In its form and layout, the Buddhist monastery had taken over all the essential features of traditional Chinese monumental architecture. In the early medieval period, and even in T'ang times, some monasteries apparently were still built according to the Indian *vihāra* tradition: the religious centre, used for meetings and cultic purposes, in the middle of a courtyard surrounded by monks' cells and service buildings such as the kitchen, the refectory and the sanitary facilities. But this type was eventually supplanted by a typically Chinese complex: an axially arranged succession of buildings separated by courtyards, the whole forming an elongated rectangle surrounded by walls, with the main entrance preferably on the south. The buildings themselves completely follow the Chinese millenarian model: impressive wooden structures erected on paved platforms; highly ornate and very complicated roof structures resting on wooden beams and pillars; ideals of complete symmetry and of harmonious proportions, effected by the application of a highly developed code of modular rules. The more important buildings – the entrance hall with protective deities; the Great Shrine hall with the main altar, used for devotions and also open to lay devotees; the Dharma hall used for preaching and study (the latter often in the library on the second floor); and sometimes also the meditation hall with its characteristic wooden platforms on which the meditators both sit and sleep – are situated on the main axis. The lateral buildings on both sides are of many different types and purposes: the service buildings like kitchen, dining-hall and bathroom; the guest department that takes care of travelling monks who, after a thorough questioning, are allowed to spend a period in the monastery; the abbot's quarters and the cells of other prominent monks and clerical officials who are entitled to have private rooms; the business department that handles the financial affairs of the monastery; and many others.

In late imperial times, such large complexes formed a kind of religious superstructure, on top of a great mass of smaller temples and monasteries. The training of novices – often young children – under a qualified *Dharma*-master was left to such smaller institutions; for full ordination the novices had to go to the large monasteries. The regular ordination was an impressive collective ceremonial, performed by the abbot and other specialized clerical officials, preferably on an 'ordination platform'. After collectively accepting the traditional 250 vows and being ordained, monks generally also made the 'bodhisattva vow' symbolizing their resolve to devote themselves to the well-being of all living creatures in accordance with the Mahāyāna; this vow was often also taken by pious laity who took part in the ceremony. After having been ordained, the monk received a printed 'ordination certificate' – a practice that had started already under the T'ang. It had originally been imposed by the bureaucracy in order better to control the Sangha: each monk had to carry this document as a kind of clerical passport. But it also acquired a religious function, as the document clearly stated the name of his original master and other particulars showing the spiritual lineage to which he belonged – another example of the way in which the traditional Chinese preoccupation with genealogy was taken over by Buddhism.

Buddhism in modern China

The modern attempt to revive the Sangha from its state of intellectual and moral decline was part of a general movement towards national regeneration which arose around the beginning of this century as a response to two oppressive forces: the general backwardness of China's 'feudal' society, and the impact of the West. It took place in an international context. The Buddhist revivalists established contacts with Japan, India and the Buddhist countries of southern and Southeast Asia, and even with Buddhist societies in the West. Some of them studied, for the first time in Chinese history, the Theravāda tradition of the Pali Canon, and occasionally, after many centuries, Chinese Buddhist scholars even took up the study of Sanskrit. Moreover, the attempted revival of Buddhism must be regarded as a reaction against one aspect of Western dominance: the impact of Christianity. The movement was deeply influenced by the presence of well-organized Catholic and Protestant missions in China, which stimulated the reformers to get themselves organized and to develop institutions and missionary methods similar to those of their Christian rivals.

The first champions of a Buddhist revival were – characteristically – cultured laymen who around the beginning of this century launched a movement to produce Buddhist scriptures and treatises using modern printing techniques and to raise the cultural level of the Sangha by founding Buddhist seminars. The political situation was unfavourable, for both the late Ch'ing and early Republican governments regarded the clergy as an easy target, and did not hesitate to confiscate Buddhist institutions to be made into schools, and to appropriate monastic landed property in order to finance their modernization programmes. Various attempts to organize the Sangha on a national scale in order better to resist the combined pressure of government policy and Christian missions finally led to the founding, in 1929, of the nationwide Chinese Buddhist Association by the two leaders of the revival movement: the venerable abbot T'ai-hsü (1899–1947), who represented the more progressive wing, and the more conservative Yüan-ying (1878–1953).

In the following decades the Association undertook a number of activities that led to a revival of Buddhist studies (notably of the old Chinese school traditions such as T'ien-t'ai and Hua-yen, and also of Yogācāra Buddhism) and to a heightened awareness of the values of Buddhism. But a real large-scale renaissance did not take place. The general intellectual and political climate in China, dominated by the forces of secular ideologies such as Nationalism, 'wholesale modernization', and Marxism–Leninism, left little room for religious activism. And, most important, the revival remained restricted to a small modernizing élite of monks and cultured laymen. The overwhelming majority of the Sangha was not touched at all. Moreover, the new Buddhist organizations generally suffered from inexperienced leadership, personal controversies and lack of funds, and the close relations between Chinese and Japanese Buddhist institutions definitely harmed the image of the movement, as such contacts were consciously used by the Japanese government for the purpose of political infiltration and 'Japan-promotion'.

After the establishment of the Chinese People's Republic in 1949, the tensions were aggravated. In general, the new regime has abstained from direct and forceful repression, as Buddhism was expected to die out by itself, like other residual phenomena of the 'feudal' past. However, violent action against the clergy and widespread vandalism have been committed during political mass campaigns, particularly in the hectic years of the Cultural Revolution (1965–9), and the Tibetan revolt in 1959 was followed by harsh repressive measures against Lamaism. In so far as Buddhism is tolerated, it clearly is a truncated Buddhism, reduced to religious worship, and divested of all the social and economic functions which monasteries used to have. The Sangha itself, of which no reliable quantitative data are available, has no doubt been decimated by laicization and lack of new ordinations. To some extent, the new Chinese Buddhist Association set up after 1949 has been politically useful as a channel for the implementation of religious policy, and as a representative 'people's organization' in entertaining formal contacts with Buddhist groups abroad.

In general, the prospects for the Buddhist clergy in China are rather gloomy. It may be argued that the Chinese Sangha has for many centuries been exposed to the pressure of hostile ideologies and still managed to survive. But the monasteries, large and small, always remained in the possession of the material means to do so. Since the early 1950s, their economic base has been destroyed. Temple lands have been confiscated and redistributed, and, apart from a few ancient temples that are at least physically preserved as historical monuments, Buddhist institutions are wholly dependent on the believers' contributions. Even if in the most recent years (since 1976) there are signs of a somewhat more liberal policy, yet the ideological pressure and the lack of means of subsistence, this time coupled with an excessive emphasis on wholesale modernization, are not conducive to the existence, let alone the flowering, of Chinese Buddhism as an organized religion.

9

This World and the Other Power: Contrasting Paths to Deliverance in Japan

ROBERT K. HEINEMANN

To the outsider, Buddhism in Japan presents strikingly new features, some of which seem in conflict with each other. Japanese thought is little preoccupied with the idea of an endless cycle of rebirth, from which the Buddha showed an escape. On the contrary, it stresses the importance of finding one's true self and realizing Enlightenment *here and now*. 'This-worldliness' is a characteristic of Japanese Buddhism as a whole. One expression of it is Zen, which in keeping with the teaching of the earliest Buddhism maintains that man can attain deliverance only through his 'Own Power' (*jiriki*). Apparently contradicting this belief are the schools of Amidism, which preach that man is powerless to save himself and must rely on the compassionate Buddha Amida, the 'Other Power' (*tariki*), who will enable him to be reborn in his 'Pure Land of the Highest Happiness', where Enlightenment will be realized.

The Sangha too has undergone great changes in Japan. The clergy of the Jōdo-shinshū, which has grown to be the largest Japanese sect, have abandoned celibacy and describe themselves as 'neither monk nor layman'. Today the great majority marry and pass on their temples to their sons; they also take other jobs. Japanese Buddhism is thus uniquely secularized. This chapter seeks to trace the historical development of these characteristics and their diversity, and tries to explain the reasons for their seeming contradictions.

The coming of Buddhism to Japan

Approximately one millennium after the death of the historical Buddha Śākyamuni, and a few centuries after the first evidence of Buddhism in China, this foreign religion started penetrating the islands of Japan by way of Korea. One of the main chronicles of ancient Japan, the *Nihonshoki*, compiled in AD 720 by imperial order, gives a detailed account of the event.

This official story of the arrival of Buddhism in Japan may be summarized thus. In AD 538, the thirteenth year of the reign of Kinmei-Tennō, 29th emperor of Japan, King Syong-Myong of the Korean state of Paikche, hoping to obtain an alliance against Korean states hostile to his own, sent a mission to Japan. With it he sent a gift to the emperor of a gold-plated bronze image of the Buddha Śākyamuni, as well as flags and umbrellas and several volumes of Buddhist sūtras. In a letter praising the merit of spreading the new religion, he called it the most excellent of all doctrines, pointing the way to the highest Enlightenment (*Bodhi*), although so difficult to comprehend that 'neither the duke of Chou nor Confucius had attained a perfect knowledge of it'. The letter concluded by citing the Buddha's alleged words: 'The Dharma shall be spread to the East.'

The emperor asked his ministers to advise him whether the new religion should be adopted. A conservative faction, represented by two powerful families, Nakatomi and Mononobe, was firmly opposed to the introduction of the 'foreign *kami*' (deity), as they called the Buddha. They feared that worshipping him would bring the wrath of the indigenous *kami* down on the nation. However, on the advice of the Soga family, who were in charge of foreign relations with Korea and one of whom, Iname no Sukune, held one of the highest governmental offices, the emperor decided that the image and the scriptures should be accepted and that the image should be 'tentatively' regarded as an object of worship. He entrusted the image of the Buddha to Iname no Sukune who, turning his house into a temple, enshrined it and worshipped it therein.

Those who dreaded the vengeance of the native deities proved to be justified in their fears: no sooner had the house of Iname no Sukune been transformed into a temple and the image worshipped there, than a horrible pestilence broke out in the country, causing the untimely death of a great many people. As the disease became worse and worse, the emperor found no other way out of the calamity than to adopt the views of those who were opposed to the foreign religion: he had the Buddhist image thrown into a canal and burnt down the newly opened temple.

However, the following year, Kinmei-Tennō had two Buddhist images made out of a log of camphorwood which had been discovered floating upon the sea accompanied by miraculous voices singing Buddhist chants. During the next three decades, several monks, a nun, a sculptor and a temple architect arrived in Japan, bringing with them further Buddhist scriptures and images. The first Japanese nuns were ordained and more temples were built.

There were a number of setbacks during the reign of Emperor Bidatsu (572–85) owing mainly to doubts about the new religion's efficacy as a means of preventing disease, and also to fear of the national *kami*. However, within only half a century Japan witnessed the firm establishment of Buddhism as a religion officially recognized and actively supported by the imperial court. The triumph of Buddhism over the factions hostile to its adoption was mainly brought about by the powerful Soga clan. They were strongly in favour of a policy of rapidly absorbing Chinese knowledge and ideas, since the Japanese state then emerging lagged far behind its mighty continental neighbour in culture and political organization.

Among the achievements of Chinese culture flowing into Japan in those early days one of the most momentous was undoubtedly the Chinese script. It was to supply the Japanese, who lacked an indigenous writing system, with the means of assimilating the vast tradition of the Chinese classics and the Chinese version of the Buddhist canon. Moreover, it enabled them to develop their own system of writing by adapting the Chinese script to the specific needs of the Japanese language. Nevertheless, very few of the Chinese texts imported from the continent were translated into Japanese (whereas the Chinese translated the Indian canon into their own language): most of them have continued, throughout history, to be used in their original version. The Buddhist canon was not translated into Japanese until the beginning of the 20th century.

The early Buddhism of Japan

The early records, such as the *Nihonshoki* cited above, tended to present things in accord with the then prevailing ideology of the state authorities and to project contemporary views and attitudes into the past. So, as history, they must be treated with caution; but as these official chronicles were to influence Japanese thought deeply, it is not surprising to find in them a number of features that characterize Japanese Buddhism. Three of them stand out particularly.

Firstly, the new religion did not come to Japan on a popular level, but was first accepted by the imperial court and then disseminated in the country from the top. In Japanese history the Buddhist faith is often connected with absolute devotion to a leader: veneration for the founders of the various sects is emphasized, and the majority of the sects stand in close relation to the central governmental authority of their times. This may account for the fact that Japanese Buddhism has less local colour than Indian or Chinese Buddhism.

Secondly, Buddhism was (and still is) often associated with magic powers and was used by the court as a means of preventing or curing disease, of preserving the peace, of bringing rainfall and abundant crops, etc. In a later, more developed state of Buddhism this aspect was referred to by the expression *chingo-kokka*, 'pacifying and protecting the state'.

Thirdly, the newly introduced religion did not replace the indigenous *kami*, but always recognized their existence and power. This led to numerous varieties of Shintō-Buddhist amalgamation: in some cases functions and responsibilities were distributed among both the members of the Buddhist pantheon and the *kami* of the native religion, but most frequently the *kami* were considered manifestations (avatars) of the Buddhas or – in later reactions (from the 14th century onwards) to this form of syncretism – it was sometimes the Buddhas who were relegated to the status of avatars of the *kami*.

Were there any specific reasons for the close link between Shintō and Buddhism? To answer this question, let us consider some of the characteristics of these two religions. From such ancient records as those mentioned above, sporadic notes in Chinese annals, and archaeological evidence it seems that the early Japanese paid reverence in local cults to things like imposing mountains, mysterious valleys, huge rocks, waterfalls, ancient trees, snakes, thunder, fire, and probably the sun – in short, to anything out of the ordinary that was felt as a manifestation of natural forces inspiring fear, admiration, or some sentiment of dependency. The forces apprehended in such phenomena were worshipped as local deities: *kami*. There was originally no comprehensive, basic principle to combine all these different local cults into a systematized whole. The *kami*, neither dependent on any transcendent, universal principle, nor mutually exclusive, were felt to be actually present, wielding power here and now. There has never been a gap between the whole world of the *kami* and the world of man; abstract speculation has not postulated a transcendental realm distinct from and beyond the concrete world we live in. This-worldliness and the assertion of reality as found in this ethnic religion (as well as in the thinking and feeling of the Japanese in general) was decisively to influence the way in which the Japanese adapted Buddhism to their own needs and tendencies.

The 'Way of the *kami*', i.e. Shintō (the word was coined after the introduction of Buddhism, by analogy with the 'Way of the Buddha', *Butsudō* in Japanese), came later to be moulded into a unified system (we find it in the 8th-century chronicles such as the one cited above) with a complex genealogy of the *kami* and everything they created: the Japanese archipelago, its natural phenomena and the nation. In this system, absolute superiority was given to the imperial lineage and their *kami* ancestors – headed by the sun goddess Amaterasu-Ōmikami – to justify the supreme position of the imperial line and the evolution of the ruling aristocracy. But even this more elaborate form of Shintō still lacked a universally valid principle, a theoretical framework strong enough to resist foreign influence. Thus Shintō proved to be open to other religions and philosophies – Buddhism, Taoism, Confucianism, in modern times even Christianity – and throughout history was disposed to borrow such elements from them as would compensate for its own structural insufficiencies in the fields of dogma, ritual and iconography.

The intrinsic nature of Buddhism, moreover, greatly favoured harmonious coexistence with indigenous beliefs and, eventually, the emergence of various kinds of Shintō-Buddhist amalgam. Fundamental principles such as the theory of Dependent Origination and the characteristically Mahāyāna doctrines of 'emptiness' and the 'two truths' (sketched in Chapters 1 and 2) were understood and accepted in Japan, but the Japanese way of thought brought about certain changes in Buddhism, much as the Chinese had adapted it to their way of thinking. The prevailing tendency of Japanese Buddhism is to search for fulfilment and ultimate truth not in any transcendental sphere, but within the structure of secular life, neither denying nor repressing man's natural feelings, desires or customs. Accordingly, in the course of history Japanese Buddhism easily assimilated indigenous beliefs and often took an especially secularized, practical form. Many Japanese arts and skills are profoundly pervaded by Buddhist spirituality. The tea ceremony (*sadō*), the arts of gardening, of calligraphy (*shodō*), and of the Nō play are well-known examples.

The Buddhism of Prince Shōtoku (574–622)

As we have seen, the triumph of Buddhism in Japan was initiated by the victory over the Mononobe won by the Soga clan. The ruling family was looking for a philosophy that would serve as an ideological basis for a centralized state. They found it in the universal principles of this foreign religion, and from that time onwards the growth of political power of the Soga was accompanied by an ever increasing promotion of Buddhism by the court.

In 592 Empress Suiko (who reigned from 592 to 628) was enthroned. She was closely related by blood to the Soga family and was a devout Buddhist. Shortly after her accession, she withdrew from her official functions and took vows as a Buddhist nun. Her nephew the Prince Shōtoku (Shōtoku-Taishi, 574–622) was appointed prince imperial and entrusted with the government as regent. He conducted the state for thirty years, and his reign is traditionally regarded by the Japanese as the period which marks the formation of an organized centralized state and of a specifically Japanese Buddhism.

'Shōtoku-Taishi', a title conferred upon him posthumously, means the 'prince of sacred virtues': all the major virtues of Japanese mentality and statesmanship were sooner or later projected onto him. It is no exaggeration to speak of a 'cult' of Shōtoku-Taishi. Even today his portrait appears on government currency. His memory is also preserved in one of the temples that he is supposed to have constructed, the Hōryūji in Nara. It contains what is said to be the world's oldest wooden structure still in use. It is now the centre of one of Japan's numerically minor congregations, the Shōtoku sect. The story – largely legendary – of his life suggests and symbolizes the enormous impact that Buddhism had on the spiritual and cultural life of that time as well as the influence his ideals had on later developments in Japanese Buddhism and political thought.

In 594, the Empress Suiko issued an edict proclaiming the state patronage of Buddhism. Many great families adopted the new religion and undertook the building of magnificent temples. Prince Shōtoku was instructed in the Buddhist doctrine by one of the naturalized monks who had come from the Korean kingdom of Koguryo and who played an important role in the formation of Buddhist ideas at this period. Shōtoku's learning also comprised the so-called Outer Doctrine, i.e. Confucianism. In his *Constitution in Seventeen Articles*, issued in 604, Buddhist and Confucian ideas are mingled. Intended as a moral guide for the conduct of the high officials of the imperial government, it starts out with these words: 'Harmony is to be esteemed above anything else.' It emphasizes that everybody in the state should act appropriately to his status, in accordance with Buddhist and Confucian principles. What is expressed in the seventeen articles is not blind obedience, but concord based on mutual understanding. 'Who is wise enough to judge which of us is good or bad? We are all wise and foolish by turns, like a ring without an end' (Article 10). This tenet is profoundly Buddhist: it resembles ideas to be found in the Chinese T'ien-t'ai teaching of Chih-i (538–97).

In 607, Shōtoku dispatched an embassy to the court of Sui China. This was the beginning of official contact with the Chinese court, which was to be maintained until 838. A large number of Japanese scholars, Buddhists and others, accompanied these embassies for study and training in China. The significance for later Japanese history of the consequent flow of Chinese culture – comprising Buddhism, philosophy, art and science as well as agricultural, architectural and other techniques – into Japan can hardly be overestimated.

For Shōtoku the possibility of becoming a Buddha was not limited to those who have left secular life and become monks; all mankind was predisposed to attain the highest Enlightenment. Accordingly, lay Buddhism was to play a particularly important part in Japanese cultural life. Shōtoku strongly emphasized work for the benefit of others, which is not surprising, considering that he was a statesman and ruler. There is certainly a discrepancy here between the quietist tendency found in the Indian scriptures and his own this-worldly ideals dictated by the practical necessities of state and society, and Shōtoku must have been conscious of this. However, his reinterpretations, far-fetched and utilitarian as some of them may seem, are by no means inconsistent with the spirit of Far-Eastern Mahāyāna, which calls for an active life for the benefit of all beings.

The practicality of Buddhism in Shōtoku's day is shown by the Temple of the Four Heavenly Kings (Shitennōji), in what is now the city of Ōsaka. Although it has since become a place of worship like

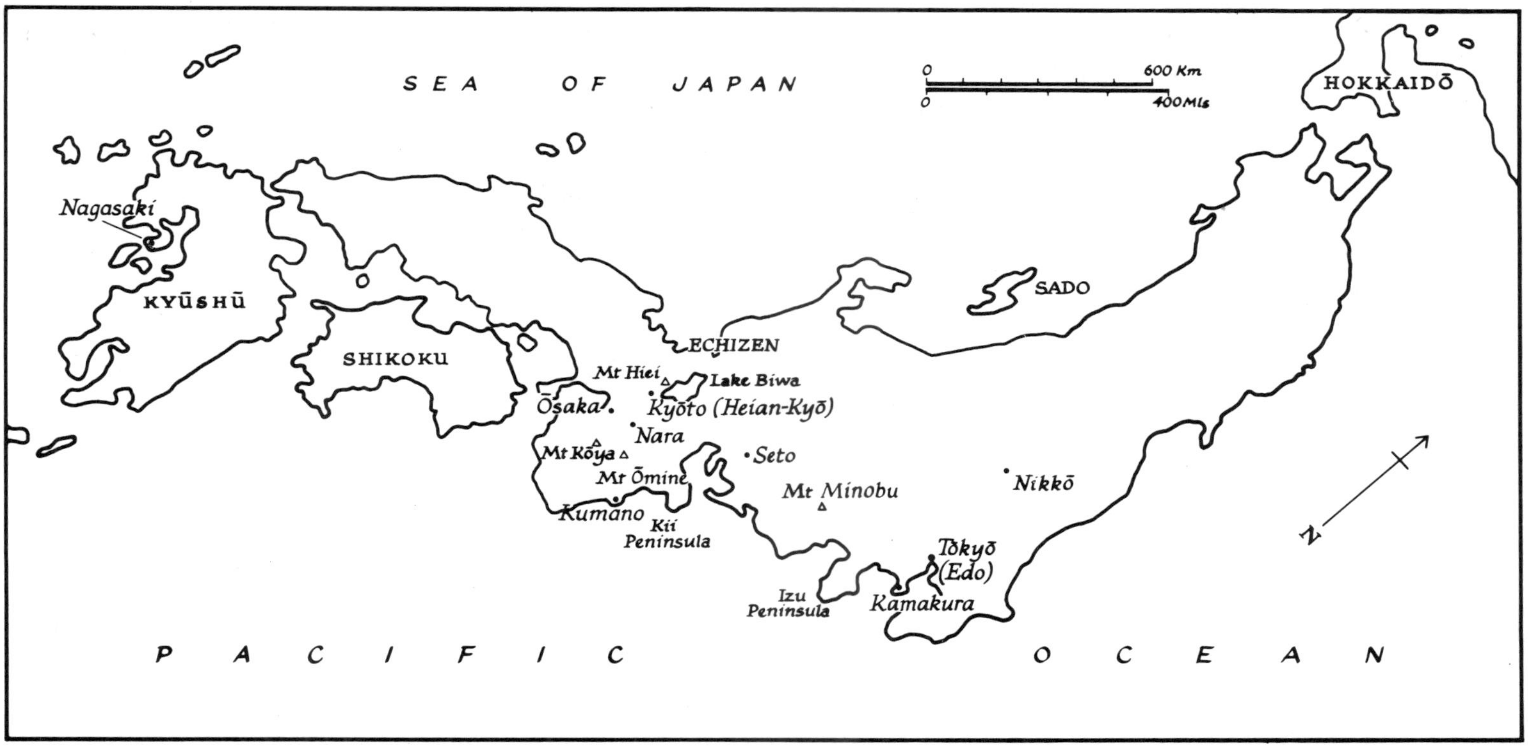

Japan, showing the areas and sites mentioned in this chapter.

other temples, when it was founded it comprised four main institutions: a religious sanctuary used for worship and training in Buddhist discipline and learning, including philosophy, science, and aesthetic pursuits; a dispensary for the collection and distribution of medical herbs; an asylum for the poor and helpless; and a hospital where treatment was given free of charge. It can be said to have been the centre of social welfare activities in those days.

Fundamental to Shōtoku's ideals are the twin virtues of tolerance and compassion. Tolerance is the ethical gist of the *Lotus Sūtra*, which embraces and harmonizes all doctrines and practices within the One Vehicle, taught by the Chinese Master T'ien-t'ai to transcend the distinction between Hīnayāna and Mahāyāna schools. The *Lotus Sūtra* has remained ever since one of the most popular and influential Buddhist scriptures of Japan. It has instilled an extremely conciliatory attitude towards different ideas that might be considered by Westerners to conflict. Tolerance is shown in the co-existence of Shintō, Buddhism, Confucianism (and in modern times also Christianity), all of which are felt by the Japanese to be harmoniously compatible. The great majority of the Japanese are Buddhists and Shintōists at the same time. In modern times there were and still are people who do not feel the slightest incompatibility between Christianity and traditional Japanese religion. Conflicts have been due rather to competition for political power, than to any contradiction that might be felt between different religious or ideological systems. Universal compassion is Mahāyāna's bodhisattva ideal *par excellence*.

The chronicles have it that in 623, the year after Shōtoku's death, there were 46 Buddhist temples, 816 monks and 569 nuns in Japan. On the broad basis created during the regency of Prince Shōtoku there gradually grew up a Buddhism that in many ways diverged from its Chinese model. Its development in the 7th and 8th centuries is noteworthy from three points of view – doctrine, politics and practice.

Doctrine

People had originally contented themselves with an understanding of the general principles of Buddhist doctrine. Now an effort was made to investigate the peculiarities of the various schools. The Sangha adopted the teaching of six Chinese schools, which were established in Nara, the capital between 710 and 784, and were known as the 'Six Sects of Nara' (*Nara-rokushū*). 'Sects' is something of a misnomer. They were not closed institutions but teaching centres open to each other and visited by learned priests of all persuasions.

1. By 625, three years after the prince's death, the Sanron sect had been introduced into Japan. It was the first real sect to arrive there. It was based on three authoritative treatises of the Indian Mādhyamika school (hence its name: 'Sanron' means 'the Three Treatises'). Its doctrine revolves round the central Mahāyāna themes of 'Emptiness' and the 'Middle Path'. In the 7th century this school assumed a leading position in the learned Japanese Sangha, but in the 8th century the Avataṃsaka ('Kegon' in Japanese; see below) sect took the lead.

The doctrine and writings of the Sanron sect were gradually absorbed by the other schools as the common basis of the Mahāyāna until it ceased to exist as an independent school.

2. The Jōjitsu sect is based on a treatise by the Indian Harivarman (*c.* 250–350) and, like the Sanron sect, puts 'Emptiness' in the centre of its reflections, though from a Hīnayāna point of view. It was transmitted to Japan with the Sanron sect and its principles were taught there together with those of the Sanron.

3. The Hossō sect first came to Japan in 660. Its doctrine, derived from the Indian Yogācāra school, is often described as Buddhist idealism. At its centre stands a fundamental analysis of consciousness, the deepest layer of which, the 'storage consciousness' (*ālaya-vijñāna*), is posited as the original ground of all being, from the unfathomable depths of which, in a continual stream of actualizations of the 'seeds' (*bīja*) stored there, phenomena proceed. A complex system of spiritual exercises leads from the supposed self and things to the recognition of true being (*tathatā*): everything is empty of substance; subject and object are not separated. This world view of a 'great self' ('*daiga*' in Japanese), that is nothing less than total being, plays a fundamental role in Japanese Buddhism, especially clearly in Zen, and has also left its imprint on certain Japanese arts in which subject and object are felt as coinciding. Like the 'Emptiness' of the Sanron sect, the essential elements of this doctrine have been adopted and worked over by later sects, while the Hossō sect itself has declined in importance during the course of history. Today it is small, and tends its material and spiritual inheritance in a few big temples in Nara.

This sect has left several traces in the religious practice of the country. In the year 700 the priest Dōshō, who was responsible for bringing further Hossō doctrine to Japan after eight years of study in China, was cremated in accordance with the wish expressed in his will. According to some sources this was the start of cremation, now generally practised in Japan. In addition many of the Buddhist customs generally followed today – for example, commemorative ceremonies for the dead celebrated every seventh day until the forty-ninth day – come from the doctrine of this sect (or, to be more precise, from the doctrine of the Kusha sect transmitted with it to Japan).

4. The Kusha sect is based on the *Abhidharmakośa* of Vasubandhu (*c.* 320–400). Its extremely complex system of analysis of all that is, for which it assumes 75 actually existing elements (*dharma*), was the point of departure of the Hossō doctrine and together with this doctrine is still regarded as the indispensable basis of knowledge for all Buddhist studies.

5. The Kegon sect, whose doctrine forms one of the finest edifices of the Buddhist philosophy of China, was transmitted to Japan in 736. It bases itself on the Indian *Avataṃsaka-sūtra*, according to which the whole universe, all being, *is* the Buddha Vairocana (known as Birushana-butsu in Japan). The deep symbolic content of the sūtra is often summarized in the concept that 'one is contained in all' and 'all in one'. Every individual phenomenon is a 'symbol' of the totality, both in the spatial and in the temporal dimension: a grain of dust contains a universe, a moment, eternity. The Chinese development of this teaching specified that everything should be considered as a part of a whole, and at the same time as a whole constituted by parts. Thus it showed in a rationally practicable way how it is possible to understand the mutual containment of the individual and the whole without having recourse to any abstract, transcendental principle. This doctrine's influence on the Buddhism of the Kamakura period (1185–1333), and particularly on the teaching of the Zen master Dōgen (1200–1253), was immense.

6. The Ritsu sect (Risshū in Japanese) puts the rules of the monks' discipline (*vinaya*) at the centre of its teaching. It attaches particular value to the 'transmission of the commandments', which accordingly becomes the most important element in ordination. As the Japanese Sangha was increasingly concerned to have proof of the authenticity of its tradition, this new school came at a very convenient moment. In 754 the Chinese monk Chien-chên (called Ganjin in Japanese) succeeded after many failures, in which he had lost his eyesight, in crossing the sea and bringing the Ritsu sect to Japan. (His contemporary statue is preserved in the sect's main temple, the Tōshōdaiji in Nara.) Previously Buddhist ordination had been carried out less formally; the tradition of this sect prescribes a complex ritual which is to be carried out by three masters in the presence of seven witnesses in an ordination hall known as the 'commandment platform' (*kaidan*). Under the direction of Ganjin three such *kaidan* were built immediately, first in Nara and then in central Japan and Kyūshū, in one of which henceforth all Buddhist priests had to 'receive the commandments' to legitimate their ordination. However, the Risshū spread much less widely in Japan than in India or China. It may be that the 250 rules for monks and 348 rules for nuns did not correspond in their formalistic rigidity to the Japanese tendency to the immediate affirmation of reality. But many spiritual leaders have, throughout Japanese history, called for the observance of monastic discipline.

Politics

Prince Shōtoku's ideal of a centralized state inspired by China was not realized in his lifetime, but was pursued after his death. In 645 the power of the Soga clan was broken by a *coup d'état* and their position taken over by the Nakatomi family (whose name was later changed to Fujiwara). The government immediately began to introduce major reforms based on Chinese models. Private land was declared public property; all households were registered and allotted rice fields for their upkeep; taxation was introduced. A code of civil and criminal law, the *ritsuryō*, was promulgated; particularly elaborate forms date from 701 and 718. The Sangha was granted immunity from taxation and the big temples were continually granted land by the central government. In return, Buddhism had the duty (again on the Chinese model) of protecting the state and ensuring public prosperity – a duty it shared with Shintoism and Confucianism. A corollary of this centralized state control was that the legal code strictly regulated the conduct of the Sangha. Some of its provisions conflict with Buddhist principles. For instance, an important text, the *Bonmōkyō* (Sanskrit *Brahmajāla-sūtra*) calls on the bodhisattva to spread Buddhist teaching among the population and to erect temples and places of religious practice. The code puts severe restrictions on this. The *Bonmōkyō* forbids the bodhisattva to approach kings or officials, or to enter their service, whereas the code lays down in what form monks and nuns must show respect to high officials of the state.

The best example of the intermingling of Buddhist and political ideas is provided by the reign of the Emperor Shōmu (724–49), who described himself as the 'servant of the Three Jewels' (Buddha, Dharma, Sangha). He ordered the construction of a state provincial temple for monks and one for nuns in every province, and had prayers said in each one for the peace and prosperity of the nation. In the capital, Nara, he erected the Tōdaiji (Great Temple of the East) with a statue (now forty-seven feet high) of the Buddha Vairocana in gilded bronze, as the main temple of all provincial monasteries, and the Hokkeji (Temple of the Dharma Blossom) as the main temple of all provincial nunneries. The 'Great Buddha Hall' of the Tōdaiji, which contains the 'Great Buddha of Nara' (*Nara-no Daibutsu*) is reckoned today to be the biggest wooden building in the world. This system of state Buddhism extended into the most remote provinces under the unifying symbol of the central Buddha, Vairocana. Vairocana, symbol of the Universal All, according to a passage in the *Bonmōkyō*, sits in the middle of a lotus blossom with a thousand petals. Each of the petals symbolizes a world, in the middle of which a great Sākyamuni sits as a manifestation of the Buddha Vairocana. Each world again embraces ten thousand million worlds with ten thousand million little Sākyamuni, manifestations of the great Śākyamuni. The hierarchical arrangement became a symbol of the ideal centralized Buddhist state at which Shōmu aimed, with the omnipotent might of the imperial house at the top of a huge administrative pyramid.

Buddhist activity not associated with the state was frowned on and even punished. Gyōgi (668–749), a monk ordained in the Hossō sect, tried to popularize Buddhism by helping the common people. He travelled widely through Japan, both preaching and helping with the construction of roads, bridges, reservoirs, etc. He made the first map of Japan. In 717 he was convicted on the charge of leading the people astray by carrying out social work. Later, however, Emperor Shōmu enlisted his help for the execution of his vast projects.

Practice

The Buddhism of the Nara period, as embodied in the Six Sects, was essentially not a *practical* religion; it was a Buddhism of learned priests. Their official function was

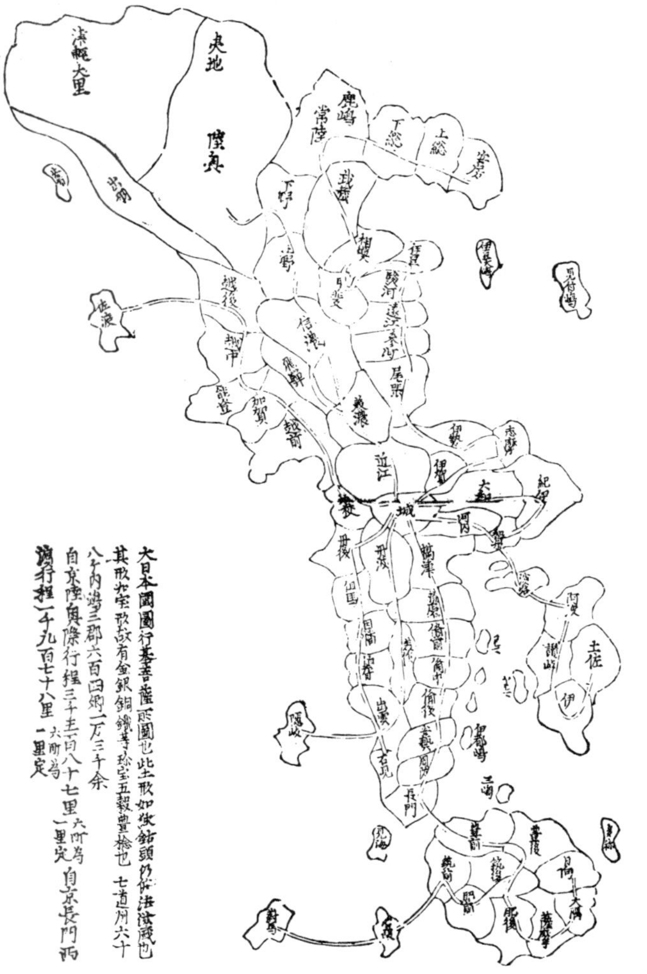

The first map of Japan was made in the 7th–8th century AD and is attributed to the monk Gyōgi. The original is lost, but several 17th-century versions, of which this is one, survive. The inscription states that it was drawn by 'Bodhisattva Gyōgi', and that the shape of the land resembles a vajra.

to pray for the peace and prosperity of the state and the imperial house; for this they were rewarded by the court. This kind of Buddhism had little to offer the ordinary, simple people who could not read or write. The best priests stayed behind the doors of the temples and devoted themselves to the study of the scriptures. Others, however, following native and Taoist usage, withdrew to live ascetic lives in the mountains.

A popular Buddhist movement developed with the *ubasoku* (Sanskrit *upāsaka*, lay followers). These 'people's priests' were not ordained and had no formal Buddhist training. Their practice combined Buddhist and Taoist elements with shamanistic features of the old indigenous religion. They travelled from place to place giving help to the sick and needy, and organizing improvements in living conditions. Sometimes they too withdrew to the mountains to steel their powers of resistance and to develop their wonder-working powers. This type of lonely sage was immensely popular and soon entered literature as the *hijiri* (the 'saint', the wise man). It is not surprising that from the ranks of these *ubasoku* rose voices criticizing the sects of Nara, for this manly, vital form of religious faith formed a sharp contrast to the sophisticated academic and bureaucratic Buddhism of the capital.

A further bridge to the people was provided by the connection between Buddhism and Shintō. Buddhism taught that the native divinities were dependent on it: the *kami* were said to long for Buddhist redemption. So little Buddhist temples, the 'kami-shrine-temples' (*jingū-ji*), were erected for them in their shrines and sūtra readings were held there for their salvation. Conversely, certain *kami* were raised to the rank of protective divinities (*chinju*) of Buddhist temples and worshipped in temple shrines dedicated to them inside the temple precincts. There are already signs in the Nara period that the process of the harmonization of *kami* with Buddhas had begun. When, according to legend, the sun goddess Amaterasu was asked if she was opposed to the erection of the 'Great Buddha' Vairocana in Nara, her reply was that she herself was nothing other than a manifestation of this Buddha.

The Heian period (794–1185)

Japanese culture now began to free itself from Chinese tutelage. The cultural shift was symbolized in space by the move of the imperial palace in 784 from Nara to Nagaoka and then in 794 to Heian-kyō, present-day Kyōto. A decisive reason for this move was a wish to escape the growing influence of the senior Buddhist clergy. The headquarters of the Six Sects was now no longer at the political centre. To preserve the continuity of the country's protection by Buddhism, just two official temples – the 'Western' (Saiji), and the 'Eastern' (Tōji) – were erected in the new imperial capital. The move was thus at first a setback for Buddhism. But the deep understanding of Buddhist teaching which the learned monks of Nara had made possible, together with the gradual liberation of the intellectual and spiritual world from dependence on this authoritarian Nara Buddhism, provided the essential preconditions for the flowering of a new, deeper religious feeling.

It was two monks – two of the most important figures in Japanese history – who effected this change and so decisively affected the future of Japanese Buddhism. The monks were Saichō (767–822) and Kūkai (774–835), better known by their posthumous titles of Dengyō-daishi, 'grand master of doctrinal transmission' and Kōbō-daishi, 'grand master of the dissemination of the Dharma'. They created in two comprehensive syntheses of the doctrine transmitted from China two systems of teaching and practice which furnished all the essentials for the whole further development of Japanese Buddhism. What came later consisted simply of variations on, simplifications of, or selections from, the doctrinal edifices erected by these two great religious thinkers.

Saichō took his first vows as a monk at the age of fourteen. After several years of study he withdrew to the loneliness of Mount Hiei, near the future capital, Heian-kyō, and there gave himself to the study and practice of Mahāyāna doctrines. He devoted himself particularly to the work of the Chinese grand master Chih-i (538–97) of the T'ien-t'ai mountains. Soon from the simple hermit's cell there arose the first temple on Mount Hiei, which was to become the biggest and most important temple area in Japan and the 'cradle of Japanese Buddhism'. In 794 the Emperor Kanmu took part in one of the big consecration ceremonies of the new temple, which was immediately declared the 'place of practice for the protection of the state'. The absolute authority of the old Six Sects was thus shattered. In 804 Saichō was commissioned by the emperor to go to China on a study trip, which he used mainly to deepen his knowledge of the T'ien-t'ai doctrine. After his return to Japan he soon received imperial permission to ordain two novices every year, and also official recognition of his sect, which now became, as the Tendai-Hokke sect (after the Japanese name for the Chinese T'ien-t'ai doctrine and for the *Lotus Sūtra* on which it was based) or, for short, Tendai sect, one of the two schools that dominated the Heian period. The doctrine of the Chinese master Chih-i forms in itself a far-reaching synthesis of Buddhist tradition inspired by the spirit of the *Lotus Sūtra*, but Saichō added to it three further elements: the practice of *Ch'an* (*Zen* in Japanese); the commandments of the Mahāyāna, which are based in essentials on the *Bonmōkyō*; and parts of the esoteric teaching of the 'True Word', *Chên-yen* (*Shingon* in Japanese). With that, the decisive step had been taken from the academic Buddhism of the Six Sects of Nara to a revived, active kind of religion based on belief. The choice of Zen reflects the will to true striving for Buddhist fulfilment; the Mahāyāna commandments are a turning away from the rigid system of formalized *vinaya* prescriptions to universally valid, adaptable principles which mirror the altruistic spirit of the bodhisattva path; and finally the esotericism of the 'True Word' was soon to become through Saichō's successors the most important element in Tendai practice. Its truly religious content leads to the recognition of the highest reality in the concrete Here and Now; on the other hand, its highly developed system of ritual and its symbolism provide an ideal basis for a religious practice promoted by the central government and later by the aristocracy for the 'protection of the state' and the realization of worldly interests. During the course of the Heian period this practice in fact gradually grew more and more shallow and finally degenerated into chicanery and magic that could be purchased for money and property. However, Saichō himself was filled with the idea that the man who truly practised his religion and strove for awakening, that is, the bodhisattva, was the best servant of the state and of society; he was the 'treasure of the state'. How seriously he took practice is shown by his demand, approved by the emperor in 822, that every novice should spend twelve years in study and practice on Mount Hiei without leaving the mountain even once. This rule, at first strictly observed, was gradually forgotten. After an attempt to revive it in the 17th century, this rigorous practice depends today on the initiative of the individual. From time to time there are still periods during which a 'monk abiding on the mountain' (*rōzan-biku*) preserves this old tradition.

Saichō was a determined opponent of any guardianship by the secular authorities. In 820 he attacked the regulations for monks and nuns drawn up in the Nara period, which gave the imperial authority power over the Buddhist clergy. He aimed at independence from the Six Sects of Nara, especially the *Vinaya* sect, by seeking imperial approval for the erection of a hall in which to carry out his sect's own ordinations; and soon after his death such a chapel, the Kaidan-in on Mount Hiei, was constructed. With this the complete independence of the Tendai sect was attained.

An essential element in the doctrine of the Tendai sect was the teaching of the *Lotus Sūtra* that the possibility of salvation is given to *all* men, whereas the dogma of the all-powerful Hossō sect of the Nara period, with a kind of doctrine of predestination, had denied salvation to a certain category of men. This view later became, together with the principles of the esotericism of the 'True Word', the point of departure for the Buddhism of the Kamakura period (1185–1333).

Kūkai out-shines his senior contemporary Saichō in the popular mind. Even today a sort of Kōbō-daishi cult is kept alive by innumerable monuments in all parts of the country. From the point of view of its civilizing effect Kūkai's work was more many-sided than that of Saichō and his secret doctrine of the 'True Word', Shingon, gave him a mysterious radiance and encouraged the formation of legends about him.

Arriving at the age of fifteen in the new capital, Nagaoka-kyō, to study Confucianism, he was soon attracted by Buddhism. He wrote a critical work, the *Sangō-shiiki*, on the 'Three Dogmas', Confucianism, Buddhism and Taoism. He showed that Buddhism goes deeper than Confucianism and Taoism and includes the essential elements of these two doctrines. He too then withdrew to lead a lonely and ascetic life in the mountains, where he practised concentration and the recitation of mantras. At the age of nineteen he became a monk and during his studies in the old capital, Nara, he soon came to know one of the principal texts of the esoteric canon, the *Dainichikyō*, the sūtra of the 'Great Enlightener' (*Mahāvairocana* in Sanskrit) without, however, reaching deeper understanding of it.

In 804 he travelled on the same embassy as Saichō to China and was kindly received in the capital of the T'ang empire, Ch'ang-an. There he met Hui-kuo (known in Japanese as Keika, 746–805), the seventh patriarch of the school of the 'True Word' and the highest authority of the time on this secret doctrine. Under his direction all the doubts and questions which Kūkai had come with were resolved. A few months after Hui-kuo had transmitted the doctrine to his pupil Kūkai, he died. With that, the orthodox line of the transmission of the teaching passed over to Japan with Kūkai. Kūkai was regarded in Japan as the eighth patriarch of this esoteric tradition, which had begun in India in the legendary past.

When Kūkai returned to Japan in 806 he took with him an abundance of knowledge, skills, sacred vessels, sūtra rolls and pictorial representations. He had had himself initiated not only into ritual practice but also into the esoteric symbolic script *siddham* (*shittan* in Japanese). In popular legend Kūkai is regarded as the inventor of the *kana* syllabary, the Japanese syllabic system of writing, for the arrangement of these signs in accordance with phonetic principles corresponds to that of the writing system of Sanskrit, *devanāgarī*, to which *siddham* is related.

Unlike Saichō, Kūkai began his work as a religious leader in the midst of the Six Sects of Nara, as abbot of the influential Tōdaiji (Kegon temple) in the old capital. However, he soon created an independent centre of his own for his teaching in the mountains near Heian-kyō. He thus followed the tendency, which had recently arisen, of situating temples in the remoteness of mountains, not in political centres. Although this was no novelty in Indian and Chinese tradition, people today see the temple harmoniously set in the mountains and its life there as characteristically Japanese, especially since this harmony with nature was elevated into an aesthetic principle. Kūkai introduced the rite of the esoteric consecration, the *abhiṣeka*, for the reception of which numerous high-ranking monks appeared, including Saichō. In 816 Kūkai founded on Mount Kōya, on the peninsula of Kii, the main temple of his sect, the Kongōbuji, as 'a place of practice in [esoteric] meditation', and in 823 one of the two state temples in the new capital, the 'Eastern Temple', Tōji, was handed over to him. His steeply ascending career reached its zenith when he was allowed to construct a 'Temple of the True Word', Shingon-in, inside the imperial palace. Here there took place every year in January, first in 834 under Kūkai's direction, splendid esoteric rites for the welfare of the emperor. A year later, in 835, Kūkai, sitting in deep meditation, fell into complete silence. In the eyes of his devotees he is not dead but still sits in timeless meditation behind the locked doors of his sanctuary on Mount Kōya.

The effect of his esoteric practices, even more than his philosophical work, must have held a magical attraction for his age and the following centuries. Twice (in 824 and 827) he had succeeded, by means of esoteric rites, in making it rain, in return for which the court had bestowed on him one of the highest ranks then existing in the Buddhist clergy. Kūkai as calligrapher, Kūkai as the creator of numerous statues, Kūkai as founder of the first Japanese private school for Buddhism and Confucianism, Kūkai as civilizer: all these facets of his work doubtless promoted the cult of his person and facilitated the spread of his teaching.

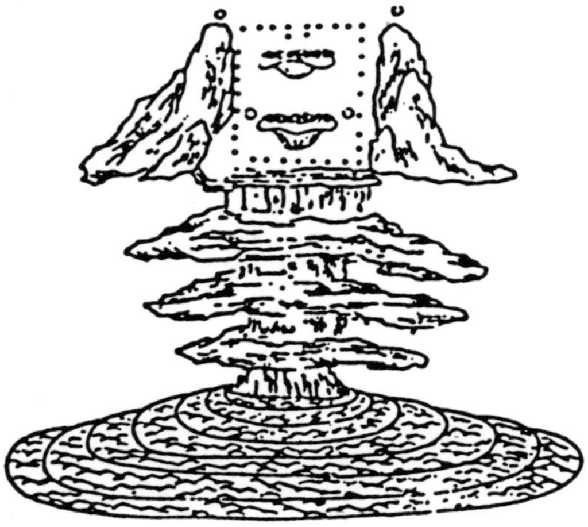

A 10th- or 11th-century picture of Mount Meru, a diagrammatic representation of the universe. Our world is one of four islands located in the sea round its base (not shown in this simplified version). Some Indian thinkers had seen spiritual progress as an ascent of the mountain and then through the heavenly spheres above it to Nirvāṇa. Japanese Buddhism, less concerned with transcendental speculation, tries to depict spiritual attainment within the forms that appear in this world.

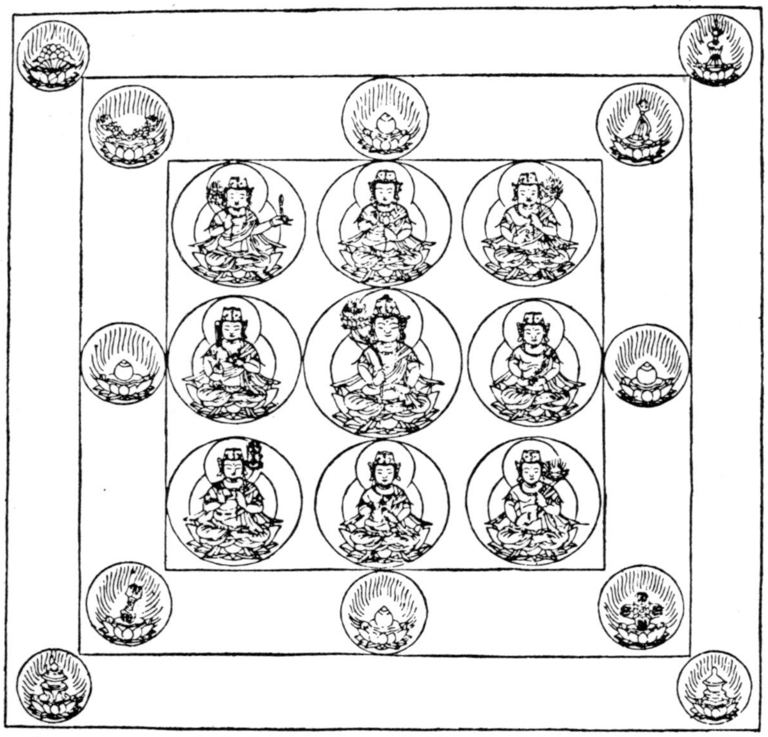

A maṇḍala with Dainichi-nyorai in the middle. Dainichi-nyorai, a symbolic personification of the universe, is identified with the illuminated mind, and is therefore represented as the Buddha. Spiritual perfection is not a state separated from the present world.

Esoteric theory and practice are among the most complicated parts of the whole Buddhist teaching. However, their basic principles – common to both the Tendai and Shingon sects in spite of their doctrinal disputes – are simple: so simple that they contained the power to dominate the Heian period and to influence decisively the Buddhism of the Kamakura period. At the start stands the conviction that the concrete world, as man experiences it Here and Now, is the highest reality. Thus there is no striving for the beyond, but for understanding of this world. This 'universe of consciousness' (perceiving consciousness and perceived world are one) is personified in the symbolic figure of the Buddha (or Tathāgata) Dainichi-nyorai (called Mahāvairocana in Sanskrit), the 'Great Enlightener'. He stands for the totality of all being and forms the centre of the *maṇḍala* (graphic representation of this view of the world), surrounded by a number of other symbolic figures, which are simply the various aspects of the central figure, the totality. The world is therefore no longer depicted, in accordance with Indian tradition, as Mount Meru, surrounded by seas, mountains and islands, but as a world of consciousness, the symbolism of which is placed in close relationship to esoteric practice.

The goal of practice is to become a Buddha oneself – in the esoteric school, Dainichi-nyorai. One need not flee one's own being or the world, for one 'becomes Buddha in this very body' (*sokushin-jōbutsu*). This principle is ritually realized in the practice of *sanmitsu-kaji*: roughly 'standing upon' or figuratively 'coinciding with' (*kaji*, in Sanskrit *adhiṣṭhāna*) the 'Three Mysteries' (*sanmitsu*, in Sanskrit *tri-guhya*): the 'Three Actions' of the believer are symbolic movements of the arms, hands and fingers (in Sanskrit, *mudrā*), the recitation of short formulas (*shingon* or *myō*; in Sanskrit, *mantra*) and the pursuit of symbolic trains of thought (*kanjō*). Properly performed, these 'Three Actions' coincide with the 'Three Mysteries' – body, speech and mind – of the personified All, with Dainichi-nyorai. The believer comes to the realization that he is one with the All, that he himself is Dainichi-nyorai.

The oneness of man with the all is symbolized in another, figurative way in a ritual act which is accompanied by the notion on the part of the believer that his body and spirit are identical with the 'Six Great [Elements]' (*roku-dai*) – earth, water, fire, wind, space and consciousness – from which all beings are constituted. In the sitting posture of meditation, legs and the lower abdomen become the element 'earth', the upper abdomen becomes 'water', the breast becomes 'fire', the head 'wind' and what lies above it 'space'. As all six elements permeate each other the first five imply the sixth, consciousness; and as they fill the universal All, the meditator, sitting there, embodies Dainichi-nyorai, the highest reality, the All.

Before long, the *sanmitsu-kaji*, in hundreds of variant forms, was construed by those incapable of penetrating the philosophical depths of esoteric dogma as a magical practice which was almost omnipotent. So great was the prestige of the 'True Word' that after Saichō's death his successors modelled Tendai practice more and more closely on that of esotericism. Ennin (794–864) and Enchin (814–91) studied for many years in China and brought back from there those parts of the doctrine that were still missing. Annen (died late 9th century) is regarded as the man who perfected the esoteric doctrine of the Tendai sect. The dominant position of this sect was largely based on its esoteric practice, welcomed far and wide as the means to attain worldly advantages.

With Enchin a period of discord within the Tendai sect began. In 868 he took over the Miidera (or Onjōji), a temple on Lake Biwa, and after his death the rivalry between the Miidera and the main temple on Mount Hiei led to open hostilities. In the course of history there were several armed encounters between the two temples. The state had lost its formerly strict control over the Buddhist clergy. More and more ordinary simple folk shaved their heads and put on monk's clothing without permission from the state, in order to escape taxation. Many roamed through the land in armed groups, plundering. Some temples raised their own armies from the so-called *sōhei*, 'warrior monks', to protect themselves from outside interference and to settle their disputes with other temples. Often temples were set on fire and destroyed. At the beginning of the 12th century the most influential temples and Shintō shrines possessed their own armies of warrior monks for self-protection. Sometimes they would storm the capital in thousands to force the court to grant their demands. Often on these occasions the *sōhei* would carry with them the precious litter (*mikoshi*) containing the Shintō divinity, which Buddhism equated with a Buddha or bodhisattva; they were thus protected against any counter-attack by the imperial troops, for an attack on a Shintō divinity, so closely connected with the imperial house, would have been regarded as blasphemy.

Meanwhile Buddhism further penetrated the life of the court. The influence of esotericism at court is shown by the custom – attested since 1068 – that on ascending the throne the emperor should perform the main *mudrā* of esoteric consecration (*kanjō*). Quite often the emperor and members of the high-ranking nobility were practising Buddhists. Their practices included the recitation of sūtras, the reception of the Buddhist commandments, the foundation of temples and pagodas, pilgrimages to temples and sacred mountains and even adoption of the status of monk. So towards the end of the Heian period it gradually became the custom for the emperors formally to renounce the throne and to withdraw to a temple from which they governed as 'Dharma king' (*hōō*); this was the time of 'government [from the] temple' (*insei*). Women, too, participated to some extent in Buddhist activities, even though at the start they were not welcomed as practising Buddhists.

For the nobility of the Heian period Buddhism also

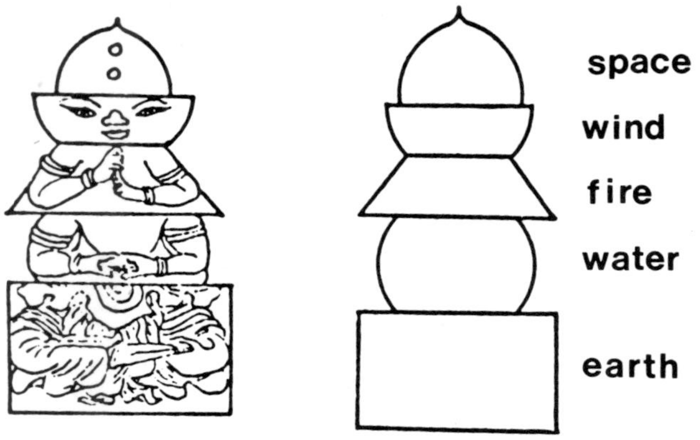

Diagram showing how the meditator becomes one with the universe in the form of a stupa, which represents the five elements. The sixth element, consciousness, permeates the other five.

meant something more than religion, philosophy and magical practice: its aesthetic side influenced the appreciation of beauty in these and the following centuries. The theatrical effect of the elaborate rites with their splended robes, artistically furnished temple halls and Buddhist chant, *shōmyō*, which corresponds to our Gregorian chant, was highly regarded from an artistic point of view. This went so far that many a practice was enjoyed as a purely aesthetic activity: competitions in the recitation of sūtras, when beauty of melody and voice were judged, were held quite frequently. In this period, too, arose the concept of 'becoming Buddha through the *shōmyō* chant', or through the art of poetry. Buddhist art also exerted a decisive influence on secular art, which was connected in even more ways than in the Western world with religious art. The *shōmyō* was one of the elements which gave rise later to the singing in the Nō theatre. Esoteric painting – for example the black-and-white pictures of symbolic figures to be found in esoteric ritual books and *maṇḍalas* – stimulated the development of a new technique of line drawing, especially in the field of the portrait, in the Kamakura period.

In the 11th century the pessimistic philosophy of a deteriorating 'final [period of the] Dharma' became widespread. On the basis of the Buddha's saying that after his death his teaching would pass through three eras distinguished by progressive decay, it was calculated that the year 1052 would introduce the last and final period. During these final ten thousand years, out of theoretical teaching, practical exercises and real Enlightenment, only the first would survive, the world being too corrupt to allow men to practise and come to Enlightenment. Thus the Indian doctrine of the redeeming power of the Buddha Amida (known in Sanskrit as Amitābha, 'Immeasurable Light', and Amitāyus, 'Immeasurable Life') was particularly welcome; for this Buddha, Lord of the Western Paradise of the 'Pure Land' (*Jōdo*: hence 'doctrine of the Pure Land', Jōdo-kyō), receives into his paradise those who

Kūya practising the invocation of the Buddha Amida, represented as tiny figures emerging from his mouth.

– even without any form of Buddhist practice – think of him with a believing heart and call on his name in the devotional formula *Namu-Amida-Butsu*, 'surrender to the Buddha Amida'. This formula, originally a meditative practice – hence its name *nenbutsu*, 'thinking on the Buddha [Amida]' – gradually became, as it passed from India via China to Japan, an invocation based on belief in the redeeming power of this Buddha.

This was not the only form of Buddhism based on faith alone which was popular during the Heian period. The belief in the bodhisattva Miroku (known in Sanskrit as Maitreya), who will be born into this world as a Buddha in the distant future for the redemption of mankind, and the belief in the bodhisattva Jizō (Kṣitigarbha in Sanskrit), who dispenses help to beings on all levels of existence, show that people did not rely on their own works but sought after a higher power. Faith in Miroku gradually declined; belief in Jizō remained deeply rooted in popular piety and is still alive today; but the belief in the power of the Buddha Amida developed in Japan into one of the most important Buddhist traditions and led to the formation of what is today the largest sect in Japan, the 'True Sect of the Pure Land', *Jōdo-shinshū*.

The two monks who did most to popularize Amidism in this period were Kūya (or Kōya, 903–972) and Ryōnin (died 1132). Kūya gained numerous devotees for the new faith by combining, during his extensive travels through the country, the practice of the invocation with social work. He helped with the building of roads and bridges and where he found corpses, which in accordance with the custom of the time had been left lying in remote spots, he collected them together, poured oil over them and cremated them. This form of funeral, introduced earlier among the Buddhist clergy, thus gradually spread among the laity. In the 'Temple of the Six Perfections' (Rokuharamitsuji) in Kyōto there still stands an impressive statue showing Kūya practising the invocation. From his half-open mouth project, arranged in a row on a little rod, a number of small figures of Amida – a symbolic depiction of the presence of Amida in the invocation.

Through Ryōnin the invocation entered the practice of the Tendai sect in ritual form; Ennin had already introduced an esoteric form of the *nenbutsu*. The belief in Amida which Ryōnin promulgated is based on the principle of Kegon philosophy according to which all things 'interpenetrate' each other: on the basis of the 'interpenetration' (*yūzū*) of the invocation, all beings are reborn in the Pure Land and attain Buddhahood even if only one human being is born again and becomes a Buddha. Ryōnin is regarded as the founder of the sect which since 1874 has been officially recognized under the name *Yūzū-nenbutsu-shū*, 'Sect of the Invocation of Interpenetration'.

How strong belief in Amida was even at the court and in the highest strata of society is shown by the example of the regent Fujiwara-no Michinaga (966–1027), who ruled the court for decades and gave his name to his century, the Fujiwara period. It is evident from his diary that he was a keen devotee of the invocation. He notes for the ninth month of the year 1008: 1st day, 110,000 times; 2nd day, 150,000 times; 3rd day, 140,000 times; 4th day, 130,000 times; 5th day, 170,000 times. The greater the number of invocations, the greater the merit. Michinaga founded, as a symbol of his worldly power, the biggest and most splendid temple of his time, the Hōjōji in Kyōto (it fell into ruins in the Middle Ages). He died in it, in the hall of Amida, holding a cord that linked him to nine gilded statues of the Buddha Amida. This custom was continued later on among the people as well; the dying person was handed a cord tied at the other end to the hand of an Amida coming to meet him in a picture. This strengthened the believer's conviction that he would be received by the merciful Buddha Amida in the paradise of the Pure Land.

The Heian period was marked by the spread of Buddhist belief and practice, not only the *nenbutsu*, to all social strata. 'Reports of rebirth' (*ōjō-den*) noted from the end of the 10th century onwards show how diverse and in part unorthodox the practices of the period were. Besides invocations in great numbers and the recitation and copying of sūtras, they mention withdrawn lives in the loneliness of the mountains, pilgrimages through the provinces and even suicide by fire and by water; and all this to achieve rebirth in the Pure Land.

The most important work of the Heian period on the doctrine of the Pure Land is considered to be the *Ōjō-yōshū*, 'Foundations of rebirth' (985), by the Tendai monk Genshin (942–1017), better known as Eshin-Sōzu. It is a collection of the most important passages from the Indian sūtras and from a commentary by the third patriarch of the Chinese School of the Pure Land, Shan-tao (in Japanese, Zendō: 613–681), on the belief in Amida. It expresses the idea that for rebirth in the Pure Land nothing more than the invocation of the name (*nenbutsu*) is required. Genshin was probably the Buddhist who most strongly influenced the whole second half of the Heian period. Not only did his work contribute to the formation of the Pure Land sects in the 12th and 13th centuries, but his colourful descriptions of the Western Paradise of the Pure Land and of the Buddhist hells stimulated the art of his time to adopt new motifs and forms. He writes that for him both the 'Impure Land' (our world of desires) and the 'Pure Land' (the paradise of the Buddha Amida) lie nowhere else than in our minds and hearts. Thus his faith had overcome the dualism that makes Amida and his paradise into 'objects' of worship and longing.

The Kamakura period (1185–1333)

From the end of the 11th century, a new military aristocracy in the provinces increasingly evaded the control of the central government. Power became concentrated in a few big families. The process culminated in armed conflict between the two mightiest of them, the Taira and the Minamoto. The Minamoto were victorious in 1185 in one of the most memorable wars in Japanese history and thereby acquired *de facto* absolute power in the country. Minamoto-no Yoritomo, their leader, set up in Kamakura, in the vicinity of present-day Tokyo – and thus in one of the eastern provinces far removed from the imperial capital of Heian-kyō (Kyōto) – a military government, the *Bakufu*, and received from the court in 1192 the title of *Shōgun* together with supreme military and police power. This transfer of power from the hands of the court aristocracy to those of the warrior class (*bushi* or *samurai*), from the luxurious, refined world of the capital to the world of coarse warriors and a hitherto plain-living provincial population, naturally changed the whole cultural climate.

Buddhism had become mature enough to adapt itself to the new social situation. Intellectualism and ritualism were replaced by simple principles and practices which lay within the capacity of ordinary people and corresponded to their needs. Buddhism became democratized as a religion of faith. The achievement of Enlightenment (*bodhi*) was accordingly no longer reserved for the monk: lay Buddhism began to become a reality.

The doctrine of 'original enlightenment' (*hongaku*) made a decisive contribution to the formation of this new Buddhism, in which the role of practice was reduced to essentials. Taken over from China, this dogma first developed as a secret 'oral tradition' in the Tendai sect but then helped to mould Kamakura Buddhism. The principle is simple. A writing of that time expresses it like this: 'Beings are the very essence of the Enlightened (*Buddha*). . . . But since they do not know this they are called the "broad mass [of the non-Enlightened]"' (*bonbu*, in Sanskrit, *pṛthagjana*). It is thus not a question of working along the path of asceticism to the state of Enlightenment, but of recognizing that one is Enlightened here and now.

The first of the three great traditions of Kamakura Buddhism, the doctrine of the Pure Land, continued a development which had begun – as we have shown – in the Heian period. However, Genkū (1133–1212), better known by his posthumous name, Hōnen-Shōnin – Hōnen for short – is regarded as the founder of an independent Japanese 'sect of the Pure Land', *Jōdo-shū*. Though learned in Buddhist doctrine, he decided that man could no longer achieve Enlightenment by his own strength and that the only possible way was surrender to the Buddha Amida and rebirth into the Western Paradise of the Pure Land. Spurred on by reading a work by Shan tao, the perfector of the Chinese doctrine of the Pure Land, and also the *Ōjō-yōshū* of Genshin, he devoted himself completely to this doctrine and recommended the 'exclusive invocation of the Buddha [Amida]' (*Senju-nenbutsu*). In 1198 Hōnen compiled his chief work, the *Shenchaku-hongan-nenbutsu-shū* (*Collection of* [*texts on*] *the Original Vow and the Invocation of the Buddha*), in which he laid the dogmatic foundation of the new sect, which was thereby created. What is new in this book and characteristic of the whole reform movement in the Buddhism of the Kamakura period is that Hōnen recognizes the scholastic apparatus of Mahāyāna philosophy, but concentrates on an intensified religious feeling which finds expression in the simple invocation of the name, *Namu-Amida-Butsu*, and is stamped by unshakeable faith in rebirth into Amida's paradise. There were soon followers of this simple, hopeful doctrine in all strata of the population. It is said of the Emperor Go-Shirakawa (died 1192), who abdicated, that he founded a *nenbutsu* rite in which *Namu-Amida-Butsu* was recited a million times and that he himself died with the invocation of the Buddha Amida on his lips. The *nenbutsu* movement took hold of senior civil servants and warriors, and swiftly spread among the people. The envy of the old sects of Nara and Mount Hiei led to more and more violent protests against the unorthodox character of the new doctrine and finally to the banning of the *nenbutsu*. Hōnen himself was exiled for ten months to the southern part of the island of Shikoku.

Shinran-Shōnin (1173–1262) was the most important of Hōnen's disciples, for he founded the largest Buddhist sect in Japan today, the 'True Sect of the Pure Land', *Jōdo-shinshū*. The son of a noble, but orphaned in childhood, he studied, like Hōnen, in the Tendai sect on Mount Hiei and in the old schools of Nara. Twenty years of study did not resolve all his doubts. He then joined the circle of disciples around Hōnen. At the age of 35 he was punished with his teacher because of the spread of the 'exclusive invocation of the name' and sent into exile in a remote province on the Sea of Japan. Pardoned by the emperor after four years, he remained for another twenty years in the eastern provinces, where he disseminated his teaching, mainly among the country people. In 1224 he wrote his chief work, the *Kyōgyōshinshō* (*Doctrine, Practice, Belief, Realization*), in which he explains that the doctrine (as written down in the Indian Amida sūtras), the practice (the invocation of the name, *Namu-Amida-Butsu*), the belief and the realization (rebirth into the Pure Land) are all given by Amida, and that nothing depends on man's 'own power' (*jiriki*); everything depends on the 'power of the other' (*tariki*), namely on that of the Buddha Amida. Shinran emphasizes that the recitation of the *Namu-Amida-Butsu* is not a real practice, by virtue of which rebirth can be attained, but the expression of thanks for joy at everything received from Amida. With this refinement of Hōnen's teaching Shinran did not intend to found a new sect in opposition to his teacher, but to make it clear against all heresies how the '*true* sect of the Pure Land' was constituted. In modern times this became the official name of the school that goes back to Shinran (previously it was known as the Ikkō sect), while Hōnen's school and its various branches still continue to exist in parallel today. Shinran spent the last decades of his life in the imperial capital of Heian-kyō (Kyōto), surrounded by his followers, whom he did not call 'disciples' but 'friends' and 'travelling companions'. He described himself as an 'ignorant baldhead' and stated that he was 'neither monk nor layman'. In spite of his religious mission he did in fact live as a layman: tradition has it that he married the 'nun Eshin' (Eshin-ni) and had five children by her.

Although Shinran was not the first monk to take a wife, his marriage nevertheless symbolizes the decisive turn in Japan towards lay Buddhism. In contrast to the other founders of sects in the Kamakura period, Shinran emphasizes that obedience to the Buddhist commandments and the performance of good deeds are not necessary to attain deliverance; and that on the contrary it is precisely the bad man who can be sure of being born into Amida's paradise. This doctrine of the 'power of the other' (the absolute), taken to its logical conclusion, enabled Shinran to overcome the opposition between 'self' and 'other'. In one of his late letters he explains that Amida and the Pure Land lie in ourselves.

A third, parallel development of the belief in Amida came in the second half of the 13th century with the monk Ippen-Shōnin (1239–1289). Ippen-Shōnin learned through a dream of the wonderful power of the invocation of the name. From then onwards he wandered through the country with a crowd of followers and spread among the population the practice of the '*nenbutsu* dance'. Since he recited the *Namu-Amida-Butsu* during the 'six hours' (our present-day twenty-four hours), his followers later came to be known as the *Ji-shū*, literally the 'Hours sect': each hour is to be regarded as the last of one's life. With Ippen-Shōnin, too, the opposition between 'self' and 'other' disappears; the invocation itself becomes absolute being. 'The *nenbutsu* utters the *nenbutsu*' is one of his bold formulations, closely related to the sayings of Zen Buddhism. After his death the tradition founded by him lived on; it became a regular custom for groups of believers to travel on pilgrimage through the country and collect donations for religious aims.

While the belief in Amida proceeds from the 'strength of the other' (*tariki*), Zen Buddhism teaches that man can come to deliverance and Enlightenment only from his 'own strength' (*jiriki*). 'Zen' (Chinese *Ch'an*, from Pāli *jhāna*, Sanskrit *dhyāna*, 'reflection, meditation') is the appropriate way to arrive spontaneously at an insight into our entanglement with the totality of being and to experience *satori* (a Japanese expression for the moment of Enlightenment, *bodhi*), when a sovereign freedom from attachment to all things and ideas prevails and the absolute is not distinct from the world of phenomena.

Japan had had contacts with the Zen doctrine through monks of the old sects since the 7th century. At the beginning of the 9th century Saichō included it in his Tendai doctrine. However, a lasting tradition that concentrated on Zen practice and that led to the formation of a separate sect was first created by the Tendai monk Eisai (or Yōsai, 1141–1215). A short journey to China in 1168 served mainly to give depth to his Tendai studies, but also awoke an interest in Zen, which drew him back to China for a longer stay (1187–91). He arranged to be introduced to the practice and doctrine of that branch of Zen which went back to Lin-chi (called Rinzai in Japanese; died 867) and on his return to Japan he started to disseminate the new doctrine. In 1194 the Tendai monks of Mount Hiei caused his missionary activity to be forbidden. But Eisai did not yield to this opposition and he succeeded in establishing firm relations with the military government (*Bakufu*) in Kamakura and the military caste that held sway there, which found the simple, hard, manly discipline of the new doctrine more to its taste than the ritualism and dogmatism of the old schools. Eisai emphasized the basic role for all Buddhist practice of meditative absorption (*zen*), which, if practised by all, must lead to sound order in the state and society.

Eisai's name is linked to the introduction of the habit of tea-drinking in Japan. In 1168 he brought back with him from his first trip to China some seeds of the first tea bush and grew the first plants. It was he who started the tradition that led – as already in China – via the use of tea in temples to its spread among wider sections of the population, to tea games (competitions in guessing variety and origin) and finally to a peculiarly Japanese development, the creation of the 'tea-way' (*sa-dō* or *cha-dō*), which though non-religious was strongly influenced by the spirit of Zen, and the so called 'Tea

Ceremony', modestly called in Japanese *cha-no yu* ('hot water for the tea').

A second Chinese school of Zen, the Ts'ao-tung (in Japanese, Sōtō) sect, was brought over to Japan by Dōgen (1200–1253). The scion of an aristocratic family related to the imperial house and an orphan from early youth, Dōgen at first studied in the main temple of the Tendai sect on Mount Hiei. After a four-year stay in China, Dōgen returned to Japan and in 1244 he withdrew to the remote province of Echizen where he founded a temple of his own, the Eiheiji, and devoted himself to the training of a first generation of Sōtō monks. He rejected all worldly honours, even a seductive invitation to Kamakura. Dōgen's style is marked by relentless severity. His writings, especially his chief work, the *Shōbō-genzō* (*The Eye and Treasury of the True Dharma*), are characterized by such terseness and mordancy that today they are among the most fascinating literary documents of Japanese Buddhism. The foundation of Dōgen's Zen is the constantly emphasized principle that practice does not *lead* to Enlightenment, but is carried out in the *state* of being Enlightened; otherwise it is not practice. In a logically constructed picture of the world he equates all being – the believer, his practice and the world – with the present moment, the moment of Enlightenment. Striving for Enlightenment would be going astray. The energy and inner 'presence' which this ideal ceaselessly demands from the monks undoubtedly contributed to the Sōtō sect's standing much further away than the Rinzai sect from Japanese arts and 'ways'. When the arts, 'ways' and culture of Japan are mentioned together with Zen, it is almost always Rinzai Zen that is meant. But it is precisely Dōgen's insistence on the coincidence of practice with the goal of practice (Enlightenment) that characterizes many 'ways' that arose later – the tea way, the flower way, the way of archery and others. It is not a question of a success to be achieved; the performance contains its own value; way and goal coincide in every phase.

To understand the aesthetic tendency of the Rinzai sect, especially after the end of the Kamakura period, it should be noted that from the start many Japanese Zen masters have been strongly attracted to Chinese culture in general. Eisai brought some Chinese actors to Japan; Dōgen brought potters and carpenters; and others have introduced Chinese pharmacy, dyeing techniques and weaving. A lay disciple of Dōgen brought back with him the art of making ceramics. He settled down in the town of Seto, where he started producing ceramic ware making use of the newly imported techniques. This tradition has been perfected and handed down from generation to generation to the present day and has become so famous that the name of 'Seto ware' (*setomono*) is now used in Japan as a synonym for porcelain and ceramics in general. Architecture, gardening, and Chinese water-colour painting and literature are other fields in which Chinese influence came to Japan in the train of Zen.

The Japanese Zen monks who travelled to China to study were instructed, as was usual in China at that time, not only in the practice and doctrine of Zen but also in Neo-Confucianism, which was itself strongly influenced by Zen Buddhism and by Hua-yen philosophy. For four centuries (until about 1600) the big Rinzai temples became centres of Chinese learning in general and Neo-Confucianism in particular. To Buddhist spirituality the Zen masters added a Confucian moral code, which appealed to the warrior class. In 1256 the fifth regent, Hōjō Tokiyori (1227–63), who held the real power in the military government at Kamakura, became a monk under the auspices of a Rinzai monk from China. At that time numerous samurai became monks, but Tokiyori remained a pre-eminent example: he realized *satori* and received from his master the seal confirming his Enlightenment. During this period Zen Buddhism also gained access to the imperial court in Kyōto. The emperor Hanazono (ruled 1308–18) was converted to Rinzai Zen and became one of the great promoters of Zen Buddhism by financing the Myōshinji, a famous temple in Kyōto.

The last great reformer and sect founder of the Kamakura period was Nichiren (1222–82), the son of a poor fisherman. After several years in Kamakura and ten years training in Tendai doctrine and practice on Mount Hiei, he came to the conclusion that the highest, all-embracing truth lay in the *Lotus Sūtra* (known in Japanese as *Myōhō-renge-kyō*, *Hokekyō* for short), the fundamental canonical text of the Tendai sect, but that for a simple, ordinary person, especially in the 'final [period of the] Dharma', the Tendai dogma and the reading of the *Lotus Sūtra* were too difficult. He proclaimed that the title *Myōhō-renge-kyō* was the essence of the whole Sūtra and that it was in fact identical with the state of Enlightenment of the Śākyamuni and with the 'true state' (*jissō*) of the totality of the All. It was therefore sufficient, he said, to utter the 'title' (*daimoku*) of the *Lotus Sūtra* in the form *Namu-Myōhō-Renge-Kyō*, 'Homage be paid to the *Lotus Sūtra* of the Wonderful Dharma', to find oneself in the state of the highest Enlightenment of the Śākyamuni. This condition gave rise spontaneously to all morally right behaviour, so that it was necessary for the state and society that all should follow the practice of the 'invocation of the title' (*shōdai*). A country in which this idea was realized was the true 'platform of the commandments' (*kaidan*). Nichiren represented the essence of this doctrine graphically as the 'main object of worship' (*honzon*) in the form of a 'great *maṇḍala*' (*dai-mandara*): the characters which spell out the title are surrounded by a multitude of names of Buddhist symbolic figures (Buddhas and bodhisattvas among others) and Shintō divinities. This picture, which became the focus of the belief, expresses the fact that the truth of the Sūtra and of the title is all-embracing.

From the words of the *Lotus Sūtra* Nichiren drew the conviction that Japan was the country from which its doctrine was to spread throughout the world, and that

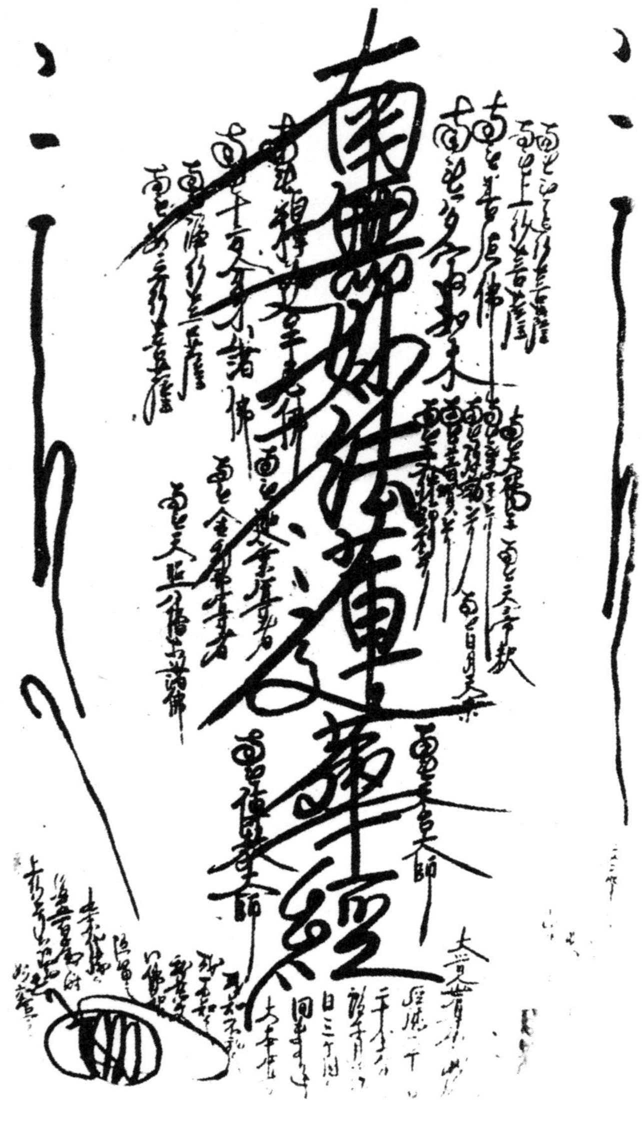

One of the maṇḍalas by Nichiren. The syllables make up the phrase 'Homage be paid to the Lotus Sūtra of the Wonderful Dharma' and are surrounded by the names of many Buddhas, bodhisattvas and Shintō divinities – including the bodhisattva of whom Nichiren considered himself an avatar (reincarnation).

he himself was the incarnation of a bodhisattva who appears in it (Viśiṣṭacāritra; in Japanese, Jōgyō-bosatsu, 'bodhisattva of outstanding practice') and who was 'suited to the dissemination of the Sūtra'. Nichiren did not turn his attention away from the world of appearances to the transcendent but related the religious statement of the *Lotus Sūtra* to his own time and country. The energy and self-confidence with which he devoted himself to political and social events soon aroused the distrust of the government and of the other sects. In several tracts – e.g. *Risshō-ankoku-ron* (*On the Security of the Country through the Establishment of the Right [Doctrine]*), 1260 – he warned people against the spread of false doctrines, especially the doctrine of the Pure Land, and against moral decline, and predicted the Mongol invasions. Only the observance of his teaching, he said, and the practice of the invocation of the title could save the country from catastrophe. In 1260 he handed over his *Risshō-ankoku-ron* to the former regent, Hōjō Tokiyori, and preached his doctrine in the streets of Kamakura. Followers of the Pure Land doctrine set fire to his house and in 1261 the government banished him to the peninsula of Izu. After he had been pardoned he increased his attacks on the other sects and wrote memoranda criticizing the government. His unyielding attitude finally so provoked the clergy and the government that he was condemned to death; however, he escaped execution as though by a miracle and was finally sent into exile on the island of Sado in the Sea of Japan (1271–4). There he developed his teaching in a series of writings and after his return from Sado spent the rest of his life on Mount Minobu (today the site of the main temple of the Nichiren sect, not far from Mount Fuji), where he devoted himself to his missionary activity and to the training of monks of his sect. While the other religious leaders of the new Kamakura Buddhism mainly emphasized the salvation of the individual, Nichiren strove for a socio-religious reform at the national level. It is thus understandable that in recent times certain branches of his sect should have been connected with nationalistic tendencies, distortions of his religious feeling for his country.

The religious revival of the Kamakura period was not limited to the 'new sects': the decadence of monks and lay believers was felt and deplored by the sects established in the 8th and 9th centuries. Many leading monks called for a revival of the Buddhist precepts and for Buddhist altruism in the form of charitable social work. The monk Eizon (1201–90) and his disciple Ninshō (1217–1303), both of the Ritsu sect, are known for having stressed the need to help the very poor and lepers. Ninshō is said to have been so unselfish that the people called him the 'Living Buddha'. Jōkei (1155–1213) of the Hossō sect opposed the practice of *nenbutsu* and called for the revival of monastic discipline. He was engaged in a famous controversy with Hōnen, the founder of the Jōdo sect. He is known as the 'Restorer of the Hossō Sect'. Another of the famous 'restorers' of the old sects is Kōben (also called Myōe-Shōnin, 1173–1232), a priest of the Kegon sect. He was an outstanding scholar who was introduced to Zen Buddhism by contact with Eisai. He also received tea-plant seeds from Eisai and cultivated tea for himself. His plan to travel to India to pay a visit to the Buddha's land was abandoned because of ill health. Two facts illustrate his eccentricity. He wrote a letter to an island, and practised Zen meditation sitting on a tree, thus earning the soubriquet 'Reverend Bird's Nest' (*Chōka-Shōnin*).

During this period, every major school had its own form of Buddhist-Shintō syncretism, explaining *kami* as manifestations of figures in the Buddhist pantheon. As a reaction, counter-movements began to declare that on the contrary the Buddhas were manifestations of the *kami*.

The Muromachi period (1336–1573)

After the middle of the 14th century, regional governors and warriors gained more and more autonomy from the central government. At the same time the farmers' standard of living rose as they started selling their products at markets. There gradually emerged a new merchant class. Trade, traffic and new commercial towns developed. Thus, a new class of townspeople and a new culture came into being. These changes led to a period of social upheaval. Throughout the Muromachi period there were constant clashes between warrior groups, and Japan's unity finally disintegrated in the period known as the 'Period of War between the Provinces' (1467–1573). In this latter period numerous peasant uprisings occurred: peasants and merchants, led by the local organizations of the True Sect of the Pure Land (Jōdo-shinshū, at that time called the Ikkō-shū, 'One Direction Sect', for their mind was set solely upon faith in the Buddha Amida) fought against local military rulers and sometimes succeeded in setting up their own autonomous administrations.

By the end of the Kamakura period all sects had become active in looking for lay believers in the lower classes of society. But most of the people were still illiterate, so the sects set up local village organizations. Old people, freed from the need to work, played a leading role in such organizations as the *nenbutsu* assemblies. Women too set up their own organizations, e.g. to pray for easy delivery.

Many itinerant priests roamed through the country. A 15th-century essay tells us (with some exaggeration) that probably 'more than a third of the people' were such mendicant priests. Though unorthodox, they undoubtedly helped to propagate Buddhism among the people.

Among the outstanding Buddhist figures of this period, three may be singled out for special mention.

Ikkyū (1394–1481), priest of the Rinzai sect (Zen) is particularly known for his unconventional character. An illegitimate son of the Emperor Go-Komatsu, he led for many years the life of an itinerant priest. It is said that he wandered from door to door carrying a skeleton attached to a pole and admonishing people with the words: 'Be on your guard!' The meaning of this was: 'Throw away the thought that there is a 'Self'!' Later in life he fell in love with a blind woman attendant. He was also an accomplished poet, calligrapher and painter. In the *Kyōun-shū*, a posthumous collection of his poetry, he speaks of brothels, and concretely describes sexual desire and rapture. The safest way to interpret this might be to say that Ikkyū was a man capable of complete emancipation as well as of emancipation from emancipation; for in 1474 he became, by order of the emperor, the chief priest of a temple in Kyōto.

Nisshin (1407–88), of the Nichiren sect, was one of those who tried to stop the tendency of his sect to adapt itself to the tastes and demands of the people. (Such a tendency was prevalent in many sects from the beginning of the Muromachi period.) He was set on restoring the genuine teaching of the founder of the sect, Nichiren. But he met with resistance everywhere. Following the example of Nichiren, he made a direct appeal to the Shōgun (which was strictly forbidden). He was twice sent to jail where he suffered unbelievably cruel punishments. It is said of him that a red hot pot was put on his head, which is why he is popularly known as 'Nisshin covered with a pot' (Nabekaburi-Nisshin).

Rennyo (1415–99), the 8th patriarch of the True Sect of the Pure Land (Jōdo-shinshū), defended his sect against the attacks of the Tendai sect (which had burnt one of the main temples of Rennyo's sect). He stressed the unlimited power of the Buddha Amida, but insisted at the same time on the importance of the Confucian virtues, of harmonious co-existence within the social order, and of obedience to authority.

The privileged relations of the Rinzai branch of the Zen sect with the military government (*Bakufu*) permitted it to gain tremendous wealth. It cultivated vast estates, gained control of part of the commerce with China, and even engaged in lending money. This wealth led to the creation of what is known as the 'Culture of the Five Mountains' (i.e. of the five main monasteries of the Rinzai sect in Kyōto), which constitutes the summit of Japanese Zen culture. It included virtually all the arts, such as architecture, painting, calligraphy and sculpture, as well as printing, gardening and medicine. Its most outstanding contribution was its literature, a body of prose and verse, written in Chinese and so accessible only to a highly educated public, but which became so venerated in these monasteries that in the 15th century it was more important than Buddhism itself.

These and other arts developed later into what is known as the Japanese 'Ways' (*dō*), which may be considered as a sort of secularization of Buddhist spirituality. Practised outside strictly Buddhist institutions, they dwell on principles fundamentally characteristic of Japanese Buddhism: highest fulfilment in every instant, every thought and every gesture. The best known examples are the tea ceremony, flower arrangement, swordsmanship and archery. 'Zen and tea have the same taste' is an often cited expression of this.

The theory that we should accept things as they are and human nature as it is could also lead to abuses. Within the Shingon sect, for instance, there evolved a heretical branch called the Tachikawa (starting in the 12th century and suppressed in the 14th), and within the Tendai sect a similar movement called *Genshi-kimyō-dan*, suppressed in the Edo period, both of which ended up using sexual practices to 'realize the Enlightenment within this body'.

The Azuchi-Momoyama and Edo periods: 1573–1867

After more than a hundred years of civil war, in which not only the local rulers (*daimyō*) but also the large Buddhist sects were involved, the country regained unity and peace. Oda Nobunaga (1534–82), a powerful *daimyō*, subdued the region around imperial Kyōto and then proceeded to break the military power of the Tendai sect. After a 10 year siege, in 1580 the Honganji, temple and military stronghold of the True Sect of the Pure Land (*Jōdo-shinshū*) at Osaka, was burnt down. After Nobunaga's death by assassination, his place was taken by Toyotomi Hideyoshi (1536–98) and the unification of the country was completed under his rule. He died before his unfortunate attempt to conquer China foundered in Korea. His faithful vassal and successor, Tokugawa Ieyasu (1542–1616), defeated his enemies in a decisive battle in 1600 and, taking in 1603 the old title of Shōgun, established his new government around the castle he had built in Edo (present-day Tokyo).

The new Shōgunate's foremost aim was to establish social and political stability. By drastic measures it succeeded in securing peace, at home and abroad, for two and a half centuries, but at the cost of stagnation in some fields. Suspicious of the activities of Christian missionaries which had begun with the arrival of the Jesuit Francis Xavier in 1549, and of European traders (mainly from the Netherlands, Britain, Spain and Portugal), the military government closed Japan to foreigners. Only Chinese and Dutch merchants were granted access, and they only under supervision to the trading post at Nagasaki. This situation lasted till the arrival of the American, Commodore Perry, in 1853.

For Buddhism this meant that for 250 years very little fresh inspiration came from the Asian continent. (The arrival of Yin-yüan Lung-ch'i from China in 1654 is the major exception – see below.) Meanwhile the Buddhist clergy was placed under the strict control of the government. It was forbidden to found a new sect or build a new temple without special permission. Neo-Confucianism, which the rulers considered better fitted than Buddhism to foster civic virtue, became the official state ideology. Since it had been studied and promulgated chiefly by Rinzai Zen temples, it is not surprising that the first leading Neo-Confucian ideologues of the Shōgunate were dissident Zen priests.

While Buddhism was deprived of political influence, it was reintegrated into the state apparatus by the *danka* (parishioner) system. Everyone had to register at a Buddhist temple; this proved that he was not a Christian and also served the purposes of a census. The *danka* system largely survives to this day and affiliates most Japanese citizens to a Buddhist temple. This does not necessarily mean that they are active Buddhists throughout their lives, but it entitles them to a Buddhist funeral at their own temples.

During the stirring times of national reunification there were two outstanding figures of Japanese Zen who well represent the spiritual trends of that period. One was the Rinzai monk Takuan (1573–1645), who is particularly known for his application of the Zen spirit to the art of fencing. In his *Recordings on the Mystery of Motionless Wisdom* he says: 'To look at things without permitting the mind to stop at them is called "to be motionless". For when the mind stops all sorts of discriminatory thoughts arise. When the mind stops, it moves; when it does not stop, it does not move' (surely a marvellous adaptation of the Zen spirit to those stirring times).

The other figure is Suzuki Shōsan (1579–1655). He became a Zen monk in the Sōtō sect at the age of 42, after having participated in the battles fought by the first Shōgun, Tokugawa Ieyasu. His Zen Buddhism was far from the rigorous monastic discipline of Dōgen. He laid stress on the work one does in one's daily life saying that 'everyone can become a Buddha in his own profession. There is no practice of the Buddhist Way outside the profession.'

The Shōgunate encouraged the Buddhist clergy of the sects in scholarly pursuits, hoping thereby to divert them from politics. The Edo period thus produced a large learned literature: scholastic accounts of sectarian doctrines and biographies of leading monks for instance. In the first half of the 17th century, two editions of the Buddhist canon appeared: the first, incomplete, by the monk Sōzon; the second by the Tendai monk Tenkai. However, the edition which was to gain the widest circulation was that by Tetsugen (1630–82) of the new Zen sect Ōbaku-shū; the edition (*ban*) is accordingly known as the *Tetsugen-ban* or *Ōbaku-ban*.

The Ōbaku-shū had been founded by the Chinese master Yin-yüan Lung-ch'i (known as Ingen Ryūki in Japanese; 1592–1673), a Rinzai Zen priest. He arrived in Japan in 1654, but met with the distrust of the local Rinzai priests when he declared that he represented the 'True Sect of Rinzai' (*Rinzai-shōshū*). While the Japanese Rinzai sect had kept its pure Zen tradition (in spite of the study of Neo-Confucianism in the big monasteries, 'the Five Mountains'), its Chinese counterpart had in the meantime evolved in a different direction, assimilating elements of Pure Land Buddhism. Thus, Ingen was forced, despite his initial intention, to found a new branch distinct from the existing Japanese Rinzai branches.

Ōbaku-shū added a new flavour to Japanese Zen, not only by its syncretism with Pure Land Buddhism (Amidism), but also by the introduction of rituals, customs and a new architectural style imported from Ming China. The use of chairs was one of these innovations.

Since they no longer enjoyed privileged relations with the government, the Zen sects of the Edo period tried to make Zen more accessible to the common people. Bankei Yōtaku (or Eitaku, 1622–93) propounded the *Fushō-zen* ('Zen of Non-production'). For him, 'Non-production' (*fushō*; in Sanskrit, *anutpāda*) was the principle *par excellence* of Buddhism, triggering Enlightenment and embracing – indeed replacing – all Buddhist practice. He who has understood this principle is Enlightened without being obliged to keep the Buddhist precepts. Bankei is the most brilliant example of those who, without betraying the most profound spirit of Zen, abandoned all traditional formalism.

Hakuin (1685–1768) is considered to be the restorer of the Rinzai sect in modern times. He revived the use of the *kōan*, statements of Zen masters that are used as problems set to novices in Zen monastries. These *kōan* cannot be solved by rational thinking and are designed to help open the mind to Enlightenment. He invented new *kōan* himself, adapted to the need of the times in that they do not presuppose any scholarly knowledge of the Chinese Zen classics. One of the most famous is: 'The sound produced by the clapping of two hands is easy to perceive, but what is the sound produced by one hand only?' There are many passages in his writings that show how strong was his this-worldliness and realism. In his *Hymn on 'Zazen'* (*Sitting in Meditation*) there are passages like this: 'Outside the [non-Enlightened] beings there is no Buddha'; 'This very place is the Land of the Lotus Flower'; 'This body is the Buddha.'

Forms of Buddhism unacceptable to the state had to go underground; this happened to branches of both Amidism and Nichiren Buddhism. Members of the Clandestine Nenbutsu maintained that the teaching of Shinran was transmitted by Rennyo (1415–99) to a lay believer because he feared that if it were transmitted to a Buddhist priest it would be misused in order to earn money. Thus, the authentic teaching subsists only among the lay teachers (*zenchishiki*) of the Edo period, and can only be transmitted to those who undergo lengthy preparation and are finally initiated into the profound meaning of the teaching in complicated secret rites.

Clandestine Daimoku (Invocation of the title of the *Lotus Sūtra*) was a branch of the Nichiren tradition particularly faithful to the doctrine of their founder Nichiren. They maintained that Japan is a Buddhist country, so its real sovereign is Śākyamuni, not the Shōgun. Together with the first Christians, this branch, officially known as Fujufuse-ha, was one of the two most oppressed religious communities of the Edo period. It has survived to the present day by the fervour of its adherents.

Modern times, the Meiji, Taishō and Shōwa periods: 1868 to the present

After two and a half centuries of isolation Japan began to reopen its doors when, in 1853 and 1854, the American Commodore Perry steamed his 'black ships' into Tokyo Bay and demanded that the authorities sign a treaty permitting American ships regular trade in certain Japanese ports. The following decade and a half was a period of hesitation and turbulence. Many Japanese realized that their rigid feudal system had become centuries out of date. Unable to resist foreign demands (after the treaty with America Japan signed treaties with England, Russia, France and the Netherlands), the military government in the opinion of many had lost its *raison d'être* as a protector of the nation against foreign influence. After years of ideological and armed struggle between factions, it finally yielded its power when, on 3 January 1868, a *coup d'état* forced the restoration of imperial rule.

Part of the 'Heart Sūtra for the Illiterate', a version of one of the most widely recited texts of Japanese Buddhism made in the form of a rebus for those unable to read. Such transcriptions were in use in the Edo period and show how strong the effort was at this time to bring Buddhist teachings within reach of the common people.

Within a few decades the new imperial regime modernized the country's political and social system, industry, commerce and communications. In 1889 a constitution was promulgated. It stressed the 'sacred' and 'inviolable' character of the emperor: as a direct descendant of the sun goddess Amaterasu Ōmikami the emperor was deified and regarded as *kami* manifested in human form. In the first year of the new emperor's reign (1868), in order to purify Shintō from foreign elements and to reinforce the basis for a policy pursuing the unity of religion and state, the new government decreed the 'Separation of Gods and Buddhas': Buddhist priests attached to Shintō shrines were secularized; Buddhist images could no longer be objects of Shintō worship and had to be removed from Shintō shrines; Shintō priests and their families had to be given a Shintō (not a Buddhist) funeral. The enforcement of this edict led to a nationwide movement, originating mainly in Shintō circles, aimed not merely at severing the ties between Buddhism and Shintō but at actually suppressing Buddhism. Buddhist temples and objects of worship were destroyed. The movement was known as *haibutsu-kishaku* ('Exterminate the Buddhas and destroy Śākyamuni') and came to a climax around 1871. However, it was brought under control, and in 1875 freedom of religion was promised to all creeds. In order to preserve a special status for Shintō, ranking above Buddhism, it was officially not considered a religion, but a form of a state cult.

Though the *haibutsu-kishaku* movement was a grave setback for Buddhism, it also gave a strong stimulus to some great figures of the Buddhist world of that period. Many went to Europe for study. For instance Shimaji Mokurai (1838–1911) of Jōdo-shinshū travelled to Europe (1872–3) to study the religious situation there. On his return he strongly advocated the disestablishment of all creeds and freedom of religion.

Others derived from contact with the West an acquaintance with the methods and results of modern scholarship; through studying Pali and Sanskrit they gained direct access for the first time to Buddhism's Indian source. This led at the beginning of this century to the founding of Buddhist universities. In the Taishō period (1912–26) the new liberal attitude of scholars towards the study of Buddhism contributed considerably to its modernization. Buddhist thought was introduced into literary and philosophical works. The most important philosopher influenced by Buddhism was Nishida Kitarō (1870–1945), now one of the world's famous philosophers. Inevitably, however, modernists were often criticized by their sects; some were expelled from them, some of them lost their university positions.

During the last fifty years the evolution of Buddhism has been closely linked to Japan's history. We have already seen how the militaristic and ultranationalistic movement that began in the late 1880s had its ideological roots partly in the philosophy of the Nichiren sect. In the 1930s this culminated in two acts of violence linked with Nichirenism. In May 1932, the prime minister, Inukai, was assassinated by a group of extremist naval officers whose mentor was Inoue Nisshō (1886–1967). And less than four years later, in February 1936, another devotee of the *Lotus Sūtra*, Kita Ikki (1883–1937), was similarly involved in the assassination of two ministers and an admiral. Kita was sentenced to death and executed.

After the invasion of China in 1937 and Japan's subsequent participation in the Second World War, the government's grip on Buddhist institutions tightened. Those sects whose writings contained passages where Buddhism was placed above the authority of state or emperor were forced to change or suppress them. There was little open opposition. The only important exception was the Sōka-gakkai (Value-creating Association), founded in 1930 as a non-religious society of teachers but quickly becoming a lay movement of one of the Nichiren sects. This bravely endured official persecution and its founder, Makiguchi Tsunesaburō, died in prison.

With the end of the war Buddhist activities revived, in spite of financial difficulties (when monasteries lost much of their land in the process of agrarian reform) and widespread indifference to religion. Religious bodies became more democratic in their composition. Links with other countries multiplied – there were missions to North and South America and to Europe, as well as renewed contacts with Buddhist countries in Southeast Asia and elsewhere. Social and cultural activities also flourished, mostly run by lay people. At the same time Japan was becoming the foremost 'Buddhological' country in the world, as academic studies advanced with a stream of scholarly publications of the highest standards.

Most interesting of all, perhaps, has been the foundation of new sects. Many of them go back to the prewar period, but it was not until after 1945 that they were able to play a major role in Japanese society. The reasons for their popularity are fairly clear: they answer a need in such areas as illness, lack of personal fulfilment and psychological problems; they make little distinction between priest and laymen (it is the layman who mostly makes converts); and they are sufficiently flexible to adapt themselves to social change. Two of the biggest, both of which – like nearly three-quarters of the new sects and lay organizations – belong to the Nichiren tradition, may serve as examples.

The Risshō-kōseikai (Society for the Establishment of Righteousness and Friendly Intercourse) was founded in 1938. By the 1950s it was among the most active religious groups. In the 1960s, when Japan was experiencing tremendous economic growth, many people began to look for a meaning and purpose in life beyond material well-being. Risshō-kōseikai, which has managed to penetrate all levels of society, including the working classes, stresses the perfectability of the individual and the need for social involvement.

Sōka-gakkai, already mentioned in connection with wartime oppression, seized public attention after the war by its outspoken propaganda. In 1964 a political arm, the Kōmei-tō (sometimes translated as 'Clean Politics Party') was formed. Six years later this separated itself from the parent sect and proclaimed separation of politics and religion. However, the Kōmei-tō continues to be a religiously inspired party, the organization of which is closely related to that of the Sōka-gakkai.

The older sects have responded to the challenge of the new by organizing movements to reinvigorate lay religious life in the community – meetings for groups of all ages and social classes, discussions, lectures and pilgrimages to the holy places of each sect. The purpose is to induce believers to practise Buddhism actively at home in order to make their families truly Buddhist families.

Compared to other Buddhist countries, Japan impresses the visitor by the tremendous variety and enormous wealth of its Buddhist life. New sects do not replace older ones but simply take their places alongside them. Thus, tradition becomes even richer, and the Japanese Buddhist world (indeed Japanese culture as a whole) can be seen as a living museum of its own past. Of course it includes seeming contradictions – high spirituality and cheap magic, deep religious feeling and superficial practice. ... Such contradictions are not unperceived by the Japanese themselves, but are they not part of any religion anywhere in the world?

10

Tibet: the Rise and Fall of a Monastic Tradition

TIBETAN BUDDHISM deserves a section to itself, for no other culture has been so deeply imbued with Buddhism as the Tibetan. Here, for over a thousand years, Buddhism permeated life. Though Buddhism came to Tibet from India over a long period, and had contacts with cultures to the north and east, the country became increasingly isolated so that Tibetan Buddhism developed independently. Throughout most of its history it was virtually unknown to the West.

It is in Tibetan translation that the classical literature of Indian Buddhism has been most accurately preserved. But Tibetans are all Mahāyāna Buddhists, in their philosophy continuing the Indian schools of *Madhyamaka* ('Centrist') and *Vijñānavāda* ('Consciousness Doctrine') thought, in ritual and organization overwhelmingly influenced by tantra. Nevertheless, there is great variety. The Yellow Hat Buddhists, headed by the Dalai Lama, followed the monastic Rule in huge monasteries which in their discipline and learning are perhaps the closest we can come to recapturing Indian Buddhism at its glorious height. On the other hand, tantric masters, some living wholly lay lives with wives and families, some part-time monks, preserve and recreate magic and yogic powers. A lama is a spiritual teacher, what Indians call a guru, but he need not be a monk or celibate, and he may or may not live in a monastery. Monks and nuns, on the other hand, preserve their tradition of celibacy.

A peculiarity of tantric Buddhism is that meditation is indissolubly associated with ritual action. Esoteric rituals may involve gratification of all the senses. Religious art and music play essential parts as props in the drama of seeking salvation. The most conspicuous tantric artefact is the *maṇḍala* (literally 'circle'). The *maṇḍala* is a cosmogram, peopled with the Buddhist pantheon, and at the same time a map of the microcosm, of man himself. When it is interpreted macrocosmically the deities are conceived mythologically; when it is interpreted microcosmically they are conceived symbolically, e.g. as personifications of emotions. The meditator visualizes and identifies with these deities. But his goal is to realize the ultimate unreality of the whole, to cut through the network of illusion with his adamantine wisdom and thus escape the round of birth and death.

Tibetan Buddhism is immensely colourful, rich in ritual and apparently as crowded with the supernatural as a *tanka*. But here, as in Buddhism everywhere, the real religion is in the life of the mind, not susceptible to illustration. The Dalai Lama preaches the same Four Noble Truths as the Theravādin from Burma or Sri Lanka.

The authentic life of Tibetan Buddhism can now be found only in such areas as Ladakh and Bhutan, culturally part of Tibet but politically separate. Ladakh, formerly a small state, is now part of Kashmir and was until recently very isolated from the rest of the world. Although never subject to the Dalai Lama's rule, its culture and religious life are virtually the same as that of Tibet. *Opposite:* country near the monastery of Tiktse, a dGe-lugs-pa monastery whose foundation goes back to the 15th century, impressively placed on the top of a rocky outcrop in the distance. Tiktse is an accumulation of buildings without an overall plan, containing dormitories for monks, courtyards for dances and ceremonies and several temples. In the foreground is a group of Tibetan stupas, or *chortens*, each holding a relic of a lama. (1)

The Sangha's garrisons

At Gyantse, one of the three towns in central Tibet that can qualify as more than villages, stands the famous Stupa of a Thousand Images (*left*), built in the 15th century. Each 'step' of the substructure houses a chapel. (2)

Before 1959, monks accounted for a large proportion of the adult male population. The head lamas of the main monasteries were powerful authorities in the secular world and the Dalai Lama, himself a monk, drew most of his ministers from their ranks.

The most splendid monument of Tibetan culture, secular and religious, is the Potala in Lhasa (*above*), the seat of the Dalai Lama. This unique building, set on a rock on the middle of a fertile plain, became the very symbol and embodiment of Tibet for the outside world. Founded by the 'Great Fifth' Dalai Lama and his chief minister between 1645 and 1653, it rises to thirteen storeys containing courtyards, halls and temples as well as palatial apartments for the Dalai Lama. (3)

Provincial fortresses (*left*) formed the old centres of Tibetan administration. The governorship of a region would be vested jointly in a monastic official and his lay counterpart. (4)

The festivals that punctuated the Tibetan year and loom large in the accounts of travellers often went back to folk-beliefs. In this ceremony outside the Jo-khang temple in Lhasa (*right*) monks are chasing away scapegoats representing the evils of mankind. The Jo-khang temple, the 'cathedral' of Lhasa, is one of the oldest and holiest temples in Tibet; beneath it a mysterious gate is said to lead down to the underworld. (5)

The undying search

Before 1950 Tibet was unique in the degree of dedication among its people to the spiritual quest. Monks and laity were totally at one in this respect.

Burnt offerings are presented to certain tantric deities. The bell symbolizes wisdom, the *vajra* (or sceptre) 'skilful means', the two constituent parts of Buddhahood. The splendid crown consists of five parts, each decorated with the image of one of the five cosmic Buddhas. (6)

A *maṇḍala* (literally 'circle') is essential to tantric meditation, a prop in the drama of seeking salvation. In this 19th-century painted *maṇḍala* (*right*), Akṣobhya, one of the five cosmic Buddhas, sits in the centre with the other four around him in the small circle-inscribed cross. The sceptre-like shape that recurs on the borders is the *vajra*. Outside the circle are bodhisattvas, in four divisions differentiated by colours. In the corners of the square, whose gates are guarded by fierce divinities, are four of the five goddesses of the senses (the fifth is the consort of Akṣobhya). *Below:* Tibetan monks tracing a *maṇḍala* in coloured sand, in preparation for an initiation ceremony. (7, 8)

The 'god-kings'

The doctrine of the reincarnated priestly ruler, the Dalai Lama, is to Westerners perhaps the most puzzling aspect of Tibetan life. In essence it is no more than the ordinary Buddhist idea of the cycle of rebirth, but given a special application. The Dalai Lamas were originally, and still are, the leaders of the dGe-lugs-pa, or Yellow Hat School, and were regarded, like the head lamas of other schools, as reincarnations of a bodhisattva. In the Dalai Lama's case this was Avalokiteśvara, the legendary ancestor, patron, protector and national deity of the Tibetan people.

The Great Fifth Dalai Lama (1617–82) consolidated the power of the Yellow Hats and made Lhasa the capital of a centralized state. *Left:* Mongol and Chinese deputations do him homage. (9)

Avalokiteśvara (*opposite*), himself an emanation of the Buddha Amitābha, is a god of mercy and compassion, working for the good of all sentient beings. The notion of multi-armed deities goes back to Hinduism; in this statue each hand conveys a meaning through the use of a formal gesture, or *mudrā*. Avalokiteśvara underwent many transformations in different cultures and, as we have seen, in China actually became female. (11)

The present Dalai Lama is the fourteenth. In exile in India (*below*) he is still revered by his people and still maintains his sacred functions intact. (10).

A unique achievement

The translation of the Buddhist scriptures into Tibetan was a vast and daunting prospect. Not only was Tibetan an unsophisticated language, lacking the terminology necessary for theological distinctions, but the Tibetans were only just becoming familiar with the art of writing. Yet in a relatively short period they succeeded triumphantly, creating a body of sacred literature comparable to any in the world.

The translators became revered as saints, and copying was a work of merit. Here (*below*) rTa-nag-'gos hands down texts to copiers. Note the typically Tibetan piles of oblong incised leaves behind him, held down by a board. Buddhas and bodhisattvas watch over the divinely favoured work. (12)

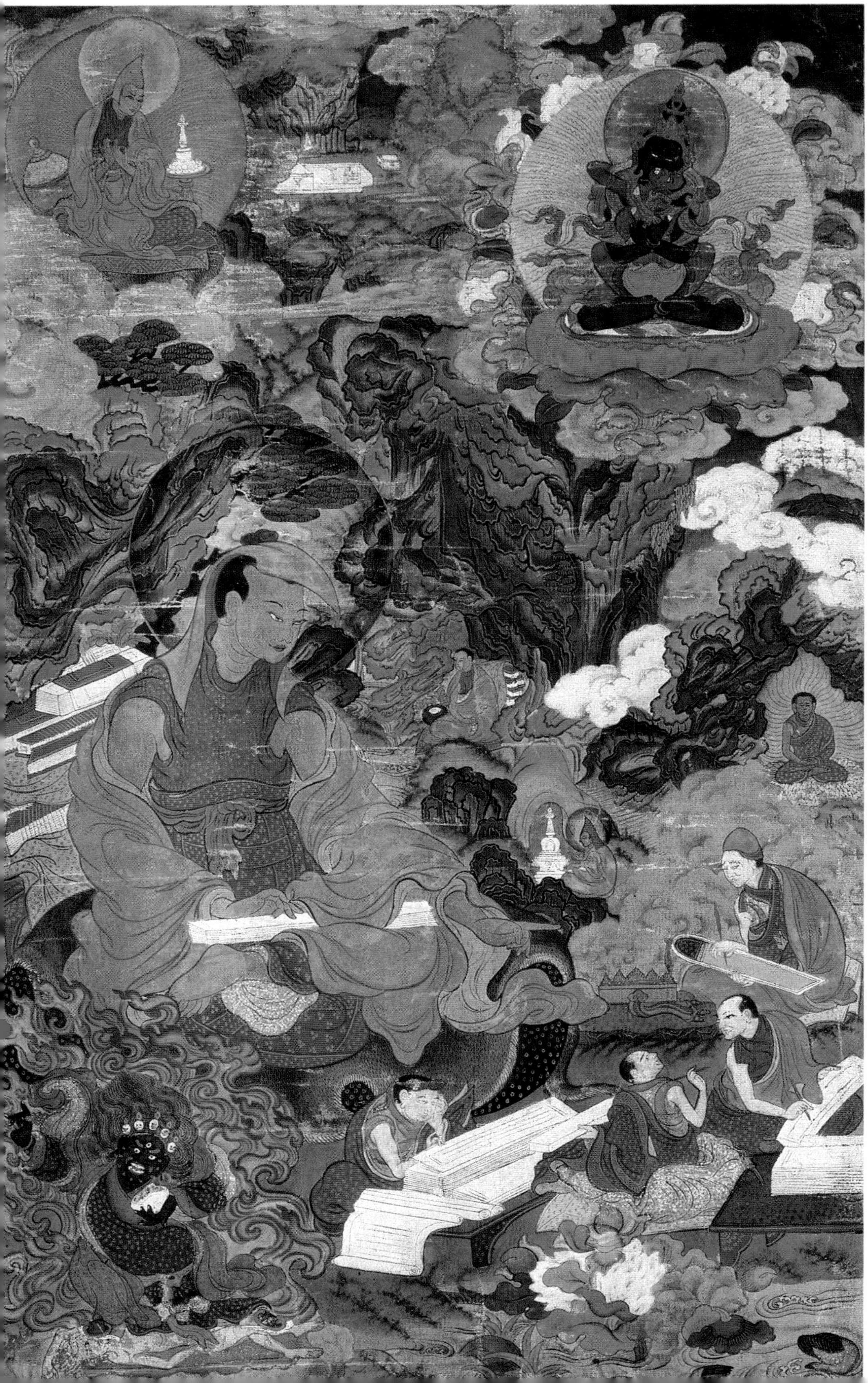

The making of books required elaborate organization. In this detail from an 18th-century *tanka* showing a monastery of the Sa-skya-pa school, the walls have been omitted by the artist so that we can see the various activities taking place: in the upper left the copying of texts, in the centre the reception of guests, on the lower right painting. (13)

Copying and caring for the scriptures still goes on, though dealt a tragic blow by their wholesale destruction in Tibet itself of the last twenty years. *Right:* Nepalese monks of the monastery of Thangpoche clean and check the 108 volumes of the Kanjur, the translation of the 'Words of the Buddha', as the Buddhist canon is known to Tibetan Buddhists. (14)

Cosmic dance

Tibetan dance ceremonies are peculiar to the country and play a prominent part in religious ritual. They are a form of narrative drama in which episodes from sacred history are re-enacted, and for both dancers and spectators are powerfully emotive occasions.

The coronation in 1974 of a new king of Bhutan was accompanied by spectacular displays of religious dancing (*below*). They took place within the walls of the Tashichodzong, the residence of the head abbot and state monks and the seat of the Bhutanese government, which dominates the capital, Thimphu. (15)

Masks help the dancers to 'generate' a chosen deity who is in some sense 'present' in the dancer's own body. *Above left:* a Bhutanese monk assuming one of the aspects of Padmasambhava, who traditionally introduced Buddhism into Tibet. *Above right:* a masked dancer in Thimphu, Bhutan, impersonating a fierce deity, his head crowned with miniature skulls. *Below:* the 'Black Hat' dance in the Potala at Lhasa, commemorating the murder in 842 of King Glang-dar-ma by a Buddhist monk. On the ground is the *linga*, a symbolic representation of the forces of evil. (16, 17, 18)

The word as icon

The Tibetan alphabet was adapted from an Indian model in order to translate the Buddhist canon into the Tibetan language. Virtually all Tibetan literature is religious. It is not surprising, therefore, that writing is surrounded by an aura of the supernatural and that 'sacred syllables' (*mantras*) appear everywhere as charms and invocatory spells.

On a ritual headdress (*left*) words in the beautiful decorative script known as 'Lantsa' appear on the panels making up a ceremonial crown. (19)

On stones the sacred *mantra* 'Oṃ maṇi padme huṃ', exquisitely carved, lines the paths to shrines and sanctuaries. *Below:* a wall of carved stones leads to Hemis monastery, Ladakh. (20)

On temples (*left*) patterns embodying ten sacred characters are displayed as ornate gilded discs. This detail is taken from the exterior of the main hall of the Drepung monastery, a famous centre of the 'Yellow Hats'. (21)

On the golden finials of Tiktse (*right*), one of the largest monasteries of Ladakh, the sacred syllables shine out across the valley. Tiktse (shown also in pl. 1 of this section) dominates its surroundings from a steeply sloping site. Far below can be seen three bell-shaped stupas or chortens. (23)

On the roof-beams of the Jo-Khang temple in Lhasa (*below*) almost every surface is inscribed with protective and sanctifying texts. The architecture of the Jo-Khang is more lavish than usual in Tibet, the whole roof being gilded and the walls covered in carvings and paintings of gods. (22)

A diverse order

Beneath the apparent regularity and conformity of Tibetan life lay a surprising degree of differentiation. Tibetan monasteries fell into a number of 'schools', each stressing different aspects of Buddhist doctrine and practice, and there are many degrees of holiness outside the Sangha altogether.

A professional reader of scriptures, often called in cases of sickness, chants from a book. He may not be ordained; he may not even live in a monastery. (24)

Popular art included images and *maṇḍalas* made of butter, which in the cold Tibetan air easily lasted one or two days. In India (*below*) they are duplicated now in plasticine. (28)

The lama is a Tibetan speciality – priest, monk, spell-binder, meditator, or all together. This one holds a portable prayer-wheel by whose movements sacred spells are incessantly activated. (29)

The Bon-po, while sharing a number of basic beliefs with the Buddhists, form a distinct religion, claiming to antedate Buddhism in Tibet. *Above:* a Bon-po abbot. (25)

The hermit belongs to a type as old as Buddhism. During the years between its suppression in the 9th century and the 'second propagation' (11th century) they kept the religion alive. (26)

The 'Yellow Hats', or dGe-lugs-pa, were the last and most powerful of the schools. Established at Lhasa in the 15th century, they moulded the later course of Buddhism in Tibet. (27)

The Sa-skya-pa school was founded in the 10th century by a monk who had spent many years in India. In the 13th century its head lama became regent of all Tibet. (30)

The 'Followers of Transmitted Command', or bKa'-brgyud-pa, stress the importance of a spiritual lineage deriving, through such teachers as Mar-pa, from the Buddha Vajradhara. (31)

Married lamas have their place in the flexible Tibetan system. This man belongs to the rNying-ma-pa, a school which has kept close to the village level. (32)

Tibet's heroic age

From the 7th to the 9th century Tibet was one of the dominant powers of Asia, with a prosperous economy and a strong army. Buddhism, adopted from India at this period, was becoming a national ideology, destined to last for a thousand years. Much of Tibetan ritual and art looks back to, and perpetuates, this heroic age.

'The lotus-born', Padmasambhava (*left*), was by tradition an Indian tantric adept at controlling demons. Later, by a familiar process, he took his place in the pantheon of Tibetan Buddhism. Here he carries a *vajra*, a symbol with many meanings, including the unity that underlies duality. (33)

'The cotton-clad', Mi-la-ras-pa, who lived from 1052 to 1135, is the most famous of Tibetan hermits. Among various powers, he was believed to have the secret of 'internal heat' which enabled him to keep warm in his mountain hermitage during the bitterly cold winters. This 19th-century *tanka* shows him dressed in his thin robe of cotton with scenes from his life in the background. (34)

A monastic land. During the early period of Buddhism in Tibet, known as the 'first propagation of the Doctrine', the country was ruled by kings. After a long spell of success the monarchy declined in the 9th century, to be followed by more than a hundred years of confusion and anarchy. The 'second propagation of the Doctrine' began in the 11th century and resulted in a new system of government in which power was held mainly by the monasteries, though disputed between the different schools. This movement culminated in the triumph of the dGe-lugs-pa school, the 'Yellow Hats', in the 17th century, whose leaders had assumed the title of Dalai Lama in the 16th. This *tanka* displays the wealth and power of the school, with its founder Tsong-kha-pa (1357–1419) seated in the centre on a lotus throne beneath a canopy held up by figures in the clouds, and all around the great 'Yellow Hat' monasteries. (35)

China, the giant neighbour

For centuries Tibet was subject to Mongol pressure. Khubilai Khan included it within his empire. But Mongol overlordship soon became a formality and by the 14th century the country was once more wholly independent.

A meeting of equals: the fifth Dalai Lama travelled to Peking in 1653 and met the Chinese emperor (*above*). Here he was received as a head of state and delivered a religious address to the emperor. The scene is commemorated in this fresco inside the Potala, the magnificent palace that the Great Fifth built for himself at Lhasa. (36)

For half of the 20th century Tibet remained a theocratic state, balanced between the rival powers of British India, Russia and China, each of whom had their own reasons for checking the expansion of the other two. Administration was shared between religious and secular authorities, the religious having the greater weight. Even such areas as military command were divided in this way and the army had two commanders-in-chief (*right*), one a lama, the other a civilian. And since monasteries were the only large institutions in the country, their abbots were inevitably influential figures. After 1945, the success of the Chinese Communist revolution together with the withdrawal of the British from India gave China the opportunity to reassert its old claims. (37)

The two abbots of Drepung monastery (*left*), with their ceremonial hats and staves of office. Chinese attempts to disguise their claims as the freeing of the Tibetan peasantry from monastic exploitation seem totally unfounded. There has been no social revolution in Tibet and no voluntary abandonment of Buddhism. (38)

The first invasion by China after the foundation of the People's Republic came in 1950. The Dalai Lama left Lhasa (*above*) and fled south, but was persuaded to return after an agreement had been signed giving China the right to garrison Tibet. (39)

During the 1950s resentment against foreign occupation flared up in popular movements. *Top right:* a vast crowd of Tibetan women converge on the Potala as a protest against the Chinese presence. In 1959 armed revolt broke out. It meant the end of the Dalai Lama's rule. He fled to India, and China took over the whole country, attempting to eradicate Buddhism altogether. Most of the monasteries and temples were destroyed; the monks were either imprisoned or forced to retire to lay life. (40)

Resistance persisted for some time but could not be sustained. *Right:* a guerilla leader, formerly a monk, sadly inspects the remains of the monastery's sacred books destroyed by the Chinese. *Below right:* Tibetan monks who took part in the uprising in 1959 are forced to hand over their weapons to Chinese soldiers. (41, 42)

The first monastery in Tibet is traditionally identified as that of Samye, south-east of Lhasa. Around its building, *c.* AD 779, legends have gathered, represented (*above*) in this colourful *tanka*. The evil omens that threatened the project may reflect political opposition, and the two masters who are associated with its foundation, Śāntirakṣita and Padmasambhava, seem to symbolize the two strands that go to make up the specific form of Tibetan Buddhism – conventional *vinaya*-based monasticism and the ritualistic and mystical tantra. (43).

New monasteries are now being built only in the 'fringe' countries of Ladakh and Bhutan (*left*). Constant in its beliefs and in most of its practices, Tibetan Buddhism is materially in decline. But as all the previous chapters in this book have shown, the story of Buddhism is one of recovery after apparent defeat and stubborn survival in the face of what seems like disaster. (44)

10

Tibet: the Rise and Fall of a Monastic Tradition

PER KVAERNE

TIBET IS OFTEN CALLED the 'Roof of the World', and the Tibetans themselves call their country the 'Land of Snows'. While there is no denying that the greater part of Tibet is situated at extremely high altitudes – the mean altitude of western and central Tibet is some 4,000 to 5,000 metres (13,000 to 16,400 feet) above sea level – the picture of Tibet as a bleak and barren land, swept by icy winds and almost completely shut off from the rest of the world by impenetrable mountain ranges, is nevertheless only part of the truth.

The mountains, of course, dominate the landscape. Towering pyramids of eternal snow, soaring high above the world of men, the mountains have from time immemorial been considered by the Tibetans as the abode of gods. The once-divine kings were believed to have descended from heaven to the summit of a holy mountain, and to this day certain mountains, now the seat of Buddhist deities, have been the object of worship and the goal of pilgrimage.

Nevertheless, Tibet is intersected by broad and fertile valleys, which in the centre and west are watered by the Brahmaputra, flowing from west to east, and its tributaries, and in the east by the upper reaches of the great rivers of Southeast and eastern Asia flowing, generally, southwards: the Yellow river, the Yangtse, the Mekong and the Salween. In these valleys is found a large agricultural population, growing barley, the staple crop of Tibet, as well as peas, buckwheat and various kinds of fruit and vegetables. Tibetans have normally been able to produce a surplus of grain which could be stored for many years in the dry climate; in times of need this provided a reserve of food so that, in contrast to the surrounding countries, widespread famine was unknown in Tibet. In recent years, however, Chinese taxation and the presence of a large foreign army has completely upset the economic balance of the country, causing a chronic shortage of food.

In the valleys, too, are situated the towns of Tibet, few in number and all of them small: Lhasa, the capital, has probably never had more than forty thousand inhabitants. Other towns are Shigatse, west of Lhasa and to the south of the Brahmaputra; Gyantse, on the route from Lhasa to Sikkim and India; and Chamdo, in eastern Tibet. The towns, like the rest of Tibet, were entirely pre-industrial until the Chinese occupation in the 1950s, and were, above all, centres of trade.

Above the valleys stretch rolling grasslands, the home of the Tibetan nomads and their herds of yak and sheep. Of an independent spirit, the nomads tend to regard themselves – and to be regarded by the sedentary farmers – as somehow the 'true Tibetans', their life-style closer to that of the 'heroic age' in Tibetan history, the 7th to the 9th century AD, when Tibetan armies dominated the whole of Central Asia. However, the nomads are fully integrated into Tibetan society, dependent as they are on bartering meat, butter and wool for grain according to firmly established, centuries-old patterns of trade.

More than one half of Tibet consists of a vast, wind-swept plateau, dotted by shallow salt lakes and stretches of shimmering soda-encrusted soil. The Tibetans call this empty wilderness the 'Northern Plain'; apart from an occasional hunter, it is completely uninhabited.

In the West, Tibet has been regarded as a closed land, and in fact it still is, in spite of a limited number of tourists who have been allowed by the Chinese to visit Lhasa and certain other areas in recent years. However, this has not always been so. During Tibet's 'heroic age' of political and military greatness, and probably earlier, too, the Tibetans assimilated many elements of culture from neighbouring peoples, above all the Chinese, but also the Iranians and the Turcs of Central Asia. Contact with Buddhism, beginning in the 7th century AD, opened Tibet to Indian culture, and, until the disappearance of Buddhism in northern India in the 13th century, there was a steady stream of pilgrims and scholars across the Himalayan passes, eventually transforming Tibet into the profoundly Buddhist country which it has remained to this day. Indeed, before long the Tibetans themselves became missionaries of the new religion, and by the 16th century they were able to convert an entire people, the Mongols, to the Tibetan form of Buddhism. At about the same time, large parts of the Himalayas were drawn into the cultural sphere of Tibetan Buddhism, resulting in the formation of the states of Sikkim and Bhutan; the latter has succeeded in maintaining its sovereignty, and is today the only country in Asia in which Mahāyāna Buddhism is still the official religion. Thus Tibet, far from being a secluded Shangri-la, has through long periods of its history played a crucial role in the history of Central and eastern Asia.

Since the 18th century, however, the Tibetans,

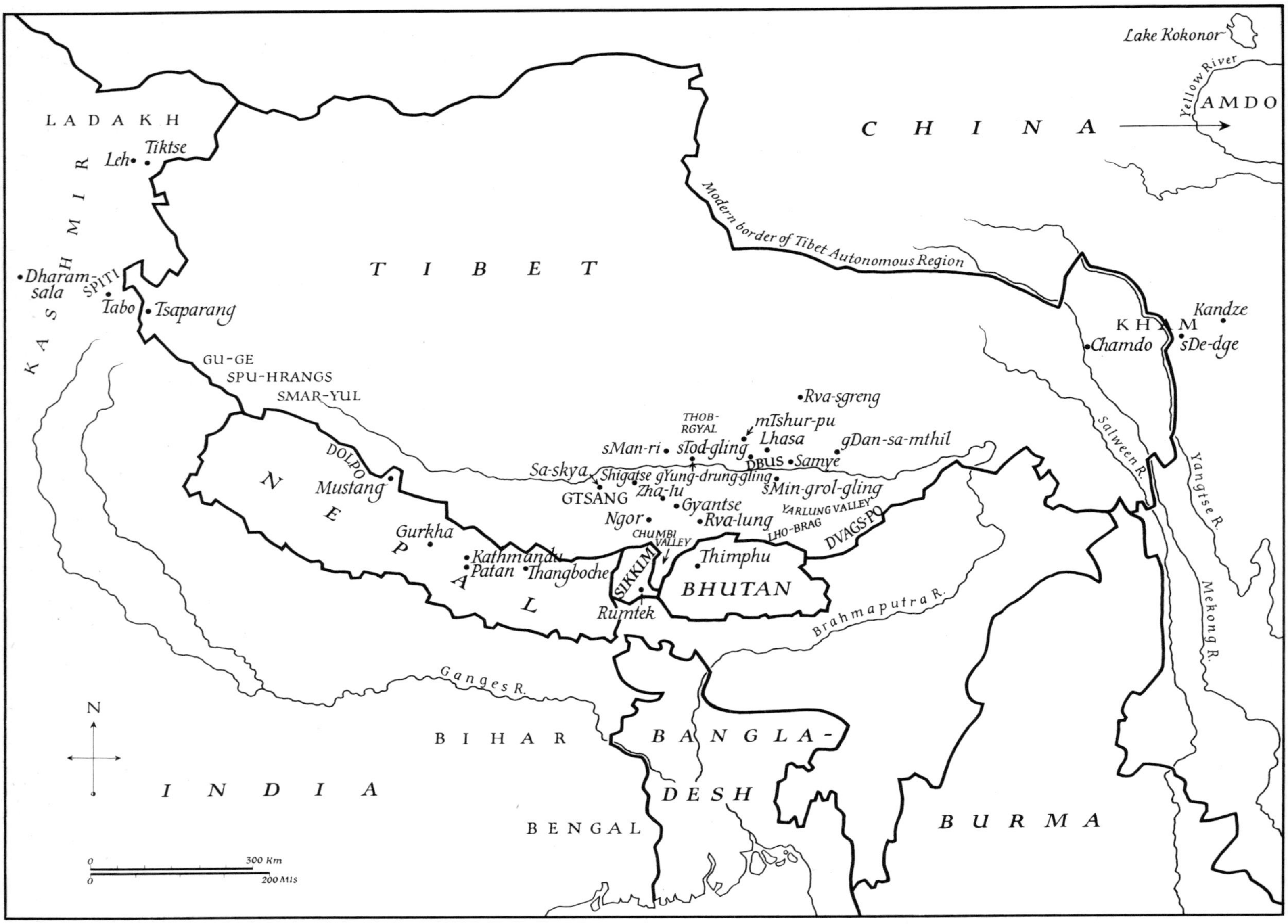

Tibet, showing the towns and sites mentioned in the text

encouraged by the Manchu emperors of China, sought to protect their distinctive way of life, above all their religion, by rigidly pursuing an isolationist policy, particularly towards the European powers which were becoming increasingly dominant in Asia. From the Tibetan point of view this policy must, on the whole, have appeared to be a success, in spite of the British military expedition led by Sir Francis Younghusband, which fought its way to Lhasa in 1904 – only to withdraw once a treaty with the Tibetans had been signed; for alone among Asian countries, Tibet completely escaped the direct influence of the Western presence in Asia during the 19th and the first half of the 20th century. However, the Tibetans eventually had to pay a heavy price for their long period of isolation, for they were totally unprepared, socially, militarily and above all politically, when a newly unified, militant and self-asserting China, armed with the ideological zeal of Marxism and exploiting the earlier tenuous link between the Manchu emperors and the Dalai Lamas, occupied Tibet in 1950–51.

Except in the earliest period (7th to 9th century AD), when the introduction of Buddhism conflicted with existing religious beliefs at the time of Tibet's greatest expansion under its own rulers, the Buddhist faith has always provided the norm quite free of competition from any other major system of belief. The complexity of monastic endeavour in this last major region to receive the Buddhist Doctrine with wholehearted acceptance (and here one must include Mongolia and other adjacent territories which were still later turned to the faith by Tibetan monks) stems in the beginning from the lateness of its conversion and its consequent absorption of the fully developed Indian Buddhist tradition. Tibetan monks followed the same disciplinary code as the Hīnayāna Schools, their philosophy was unquestionably that of the Mahāyāna School (the Madhyamaka in particular), and their meditative and ritual practices were mainly those of the tantric Vajrayāna School. This 'complete' Buddhism, as it has been characterized, was subjected to numerous adaptations and developments in a cultural and geographical setting very far removed from its place of origin, to the extent that a genuine hybrid arose. The final growth is so specifically Tibetan that it is often referred to as 'Lamaism', a term which underlines the central role of the spiritual preceptor ('lama') in the religious society of Tibet. The term has on occasion acquired a pejorative tone suggestive of 'degraded' Buddhism, but if that sense is consciously eliminated it retains value for its allusion to a fact of fundamental importance: the lama in Tibet is not necessarily a fully ordained monk and consequently the monk does not monopolize the Dharma as he does in other Buddhist countries. A host of quasi- or semi-monastic priestly types is found with overlapping aims and conventions. Whether living in settled communities or not, these yogins, spell-binders and meditators are broadly considered to belong to the Sangha and are treated as such even if married. This formal inclusiveness, marked at the lower end of the occupational spectrum by the activities of a vast population of menial monks, tends to set the Tibetan monastic tradition apart from other Asian traditions, where monastic life conforms to a single model with few variations. The diversity of professional types found in Tibet, each sanctioned either by scriptural authority or by historical precedent, is in turn a reflection of the belief that all human activity can be directed to achieving Enlightenment on the interim level where 'relative' truth and 'ultimate' truth are seen as dualities. The same notion makes it possible for the complex symbolism of Tibetan religion to have meaning and validity on many levels of spiritual experience and also for many apparently conflicting attitudes and methods to coexist within the same norm.

The only other 'renouncer' found in Tibet, besides the monk, the nun and their associated types, is the professional brigand, a figure who regularly looms through the mist on the edge of society from the earliest times, always in the company of his fellows and governed by his own peculiar conventions and folk laws. To achieve a true picture of Tibetan society in each period it would be necessary to juxtapose the figures of the monk and the brigand under successive regimes against the timeless backcloth of the Tibetan peasantry, both sedentary and semi-nomadic. However, brigands, robber tribes and marauding rebels never left documentary records to tell us of their rise and fall. Consequently, our knowledge of Tibetan history is nearly always limited to the viewpoint of the monk. No doubt if there had survived as many biographies of brigands as of lamas, these would have been hailed by the Chinese authorities who now rule Tibet as great testaments of revolutionary heroism. As it is, the only knowledge we have of a truly spontaneous popular uprising concerns the one that occurred in 1959 against the Chinese in Lhasa, which resulted in the total destruction of Tibet's religious society and the exodus of 80,000 refugees to the Indian sub-continent.

The interconnections of religion and politics in Tibet are so tight and organic that any historical survey of monastic developments falls quite naturally into the same basic periods that mark the different phases in the life of the Tibetan state as a whole; the fortunes of monks and their monasteries strongly reflect the upheavals in the body politic. At the same time there are so many elements of continuity which transcend the sharp periodization of history that by the mid-20th century monastic institutions appeared to all observers as part of a huge and complicated medieval relic frozen in time and space. The physical remoteness of many communities in this most isolated of countries added to the sensation of anachronism.

The politics of conversion

When dealing with the introduction of Buddhism into Tibet, there are two types of source at our disposal: contemporary sources, including various documents, inscriptions and architectural monuments as well as Chinese historical annals; and later literary sources, generally dating from the 14th century onward, which frequently contain detailed information, but which are to be used with caution, coloured as they are by the expectations and ideas of later generations.

It is in one of the later literary sources that we find a story of how one of the earliest Tibetan kings, Lha-tho-tho-ri (6th century AD?), received the first elements of Buddhism in the form of a Buddhist text and a miniature stupa which fell from the sky on to the top of his palace. The story, which may be modelled on similar Chinese accounts of the introduction of Buddhism into China, is of course nothing but pious fiction, serving to provide a fitting background to subsequent events.

With the great king Srong-btsan-sgam-po (who died in AD 650), Tibet enters the full light of history. His father had, by the time he was assassinated (*c.* 627), succeeded in securing the allegiance of the warring noble families and thus unifying Tibet into a powerful state. Under Srong-btsan a period of aggressive military expansionism began, which (with occasional setbacks) lasted until the middle of the 9th century. This brought the Tibetans into closer contact with their neighbours than they had been before: the Chinese, the Turcs, the Uighurs, the Arabs, the Indians. As part of his policy towards these peoples, Srong-btsan married – among other wives – a Chinese princess and a Nepalese princess. According to later tradition, these ladies were Buddhists; they brought Buddhist images with them, and for their benefit the king erected Buddhist temples in Lhasa and elsewhere.

Now (still according to later tradition), all this was part of a divine plan. The great bodhisattva Avalokiteśvara, wishing to convert the 'Land of Snows' to the Doctrine of the Buddha, had in past ages taken the form of a monkey, which went to Tibet to meditate in solitude. The monkey eventually copulated with a female rock-demon, and from this union were born the ancestors of the Tibetan clans. With Srong-btsan, so the later chronicles maintain, the time had come for the conversion of Tibet, for Srong-btsan himself was an emanation of Avalokiteśvara, and his Nepalese and Chinese wives were the emanations of Tārā, the divine consort of the bodhisattva. The Buddhist temples were therefore constructed at spots geomantically determined so as to pin down and tame a female demon believed to be prostrate on her back beneath the territory of Tibet. This model, which finds its first mention in a compilation of the 12th to the 13th century, may perhaps be of Chinese inspiration, but was taken over by the Tibetans to express the civilizing force of Buddhism, the prostrate demoness being in reality Tibet itself, whose inhabitants, in this later literary view, are described as 'red-faced demons, eaters of raw flesh and drinkers of red blood'. In accordance with his divine nature, at his death the king was absorbed together with his spouses into the statue of Avalokiteśvara in the main temple of Lhasa (the Jo-khang, the 'House of the Lord'). Srong-btsan is also regarded as the author of collections of religious instruction and civil laws, as well as prophesies regarding the final establishment of Buddhism five generations after himself.

If we turn to contemporary sources, a different picture emerges. Although there is contemporary evidence for only one of Srong-btsan's wives, the Chinese princess Wen-cheng, it is possible that Buddhism was introduced during his reign. Apart from the Jo-khang, which has been greatly enlarged and transformed over the centuries, several other early temples, perhaps dating from the 7th century, have been preserved to our time: dBu-ru-ka-tshal east of Lhasa, Khra-'brug in the Yarlung valley, and perhaps Ra-mo-che in Lhasa itself. However, there are no signs of the king himself having adopted Buddhism, nor in fact any mention at all of Buddhism in contemporary literary sources. On the contrary, the king seems to have been loyal to his ancestral religion, a religion in which the cult of the king, regarded as a divine being, played a crucial part. In particular, complicated rituals on a vast scale, involving animal as well as human sacrifice, took place in connection with the burial of the kings, and Srong-btsan was buried in the traditional way in the Yarlung valley, where the enormous burial mound is still to be seen. In fact, recent research indicates that the cult of royal divinity was considerably developed during the reign of Srong-btsan.

In introducing Buddhism, the true motives of the Tibetan king were certainly not religious. It is far more likely that he wished to acquire for his government certain elements of culture, so prominent in neighbouring civilizations, without opening the country to foreign political influence. For this purpose Buddhism, with its universalist perspective, must have seemed the ideal instrument. An analogous process, it may be noted, was going on at the same time in Japan. There, too, the ruler imported elements of a more sophisticated culture, chiefly through the medium of Buddhism. But while Japan had no choice but to turn to China, Tibet was in a position to choose – and finally chose (for reasons that were probably political rather than religious) to receive Buddhism from India, and, with it, many other aspects of Indian culture, above all the art of writing. Thus instead of adopting the Chinese ideographic script, Tibetans have since the 7th century AD used an alphabet of only thirty consonants and four vowel signs, at the same time assimilating Indian stylistic conventions, literary genres and grammatical theory, with profound consequences for their entire cultural orientation.

In fact, it is still uncertain whether Buddhism was really present at all in Tibet during the reign of Srong-btsan; contemporary documents make no mention of the Doctrine of the Buddha. It is only in the following century, during the reign of King Khri-srong-lde-btsan (740 to *c.*798), that Buddhism appears in official documents. Khri-srong was favourably inclined to Buddhism, presumably for the reasons mentioned above, and by the later tradition he is regarded as the second 'King of the Law' and as an emanation of the bodhisattva Mañjuśrī.

In any case, it is clear that Buddhism was established under royal patronage and that it served to increase royal power. Therefore, it is not surprising that the indigenous priesthood made common cause with certain noble families against the king and the new religion. After a bitter struggle, which seems to have taken the form of ruthless palace intrigues, the king and the Buddhist party got the upper hand, and the task of providing the Good Law, the Dharma, with a firmer basis could begin.

Later tradition reflects a legendary, almost epic vision of how the first Buddhist monastery in Tibet was founded and the first Buddhist monks ordained. Having rid himself of those ministers who were opposed to Buddhism, the king invited the Indian scholar Śāntirakṣita to Tibet. He determined that the first monastery should be founded at Samye, south-east of Lhasa and near the north bank of the Brahmaputra. Evil omens, however, occurred while the construction of the monastery was under way (perhaps the legend expresses at this point opposition to the new religion), and under pressure from his anxious subjects, the king had to send Śāntirakṣita back to India. However, a new Indian master was invited: Padmasambhava, the 'Lotus-born', probably a native of Swat in the extreme north-west of India (present-day Pakistan), a crucial but enigmatic figure in the introduction of Buddhism in Tibet. While Śāntirakṣita was a representative of the conventional *vinaya*-based monasticism and the *sūtra*-inspired philosophical tradition in Mahāyāna,

Padmasambhava was a tantric *siddha*, an adept in magical rites and techniques of coercing demonic forces. These two masters represent two different forms of Buddhist practice, one based on the *vinaya*, the *sūtras* and scholastic philosophy, the other on the ritualistic and mystical *tantras*. Both forms, the one often more or less permeating the other, have remained characteristic of Buddhism in Tibet.

According to an epic account which only appeared in fully developed form in the 14th century, Padmasambhava turned his journey to Tibet into a veritable *via triumphalis*. Sensing that their sway over the Land of Snows was coming to an end, inimical demons continually blocked his way; however, without exception they were suppressed by the great *siddha*. One after the other they 'offered up their life-essence', and their continued existence was only ensured when they swore an oath to become the protectors of the Doctrine of the Buddha.

Under the surface of this colourful legend, however, is described a process which has everywhere been of fundamental importance in the history of Buddhism: the assimilation, or rather accommodation, of local deities. Padmasambhava could surely, *mutatis mutandis*, have spoken with the words of the Gospel: 'I did not come to abolish, but to complete' (Matthew 5:17). This has been true of Buddhism all over Asia; purged of elements (especially human and animal sacrifice) which are incompatible with basic Buddhist values, the cult of the deities of the local religions has been assigned a secure, though often modest, place in religious life. In Tibet these deities are generally regarded as being 'of this world' and their power is limited to granting worldly blessings, as opposed to the great bodhisattvas, Avalokiteśvara and others, who are 'beyond this world', being close to Buddhahood and able to aid their devotees towards liberation.

Padmasambhava was able to complete the construction of Samye, and it was consecrated in the presence of the king and his court, probably *c.* AD 779. Thereafter, the first Tibetans, traditionally referred to as the 'Seven Elected Ones', received ordination as Buddhist monks.

Mani stone, of uncertain date, with the 'sacred syllables' (see p. 244, pl. 20) beneath a relief of Avalokiteśvara, the patron deity of Tibet, of whom the Dalai Lama is thought to be a reincarnation.

Monks and statesmen

Although its influence must still have been restricted to court circles, Buddhism was in fact now firmly established. In an inscription preserved at Samye, and dating, perhaps, from 791, Khri-srong and his ministers swore an oath to uphold the Buddhist Law. Monks belonging to noble clans were appointed ministers and given a higher rank than their lay colleagues. It is reported that at a royal reception a monk was placed on the king's right side (the side of honour), on the dais itself, while the ministers were seated below the dais. Thus a notable characteristic of the Buddhist hierarchy in Tibet emerged from the very start: its superiority over lay authorities.

The king also ensured the material and legal basis of monastic life. The monastery was exempted from tax – here the Tibetans merely followed the Indian model – and a chronicle, which, while not contemporary, nevertheless appears to contain much ancient material, specifies that the abbot received 70 loads of grain a month, teachers received 35 and pupils 12. The monastery also received land as well as tenant farmers. Butter, paper, ink and salt are other items with which the monks were to be supplied. Of greater importance is the fact that several inscriptions of this period state that the ruler would under no circumstances resume authority over servants, villages, etc. donated to the monastery. The monks were also exempted from civil legislation, and in particular they were granted immunity from any kind of bodily punishment, such as having their eyes plucked out or nose cut off. An indication of the high status of the monks is a legal code ascribed to Khri-srong according to which theft of the king's goods had to be restituted a hundredfold, that of the clergy's eighty times, while theft of an ordinary man's goods was only to be paid for nine times.

Fragment of a Tibetan manuscript from Tun-huang, the great pilgrimage site in China described in Chapter 8, depicting a Tibetan monastery. It is clear that the basic layout changed little with the centuries. Easily recognizable are the courtyards surrounded by cells, the imposing entrance, the chortens (stupas) dotted around the vicinity of the monastery, and the high mountain ranges that surround it.

From the very start, then, the monks enter into politics: as ministers, ambassadors and mediators. Thus the treaty of peace between China and Tibet of 821–2 was negotiated by Chinese and Tibetan monks. The text of this treaty is inscribed on a pillar erected in Lhasa, where it is still preserved. It surely reflects an authentic picture of the religious situation in Tibet at the time. The concept of divine kingship is still very prominent; the king is referred to as almighty and omniscient. Reference to Buddhism is much less conspicuous: the Three Jewels and the 'saints' are invoked – together with the sun and moon, planets and stars. That the old customs were still very much alive is evident, for the inscription also states that 'the oath has been sworn with the sacrifice of animals', a fact confirmed by the Chinese annals. On the other hand, first in rank of the Tibetan ministers is the 'great Monk-Minister', before even the commander-in-chief of the army – exactly matching the situation when Tibet was invaded by China in 1950!

The treaty was signed during the reign of the third and last 'King of the Law'. Later tradition pictures him as devoted to the Buddhist monks, allowing them to sit on lengths of silk attached to his long hair, and finally entering the Order himself. This aroused strong opposition, and in 838 he was assassinated and succeeded by his elder brother Glang-dar-ma, who is described in the later tradition as an apostate and an upholder of the ancient rites. He is supposed to have launched a violent persecution of all Buddhist monks, destroying temples and images and either banishing the 'sons of the Buddha' from his realm or forcing them to marry. There does not seem to exist contemporary evidence to confirm this, but, according to tradition, after only a few years in power, Glang-dar-ma in turn was killed by a Buddhist monk (in 842). The event is still celebrated in the so-called 'Black-Hat Dance' of the monastic festivals of sacred dance. The justification of this apparently un-Buddhist act has traditionally been given as the disinterested wish to prevent the king from further accumulating evil deeds which would plunge him into hell after his death.

The murder of Glang-dar-ma did not, however, lead to a restoration of Buddhism. The royal lineage was broken up by internecine feuds; the great Tibetan empire rapidly disintegrated, and, in the ensuing turmoil, Buddhism as an organized religion disappeared, at least from central Tibet. There followed a period of almost 150 years in Tibetan history about which we know very little, except that the country was without any centre of unifying political or spiritual power.

The period of the great kings is known among the Tibetans as the 'first propagation of the Doctrine'. It might appear that it ended with near-failure for Buddhism. Yet one achievement could not be erased: the translation of Buddhist texts into Tibetan. It seems that the Tibetans were not familiar with the art of writing before the introduction of Buddhism. However, the problem was not only that of creating a suitable alphabet, but of deciding which texts to translate from. Their success in translating in a remarkably short time the vast literature of Mahāyāna Buddhism into their own language, accurately recreating in Tibetan its technical and extremely sophisticated philosophical terminology, must rank as one of the major intellectual achievements in the history of man. Initially, translations were made of Chinese as well as of Indian Buddhist texts; but it was finally decided that translations should be made from Sanskrit only. Long lists of approved renderings of Sanskrit terms in Tibet were drawn up, and earlier translations were revised accordingly by specially appointed boards of translators, including Tibetan as well as Indian scholars. Thus a Tibetan literary language was created which has remained more or less unchanged until today, making Tibetan Buddhism heir to the immense Buddhist literature of India (soon to be obliterated by Muslim invasions in its homeland), and providing a medium that enabled Tibetan monks in the course of time to add their own contribution to Buddhist thought.

One more event from this early period of Buddhism in Tibet must be mentioned: the so-called 'Great Debate' at Samye. Royal preference in the 8th century for the Indian rather than the Chinese form of Buddhism was probably much less clear than sources would have us believe. Certainly, Chinese monks were active both as translators and as propagators of the Doctrine. (Monks from Central Asian oasis states were also, though perhaps more sporadically, present in Tibet.) It is not surprising that there developed deep antagonism between Indian upholders of the conventional Mahāyāna view that final liberation could only be gradually achieved by practising the perfections of a bodhisattva for countless lives, and Chinese partisans of the so-called 'Meditation School' (Ch'an, Japanese Zen). To decide which side should be regarded as exponents of the Doctrine, King Khri-srong is reported to have summoned both parties, around 792, to a debate at Samye over which he himself presided. The debate continued for two years, and in the end the verdict went to the moralistic and 'gradualistic' Indian school. The Chinese monks were banished from Tibet. It is likely that political considerations weighed heavily in this verdict, because the Tibetan king had every reason to fear the political influence of monks from China, a country with which he was continually at war. But it should at least be mentioned that the Chinese dossier, which has been preserved, states that the Chinese side was victorious in the theological duel. However this may be, a standard of orthodoxy was established, and in later doctrinal disputes between various Tibetan Buddhist schools, the accusation of propagating 'Chinese' or 'spontanist' views was considered to be most serious.

Innovation and crisis

The upheavals following the break-up of the royal dynasty hardly signified the complete disappearance of Buddhism. Hermits and isolated communities surely continued to exist even in central Tibet, and both in western Tibet and in the east, along the Chinese border, Buddhist monks continued their activities, and the later tradition makes a point of explaining that there was no absolute break in continuity.

The restoration of Buddhism, known in Tibetan tradition as the 'second propagation of the Doctrine', received its decisive impetus in western Tibet. Here, descendants of the royal dynasty had founded three kingdoms (sMar-yul, Gu-ge and sPu-hrangs), where Buddhism was strengthened by proximity to the Indian regions of Kashmir, Gilgit and Swāt, which could still provide Buddhist scholars, yogins and artists.

Two figures stand out as renewers of Buddhism: the king of sPu-hrangs, Ye-shes-'od, and the translator-monk Rin-chen-bzang-po. Ye-shes-'od is said to have abdicated in favour of a younger brother and to have taken the vows of a monk. By later tradition he is regarded as a bodhisattva, more or less like the early kings. The story of his sacrificing his life in captivity among the Qarlug Turcs so that the gold raised as ransom to set him free could be used to further the spread of the Doctrine is in all probability a pious but unfounded legend. His concern with the moral state of the Buddhist monks in his realm is beyond doubt, however, and later sources have preserved an ordinance issued by him in which he severely criticises aberrant practices resulting from a literal interpretation of certain *tantras*. In particular, he attacks those tantrists and 'village abbots' who sacrifice goats and sheep, indulge in sexual intercourse, offer all kinds of impure substances to the deities and even perform magic rites to kill human beings – and still claim to 'follow Mahāyāna'. Probably these accusations were not unjustified; lacking monastic organization and scholarly training, many Buddhist tantric adepts must have been tempted to compete with the still-powerful pre-Buddhist priesthood on their own ground – that of magic powers.

Ye-shes-'od was concerned with re-establishing monastic discipline. Accordingly, he sent a group of young men to Kashmir and India for training. Chief among them was Rin-chen-bzang-po (958–1055), who spent a total of seventeen years in India, where he became thoroughly familiar with the conventional Mahāyāna monasticism and its regular observance of the *vinaya*, still flourishing in the north-west. On his return to Tibet, he was prolific as a translator of Indian texts; he renewed monastic discipline, and is credited with the founding of many monasteries and temples, some of which have been preserved almost intact (though generally in a rather dilapidated state). Among those monasteries genuinely attributable to Rin-chen-bzang-po are Tabo in Spiti (politically Spiti is now part of India), sTod-gling in Gu-ge, and Nyar-ma (now in ruins) in Ladakh. Another fine and remarkably well preserved example of Buddhist architecture dating from this period is the group of small temple buildings at Alchi in Ladakh, on the way to Leh; though not actually founded by Rin-chen-bzang-po, Alchi nevertheless testifies to the impetus given to Buddhism through his activities. That the influence of Central Asia also made itself felt is proved by the recently discovered presence of Manichaean elements in the murals at Alchi.

An even greater stimulus to the development of Buddhism in Tibet in the 11th century was the Indian monk Atiśa (982–1054). Atiśa was a native of Bengal and travelled widely, studying at various monasteries and becoming one of the most famous scholar-monks in India at the time. Having been repeatedly invited to Tibet by the nephew of Ye-shes-'od, he finally arrived there in 1042, where he met the aged Rin-chen-bzang-po. Atiśa was well versed in the *tantras*, and conferred initiations on Rin-chen-bzang-po as well as on his own chief disciple 'Brom-ston (1008–64). Insisting as he did on monastic discipline, Atiśa thereby secured a place for the study and practice of the *tantras* within the monasteries from this time onwards, thus continuing in Tibet the centuries-old tradition of tantric studies, which had characterized the Indian monastic universities. At the same time he stressed the cult of Avalokiteśvara, and insisted on the importance of practising the conventional Buddhist virtues and treading the long and strenuous path of a bodhisattva. From Atiśa stems the mainstream of Tibetan Buddhism, particularly of Buddhist monastic religion, in later centuries.

At the same time as Atiśa's activities, a completely different kind of Buddhist practice was introduced into Tibet from Bihar and Bengal in India. These practices were of a tantric kind, stressing certain meditative procedures and yogic powers. Known as the 'Six Doctrines of Nāropa', they were taught by the Indian *siddha* Nāropa. They were brought to Tibet by one of the most extraordinary figures in the history of Buddhism in the Land of Snows: Mar-pa (1012–96). Mar-pa travelled to Bihar where he studied for sixteen years with Nāropa; returning to Tibet, he settled in his native Lho-brag, just north of the Himalayas, and to the uninitiated apparently led the life of an ordinary, married householder, ploughing his fields and engaging in quarrels with his relatives. In India he had learned Sanskrit thoroughly, and thus in Tibet he became famous as a translator of Buddhist texts. However, to the inner circle of initiated disciples he was more: an accomplished tantric master, able to confer initiations into the most esoteric practices, tracing his spiritual lineage through Indian *siddhas* direct to the personified principle of Buddhahood, Vajradhara, 'Holder of the Vajra'.

The most famous of Mar-pa's disciples was Mi-la-ras-pa (1052–1135). Mi-la-ras-pa was a more ascetic figure, spending many years in solitude and meditating in caves on the high slopes of the Himalayas, where he practised the various yogic exercises which had been taught him by Mar-pa. Among the various powers he is believed to have developed is that of 'internal heat', which enabled him to survive the snowstorms and bitterly cold winters, clad only in a thin robe of white cotton.

Thus Mar-pa 'the Translator' and Mi-la-ras-pa 'the Cotton-clad' exemplify – each in his own way – a type of Buddhist tantric yogin very different from the monastic ideals propagated by Atiśa; in fact, neither Mar-pa nor Mi-la-ras-pa was ever ordained as a monk. In the history of Buddhist literature in Tibet, both are important because they introduced a new kind of religious, highly personal poetry, combining elements of the Indian *dohā* tradition with their own spontaneous feelings and observations. As a genre, this type of poetry, together with the cotton-clad, solitary yogin, has continued in Tibet until our own times.

When dealing with the 'second propagation of the Doctrine', contemporary sources gradually become more plentiful. Nevertheless, careful textual criticism is important. Thus the standard biography of Mi-la-ras-pa as well as the collection of his songs, both translated into European languages, were regarded until recently as the work of his immediate disciples, and the songs as authentically his own. Recent research, however, has established beyond doubt that both are the work of a 16th-century yogin; and while some of the songs, at least, may in fact have been composed by Mi-la-ras-pa himself (according to tradition they arose spontaneously in his mind as occasion required), the whole is perhaps more a kind of religious picaresque novel than anything else, reflecting Buddhist ideals of 16th- rather than 11th-century Tibet.

Six schools of Tibetan Buddhism

What was happening in Tibet in the 11th and 12th centuries was in fact the formation of different schools, all tracing their origins to the holy land of India, but at the same time stressing different aspects of Buddhist doctrine and practice. These schools rapidly developed their own hierarchies and set about founding monasteries throughout Tibet, competing for lay support, and, once sufficiently powerful, often engaged in bitter struggles for temporal power.

To begin with, 'Brom-ston, chief disciple of Atiśa, founded the monastery of Rva-sgreng north of Lhasa in 1056. The school of 'Brom-ston was known as bKa'-gdams-pa, 'Bound by Command', that is, by strict monastic rules, and in particular by abstention from marriage, intoxicants, travel and the possession of money. His followers led a secluded life of study and meditation, a small school without wealthy lay patrons. However, the bKa'-gdams-pa was destined to play a crucial role in later developments when, in the late 14th and early 15th centuries, it was transformed into the dGe-lugs-pa School, which eventually obtained both religious and temporal dominance in Tibet (see p. 265).

Mar-pa is retrospectively regarded as the founder of another school, or rather a group of related schools, the bKa'-rgyud-pa, 'Followers of the Transmitted Command'. Its name refers to the crucial importance of the unbroken spiritual lineage through which this school traces its teachings: through Mar-pa back to Nāropa, and through the latter to Tilopa, who was believed to have received them from the Buddha Vajradhara. Mi-la-ras-pa, in turn, had many disciples, but one in particular was to have far-reaching influence: sGam-po-pa, the 'Doctor from Dvags-po' (1079–1153). sGam-po-pa came from a noble family in the southern district of Dvags-po. In his youth he studied medicine, but the death of his wife when he was only twenty turned his mind towards religion. He received monastic ordination as a follower of the bKa'-gdams-pa School, but soon became a disciple of Mi-la-ras-pa. sGam-po-pa's direct disciples founded several famous schools, but the difference between them in matters of doctrine is slight.

Thus Phag-mo-gru-pa (1110–70) founded the first great bKa'-rgyud-pa monastery, gDan-sa-mthil, which rapidly grew large and wealthy, with the simple grass hut of the founder preserved in the centre. This development was possible thanks to the patronage of the noble family of Rlangs, which soon came to supply both the abbot and the lay administrative head of the monastery. While the abbot remained celibate, his lay counterpart continued the family line, including the next abbot, so that the abbots succeeded each other in a continual sequence of uncle and nephew, a pattern that was also found, as we shall see, within other schools. This symbiosis between spiritual and temporal power within a noble family was an extremely significant development, and to a large extent explains the political – at times even military – preoccupations of many great Tibetan monasteries in the following centuries.

A bKa'-rgyud-pa school which has remained extremely powerful is the Karma-pa School, founded by the disciple of sGam-po-pa, Dus-gsum-mkhyen-pa (1110–93). The principal monastery of this school was at mTshur-pu in central Tibet (founded 1185); however, Dus-gsum-mkhyen-pa was a native of eastern Tibet, and the Karma-pa connection with this region has continued to be strong. Rather than depending on a powerful family, the Karma-pa drew their support from the population in the neighbourhood of their monasteries; the hierarchs travelled widely, surrounded by armed followers, the 'men of the camp'. The Karma-pa could thus muster a considerable military force, and were to play an important part in the struggles for power in later centuries.

One more of the bKa'-rgyud-pa schools must be mentioned: the 'Brug-pa. This school originated as a branch of the Phag-mo-gru-pa. Its spiritual founder was the Tibetan *siddha* Gling-chen-ras-pa (1128–88), who founded the monastery of Rva-lung (*c.* 1180), south-east of Gyantse, not far from the Bhutanese border. The school received its name from the slightly younger monastery of 'Brug ('Dragon' – so called because a dragon is supposed to have appeared in the sky during its consecration), just north of the Brahmaputra. In the 17th century, a branch of the 'Brug-pa School established itself in Bhutan, where it has remained dominant ever since.

We next turn to a school that has also survived until today: the Sa-skya-pa, so called from the monastery of Sa-skya, to the west of Shigatse, in the province of gTsang. The school's founder was 'Brog-mi (992–1072). Like Mar-pa, he spent many years in India, studying with various masters, in particular the *siddha* Śāntipa. He was initiated into a different series of *tantras* from those that had interested Rin-chen-bzang-po and Atiśa, among them the important *Hevajratantra*, which he translated into Tibetan. His disciple, dKon-mchog-rgyal-po, founded Sa-skya in 1073. He belonged to the powerful 'Khon family, and the succession of abbots of Sa-skya has continued within the 'Khon family until today on the uncle-and-nephew pattern already noted for the Phag-mo-gru-pa. Sa-skya was strategically placed on a trade route linking the Nepal valley with Shigatse, and within a short time it had become a large and flourishing institution – with numerous affiliated monasteries – famous for the learning of its teachers, who were particularly active as translators of Indian texts.

The power of the Sa-skya-pa reached its apex in the 13th century, when Ködän, the Mongol khan, summoned the head lama of Sa-skya to his court in 1244. The khan demanded and received the submission of Tibet from the Sa-skya lama, who was then appointed regent of Tibet. The choice of a religious hierarch rather than a lay prince in this connection is not surprising; the monks had a monopoly of learning, and the main monasteries had a network of affiliated

Vajra and bell used in tantric Buddhist ritual. The vajra, which functions ceremonially as a sceptre, is a symbol of the basic unity which underlies all duality. This unity is described as indestructible and indivisible, and hence being like a diamond, for which reason 'vajra' is sometimes translated as 'diamond thunderbolt'.

A lamaist flag, with the 'Lung' horse (literally 'wind horse'), one of the most popular images among the ordinary Tibetan people. The horse itself goes back to mythical Chinese origins. Flags like these are used as good luck charms. Prayers too are commonly inscribed on flags and allowed to flutter in the breeze.

monasteries throughout Tibet, thus to some extent transcending the purely local interests of the noble families. At the same time, the Sa-skya-pa mode of succession within the 'Khon family ensured continuity of control.

The next head of the Sa-skya monastery, 'Phags-pa (1235–80), succeeded in winning the confidence of Khubilai Khan; according to hagiographic tradition, this came about after he had won a contest of magic display over Taoist and Nestorian Christian priests. Apparently the Mongols were particularly impressed by the magic powers of the Tibetan monks, powers that were also noted by Marco Polo during his stay at Khubilai's court. Khubilai, who soon became emperor of China, was a powerful patron of Buddhism, and granted freedom from taxation to the monasteries in Tibet. Thus Tibet became subject to a single political leadership for the first time since the 9th century, at the same time avoiding direct Mongol conquest; and this leadership was that of a religious hierarchy. Here, then, is the origin of that theocratic – or, more properly, hierocratic – rule, which was to become so characteristic of Tibet and which continued down to 1959. From 'Phags-pa and Khubilai, too, dates the vague but convenient concept of 'priest and patron', which defined the relationship between the Sa-skya hierarchs and the Mongol emperors of China, a concept which was later revived by the Manchu dynasty and which in our century has been exploited by Nationalist as well as Communist regimes in China.

We are, however, anticipating events. In the 14th century, Sa-skya-pa power waned with that of the Mongol dynasty in China; and when it was succeeded by the native Chinese Ming dynasty, dominance of Tibet, already a political fiction, came to an end. In Tibet, however, there followed a period of struggle for power between the various Buddhist schools, often supported by their lay patrons.

All these schools have one characteristic in common: their origin in 11th-century Buddhist India. There remains a school with a rather different background: the rNying-ma-pa, 'Adherents of the Old [*tantras*]', which traced its history back to Padmasambhava, in other words to the 'first propagation of the Doctrine'. Its background was partly that of the 'village tantrists', which King Ye-shes-'od had criticized so severely, and partly that of a school of meditation, known as the 'Great Perfection', which, tracing its practices back to Vairocana (a Tibetan disciple of Padmasambhava exiled by Khri-srong to east Tibet) as well as other early figures, had survived in east Tibet after the disintegration of royal power in central Tibet.

While the schools we have discussed earlier may perhaps to some extent be compared to the 'orders' of Christian monasticism in the West, the rNying-ma-pa present an entirely different case. They developed no centralized leadership or organized hierarchy, they avoided involvement in the political struggles of the times and their monastic centres remained small and scattered. However, it is above all doctrinally that they stand apart from the later schools. For the rNying-ma-pa, Padmasambhava was elevated to a divine figure, a second Buddha, in theory equal with and in practice eclipsing Śākyamuni; in fact, Padmasambhava came to be regarded – as was Śākyamuni – as a 'transformation-body' of the bodhisattva Avalokiteśvara, and hence became the object of a cult. While the rNying-ma-pa eventually did establish centres of conventional monastic life after the model of the later schools, they also retained the 'village tantrist' type of religious practitioner, often living as householders forming a distinctive social group or class, and only gathering in the local temple for the performance of rituals, a practice which continues today.

This somewhat diffuse movement – characterized by a modern scholar as the religious 'underground' of the period – received its name from the fact that it accepted as authoritative a group of *tantras* allegedly introduced into Tibet at the time of Padmasambhava. While some of these *tantras* may have been 'authentic' in this sense, others were clearly apocryphal. The important point, however, is that these 'old' *tantras* were rejected *en bloc* by the other schools, who instead based themselves on the 'new' *tantras*, such as the *Guhyasamāja* and the *Hevajra*, whose Indian origin was beyond doubt.

I have referred to certain texts as 'apocryphal'. By the 13th century, if not before, the rNying-ma-pa had adopted the view that Padamasambhava and his disciples, foreseeing the troubles which lay ahead for Buddhism in Tibet, had hidden away a great number of texts in caves, inside pillars, statues, etc., as well as buried in the ground, to be 'taken out' again and propagated when the time was ripe. Such 'rediscovered texts' were known as 'treasures', and the lamas who discovered them were known as 'revealers of treasure'. Among such texts were *tantras*, medicinal and ritual texts, manuals of meditation of the 'Great Perfection' type, and a detailed biography of Padmasambhava. By the more severe of its critics, this rNying-ma-pa literature was rejected out of hand as nothing but fabrications, but recent research seems to indicate that it does in fact contain much ancient material. A noteworthy trait of these 'treasures' is their national sentiment and their glorification of the ancient royalty, clearly as a reaction to Mongol overlordship.

Further rNying-ma-pa developments are partly characterized by scholastic efforts at systematization – we may mention the great Klong-chen lama (1308–64) who composed 'Seven Treasuries' providing a detailed philosophical basis for the 'Great Perfection' – and partly by visionaries transmitting 'treasures' that no longer had to have the form of written texts, but were perceived intuitively as 'mental treasures' or revealed as 'clear visions'. The discovery of such 'treasures' has continued till now, and not only within the rNying-ma-pa School.

Succession by reincarnation: the formative period

While the rNying-ma-pa were busy constituting a literature of their own, the other schools remained in constant contact with Buddhist centres in Kashmir, Nepal, Bihar and Bengal. A steady flow of Tibetan pilgrims crossed the Himalayas – frequently via the Nepal valley – in search of texts, relics and, above all, spiritual instruction. In the opposite direction travelled Indian 'saints' and scholars. The Muslim invasions of Bihar and Bengal towards the end of the 12th century, and of Kashmir about a century later, brought about the virtual disappearance of the Doctrine of the Buddha in the land of its origin. Although it never quite ceased, the flow of Tibetan pilgrims to India gradually dwindled to a mere trickle; and gradually Tibetans came to regard their own country as the centre of the Buddhist world, a role which they now believed had been prophesied by the Buddha himself. It is from this period that belief in Avalokiteśvara's involvement in the birth of the ancestors of the first Tibetans (referred to above), as well as in the early history of the Tibetan state, finds full expression. Henceforth, Avalokiteśvara was to remain, in a profound sense, the patron deity of Tibet.

By the end of the 14th century, the period of translation had by and large come to an end. It was now up to the Tibetans to make what use they could of their vast Indian patrimony. The Tibetan genius for analyzing and cataloguing, for elaboration and compilation, now came fully into its own. The most important result of this work was the editing of the enormous mass of accumulated translations into a canonical collection of texts accepted as the 'Word of the Buddha'. This compilation, known as the Kanjur ('Translation of the Word of the Buddha'), consisting of 108 volumes, was above all associated with the great scholar Bu-ston (1290–1364). The Kanjur contains *vinaya* texts, Mahāyāna *sūtras*, and *tantras*. Bu-ston was also responsible for the prodigious task of compiling the collection of commentaries and treatises, the Tenjur ('Translation of the Treatises'), consisting of 225 volumes. Together the two collections contain more than 4,500 works. A master copy of the Tenjur was completed and deposited in 1334 in the temple of Zhalu, between Shigatse and Gyantse. Over the centuries, different editions of the Kanjur and the Tenjur have been prepared. There is no need to go into the complicated and still obscure history of these editions, beyond noting that a printed edition of the Kanjur was made in Peking as early as 1410. The Kanjur and the Tenjur were translated into Mongolian, the translation (or perhaps redaction) of the Tenjur being completed only in 1749. In the course of the 14th century, the rNying-ma-pa compiled a voluminous 'Compendium of Old Tantras', thus codifying their own doctrines to which they firmly continued to adhere.

It is, finally, during this formative period of the Tibetan schools that the peculiar mode of religious succession developed that has become one of the most characteristic aspects of Tibetan Buddhism: succession by reincarnation. This term in fact covers two somewhat different ideas. We have already seen that the great 'religious kings' came to be regarded as the emanations of bodhisattvas. On the same pattern the Sa-skya-pa lamas were all regarded as the incarnation of some holy person, and the same idea soon appeared within other schools, furthered by the universal tendency to regard one's spiritual preceptor, one's lama, as the visible manifestation of universal Buddhahood. However, within the Karma-pa School the successor of a deceased head lama was sought in a child showing certain signs indicating that he was indeed the reincarnation of the former. It is significant that this idea developed within a school where there was no dominant family line. Within the Karma-pa School there developed several lines of reincarnating lamas, the 'Black Hat', the 'Red Hat' – both of which still exist – and others. Likewise, the head lamas of the 'Bri-khung-pa, another bKa'-rgyud-pa school, succeeded each other by reincarnation, complicating the system by allowing three incarnations of each head lama, one of 'body', one of 'speech' and one of 'mind'. Reincarnated lamas are known as 'transformation bodies' (*nirmāṇakāya* in Sanskrit), the Tibetans making use of the concept of the three bodies of the Buddha (see p. 92) to provide a doctrinal basis for this practice.

'The Way of Virtue'

The last of the Buddhist schools to develop in Tibet was the dGe-lugs-pa, the 'Followers of the Way of Virtue', also called – originally by the Chinese, later, and very commonly, by Western writers – the 'Yellow Hats', from the colour of their head-dress. This school was founded by Tsong-kha-pa (1357–1419), a monk whose influence has probably been more far-reaching than any other 'son of the Buddha' in Tibet. Tsong-kha-pa was born in the neighbourhood of the great lake of Kokonor in north-east Tibet, and as a young man he travelled – as was usual in his time – from monastery to monastery in central Tibet, studying with teachers of different schools. However, at the age of forty he joined the great bKa'-gdams-pa monastery of Rva-sgreng. Tsong-kha-pa was by now extremely influential as a religious teacher. He emphasized the bKa'-gdams-pa ideals of monastic discipline, insisting on celibacy and abstention from intoxicants, and based his religious instruction on the works of great Indian philosophers such as Nāgārjuna, Asanga and Dignāga, expounding his views in a masterly exposé of Mahāyāna Buddhism entitled 'The Great Exposition of the Stages of the Way'.

In 1409 Tsong-kha-pa founded his own monastery, Ganden, a short distance from Lhasa, and as his school expanded, finding eager support both among monks of the older schools as well as among the lay people, his disciples founded two more monasteries in the immediate vicinity of Lhasa – Drepung in 1416 and Sera in 1419. In 1408 he instituted the annual New Year celebration, called the Great Prayer, in the ancient Jo-khang temple in Lhasa, intending it as a yearly rededication of Tibet to Buddhism. Thereafter, the Great Prayer continued every year without interruption until 1959. Thus Tsong-kha-pa made Lhasa and the surrounding province of dBus the stronghold of his school, a fact which was to be significant for the development of dGe-lugs-pa power. However, his own learning and, above all, the strictly regulated and austere religious life of the monks were no doubt very real factors in securing popular support for his school, which soon completely engulfed the bKa'-gdams-pa School so that it ceased to have a separate existence.

Tsong-kha-pa is sometimes represented as a kind of self-appointed reformer of Tibetan Buddhism, as a kind of Tibetan Luther. However, this is quite misleading. He did not question the basic doctrinal validity of the other schools, and there was in fact no all-embracing 'church' to reform. He did found a new school, but its rise to power only occurred several centuries later. Nor did he, as is sometimes suggested, ban the *tantras*; he did, as we have seen, emphasize the early, non-tantric Mahāyāna philosophers, but he also composed commentaries on the *tantras*, reserving for them a place at the highest level of monastic studies, and eventually two dGe-lugs-pa monasteries specially devoted to tantric studies were founded in Lhasa, 'Upper' and 'Lower Tantra'. They drew their inmates only from the most accomplished monks of the capital. This élite was traditionally subjected to an extremely rigorous code of discipline – a fact which should be sufficient to dispel the popular notion that tantric practitioners always represented a corrupt and degenerate group in Tibet.

A feature common to all schools as they developed in Tibet, and one which links them by turn to all the regional variations of Buddhist monasticism throughout Asia, was their adoption of the same *vinaya* code governing ordination and the regulation of daily life. But superimposed on this basic code is a diverse curriculum of mainly tantric inspiration which serves to distinguish the Tibetan monk from most of his neighbours to the east and south-east. Practically all of the art and music and most of the literature of Tibetan monasteries are the product of the complex ritual cycles which punctuate the life of the monk according to the traditions of his school. If one were to choose one of the most typical of ritual activities to illustrate this point, one might focus on the aim to 'generate' a chosen deity. Whether it is a specifically Buddhist deity or one selected from the Hindu or pre-Buddhist pantheon (with their primary characters more or less neutralized), the devotee seeks to visualize the god first within his own body. He then creates an external image of the same deity before dissolving him back into the void from which he was created. Both stages, internal and external, revolve around the creation of the deity's mandala, a circumscribed area rendered safe from hostile influences into which the god is led by his divine attendants. The visual and aural 'supports' for this process account for almost all the art and ritual paraphernalia found in Tibetan monasteries. The whole purpose of sacred dance as performed during monastic festivals centres on the quest to 'generate the deity in front' as a dramatic extension of the liturgy taking place within the precincts of the temple. Most dances, even some of those with an auxiliary or didactic purpose peripheral to the main concern, serve to create a mandala in the centre of which the deity is invited to take his place. There, if the deity is a wrathful one as is often the case, a dough image is dismembered and strewn to the four quarters, an act which can be viewed either as the destruction of the ego principle or as the annihilation of the external enemies of the Doctrine.

With the emergence of the dGe-lugs-pa School it may be fairly said that Buddhism in Tibet had found its final form. Although certain branches of established schools were still to appear – one could especially mention the monastery of Ngor – and although several of the bKa'-rgyud-pa schools eventually disappeared, hereafter there were to be hardly any changes at all either in monastic life or in general religious beliefs, nor any significant philosophical or intellectual renewal. The Tibetans seemed content to restate what they had learned, moving intellectually within a framework of ideas which became gradually more and more rigid. Their lack of interest in the cultures of the surrounding countries, India as well as China, contrasts with their apparent openness to foreign influence and willingness to learn and assimilate during the earlier royal period. It became rare for Tibetans to know other languages than their own; in the monasteries, while the knowledge of Sanskrit never entirely disappeared, it was generally used merely for magic formulas. With Chinese Buddhists, the Tibetans had – apart from occasional visits to places of pilgrimage like the holy mountain of Wu-tai-shan associated with the bodhisattva Mañjuśrī – little or no contact since the Chinese texts were written in a language and a script they could not read, and their entire religious terminology had a completely different origin.

The age of the Dalai Lamas

The history of Buddhism in Tibet from the 15th century onward is therefore largely a matter of *political* history, the history, above all, of the dGe-lugs-pa School and its rise to power. When the question of succession arose within the dGe-lugs-pa School, it followed the model of the Karma-pa. The third successor of Tsong-kha-pa was his nephew dGe-'dun-grub (1391–1475), an energetic and ambitious leader. By the time of his death, Drepung housed at least 1,500 monks and had become the largest monastery in the whole of Tibet. He was also the founder of the Tashilhunpo monastery outside Shigatse. His successor was found in a child born soon after his death, and this child was regarded as the reincarnation of dGe-'dun-grub. Retrospectively, he was regarded as the second Dalai Lama, dGe-'dun-grub being regarded as the first. The title of Dalai Lama ('Ocean Lama', presumably 'Ocean of Wisdom') was, however, first bestowed on the second successor of dGe-'dun-grub, bSod-nams-rgya-mtsho (1543–88), by Altan Khan, chief of the Tümed branch of the Mongols.

bSod-nams-rgya-mtsho met Altan Khan near the Kokonor in 1578. For Tibet, this meant the eventual renewal of Mongol involvement in Tibetan affairs; but for the Mongols, the consequences were perhaps even more far-reaching. The Mongol contact with Tibetan Buddhism had never been completely broken off since the days of Khubilai Khan, and in the Mongols the Dalai Lama now saw the possibility of a vast missionary field. Altan Khan was converted and set about suppressing blood-sacrifices and the worship of ancestral images. Although the traditional Mongol religion obviously did not disappear overnight, the Mongols now became firm adherents of the dGe-lugs-pa School, and adopted Tibetan Buddhism with its texts, rituals and art, as well as literary Tibetan as their sacred language.

Mongol support of the dGe-lugs-pa was strengthened when the fourth Dalai Lama was discovered in a great-grandson of Altan Khan. However, it was only with the fifth Dalai Lama, Ngag-dbang-blo-bzang-rgya-mtsho (1617–82), that the Mongols interfered in Tibet in a decisive way. With the help of Gushri Khan, the leader of the Qoshot Mongols, who had established themselves in the Kokonor region, the fifth Dalai Lama won a final victory over his opponents, in particular the king of gTsang and the Red Hat Karma-pa. By the time of Gushri's death in 1656, the Dalai Lama was the undisputed master of Tibet.

Once in control, he showed considerable generosity towards the other schools, and while the position of the Karma-pas in central Tibet was greatly reduced (their stronghold from now on being in Kham), the rNying-ma-pas were favoured; their monastery of sMin-grol-gling, formerly a small centre, was turned into a large monastic establishment (pillaged, however, by the Dzungar Mongols in the 18th century), and there were even rumours to the effect that the Dalai Lama, born as he was in a rNying-ma-pa family, was a secret follower of that school.

Ngag-dbang-blo-bzang-rgya-mtsho is known to the Tibetans as the Great Fifth, and beyond any doubt he was an unusually intelligent, strong-willed and at the same time generous-minded ruler. He travelled to Peking at the invitation of the emperor, and their meeting in 1653 was that of two equal heads of state. Lhasa itself now finally became the centre of Tibet, symbolized by the magnificent Potala palace, which the Dalai Lama had built on the basis of earlier constructions. The choice of the name 'Potala' was significant, for it is the name of the mountain in south India that is regarded as the seat of Tibet's patron bodhisattva Avalokiteśvara. The Dalai Lama was already regarded as the reincarnation of his predecessor; now, in the person of the Great Fifth, he was also believed – as in the case of the 'Religious Kings' – to be the manifestation of Avalokiteśvara. Thus the two types of incarnation discussed above came to be united in one person for the first time, and have remained so down to the present Dalai Lama, the fourteenth. This helps to explain the combination of national sentiment and religious fervour with which present-day Tibetans regard him.

The period of greatness under the fifth Dalai Lama was, however, to be short-lived. After his death, which was kept secret for thirteen years until 1695, exactly two hundred years were to pass before a strong Dalai Lama was once more to play a decisive role in the destiny of Tibet. During these two hundred years, the Tibetans preserved practically unchanged their system of government and their religious and social life; however, they were constantly subjected to pressure and intervention from neighbouring powers. In 1644, the Manchus, originally a Tungusic people of hunters and nomads living to the north-east of China, were able to establish a new dynasty in Peking; the Manchu dynasty, though rapidly assimilated to Chinese culture, like the Mongol dynasty four hundred years before, remained in power until 1911. Profiting from the general turmoil caused by the continual intervention of various Mongol princes in Tibet, the Manchus were able, in the course of the 18th century, to re-establish the 'patron-and-priest' relationship which has already been noted in connection with 'Phags-pa and Khubilai Khan in the 13th century. This time, however, it was to define the relationship between the Dalai Lama, already the ruler of Tibet, and the Chinese emperor. At no time was there any question of direct Chinese administration.

At the same time, European powers were busy creating colonies and establishing trade throughout Asia. In contrast to India, and even to China, Tibet never came under direct European dominance. Nevertheless, some European contacts did occur. As early as 1624, a Jesuit, Father Antonio d'Andrade, reached Tsaparang in the western Tibetan kingdom of Gu-ge and established a small mission, which continued until 1640. In 1707, a Capuchin mission was established in Lhasa, and maintained until 1745. While the Capuchins seem to have had little or no understanding of Tibetan religion, the Jesuit Ippolito Desideri, who lived in Lhasa from 1716 to 1721, acquired a mastery of Tibetan and a practical familiarity with Tibetan Buddhism, as few Westerners have done either before or since; he won the respect of Tibetan nobles, entered into disputation with dGe-lugs-pa monks on their own terms and wrote – in Tibetan – a refutation of their doctrines. However, the Capuchins showed little respect for Tibetan ways and religious beliefs, and when the last missionary, Father Orazio della Penna, left Lhasa in 1745, their chapel was razed. The last that was heard of the small group of Christian converts was a message in 1769 asking for a priest to be sent to them.

While these missionary efforts did not lead to any lasting results, the commercial interests of the British in India had more far-reaching consequences. Already, in 1775, Warren Hastings had sent an emissary, George Bogle, to Shigatse to investigate ways of increasing trade between India and Tibet. The friendship which arose between the Head Lama of the Tashilhunpo monastery and the young Scotsman might have seemed an auspicious beginning to British–Tibetan relations. A second envoy, Samuel Turner, was sent in 1783. However, the Gurkha invasion of Tibet in 1792, driven back almost to Kathmandu by a Chinese army, led to the virtual closing of Tibet to all foreigners; when the British again took an interest in Tibet in the 19th century, it was as a pawn in what was called the 'Great Game', the drive of tsarist Russia for supremacy in Central Asia countered by Britain's determination to protect the northern borders of her Indian empire. Mounting frustration with the refusal of the Tibetans to open their borders to trade, and a deep-seated suspicion of Russian designs on Tibet, finally led to the British military expedition to Lhasa in 1904.

By this time, the thirteenth Dalai Lama, Thub-bstan-rgya-mtsho (1876–1934), had assumed power. Like the Great Fifth, he was a forceful personality and an able politician. He re-established complete Tibetan independence of China after the Chinese Revolution in 1911. The Chinese garrison in Lhasa was expelled (returning to China via India, by far the easiest route), and Tibet enjoyed a period of freedom, lasting until 1951.

Deeply affected by the persecution of Buddhist monks in Mongolia after the Communist take-over in that country in the 1920s, the thirteenth Dalai Lama wrote what has been called his 'political testament', in 1933, in which he foresaw a similar fate for Tibet:

> It may happen that here in the centre of Tibet the Religion and the secular administration may be attacked both from the outside and from the inside. . . . As regards the monasteries and the priesthood, their lands and other properties will be destroyed. The administrative customs of the Three Religious Kings will be weakened. The officers of the state, ecclesiastical and secular, will find their lands seized and their other property confiscated, and they themselves made to serve their enemies, or wander about the country as beggars do. All beings will be sunk in great hardship and in overpowering fear; the days and the nights will drag on slowly in suffering.

The destruction of Tibetan Buddhism

Less than twenty years later, this prophecy was to be fulfilled. In the autumn of 1950, the Communist regime in China, having emerged victorious from the civil war, sent its army into Tibet. Organized resistance was soon fought down, and in 1951 Chinese troops again – for the first time since 1911 – entered Lhasa. The fourteenth Dalai Lama, bsTan-'dzin-rgya-mtsho (b. 1935), was hastily invested with full powers as head of state, at the age of sixteen. We cannot here trace the political developments which followed the annexation of Tibet and its subsequent transformation into a Chinese colony. We must restrict ourselves to stating the basic facts: the growing opposition to Chinese rule leading to a full-scale revolt in eastern Tibet in 1956; the uprising in Lhasa in March 1959, soon after the Great Prayer had been performed for the last time; the flight of the Dalai Lama to India; and the subsequent subjection of the whole of Tibet to direct Chinese rule, formalized by the establishing of a so-called 'Tibet Autonomous Region' in 1965, more or less comprising the regions traditionally under Lhasa rule, leaving the greater part of Kham and Amdo to be engulfed by neighbouring Chinese provinces. Thus, by the end of the 1970s, the long story of the interrelationship of China and Tibet would seem to have come to an end with the total obliteration of the latter.

What have been the consequences of the total disruption of the traditional social fabric for the 'sons of the Buddha'? On the face of it, the consequences would seem to have been disastrous. The Chinese have been utterly ruthless in their efforts to stamp out the influence of Buddhism in the Land of Snows. Monasteries have been systematically looted, turned into military barracks, or razed to the ground. Whole libraries and countless religious images have been wantonly destroyed. A large number of monks have been executed, often after public humiliation and appalling torture. Thousands have been imprisoned or sent to labour camps. The anti-religious campaign was particularly intense during three periods: in eastern Tibet (Kham and Amdo) from 1954–5 to 1959; in central and western Tibet in 1959 and 1960; and finally – by some accounts the most destructive campaign – during the years of the Cultural Revolution, which was launched in Tibet in 1967. No one can measure the sum of human suffering which these attempts at eradicating the Doctrine of the Buddha in Tibet have caused.

Nevertheless, from 1978 onward there has been a gradual change of Chinese policy towards religion in Tibet. A few temples and monasteries have been restored, murals and wooden beams repainted in the traditional style, and images installed once more. Drepung and Tashilhunpo are among the monasteries which have been at least partially restored. In these monasteries, a certain number of monks are now maintained – officially some two hundred monks were living in Drepung by 1980 (compared with more than ten thousand before 1959). The Jo-khang has been opened for public worship on certain days of the week, and the Potala has been turned into a museum.

The reports of visitors to Lhasa make it quite clear that this limited easing of the former state of total suppression has resulted in the surfacing of a strong religious sentiment among the Tibetans. Pilgrims from all over the country once more flock to the Jo-khang to prostrate themselves before the image of Avalokiteśvara – no matter that the present image is said to be a copy recently installed by the Chinese. Private devotions by individual lay people can now apparently be carried out quite openly, and it is reported that sacred texts hidden away or buried underground in the 1950s and 1960s are now being retrieved, exactly as Tibetans believe was done during the persecution of Buddhism in ancient times. Groups of pilgrims have even been allowed to journey to India to attend religious ceremonies and receive blessings from the Dalai Lama.

On the other hand it does not seem that new monks have yet been ordained, and the restoration of perhaps twenty or thirty monasteries must be seen in the perspective of the thousands of flourishing religious institutions that existed before 1959. Thus it still seems uncertain who will finally triumph in Tibet: Marx or Buddha.

Following the uprising of 1959, some 80,000 Tibetans have sought refuge in India, Nepal and Bhutan. Several thousand have also settled in Europe (mostly in Switzerland) and North America. The refugees immediately set about reorganizing their religious life along traditional lines, and by 1981 they had established a considerable number of temples and monastic centres, all of them connected with one or another of the traditional schools. Young monks are constantly being ordained and 'incarnations' discovered and duly installed. Thus there would seem to be no danger of Buddhist monastic life disappearing among the refugees, at least in the foreseeable future.

The focal point of religious faith and national sentiment among the exiles – and by all accounts, among the vast majority of Tibetans in Tibet – is the Dalai Lama, who since 1960 has had his headquarters in the 'hill station' of Dharamsala in the Himalayan foothills north-west of New Delhi. Repeatedly invited by the Chinese in recent years to return to Tibet, he has refused to do so until the Tibetans have been allowed to express freely what kind of government they wish to have. Combining the austere life of a devout dGe-lugs-pa monk with a universal appeal for non-violence and peace, based on compassion and tranquillity of mind, he has become perhaps the leading spokesman of Buddhism in the world today.

Tibetan Buddhism outside Tibet

In the course of history, Buddhism was propagated by Tibetans among various non-Tibetan peoples. Wherever this has happened, Buddhism has retained its specifically Tibetan form, rather than becoming assimilated to local cultures. By far the most important conquest of the Tibetan Buddhist mission has been the Mongols. We have already noted the close contact which existed between Tibetan hierarchs and the Mongol court in China during the 13th and 14th centuries, and the conversion of the Mongols due to the efforts of the third Dalai Lama in the 16th. Since then, the vast majority of the Mongols have been staunch adherents of the dGe-lugs-pa School. Religious and in particular monastic life developed entirely according to the Tibetan model. The Mongols soon took up the Tibetan practice of ecclesiastical succession by reincarnation, so that, by 1900, some 240 reincarnated lamas were to be found among them. The most powerful of these lineages was that of the rJe-btsun-dam-pa in Urga (present-day Ulaan Baator). In 1911 'Outer Mongolia' declared its independence and installed the eighth rJe-btsun-dam-pa as head of state. On his death in 1924, however, 'Outer Mongolia' became, with Russian help, a 'People's Republic', and in 1930 a violent campaign against the monasteries and religion in general was launched by the Communist regime. The result was that more than seven hundred monasteries and temples were destroyed, and only in Ulaan Baator has the state-supported Buddhist monastery of Ganden (dGa'-ldan) been maintained. However, there are indications that Buddhist belief has remained strong among the Mongols, and a crowd estimated at 200,000 attended a sermon given by the Dalai Lama when he visited Ulaan Baator in June 1979.

'Inner Mongolia' has remained a part of China, and since 1949 Buddhism has suffered the same fate there as in Tibet. The Mongols in China, fewer in number than the Tibetans and inhabiting a vast but fragmented territory, have been far less able than the Tibetans to withstand the process of Sinification.

In the Soviet Union, there are two branches of the

Mongols: the Kalmuks and the Buryats. The Kalmuks migrated to the Volga region in the 17th century, thus forming a nation adhering to Tibetan Buddhism on European soil. A small exile community with a temple and resident lamas has been established in the USA.

The Buryats live in the region surrounding Lake Baikal. They were brought to Buddhism fairly late, in the 18th century, and many of the Buryats retained their ancient beliefs and practices until recent times, in open defiance of Buddhism. In spite of severe repression of Buddhism in the USSR in the 1930s and the imprisonment of leading Buddhists in recent years – thus the famous Lama Dandaron died in a labour camp on the shores of Lake Baikal in October 1974 – there are several monasteries maintained by the state. Well known are the Ivolginsky monastery, constructed in 1948, twenty-five miles outside Ulan-Ude, seat of the Hambo Lama; and especially the Aginsky monastery, founded in 1811–16 and particularly famous as a centre of scholarship.

Since the early 1960s, Tibetan lamas in exile have vigorously established religious centres in the West. Here, too, each school has operated on its own. In particular, the Karma-pa have been extremely active; the last hierarch, the sixteenth 'Black Hat' incarnation (Rang-'byung-rig-pa'i-rdo-rje, 1924–81), established a flourishing monastery at Rumtek in Sikkim, with affiliated centres throughout the Western world. Certain rNying-ma-pa teachers have also had great success as spiritual masters. Sa-skya and dGe-lugs-pa centres are less numerous, but nevertheless firmly established. It is certainly too early to say if all this activity, in itself quite impressive and involving tens of thousands of sympathizers, will have lasting results in the West. Meditation in particular has been taken up with great enthusiasm, and there is a great demand for 'blessings', 'precepts' and 'initiations'. On the other hand, there has been relatively little interest among Western adherents of Tibetan Buddhism in the basic intellectual training which has traditionally formed the backbone of monastic life, and more than superficial knowledge of Tibetan is generally rare. Nevertheless, this unprecedented interest in Tibetan Buddhism in the West is a remarkable phenomenon, which may yet have a lasting impact.

Tibetan Buddhism is also firmly established in areas of the Himalayas which have at one time or another been part of Tibet but which today are politically part of India or Nepal, or which are inhabited by a population that emigrated from Tibet in historical times, or are otherwise more or less fully Tibetanized. Starting from the western end of the Himalayan range and working east, the most important of these areas will be mentioned briefly.

Ladakh is an ancient Tibetan kingdom conquered by the Indian state of Jammu in 1834, and since then a part of India. There are numerous monasteries in Ladakh, most of them founded in dependence upon Tibetan schools. Some are dGe-lugs-pa monasteries, and the other major order in Ladakh is the 'Brug-pa. Lamayuru, however, belongs to the 'Bri-khung order of the bKa'-rgyud-pa. The destruction of monastic institutions in Tibet itself has brought about the cultural isolation of Ladakh, and the cessation of trade with Tibet has led to complete economic dependence on India. There is also a large and increasingly influential Muslim population in Ladakh, so that in a long-term perspective the future of Buddhism in Ladakh seems problematic.

Further to the east, the sparsely populated districts of Zangskar and Spiti are entirely Tibetan, though politically part of India. Moving into Nepal, Dolpo is a completely Tibetan area where life as late as the 1970s was still practically untouched by the 20th century. East of Dolpo lies the ancient kingdom of Mustang with several sizable monasteries; though part of Nepal, Mustang is unique in that it is the only example of an ancient Tibetan principality surviving as a political unit today. Another Tibetan Buddhist population in Nepal is the Sherpas further to the east, the descendants of immigrants from Tibet, perhaps in the 16th century. The Sherpas, of course, are well known as guides and porters for several generations of Western mountaineers and tourists. Their monasteries are small, founded during this or the previous century, but often with energetic and able leaders.

Sikkim since the 17th century has been a Tibetan kingdom ruled by a line of kings known as 'Kings of the Doctrine'. Sikkim became a British protectorate in 1890, and was annexed by India in 1975, the king being deposed. There are several small monasteries in the north of Sikkim, as well as the large Rumtek monastery.

East of Sikkim lies Bhutan (separated from it by the Chumbi valley of Tibet and the Darjeeling/Kalimpong area of West Bengal with its considerable Tibetan population), which since the 17th century has been a stronghold of the 'Brug-pa School. Bhutan is an independent country, a member of the United Nations, and pursues a firm policy of preserving its traditional culture and religious institutions. The country was ruled by a line of 'Brug-pa hierarchs until 1905, when the country's first hereditary king seized effective power. Monastic life in Bhutan is still flourishing, the larger monasteries having up to five hundred monks; a characteristic trait of Bhutanese monasticism is the function of the main monasteries as fortified centres of administration. Alone among the Himalayan areas, Buddhism in Bhutan would seem to have the economic resources and political support which can ensure its undiminished vigour in the foreseeable future.

The enigmatic Bon-po

To the Tibetans themselves, Tibet is in a unique sense the Land of Religion, the land in which the Good Law has flourished for centuries in accordance with a prophecy made by the Buddha himself. Accordingly, the Tibetans designate themselves – as well as others, especially Mongols, who practise the Tibetan form of

Today Tibetan Buddhism in its traditional form survives only in small areas lying close to the borders of historic Tibet: Ladakh, Zanskar, Nepal, Sikkim and Bhutan. Here the ancient monastic life continues and can be seen as a living force. This wall painting from the New Temple at Tangshji, Bhutan, shows a monk receiving gifts from lay patrons.

Buddhism – as 'insiders', as opposed to all other people who are 'outsiders'. All this is well known. It is, however, less well known that there are, in fact, two distinct religions in Tibet. Besides Buddhism, which Tibetans call *chos* (a word which translates the Indian term *dharma*, 'law, doctrine'), there exists another religion, called *bon*, its adherents being called *bon-po*.

The term *bon-po* was the name of a type of priest within the pre-Buddhist religion in Tibet, a religion frequently referred to as 'shamanism', which is, however, an entirely misleading term. At this point it will be useful to keep in mind once more the distinction between the oldest sources, contemporary with the introduction of Buddhism, and the later, retrospective ones. Thus, judging from the oldest sources, the chief function of the *bon-po* seems to have been connected with the funeral ceremonies of the kings and the subsequent cult which took place at the burial mound. This cult was apparently extremely complicated and need not be described in detail here, but we may at least note that we nowhere find any indication of what might be called 'shamanistic' elements. There is no indication of trances of any kind; on the contrary, the cult was entirely ritualistic, strictly regulated down to the smallest detail, its efficacy depending on the correct performance of each element. An important part in this religion was played by the sacrifice of many animals, a fact also attested by Chinese sources. Besides the *bon-po* priests there were other priests styled *gshen*.

It is clear that many elements of this ancient religion survived the introduction of Buddhism (which bitterly opposed and gradually succeeded in abolishing such practices as blood-sacrifices) and became part of a broad religious substratum, finding expression in many kinds of popular religious beliefs and practices which survive among Tibetans – monks included. With the triumph of Buddhism, however, the *bon-po* of the royal period completely disappeared as an organized body of priests.

What causes confusion is the fact that in the 11th century, if not before, a religion appears on the scene, styling itself *bon* and its adherents *bon-po*, but it is manifestly not identical with the ancient faith. In fact, not only does this new religion appear simultaneously with the various Buddhist schools introduced from India – the bKa'-rygud-pa, the Sa-skya-pa and so on – but in doctrine and practice it is, at least at the present stage of research, difficult to discern any really significant differences between *bon* and *chos*. In particular, there is a very clear and profound relationship between the post-11th-century Bon-po and the rNying-ma-pa, both schools tracing their history back to the crucial period of the introduction of Buddhism in the 8th century.

Nevertheless, the fact remains that the Bon-po regard themselves as forming a distinct religion, and are also thus regarded by the Buddhists. And in a fundamental respect the two are quite opposed: while Buddhists ultimately derive the authority of their doctrines from the Indian Śākyamuni, the Bon-po deny that he was the Buddha, the Awakened One. They maintain instead that the true Buddha of our age was a certain sTon-pa-gshen-rab, 'the Teacher, Master-gShen', who lived long before Śākyamuni, in the land of sTag-gzig, situated somewhat vaguely to the west of

Tibet. sTon-pa-gshen-rab is held to have propagated *bon* throughout the world, including Tibet; and it was this doctrine of *bon*, so the later (post-11th-century) Bon-po tradition insists, that was suppressed by the kings, in particular by Khri-srong-lde-btsan. Accordingly, the later Bon-po sources manifest a deep antagonism to *chos*, the doctrine which under royal patronage was brought to Tibet from India; it is represented as a pernicious heresy. Thus a 19th-century Bon-po scholar, Nyi-ma-bstan-'dzin, has this to say concerning the introduction of *chos*:

> In the Earth-Ox Year (AD 749), the perverse prayer of a demon (being the ultimate cause), and he who acted like a monk but retained the Five Poisons [ignorance, hate, lust, etc. – Śāntirakṣita is referred to] providing the immediate cause of the coming of the pernicious Buddhist [i.e. *chos-pa*] monks, a demon having entered the heart of the king and the merit of the realm of Tibet being low, the time came when the sun of the Doctrine [i.e. *bon*] was made to set.

It is indeed startling to see the appearance of Buddhism described as a catastrophe by an author who is in every other respect profoundly Buddhist!

Bon-po religious centres – like those of the rNying-ma-pa – were very modest to begin with, being hermitages or local family lineages on the Sa-skya-pa pattern, although neither seeking nor obtaining political power. Thus the Bon-po were left in peace as a small and aberrant school, more often ignored than explicitly tolerated. Several such family lineages are known, and some continue.

By the 15th century, the Bon-po were organizing their monastic life along the same lines as the Buddhist schools. The foremost figure in this connection is Shes-rab-rgyal-mtshan (1356–1415), who founded the monastery of sMan-ri in the district of Thob-rgyal in gTsang in 1405. The abbots of sMan-ri (who succeeded each other by vote, not by reincarnation or family lineage) were thenceforth regarded as the spiritual heads of the Bon-po. In 1834, the monastery of gYung-drung-gling was founded, likewise in gTsang, and the abbot of that monastery now took over the religious leadership. Both these monasteries were flourishing institutions, each housing several hundred monks in 1959. Other Bon-po monasteries existed in Kham, in rGya-rong, on the Chinese border, and in Amdo. Lacking political power of any kind, the Bon-po monasteries seem to have been entirely dependent on the gifts of the lay people.

It has often been remarked, not least by Western writers, that the Bon-po perform certain ritual acts in a manner opposite to that of the Buddhists. Thus they turn their prayer-wheels towards the left instead of towards the right; they circumambulate holy objects in the same fashion but they recite different *mantras*; and the iconography and names of their deities are different from those of Buddhism. It is important to realize, however, that this is not, as has been so often asserted by Western writers, an expression of 'wilful distortion or perversion', nor does the essence of their doctrines lie 'largely in contradiction and negation'. On the contrary, the Bon-po – exactly like the Buddhists – perform ritual acts as prescribed by their religion with the pious intention of eventually becoming 'awakened' and with unquestioning faith in the Buddha (that the Buddha in their view is sTon-pa-gshen-rab is another matter), so that in this sense they may be considered as profoundly 'Buddhist' as any other Tibetans. Certainly their monks (who are strictly celibate) would consider themselves – in the perspective of their own tradition – as 'sons of the Buddha'.

Bon-po refugees have established a well organized and flourishing monastery in Himachal Pradesh in India, housing some sixty monks who carry on traditional monastic life and give instruction to novices, including some from Dolpo. Thus it would seem that the tradition of *bon* will be continued, maintaining its claim to be, in a special sense, the true religion of Tibet.

The 'Non-aligned'

The picture which has been unfolded of Tibetan Buddhism has perhaps left an impression of constant rivalry between different schools and of continual struggle for political power or – at best – spiritual supremacy. However, of greater fundamental importance has been a basic doctrinal unity and a common cultural idiom, transcending political borders and factional rivalries, uniting Tibetans into what is nothing less than a Tibetan nation, profoundly committed to Buddhism.

Accordingly, this survey of Buddhism in Tibet shall end with a brief mention of a movement which, starting in the 19th century in eastern Tibet, has sought to unite the various religious schools on a common doctrinal basis, stressing those beliefs and practices that are held in common by all. This Ris-med ('Impartial' or 'Non-aligned') movement arose in rNying-ma-pa circles in Kham, especially in the independent principality of Derge. The Ris-med movement basically remained a rNying-ma-pa development, but did influence monks belonging to other schools. An example is the Bon-po lama, bKra-shis-rgyal-mtshan (1859–1935), from Shar-rdza. Another is a pupil of the latter, the dGe-lugs-pa lama, who became the abbot of the Brag-dkar monastery in Kandze. He was in contact with the Norwegian missionary Theo Sörensen (1873–1959), in whose Christian religion he took a friendly interest.

The total disruption of religious life under the Chinese intervened while this movement was still under way. Yet the Ris-med movement perhaps somehow pointed out the direction in which Tibetan Buddhism – the power of its thousands of monasteries irrevocably a thing of the past – will have to evolve if it is to remain the 'ultimate concern' of future generations of Tibetans.

Buddhism in the Modern World

11

Buddhist Revival in East and West

The Buddhistisches Haus at Frohnau, Berlin. This was among the earliest, and is still one of the most elaborate, Buddhist temples built in the West. It was founded by Dr Paul Dahlke between 1922 and 1924 for the benefit not only of the Buddhist community of which he was the leader but also for interested visitors of all beliefs. It is now administered by the German Dharmaduta Society of Sri Lanka. KEY *1. Entrance. The Buddhistisches Haus is open all day, free of charge;* 2. *The Elephant Gate, a portal based on the Indian* toraṇa, *carved with Eastern emblems and inscriptions;* 3. *Flight of stone steps, divided into eight levels, symbolizing the eightfold path to Nirvāṇa. The temple stands on the eighth level;* 4. *Way in to the temple;* 5. *Path going round the Buddhistisches Haus and temple;* 6. *Statue of Kannon (Kuan-yin), presented by the Japanese town of Nagoya in 1959;* 7. *Entrance to the temple;* 8. *Small ante-chamber to the prayer-hall;* 9. *The temple area, a consecrated place;* 10. *Meditation path;* 11. *Stone Buddha image;* 12. *Garden shrine;* 13. *Another part of the encircling path, with steps to the garden;* 14. *Entrance to the Buddhistisches Haus;* 15. *Ante-chamber with Buddha tapestry;* 16. *Office;* 17. *Sitting room for members and visitors;* 18. *Library. This was enlarged in 1968 and is open to members and to the public;* 19. *Sculpture of the Buddha;* 20. *Guest rooms for Buddhists from all over the world;* 21. *Inset showing position of the Buddhistisches Haus in the suburb of Frohnau in the northern part of west Berlin.*

11

Buddhist Revival in East and West

HEINZ BECHERT

THE EXPANSION of Buddhism had already come to an end about a thousand years ago when the forces of the Muslim conquerors entered Afghanistan and the north-western parts of India. Though Buddhist missions were successful in converting the Mongols and some other peoples in northern and Central Asia even after this period, Buddhism lost its influence in several parts of Asia. In India itself, it had totally disappeared by about AD 1500 after receiving a deadly blow from Islamic conquerors during the 12th century. Some small remaining Buddhist groups were increasingly assimilated to Hinduism. At about the same period, Buddhism lost Eastern Turkestan (Sinkiang) to Islam. Islam also spread in Malaya and Indonesia at the cost of Buddhism, and by the early 17th century practically all of Java had become Islamic.

With the rise of colonialism, a new enemy of Buddhism appeared on the scene: the early 16th century brought Christian missions. The close relation between colonial interests and the missionary activities of the churches is only too well known, and it may suffice here to quote the example of Ceylon where the Portuguese forced the whole population under their control in the coastal areas of the island to accept Roman Catholicism. The Dutch, who took over from the Portuguese in 1636, followed the same policy in principle: they forced the population to become Protestants and persecuted not only Buddhists and Hindus, but also Roman Catholics. Some Catholics took refuge in the Kandyan kingdom which had remained independent in the interior of the island; its Buddhist ruler guaranteed religious freedom in accordance with ancient Buddhist tradition. In the late 18th century, however, when the Dutch granted religious freedom to their subjects, a large part of the population of Ceylon reverted to Buddhism and Hinduism, the religions of their ancestors.

The British and the French who came to rule over south Asia and mainland Southeast Asia in the 19th century with only the exception of the kingdom of Siam (now Thailand) generally avoided direct interference in religious matters in their colonial possessions. During the early phase of British rule, however, conversion to Christianity gave access to a number of privileges. In the treaty between the Kandyan Chiefs and the British Crown which is known as the Kandyan Convention of 1815, the British administration of Ceylon agreed to 'maintain and protect' the religion of the Buddha as a responsibility of the government. However, this agreement was opposed by the churches in England, and, as a consequence, the administration gradually 'disestablished' Buddhism during the period 1818–53, i.e. it severed most ties between government and the Sangha. A new élite emerged who adapted their values and ways of life to those of the new rulers.

Buddhist resurgence: the early phase

In spite of the development described above, conversions of Buddhists to Christianity remained rather the exception than the rule. Towards the end of the 19th century the trend towards the assimilation of Western values was arrested, and a new feeling of cultural identity began to emerge. The so-called Buddhist revival started amongst the educated middle class almost at the same time as the beginnings of the movement towards national independence.

Sri Lanka has played a key role in this development. Buddhist culture there had survived the onslaught of Western domination for centuries. The reform of the Sangha at the instigation of Saraṇaṃkara in the 18th century and the foundation of reformist *nikāyas* (Amarapura Nikāya and Rāmañña Nikāya, see above, p. 144) during the 19th century were early signs of the vitality of Buddhist tradition in the island. In 1849 the monk Valānē Siddhārtha founded the first *piriveṇa* or monastic school of modern Ceylon in Ratmalana, a few miles south of Colombo. In 1873 and 1875 two great seats of Buddhist learning, the Vidyodaya Pirivena in Colombo and the Vidyālankāra Pirivena in Kelaniya near Colombo, were opened. Since 1865 a number of public debates between Buddhist monks and Christian clergy on the merits of both religions have been held. The text of the 'Great Debate of Panadura' of 1873 between Mohoṭṭivattē Guṇānanda Thera on the Buddhist side and the Reverends David de Silva and F. S. Sirimanne on the Christian side was a turning-point for Christian-Buddhist relations in Ceylon.

Within the same year the text of this debate was translated into English and published by the American J. M. Peebles in Battle Creek, Michigan. It was this book which drew the attention of Colonel Henry Steel Olcott (1832–1907) to Buddhism. Together with

Madame Blavatsky (originally Helene Hahn von Rottenstern, 1831–91), Olcott founded the Theosophical Society in 1875. Though Theosophy was, of course, unlike Buddhism in many respects, the high esteem in which Buddhism was held by the founders of Theosophy gave a strong impetus to interest in Buddhism amongst many Americans and Europeans, and in many books of that period Theosophy is termed 'Esoteric Buddhism'.

In 1880 Madame Blavatsky and Colonel Olcott visited Ceylon, and this event is still considered as the commencement of the modern Buddhist revival on the island. The fact that two prominent Westerners came to Sri Lanka out of sympathy and admiration for Buddhism restored the self-confidence of the Buddhists in a period when Christian powers seemed to dominate the whole world. Olcott founded the Buddhist Theosophical Society in Ceylon with the aim of preserving the heritage of Buddhism and spreading Buddhist education by setting up Buddhist schools.

A leading personality of the early phase of Buddhist resurgence was David Hewavitarne (1864–1933) who became known by his name in religion, Anagārika Dharmapāla. Born in a Buddhist family in Colombo, he was educated in an Anglican school at a time when higher education in Buddhist schools was not yet available, and there he was subjected to the disgusting combination of Christian missionary fanaticism, intolerance and disregard for the values dear to Buddhist tradition which was characteristic of many such institutions during the earlier phases of the colonial period. His deep aversion to all forms of 'Christian barbarism' was definitely formed by these experiences of his early youth. In 1880 Hewavitarne met Colonel Olcott during his visit to Colombo.

With Olcott he travelled to Japan in 1889, a visit which established the first relations in modern times between Buddhists of Japan and Sri Lanka. When Dharmapāla visited Bodh-Gayā in 1891, he witnessed the deplorable state into which the site most sacred to Buddhists had fallen, and he decided to work for its restoration. In the same year, Dharmapāla initiated the Budh-Gaya-Mahabodhi Society in Colombo; it was the first international Buddhist organization, and aimed to unite Buddhists of all countries and to make Bodh-Gayā a centre of Buddhist religious devotion again. In 1892, the Maha Bodhi Society, as it was generally known, moved its headquarters to Calcutta and the reconversion of Indians to Buddhism became one of its main concerns.

No less important as a force of Buddhist resurgence was the Young Men's Buddhist Association (YMBA), modelled on the Young Men's Christian Association. The YMBA was founded by C. S. Dissanayake, a convert from Roman Catholicism, in Colombo in 1898, and many branch associations were opened in the following years. The umbrella organization of all YMBA branches was later renamed the All-Ceylon Buddhist Congress and it became the country's leading Buddhist organization. The great importance of the YMBA in Burma (started in Rangoon in 1906) has already been mentioned in the chapter on Burma.

The beginnings of Western Buddhism

The last two decades of the 19th century saw interest in Buddhism as a religion spread to many countries where it had previously been only the subject of purely academic interest. Of course, a few independent thinkers had earlier recognized the validity of Buddhist thought. The German philosopher Arthur Schopenhauer (1788–1860) must here be given pride of place. For Schopenhauer, Buddhism is the best of all religions, because it is preferable to 'Brahmanism' with its caste system, and even more to Christianity with its fallacious ideas about god and its defective code of ethics which has no consideration of animals. Schopenhauer claims that his own philosophy agrees with the Buddha's teaching. Though Schopenhauer's knowledge of Buddhism was based on the rather incomplete and inaccurate source material available in the first half of the 19th century, the affinity between his philosophy and Buddhism is in many ways striking, and a close review of Schopenhauer's teachings reveals it as a kind of incomplete Buddhism. Schopenhauer's philosophy became popular during the latter part of the 19th century, and his high regard for Buddhism has definitely contributed towards the interest in it not only as a subject of study, but also as a way of thought and life with which one can identify.

In England, Sir Edwin Arnold (1832–1904) published his famous poem *The Light of Asia, or the Great Renunciation, being the Life and Teaching of Gautama, Prince of India and Founder of Buddhism, as told in verse by an Indian Buddhist* in 1879. Colonel H. S. Olcott's *Buddhist Catechism According to the Canon of the Southern Church* was first published in Colombo in 1881. Its first American edition appeared in Boston in 1885. Only three years later, the German Buddhist Friedrich Zimmermann, using the pseudonym Subhadra Bhikshu, wrote *A Buddhist Catechism: an Introduction to the Teaching of the Buddha Gotama* which was soon translated into ten other languages. It was the author's aim to present Buddhism in 'the spirit and essence of the true teaching of the Buddha, omitting all additions with which scholastic learning of later times has amplified the words of the Master, and superstition and the imagination of the people have encumbered them'. The understanding of Buddhism by these early Western Buddhists was based on the Pali Canon as handed down by Theravāda Buddhism.

The evaluation of the early Buddhist sources was immensely helped by the rapid progress of Buddhology as an academic subject in the last quarter of the 19th century. Detailed academic research based on original sources was begun by the French scholar Eugène Burnouf (1801–52), whose famous *Introduction à l'histoire du bouddhisme indien* appeared in 1845. Burnouf mainly worked with Sanskrit sources of Mahāyāna

Buddhism, and he also translated the *Saddharma-puṇḍarīka-sūtra* or *Lotus Sūtra* (1852). It was only with the systematic evaluation of the Pali sources that the historical Buddha and his teachings were presented to the Western reader in an authentic way. The two scholars who initiated this development were the Englishman Thomas Williams Rhys Davids (1843–1922) and the German Hermann Oldenberg (1854–1920). Rhys Davids' *Buddhism, Being a Sketch of the Life and Teachings of Gautama, the Buddha* (1877) and Oldenberg's *Buddha: Sein Leben, Seine Lehre, Seine Gemeinde* (1881) mark the beginning of modern Buddhist studies. Oldenberg, who also edited the complete Pali text of the *Vinaya Piṭaka* in five volumes (1879–83), succeeded in presenting a description of early Buddhism based on the sources which has remained valid as the classic treatment of this subject to the present day. Also in 1881, T. W. Rhys Davids founded the Pali Text Society for the publication and translation of the texts of the Pali Canon and the commentaries of the Theravāda school. In co-operation with scholars from many countries, this society succeeded in publishing critical editions of most of the canonical works during the first three decades of its existence. So far 154 volumes of editions of text, seventy-eight volumes of translations and a number of other publications have been issued by the Pali Text Society.

Practising Western Buddhists became both more numerous and more active *c.* 1900. The first European to enter the Sangha was the Englishman Allan Bennett McGregor (1872–1923). He had first been a follower of an occultist movement, but he severed those connections, travelled to Ceylon, and in 1902 was ordained in Akyab in Burma and received the ecclesiastical name of Ānanda Metteyya. Two years later, in Rangoon, the German violin virtuoso Anton Gueth (1878–1957) became the second European-born member of the Sangha; under his name as a monk, Nyanatiloka, he became world-famous as an authority on Buddhist learning and practice. He spent most of his life in Sri Lanka, where in 1911 he became the founding abbot of a monastery on the island Polgasduwa near Doḍanduwa. Many Europeans of several nations became members of the Sangha there, and Nyanatiloka's most famous disciple, Nyanaponika, is still active as a Buddhist scholar.

As early as 1897, Anagārika Dharmapāla founded the first Buddhist organization in the West, an American branch of the Maha Bodhi Society, when he visited the United States at the invitation of the American Buddhist Paul Carus. In 1903, the first Buddhist association in Germany, the Buddhistischer Missionsverein für Deutschland (Society for the Buddhist Mission in Germany), was initiated in Leipzig by the Pali scholar Dr Karl Seidenstücker. During the same year, the above-mentioned British *bhikkhu* Ānanda Metteyya formed 'an International Buddhist Society, to be known as the Buddhasasana Samagama' in Rangoon; it was to have branches in various countries. The first British Buddhist association was the Buddhist Society of Great Britain and Ireland. It was initiated in London in 1907, with T. W. Rhys Davids as its first president, and it existed until 1926. Most Buddhist associations which were started in Western countries during this early period were rather short-lived, and co-operation between the various regional Buddhist groups had yet to be developed.

One of the leaders of the Buddhist revival was the Sinhalese Anagārika Dharmapāla. Born in 1864 and educated in an Anglican school in Colombo (which gave him a lasting distaste for Christianity) he dedicated himself to the Buddhist cause. In 1891 he visited the site of the Buddha's Enlightenment in Bodh-Gayā which was under the control of Hindus at that time. In order to achieve its restoration to the Buddhists, he founded the Mahābodhi Society which was the first international Buddhist association.

Buddhist modernism

As can be seen from the foregoing remarks, there was a close interrelation between Buddhist resurgence in the East and the early phases of the spread of Buddhism in the West. This interrelation was not only organizational; essentially it concerned trends towards reinterpretation of Buddhism as a system of thought. We may refer to these trends as 'Buddhist modernism'.

Buddhism as it existed in Asia in the early 19th century consisted of a multitude of different forms of religious thought and practice in which Buddhism had combined with various forms of traditional cosmology etc. Now, under the influence of the general aims and methods of 19th-century scholarship, the earliest sources were evaluated as a means to discover the Buddha's original teachings. Scholars and modern Buddhists rediscovered 'original' Buddhism as a system of philosophical thought with the sole aim of showing a way to salvation from suffering and rebirth. Traditional cosmology, the belief in miracles, and other elements which were unacceptable to a modern thinker were now identified as inessential accretions or modifications of Buddhism accumulated during its long historical development.

In this way, Buddhism was understood as a rational way of thought, and it was particularly stressed that the Buddha did not demand belief in his teachings, but invited people to find out by way of reason and to test by religious practice and meditation that it was the truth. Therefore, modernists describe Buddhism as 'the religion of reason' as opposed to the religions of blind belief in dogmas like Christianity, Islam or Judaism. The ideas about god and soul propagated by the Western religious traditions are criticized as incompatible both with reason and with a realistic view of the world.

I shall mention here only three names out of a large number of writers on Buddhist modernism. Anagārika Dharmapāla was also famous as an author whose critical essays were reprinted in 1965 under the title *Return to Righteousness*. The Japanese scholar Hajime Nakamura, the author of *Ways of Thinking of Eastern Peoples* (Honolulu 1964), became world-famous as the leading interpreter of Buddhist thought for our times. The philosopher K. N. Jayatilleke (1920–1970) of Peradeniya University in Sri Lanka has contributed the most consistent interpretation of early Buddhism as a philosophy in relation to contemporary philosophical thought.

Buddhist modernism is by no means a uniform movement. Naturally, in most forms of Buddhist resurgence, some elements of traditionalism lived on. In addition, Buddhist modernism in the countries of south Asia, particularly Ceylon and Burma, was linked to political and social issues from the very beginning. Social reform became one of the aims of modern Buddhists there, and the reassertion of Buddhism as the national religion, restoring it to its 'due place' in state and society, was demanded in the early writings of Anagārika Dharmapāla and other Asian Buddhist leaders. They described how the colonial administration had tried to destroy Buddhism, and their efforts for the revival of Buddhism were closely related to their participation in the struggle to regain national independence for their countries.

In the case of Sri Lanka, 'Buddhist nationalism' has a very long history. The special connection between the Buddhist religion and the Sinhalese people was emphasized in the ancient chronicles of the island, particularly in the *Mahāvaṃsa*, which embodies the so-called 'Duṭṭhagāmaṇī epic', the story of the liberation of the island from foreign (Tamil) domination by King Duṭṭhagāmaṇī during the 2nd century BC. The chronicle stresses the particular role of the Sinhalese people as the custodians of the religion of the Buddha, and the Sangha was understood to have the function of upholding the tradition of this 'religio-nationalism' as a part of the cultural heritage of the Sinhalese.

In Burma, the degree of identification of Burmese with Buddhist interests was no less than in Ceylon, as has been discussed above in the chapter on Burma. In both countries, many differences arose between the supporters of modernism and the defenders of traditionalist views, and these differences are also reflected in the political controversies that arose from the attempts to reform the Sangha by legislation.

Notwithstanding these problems, the Buddhist Sangha continues to play a leading role in nation-building in Sri Lanka as well as in Southeast Asia. Through the centuries, the *bhikkhus* served the needs of community relations at all levels, particularly at that of the village. The relation between monastic community and village population remains the focus of the structure of village life in Buddhist countries. For the newly emerging urban and semi-urban population of the late colonial and the post-colonial period, Buddhism has become a symbol of national identity during the struggle against foreign political and cultural domination. An idealistic image of life in the pre-colonial Buddhist kingdoms was depicted by the writers of Buddhist modernism, and these writings were widely read by the new middle class. Their growing self-confidence finds visible expression in new forms of Buddhist symbolism, for example the erection of large Buddha images at cross-roads, hills and other prominent places. This new symbolism has been termed 'the Buddha in the market place' by Gananath Obeyesekere.

Another important element of Buddhist modernism is the revival and popularization of meditation techniques. The practice of Buddhist meditation was handed down through the centuries without break. Traditionally, instructions for meditation were not given to the general Buddhist public, but only by a teacher to his carefully selected personal disciples. The number of monasteries where meditation was practised remained rather limited, and in Ceylon the old tradition of practising meditation had died out in the middle of the 19th century. In about 1890 Anagārika Dharmapāla discovered the manuscript of a handbook on meditation in the Sinhalese language in Bambaragala monastery; it was later published by the Pali Text Society as *The Yogāvachara's Manual* and translated as *The Manual of a Mystic*. Dharmapāla decided to renew the practice of meditation after studying this book. In Burma too, a Thera by the name of Nārada revived the practice of *satipaṭṭhāna* ('awareness of mindfulness') meditation at about the same period after studying ancient texts, and he became the founder of the still existing 'Burmese School' of *satipaṭṭhāna* meditation. The famous Mahasi Sayadaw (see chapter on Burma, p. 154) follows this tradition. In this rather unorthodox way, these and other new meditation traditions have been started by modern Buddhists. They have also been spread in a way unknown in earlier times: meditation centres have been opened, where Buddhist lay followers can attend meditation classes and be instructed in practices hitherto reserved for specially selected and initiated monks.

In the course of the growth of Buddhist modernism,

this new tendency has not remained restricted to these newly founded schools of meditation; a number of meditation teachers who have been initiated in unbroken ancient traditions have also instructed lay Buddhists. Whereas the earliest phase of modernist Buddhism was still dominated by intellectual and philosophical interests, the practice of several forms of meditation has become a leading feature in almost all the more recent developments of modern Buddhism. That is why teachers and centres of meditation will be mentioned again and again in the following pages, in which I discuss the Buddhist revival in a few countries selected to serve as paradigms.

Without these intellectual and spiritual achievements of Buddhist modernism, neither the Buddhist revival in the East not the spread of Buddhism in the West would have been possible. By the extension and modernization of monastic schools in the Buddhist countries, large parts of the Sangha came under the influence of the ideals of Buddhist modernism and, for their part, also contributed to the spread of these ideals amongst the general public in these countries.

The revival of Buddhism in India

When India became partitioned and independent in 1947, few Buddhists lived in the sub-continent. There was a Buddhist minority of about 300,000 in the districts of Chittagong and Chittagong Hill Tracts, the south-eastern parts of East Bengal which had now become East Pakistan. These Bengali Buddhists were Theravādin, and they had succeeded in carrying out a reform of their Sangha after 1856. In 1887 they had formed the Chittagong Buddhist Association which was the earliest Buddhist society of a modern type to be formed in the sub-continent. Some Tibetan Buddhists lived in Ladakh, Sikkim and in other areas near the Tibetan border. From 1892 on, the Maha Bodhi Society attracted the intellectual interest of some educated Indians, but very few of them actually converted to Buddhism.

The reintroduction of Buddhism into India as a mass movement had different roots. It was the work of Dr Bhimrao Ramji Ambedkar (1891–1956) who was born in Ambavade in Maharashtra as the fourteenth child of a family belonging to the Mahar caste. The Mahars are one of the lowest social groups, being considered 'untouchable' and traditionally restricted to cleaning and maintaining streets or cremation grounds and similar occupations. Ambedkar's family followed the Hindu reformist movement of the Kabir Panth. By a coincidence of fortunate circumstances, he was able to receive a high school and college education, and, with a scholarship offered by the Maharaja Sayajirao Gaekwad of Baroda, he studied at Columbia University in New York, where he received his Ph.D. in 1916. After further studies in England and his return to India, he practised law and began to work for the emancipation of the Untouchables.

Dr Bhimrao Ramji Ambedkar is the dominant figure of resurgent Buddhism in India. He was born, in 1891, into a family belonging to the Mahar caste which was one of the many groups of 'Untouchables', and he spent all of his life fighting for the human rights of the repressed castes in India. In 1950 Dr Ambedkar formally embraced Buddhism. In October 1956 he and his numerous followers were officially converted, but he died less than two months later.

As early as 1930, many of the Untouchables considered Ambedkar as their spokesman and their political as well as spiritual leader. His views were opposed to those of Mahatma Gandhi. Gandhi considered the caste system of Hindu India a beneficial institution which ought to be reformed to get rid of abuses like untouchability, but should not be abolished. For him, the integration of the 'Harijans' (men of god) as he called the Untouchables would be possible without a complete break-down of the Hindu social system by granting them the status of a fifth caste within this system. Ambedkar, on the other hand, had come to the insight that the Hindu caste system as such remains the root of the evils presently inherent in Indian society, because 'the outcaste is a necessary by-product of the caste system', and therefore he believed that 'nothing can emancipate the outcaste except the destruction of the caste system'.

In 1936 Ambedkar formed the Independent Labour Party, and in 1947 he was appointed Minister of Law of the first government of independent India. As the chairman of the Constitution Drafting Committee, he was the author of large parts of the Indian constitution, and hence he is often called 'the Father of the Indian Constitution'. However, his attempt to bring about a thorough reform of Indian civil law met with strong opposition, and in 1951 he withdrew from the government.

Ambedkar's contribution to the new social order of India remains remarkable though he could not implement all of his ideas. The Untouchables or 'Scheduled Castes', as they are now officially called, were given equal rights in all public institutions, and, until their full integration into society could be achieved, a number of privileges was granted to them in the field of education, in the distribution of posts in government service etc.

According to the beliefs of his Indian followers, Ambedkar's role in the renewal of Buddhism was predetermined from the day of his birth. Legend has already grown around the events of his early youth, but it seems that his intellectual interest in Buddhism dated back at least as far as 1927. In 1935 Ambedkar publicly declared that he would convert to another religion, and religious leaders of all major creeds courted Ambedkar in the hope of winning over the Untouchables with him, but it was only in 1950 that he made his allegiance to Buddhism known. Buddhism is preferable to all other religions because it is based on wisdom and understanding, not on superstition and supernaturalism, because the concepts of love, equality and spiritual freedom are essential parts of its message and therefore the inequalities inherent in the caste system find no place in it, and it is also part of the great cultural heritage of India so that it is nearer to the people than any Western religion could be.

Ambedkar now called upon the Untouchables to accept it. On 14 October 1956, the symbolic 'consecration' (*dīkṣā*) of Ambedkar and his followers took place in Nagpur, and with this event India's 'New Buddhism' became a strong force in Indian sociopolitical life. It was very unfortunate that Ambedkar died soon thereafter, on 6 December 1956, without leaving behind an equally charismatic leader to follow in his steps. Ambedkar is revered by his followers as a bodhisattva and as the fourth refuge besides the Buddha, the Dhamma and the Sangha.

There have been mass conversions of members of the Scheduled Castes to Buddhism in Madhya Pradesh, Maharashtra, Uttar Pradesh, Panjab and in some areas of Kashmir, Tamilnadu and Karnataka. However, there are also considerable problems for India's new Buddhists arising from the want of trained teachers of religion and from the need to build up a structure of Buddhist education and to develop new conventions and forms of social and communal life within a short period. Another problem is created by the fact that with conversion to Buddhism the former Untouchables also give up most of their privileges, because Indian courts have decided that caste is an institution of Hinduism so that a convert to another religion loses rights derived from his belonging to one of the Scheduled Castes.

Ambedkar's Buddhism is essentially a philosophy of ethical and social reform, aiming to achieve moral reconstruction in this world. Dharma is nothing else than this principle of morality, and Nirvāṇa is understood as the final establishment of the moral order. This moral order must be created within each of us as an individual and within society as a whole, and it can only be attained by non-violent means, never by force. Ambedkar fully accepted Buddhist soteriology as handed down in the tradition of the Pali Canon, but he emphasized the social aspects of the message of Buddhism, because it was particularly this emphasis which was needed by his people on their road towards emancipation.

Resurgence of Buddhism in Indonesia

Buddhism was introduced into Indonesia in the course of what scholars call the Hinduization of Southeast Asia and it existed side by side with Hinduism in Sumatra and Java as early as the first half of the 5th century. Several forms of Hīnayāna and Mahāyāna were encountered by Chinese pilgrims, and many monuments and inscriptions attest to Buddhism's importance there over a long period. Later, Mantrayāna or Vajrayāna of a particular Indonesian form became predominant, and Borobudur, the largest Buddhist monument of Southeast Asia, bears testimony to Buddhism's vitality and creativity as the source of inspiration of some of the greatest artists of all time. Of the literature of early Indonesian Buddhism only a limited number of works survive. Among these is the *Sang hyang Kamahāyānikan* in Sanskrit and Old Javanese, which is one of the main sources for an understanding of mediaeval Javanese Tantric Buddhism.

During the centuries preceding the advent of Islam on the islands, Buddhism and Śaivism merged in a peculiar form of syncretism which scholars have termed Śiva-Buddhism. It is characterized by the doctrine of the identity of Śiva and Buddha. In this religion, which has survived on the islands of Bali and Lombok to the present day, the Hindu elements of the tradition are so much stronger than the survivals of Buddhism that it is now officially termed a 'Hindu religion' (*agama Hindu*) of Indonesia. Although the Buddhist element became integrated into a system which is dominated by Hindu tradition, it is by no means negligible, and the 'Buddha priest' must still be present at the great rituals and there recite holy incantations of the Buddhist tradition.

In the 15th century Islam began to spread into Indonesia, and by the beginning of the 17th century the whole of Sumatra and Java (with only the exception of the rather small region of the Tengger around Mount Bromo) had been converted. However, the tradition of *kebatinan*, Javanese mysticism, gave Indonesian Islam its particular character, and Hindu tradition survived beside Islam in the shadow-plays as well as in Javanese mysticism. The concept of 'emptiness' (*śūnyatā*) which stands for the absolute in Mahāyāna and Tantric Buddhism, also deeply influenced the way in which god was described as *kesunyataan* – a word derived from *śūnyatā* – by the Islamic mystics of Java.

Buddhism as a separate religion has reappeared in Indonesia only during the last few decades. One of the roots of this new development was the religion of Chinese immigrants, which originally consisted mainly of syncretistic practices combining Confucian, Buddhist and Taoist elements. In educated Chinese circles, Theosophy became known, giving an impetus towards the study of Buddhist sources.

The revival of Buddhism as a distinct religion was largely achieved by the charismatic personality of Jinarakkhita Thera, whose lay name is The Boan An. Born in Bogor, he studied physics at Groningen (Netherlands), but in 1953 he entered the Sāsana

Yeiktha, a well-known monastery and meditation centre in Rangoon, studied *satipaṭṭhāna* meditation under the aforementioned Mahasi Sayadaw and was ordained as a *bhikkhu* there. After his return to Java in 1955, he successfully worked for the establishment of Buddhist monasteries and places of worship, and Buddhist associations were founded in many parts of the country. The Buddha Jayanti celebrations of 1956 gave a great impetus to the spread of Buddhism. Several Buddhist missions from Thailand and Sri Lanka visited the country to teach the local Buddhists and in 1970 a Buddhist mission headed by Phra Sāsana Sobhana of Wat Bovoranives in Bangkok was instrumental in ordaining Indonesian *bhikkhus* so that an autonomous Sangha in Indonesia could come into existence.

Indonesian Buddhists encountered some problems over the question of Buddhist 'atheism'. The controversy arose when the English version of Helmuth von Glasenapp's book *Buddhism, a non-theistic religion* (written in 1954, English version published in 1970) became known, because 'belief in god' (*maha esa*) is one of the fundamental principles of *pancasila*, formulated on 29 May 1945 as part of the fundamental laws of the Republic of Indonesia. If Buddhism was 'atheistic' in the strict sense of the word, its recognition as a religion under Indonesian law would have been jeopardized. The two solutions to this question found by Indonesian Buddhists led to a division within their ranks. The minority group reinterpreted Nirvāṇa as being *maha esa*; as scriptural justification for this interpretation they quoted the famous passage in the *Udāna* (VIII.3): 'Verily, there exists an Unborn, Unoriginated, Uncreated, Unformed. If there were not this Unborn, Unoriginated, Uncreated, Unformed, escape from the world of the born, the originated, the created, the formed, would not be possible.' Here, Nirvāṇa is the 'transcendent' in Buddhism, corresponding to the concept of god in other religions.

But the majority of the Indonesian Buddhists who had joined the original Theravāda groups preferred a different answer and thereby reaffirmed the character of Buddhism as a religion of indigenous Indonesian tradition. They created a new combination of Theravāda and of ancient Javanese Buddhism by claiming that the concept of the *Ādibuddha* ('Primeval-Buddha') can be derived from ancient Javanese traditions and is the Buddhist concept of God. Under the leadership of Jinarakkhita Thera, this group organized itself as *Majelis Upasaka Pandita Agama Buddha Indonesia* (abbreviated to *Muabi*) also called *Majelis Agung Agama Buddha Indonesia*. It is also called *Buddhayana*, emphasizing its universal character comprising Theravāda, Mahāyāna and Javanese Vajrayāna traditions. The study of the *Sang hyang Kamahāyānikan* was revived along with that of the Pali scriptures and the main texts of Mahāyāna. In this way, the syncretistic tendencies which are so characteristic of Javanese tradition have again made their impact on Javanese Buddhism, and many followers of Javanese mystic movements as well as Chinese Buddhists can identify with the *Buddhayana* movement. In 1977 a *Buddhayana* monastery was opened in Holland in The Hague.

Another group of Indonesians went one step further in the reassertion of ancient Javanese traditions. They are the followers of *Kasogatan*, headed by Pandita Dharmaduta Kasogatan Giriputra Soemarsono. The aim of *Kasogatan* (named after *kasaugatan*, the title of the Buddhist head priest of pre-Islamic East Java) is the revival of the indigenous Javanese Buddhism which existed before the arrival of Islam and found expression in the gigantic structure of Borobudur. Mystic prophecies about a revival of the old religion in our times, which are believed to have been revealed by the Javanese Buddhist saint Sabdopalon almost five hundred years ago, have also contributed to the spread of Buddhist revivalism.

Chinese Buddhists have organized a Mahāyāna Sangha and lay community in Indonesia, and the followers of the traditional syncretism of the 'three religions' (Buddhism, Confucianism, Taoism) have organized themselves in the Tridharma Association. The Buddhist element in this syncretism has been effectively strengthened as has the tendency to Indonesianization of the religion. A small group of followers of the cult of the future Buddha Maitreya and the Indonesian branch of *Sōkagakkai* which has organized itself as the Nichiren Shoshu of Indonesia must also be mentioned.

Several earlier attempts to create a federation of the various Buddhist groups in Indonesia had no lasting success, but in 1978 all the seven denominations of Indonesian Buddhism described above joined together to co-operate in the *Perwalian Umat Buddha Indonesia* or All-Indonesian Federation of Buddhist Organizations.

Buddhism in Germany

One of the most remarkable personalities of the early history of German Buddhism was Karl Eugen Neumann (1865–1915). His interest in the Dharma was aroused, like that of many other German Buddhists, by reading Schopenhauer's works. After studying Sanskrit and Pali he received a Ph.D. from Leipzig University in 1890, and in 1894 he travelled to Ceylon and India. During the following years Neumann translated large parts of the Pali Canon into German. The solemn style of his translations is considered to be particularly suitable for these texts. His translations were widely read by the educated public in Germany and they have contributed immensely to the spread of knowledge about Buddhism.

In the German Buddhist movement, a kind of schism arose as a consequence of different interpretations of the Buddhist doctrine of *anātman* ('No-Self'). The leading personalities of the two schools were Paul Dahlke (1865–1928) and Georg Grimm (1868–1945). Dahlke, who had come into contact with Buddhism during a journey to Ceylon in 1900, termed his interpretation of Buddhism 'Neo-Buddhism'. His ways of thinking were very close indeed to those of other Buddhist modernists, but he retained the essence of original Buddhism as found in the sources, and, in his understanding of the Buddha's teaching about the non-existence of the Self (*ātman*), he followed orthodox Theravāda tradition as handed down through the centuries.

Grimm, on the other hand, believed that tradition had completely misunderstood the Buddha's words in this respect. In Grimm's opinion, the Buddha never denied the eternal existence of a transcendent soul, and the Buddhist doctrine of 'No-Self' had to be understood quite otherwise than it had previously been understood: everything which we can describe or recognize is not the Self, but the Self exists beyond the sphere of intellectual comprehension. Since Grimm claimed thus to have rediscovered the original teachings of the Buddha which had been lost in later Buddhist tradition, he coined the term 'Old Buddhism' (in the sense of 'original Buddhism') for the particular form of Buddhism which he propagated. His book *The Doctrine of the Buddha, the Religion of Reason* (first German edition 1915) was translated into several languages and became one of the most widely read works on Buddhism. The centre of the Old Buddhism movement and the headquarters of the association founded by Grimm in 1921 remains in Utting near Munich, where he lived for many years.

Grimm's interpretation was, however, rejected by the majority of German Buddhists as well as by Nyanatiloka and most of the other German Buddhist monks living in Ceylon. Old Buddhism then established itself as something like a Buddhist sect denying the validity of the other Buddhist traditions. For a long time, the other groups did not establish a centralized association, but only a number of regional societies. In 1955 the German Buddhist Society was founded as a union of several smaller Buddhist groups. In 1958 it was renamed the German Buddhist Union, and now all Buddhist groups in Germany, including the community of Old Buddhism, have joined in this union.

In 1924 Paul Dahlke built the 'Buddhist House' in Berlin-Frohnau; it consists of the essential parts of a Buddhist monastic complex. After Dahlke's death it was used for other purposes but in 1957 it was taken over by the German Dhammaduta Society, and since 1958 it has regularly housed *bhikkhus* from Sri Lanka. A Buddhist meditation centre was established in Roseburg near Hamburg in 1961, and courses on *satipaṭṭhāna* meditation are regularly given there.

Though the followers of Theravāda still remain the largest among the German Buddhist communities, other schools of Buddhist thought have also spread. The Arya Maitreya Mandala was founded by Lama Anagārika Govinda (E. L. Hoffmann) who was initiated in the 'Brug-pa branch of the bKa'-rgyud-pa school of Tibetan Buddhism (see above, chapter 9, p. 261) in 1947, but considers himself a follower of the Ris-med movement (see above, p. 270). The Arya Maitreya Mandala is organized as a 'laymen's order', and all members are initiated by particular rituals based on certain traditions of Vajrayāna Buddhism. Some smaller groups of followers of other forms of Mahāyāna including Zen and Jōdo Shinshū have also been formed recently in Germany.

Buddhism in Great Britain

Buddhist activities in Great Britain can look back on an unbroken tradition of 75 years since the foundation of the Buddhist Society in 1907. Progress was slow at first, but in 1909 the first issue of the *Buddhist Review* was published in London. The first Buddhist mission from an Asian country to England arrived in 1908. It came from Burma and consisted of the above-mentioned British-born *bhikkhu* Ananda Metteyya and three Burmese Buddhists. In 1925 Anagārika Dharmapāla visited London and his presence gave a great impetus to the British Buddhists. They were also supported by a number of young Ceylonese Buddhists who studied in England.

As was the case with Buddhism in Germany, the impact of Theravāda and the orientation towards modernistic interpretation were very strong during the first decades of British Buddhism. However, the Buddhist movement in England had deep roots in the Theosophic movement too, and this was particularly the case with the second Buddhist society, which succeeded the original association. This was the Buddhist Centre of the Theosophical Society, which was organized as the Buddhist Lodge of the Theosophical Society in 1924. It absorbed the earlier Buddhist Society of 1907 in 1926 and was later transformed into the Buddhist Society which still exists today, with 25 affiliated groups. 1926 also saw the foundation of the British Maha Bodhi Society during the presence of Anagārika Dharmapāla in England. Ever since those years, British Buddhists have received many missions from all Buddhist countries and played a leading role in the promotion of international co-operation between Buddhists. In 1928 a *vihāra* was opened in Hampstead. It was founded by Anagārika Dharmapāla and existed until 1939.

Buddhists in Great Britain have long been more open-minded than their German counterparts in their attitude towards different forms of Buddhism. Christmas Humphreys, the founder-president and the historian of the Buddhist Society, describes most English Buddhists as 'frankly eclectic, choosing and using those principles found to be most helpful in their search for enlightenment' (*Sixty Years of Buddhism in England*, p. 80). In this way, Theravāda as well as Tibetan, Japanese and Chinese Buddhism have had their place within British Buddhism without causing serious conflicts. 'Why should there not be in time a Western Buddhism, a Nava-yana or "new vehicle" as Captain Ellam called it, not deliberately formed as such but a natural growth from the same roots of Buddhism as all

'Buddhism in England' was first published in 1926, the year in which Anakārika Dharmapāla visited England and the present Buddhist Society was founded. The lotus on its cover, designed by Aileen M. Faulkner (later Mrs Christmas Humphreys), was adopted as the Society's seal. At the bottom are the 'sacred syllables' of the mantra AUM (or OṂ) MAṆI PADME HUM (see p. 244).

others, that is, the record of the Buddha's Enlightenment?' asks Humphreys, and he answers the question in this way: 'There is no reason why it should not grow happily alongside, and even blend with the best of Western science, psychology and social science, and thus affect the ever-changing field of Western thought. It will not be Theravāda or Zen, Prajñāpāramitā intuitive philosophy or Tibetan ritual. Just what it will be we do not know, nor does it matter at the present time. The Dhamma as such is immortal, but its forms must ever change to serve the ever-changing human need.' (Ibid.)

Most Buddhist organizations in England describe themselves as 'non-sectarian' and accept adherents of all schools of Buddhism. Some groups (for example the Aberdeen Buddhist Group) use the term 'eclectic' to describe their orientation. This non-denominational orientation is also a characteristic of the Hampstead Buddhist Vihara in London which was opened in 1962. The two other *vihāras* in London are Theravāda institutions: the monastery in Chiswick which houses Sinhalese monks and the Buddhapadipa Vihara in East Sheen inhabited by *bhikkhus* from Thailand. A monastery and meditation centre for Tibetan monks, Samyeling, exists in Dumfries in Western Scotland. It was founded in 1967 by Chögyam Trungpa who later established the Vajradhatu and Nalanda Foundation in the United States (see below).

Buddhism in the United States

The history and situation of Buddhism in the United States of America differs in several respects from what we observe in Europe. The earliest phase of American Buddhism was characterized by its introduction by East Asian immigrants during the later decades of the 19th century. Some Buddhist immigrants from both China and Japan came to the United States and to Hawaii (which was formally annexed by the U.S. only in 1898) before 1868, but it was only after that date that their number grew considerably so that they became a significant factor in American life. In Hawaii it was particularly difficult to assimilate these immigrants into the local population, as the organizers of the immigration had hoped when they brought them into the country as a cheap labour force. In particular, very few of them were ready to convert to Christianity. The Chinese brought with them ancestor worship and the cult of Chinese popular deities as well as Chinese forms of Buddhism. In the earlier period, however, their temples, including some temples of Kuan-yin, the popular female form of Avalokiteśvara, had no institutional affiliations, and most of them were community centres where sycretistic cults rather than Buddhist traditions in the strict sense were cultivated.

Organized East Asian Buddhism entered Hawaii in 1889 when the young Japanese priest Sōryū Kagahi of the Honpa (or Nishi) Hongwanji (West School of the Original Vow of Amida Buddha) Branch of Jōdo Shinshū (True Pure Land School) arrived in Honolulu. He had received the blessings of Myōnyo Shonin (1850–1903), the Monshu (Lord Abbot) or spiritual leader of the Honpa Hongwanji in Kyoto, for his mission. This branch of Jōdo Shinshū grew into what was for long the largest denomination of Hawaiian and American Buddhism, and it has always retained its original character as consisting mostly of Americans of Japanese descent. In April 1889 the first Japanese Buddhist temple on the Hawaiian islands was opened. Kagahi soon returned to Japan to enlist more support for his mission, but his advocating a kind of Buddhist-Christian syncretism met with the strongest objections from the Japanese religious authorities so that he could not accomplish his intended second mission to Hawaii.

In the following years, only two Japanese Buddhist priests of the same denomination, Dōrin Nishizawa and Gyōya Gama, officiated on the islands. The formal establishment of a 'Buddhist Church' in Hawaii was achieved in 1899, and Yemyō Imamura was then

The United States has been a fertile ground for the propagation of Buddhism, largely inspired by China and Japan. This building in New York was built as a Buddhist centre; its stained glass windows incorporate traditional symbolism.

appointed the first 'Bishop of the Honpa Hongwanji Mission of Hawaii'. In 1900 he organized a Young Men's Buddhist Association in Honolulu. Almost at the same time, missions of Jōdoshū (Pure Land School) and of the Sōtō branch of Zen Buddhism also became active amongst the ethnic Japanese living on the islands, and they succeeded in establishing several temples.

The Jōdo Shinshū, and in particular the Honpa Hongwanji mission, played an equally important role amongst Japanese-Americans on the continent, because their Japanese ancestors had largely belonged to this religious group. This denomination is estimated to have formed more than eighty per cent of Japanese-American Buddhists during the early years of our century. The followers of this tradition formed the North American Buddhist Mission in 1899 with its headquarters in San Francisco. Until 1944 it remained an overseas branch of the Japanese Honpa Hongwanji 'sect' under the organizational control of the headquarters in Kyoto. With the Second World War, the establishment of an autonomous structure became necessary, and the influence of the Japanese parent organization was greatly reduced. In 1944 it was reorganized as the Buddhist Churches of America, or, more exactly, the Buddhist Churches of Jōdo Shinshū. A step forward in the emancipation of American Jōdo Shinshū Buddhism was the foundation of American institutions for the training of new priests; first, soon after the end of the war, the American Buddhist Academy in New York, then in 1966 the Institute of Buddhist Studies at Berkeley. The higher levels of theological training are, however, still available only in Japan. The estimated total membership of the Buddhist Churches of America was 43,500 in 1972, and it employs about eighty priests under the leadership of a 'bishop' (*socho*) of the Church.

The Japanese-American Buddhists experienced considerable difficulty in handing on their cultural heritage to the younger generation; to arrest the decline of Buddhism, they organized so-called Buddhist 'Sunday schools' (later on often called 'Dharma schools'), as well as Buddhist women's societies, orphanages and other social institutions. This adoption of Western techniques of religious propaganda was, however, not invented by the Buddhists of America. It had already started in Japan during the years of Buddhist resurgence after 1876 when the suppression of Buddhism in the first years of the Meiji era was replaced by a policy of religious tolerance. It seems that these modern forms of religious propaganda were introduced into America from there, and early observers described the American Buddhist Sunday schools as a rather faithful copy of the Jōdo Shinshū Sunday schools in Japan.

Apart from these 'Buddhist Churches' there are many other Buddhist groups and organizations in the United States, and some of them have a rather long history. American Buddhists have never attempted to create a forum to formulate their common interests or even systematically to develop mutual contacts, still less to form a common organization. Thus American Buddhism has always been characterized by an extraordinary degree of individualism, pluralism and decentralization. The *List of Buddhist Institutions* issued by the World Fellowship of Buddhists lists fifty-eight separate Buddhist organizations in the United States, the largest number it gives for any country. American sources tell of several hundred Buddhist groups and circles in the United States. Practically all existing forms of Buddhism are represented, and it is impossible to give an adequate account of even the more important of them in a short survey. Apart from the Jōdo Shinshū and Jōdoshū traditions, there are all other important forms of Japanese Buddhism as well: Zen Buddhism of the Sōtō and Rinzai Schools, Shingon School, and recently the so-called 'Lotus Sects'. Also present are the main traditions of Tibetan Buddhism, which attract growing numbers of young people who are fascinated by its mysticism, symbolism and ritualism as well as by its insights into depth psychology. Theravāda flourishes, not only as an intellectual movement, but also through the practice of meditation as taught by masters from Thailand. Finally, new eclectic and syncretistic forms of Buddhism are emerging, which aspire to unite the various traditions into what some term the 'One Vehicle' or *Ekayāna*. Buddhism has for long ceased to be the religion only of certain ethnic groups like Japanese-Americans and Sino-Americans: Americans of Caucasian descent and other races are found in practically all Buddhist denominations. As a consequence of the weak organizational structure of most Buddhist groups, exact figures for the number of Buddhists in the United States are not available. Estimates range from 300,000 to more than 500,000, but approximately 400,000 seems to the present author to be a realistic estimate. The number of registered Buddhist places of worship was fifty-five in 1961, and it is estimated at more than three hundred now.

The World's Parliament of Religions which was held in Chicago on the occasion of the Chicago World's Fair of 1893 has probably had greater importance for the early development of American Buddhism than any other single event, though Theosophy had earlier drawn the attention of some Americans to Buddhist tenets. On that occasion, two Buddhists delivered speeches: Anagārika Dharmapāla and Sōen Shaku, a master of the Rinzai school of Zen. Paul Carus (1852–1919), the owner of the Open Court Publishing Company in LaSalle, and later on author of the famous book *Kalyāṇo Dhammo, the Gospel of Buddha* (1894), was so impressed by what he learnt there about Buddhism that he decided to patronize the spread of knowledge about it, particularly Zen. He invited Daisetzu T. Suzuki (1870–1966), a disciple of Sōen Shaku, to work for his publishing house. D. T. Suzuki, through his numerous works on Zen and on Mahāyāna, which have been translated into many languages, has probably done more than any other person to bring knowledge about Zen to the West and particularly to the United States.

Zen has played a great role in American Buddhism since that time; several Zen masters came over from Japan and educated American disciples. There was a period when a kind of degenerate Zen called 'Beat Zen' became fashionable in the 'counterculture' of the protest movement of the 1960s and 1970s, and there were also popularized variations (or, at least partially, misrepresentations) of Zen, like that propagated by Alan Watts ('Square Zen'), but true Zen Buddhism can be found now in several centres. Amongst these is the impressive San Francisco Zen Center which was opened in 1961 by the Japanese Zen master Shunryu Suzuki (1904–71). It belongs to the Sōtō school of Zen, and its present head is the American-born 'master' (*rōshi*) Richard Baker. Another famous Zen institution in the United States is the Shasta Abbey in northern California. Its tradition is also based on that of the Sōtō Zen school, and it was founded by the British-born Peggy Teresa Nancy Kennett who had been a follower of Theravāda when young, but was ordained as a *bhikṣuṇī* of the Chinese Sangha in Malacca, Malaysia, in 1962. Later she became the first woman for several centuries to be admitted into the Sōjiji Temple, one of the main training centres of Sōtō Zen in Japan, and in 1963 she was given the rank of abbess. In 1969 she moved to the United States to become the founder-abbess of the Shasta Abbey.

The Sino-American Buddhist Association in San Francisco was founded by the *tri-piṭaka* master Hsüan Hua in 1968. Hsüan Hua had come over from Hongkong in 1962 at the invitation of his American disciples. The headquarters of the association has been in the Golden Mountain Dhyāna Monastery since 1971. The Sino-American Buddhist Association is characterized by emphasis on strict discipline and full application of the *vinaya* rules in its monastic institutions. The study of Chinese Buddhist traditional texts is strongly encouraged, and a Buddhist Text Translation Society has been set up in order to translate the sacred texts with explanations by the master Hsüan Hua.

Tibetan Buddhism is present in the United States in several forms. Before 1959 very few Tibetan lamas had lived in the United States. After the suppression of Tibetan Buddhism by the Chinese Communists which began in 1959, a considerable number of Tibetan refugees moved on from Nepal and India to the United States, and a number of refugee communities and monasteries were established. Most of these centres have taken up the task of teaching the Tibetan form of Buddhism to interested Americans. The lamas belong to all major schools of Tibetan Buddhism, and mainly represent the traditions of rNying-ma-pa, the Karma-pa branch of the bKa'-rgyud-pa, Sa-skya-pa and dGe-lugs-pa.

Two Tibetan spiritual leaders have shown themselves to be charismatic personalities, and have been particularly active both in the establishment of meditation centres attracting many young Americans and in the writing of a large number of books which are widely read by Americans interested in Buddhism. These are the Chögyam Trungpa (full Tibetan name: Chos-kyi rgya-mtsho drung-pa) Rinpoche of the Karmapa branch of the bKa'-rgyud-pa tradition, and the Tar-thang Tulku (Dar-thang sprul-sku) Rinpoche, who before 1959 was the abbot of a large rNying-ma-pa monastery in Tibet.

Chögyam Trungpa, who has described his youth in his autobiography *Born in Tibet*, escaped from Tibet to India in 1959, and later proceeded to England where he established the Samye-ling Meditation Centre. He gave up the monk's robe in 1969 after a serious car accident, and then moved to the United States to the 'Tail of the Tiger' or Karme Chöling Meditation Center near Barnet, Vermont, which had been started by some of his students. Soon after, he founded the Karma Dzong in Boulder, Colorado, and within a few years the Vajradhatu and Nalanda Foundation had extended to comprise a number of other meditation centres, a Naropa Institute for learned Buddhist studies and many affiliated groups. Chögyam Trungpa has also been exceptionally productive as a writer. His interpretation of Buddhism largely concentrates on the basic tenets of the Dharma, but he explains them in his own ways, often using uncommon translations of the Buddhist terms and thereby changing some of the original meanings and concepts. Here, transposition of traditional ideas into a new cultural setting and using a new kind of language seems to pave the way for new trends of thought – a development which will be a fascinating subject for further studies.

The other charismatic personality within Tibetan-American Buddhism, Tarthang Tulku, also fled from Tibet in 1959, and he was selected by the Dalai Lama as a teacher of the rNying-ma-pa tradition at the Institute of Higher Tibetan Studies at the Sanskrit University in Varanasi in 1962. He too gave up the monk's robes before he came to America in 1968, where he established the Nyingma Meditation Center in Berkeley, the Nyingma Institute for academic studies, Dharma Publishing for the publication of Buddhist literature and the Tibetan Relief Foundation to help Tibetan refugees in India. The form of Buddhism taught in the Nyingma Center is firmly based on the traditions of the rNying-ma-pa school, and it is presented and practised in a way that allows Americans to combine its study and practice with daily professional life. The learning of Tibetan and Sanskrit is encouraged, to open the way for a proper understanding of the sources, and the Nyingma Institute has succeeded in gaining high recognition for its achievement in the field of learned Buddhist studies.

There are various groups of Theravāda Buddhists; monasteries with Sinhalese, Thai and American *bhikkhus* professing this tradition exist in the United States as well as a number of *satipaṭṭhāna* meditation centres. Finally, a few words must be said about the so-called 'Lotus Sects' which have recently spread to America from their Japanese home-country. The *Reiyukai* or Spiritual Friendship Society, started in 1919 on the basis of Nichiren Buddhism and characterized by its engagement with society as well as by its spirit of tolerance, has found a few followers in the United States. The Sōka-gakkai, however, which is known for its rather aggressive methods of mission, has exploded into a mass movement in America within a few years. It is called Nichiren Shoshu of America and has its separate national organization headed by George Williams whose original Japanese name was Masayasu Sadanaga. Beginning with a small number of followers in about 1960, Nichiren Shoshu of America had a membership of nearly 200,000 in 1970, and in the next decade it must have increased to more than 250,000.

The international Buddhist movement

The aim of bringing together Buddhists from all countries and from all denominations for the renewal of their religion has been formulated by Buddhist reformers since the beginnings of the revival movement in about 1880. The first international Buddhist organization was the Maha Bodhi Society (founded by Anagārika Dharmapāla in 1891; see above, p. 274). In the same year, Colonel Olcott convened the first International Buddhist Conference with participants representing Ceylon, Burma, China, Japan and Buddhists of the Chittagong Hill Tracts (in East Bengal). The conference was held in Adyar, a suburb of Madras (where the Indian headquarters of the Theosophical Society was installed), and it formulated 'Fourteen Fundamental Buddhist Beliefs' as a common platform which would be acceptable to all schools of Buddhism.

Since then there have been several attempts to bring about closer co-operation between the various forms of Buddhism. It may suffice to mention the Japanese efforts which led to the establishment of the International Buddhist Young Men's Association in Tokyo in 1903, the General Conferences of the Pan-Pacific Young Buddhist Associations in Hawaii and in Japan since 1930, and the first European Buddhist Congress in London in 1934, which was followed by a second European congress in Paris in 1937.

Political developments and the war interrupted progress towards international Buddhist co-operation. It was only in 1950 that Buddhists succeeded in forming a world-wide union, the World Fellowship of Buddhists (WFB). Preparations for the Buddhist World Conference which was held in Colombo in 1950 were made by the All-Ceylon Buddhist Congress, and the architect of success was the world-famous Sinhalese Buddhist scholar Dr G. P. Malalasekera (1899–1973) who was also elected the first president of WFB. This organization has held regular conferences ever since (1956 in Kathmandu, 1958 in Bangkok, 1961 in Phnom Penh etc.), and it has served effectively as a forum for nearly every country in the world to discuss, co-ordinate, express and spread Buddhist view-points. Apart from being a common platform for the promotion of Buddhism, Buddhists have understood the mission of their international organization as a contribution towards a solution of the problems of the world today. Let me quote from the 'keynote address' delivered by one of the greatest Buddhist scholars of the world, Professor Hajime Nakamura, to the 12th General Conference of the WFB in Tokyo on 1 October 1978:

> There is no doubt that from now on, all the nations on earth will interact and influence one another more intensely. Precisely because of this state of affairs, mankind is now confronted with the crisis as to whether it will survive or perish. The teaching of Buddhism which has been transmitted through various countries should reveal the path which mankind is obliged to follow. We Buddhists are obliged to reflect upon ourselves from the point of view of this task and put it into practice so that we are able to expect a brighter future.

In 1980 a party of Japanese Buddhist monks came to Britain and at Milton Keynes in Buckinghamshire built this memorial, the Peace Pagoda, as a symbol of universal harmony. It deliberately combines elements belonging to various cultures, from India to Japan, with lions recalling those of Aśoka.

In the last decades, many additional international Buddhist undertakings and institutions have been successfully initiated. As examples, the World Buddhist Sangha Council and the *Encyclopedia of Buddhism* may be mentioned here. The World Buddhist Sangha Council was established in Colombo in 1966 as an international organization of Buddhist monks and nuns. Its aim is defined as the effort to 'unite all Buddhist monks in the world today, both Theravada and Mahayana, as one solid organization in spite of superficial minor differences and in order to develop their ethical, intellectual and spiritual standards and adapt themselves to changing social and economical conditions in the modern world'. The World Buddhist Sangha Council also feels the obligation to oppose war and to contribute towards achieving world peace 'by spreading the Buddha's message of compassion and wisdom against violence and materialist thinking devoid of moral values'. Compilation of the *Encyclopedia of Buddhism* began in 1956 as an international academic venture to 'give a comprehensive account of the origins of this World-Religion and of the developments that have taken place during a period of more than 25 centuries of its history'. In Japan, another encyclopaedic dictionary of Buddhism is being compiled under the title *Hōbōgirin*. It is mainly based on Chinese and Japanese sources. Since 1976, scholars of all countries who are engaged in research on Buddhism have been co-operating in the International Association of Buddhist Studies.

Glossary

by Richard Gombrich

Technical and foreign terms are explained where they first occur in the text. This glossary includes only those which recur. Most proper names are not to be found here; they are included in the index. Words in inverted commas at the beginning of an entry represent a literal translation of the term.

Abbreviations: B = Burmese; C = Chinese; J = Japanese; P = Pali; S = Sanskrit; Si = Sinhalese; T = Tibetan.

abhidhamma (P) see *abhidharma.*
Theravādin *abhidhamma* occupies its own section of the Pali Canon, the *Abhidhamma Piṭaka*. It consists largely of schematizations of material presented more discursively in earlier texts.

abhidharma (S)
Buddhist systematic philosophy.

abhiṣeka (S)
'consecration', a high grade of tantric initiation. The term is taken from the consecration of a king.

āgama (S)
'[religious] tradition', a term used especially in tantra; the *āgama* house in a Newari Buddhist *vihāra* contains the shrine of esoteric tantric deities.

Aggregates see *skandha.*

anagārika (S and P)
'homeless'. Originally an epithet of a Buddhist monk, the term was borrowed by David Hewavitarne to create a new religious status – a layman who has dedicated his life to Buddhism.

anātman (S)
'no self', lacking any soul or enduring essence. It is a cardinal doctrine of Buddhism that this is one of the three fundamental characteristics of all phenomenal existence – the other two are *duḥkha* and impermanence.

anatta (P) see *anātman.*

arahat (P) see *arhat.*

arhat (S)
Enlightened person, sometimes referred to by Westerners as 'a Buddhist saint'.

ātman (S)
'self', an entity to which Buddhism denies ultimate reality.

avadāna (S)
exploits of Buddhist saints; a genre of literature describing such exploits.

avatāra (S)
'descent', the manifestation on earth of a Buddha or other transcendent being.

bakufu (J)
the military government which dominated Japan 1185–1868.

bandya (S) = *vandya*
'honourable', a term for a Newari *śākya-bhikṣu.*

bhāvanā (S and P)
'development'. Buddhist meditation.

bhikkhu (P) see *bhikṣu.*

bhikkhunī (P) see *bhikṣuṇī.*

bhikṣu (S)
Buddhist monk.

bhikṣuṇī (S)
Buddhist nun.

bKa'-gdams-pa (T)
'Those Bound by Command', a Tibetan monastic school founded in the 11th century by 'Brom-ston, later transformed into the dGe-lugs-pa.

bKa'-rgyud-pa (T)
'Followers of the Transmitted Command', a group of Tibetan monastic schools tracing their origin back through Mar-pa (11th century) to the Buddha Vajradhara.

bla-ma (T) see *lama.*

bō (Si) see *bodhi.*
'Bo tree' = 'Bodhi tree', the tree under which the Buddha achieved Enlightenment, or a tree (theoretically) descended from that tree.

bodhi (S and P)
Enlightenment.

bodhisatta (P) see *bodhisattva.*

bodhisattva (S)
future Buddha, one who has taken a vow to become a Buddha. Gautama Buddha too was a *bodhisattva* until he attained Enlightenment.

bodhisattvayāna (S)
'vehicle/career of the bodhisattvas'. Term for Mahāyāna.

bon-po (T)
priest in a pre-Buddhist Tibetan religion which is long obsolete. Distinguished typographically in this book from Bon-po, a monastic religion which distinguishes itself from Buddhism but appears to outsiders rather similar to rNying-ma-pa.

'Brug-pa (T)
a Tibetan monastic school in the bKa'-rgyud-pa tradition, founded *c.*1180 by Gling-chen-ras-pa and now dominant in Bhutan.

Buddha (S and P)
Enlightened. Especially used as a title for Gautama Buddha, the historical founder of Buddhism. According to Buddhists, however, Gautama is but one in an infinite series of Buddhas who rediscover and preach the Dharma. The Buddha is one of the Three Jewels of Buddhism.

Butsudō (J)
'the way of the Buddha', Buddhism.

caitya (S)
a term generally used as synonymous with *stūpa*, though strictly speaking the *caitya* is empty of relics.

cakra (S)
'wheel'. A common symbol for the Buddha's teaching. In tantric mystical physiology, a centre of nervous energy.

cakravartin (S)
Buddhist conception of a righteous world ruler.

caryā (S)
in Mahāyāna, a stage in the spiritual progress of a *bodhisattva.* In tantra, conduct adopted by a tantric to acquire powers or salvation.

caryāpada (S)
Genre of Buddhist tantric poetry composed in a late form of Prākrit.

cetiya (P) see *caitya.*

Ch'an (C)
from *dhyāna.* Name of a stream of Buddhism, originating in China, which rejects the scriptural tradition and preaches a sudden experience of Enlightenment as the culmination of meditation; known in Japan as 'Zen'.

chos (T) = Dharma.

dāgaba (Si)
'relic container', i.e. a stupa. In European languages often spelt dagoba.

daimoku (J)
the term referring to the Japanese title of the *Lotus Sutra* and its utterance, recommended by Nichiren (13th century) as the way to salvation.

Dalai Lama (T)
'Ocean [of wisdom?] Lama', title (in use since the late 16th century) of the head of the dGe-lugs-pa monastic school. The word Dalai is loaned from Mongolian.

dānaya (Si)
'generosity'; refers specifically to a monk's meal.

Dependent Origination see *pratītya-samutpāda.*

Dhamma (P) see Dharma.

dhāraṇī (S)
Buddhist spell which works by evoking and fixing the power of a Buddha, *bodhisattva* or high grade of realization.

Dharma (S)
in brahminism: the natural law of the universe, the way things are and should be. In Buddhism: the Law of the universe discovered and preached by the Buddha. One of the Three Jewels of Buddhism. The word can also have the quite different meaning (differentiated in this book by being spelled with a small d): any potential object of consciousness, 'thing'.

dhutaṅga (P)
ascetic practice which a monk may undertake (there are thirteen).

dhyāna (S)
Buddhist meditation exercises aimed at concentrating the mind; states achieved by those exercises.

dGe-lugs-pa (T)
'Followers of the Way of Virtue', the monastic school (often known as 'Yellow Hats') founded in 1409 by Tsong-kha-pa on the basis of the bKa'-gdams-pa.

Discipline see *vinaya.*

Doctrine see Dharma.

dohā (Prākrit)
a genre of mystical poetry in a metre of the same name.

duḥkha (S)
'suffering, unsatisfactoriness', the topic of the Four Noble Truths and one of the three fundamental characteristics of all phenomena.

dukkha (P) see *duḥkha.*

Eight Precepts
a set of vows of abstention traditionally taken by Buddhist laity on *uposatha* days, also taken for life by the pious women who in contemporary Theravādin societies are the functional equivalent of nuns.

Emptiness see *śūnyatā.*

Five Precepts
the Buddhist undertakings not to kill, steal, be unchaste, lie or take intoxicants.

Four Noble Truths
the doctrine expounded (after the Middle Way) in the Buddha's first sermon, viz. (1) life is suffering; (2) suffering has a cause; (3) suffering can be eliminated; (4) there is a path to that elimination.

Hīnayāna (S)
'the lesser vehicle/career', a Mahāyāna collective term for all older forms of Buddhism. Of those, only Theravāda now survives.

jātaka (S and P)
a genre of literature describing the former lives on earth of Gautama Buddha.

jhāna (P) see *dhyāna.*

jiriki (J)
'own power', the doctrine that salvation can come to man only by his own effort.

Jōdo (J)
'Pure Land', the western paradise of Amida Buddha, into which those who have faith in him are reborn.

Jōdo-shinshū (J)
'True Sect of the Pure Land', founded by Shinran in the early 13th century.

Jōdo-shū (J)
'Pure Land Sect', founded by Hōnen in 1198.

kaidan (J)
'commandment tribunal', Buddhist ordination hall.

kami (J)
indigenous (Shintō) deity, normally the personification of a natural phenomenon.

kamma (P) see *karman.*

kanjō (J) = *abhiṣeka.*

Kanjur (T)
'Translation of the Word of the Buddha', the Tibetan Canon, containing *vinaya* texts, Mahāyāna *sūtras* and *tantras.*

karman (S)
action; significant action. In brahminism: ritual action; in Buddhism: morally significant action, action with moral intention.

Karma-pa (T)
Tibetan monastic school in the bKa'-rgyud-pa tradition, founded *c.*1185 by Dus-gsum-mkhyen-pa and often known as 'Red Hats'.

kṣatriya (S)
the second in rank of the four Hindu social classes, the estate of nobles and warriors.

lama (T)
religious teacher. Scholarly orthography: *bla-ma.*

Lamaism
a Western term for the Tibetan form of Buddhism.

madhyamā pratipad (S)
the 'Middle Way' preached by the Buddha in his first sermon as the mean between indulging and mortifying the flesh.

madhyamaka, mādhyamika (S)
'centrist', the school of Mahāyāna philosophy which systematically seeks a middle way between assertion and denial.

Mahāyāna (S and P)
'the great vehicle/career', a vast movement in Buddhist doctrine, sentiment and practice which began in India shortly before the Christian era and embraces almost all schools and sects of later origin. It is now dominant in countries north and east of India and is therefore sometimes known as 'northern Buddhism'.

maṇḍala (S)
'circle', a cosmogram representing at the same time the macrocosm, peopled by Buddhas, deities, etc., and the microcosm of the practitioner's own psychology. An indispensable aid to tantric meditation.

mantra (S)
a formulaic religious utterance. In Buddhism the term is normally confined to tantra.

mantrayāna (S)
'spell vehicle/career', a term for tantric Buddhism.

merit see *puṇya.*

Meru (S and P)
in Hindu and Buddhist cosmology the great mountain at the centre of the earth, situated north of India.

Middle Way see *madhyamā pratipad.*

mudrā (S)
'seal', in tantra, the seal of approval of the deity with whom the practitioner is identifying, made visible in ritual gesture.

nairātmya (S)
'soullessness', the fact of *anātman.*

nat (B)
from S *nātha,* 'lord': Burmese god. There are thirty-seven national and many local ones.

nenbutsu (J)
'thinking of the Buddha [Amida]', the formula of faith in Amida ('Namu Amida Butsu'); its utterance.

nibbāna (P) see *Nirvāṇa.*

nikāya (S and P)
sect of the Sangha, a body of monks sharing an ordination tradition and in agreement on matters of Discipline. Also part of the name of five sections of the Pali Canon. In transcription from Thai the word is spelled *nikai.*

nirmāṇakāya (S)
'transformation body', the form of a Buddha created (according to Mahāyāna) for his appearance on earth.

Nirvāṇa (S)
'blowing out' the fires of greed, hate and delusion, which is tantamount to Enlightenment. While it is best to think of Nirvāṇa as a negatively defined state, Buddhist scholasticism came to define it as a 'thing' (*dharma*), the only thing which is unconditioned, not part of the causal chain. The physical death of an Enlightened being, also sometimes referred to as Nirvāṇa, is in this book called 'Final Nirvāṇa' or 'complete Nirvāṇa'.

rNying-ma-pa (T)
'Adherents of the Old [Tantras]', a Tibetan school of Buddhism

which is less monastic than the others and gives special veneration to Padmasambhava.

Order see Sangha.

pabbajjā (P) see *pravrajyā*.

pagoda
: a stupa. The term is used mainly when referring to countries east of India.

Pāli (S and P)
: originally 'text', i.e., a Buddhist scripture; now used as the name of an ancient language, derived from Sanskrit, in which has been preserved a complete recension of the basic scriptures, the Pāli Canon. This book treats the name of the language as an English word and spells it Pali.

paññā (P) see *prajñā*.
: In Theravāda the term refers primarily to the full apprehension of fundamental Buddhist doctrines such as the Four Noble Truths.

pāramitā (S)
: 'perfection' of a moral or mental quality. A bodhisattva develops such perfections on his path to Buddhahood.

parinirvāṇa (S)
: a term for the death of an Enlightened being, also called *nirupadhiśeṣa nirvāṇa* (S), in this book called 'Final Nirvāṇa' or 'complete Nirvāṇa'.

paritta (P) see *pirit*.

paṭicca-samuppāda (P) see *pratītya-samutpāda*.

pātimokkha (P) see *prātimokṣa*.

paṭipatti (P) see *pratipatti*.

pirit (Si)
: a collection of Buddhist texts believed to provide physical protection; the chanting of such texts.

poṣadha (S) see *uposatha*.

poya (Si) see *uposatha*.

prajñā (S)
: 'wisdom', gnosis, the insight which is tantamount to Enlightenment. The concept is much symbolized and personified, especially in tantra. The noun is feminine. In Mahāyāna the term often refers to the omniscience of Buddhas.

prajñā-pāramitā (S)
: 'perfection of wisdom'. Also the name of a class of Mahāyāna scriptures and of a goddess who personifies perfect wisdom.

Prākrit
: the group of ancient languages derived from Sanskrit, also called Middle Indo-Aryan. The term is sometimes used to include Pali, but in this book denotes only the other languages of the group.

prātimokṣa (S)
: the code of rules governing the life of the individual monk or nun. The list is arranged by the penalty set for infringement, in decreasing order of gravity. It is to be recited regularly (in theory every fortnight) by the assembled community after confessing transgressions against it. This and ordination are the most important communal acts of the Sangha.

pratipatti (S)
: 'practice' of the Buddha's way. This is the middle member of the ascending triad of learning (S: *paryāpti*), practice and realization (S: *prativedha*).

pratītya-samutpāda (S)
: 'Dependent Origination', the formula discovered by the Buddha which explains the chain of cause and effect which runs through the universe and conditions everything.

pravrajyā (S)
: 'going forth' from home, formal entry into the Buddhist Order as a novice. Also known as 'lower ordination' to distinguish it from *upasampad*. Originally however the two were the same.

puñña (P) see *puṇya*.

puṇya (S)
: merit, good *karman*; also sometimes used as a term for the results or potential results of good *karman*.

Rinzai (J)
: branch of Zen tracing its origin to the 9th-century Chinese master Lin-chi.

rōshi (J)
: advanced Zen master.

Śākya (S)
: the clan/tribe into which Gautama Buddha was born.

śākya-bhikṣu (S)
: a synonym of *bhikṣu* among the Newars, where however they are now no longer monks but constitute a hereditary class ranking second in the spiritual hierarchy.

Śākyamuni (S)
: 'the Śākyan sage', a title of Gautama Buddha.

sāmaṇera (P) see *śrāmaṇera*.

saṃsāra (S and P)
: the sequence of repeated births in the world. It has no beginning and can be ended only by Enlightenment.

Saṅgha (S and P)
: originally the community of all Buddhists: monks, nuns, laymen and laywomen; then – and now generally – the Order of ordained monks, nuns (where they exist) and novices. One of the Three Jewels of Buddhism, and the main topic of this book, in which for simplicity the word is spelled Sangha.

Sangharāja (P)
: 'King of the Order', a title used at various times in Theravāda countries for the monk heading the local Sangha.

sanmitsu-kaji (J)
: 'approaching the three mysteries', Shingon religious practice.

Sa-skya-pa (T)
: Tibetan monastic school founded in the 11th century by 'Brog-mi.

satipaṭṭhāna (P)
: 'establishing awareness', an ancient form of Buddhist meditation (based on the *Mahā Satipaṭṭhāna Sutta*, a text in the Pali Canon), re-popularized in the 20th century by Burmese masters.

satori (J) = *bodhi*.

sayadaw (B)
: 'teacher', a title given to senior monks in Burma.

Shingon (J)
: 'True Word', the Japanese Buddhist sect founded by Kūkai at the beginning of the 9th century as a continuation of the Chinese Zhen-yan sect.

Shintō (J)
: the systematized form of *kami* worship.

shōmyō (J)
: Buddhist chanting.

shū (J)
: sect in Japanese Buddhism.

siddha (S)
: tantric adept who has acquired magical powers.

sīmā (P)
: 'boundary'. Formally drawn around monastic territory.

skandha (S)
: the five groups of phenomena into which the Buddha analysed the flux we conventionally call a sentient being: body, feelings, perceptions, volitions and consciousness. This analysis is exhaustive and leaves no room for a soul. These are also called the impure (*sāsrava*) aggregates when they are contrasted with the five elements of holiness (*anāsrava skandha*).

smṛtyupasthāna (S) see *satipaṭṭhāna*.

Sōtō (J)
: branch of Zen brought to Japan by Dōgen *c.*1244.

śramaṇa (S)
: wandering ascetic, not necessarily Buddhist.

śrāmaṇera (S)
: Buddhist novice.

śrāvakayāna (S)
: 'disciples' vehicle/career', a Mahāyāna collective term for all older forms of Buddhism, synonymous with Hīnayāna.

Sthaviravāda (S) see Theravāda.

stūpa (S)
: monument, originally shaped like a stylized tumulus, commemorating the death of a Buddha or other Enlightened person and often containing relics. A small replica of a *stūpa* may be used as a reliquary. Used in this book as an English word and spelled stupa.

śūnyatā (S)
: 'emptiness' of a soul or abiding essence, synonymous with *nairātmya*. See *anātman*. In late Buddhism this 'emptiness' is sometimes hypostatized as the Absolute.

sūtra (S)
: Buddhist scripture, usually one dealing with doctrine.

sutta (P) see *sūtra*.
Svayambhū (S)
'Spontaneous', a manifestation of the Buddha, worshipped especially in Nepal.
tantra (S)
form of Buddhism, and of other religions indigenous to India, in which the means to both salvation and magical power is to link meditation with an elaborate ritual. The teachings are transmitted esoterically. In a religious context the word basically designates a type of scripture. The Sanskrit adjective is *tāntrika*, whence English tantric.
tariki (J)
'power of the other', the doctrine that man is powerless to save himself and can be saved only by e.g. Amida Buddha.
Tathāgata (S and P)
title of a Buddha (see p. 41).
tathatā (S)
'thusness', the way things really are (according to Buddhism), which language is inadequate to express.
Tendai (J)
school of Buddhism founded by Saichō in the early 9th century on the basis of Chinese T'ien-t'ai doctrine.
Tenjur (T)
'Translation of the Treatises', the Tibetan corpus of commentaries and non-canonical treatises.
Theravāda (P)
'the Doctrine of the Elders', the form of Buddhism based on the Pāli Canon. It was preserved in Sri Lanka and spread from there to the Southeast Asian mainland, so it is sometimes known as 'southern Buddhism'. The only form of non-Mahāyāna Buddhism still extant.
Three Jewels
the Buddha, the Dharma and the Sangha, traditionally constitutive of Buddhism.
thudong (Thai) see *dhutaṅga*.
Thusness see *tathatā*.
Tipiṭaka (P) see Tripiṭaka.
Tripiṭaka (S)
'[comprised of] Three Baskets', name of the Buddhist Canon, the earliest scriptural corpus.
ubasoku (J) see *upāsaka*.
upāsaka (S and P)
Buddhist layman.
upāsikā (S and P)
Buddhist laywoman.
upasampad (S)
ordination as a Buddhist monk or nun, also called 'higher ordination' or 'full ordination'. It must follow the *pravrajyā* and the minimum age for it is 20.
upasampadā (P) see *upasampad*.
upāya (S and P)
'means', especially to bring to salvation. The concept is much symbolized and even personified in tantra. The noun is masculine.
uposatha (P)
the quarter-month day of the lunar calendar, a time of heightened Buddhist observance. The *uposatha* of the new and full moon are the more important ones; on them the monks are supposed to recite the *prātimokṣa*.
vajra (S)
'thunderbolt/diamond', symbol of the Emptiness of this world of appearances; symbol also of the Buddha's teaching of this truth.
vajrācārya (S)
'thunderbolt/diamond teacher', tantric master qualified to initiate others.
vajrayāna (S)
'thunderbolt/diamond vehicle/career', a term for tantric Buddhism.
vihāra (S and P)
Buddhist monastery or nunnery.
vijñāna-vāda (S)
'consciousness doctrine', a major school of Mahāyāna doctrine and philosophy, which stresses manipulation of one's consciousness as the means to Englightenment.
vinaya (S and P)
the Discipline, the Rule of the Buddhist Order; also the scripture containing that Rule.
wat (Thai) see *vihāra*.
yogācāra (S)
a term for *vijñāna-vāda*.
Zen (J) see Ch'an.
A major current of Japanese Buddhism (see p. 224).

Select Bibliography

by Heinz Bechert

GENERAL STUDIES AND REFERENCE WORKS

Some general surveys of the history of Buddhism: E. Conze, *A short history of Buddhism* (2nd ed.; London, 1981); id., *Buddhism, Its essence and development* (New York, 1951; repr. 1959); R. A. Gard, *Buddhism* (New York, 1961); H. Hackmann, *Buddhism as a religion, Its historical development and its present condition* (n.p., 1910; repr. 1981); C. Humphreys, *Buddhism* (4th ed.; Harmondsworth, 1955); R. H. Robinson, *The Buddhist religion, A historical introduction* (Belmont, Calif., 1970); Sangharakshita, *A survey of Buddhism* (3rd ed.; Bangalore, 1966); Secretariatus pro non-christianis (ed.), *A la rencontre du bouddhisme* [by E. Lamotte et al.], 2 vols. (Rome, 1970); H. W. Schumann, *Buddhism, An outline of its teachings and schools* (Wheaton, Ill., 1974); E. Zürcher, *Buddhism, Its origin and spread in words, maps and pictures* (London, 1962).

The following three works are mentioned here in their first editions on account of their outstanding importance in the history of Buddhist studies: E. Burnouf, *Introduction à l'histoire du bouddhisme indien* (Paris, 1844); T. W. Rhys Davids, *Buddhism* (London, 1877); H. Oldenberg, *Buddha, sein Leben, seine Lehre, seine Gemeinde* (Stuttgart, 1881; for an English translation see below).

Collections of essays: P. V. Bapat (ed.), *2500 Years of Buddhism* (2nd ed.; Delhi, 1964; repr. 1976); R. de Berval (ed.), *Présence du bouddhisme* (Saigon, 1956); A. K. Narain (ed.), *Studies in the history of Buddhism* (Delhi, 1980).

Encyclopaedias and dictionaries: P. Demiéville et al., *Hôbôgirin, dictionnaire encyclopédique du bouddhisme d'après les sources chinoises et japonaises* (Tokyo, 1929ff.; latest published part is fasc. 5, 1979); C. Humphreys, *Popular dictionary of Buddhism* (2nd ed.; London, 1976); T. O. Ling, *A dictionary of Buddhism* (New York, 1972); G. M. Malalasekera et al. (ed.), *Encyclopaedia of Buddhism*, vol. 1ff. (Colombo, 1961ff.; latest published part is vol. 4, fasc. 1, 1979); Nyanatiloka, *Buddhist dictionary* (3rd ed.; Colombo, 1972).

Bibliographies: F. E. Reynolds, *Guide to Buddhist religion* (Boston, 1981); R. Gard, 'Buddhism' in *A reader's guide to the great religions*, ed. C. Adams (New York, 1965), pp. 83–160; S. Hanayama, *Bibliography on Buddhism* (Tokyo, 1961); A. C. March, *A Buddhist bibliography* (London, 1935); C. Regamey, *Buddhistische Philosophie* (Bern, 1950).

Some other titles of general interest: H. von Glasenapp, *Buddhism, A non-theistic religion* (London, 1970); K. W. Morgan (ed.), *The path of the Buddha, Buddhism interpreted by Buddhists* (New York, 1956); D. Seckel, *Kunst des Buddhismus* (2nd ed.; Baden-Baden, 1964; repr. 1980); S. Tachibana, *The ethics of Buddhism* (new ed.; London, 1975); J. Takakusu, *The essentials of Buddhist philosophy* (3rd ed.; Honolulu, 1956; repr. 1975); Government of India (ed.), *The Way of the Buddha* (Delhi, *c.*1956); L. de La Vallée-Poussin, *Le dogme et la philosophie du bouddhisme* (Paris, 1930).

For want of space, it is not possible to list translations of original Buddhist texts in this bibliography. However, it should be mentioned that practically all the scriptures in Pali have been published in English translation by the Pali Text Society (London). In addition, many Buddhist Sanskrit texts and a fair number of canonical texts, as well as some non-canonical works, have been translated from Sanskrit, Chinese and Tibetan into English, French and German. Out of the rather large number of anthologies a few English works may be mentioned here: S. Beyer, *The Buddhist experience, Sources and interpretations* (Encino and Belmont, Calif., 1974); E. Conze, *Buddhist scriptures* (6th ed.; Harmondsworth, 1959; repr. 1971); id., *Buddhist texts through the ages* (New York, 1954); D. Goddard, *A Buddhist bible* (new ed.; Boston, 1970); Nyanatiloka, *The word of the Buddha, An outline of the teaching of the Buddha in the words of the Pali canon* (14th ed.; Kandy, 1967); Bukkyo Dendo Kyokai (ed.), *The Teaching of Buddha* (33rd ed.; Tokyo, 1977); H. C. Warren, *Buddhism in translations* (9th ed.; New York, 1977).

For a history of Buddhology see J. W. de Jong, *A brief history of Buddhist studies in Europe and America* (Varanasi, 1976).

ANCIENT BUDDHISM AND THE HISTORY OF BUDDHISM IN INDIA

The most comprehensive scholarly study of early Buddhism is provided by E. Lamotte, *Histoire du bouddhisme indien, des origines à l'ère śaka* (Louvain, 1958; repr. 1976).

Other important scholarly surveys of Buddhism in India: A. Bareau, 'Buddhismus' in *Die Religionen der Menschheit*, vol. 3 (Stuttgart, 1964), pp. 1–215; H. Nakamura, *Indian Buddhism, A survey with bibliographical notes* (Hirakata, 1980); A. K. Warder, *Indian Buddhism* (2nd ed.; Delhi, 1980).

Literature on 'original' and early Buddhism: E. Lamotte, *The spirit of ancient Buddhism* (Venice, 1961); id., *Le bouddhisme de Śākyamuni* (Göttingen, 1983); Narada, *A manual of Buddhism* (4th ed.; Colombo, 1953); H. Oldenberg, *Buddha, His life, His doctrine, His order* (London, 1882; repr. Delhi, 1971); W. Rahula, *What the Buddha taught* (2nd ed.; New York, 1974); C. A. F. Rhys Davids, *A manual of Buddhism for advanced students* (London, 1932; repr. 1978); H. Saddhatissa, *Buddhist ethics, Essence of Buddhism* (London, 1970); D. Schlingloff, *Die Religion des Buddhismus*, 2 vols. (Berlin, 1962); L. de La Vallée-Poussin, *The way to Nirvāṇa, Six lectures on ancient Buddhism as a discipline of salvation* (Cambridge, 1917).

On early Buddhist philosophy, psychology and the meaning of Nirvāṇa: E. Frauwallner, *History of Indian philosophy*, vol. 1 (Delhi, 1973); A. Govinda, *The psychological attitude of early Buddhist philosophy* (new ed., 2nd printing; London, 1970; repr. Delhi, 1975); I. B. Horner, *Early Buddhist theory of man perfected* (London, 1936; repr. 1975); K. N. Jayatilleke, *Early Buddhist theory of knowledge* (London, 1963); R. E. A. Johansson, *The psychology of Nirvana* (London, 1969); E. J. Thomas, *The history of Buddhist thought* (London, 1931; repr. 1971); G. R. Welbon, *The Buddhist Nirvāṇa and its western interpreters* (Chicago, 1968).

On early Buddhist meditation: Nyanaponika, *The heart of Buddhist meditation* (5th ed.; London, 1975); Vajirañāṇa, *Buddhist meditation in theory and practice* (2nd ed.; Kuala Lumpur, 1975; see also L. Schmithausen, 'Die vier Konzentrationen der Aufmerksamkeit' in *Zeitschrift für Missionswissenschaft und Religionswissenschaft*, vol. 60, 1976, pp. 241–66.

Life of the Buddha: A. Bareau, *Le Bouddha* (Paris, 1962); A. Foucher, *The life of the Buddha according to the ancient texts and monuments of India* (Middletown, Conn., 1963); Ñāṇamoli, *The life of the Buddha as it appears in the Pāli canon* (Kandy, 1972); J. Naudou, *Le Bouddha* (Paris, 1973); H. W. Schumann, *Der historische Buddha* (Cologne, 1982); E. J. Thomas, *The life of the Buddha as legend and history* (6th ed.; London, 1960; repr. 1975); E. Waldschmidt, *Die Legende vom Leben des Buddha* (Berlin, 1929; repr. Graz, 1982); id., *Die Überlieferung vom Lebensende des Buddha*, 2 vols. (Göttingen, 1944–8); K. D. P. Wickremasinghe, *The Biography of the Buddha* (Colombo, 1972).

On the date of the historical Buddha: H. Bechert, 'The date of the Buddha reconsidered' in *Indologica Taurinensia*, vol. 10, 1982, pp. 29–36.

Further studies of the various aspects of Buddhist thought and institutions in ancient and medieval India: A. Aiyappan and P. R. Srinivasan, *Story of Buddhism with special reference to South India* (Madras, 1960); D. K. Barua, *Viharas in ancient India, A survey of Buddhist monasteries* (Calcutta, 1969); id., *Buddha Gaya temple, Its history* (Bodh-Gayā, 1981); E. Conze, *Buddhist thought in India* (London, 1962); S. Dutt, *Buddhist monks and monasteries in India* (London, 1962); A. Ghosh, *Nālandā* (4th ed.; Delhi, 1959); L. M. Joshi, *Studies in the Buddhistic culture of India during the 7th and 8th centuries* (2nd ed.; Delhi, 1977); D. J. Kalupahana, *Buddhist philosophy, A historical analysis* (Honolulu, 1976); A. B. Keith, *Buddhist philosophy in India and Ceylon* (Oxford, 1923; repr. Varanasi, 1963); J. Naudou, *Buddhists of Kaśmir* (Delhi, 1980).

On Buddhist 'sects' or schools, 'councils', and the growth of early Buddhist literature: A. Bareau, *Les sectes bouddhiques du petit véhicule* (Saigon, 1955); id., *Les premiers conciles bouddhiques* (Paris, 1955); H. Bechert, 'The importance of Aśoka's so-called schism edict' in

Indological and Buddhist Studies, Volume in Honour of Prof. J. W. de Jong (Canberra, 1982) pp. 61–8; id. (ed.), *The language of the earliest Buddhist tradition* (Göttingen, 1980); E. Frauwallner, 'Die buddhistischen Konzile' in *Zeitschrift der Deutschen Morgenländischen Gesellschaft*, vol. 102, 1952, pp. 240–61; id., *The earliest Vinaya and the beginnings of Buddhist literature* (Rome, 1956).

Though largely outdated in contents, the following books are still widely used: N. Dutt, *Early history of the spread of Buddhism and the Buddhist schools* (new ed.; Delhi, 1980); id., *Buddhist sects in India* (2nd ed.; Delhi, 1978); S. Dutt, *Early Buddhist monachism* (new ed.; Delhi, 1960); H. Kern, *Manual of Indian Buddhism* (Strasbourg, 1896; repr. Delhi, 1974).

Though there are many learned studies of **Aśoka's inscriptions**, no up-to-date complete edition and translation of all of them is available. For an introduction and translation of most of them, see R. McKeon and N. A. Nikam, *The edicts of Asoka* (Chicago, 1966); cf. also E. Hultzsch, *The inscriptions of Asoka* (Oxford, 1925); J. Bloch, *Les inscriptions d'Asoka* (Paris, 1950).

Mahāyāna Buddhism and its history: H. Dayal, *The Bodhisattva doctrine in Buddhist Sanskrit literature* (London, 1932; repr. Delhi, 1975); N. Dutt, *Mahayana Buddhism* (new ed.; Calcutta, 1976); A. Getty, *The gods of northern Buddhism* (3rd ed.; Rutland, Vt., 1962; repr. 1977); E. Lamotte, *Der Verfasser des Upadeśa und seine Quellen* (Göttingen, 1973); id., 'Mañjuśrī' in *T'oung Pao*, vol. 48, 1960, pp. 1–96; W. M. McGovern, *Introduction to Mahayana Buddhism* (London, 1922; repr. Varanasi, 1968); T. R. V. Murti, *The central philosophy of Buddhism, A study of the Mādhyamika system* (London, 1955); R. H. Robinson, *Early Mādhyamika in India and China* (Madison, 1967; repr., Delhi, 1976); L. Schmithausen, *Der Nirvāṇa-Abschnitt in der Viniścayasaṃgrahaṇī der Yogacārabhūmiḥ* (Vienna, 1969); D. Seyfort Ruegg, *La théorie du tathāgatagarbha et du gotra, Étude sur la sotériologie et la gnoséologie du bouddhisme* (Paris, 1969); F. J. Streng, *Emptiness, A study in religious meaning* (Nashville, N.Y., 1967); D. T. Suzuki, *Studies in the Lankavatara Sutra* (London, 1930).

From the large number of **translations of Mahāyāna texts**, only the following examples need be quoted: E. Lamotte (transl.), *Le traité de la grande vertu de sagesse de Nāgārjuna, Mahāprajñāpāramitāśāstra*, 5 vols. (Louvain, 1944–80); id. (transl.), *Vimalakīrtinirdeśa, The teaching of Vimalakīrti* (London, 1976); D. T. Suzuki (transl.), *Lankavatarasutra* (London, 1932). For Prajñāpāramitā texts, see E. Conze, *The Prajñapāramitā literature* (2nd ed.; Tokyo, 1978).

On Buddhist tantras: B. Bhattacharyya, *Introduction to Buddhist esoterism* (2nd ed.; Varanasi, 1964); id., *The Indian Buddhist iconography* (2nd ed.; Calcutta, 1958; repr. 1968); S. B. Dasgupta, *An introduction to tantric Buddhism* (Calcutta, 1958; repr. Berkeley, 1974); A. Wayman, *The Buddhist tantras, Light on Indo-Tibetan esotericism* (New York, 1973).

Mythology: G. Grönbold, 'Die Mythologie des indischen Buddhismus' in *Wörterbuch der Mythologie*, ed. H. W. Haussig, vol. 1, pp. 287–508 (Stuttgart, n.d.).

Buddhist symbols: W. Kirfel, *Symbolik des Buddhismus* (Stuttgart, 1959).

Records of Chinese Buddhist pilgrims to India: S. Beal (transl.), *Su-yu-ki, Buddhist records of the western world* [by Hsüan-tsang], 2 vols. (Oxford, 1884; repr. Delhi, 1969); id. (transl.), *The life of Hsüan-tsang* [by Hui-li] (London, 1888); H. A. Giles (transl.), *The travels of Fa-hsien, or records of the Buddhist kingdoms* (3rd ed.; London, 1959); R. Grousset, *Sur les traces du Bouddha* (Paris, 1957); J. Takakusu (transl.), *A record of the Buddhist religion as practised in India and the Malay archipelago by I-tsing* (Oxford, 1896; repr. Delhi, 1966); T. Watters, *On Yuan Chwang's* [*i.e. Hsüan-tsang's*] *travels in India*, 2 vols. (London, 1904–05; repr. Delhi, 1961).

Some important primary sources in translation: Lama Chimpa and A. Chattopadhyaya (transl.), *Tāranātha's History of Buddhism in India* (Simla, 1970); E. Obermiller, *History of Buddhism in India by Bu-ston* (Heidelberg, 1931; repr. Tokyo, 1964); G. N. Roerich (ed. and transl.), *Biography of Dharmasvāmin* (Patna, 1959).

For want of space, literature on art and archaeology is not listed here. See, however, D. L. Snellgrove, *The image of the Buddha* (London, 1978), which has a relevant bibliography.

BUDDHISM IN AFGHANISTAN AND IN CENTRAL ASIA

F. R. Allchin and N. Hammond, *Archaeology of Afghanistan from the earliest times to the Timurid period* (London, 1978); P. C. Bagchi, *India and Central Asia* (Calcutta, 1955); M. Bussagli, *Central Asian Painting* (Geneva, 1963); J. A. Dabbs, *History of the discovery and exploration of Chinese Turkestan* (The Hague, 1963); R. E. Emmerick (ed. and transl.), *The Book of Zambasta, A Khotanese poem on Buddhism* (London, 1968); id., *A guide to the literature of Khotan* (Tokyo, 1979); G. Frumkin, 'Archaeology in Soviet Central Asia', in *Handbuch der Orientalistik*, vol. 7, part 3.1 (Leiden, 1970); G. Fussmann, 'Documents épigraphiques Kouchans' in *Bulletin de l'École Française d'Extrême-Orient*, vol. 61, 1974, pp. 1–77; id. and M. LeBerre, *Le monastère de Gul Dara* (Paris, 1976); A. v. Gabain, 'Buddhistische Türkenmission' in *Asiatica, Festschrift Friedrich Weller* (Leipzig, 1954), pp. 161–73; id., *Das Leben im uigurischen Königreich von Qočo*, 2 vols. (Wiesbaden, 1973); id., *Einführung in die Zentralasienkunde* (Darmstadt, 1979); S. Gaulier, R. Jera-Bezard and M. Maillard, *Buddhism in Afghanistan and Central Asia*, 2 vols. (Leiden, 1976); H. Härtel, *Turfan und Gandhara* (Berlin, 1957); A. v. LeCoq and E. Waldschmidt, *Die buddhistiche Spätantike in Mittelasien*, 7 vols. (Berlin 1922–33; repr. Graz, 1973–4); M. A. Stein, *Ancient Khotan*, 2 vols. (London, 1907); D. A. Utz, *A survey of Buddhist Sogdian studies* (Tokyo, 1978); E. Waldschmidt, *Gandhara, Kutscha, Turfan, Eine Einführung in die frühmittelalterliche Kunst Zentralasiens* (Leipzig, 1925).

BUDDHISM IN NEPAL

J. Brough, 'Nepalese Buddhist rituals' in *Bulletin of the School of Oriental and African Studies*, vol. 12, 1948, pp. 668–76; K. R. van Kooij, *Religion in Nepal* (Leiden, 1978); S. Lévi, *Le Népal*, 3 vols. (Paris, 1905–08); S. Lienhard, *Nevārigītamañjarī, Religious and secular poetry of the Nevars of the Kathmandu valley* (Stockholm, 1974); id., 'Problèmes du syncrétisme au Népal' in *Bulletin de l'École Française d'Extrême-Orient*, vol. 65, 1978, pp. 239–70; id., *Die Legende vom Prinzen Viśvantara, Eine nepalesische Bilderrolle* (Berlin, 1980); A. W. Macdonald and A. Vergati Stahl, *Newar art, Nepalese art during the Malla period* (Warminster, 1979); G. S. Nepali, *The Newars* (Bombay, 1965); L. Petech, *Mediaeval history of Nepal* (Rome, 1958); D. L. Snellgrove, *Buddhist Himalaya* (Oxford, 1957); id., 'Shrines and temples of Nepal' in *Arts asiatiques*, vol. 8, 1961, pp. 3–10 and 93–120; E. and R. L. Waldschmidt, *Nepal, Art treasures from the Himalayas* (London, 1969).

THERAVĀDA BUDDHISM

Translation of important sources: W. Geiger (transl.), *Mahāvaṃsa, The great chronicle of Ceylon* (London, 1934; repr. Colombo, 1960); id. (transl.), *Cūlavaṃsa, being the more recent part of the Mahāvaṃsa*, 2 vols. (London, 1929–30; repr. Colombo, 1953); Ñāṇamoli (transl.), *The Path of purification, Visuddhimagga by Buddhaghosa* (4th ed.; Kandy, 1979).

History of Theravāda, its teachings and development: H. Bechert, *Buddhismus, Staat und Gesellschaft in den Ländern des Theravāda-Buddhismus*, 3 vols. (Frankfurt, Wiesbaden, 1966–73); id., 'Theravāda Buddhist Sangha' in *Journal of Asian Studies*, vol. 29, 1970, pp. 761–78; id., 'Einige Fragen der Religionssoziologie und Struktur des südasiatischen Buddhismus' in *Internationales Jahrbuch für Religionssoziologie*, vol. 4, 1968, pp. 251–95; W. L. King, *In the hope of Nibbana, An essay on Theravada Buddhist ethics* (La Salle, Ill., 1964); id., *Theravada meditation, The Buddhist transformation of Yoga* (London, 1980); M. Nash (ed.), *Anthropological studies in Theravada Buddhism* (New Haven, 1966); B. L. Smith (ed.), *The two wheels of dhamma, Essays on the Theravada tradition in India and Ceylon* (Chambersburg, 1972) [with a bibliographical essay by F. Reynolds]; id. (ed.), *Tradition and change in Theravada Buddhism, Essays on Ceylon and Thailand in the 19th and 20th centuries* (Leiden, 1973).

Buddhism in Sri Lanka: E. W. Adikaram, *Early history of Buddhism in Ceylon* (Colombo, 1953); H. Bechert (ed.), *Buddhism in Ceylon and studies on religious syncretism in Buddhist countries* (Göttingen, 1978); id., 'Mythologie der singhalesischen Volksreligion' in *Wörterbuch der Mythologie*, ed. H. W. Haussig, vol. 1, pp. 511–656; id., 'Buddha-Feld und Verdienstübertragung: Mahāyāna-Ideen im Theravāda-Buddhismus Ceylons' in *Bulletin de la Classe des lettres et des sciences morales et politiques, Académie royale de Belgique*, vol. 62, 1976, pp. 27–51; id., 'On the identification of Buddhist schools in early Sri Lanka' in *Indology and law, Studies in honour of Prof. J. D. M. Derrett* (Wiesbaden, 1983), pp. 60–76; M. B. Carrithers, *The forest monks of Sri Lanka, An anthropological and historical study* (Delhi, 1983); H.-D. Evers, *Monks, priests and peasants, A study of Buddhism and social structure in central Ceylon* (Leiden, 1972); W. Geiger, *Culture of Ceylon in mediaeval times* (Wiesbaden, 1960); R. F. Gombrich, *Precept and practice, Traditional Buddhism in the rural highlands of Ceylon* (Oxford, 1971); R. A. L. H. Gunawardana, *Robe and plough, Monasticism and economic interest in early* *mediaeval Sri Lanka* (Tucson, 1979); K. Malalgoda, *Buddhism in Sinhalese society, 1750–1900* (Berkeley, 1976); N. Mudiyanse, *Mahayana monuments in Ceylon* (Colombo, 1967); W. Rahula, *History of Buddhism in Ceylon, The Anurādhapura period* (2nd ed.; Colombo, 1966); N. Ratnapala, *The Katikāvatas, Laws of the Buddhist order of Ceylon* (Munich, 1971); H. L. Seneviratne, *Rituals of the Kandyan state* (Cambridge, 1978); L. de Silva, *Buddhism, Beliefs and practice in Sri Lanka* (2nd ed.; Colombo, 1980); B. L. Smith (ed.), *Religion and legitimation of power in Sri Lanka* (Chambersburg, 1978).

Theravāda Buddhism in Southeast Asia: R. Lester, *Theravada Buddhism in Southeast Asia* (Ann Arbor, Mich., 1972); M. Sarkisyanz, 'Die Religionen Kambodschas, Birmas, Laos, Thailands und Malayas' in *Die Religionen Südostasiens* (Stuttgart, 1975), pp. 384–551; B. L. Smith (ed.), *Religion and legitimation of power in Thailand, Laos and Burma* (Chambersburg, 1978).

Buddhism in Burma: J. F. Ferguson (ed.), *Essays on Burma* (Leiden, 1981); Maung Htin Aung, *Folk elements in Burmese Buddhism* (London, 1962; repr. 1978); E. M. Mendelson, *Sangha and state in Burma* (Ithaca, N.Y., 1975); N. Ray, *Sanskrit Buddhism in Burma* (Amsterdam, 1936); id., *An introduction to the study of Theravada Buddhism in Burma* (Calcutta, 1946; repr. 1977); E. Sarkisyanz, *Buddhist backgrounds of the Burmese revolution* (The Hague, 1965); D. E. Smith, *Religion and politics in Burma* (Princeton, N.J., 1965); M. E. Spiro, *Burmese supernaturalism* (2nd ed.; Philadelphia, 1978); id., *Buddhism and society, A great tradition and its Burmese vicissitudes* (New York, 1970).

Buddhism in Thailand, Laos and Cambodia: C. Archaimbault, *Structures religieuses lao, Rites et mythes* (Vientiane, 1973); F. Bizot, *Le figurier à cinq branches, Recherches sur le bouddhisme khmer* (Paris, 1976); J. Bunnag, *Buddhist monk, Buddhist layman, A study of Buddhist monastic organization in Central Thailand* (Cambridge, 1973); Prince Damrong Rajanubhab, *Monuments of the Buddha in Siam* (2nd ed.; Bangkok, 1973); Prince Dhaninivat, *A history of Buddhism in Siam* (Bangkok, 1970); M. Giteau, *Le bornage rituel des temples bouddhiques au Cambodge* (Paris, 1969); A. B. Griswold, *Wat Pra Yün reconsidered* (Bangkok, 1975); R.-I. Heinze, *The role of the Sangha in modern Thailand* (Taipei, 1977); A. Leclère, *Le bouddhisme au Cambodge* (Paris, 1899; repr. 1975); J. A. N. Mulder, *Monks, merit and motivation, An explanatory study of the social functions of Buddhism in Thailand* (2nd ed.; De Kalb, Ill., 1973); A.-R. Peltier, *Introduction à la connaissance des hlvṅ ba¹ de Thailande* (Paris, 1977); H. G. Quaritch Wales, *Siamese state ceremonies, Their history and function* (London, 1931); T. H. Silcock, *A village ordination* (Lund, London, 1976); W. Skrobanek, *Buddhistische Politik in Thailand* (Wiesbaden, 1976); D. K. Swearer, *Wat Haripuñjaya, A study of the royal temple of the Buddha's relic, Lamphun, Thailand* (Missoula, Montana, 1976); S. J. Tambiah, *World conqueror and world renouncer, A study of Buddhism and polity in Thailand* (Cambridge, 1976); id., *Buddhism and the spirit cults in North-East Thailand* (Cambridge, 1970); id., 'The ideology of merit and the social correlates of Buddhism in a Thai village' in *Dialectic in practical religion*, ed. E. R. Leach (Cambridge, 1968), pp. 41–122; B. J. Terwiel, *Monks and magic, An analysis of religious ceremonies in central Thailand* (Lund, 1975); Prince Vajirañāṇavorasa, *Ordination procedure* (Bangkok, 1963); K. E. Wells, *Thai Buddhism, Its rites and activities* (3rd ed.; Bangkok, 1975); M. Zago, *Rites et cérémonies en milieu bouddhiste lao* (Rome, 1972).

BUDDHISM IN EAST ASIA

Some general works: P. Beautrix, *Bibliographie du bouddhisme Zen* (Brussels, 1969); R. H. Blyth et al. (ed.), *Japanese–English Buddhist dictionary* (Tokyo, 1965); S. Dutt, *Buddhism in East Asia* (New Delhi, 1966); R. K. Heinemann, *Der Weg des Übens im ostasiatischen Mahāyāna* (Wiesbaden, 1979); D. Seckel, *Buddhistische Kunst Ostasiens* (Stuttgart, 1957).

Buddhism in China: P. C. Bagchi, *India and China, A thousand years of cultural relations* (2nd ed.; Bombay, 1950); K. K. S. Ch'en, *Buddhism in China, A historical survey* (Princeton, N.J., 1964; repr. 1972); id., *The Chinese transformation of Buddhism* (Princeton, N.J., 1973); P. Demiéville, 'La pénétration du bouddhisme dans la tradition philosophique chinoise' in *Cahiers d'Histoire Mondiale*, vol. 3, pp. 19–38; Fung Yu-lan, *History of Chinese philosophy*, vol. 2 (Princeton, N.J., 1953); A. F. Wright, *Buddhism in Chinese history* (Stanford, 1959; repr. 1965); C. K. Yang, *Religion in Chinese society*, (Berkeley, 1961); E. Zürcher, *The Buddhist conquest of China*, 2 vols. (Leiden, 1959).

Early history of Chinese Buddhism: H. Maspéro, 'Des origines de la communauté bouddhiste de Loyang' in *Journal Asiatique*, 1934, pp. 87–107.

Record of Ennin's travels: E. O. Reischauer (transl.), *Ennin's diary, The record of a pilgrimage to China in search of the law* (New York, 1955); cf. also id., *Ennin's travels in T'ang China* (New York, 1955).

Interrelation of Buddhism, economy, state and politics in China: K. Ch'en, 'The economic background of the Hui-ch'ang suppression of Buddhism' in *Harvard Journal of Asiatic Studies*, vol. 19, 1956, pp. 67–105; W. Eichhorn, *Beitrag zur rechtlichen Stellung des Buddhismus und Taoismus im Sung-Staat* (Leiden, 1968); J. Gernet, *Les aspects économiques du bouddhisme* (Saigon, 1956); J. J. M. de Groot, *Sectarianism and religious persecution in China*, 2 vols. (Amsterdam, 1903–04); D. C. Twitchett, 'Monastic estates in T'ang China' in *Asia Major*, vol. 5, 1956, pp. 123–46; id., 'The monasteries and China's economy in mediaeval times' in *Bulletin of the School of Oriental and African Studies*, vol. 19, 1957, pp. 526–49.

On Chinese Amidism: H. Hackmann, *Laien-Buddhismus in China* (Gotha, 1924).

Ch'an Buddhism in China: C. Luk (Lu K'uan-Yü), *The secrets of Chinese meditation* (London, 1964); P. B. Yampolski (ed. and transl.), *The Platform Sūtra of the Sixth Patriarch* (New York, 1967).

Chinese Buddhism in the 19th and in the first half of the 20th century: Wing-tsit Chan, *Religious trends in modern China* (New York, 1953); J. J. M. de Groot, *Buddhist masses for the dead in Amoy* (Leiden, 1885); id., *Le code du Mahāyāna en Chine, Son influence sur la vie monacale et sur le monde laïque* (Amsterdam, 1893; repr. 1967); K. L. Reichelt, *Truth and tradition in Chinese Buddhism* (Shanghai, 1927); H. Welch, *The practice of Chinese Buddhism, 1900–1950* (Cambridge, Mass., 1967); id., *The Buddhist revival in China* (Cambridge, Mass., 1968); id., 'Dharma-scrolls and the succession of abbots in Chinese monasteries' in *T'oung Pao*, vol. 50, 1963, pp. 93–149.

Buddhism in the People's Republic of China: H. Welch, *Buddhism under Mao* (Cambridge, Mass., 1972); id., 'Buddhism since the Cultural Revolution' in *China Quarterly*, vol. 40, 1969, pp. 127–36.

Buddhist art and architecture in China: E. Boerschmann, *Die Baukunst und religiöse Kunst der Chinesen*, vol. 3: *Pagoden* (Berlin, 1931); D. LeRoy Davidson, *The Lotus Sūtra in Chinese art* (New Haven, 1954); W. Eberhard, 'Temple building activities in mediaeval and modern China' in *Monumenta Serica*, vol. 23, 1964, pp. 264–318; G. Ecke and P. Demiéville, *The twin pagodas of Zayton, A study of later Buddhist sculpture in China* (Cambridge, Mass., 1935); B. Gray, *Buddhist cave painting at Tunhuang* (London, 1959); S. Mizuno and T. Nagahiro (ed.), *Yünkang, The Buddhist cave-temples in the 5th century A.D. in North China*, 16 vols. (Kyōto, 1952); P. Pelliot, *Les grottes de Touen-houang, Peintures et sculptures bouddhiques des époques des Wei, des T'ang et des Song*, 6 vols. (Paris, 1914–24); J. Prip-Møller, *Chinese Buddhist monasteries* (Copenhagen, 1937); E. Rousselle, *Vom Sinn der buddhistischen Bildwerke in China* (Darmstadt, 1958); L. Sickman and A. Soper, *The art and architecture of China* (London, 1956); I. Vincent, *Sacred oasis* (Chicago, 1953).

Some additional titles: H. Maspéro, 'Le Taoïsme et les débuts du bouddhisme en Chine' in *Essay sur le Taoïsme, Mélanges posthumes*, vol. 2 (Paris, 1950), ch. III; R. Shih (transl.), *Biographies des moines éminents (Kao Seng Tchouan) de Hoei-kiao* (Louvain, 1968).

Buddhism in Japan: M. Anesaki, *History of Japanese religion* (Tokyo, 1963); S. Hanayama, *A history of Japanese Buddhism* (Tokyo, 1966); id., *A guide to Buddhism* (Yokohama, 1970); J. M. Kitagawa, *Religion in Japanese history* (New York, 1966); H. Nakamura, *History of the development of Japanese thought*, 2 vols. (Tokyo, 1969); E. Saunders, *Buddhism in Japan* (Philadelphia, 1964); D. T. Suzuki, *Japanese spirituality* (Tokyo, 1972); S. Watanabe, *Japanese Buddhism* (Tokyo, 1964).

Zen Buddhism: R. H. Blyth, *Zen and Zen classics*, 8 vols. (Tokyo, 1960); H. H. Coats and R. Ishizuka, *Hōnen, The Buddhist saint, His life and teaching* (Kyōto, 1949); E. Fromm, D. T. Suzuki and R. D. Martino, *Zen Buddhism and psychoanalysis* (New York, 1960); E. Herrigel, *Zen in the art of archery* (London, 1957); P. Kapleau, *The three pillars of Zen* (new ed., London, 1980); R. Masunaga (transl.), *A primer of Sōtō Zen* [by Dōgen] (Honolulu, 1971); K. Nishiyama and J. Stevens, *Shōbōgenzō by Dōgen Zenji* (Tokyo, 1977); S. Sekiguchi, *Zen, a manual for westerners* (Tokyo, 1970); B. L. Smith (ed.), *Unsui, a diary of Zen monastic life* (Honolulu, 1973); D. T. Suzuki, *Zen and Japanese culture* (New York, 1970); id., *Zen Buddhism* (New York, 1956); P. B. Yampolski, *The Zen master Hakuin* (New York, 1971); E. Wood, *Zen dictionary* (Tokyo, 1972).

'Pure Land' Buddhism: A. Bloom, *Shinran's gospel of pure grace* (Tucson, 1965); N. Kikukawa, *Shinran, His life and thought* (Los Angeles, 1972); K. Yamamoto, *An introduction to Shin Buddhism* (Yamaguchi, 1963).

Tendai school: B. Petzold, *Tendai Buddhism* (Yokohama, 1979).

Shingon school: Y. S. Hakeda, *Kūkai, Major works* (New York, 1972).

Shinto–Buddhist syncretism: R. Heinemann, 'Buddhistisch–schintoistischer Synkretismus' in *Buddhism in Ceylon and studies in religious syncretism in Buddhist countries*, ed. H. Bechert (Göttingen, 1978), pp. 199–213; A. Matsunaga, *The Buddhist philosophy of assimilation* (Tokyo, 1969).

Nichiren school: M. Anesaki, *Nichiren, the Buddhist prophet* (Gloucester, 1966); S. Murano (transl.), *Rissho Ankoku Ron, or Establish the right law and save our country* [by Nichiren] (Tokyo, 1977).

Contemporary developments: K. Takada, *The spirit of Buddhism today* (Tokyo, 1973); Y. Tamura, *Living Buddhism in Japan* (Tokyo, 1960); H. Thomsen, *The New religions of Japan* (Rutland, Vt., 1963).

Buddhist art in Japan: T. Sawa, *Art in Japanese esoteric Buddhism* (Tokyo, 1972); Y. Yashiro, *2000 Years of Japanese art* (New York, 1958).

Buddhism in Korea: Chun Shin-Yong (ed.), *Buddhist culture in Korea* (Seoul, 1974); C. A. Clark, *Religions of old Korea* (New York, 1932; repr. Seoul, 1982).

Buddhism in Vietnam: Thich Thien-An, *Buddhism and Zen in Vietnam in relation to the development of Buddhism in Asia* (Rutland, Vt., 1975).

TIBETAN BUDDHISM

C. Bell, *The religion of Tibet* (Oxford, 1931; repr. 1968); A. M. Blondeau, 'Les religions du Tibet' in *Histoire des religions*, ed. H. C. Puech, vol. 3 (Paris, 1976), pp. 233–329; H. Hoffmann, *The religions of Tibet* (London, 1961; repr. 1979); P. Kvaerne, 'Aspects of the origins of the Buddhist tradition in Tibet' in *Numen* 19, 1972, pp. 22–40; M. Lalou, *Les religions du Tibet* (Paris, 1957); G. Schulemann, *Geschichte der Dalai-Lamas* (2nd ed., Leipzig, 1958); D. L. Snellgrove and H. E. Richardson, *A cultural history of Tibet* (London, 1968; repr. 1980); R. A. Stein, *Tibetan civilisation* (London, 1972); G. Tucci, *The religions of Tibet* (London, 1980); L. A. Waddell, *Buddhism and Lamaism of Tibet* (London, 1895; repr. 1974).

On schools or 'sects', councils and religious masters: A. Chattopadhyaya, *Atīśa and Tibet, Life and works of Dīpaṃkara Śrījñāna* (Calcutta, 1967); P. Demiéville, *Le concile de Lhasa* (Paris, 1952); W. Y. Evans-Wentz, *Tibet's great yogi Milarepa* (London, 1928; repr. 1963); R. Kaschewsky, *Das Leben des lamaistischen Heiligen Tsongkhapa Blo-bzaṅ-grags-pa (1357–1419)*, 2 vols. (Wiesbaden, 1971); L. P. Lhalungpa (transl.), *The Life of Milarepa* (New York, 1977); D. L. Snellgrove, *Four Lamas of Dolpo*, vol. 1 (Oxford, 1967); R. A. Stein, *Vie et chants de 'Brug-pa-kun-legs le yogin* (Paris, 1972).

Ritual and meditation: S. Beyer, *The cult of Tara, Magic and ritual in Tibet* (Berkeley, 1973); R. B. Ekvall, *Religious observances in Tibet, Patterns and functions* (Chicago, 1964); G. Tucci, *The theory and practice of the mandala* (4th ed., New York, 1974).

Interpretation of Buddhism by the present Dalai Lama: Tenzin Gyatsho, the 14th Dalai Lama, *The opening of the wisdom-eye and the history of the advancement of Buddhadharma in Tibet* (Bangkok, 1968).

Art, iconography and symbols: L. S. Dagyab, *Tibetan religious art*, 2 vols. (Wiesbaden, 1977); H. Hoffmann, *Symbolik der tibetischen Religionen und des Schamanismus* (Stuttgart, 1967); D. I. Lauf, *Tibetan sacred art, The heritage of Tantra* (Boulder, Col., 1976); G. Tucci, *Tibetan painted scrolls*, 3 vols. (Rome, 1949; repr. Kyōto, 1980).

On the Tibetan Bon religion: S. G. Karmay, *The treasure of good sayings, A Tibetan history of Bon* (London, 1972); D. L. Snellgrove, *The nine ways of Bon* (London, 1967).

Buddhism in Mongolia: C. A. Bawden, *The Jebtsundamba Khutukhtus of Urga* (Wiesbaden, 1961); W. Heissig, *The religions of Mongolia* (Berkeley, 1979); R. J. Miller, *Monasteries and culture change in Inner Mongolia* (Wiesbaden, 1959).

BUDDHISM IN THE MODERN WORLD

Buddhist revival and modernism: H. Bechert, *Buddhismus, Staat und Gesellschaft in den Ländern des Theravāda-Buddhismus*, vol. 1 (Frankfurt, 1966); H. Dumoulin and J. C. Maraldo (ed.), *Buddhism in the modern world* (New York, 1966); D. Swearer, *Buddhism in transition* (Philadelphia, 1970).

Some original sources: Sir E. Arnold, *The light of Asia, or the great renunciation, being the life and teaching of Gautama* (London, 1879; many reprints); A. Dharmapala, *Return to righteousness, A collection of speeches, essays and letters* (Colombo, 1965); H. Nakamura, *The ways of thinking of eastern peoples* (Honolulu, 1964; repr. 1978); H. S. Olcott, *A Buddhist catechism* (44th ed., Madras, 1915); J. M. Peebles (transl.), *The great debate, Buddhism and Christianity, being an oral debate held at Panadura between M. Gunananda and D. de Silva* (Colombo, 1955); W. Rahula, *The heritage of the bhikkhu* (New York, 1974); Subhadra Bhikshu, *A Buddhist catechism, An introduction to the teaching of the Buddha Gotama* (rev. ed., Kandy, 1970); D. C. Vijayavardhana, *Triumph of righteousness, or the revolt in the temple* (Colombo, 1953).

Revival of Buddhism in India: A. C. Ahir, *Buddhism in modern India* (Nagpur, 1972); W. N. Kuber, *B. R. Ambedkar* (New Delhi, 1978); T. Ling, *Buddhist revival in India* (London, 1980). Original source: B. R. Ambedkar, *The Buddha and his dhamma* (2nd ed., Bombay, 1974).

Buddhism in Indonesia: For the Buddhist element in traditional Javanese and Balinese religion, see J. Ensink, 'Śiva-Buddhism in Java and Bali' in *Buddhism in Ceylon and studies on religious syncretism in Buddhist countries*, ed. H. Bechert (Göttingen, 1978), pp. 178–98; C. Hooykaas, 'Buddhism in Bali' in *Felicitation volumes on southeast Asian studies presented to Prince Dhaninivat*, vol. 1 (Bangkok, 1965), pp. 25–34; id., *Balinese Bauddha Brahmans* (Amsterdam, 1973); K. Wulff, *Sang hyang Kamahāyānan Mantrānaya, Ansprache bei der Weihe buddhistischer Mönche* (Copenhagen, 1935).

Buddhist revival in Indonesia, Malaysia and Singapore: H. Bechert, 'Buddhayana in Indonesia, A syncretistic form of Theravada' in *Journal of the Pali Text Society* 1981, pp. 10–21; Khantipalo, *A record of journeys in Indonesia* (Bangkok, 1971); C. McDougall, *Buddhism in Malaya* (Singapore, 1956); V. Wee, 'Buddhism in Singapore' in *Singapore: Society in transition*, ed. R. Hassan (Kuala Lumpur, 1976), pp. 155–188.

Buddhism in Germany: H. Hecker, *Buddhismus in Deutschland, Eine Chronik* (2nd ed., Hamburg, 1978). Original sources: P. Dahlke, *Buddhism and its place in the mental life of mankind* (London, 1927); A. Govinda, *Foundations of Tibetan mysticism* (5th ed., London, 1975); G. Grimm, *The doctrine of the Buddha, The religion of reason and meditation* (2nd ed., Berlin, 1958, repr. 1973).

Buddhism in Great Britain: C. Humphreys, *Sixty years of Buddhism in England* (London, 1968); id., *Both sides of the circle* [autobiography] (London, 1978).

Buddhism in America: R. Fields, *How the swans came to the lake: A narrative history of Buddhism in America* (Boulder, Col., 1981); L. H. Hunter, *Buddhism in Hawaii* (Honolulu, 1971); T. Kashima, *Buddhism in America* (Westport, Conn., 1977); E. M. Layman, *Buddhism in America* (Chicago, 1976); C. S. Prebish, *American Buddhism* (North Scituate, Mass., 1979). Some original writings: Chögyam Trungpa, *Cutting through spiritual materialism* (Berkeley, 1973); id., *The myth of freedom and the way of meditation* (Berkeley, 1976); id., *Born in Tibet* [autobiography] (London, 1966); Tarthang Tulku, *Reflections of mind, Western psychology meets Tibetan Buddhism* (Emeryville, Calif., 1975); id., *Time, space and knowledge, A new vision of reality* (Emeryville, Calif., 1977).

Sources of Illustrations

The Buddhist Way

17 1. Detail from a Tibetan *tanka*, depicting the Three Jewels. 19th century. Museum für Völkerkunde, Munich.

18 2. The Three Jewels. Gandhāra relief. 2nd–3rd century AD. British Museum, London.

3. Queen Māyā's dream. Sandstone relief from Bhārhut. 2nd century BC. Indian Museum, Calcutta. *Photo: Josephine Powell.*

4. The future Buddha leaves his palace. Marble relief from Amarāvatī. 2nd–3rd century AD. British Museum, London. *Photo: Werner Forman.*

19 5. The Buddha's Enlightenment. Detail of the East Gate pillar, Sāñcī. 1st century AD. *Photo: Josephine Powell.*

6. The Buddha's first sermon. Relief from Amarāvatī, 2nd–3rd century AD. British Museum.

7. The Buddha's Final Nirvāṇa. Detail from the East Gate at Sāñcī. 1st century AD. *Photo: Josephine Powell.*

8. Deer and the wheel. Detail from a preaching Buddha figure. Nālandā Museum. *Photo: Stella Snead.*

20 9. Tibetan *tanka* from a series on the life of the Buddha. 18th century. Musée Guimet, Paris.

21 10. The future Buddha leaves his palace. Illustration from a Burmese folding manuscript on the life of the Buddha. 19th century. Ms. Or. 4762, British Library, London.

11. The future Buddha encounters old age and sickness. Painting on silk from Tun-huang. 9th–10th century. British Museum, London.

12. The Buddha's Enlightenment. Modern postcard from Thailand. By courtesy of S. Dhumpakdi and Sons, Bangkok.

22–23 13. The Buddha's Final Nirvāṇa. Rock carving at Ajaṇṭā, Cave 26, *c.*6th century AD. *Photo: Hans Hinz.*

24 14. Monk meditating on a skull. Wall-painting from Qizil, *c.*AD 500. Museum für Indische Kunst, Berlin.

15. Meditation walk, Sri Lanka. *Photo: Michael B. Carrithers.*

25 16. Skeleton dance, Bhutan. *Photo: Martin Brauen.*

26 17. A novice monk. Painted clay figure at Tun-huang. 6th–7th century AD. *Photo: Martin Hürlimann.*

18. A novice monk. Gandhāra relief. 3rd–4th century AD. British Museum, London.

19. Novices mourn over the Buddha. Detail from Gandhāra relief. Peshawar Museum. *Photo: Josephine Powell.*

27 20. A novice monk with begging bowl. Marble statuette. Burmese, 19th century. British Museum, London.

21. Tibetan child at a religious ceremony at Dharamsala, India. *Photo: Ernst Haas.*

28 22. The path to Enlightenment. Wall-painting from the monastery of Likir, Tibet. *Photo: Martin Brauen.*

23. The twenty-four previous Buddhas. Section of mural. Early 19th century but heavily restored. Liyangastänna Vihāra, Kandy District, Sri Lanka. *Photo: Richard Gombrich.*

29 24. The cycle of Dependent Origination. Wall-painting from the monastery of Likir, Tibet. *Photo: Martin Brauen.*

30 25. Sandstone figure of the Buddha preaching. Gupta, 6th century AD. Archaeological Museum, Sārnāth. *Photo: Josephine Powell.*

26. The cowherd and the frog. Wall-painting from the Cave of the Statues, Qizil, *c.*AD 500. Museum für Indische Kunst, Berlin.

30–31 27. Detail from a painted scroll showing the history of the Yuzunembutsu sect. 14th century. Freer Gallery of Art, Washington, DC.

31 28. Monk preaching in the prayer hall of Namtok monastery, Burma. *Photo: Popperfoto.*

29. Preaching monk, Mandalay. *Photo: John Okell.*

32 30. Library of the Lamayuru monastery, Ladakh. *Photo: Felicitas Vogler.*

31. Tibetan book. Museum für Völkerkunde, Zürich. *Photo: István Rácz.*

33 32. Marble stelae at the Kuthodaw pagoda, Mandalay. *Photo: Heinz Bechert.*

34 33. Children dressed for lower ordination ceremony, Rangoon, *c.*1900. *Photo: Popperfoto.*

34. Novices carried by their fathers, Rangoon. *Photo: Popperfoto.*

35. Boy being shaved before ordination, Burma. *Photo: Popperfoto.*

35 36. Ordination ceremony, Kandy, Sri Lanka. *Photo: Richard Gombrich.*

37. Wall-painting in Ordination Hall of monastery, Pagan. 18th century. *Photo: Patricia Herbert.*

38. Ordination text and its lacquered cover. Burma, 19th century. Ms. Or. 4949, British Library, London..

39. A monk receives his robes in an ordination ceremony, Thailand. *Photo: Henry Ginsburg.*

36 40. The Buddha receives alms. Illustration from a 19th-century Burmese manuscript of the life of the Buddha. Ms. Or. 5757, British Library, London.

37 41. The Buddha receives donations. Illustration from a 19th-century Burmese manuscript of the life of the Buddha. Ms. Or. 13534, British Library, London.

42–43. Laymen offer gifts to a monk. Illustrations from a 19th-century Thai manuscript. Ms. Add. 15347, British Library, London.

44. Almsgiving, Rangoon. *Photo: Henry Wilson.*

38 45. Monks chanting in the

monastery of Gyantse, Tibet. *Photo: Fosco Maraini.*

39 46. A monk honours his teacher. Wall-painting from Karashahr, *c.*10th century. British Museum, London.

47. Monk and pupil. Illustration from a Thai meditation manual. 19th century. Ms. Or. 13703, British Library, London.

48. Master and disciple, Korea. *Photo: Roland Michaud.*

49. Forest monastery, Sri Lanka. *Photo: Michael B. Carrithers.*

40 50. A monk's possessions. Wall-painting from Samskar monastery, Ladakh. *Photo: Martin Brauen.*

42 Śākyamuni as ascetic. Gandhāra sculpture. 2nd century AD. Lahore Museum, India.

44 Elephants worshipping stupa. Stone relief from Amarāvatī. 2nd century AD. British Museum, London.

46 *Mudrās* used in Tibetan figures of the Buddha. British Museum, London.

49 The first sermon in the Deer Park. Stone relief from Ali Masj'd. British Museum, London.

51 Central detail from a Wheel of Life from Tibet. 19th century. Museum voor Land en Volkenkunde, Rotterdam. *Drawn by Georgie Glen.*

52 The Final Nirvāṇa of the Buddha. Gandhāra relief. 10th century. British Museum, London.

56 The monks' possessions. Tibetan blockprint. Toyo Bunko Library, Tokyo.

The Indian Tradition

61 1. Head of the Buddha from Haḍḍa, Central Asia. Victoria and Albert Museum, London. *Photo: István Rácz.*

62 2. A monastic courtyard. Illumination from Nepalese manuscript, AD 1015. Ms. Add. 1643, University Library, Cambridge.

3. Adoration of a stupa. Gandhāra relief. 2nd–3rd century AD. British Museum, London.

63 4. Stupa at Svayambhunath, Nepal. *Photo: Josephine Powell.*

62–63 5. Aerial view of Borobudur. *Photo: Brian Brake/John Hillelson Agency.*

64 6. Bhājā. *Photo: India Office Library, London.*

64–65 7. Inner face of the East Gate, Sāñcī. *Photo: Martin Hürlimann.*

64 8. Nālandā. *Photo: Josephine Powell.*

9. Nālandā. *Photo: Josephine Powell.*

65 10. The North Gate, Sāñcī. *Photo: Josephine Powell.*

11. Bodh-Gayā. *Photo: Josephine Powell.*

12. Sārnāth. *Photo: Josephine Powell.*

66 13. Kārle, *caitya*-hall. *Photo: Roloff Beny.*

67 14. Ajaṇṭā, entrance to Cave 19. *Photo: Colour Library International.*

15. Ellora. Entrance to Cave 10. *Photo: Scala.*

16. Bezeklik. *Photo: Yolande Crowe.*

68 17. Giant Buddha at Bāmiyān. *Photo: Josephine Powell.*

69 18. Group of monks. Detail of wall-painting from Mirān, *c.*AD 300. Central Asian Museum, Delhi. *Photo: Josephine Powell.*

19. Stucco head of a monk. Srinagar Museum. *Photo: Josephine Powell.*

68–69 20. Haḍḍa. *Photo: Josephine Powell.*

70–71 21–24. Wall-paintings from a ruined monastery at Karashahr. British Museum, London.

72 25. A series of Buddhas. Wall-painting at Bezeklik. 8th–10th century. From F. Andrews, *Wall paintings from ancient shrines in Central Asia* (London, 1948).

26. The bodhisattva Mañjuśrī. Illumination from palm-leaf manuscript, AD 967 from Vikramaśilā. Ms. Or. 6902, British Library, London.

73 27. Fire-gilded bronze figure from Veheragala, Sri Lanka, 11th century. Archaeological Department, Colombo. *Photo: Roloff Beny.*

28. Kuan-yin. Painted and gilded wood figure. Chinese, 13th century. Museum Rietberg, Zürich. *Photo: István Rácz.*

29. Mañjuśrī. Japanese 18th-century figure. Museum für Völkerkunde, Zürich. *Photo: István Rácz.*

30. Mahākāla. 18th-century Tibetan terracotta. *Photo: Werner Forman.*

74 31. Takht-i-Bahi. *Photo: Josephine Powell.*

75 32. Monks or disciples. Detail of wall-painting from Ming-öi, 8th–9th century. Central Asian Museum, Delhi. *Photo: Josephine Powell.*

33. Pilgrims mourn the Buddha's death. Detail of wall-painting from Bezeklik. 8th century. Central Asian Museum, Delhi. *Photo: Josephine Powell.*

76 34. The Golden Vihara (Hiraṇyavarṇamahāvihāra), Patan, Nepal. *Photo: Anne Vergati.*

35. A *vajrācārya* performs the *aṣṭamīvrata*. Detail from Nepalese picture roll, 1837. Museum für Indische Kunst, Berlin.

78 Fragment of figure of Kaniṣka, Kabul Museum. *Photo: Josephine Powell. Drawn by Georgie Glen.*

79 Glazed tile depicting the Second Buddhist Council. Made in Rangoon, 19th century. British Museum, London.

80 Part of a *Perfection of Wisdom Sūtra*, Bihar, 1150–75. British Library, London.

82–83 Tibetan block-prints illustrating the *vinaya* rules. Toyo Bunko Library, Tokyo.

84 *Above:* Hsüan-tsang on his travels. Wall-painting at Tun-huang. 8th century. *Below:* the Sanskrit text of the *Heart Sūtra* written in Chinese characters. Ms. Or. 8218(195), British Library, London.

85 *Perfection of Wisdom Sūtra.* Chinese manuscript, 8th century AD. Bibliothèque Nationale, Paris.

87 Map of India. *Drawn by Hanni Bailey.*

90 Tibetan blockprint. Toyo Bunko Library, Tokyo.

91 'Thousand Buddhas'. Chinese blockprint, 9th century. Bibliothèque Nationale, Paris.

93 *Maṇḍala* of Mañjuśrī. Nepal, 19th century. Musée Guimet, Paris.

95 *Above:* the Great Stupa at Sāñcī. *Below:* Japanese pagoda, Hōryūji. Drawing after F. Baltzer, *Die Architektur der Kultbauten Japans* (Berlin, 1907).

96 Lion capital from Sarnath. *c.*250 BC. *Photo: Martin Hürlimann.*

98 Plan of Ajaṇṭā and its caves.

100 Sketch of donors from a small

book found at Tun-huang. 9th–10th century. British Museum, London.

101 Map of Central Asia. *Drawn by Hanni Bailey.*

103 *Top:* Sanskrit manuscript. Mainz 705, State Library, West Berlin; *centre:* Uigur manuscript, dated 1350. Ms. Or. 8212, British Library, London; *bottom:* Sogdian manuscript. Ms. Or. 8212 (158), British Library, London.

105 Painted panel from Khotan. British Museum, London. *Drawn by Georgie Glen.*

106 *Above:* details of a wall-painting from Qočo. *Below:* Uigur and Tokharian monks from wall-paintings in the Kučā region. Drawings after A. von Gabin, *Das Uigurische Königreich* (Berlin, 1960).

112–13 Festival in Patan. Late 19th-century drawing. Musée Guimet, Paris.

Theravāda Buddhism

117 1. Meditating monk, Bangkok. *Photo: Henry Wilson.*

118 2. Meditation discs, Sri Lanka. *Photo: Michael B. Carrithers.*
3. Illustration from a Thai meditation manual. 19th century. Ms. Or. 13703, British Library, London.

118–19 4. Forest monastery in Sri Lanka. *Photo: Michael B. Carrithers.*

119 5. Forest monastery in Sri Lanka. *Photo: Michael B. Carrithers.*

120 6. Monk collecting alms by boat, Bangkok. *Photo: Sarah Errington/Alan Hutchinson.*
7. Monks given offerings at funeral, Colombo. *Photo: Michael B. Carrithers.*
8. Monks pouring concrete, Thailand. *Photo: Tim Page.*
9. Centre for drug addicts, Thailand. *Photo: Sarah Errington/Alan Hutchinson.*

121 10. Monk teaching in refugee camp near Thai border. *Photo: Tim Page.*
11. Monks working in vegetable garden, bank of the Mekong river, Thailand. *Photo: Tim Page.*

122 12. Ayudhya. *Photo: Henry Wilson.*

123 13. Buddha image in Shwedagon pagoda, Rangoon. *Photo: Henry Wilson.*
14. Wat Phra That Doi Suthep. Chiang Mai, northern Thailand. *Photo: Henry Wilson.*

124 15. Crumbling *caityas* on shores of Lake Inle, Shan States, Burma. *Photo: Patricia Herbert.*
16. Great pagoda at Prome, Burma. *Photo: Popperfoto.*

124–25 17. Pagan, Burma. *Photo: John Okell.*

125 18. Pegu, Burma. *Photo: Popperfoto.*
19. Laying foundation stone of new monastery, Sri Lanka. *Photo: Richard Gombrich.*

126 20. Shwedagon pagoda under scaffolding. *Photo: Heinz Braun.*

126–7 21. Illustration from the *Book of Royal Donations*, Burma, 1853–7. Ms. Or. 13681, British Library, London.

127 22–23. Illuminations from a Thai devotional manual. 19th century. Ms. Or. 14026, British Library, London.

128 24. Mural painting showing conversion of Aśoka. 20th century. Asokārāma, Colombo. *Photo: Richard Gombrich.*
25. Procession of King Mindon. Burmese folding book, 1865. Ms. Or. 12013, British Library, London.

129 26. Image of the Buddha as ruler of the world. 19th century, Burma. British Museum, London.
27. Mural painting showing the Venerable Saraṇaṃkara being made king of the Sangha. By S. Mendis, *c.*1938. Kelaniya, Sri Lanka. *Photo: Richard Gombrich.*
28. Mrs Bandaranaike at the Temple of the Tooth, Kandy. *Photo: Kenneth Somanader/Camera Press.*
29. Meeting of Buddhist monks in Mandalay, 1961. *Photo: Popperfoto.*

130–31 30. Karavika barge on Lake Inle. *Photo: Patricia Herbert.*

130 31. Monks at the Temple of the Tooth, Kandy. *Photo: Tim Page.*

131 32. Buddha image, Thailand. *Photo: Henry Wilson.*
33. Buddha images on Karavika barge. *Photo: John Okell.*
34. Procession of the Sacred Tooth, Kandy. 18th-century illustrated manuscript from Sri Lanka. Ms. Or. 11901, British Library, London.

132 35. Monk's funeral, Burma, *c.*1900. *Photo: Popperfoto.*

135 Detail from a palm-leaf manuscript illustrating *jātaka* stories. 18th century, Ceylon. Ms. Or. 11666, British Library, London.

137 Map of Sri Lanka, Burma and Thailand. *Drawn by Hanni Bailey.*

140 Detail from palm-leaf manuscript illustrating *jātaka* stories. 18th century, Ceylon. Ms. Or. 11666, British Library, London.

143 Toilet stone from the Jetavana monastery, Sri Lanka. Photo by courtesy of the Commonwealth Institute. *Drawn by Georgie Glen.*

145 Buddha image made of coconut leaves. *Photo: Sri Lanka National Tourist Organization.*

148 Shin Arahan. A 12th-century statue in the Ānanda Temple, Pagan. From *Handbuch der Formen- und Stilkunde Asien* (Verlag W. Kohlhammer).

149 The fighting in Burma. *Illustrated London News*, 1887. Mansell Coll.

150 Burmese cartoon. British Library, London.

152 The Upali Thein, Pagan. From *Burma, Korea, Tibet* (Holle Verlag).

155 The Buddha and the places he visited in his earthly life. Burmese palm-leaf manuscript. 19th century. Ms. Add. 17699/A, British Library, London.

156 Standing Buddha, Mandalay style, 19th century. See pl. 148.

157 Two glazed terracotta panels from the Ānanda Temple, Pagan. See pl. 148.

158 Buddha's footprint. Burmese, 19th century. British Museum, London.

160 Detail of the inscription of Rama Khamheng, 1292. British Library, London.

163 Thai good luck amulet. British Library, London.

165 Cosmogram with Thai and Cambodian text. British Library, London.

166 Thai amulet for obtaining one's wishes. British Library, London.

169 Three Thai amulets. British Library, London.

Buddhism in East Asia

173 1. The monk Myōe-Shōnin meditating. Hanging scroll, early 13th century. Kōzanji, Kyōto.

174 2. Giant Buddha at Yün-Kang. *Photo: China News Agency.*

3. Giant Buddha and attendant at Yün-Kang. British Museum, London.
4. Inside one of the caves at Yün-Kang. *Photo: Werner Forman.*

175 5. Interior of a cave at Lung-mên. *Photo: Werner Forman.*
6. Rock of the Thousand Buddhas at Lung-mên. *Photo: Werner Forman.*
7. Bodhisattva and guardians at Lung-mên. *Photo: China News Agency.*

176–77 8. The return of Hsüan-tsang with the Buddhist scriptures. Chinese painting on silk scroll. Fujita Art Museum, Ōsaka.

176 9. Fragment of the *Bhadra Kalpa*, found at Tun-huang. British Museum, London.

177 10. Hsüan-tsang on his pilgrimage. Coloured woodcut found at Tun-huang. 10th century. Bibliothèque Nationale, Paris.

178 11. Reliefs of donors from the Buddhist cave temples at Kung-Hsien, in Honan province, Northern Wei. 6th century. Freer Gallery of Art, Washington, DC.
12. Donors. Detail from a Chinese tombstone, 9th century. Museum für Völkerkunde, Zürich. *Photo: István Rácz.*
13. Empress and court ladies bring offerings. Detail of a relief from Freer Gallery of Art, Washington, DC.

179 14. Prince Shōtoku with his two sons. 7th-century painting. Imperial Household Collection, Kyōto, Japan.
15. Modern Japanese banknote. *Photo by courtesy of Professor Robert K. Heinemann.*
16. Large bronze Buddha from Tōdaiji, Kegon temple at Nara. *Photo: Pierre-Gilles Delorme.*
17. Modern war-memorial statue of Kannon. *Photo: Popperfoto.*

180 18. Lao-tsu and Confucius protect the infant Śākyamuni. Chinese painting on silk. 14th century. British Museum, London.

181 19. Kasuga deer *maṇḍala*, Japan, *c.*1400. By courtesy of Colnaghi's, London.
20. Thirteen deities of Kumano in their Buddhist form. Japanese silk paintings. Late 14th century. Smithsonian Institution, Washington, DC.

182 21. Detail from the *Diamond Sūtra*, printed AD 868. British Library, London.
22. Chinese folding book. British Library, London.
23. The library of the monastery of the Ocean Insignia, Korea. *Photo: A. R. Michaud.*
24. Wooden printing-block held by Korean monk. *Photo: N. Bouvier.*

183 25. Drawers in the octagonal library, Hopei, Peking. *Photo: J. Prip-Møller, Royal Library, Copenhagen.*
26. Wooden printing-block found at Tun-huang. Musée Guimet, Paris.
27. Travelling monk studying in library, Szechuan. *Photo: J. Prip-Møller, Royal Library, Copenhagen.*
28. Storing printing-blocks in the library, Szechuan. *Photo: J. Prip-Møller, Royal Library, Copenhagen.*

184 29. Silk scroll painting found at Tun-huang. 10th century. British Museum, London.

185 30. Amida Buddha. Painting on silk. 13th or 14th century. Staatliche Museen, Berlin-Dahlem.
31. Japanese scroll-painting of hell. 11th or 12th century. Horniman Museum, London.

186 32. Buddhist priests at prayer, Ikegami, Japan. *Photo: Popperfoto.*
33. The main gate to the monastic complex of Anchin, China. *Photo: J. Prip-Møller, Royal Library, Copenhagen.*
34. Hōryūji, Hossō temple at Nara, Japan. *Photo: Martin Hürlimann.*

187 35. Nanking monastery, China. *Photo: J. Prip-Møller, Royal Library, Copenhagen.*
36. Main hall of the Ling-yen monastery, China. China News Agency.
37. Aerial view of Chin Shan monastery. *Photo: J. Prip-Møller, Royal Library, Copenhagen.*

188–89 38. Nichiren searching for a temple site. Silk scroll painting. 15th century. Freer Gallery of Art, Washington, DC.

188 39. Detail from picture-scroll on the life of Dengyō Daishi. Coloured woodcut. Private collection, Japan.

189 40. Monk of the Tendai sect conducting a fire ceremony. *Photo by courtesy of Enryakuji, Tendai sect.*

190 41. Members of the Jōdo Shū (Pure Land sect). *Photo: Popperfoto.*
42. Member of the Fuke sect. *Photo: N. Bouvier.*
43. Zen monastic garden, Manpukuji, Ōbaku temple near Kyōto. *Photo: P. Rambach.*
44. Zen training for girls. *Photo: Camera Press.*

191 45. Bodhidharma in meditation. Drawing by Hakuin. Eisei Bunko, Tokyo.
46. Kenzō catching prawns. 14th-century drawing. National Museum, Tokyo.
47. Kanzan and Jittoku by Yamada Doon. Andrew Dickson White Museum, Cornell University.
48. Zen garden, Nanzenji, Rinzai temple at Kyōto. *Photo: Martin Hürlimann.*

192 49. Japanese pilgrim at Nikkō, near Tokyo, *c.*1900. *Photo: Popperfoto.*

195 Map of China. *Drawn by Hanni Bailey.*

196 Envoys returning to China. 19th-century drawing. British Museum, London.

201 Inscription about an image of Śākyamuni, donated by Yuan Hsieh, Prince of An-ting. Ku-yang cave. AD 511. *Photo: British Museum, London.*

204 Text of the Vinaya, 6th century AD. *Photo: Bibliothèque Nationale, Paris.*

207 Six drawings showing life in a Buddhist monastery. 19th century. British Museum, London.

208 Symbolic representation of the Unity of the Three Religions. Rubbing of a stela in the Shao-lin Temple, Honan. British Museum, London.

210 Chinese printed book of legends of Kuan-yin. British Library, London.

215 Map of Japan. *Drawn by Bryan Woodfield.*

217 Woodcut version of Gyōgi's map of Japan. 17th century.

220 *Above:* diagrammatic picture of Mount Meru by the Tendai priest Kakuchō (died 1037) from his work *Tō-mandara-shō.* Reproduced from *Taishō-shinshū-*

Tibet

Index

Page numbers in *italics* refer to illustrations

H

I

J

K

T

U

V

W

Y

Z